# THE RECOVERED
# MEMORY/FALSE MEMORY
# DEBATE

# THE RECOVERED
# MEMORY/FALSE MEMORY
# DEBATE

Edited by

## KATHY PEZDEK

*The Claremont Graduate School*
*Claremont, California*

## WILLIAM P. BANKS

*Pomona College and*
*The Claremont Graduate School*
*Claremont, California*

## ACADEMIC PRESS

San Diego   London   Boston   New York   Sydney   Tokyo   Toronto

**Find Us on the Web! http://www.apnet.com**

This book is printed on acid-free paper. ∞

Copyright © 1996 by ACADEMIC PRESS, INC.

All Rights Reserved.
No part of this publication may be reproduced or transmitted in any form or by any
means, electronic or mechanical, including photocopy, recording, or any information
storage and retrieval system, without permission in writing from the publisher.

Academic Press, Inc.
A Division of Harcourt Brace & Company
525 B Street, Suite 1900, San Diego, California 92101-4495

*United Kingdom Edition published by*
Academic Press Limited
24-28 Oval Road, London NW1 7DX

Library of Congress Cataloging-in-Publication Data

The recovered memory--false memory debate / edited by Kathy Pezdek,
   William P. Banks.
          p.          cm.
   Includes index.
   ISBN 0-12-552975-9 (hardcover : alk. paper)
   1. False memory syndrome.   2. Recovered memory.   3. Memory in
children.   I. Pezdek, Kathy.   II. Banks, William P.
RC455.2.F35R43     1996
616.85'8369--dc20                                                              96-12262
                                                        CIP

PRINTED IN THE UNITED STATES OF AMERICA
96   97   98   99   00   01   MM   9   8   7   6   5   4   3   2   1

*This book is dedicated to all victims of childhood abuse:*
*to the adults who were those children*
*and the children who were adults too soon;*
*to the falsely accused*
*and the silent abused.*

# CONTENTS

## I

## Childhood Trauma and Memory

## II

## The Development of Self and Autobiographical Memory

# III

## Childhood Memory: Distortion and Suggestibility

# IV

## Repressed Memory and Recovered Memory

# CONTRIBUTORS

*Numbers in parentheses indicate the pages on which the authors' contributions begin.*

JUDITH L. ALPERT (325), New York University, New York, New York 10011

JENNIFER M. BATTERMAN-FAUNCE (3), Department of Psychology, State University of New York at Buffalo, Buffalo, New York 14260

LAURA S. BROWN (341), Independent Practice and Department of Psychology, University of Washington, Seattle, Washington 98105

CATHERINE CAMERON (41), Behavioral Science Department, University of La Verne, La Verne, California 91750

STEPHEN J. CECI (225), HDFS, Cornell University, Ithaca, New York 14853

NEAL J. COHEN (81), Beckman Institute, University of Illinois, Urbana, Illinois 61801

MARY L. COURAGE (121), Psychology Department, Memorial University of Newfoundland, St. John's, Newfoundland Canada A1B 3X9

CHRISTINE A. COURTOIS (355), Washington, District of Columbia 20037

MARY LYNDIA CROTTEAU HUFFMAN (225), HDFS, Cornell University, Ithaca, New York 14853

ROBYN FIVUSH (151), Department of Psychology, Emory University, Atlanta, Georgia 30322

GAIL S. GOODMAN (3), Department of Psychology, University of California, Davis, Davis, California 95616

MARY R. HARVEY (29), Psychiatry Department, The Cambridge Hospital Department of Psychiatry, Harvard Medical School, Cambridge, Massachusetts 02139

JUDITH LEWIS HERMAN (29), The Cambridge Hospital Department of Psychiatry, Harvard Medical School, Cambridge, Massachusetts 02139

MARK L. HOWE (121), Psychology Department, Memorial University of Newfoundland, St. John's, Newfoundland Canada A1B 3X9

JOHN F. KIHLSTROM (297), Yale University, New Haven, Connecticut 06520

JERALD KUHN (3), Children's Hospital of Buffalo, Buffalo, New York 14222

D. STEPHEN LINDSAY (267), University of Victoria, Victoria, British Columbia V8W 242 Canada

ELIZABETH F. LOFTUS (225), University of Washington, Seattle, Washington 98195

SUSAN MOAN-HARDIE (245), Department of Psychiatry, University of California Los Angeles School of Medicine, Harbor/University of California Los Angeles Medical Center, Torrance, California 90509

JENNIFER T. MYERS (211), Psychology Department, University of North Carolina at Chapel Hill, Chapel Hill, North Carolina 27599

KATHERINE NELSON (101), Department of Psychology, Lehman College, City University of New York, Bronx, New York 10468

PETER A. ORNSTEIN (211), Psychology Department, University of North Carolina at Chapel Hill, Chapel Hill, North Carolina 27599

CAROLE PETERSON (121), Psychology Department, Memorial University of Newfoundland, St. John's, Newfoundland Canada A1B 3X9

KATHY PEZDEK (197), Center for Organizational and Behavioral Sciences, The Claremont Graduate School, Claremont, California 91711

JODI A. QUAS (3), Department of Psychology, University of California, Davis, Davis, California 95616

M. M. RIDDLESBERGER (3), Children's Hospital of Buffalo, Buffalo, New York 14222

CHANTAL ROE (197), Center for Organizational and Behavioral Sciences, The Claremont Graduate School, Claremont, California 91711

KAREN J. SAYWITZ (245), Department of Psychiatry, University of California Los Angeles School of Medicine, Harbor/University of California Los Angeles Medical Center, Torrance, California 90509

JONATHAN W. SCHOOLER (279), Learning Research and Development Center, University of Pittsburgh, Pittsburgh, Pennsylvania 15260

ELLIOTT SMITH (225), HDFS, Cornell University, Ithaca, New York 14853

NANCY L. STEIN (169), Department of Psychology, The University of Chicago, Chicago, Illinois 60637

LENORE C. TERR (69), University of California, San Francisco, San Francisco, California 94108

MINDA TESSLER (101), Department of Psychology, Lehman College, City University of New York, Bronx, New York 10468

MICHAEL P. TOGLIA (313), Department of Psychology, State University of New York, Cortland, New York 13045

# PREFACE

We count ourselves among those cognitive psychologists who are pleased to see that their work and their field have some tangible benefit to humankind or a relation to personally or socially important issues. It was therefore with considerable interest and anticipation that we entered into this project. Here we have a central question that is essentially cognitive: Can long-forgotten memories of sexual abuse be recovered with any accuracy? This question touches on a number of fundamental cognitive questions and would seem to be approachable, and answerable, by good, basic cognitive research. The specific mission of this book, consciousness, volition, and the self, is also engaged by the basic questions regarding the topics of psychogenic loss of memory, recovery of memory, autobiographical memory, and the possible psychological effects of memories not available to consciousness. Clearly we have a question and a set of issues close to the theoretical core of the field.

Furthermore, the social and personal ramifications of the topic are deep and important beyond question. They can be found in diverse areas, from the intimacy of the psychotherapeutic session to quiet personal tragedy and psychological distress, to the breakup of families, to lurid news items and public blame and accusation and retraction. Some large minority of us may have been sexually abused in our childhood; many of this minority may have lost access to this episode and may be suffering psychological anguish as a result. On the other hand, any one of us could be the innocent target of an illusory "recovered memory" that permanently damages our life. Because they were not believed, children have been returned to the tender mercies of their abusers; because they were believed, children and adults have brought untold miseries to the accused. These are riveting, consuming issues that have widespread potential for damage and healing.

It seemed too good to be true. Now, after having spent the better part of two years planning and assembling this volume and being immersed in these issues, we feel a bit like the character in a fable who gets his wish just as promised, but with a catch. The catch here is that we got a lot more than we wanted. We wanted questions that grabbed people, but these questions can rend people with a terrible and destructive fury. We wanted vital social interests, but we got something closer to a religious war.

The most difficult part of this project, for our authors as well as ourselves, was keeping the emotional power of the issues from clouding the scientific questions. We tried to hew to a middle course, looking for value in all sides, but the middle road here is more like a tightrope than a broad viaduct. To keep in the middle is to do battle with an unstable equilibrium. Look at one set of evidence, and the damage done by false memories seems of overwhelming importance. Look at another set, and anger boils at the perpetrators who are able to humiliate and dismiss their victims with accusations of false memories. An additional lure pulling us away from the center is the chemistry of debate on the issues and the temptation to use evidence to battle an opponent rather than to find the truth.

We used several devices to strive for objectivity. One was to invite authors from all sides of the issue. Although many were unable to contribute, the resulting balance reflects the breadth of the net we initially cast. A second device was to use preparation of this volume as an aid to our own education. Both of us have learned a considerable amount about the complexity of the issues. We have modified positions we began with, and we found ourselves coming to grips with issues we did not even see before. More than that, we have learned the hard truth that the resolution of burning questions sometimes has to be deferred. It would be satisfying, and relatively easy, to plant our flag in one camp or the other and then to do battle from there. This is a satisfaction we must forego for the present.

One thing we have learned is that objectivity is not a simple thing. This is partly because there are several different perspectives, each with its own predominant importance in its arena and its own working definition of objectivity. We began with a scientific perspective, which we still believe will ultimately be the most important. But with the present state of knowledge, perhaps even with most of the basic scientific questions answered, we must still confront other questions on different grounds. For example, the question of reasonable doubt in a court of law puts an entirely different slant on the evidence we might otherwise use to verify a scientific hypothesis. Psychotherapy brings another perspective. Both the legal and the therapeutic contexts force us to grapple with whether *this* theory or *this* observation applies to *this* individual, in the one case to establish guilt beyond reasonable doubt and in the other to get to the root of a client's psychological problem. The scientific perspective will always be of limited help in this area. Still another perspective comes from a public health concern about sexual abuse of children. Here, we might be concerned less about the sort of uncertainty that would be devastating in a legal context and more with the statistical impact and analysis of various causes and remedies.

These different perspectives have caused us to note certain arguments that seem to work in one area (or at least that are persuasive there) but that do not translate well to others, or that simply are invalid. For example, we have heard and read implications and direct assertions to the effect that because a patient improved after coming up with a memory of childhood sexual abuse, the recovered memory must reflect something that actually happened. We call the principle behind this reasoning the *aspirin deficiency fallacy* because it leads to absurd conclusions such as because aspirin cures headaches, then headaches are caused by aspirin deficiency. There are many reasons for which the apparent recovery of memories could lead to a remission of presenting clinical symptoms, even when the memories are completely imaginary. Even though faith healing sometimes results in lasting cures, few of us are thereby persuaded to a belief in such divine intervention. The issue of repression leads to some problematic reasoning and outright errors. Recovered memory is sometimes said to be impossible because there is no support for the concept of repression. This argument is flawed: it assumes that repression is the only mechanism by which psychogenic forgetting can happen and, further, that recovery can happen only when this repression is lifted. There may be many mechanisms of psychogenic forgetting other than repression; whatever the mechanism may be, available research does not exclude recovery on the basis of any assumed mechanism. On the other hand, to invoke the concept of repression as a mechanism that seals memories intact to be recovered in full, accurate detail in adulthood goes beyond the available evidence. There is at present no reason to believe that memories that were unavailable for some time and then were "recovered" are any more accurate than memories that were available all along for the same period.

Another error is to overgeneralize from individual cases. The literature now provides a number of reports of single cases of accurately recovered memories and, as well, of successfully planted fabrications. These may be crucial in a legal context or seem in the popular press to provide decisive evidence on one side or the other, but they provide demonstrations of existence and nothing more. Yes, recovered memories can be accurate, and, yes, vivid and compelling memories can be completely unfounded. Once these demonstrations have been made, and we believe that they have been, we need to go beyond them and ask more precise questions about the incidence, characteristics, circumstances, and so on of these memories. We also need to go beyond these statistical questions to the scientific questions about memory in this domain: What causes childhood amnesia? What is or are the mechanism or mechanisms behind psychogenic forgetting? Can memory be recovered in either case, or after "normal" forgetting for that matter? What are the mechanisms of recall or reconstruction of memory? Are there "raw data" of memory? Are they ever directly accessible or are all conscious memories filtered and constructed? Our hope in assembling this volume was to make some advances on the basic questions and to report data on the central issues.

We began this project excited about the possibility of integrating the research in this area and finding a useful application of these findings to a personally and socially important issue. Now, two years later, we have learned a tremendous amount and have amassed an impressive volume of research. And although we feel that we have identified the most relevant research from the most relevant topics in psychology, we were surprised to find ourselves admitting, in honest conversations with each other, that little of this work has much direct unqualified application to sorting out when memory for traumatic sexual abuse is likely to be reliable and when it is not. Rather, and as is typically the case with lofty goals and complex problems, the exercise of editing this volume has highlighted for us the *unanswered* questions that remain in this area and some efficacious directions for future research.

## THE CHAPTERS

We used several criteria in recruiting contributors and editing their chapters. The first requirement was that the research and positions be based on replicable data of some generality. From the outset, we encouraged reports of original experiments or observational studies; we required at least that arguments and positions be grounded in such data. A second set of criteria was designed to achieve balance in coverage of the areas related to our topic. We wanted to include studies of trauma and case studies of abuse survivors from clinical psychology, research—laboratory or otherwise—by cognitive psychologists who study memory, and research from developmental psychology that relates to children's memory. Although several of the people we tried to enlist in this volume were ultimately not able to contribute a chapter, looking back on the chapters we have included, we think little in the area is left uncovered and that all positions are heard in some form.

The chapters are conceptually organized around four key aspects of this debate. The first section presents research and theory regarding *childhood trauma and memory*. Although there is a significant amount of research on the effects of emotion and stress on memory, little of this research pertains to these effects on children, and few of these studies have investigated stressors of the caliber of sexual abuse. The chapters included examine the memory for real-world traumatic events, primarily in clinical contexts.

The chapters in the second section address *children's autobiographical memory*. As we planned this book, it was clear to us that it was important to present research on how children remember the regular events of their lives as a context for understanding how they might remember the irregular traumatic events both as children and later as adults. These chapters present several different accounts of the development of autobiographical memory and the concept of self.

The chapters in the third section present research relating to *childhood memory: distortions and suggestibility*. Suggestibility is central to the recovered memory/false memory debate. Assumed in this debate is the presumption that if the recovered memory is not real, then it was suggested by, for example, a therapist or a self-help book. A rather strong notion of the construct of suggestibility is thus invoked by the false memory claims. A secondary issue of suggestibility has to do specifically with sexual abuse by a close adult. Often the abuser will use a form of suggestion enforced by personal intimidation, saying such things as "this didn't happen." The effect may be to block or eradicate the memory rather than merely to cause the child to be silent about the event.

The chapters in the final section, *Repressed Memory and Recovered Memory,* present a range of issues relevant to the veracity of claims regarding repressed and recovered memory. The last two chapters in this section include the reports of the American Psychological Association and the British Psychological Association regarding the recovered memory/false memory debate. Each of these reports was produced by a task force of distinguished psychologists who reviewed the scientific evidence on the topic and who offer a summary of their findings. These two reports present interesting notes on which to end our book. As with the process of developing our own book, both of these reports reflect the groups' struggles to come to terms with the unanswered questions and conflicting findings in the literature.

# I. CHILDHOOD TRAUMA AND MEMORY

At the most general level, the process of editing this volume has reminded us of the apparently inescapable dialectic of *control versus applicability*. That is, the research programs that on the surface seem so promising because they come closest to investigating actual memory for childhood sexual abuse, are riddled with problems of experimental control and validation. On the other hand, there are research programs with high ratings in validation and experimental control, but the generalizations of these findings to memory for traumatic childhood abuse are suspect because the domain investigated is such a far cry from traumatic abuse. The chapters in the first part of this volume bring us face-to-face with this dialectic.

It is no longer productive to debate whether recovered childhood memories are true or false. It now seems clear that *some* recovered memories for childhood abuse are true and *some* are suggestively planted. We feel that the most compelling course for future research on the recovered memory/false memory debate is in the direction of investigating the conditions under which traumatic events are or are not likely to be repressed and the conditions under which recovered traumatic memories are or are not likely to be true, using, whenever possible, memory for real-world traumatic events. We have identified several factors that appear to be essential to the generalization of research findings to real-world memory for traumatic events, specifically, memory for childhood abuse. Although these factors are found to various degrees in some of the research presented in this volume, we hope to motivate a more widespread consideration of these factors in future research.

An important earmark of childhood abuse is the fact that it is secretive, private, often repetitive, and often occurs at the hand of a caregiver with whom the child is likely to need to maintain his or her attachment. As a result, the child is alone in dealing with the consequences of the abuse, knowing that it is likely to reoccur. And, because the perpetrator often denies that anything inappropriate has occurred, the child is forced to carry on an "otherwise normal" relationship with the perpetrator on a daily basis. This convoluted situation is a common way of life for abused children and is likely to be at the heart of the difficulty in finding researchable real-world opportunities for investigating repression and recovery of traumatic memories.

Goodman's research, reported in this part, comes impressively close to approximating the experience of childhood sexual abuse by assessing memory for an undesirable traumatic event that involves genital exposure and genital contact in an embarrassing setting. Also, Goodman was able to examine memory as a function of how frequently the child had experienced the procedure, once versus multiple times. However, the children in Goodman's study had a parent present to validate their experience and provide various degrees of emotional support. The event was thus not secretive and private for these children; the occurrence of the event was certainly not overtly denied by the parents. These conditions are likely to distinguish Goodman's results regarding children's memory for the voiding cystourethrogram test from children's memory for sexual abuse.

Another requirement of the research in this area is that some degree of validation exist regarding how the actual event being remembered took place. However, in many situations in which validation is available, we have the confounding effect of memory contamination by publically available information. Terr's research on the Chowchilla children is a case in point. The Chowchilla kidnapping actually did occur, and there is a significant amount of evidence about what in fact happened. However, there was a tremendous amount of public information available subsequent to the incident. Thus, it is impossible to determine what any child remembered from the kidnapping event itself as opposed to the less interesting alternative that they remembered information from media treatments of the event or from the ensuing conversations with the other children. Furthermore, the event was not secretive and private for these children and their parents did not systematically and overtly deny that the kidnapping occurred.

We suggest that to generalize from any research on memory for trauma to the specific situation of remembering childhood sexual abuse, it is important to include in the research the critical aspects of childhood sexual abuse. However, we recognize the difficulty in carrying out this directive. For example, the research conducted by Cameron and by Harvey and Herman offer very good first steps toward understanding the process of recovering repressed memories by actual victims of sexual abuse. But this research puts a fair amount of faith in the metamemorial ability of participants to remember if and when in the past they had not remembered something that they did at present remember. We recognize that no single study will be able to capture all of the critical elements of real-world memory for childhood abuse and also satisfy all of the requirements of good scientific research. However, we seek to motivate converging studies using a variety of methodologies, in clinical as well as experimental domains, to investigate memory for a variety of childhood traumas possessing the critical components of childhood sexual abuse. The chapters in the first part of this volume take us in this direction.

# Predictors of Accurate and Inaccurate Memories of Traumatic Events Experienced in Childhood

Gail S. Goodman[1] and Jodi A. Quas

*Department of Psychology, University of California, Davis, California 95616*

Jennifer M. Batterman-Faunce

*Department of Psychology, State University of New York at Buffalo, Buffalo, New York 14260*

AND

M. M. Riddlesberger and Jerald Kuhn

*Children's Hospital of Buffalo, Buffalo, New York 14222*

How likely is it that traumatic childhood events are misremembered or forgotten? Research on children's recollections of painful or frightening medical procedures may help answer this question by identifying predictors of accurate versus inaccurate memory. In the present study, 46 3- to 10-year-old children were interviewed after undergoing a stressful medical procedure involving urethral catheterization. Age differences in memory emerged, especially when comparing 3- to 4-year-olds with older children. Children's understanding of the event, parental communication and emotional support, and children's own emotional reactions also predicted accuracy. Memory did not reliably vary for children who endured the medical procedure once versus multiple times. Results are discussed in relation to possible precursors of accurate and false memories, and forgetting, of traumatic events experienced in childhood.

Many professionals, and even some poets, believe that an experience can be so painful that memory of it becomes barred from awareness. Or, in Emily Dickinson's (1890/1955) words, there can be "a pain/so utter/it swallows substance up/then covers the Abyss with trance/so memory can step around, across, upon it/as one within a swoon goes safely/where an open eye/would drop him/bone by bone." For many psychologists, the hypothesized mechanism permitting one's memory to "step around, across, upon it" and yet still "go safely" is repression, a hallmark of psychoanalytic theory. Repression is widely believed to explain lack of conscious awareness of a traumatic event. In recent years, the notion of repressed memory of trauma has become particularly controversial as adults claim to regain lost memories of early childhood sexual abuse. Although the clinical literature is rich with examples of "repressed memories" of traumatic childhood experiences (e.g., Courtois, 1992; Freud, 1915/1957; Goodwin, 1993;

This article is reprinted by permission from *Consciousness and Cognition*, Volume 3, pp. 269–294 (1994).

Herman & Schatzow, 1987), surprisingly little scientific research exists on this important topic.

The dearth of research is due not to disinterest, but to a lack of relevant scientific methods and research paradigms. Rather than focusing on repression per se, perhaps the field could make greater progress by concentrating on mechanisms that influence children's accurate or inaccurate memories of stressful experiences and by tracking whether such memories are later forgotten. In this way, we may be able to identify important predictors of accurate or false memories of childhood traumas, and of forgetting, and begin to understand the mechanisms involved.

In this article, we first discuss evidence suggesting that traumatic childhood events can be forgotten. We then examine how basic research on memory development relates to children's forgetting and accurate or inaccurate recollection of personally experienced events. We also consider the literature on children's reactions to traumatic experiences for insight and explore how individual differences in children's processing of a trauma might influence memory retention. The goal is to answer the following questions: Can early traumatic memories be forgotten? Can we identify important factors—for example, those associated with normal cognitive development—that influence retention of traumatic events? What might cause a child to misremember all or part of a stressful incident?

We propose that several key factors in addition to age influence whether a child accurately remembers or misremembers a traumatic experience. Specifically, we propose that the child's understanding of and emotional reaction to the event, as influenced by parental communication and emotional support, play important roles in determining the accuracy, inaccuracy, or loss of a child's memory for a traumatic experience. In support of our proposal, we describe recent research in which we identify precursors of children's accurate versus inaccurate memory of a stressful event which partially mimics sexual victimization.

## DO ADULTS FORGET CHILDHOOD TRAUMAS?

There is widespread agreement that people forget at least some traumatic events from early childhood. Studies of infantile amnesia show convincingly that if a trauma is experienced early enough, before an autobiographical memory system is fully functioning, consciously accessible explicit memory of the early trauma becomes lost (e.g., Pillemer & White, 1989; Schactel, 1947; Terr, 1988; Usher & Neisser, 1993). But once an autobiographical memory system has developed, does a person necessarily form a memory of traumatic or abusive events that lasts into adulthood?

Many would agree that the most important recent study to examine adults' memory for traumatic childhood events is the one conducted by Linda Williams (1993). She interviewed women who as children were evaluated for child sexual assault at a hospital emergency room, finding that 38% of the women failed to remember the documented abuse. Even when women who experienced maltreatment in infancy and toddlerhood were excluded, the proportion who forgot their abuse experiences did not change markedly. Although some women may have chosen not to disclose abuse that they could actually remember, this fails to fully account for Williams's findings because many of the women who did not remember the abuse described other highly personal sexual experiences. Retrospective survey studies of adults who claim they were sexually assaulted as children also indicate that the abuse was sometimes forgotten for extended periods of time (Briere & Conte, 1993; Loftus, Polonsky, & Fullilove, 1994).

Thus, according to the best evidence available, at least some childhood traumas may be lost from adult memory. If so, can we identify precursors to accurate, inaccurate, or forgotten memories of childhood traumas? We first look to basic research on memory development for possible answers.

## THE DEVELOPMENT OF MEMORY

It is well accepted that children often have fewer cognitive resources than adults to help them retain and recall complex information. Children also are less likely than adults to operate strategically on memory, and they have a less well-developed knowledge base to impute meaning to events (Case, 1985; Chi, 1978; Fischer, 1980). With development, children evidence more complete memory, less memory distortion due to external influences, and greater conscious control of the memory process (Kail, 1990). Current research also suggests that young children's memories often fade relatively quickly and thus are more fragile (e.g., open to false suggestions) than the memories of older children and adults (Brainerd & Reyna, 1991; Flin, Boon, Knox, & Bull, 1992). Nevertheless, some memories are retained well by children over long periods of time (Fivush, 1993; Hudson & Fivush, 1987), and at least by the age of 4 or 5 years, children can often, although not always, resist some false suggestions about personally significant acts (Goodman & Aman, 1991; Lepore & Sesco, in press; Rudy & Goodman, 1991).

Even when young children have retained substantial amounts of information in memory, considerable cuing and contextual support may be necessary for them to reactivate and retrieve this information (e.g., Fivush, 1993; Price & Goodman, 1990). One of the most reliable findings in the memory-development literature is that young children have difficulty retrieving detailed episodic memories on their own. With development, children become better at accessing memories without cues from others (Price & Goodman, 1990). Increased use of memory strategies, such as rehearsal and retrieval by category membership (Kobasigawa, 1974; Ornstein & Naus, 1985), may serve as a form of self-cuing. Such strategies may influence memory of emotion-laden events, for example, by facilitating covert or overt reactivation of affectively charged information in memory (Bohannon & Symons, 1992) and by providing access to memories via trauma-related categories (e.g., being hurt, being punished, or getting in trouble; Liwag & Stein, 1993).

If an event is repeated, as are some traumatic events, would a child be more likely to remember it? Basic research on memory development suggests that the answer is "yes." Young children develop rudimentary scripts of repeated life experiences (Nelson, 1986), including traumatic ones (Bearison & Pacifici, 1989). However, their early scripts may be driven more by semantic than episodic memory, making it difficult for children to recount a single occurrence of a repeated event and more likely for children to merge similar events in memory (Farrar &

Goodman, 1992; Fivush, 1984; Nelson, 1986). Moreover, young children's script reports are often limited, containing an accurate core along with disjointed bits and pieces of what occurred. However, because there has been little research on the development of script memory for repeated, traumatic events, we do not know for sure whether children are more or less likely to merge traumatic than neutral events in memory or whether they form distinct "flashbulb" memories (Warren & Swartwood, 1992).

Recent research suggests, in any case, that advances in memory development, such as those mentioned above, do not occur in an interpersonal vacuum and that social influences on memory must be considered (Tessler & Nelson, this issue). Adults help children learn how to perform acts of remembering, in part by discussing past events with them. Although a rudimentary memory system exists in infancy, children may need to learn discourse and memory-search skills, and also learn that remembering is a goal in itself (Fivush, 1993; Hudson, 1990; Nelson, 1993). Nelson (1993) has argued that children acquire these skills and obtain such knowledge through conversation with others, particularly parents. Providing empirical support for this claim, Tessler (cited in Nelson, 1993) found that young children who talked with their mothers about specific parts of an event were the only ones who remembered those parts of what occurred. Not only "whether" but also "how" parents talk to their children appears to be important. Hudson (1990) studied conversations between 24- and 30-month-old children and their mothers about events in the recent and remote past, and she noted the ways in which such conversations affected memory. She reports that the way, "mothers talked about the past was more important than the specific content of what they mentioned" (p. 190). Thus, certain maternal conversation styles may facilitate recall of past events more than others.

In summary, normal cognitive- and social-development processes influence children's memories. Regarding memory for early traumatic events, younger children should be particularly likely to forget or misremember parts of autobiographical experiences, including traumatic ones. To the extent that young children may have more difficulty understanding an event in the first place, holding the event in memory, bringing the event back to mind, and rehearsing the event, they might be expected to forget or misremember stressful life experiences. Moreover, the extent to which a parent helps a child discuss and process a traumatic event might also influence the child's subsequent ability to recall the trauma. However, these principles are based primarily on research concerning nonemotionally charged information. We next consider research that bears more directly on memory for stressful childhood experiences.

## CHILDREN'S MEMORY FOR TRAUMATIC EVENTS

Scientific research on children's memory for stressful events is still relatively new, and most studies have taken advantage of stressful experiences that virtually all children undergo, such as inoculations or dental examinations. This body of research indicates that differences in the amount and accuracy of information retained about stressful events generally follows typical developmental patterns (e.g., Goodman, Hirschman, Hepps, & Rudy, 1991; Ornstein, Baker-Ward, Gordon, & Merritt, 1993). For example, younger compared to older children tend to evidence less complete and less accurate memories. Moreover, memory for stressful events, like memory for neutral ones, becomes less detailed over time (Goodman et al., 1991; Ornstein et al., 1993).

When adults are questioned about events from early childhood, they often mention events that evoked strong emotions (Main, Kaplan & Cassidy, 1985; Pillemer & White, 1989), indicating that affectively charged memories (at least those that fall within normal experience) are more likely to be retained over time than mundane ones (but see Howe, Courage, & Peterson, this volume). Compatible with this trend, some research indicates that highly stressful events are retained particularly well by children (Goodman et al., 1991; Warren-Leubecker, 1991). However, other research indicates detrimental effects of negative emotional states on children's memory (Bugenthol, Blue, Cortez, Fleck, & Rodriguez, 1992; Peters, 1989). It is worth noting that the former studies tend to focus on central features of stressful events, whereas the latter studies tend to focus on information peripheral to the stressor, and that the pattern of results is thus consistent with Christianson's (1992) recent proposal, formulated for adult memory, that information integral to a stressor is retained well, whereas information peripheral to a stressor is retained poorly. Nevertheless, still other studies indicate complex relations or no relation between stress and memory (Goodman et al., 1991; Steward, 1993; Vandermaas, Hess, & Baker-Ward, 1993), suggesting that perhaps stress alone is an insufficient predictor of retention.

In an attempt to clarify possible relations between stress and memory, some researchers propose that new distinctions are needed. For example, Pynoos (1992) and Yuille and Tollstrup (1992) suggest that the relation between stress and memory might be better understood if a distinction were made between external versus internal focus of attention during a traumatic event. According to this view, once a person is injured or penetrated, attention may become focused on internal sensations rather than external reality, a focus that could result in relatively poor memory for external events, at least for part of the experience. Other researchers propose that individual differences in children's interpretation of a traumatic event need to be considered in understanding the relation between stress and memory (Bretherton, 1993; Goodman, 1993).

However, because many of the stressful experiences studied to date are common to most children and are not, for example, life threatening, one might ask whether the above findings and formulations would hold for highly traumatic events. Few careful studies have addressed this question. The most notable exception is Terr's (1988) landmark research on children who experienced traumas between the ages of 6 months and 4 years 5 months and for whom documentation of the traumas existed. Consistent with the infantile amnesia literature, Terr (1988) reports that if the trauma occurred before the age of about 28 to 36 months, children did not evidence consciously accessible, verbalizable episodic memory (although some children had "spot" memories). Interestingly, even if the trauma occurred before 28 months, many children exhibited "behavioral memories," post-traumatic play, and trauma-associated personality change. Terr (1991) concluded that children have vivid memories for single, startling traumas, but more spotty or absent memory for repeated, prolonged traumatic experience.

Terr's research is an important starting point, but a number of potentially important factors were uncontrolled in her study (e.g., number of other traumas in the child's life, intra- vs extrafamilial sources of the trauma, the child's involvement in the event). If, for example, a child's exposure to repeated traumas is associated with greater family dysfunction (e.g., an abusive parent or parents who fail to protect the child), it is unclear whether the adverse effects on memory are associated with repetition of a trauma or more pervasive parenting factors. Thus, many important questions remain about children's memories for highly traumatic events.

Although scientific research on children's memory for highly traumatic events is limited, studies of children's emotional reactions to traumatic events may provide important insights. For example, studies of post-traumatic stress disorder (PTSD) in children reveal several core reactions that may influence later memory, such as avoidance of reminders, reenactment, nightmares, and denial. Nader, Pynoos, Fairbanks, and Frederick (1990) examined children's PTSD reactions 14 months following a sniper attack on their school playground. Children who were directly exposed to the initial trauma displayed more severe symptoms (nightmares, intrusive imagery) than children who were inside the school or not in attendance when the attack occurred. A majority of the children avoided reminders of the attack. Interestingly, the researchers presented no evidence that children failed to recall, forgot, or repressed the experience, although some children remembered parts of it inaccurately (Pynoos & Nader, 1988). A somewhat different pattern was found for children who experienced a prolonged, invasive, and painful medical procedure (bone-marrow transplant) (Nader, Stuber, & Pynoos, 1991; Stuber, Nader, Yasuda, Pynoos, & Cohen, 1991). Although these children also demonstrated strong avoidance of reminders, they exhibited denial of the traumatic experience and reenacted portions of their traumas in play.

How might PTSD-associated reactions influence memory? The research on PTSD indicates that some children, particularly children who suffer extended traumatic events, may be prone to denial as a defense mechanism, a finding consistent with Terr's (1991) formulation that prolonged stressful events are less likely to be recalled. Intuitively, one might suspect that denial combined with avoidance of reminders would be associated over time with loss of consciously accessible traumatic memories. In contrast, other symptoms, such as post-traumatic play, nightmares, and intrusive imagery, might reactivate traumatic memories, keeping such memories alive. Accurate memory is by no means guaranteed by these processes, however. (For example, post-traumatic play may not be consciously related to the trauma in children's minds and may be used to master the event through reworking of memory, possibly altering it in the process; see Terr, 1988.)

## INDIVIDUAL DIFFERENCES IN MEMORY FOR STRESSFUL EVENTS

Despite the overall trends mentioned above, there is considerable variation in children's reactions to and ability to recall stressful experiences. Several researchers who studied children's memory for stressful events have commented that there are substantial individual differences, in addition to age trends, in children's recall of past events (Goodman, Bottoms, Schwartz-Kenney, & Rudy, 1991; Steward, 1993). Perhaps such variation will hold part of the key to understanding the effects of stress on memory and the likelihood of accurate, false, or forgotten memory later on. One potentially important individual difference factor, identified by Steward (1993), is gender. In her study of children who experienced stressful medical procedures, boys were particularly likely to deny feelings and actions associated with victimization. For example, a number of boys who cried and struggled during invasive medical procedures later denied that they cried or that the procedure hurt. Temperament may be another factor related to later memory: Gordon, Ornstein, Nida, Follmer, Crenshaw, and Albert (1993) found that a measure of temperament predicted children's memory for a medical examination. Can we identify other individual difference factors that may influence children's memories of traumatic events?

Recent emphasis on social, specifically parental, influence on autobiographical memory development points to differences in parent–child interaction as a potential source of individual differences in memory for a traumatic event. Consistent with this possibility, Williams (personal communication, May, 1994) found that one predictor of adults' lack of recall of childhood abuse was having a nonsupportive mother. Nonsupportive mothers would likely fail to comfort their children or fail to help them understand and cope with a traumatic event. What happens to a child's memory if a parent refuses to talk to the child about a stressful experience or refuses to comfort the child? When a child suffers a traumatic event, some parents express the hope that the child will simply forget about it. They may specifically tell their child "don't think about it," "put it behind you," or "just forget it." Other parents may comfort their child, strengthen his or her self-esteem, and help the child better understand why the event occurred. Because relatively little is known about parental supportiveness or communication in relation to memory for emotional events, we were interested in exploring how differences in parent–child interaction affect children's memory for a stressful experience.

## THE PRESENT STUDY

In the study reported here, we examined children's memory for an invasive medical procedure called Voiding Cystourethrogram Fluoroscopy (VCUG). We were particularly interested in children's memory for this procedure because it involves painful, forced genital contact (i.e., catheterization through the urethra, infusion of liquid into the bladder) and thus in certain ways mimics sexual assault on a child. Of course, we did not recruit children to undergo this procedure for our study. Family doctors order the VCUG test when children have urinary tract infections, urinary tract abnormalities, or incontinence. The VCUG test identifies "reflux," which can lead to serious medical problems (e.g., kidney failure) if uncorrected.

Because an objective record of the VCUG test can be obtained, the procedure provides an opportunity to examine chidren's memory for a stressful, embarrassing, and painful experience involving genital touch. Additionally, because some children undergo more than one VCUG test while growing up, children's memory for a repeated stressful event can be examined. Thus, studying children's memory for the VCUG test may offer insight into mechanisms influencing accuracy, inaccuracy, and forgetting of traumatic childhood events.

## Method

### Subjects

Forty-six children ($M$ = 5 years 6 months; range 3 to 10 years) participated. There were initially 48 participants, but one child was eliminated from the study because he had been previously diagnosed with attention deficit disorder and could not attend to the interview, and another was eliminated because her parent crossed out 55 of the 63 questions on the memory test. There were 28 females and 18 males in the final sample. Children were divided into three age groups, 3- to 4-year-olds ($n$ = 17), 5- to 6-year-olds ($n$ = 16), and 7- to 10-year-olds ($n$ = 13). Twenty-nine of the children were experiencing their first VCUG, whereas the remaining 17 had undergone at least one previous VCUG test (range = 1 to 6 VCUGs).

### Questionnaires[2]

*VCUG checklist.* A checklist was used to help document the child's experiences and reactions during the VCUG test. It listed standard features of the medical procedure and contained sections for noting the specifics of each VCUG test. The checklist also contained six stress-level scales and six crying scales to be completed by the researcher regarding the child's reactions at prescribed times: when the child entered the X-ray room, during the initial X-ray, during catheterization, when the parent left the room, when the child voided on the table, and when the parent and child were reunited at the end of the procedure. The 6-point stress scale ranged from "extremely happy" (1) to "extremely unhappy" (6). The crying scale ranged from "no crying at all" (1) to "hysterical crying" (6).

*Mother's Reaction Questionnaire.* The mother's response to her child's reaction following the VCUG test was assessed through a series of "yes" or "no" questions. The questions were designed to identify, through self-report, whether the mother discussed the exam with the child, explained the exam to the child, did not have time to attend to the child's reaction to the exam, sympathetically talked about the exam with the child, physically comforted (e.g., hugged) the child because of the child's reaction to the exam, and asked the child questions about the exam.

*Child's VCUG Reaction Questionnaire.* This questionnaire dealt with the way the child reacted to the VCUG after it occurred. Parents responded either "yes" or "no" to 26 questions concerning their child's behavior since the VCUG (e.g.,

---

[2] Several additional questionnaires were administered, such as the Peabody Picture Vocabulary Test, but are not dealt with in the present paper.

child cried since the VCUG exam; child had nightmares since VCUG; child has been concerned about result of the exam; child has been concerned about touching since the exam; child has asked questions about the exam; child has seemed or expressed embarrassment about the exam; child expressed feeling proud of self for undergoing the exam; child expressed feeling sad about the exam; child seemed to have understood the exam; child has played acted the exam by self, with friends, adults, or dolls).

*Memory questionnaire.* The memory questionnaire consisted of three parts: free recall, doll demonstration, and directive questions.[3] The initial free recall question was: "I want to ask you some questions about the last time you went to Children's Hospital. Remember, you went there for a medical test. Tell me everything you can remember about what happened." Further prompts included "What else happened when you got that medical test?" and "I need to know everything that happened when you got that test." If necessary, more specific prompts were used: "The time I need to know about was when you had the medical examination/test to see about the problems you are having going to the bathroom. Tell me everything you can about what happened that time."

The final part of the memory questionnaire was composed of 61 direct questions; 33 of these were specific questions (e.g., "Was the doctor a man or a woman?" "How did you get up onto the table?") and 15 were misleading questions (e.g., "What color was the rug on the floor in that room?" "Didn't the doctor look in your ears when he gave you that test?"). Misleading questions were included because of their special relevance to children's suggestibility. There were also 3 questions that were either misleading or correctly leading depending on each child's specific VCUG test and 1 question that was either specific or misleading, again depending on each child's specific VCUG experience. Additionally, there were 9 questions that were open-ended (e.g., "What did the doctor look like?").

### Procedure

Parents of children scheduled to undergo a VCUG were contacted by phone. Parents were told that the study concerned children's reactions to medical tests. Although parents were also told initially that, during Session 3, a researcher would talk to the children about the VCUG test, only at the start of Session 3 did we explicitly mention our interest in memory.

Parents who agreed to allow their child to participate were scheduled for an initial interview (Session 1) at a university laboratory prior to the child's scheduled VCUG. When the initial session was not possible due to time constraints, the information obtained from the initial interview was gained at Session 3.

*Session 1.* First, parental consent and child assent were obtained. A research

---

[3]Reliability of coding of units of information in free recall and answers to open-ended questions was established by two researchers who scored a subset of the free recall protocols and achieved proportion of agreement of .89. The coding system was an adaptation of that used in several previous studies (e.g., Rudy & Goodman, 1991; Tobey & Goodman, 1992). Results of the doll demonstration will be reported in a future paper.

assistant (RA) then administered various standardized questionnaires to the parent and child. The VCUG test was not mentioned to the child.

*Session 2.* An RA met the child and parent(s) in the waiting room of the Radiology Department at the hospital on the day of the VCUG test to observe and videotape the VCUG procedure. Thirty-three of the children had other tests the same day as the VCUG. These included either a sonogram ($n = 25$) or Intravenous Pyelogram (IVP, $n = 7$). One child had a renal scan.

For the VCUG test, the child first changed into a hospital gown. Then the child and parent were brought into an X-ray room by a technician for initial X-rays. Once the child was on the examination table and the X-ray camera was in place, the parent, RA, and technician stood at the doorway outside the room while the X-ray was being taken. Next, a nurse and technician prepared the child to be catheterized by washing the child's genitals with soap. For girls, this entailed bringing their legs up to a "frog-like" position while lying on their backs. After the cleansing, some boys were given the benefit of an anesthetizing gel inserted into the tip of the penis to numb it slightly; however, the gel was only partially effective. Next, most children were given a pinwheel to blow on; this served both to distract them and to facilitate relaxation of the stomach muscles. The technician and parent held the child down and tried to comfort her or him while the nurse performed the catheterization (insertion of a 12" to 15" plastic tube up through the urethra into the middle of the child's bladder). If a child struggled excessively, extra technicians helped restrain the child or the child was physically restrained with special equipment (e.g., tied onto a "papoose board").

After the catheter was inserted, the parent was required to leave the room before the doctor entered. A liquid dye (contrast medium) was then infused through the catheter into the child's bladder as the doctor took X-rays. Once the child's bladder was full, he or she was asked to void on the examination table. X-rays were taken as the child voided; the catheter slipped out nonpainfully at that time. When children would or could not urinate on the table, a nearby water faucet was turned on or warm water was poured over their genitals. Two girls who still refused were eventually permitted to urinate in the bathroom. Following urination, children and their parents were reunited.

The RA completed the stress and crying ratings at the prescribed times during the procedure. The RA also completed the checklist and took notes on what occurred. In most cases, the entire event was videotaped.

*Session 3.* After a delay ($M = 11.63$ days; range 6 to 27 days), children returned to the university laboratory for a memory test. At the start of the session, our interest in memory was explained to the parent. The parent was shown all questions to be asked of the child and encouraged to cross out any that the parent did not want asked. Informed consent was again obtained; no parent objected to our procedure or withdrew from the study. Before the memory interview began, the parent also privately indicated the child's terms for various parts of the medical procedure (e.g., "tube" for catheter) and the child's genitals.

A researcher who had not been present at Session 2 conducted the memory interview. Rapport was carefully established with the child, who was informed that she or he did not have to answer any questions and could stop at any time.

The child's assent for the interview was obtained. Using the child's terms when possible, the interviewer then asked the memory questions, with the parent in a separate room. At this same time, the parent completed the Mother's Reaction Questionnaire and the Child's Reaction Questionnaire. The parent and child were then thanked, debriefed, and paid, and the child was given a small toy.

## Results

Preliminary correlational analyses revealed no significant relations between memory measures and the following variables: the child's gender, the delay between the VCUG and the memory test, or the child's having experienced other medical procedures on the day of the VCUG. Data were therefore collapsed across these variables. Neither delay nor number of VCUGs was significantly related to age, $r = .15$ and $r = .08$, respectively.

### Age and Number of VCUGs

Effects of age and repeated VCUG tests on memory were first examined through a series of 3 (age group) $\times$ 2 (number of VCUGs) analyses of variance (ANOVA). Children were divided into two groups based on the number of VCUGs they had experienced (i.e., one versus more than one previous VCUG). As can be seen in Table 1, main effects of age were significant for most memory

TABLE 1
Memory Performance for Each Age and Number of VCUG Group

| | 3- to 4-years | | | 5- to 6-years | | | 7- to 10-years | | | Age | |
| --- | --- | --- | --- | --- | --- | --- | --- | --- | --- | --- | --- |
| | One VCUG ($n = 12$) | Multiple VCUGs ($n = 5$) | $M$ | One VCUG ($n = 10$) | Multiple VCUGs ($n = 6$) | $M$ | One VCUG ($n = 7$) | Multiple VCUGs ($n = 6$) | $M$ | Effect $F(2, 40)$ | $p$ |
| Free recall (mean number of units) | | | | | | | | | | | |
| Correct | 9.67 | 7.00 | 8.88[a] | 16.20 | 18.33 | 17.00[ab] | 26.86 | 25.50 | 26.23[b] | 5.58 | .01 |
| Incorrect | 3.17 | 1.20 | 2.59 | 2.00 | 0.33 | 1.38 | 1.14 | 0.83 | 1.00 | n.s. | |
| Don't know* | 0.17 | 0.40 | 0.24 | 0.20 | 0.33 | 0.25 | 0.00 | 0.00 | 0.00 | — | |
| Specific questions (mean proportions) | | | | | | | | | | | |
| Correct | 0.48 | 0.44 | 0.47[a] | 0.60 | 0.68 | 0.63[b] | 0.83 | 0.81 | 0.82[c] | 20.30 | .001 |
| Commission | 0.13 | 0.20 | 0.15[a] | 0.08 | 0.09 | 0.08[b] | 0.06 | 0.07 | 0.06[b] | 8.90 | .001 |
| Omission | 0.17 | 0.16 | 0.16[a] | 0.10 | 0.10 | 0.10[b] | 0.06 | 0.03 | 0.04[c] | 13.50 | .001 |
| Don't know | 0.20 | 0.17 | 0.19[a] | 0.20 | 0.13 | 0.17[a] | 0.03 | 0.03 | 0.03[b] | 4.74 | .025 |
| Misleading questions (mean proportions) | | | | | | | | | | | |
| Correct | 0.52 | 0.38 | 0.48[a] | 0.65 | 0.71 | 0.67[b] | 0.81 | 0.83 | 0.82[c] | 13.59 | .001 |
| Commission | 0.22 | 0.33 | 0.26[a] | 0.12 | 0.10 | 0.11[b] | 0.10 | 0.02 | 0.06[b] | 14.93 | .001 |
| Omission | 0.15 | 0.16 | 0.15[a] | 0.08 | 0.07 | 0.08[b] | 0.08 | 0.03 | 0.06[b] | 6.34 | .01 |
| Don't know | 0.09 | 0.11 | 0.10 | 0.14 | 0.13 | 0.13 | 0.02 | 0.11 | 0.06 | n.s. | |
| Open-ended questions (mean number of units) | | | | | | | | | | | |
| Correct | 9.00 | 4.80 | 7.76[a] | 18.60 | 20.83 | 19.44[b] | 37.71 | 49.17 | 43.00[c] | 22.91 | .001 |
| Incorrect | 5.42 | 7.80 | 6.12 | 8.00 | 7.33 | 7.75 | 7.43 | 2.67 | 5.23 | n.s. | |
| Don't know* | .61 | .48 | .57[a] | .49 | .45 | .47[a] | .18 | .25 | .21[b] | 7.60 | .01 |

*Note.* Proportions may total less than 1.00 due to ambiguous and unscorable responses. Across rows, a different suprascript letter indicates a significant planned mean comparison, all $Fs(1, 40) \geq$ 5.04. "Don't know" responses in free recall violate analysis of variance assumption of homogeneity of covariance.

* Proportion of "don't know" responses based on dichotomous 0 vs 1 scoring.

measures, except number of incorrect units to free recall and open-ended questions. Planned comparisons revealed that 3- to 4-year-olds generally answered significantly fewer questions correctly and made more errors of commission and omission than older children. The 5- to 6-year-olds provided significantly fewer correct answers to specific and misleading questions than older children, but did not generally make significantly more errors, with the exception of errors of omission to specific questions.

Main effects of number of VCUGs did not reach statistical significance in any of the analyses, all $Fs(1, 40) \leq 2.45$, and none of the interactions were significant. However, the age X number of VCUGs interaction approached significance for commission errors to misleading questions, $F(2, 40) = 2.80, p = .07$. The 3- to 4-year-olds who experienced multiple VCUGs produced a higher proportion of commission errors than did agemates who experienced only one VCUG, while the opposite was true for the oldest age group, whose commission errors decreased with number of VCUGs.

A series of one-way analyses of covariance was also conducted on the memory measures with number of VCUGs divided into three categories: one ($n = 29$), two ($n = 8$), or more than two ($n = 9$). Age was covaried. There were no significant effects of number of VCUGs, all $Fs(2, 42) \leq 1.47$.

In conclusion, there were clear age differences in memory performance, with older children providing more correct information and making fewer errors of commission and omission to both specific and misleading questions. The most marked differences in accuracy were between 3- to 4-year-olds and the two older age groups. The 5- and 6-year-olds made fewer correct responses than 7- to 10-year-olds, but they did not usually make significantly more incorrect responses. There were no clear effects of repeated VCUGs on memory performance.

Experiencing multiple VCUGs was associated with adverse emotional consequences, however. Correlational analyses revealed that children who experienced more than one VCUG displayed more negative affect following the VCUG test. Specifically, with age partialled, there was a significant correlation between number of VCUGs and parental report that the child expressed fear of the VCUG test, $r = .44, p < .01$, and embarrassment about it, $r = .50, p < .001$. Additionally, parents of children who had more than one past VCUG were somewhat more likely to indicate that their children cried about their most recent VCUG test since its occurrence, $r = .29, p = .057$.

*Mothers' Interaction with Their Children*

We predicted that parent–child discussion and maternal support might affect children's accuracy. These possibilities were explored through correlational analyses, with age statistically controlled. Results indicated, interestingly, that parent–child interaction did not predict correct answers but did predict incorrect answers children provided on the memory test (see Table 2).

Mothers who did not sympathetically talk to or physically comfort their children (e.g., did not hug them) after the VCUG test had children who provided

TABLE 2
Correlations between Measures of Children's Memory Performance and Mothers' Reactions to the Child Since the VCUG Test, with Child's Age Partialled ($n = 42$)

| | Discussed VCUG with child | Explained VCUG to child | Asked child questions about VCUG | Had no time to attend to child | Sympathetically talked to child | Physically comforted child |
|---|---|---|---|---|---|---|
| Free recall correct | .03 | −.09 | .06 | −.11 | .12 | −.11 |
| Free recall incorrect | −.11 | −.21 | −.16 | .12 | −.39** | −.43** |
| Free recall don't know | −.14 | −.11 | −.24 | .04 | .11 | .14 |
| Specific correct | −.04 | −.15 | −.04 | −.24 | .15 | .08 |
| Specific commission | −.05 | .11 | −.01 | .22 | .06 | .00 |
| Specific omission | −.20 | −.22 | .11 | .48** | −.28* | −.24 |
| Specific don't know | .11 | .18 | −.06 | −.07 | −.05 | −.03 |
| Misleading correct | .25 | −.01 | .10 | −.29* | .14 | .19 |
| Misleading commission | −.33** | −.07 | −.06 | .30** | −.03 | −.29** |
| Misleading omission | −.33** | −.32** | −.18 | −.38** | −.26* | −.29* |
| Misleading don't know | .16 | .28* | −.10 | −.12 | .10 | .15 |
| Open-ended correct units | .03 | −.05 | −.17 | −.05 | .14 | .12 |
| Open-ended incorrect units | .09 | .05 | .12 | .20 | .16 | .01 |
| Open-ended don't know | .11 | .26* | .11 | .05 | .06 | −.05 |

* $p < .10$.
** $p \leq .05$.
*** $p < .01$.
Two-tailed tests.

significantly more units of incorrect information during free recall. Failing to physically comfort the child was associated with increased commission errors to misleading questions. Additionally, having no time to attend to the child was associated with a significantly greater proportion of omission errors to the specific questions and to the misleading questions, and a significant increase in commission errors to misleading questions.

As can also be seen in Table 2, not discussing and not explaining the VCUG test to children were associated with more omission errors to the misleading questions, indicating greater suggestibility (e.g., giving the answer "no" in response to the question "While you were in the room getting the medical test, a nurse didn't come into that room, did she?"). Not discussing the VCUG exam with the child was also related to the child making a greater proportion of commission errors to misleading questions. Thus, inaccurate responses were associated with having a nonsupportive mother who, after the VCUG test, did not talk to the child, spent little time attending to the child's reactions, and failed to explain the procedure to the child. (Mothers who reported that, after the VCUG procedure, they discussed the VCUG with their children also tended to be the ones who explained the procedure to the child, talked sympathetically to the child, asked the child questions, and physically comforted the child, all $r$'s $\geq$ .31, $p <$ .05, with age partialled.)

The only indication that the mother–child interaction influenced memory accuracy was a correlation that approached significance: Mothers who reported that they had no time to attend to their child had children who produced fewer correct responses to the misleading questions.

In summary, mothers' self-reports of their post-VCUG interactions with their children, while not predicting memory accuracy, did predict memory inaccuracy. Discussing the VCUG test and having time to attend to the children's reactions decreased memory errors and suggestibility.

### Children's Reactions after the VCUG Test

We were also interested in examining whether children's understanding of the VCUG test and their emotional reactions after the VCUG test predicted their memory performance. Several significant predictors of children's accuracy were uncovered (see Table 3).

Whether or not children understood the VCUG test predicted accuracy. Again based on parent report, children who seemed to have understood the medical procedure were more correct in response to misleading questions; they also evidenced a lower proportion of "don't know" responses[4] and a somewhat higher proportion of correct responses to specific questions. These children also made fewer omission errors to specific questions and fewer commission errors to misleading questions. (Children who reportedly understood the procedure tended to have mothers who talked sympathetically to their children about the VCUG after it occurred, $r = .41, p < .01$.) In addition, children who expressed concern about the medical results of the VCUG test—perhaps an indication that they understood that the results had implications for them—provided more units of correct information in response to open-ended questions and a higher proportion of correct answers to the misleading questions. In contrast, children's tendency to ask questions about the test was associated both with greater accuracy and inaccuracy. Children who asked questions tended to be accurate in response to the initial free recall questions but then to become more incorrect once questioning began. Specifically, the child asking questions was positively correlated with a greater number of correct units of information in free recall but also positively associated

---

[4]"Don't know" responses included children's failure to respond at all to the question even when it was repeated or when children changed the subject (asked "Where's my mom?") and refused to answer.

TABLE 3
Correlations between Measures of Children's Memory Performance and Parents' Indications of Children's Reactions Since the VCUG Test, with Age Partialled ($n$ = 41 to 42)

| | Child seems to have understood | Child asked questions about VCUG | Child concerned with results | Child proud of enduring VCUG | Child seems embarrassed |
|---|---|---|---|---|---|
| Free recall correct | .22 | .29** | .21 | .33** | −.30** |
| Free recall incorrect | −.17 | .01 | −.08 | −.15 | −.06 |
| Free recall don't know | .10 | −.14 | −.13 | −.03 | .11 |
| Specific correct | .25* | .14 | .18 | .25* | −.13 |
| Specific commission | −.15 | .17 | −.07 | −.32** | .14 |
| Specific omission | −.34** | −.05 | −.19 | −.23 | −.07 |
| Specific don't know | −.06 | −.14 | −.11 | .01 | .05 |
| Misleading correct | .36** | .06 | .34** | .12 | −.15 |
| Misleading commission | −.49*** | .04 | −.12 | .02 | .01 |
| Misleading omission | −.24 | −.03 | −.25 | −.11 | −.04 |
| Misleading don't know | .17 | .00 | −.14 | −.07 | .22 |
| Open-ended correct units | .12 | .07 | .38** | .12 | −.26* |
| Open-ended incorrect units | −.03 | .35** | .12 | −.10 | −.18 |
| Open-ended don't know | −.03 | −.12 | −.20 | −.07 | .19 |

| | Child has cried about VCUG | Child has acted sad since VCUG | Child has reenacted VCUG in play | Child concerned with touch | Child had nightmares about VCUG |
|---|---|---|---|---|---|
| Free recall correct | .19 | .36** | .19 | .11 | .03 |
| Free recall incorrect | −.17 | −.12 | −.04 | −.03 | −.14 |
| Free recall don't know | −.29** | −.31** | −.23 | −.19 | .06 |
| Specific correct | .26* | .26* | .15 | .00 | .07 |
| Specific commission | .19 | .30** | .43*** | .25 | .37** |
| Specific omission | −.02 | −.02 | −.03 | .08 | .07 |
| Specific don't know | −.30** | −.35** | −.28* | −.13 | −.24 |

TABLE 3—*Continued*

| | Child has cried about VCUG | Child has acted sad since VCUG | Child has reenacted VCUG in play | Child concerned with touch | Child had nightmares about VCUG |
|---|---|---|---|---|---|
| Misleading correct | .07 | .12 | .02 | −.09 | .12 |
| Misleading commission | .20 | .11 | .33** | .32** | .07 |
| Misleading omission | .07 | .00 | −.12 | .01 | .03 |
| Misleading don't know | −.24 | −.17 | −.18 | −.11 | −.19 |
| Open-ended correct units | .21 | .33** | .22 | .28* | .31** |
| Open-ended incorrect units | .15 | .25* | .42*** | .17 | .33** |
| Open-ended don't know | −.32** | −.25 | −.30** | −.21 | −.21 |

$* \ p < .10.$
$** \ p \le .05.$
$*** \ p < .01.$
Two-tailed tests.

with incorrect units of information in response to open-ended questions. Perhaps children who asked questions had only a partial understanding of the VCUG test. What they could recount on their own tended to be accurate, but their incomplete understanding resulted in more errors later in the memory test when they were asked such questions as, "What exactly did they do to your [private parts] when they did that medical test?"

As can be seen in Table 3, children's emotional reactions to the VCUG test were also correlated with memory performance. Expression of positive emotions was related to accuracy. Specifically, children who felt proud of themselves for undergoing the VCUG test and were not embarrassed provided more units of correct information in free recall, and children who felt proud made fewer commission errors to specific questions. Perhaps these children were more willing to talk freely about the VCUG exam. In contrast, parents who indicated that their children cried about the VCUG exam well after it occurred had children who were significantly less likely to say "don't know" in response to free recall, specific, and open-ended questions. However, the meaning of this pattern is unclear given that having cried was not significantly associated with greater accuracy or inaccuracy.

Surprisingly, according to parental report, children's expression of sadness was associated both with greater accuracy and inaccuracy. Like the children who asked questions, children who expressed sadness tended to be accurate in response to the initial free recall questions but then to become more incorrect once direct questioning began (expressing sadness and asking questions were positively related, $r = .36$, $p < .025$). Specifically, expression of sadness was positively correlated with number of correct units of information provided to the free recall and open-ended questions. However, expression of sadness was also positively correlated with commission errors, and inversely related to "don't know" responses, to specific questions. We can speculate that for children who felt sad, reinstatement of that emotion during the questioning negatively affected their performance, perhaps in addition to the adverse influence of not fully understanding the VCUG test. These children apparently were willing to talk about the VCUG experience but included inaccurate as well as accurate information. As suggested by previous research (e.g., Goodman & Reed, 1986), the more a person says, the more likely the person is to provide correct and incorrect information.

Children who had symptoms that are often associated with PTSD (i.e., nightmares, reenactment in play, trauma specific fears) as defined in the *Diagnostic and Statistical Manual of Mental Disorders (3rd ed)* (American Psychiatric Association, 1987), tended to be more inaccurate (see Table 3). Although only four children reportedly reenacted the VCUG exam in play either with themselves, friends, adults, or dolls, these children made significantly more commission errors to specific questions and misleading questions and provided a greater number of incorrect responses and fewer "don't know" responses to open-ended questions than children who did not reenact the exam. The five children who were more concerned after the VCUG exam about being touched (e.g., about genital touch), which could be considered a trauma specific fear, made significantly more commission errors to misleading questions than children who did not reveal such concerns. Only four children were reported to have experienced nightmares about the VCUG test, but having nightmares was significantly associated with commission errors to specific questions and positively correlated with total units incorrect to open-ended questions. However, it was associated with total units correct to the latter questions as well. Perhaps children who displayed more adverse symptoms following the VCUG test were more motivated and willing to talk about what happened and, like the children who were sad, ended up providing more correct and more incorrect information. (Children who reenacted the event tended to have nightmares, $r = .45$, to be concerned about touch following the exam, $r = .27$, $p < .10$, to have expressed sadness, $r = .50$, $p < .01$, and to have cried after the VCUG test, $r = .38$, $p < .05$.)

Although memory performance was sporadically correlated with measures of stress during the VCUG test ($r$'s ranged from $-.37$ to $.18$), the correlations reported above did not change substantially when stress level during the VCUG test was statistically controlled.

*Regression Analyses*

We computed regression analyses to determine predictors of children's free recall performance and their suggestibility. Free recall was of particular interest because it assessed children's ability and willingness to recount the VCUG procedure with little prompting, and suggestibility was of special interest because of its relevance to children's testimony.

First, we computed regression equations predicting units of correct information provided in free recall from the post-VCUG child reaction variables that significantly correlated with free recall accuracy. Post-VCUG mother reaction variables were not included because they failed to correlate significantly with free recall accuracy. Using hierarchical regression, age was entered first and resulted in a Beta of .50, $p < .001$, and an $R^2$ change of .25, $p < .001$, $F(1, 43) = 14.53$, $p < .001$. On the second step, when the child reaction variables were entered, the $R^2$ change was .21, $p < .01$, $F(5, 39) = 6.78$, $p < .001$. The only significant or nearly significant predictors to emerge were "child has acted sad since the VCUG exam," Beta = .25, $p = .05$, and "child has seemed embarrassed since the VCUG exam," Beta = $-.28$, $p = .07$. Thus, child sadness after the VCUG exam was associated with more correct information in free recall, whereas child embarrassment was associated, at least to some degree, with less correct information in free recall.

Hierarchical regression was also conducted to examine predictors of suggestibility as indexed by commission errors to misleading questions. For predictors, we included all post-VCUG child and mother reaction variables that significantly correlated with commission errors. Age was entered by itself on the first step and, as expected, significantly predicted commission errors: Beta = $-.59$, $R^2$ change = .35, $p < .001$, $F(1, 42) = 22.67$, $p < .001$. Three significant predictors of commission errors emerged on the second step: $R^2$ change = .32, $p < .001$, $F(7, 36) = 10.44$, $p < .001$. The three predictors were: "child seems to have understood the VCUG exam," Beta = $-.31$; "mom discussed VCUG exam with child," Beta = $-.24$; and "child has reenacted VCUG in play," Beta = .31, all $p$s $< .05$. These results indicate that children who understood the VCUG exam and whose mothers discussed the VCUG exam with them were less suggestible, whereas children who reenacted the VCUG in play were more suggestible.

A third hierarchical regression was performed to examine predictors of commission plus omission errors (total errors) to misleading questions, since in the present study both types of errors can be considered indices of suggestibility. Specifically, we computed regression equations predicting total errors to misleading questions from the post-VCUG child and mother reaction variables that significantly correlated with either commission or omission errors. Age was entered on the first step and was a significant predictor; Beta = $-.61$, $p < .001$, $R^2$ change = .37, $p < .001$, $F(1, 42) = 24.69$, $p < .001$. On the second step, when the child and mother reaction variables were entered, the $R^2$ change was .30, $p < .001$, $F(8, 35) = 8.81$, $p < .001$. The following predictors were significant: "mom discussed VCUG with the child," Beta = $-.23$, and "child seems to have understood the VCUG exam," Beta = $-.23$, both $p$'s $< .05$. In addition, "mom had no time to attend to the child" approached significance, Beta = .19, $p < .10$. Thus, this analysis confirms that children were less suggestible if, after children experienced the VCUG procedure, their mothers discussed it with them and they understood it. This analysis reveals that children were somewhat more suggestible if their mothers had no time to attend to them.

## Discussion

We examined children's memory for an invasive medical procedure involving painful genital contact. The strongest findings were age differences in memory performance. As expected, younger compared to older children recalled less about the experience, answered fewer questions correctly, and made more errors. These findings held whether the children experienced only one or multiple VCUGs; in general, repeatedly experiencing a VCUG test did not affect children's memory. Instead, age was a much more powerful predictor of memory performance. Nevertheless, even when age was statistically controlled, important individual differences in children's memory for the stressful experience surfaced. These individual differences had mainly to do with children's understanding of the event, maternal communication and compassion, and children's emotional reactions.

Research on children's memory and suggestibility, whether concerning neutral or emotional events, consistently reveals age differences in performance, especially when 3- to 4-year-old children's memory reports are compared to those of older children. Most of the significant age differences in our study resulted from inferior performance by the youngest children; a mere increase in age to 5- to 6-years was associated with significantly greater accuracy and greater resistance to suggestion. The fact that age differences in memory emerged for children experiencing the VCUG test for the first time (a fairly novel experience) could be interpreted as a consequence of cognitive development rather than specific "knowledge base"; however, older children also tend to have more general experience with doctors and medical procedures, affording them more elaborate, relevant knowledge. Both advanced cognitive development and greater knowledge may contribute to age differences in memory. Both would be expected, for example, to influence a child's understanding of an event. In our study, even with age controlled, there were differences in children's understanding of the VCUG test, as reported by their parents, that were associated with memory: Children who understood the VCUG test made fewer memory errors. Children's inclination to ask their parents questions about the VCUG test was associated with greater accuracy in free recall but not in response to open-ended questions; perhaps children who had to ask questions had not received an adequate explanation and still failed to sufficiently understand the procedure. Lack of understanding (e.g., absence of an organizing framework) to interpret experience has detrimental effects on memory, even for adults (Bransford & Johnson, 1972). Our results suggest that children who lack adequate understanding of a stressful experience may have less accurate memories of it.

Repetition of the VCUG test did not significantly hinder or benefit memory. Our results do not support the prediction that children develop spot memories or amnesia for repeated or prolonged stressful events (Terr, 1991). In fact, a number of the children who had endured VCUG tests in the past had vivid and accurate memories of the particular experience we studied. For example, in response to the free recall question, one child who had three VCUGs said, "I had a catheter, and they, and they took pictures of me. And they, and you see in their, and in their big TV, laying on the table first. After they put it in they put water in my bladder. So I had to go to the bathroom. That's what they always do." To translate, this child accurately recounted being catheterized, having X-ray pictures taken, and seeing the X-ray images on the doctor's monitor (the doctor pointed out the image of the child's bladder and kidneys on a monitor screen, which was located near the child's head). This child also accurately remembered his bladder being filled with fluid and having to void. His memory may have been supported by, and in part may have reflected, a VCUG "script." Children who experienced only one VCUG and who were thus presumably relying more exclusively on episodic memory could also often recount details of the event. For example, in free recall, a 7-year-old girl who had experienced her first VCUG said, "It hurted. They stuck a tube up me. They took X-rays. I seen the inside of my kidney."

However, not all children were able to recount in detail what had occurred. Some children failed to provide any relevant information in free recall. Furthermore, in response to the free recall question and prompts, a few children even denied that they experienced the medical test. But such reactions were more closely associated with age than with repetition of the event. All children were able to answer correctly at least some of the directive questions about their VCUG experience.

Nonetheless, there was a hint in our data that age and repetition of a stressful experience might interact to influence accuracy. Younger children who endured a greater number of VCUGs evidenced somewhat more suggestibility than younger children who endured only one VCUG, whereas the opposite trend was found for older children. This pattern may reflect younger children's greater merging of repeated events compared with older children's ability to keep such events separated in memory (Farrar & Goodman, 1992).

However, for a number of reasons our results concerning the effects on memory of repetition must be treated cautiously. Because our sample size was relatively small, we may have lacked sufficient statistical power to detect differences. For obvious ethical reasons, we could not randomly assign children to number-of-VCUG groups; therefore, variables not accounted for in our study could be responsible for the one trend we detected. Moreover, the findings might differ for another type of traumatic event, for greater repetitions of the VCUG test, or for more highly stressful experiences. For example, the event we investigated did not generally seem to be interpreted by the children as life-threatening. (Although one boy in our study when first placed on the examination table asked if he was going to be killed, his parent and the hospital staff quickly assured him that he would not be injured.)

The age effects we uncovered were expected. Mere repetition alone did not seem to inhibit memory. What other factors might have contributed to accurate versus inaccurate memories? One factor was parent-child interaction about the VCUG. Correlational analyses indicated that lack of communication and emotional support predicted the inaccuracy of children's memory of the VCUG test, particularly their free recall responses and suggestibility. Exploratory regression analyses indicated that the mothers' reactions were especially related to children's suggestibility. From this analysis, the strongest predictor to emerge was whether or not mothers discussed the VCUG exam with their children. Another predictor also concerned maternal behavior; higher suggestibility was associated with having a mother with no time to attend to the child (although this relation only approached significance).

Several interpretations of these effects are possible. For example, it may be that parents who do not communicate with or take time to attend to their children do not help correct the children's misunderstandings of what occurred. Alternatively, findings from previous research indicate that children who are more intimidated or eager to please adults tend to be more suggestible (e.g., Clarke-Stewart, Thompson, & Lepore, 1989; Goodman & Reed, 1986). Perhaps children in the present study whose parents did not talk or attend to their children were more intimidated or needy of attention, and thus more suggestible, in an interview setting with an unfamiliar adult. Or children with less communicative and less supportive parents may evidence more general cognitive deficits that affected their memory performance during our interview. In any case, parent discussion and attention to children's needs may be vital influences on children's memory and suggestibility about traumatic events. Interestingly, our pattern of results is consistent with Tessler's and Nelson's (this issue) conclusions regarding the importance of maternal conversation for young children's retention of events and Williams's (personal communication, May, 1994) finding that lack of maternal support was associated with forgetting of childhood sexual abuse. Taken together, the results of these studies implicate parental communication and emotional support as important influences on accurate memory for stressful events experienced in childhood.

However, children's own emotional reactions also seemed to drive their recollections. Correlational analyses revealed that children who were proud of undergoing the medical test were more accurate and less inaccurate; while positive emotion may have affected memory directly (e.g., assuaging the desire to block the experience from memory), it is also possible that a sense of pride motivated children to tell us about what happened and to do so accurately. Being sad after the VCUG exam was also associated with greater accuracy, particularly on free recall and open-ended questions. However, commission errors to specific questions were also associated with being sad. These children appeared to be willing to talk about the VCUG test, but had a more difficult time answering specific questions correctly. A regression analysis confirmed the positive relation between children who were sad after the VCUG test and correct free recall. Interestingly, embarrassment had the opposite effect: Embarrassment about the VCUG test was associated with mention of less correct information in free recall. This latter finding is consistent with those from a study by Saywitz, Goodman, Nicholas, and Moan (1991) in indicating that children who are embarrassed are hesitant to disclose details about genital touch.

Few studies have examined the relation between children's memory and emotional responses often associated with PTSD. In our study, some children exhibited reenactment, had nightmares, and were concerned about being touched (including about genital touch), which are symptoms often associated with PTSD. Interestingly, these children were not noticeably more stressed than other children during the VCUG (e.g., as indicated by nonsignificant correlations between stress ratings during the VCUG and reenactment later). As evidenced by correlational analyses, children who displayed PTSD-like symptoms were particularly likely to make commission errors to the specific and open-ended questions. Furthermore, multiple regression revealed that reenactment of the VCUG exam was a significant predictor of children's suggestibility. Although these findings are of considerable interest, they must be interpreted with caution because relatively few children in our sample exhibited symptoms such as nightmares. Replication of these findings is needed.

Anecdotally, what stood out in many children's reports was that the medical procedure hurt. In free recall, one 6½-year-old child said, "It hurt and it stung, and it did, too, and it hurt real bad." The interviewer then asked, "Do you remember anything else?" and the child responded, "I forgot." This child's report seemed to indicate an internal focus on emotions, to use Yuille and Toolstrup's (1992) term. An internal focus might lead to a less complete memory of the external event and better memory for internal feelings. For example, one boy in our study, when asked "What happened?" said, "I don't know because I cried." However, it is also possible that these children just did not want to talk about what happened.

In summary, our study suggests that although age influences children's memory for traumatic events, several other factors are important as well, including factors that have been largely overlooked. Comprehension of the event, maternal attention and compassion, parent–child communication, and children's specific emotional reactions appear to be related to children's memory of a stressful event, at least one involving painful and invasive genital contact. However, because of the relatively small number of children included in our study and the relatively large number of correlations calculated, several of our results concerning mother and child reaction variables need to be replicated before they can be relied on with confidence.

Although our research was inspired in part by a desire to understand children's memory for a stressful experience involving their genitals, a number of caveats should be heeded in attempts to generalize our findings to children's memory for acts of victimization such as sexual abuse. Medical procedures are socially sanctioned events; the VCUG test was not as shrouded in secrecy as is much sexual violation. Moreover, even though some of the children in our study endured as many as six VCUGs, a child may experience even more frequent incidents of sexual abuse. Whereas much of the discomfort associated with the VCUG test is felt immediately, some forms of sexual abuse may not be frightening or painful when they occur but become traumatic only much later when the full meaning of the event is understood. Moreover, the children in our study were questioned after relatively brief intervals and were interviewed only once. Despite these differences, the VCUG test is in some ways like a sexual assault, even like a rape—it involves genital contact and physical penetration, it is committed against children's will, it is embarrassing for many children, and it hurts. If one were tempted to generalize our findings to actual cases, a number of such differences and similarities between the VCUG test and vitimization experiences should be considered.

Many unexplored questions about children's memory for traumatic events are raised by our research. For example, what will children remember about the VCUG procedure 5, 10, or 20 years from now? Will any of the children completely lose their memory of the VCUG test over time? If so, will it simply be the youngest children who forget or will it be children whose parents failed to provide emotional support or did not help the child "process" the experience? Will the children with more inaccurate memories initially be more susceptible to false memory later on? In an attempt to answer these and related questions, we hope in future research to follow children over time and examine changes in their memories for this and other traumatic events. In this way, we may learn more about predictors of accurate and inaccurate memories—and perhaps even about repressed memories—of traumatic events experienced in childhood.

## ACKNOWLEDGMENTS

We gratefully acknowledge the research assistance of Ann E. Tobey and Debra Dorfman Botens, as well as Bridgette Doherty, Teresa Drost, Colleen Flanagan, Felicia Katz, Michelle Larro, Holly Orcutt, Michelle Schweitzer, Cheryl Shapiro, and April Smith. We also thank James Blascovich for first bringing the VCUG procedure to our attention and Phillip R. Shaver for editorial suggestions. Without the gracious and substantial aid of the staff of the Department of Radiology at Children's Hospital of Buffalo this study would not have been possible; we are particularly indebted to Connie Ryan and Diane Deck, head X-ray technicians. This research was supported in part by grants to Gail S. Goodman from the Baldy Center on Law and Social Policy at the State University of New York at Buffalo; the University of California, Davis Discretionary Research Fund; and the National Center on Child Abuse and Neglect.

## REFERENCES

American Psychiatric Association (1987). *Diagnostic and statistical manual of mental disorders* (3rd ed.). American Psychiatric Association: Washington, DC.

Bearison, D. J., & Pacifici, C. (1989). Children's event knowledge for cancer treatment. *Journal of Applied and Developmental Psychology,* **10,** 469–486.

Bohannon, N., & Symons, V. (1992). Flashbulb memories: Confidence, consistency, and quantity. In E. Winograd & U. Neisser (Eds.), *Affect and accuracy in recall* (pp. 65–94). New York: Cambridge Univ. Press.

Bretherton, I. (1993). From dialogue to internal working models: The co-construction of self in relationships. In C. Nelson (Ed.), *Memory and affect in development: Minnesota Symposium on Child Psychology* (Vol. 26, pp. 237–263). Hillsdale, NJ: Erlbaum.

Brainerd, C., & Reyna, V. (1991). Gist is the grist: Fuzzy-trace theory and the new intuitionism. *Developmental Review,* **10,** 3–47.

Bransford, J. D., & Johnson, M. D. (1972). Conceptual prerequisites for understanding: Some investigations of comprehension and recall. *Journal of Verbal Learning and Verbal Behavior,* **11,** 717–726.

Briere, J., & Conte, J. (1993). Self-reported amnesia for abuse in adults molested as children. *Journal of Traumatic Stress,* **6,** 21–31.

Bugenthol, D. B., Blue, J., Cortez, V., Fleck, K., & Rodriguez, A. (1992). Influences of witnessed affect on information processing in children. *Child Development,* **63,** 774–786.

Case, R. (1985). *Intellectual development.* New York: Academic Press.

Chi M. (1978). Knowledge structures and memory development. In R. Siegler (Ed.), *Children's thinking: What develops?* Hillsdale, NJ: Erlbaum.

Christianson, S. A. (1992). Emotional stress and eyewitness memory: A critical review. *Psychological Bulletin,* **112,** 284–309.

Clark-Stewart, A., Thompson, R., & Lepore, S. (1989, April). Manipulating children's testimony through interrogation. In G. Goodman (Chair), *Can children provide accurate eyewitness testi-*

*mony?* Symposium presented at the Meetings of the Society for Research in Child Development, Kansas City, MO.

Courtois, C. (1992). The memory retrieval process in incest survivor therapy. *Journal of Child Sexual Abuse,* **1,** 15–31.

Dickinson, E. (1890/1955). *The poems of Emily Dickinson.* Cambridge, MA: Harvard Univ. Press.

Farrar, M. J., & Goodman, G. S. (1992). Developmental differences in event memory. *Child Development,* **63,** 173–187.

Fischer, K. (1980). A theory of cognitive development: The control of hierarchies of skill. *Psychological Review,* **87,** 477–531.

Fivush, R. (1984). Learning about school: The development of kindergartners' school scripts. *Child Development,* **55,** 1697–1709.

Fivush, R. (1993). Developmental perspective on autobiographical recall. In G. S. Goodman & B. L. Bottoms (Eds.), *Child victims, child witnesses: Understanding and improving testimony* (pp. 1–24). New York: Guilford Press.

Flin, R., Boon, J., Knox, A., & Bull, R. (1992). The effects of a five month delay on children's and adults' eyewitness memory. *British Journal of Psychology,* **83,** 323–336.

Freud, S. (1915/1957). Repression. In J. Strachey (Ed.), *The standard edition of the complete psychological works of Sigmund Freud* (Vol. 14). London: Hogarth.

Goodman, G. S. (1993, March). Children's memory for stressful events: Theoretical and developmental considerations. In N. Stein (Chair), *Emotional events and memory.* Symposium presented at the Society for Research in Child Development, New Orleans, LA.

Goodman, G. S., & Aman, C. J. (1991). Children's use of anatomically detailed dolls to recount an event. *Child Development,* **61,** 1859–1871.

Goodman, G. S., Bottoms, B. L., Schwartz-Kenney, B. M., & Rudy, L. (1991). Childrens' testimony for a stressful event: Improving children's reports. *Journal of Narrative and Life History,* **1,** 69–99.

Goodman, G. S., Hirschman, J. E., Hepps, D., & Rudy L. (1991). Children's memory for stressful events. *Merrill-Palmer Quarterly,* **37,** 109–158.

Goodman, G. S., & Reed, R. S. (1986). Age differences in eyewitness testimony. *Law and Human Behavior,* **10,** 317–332.

Goodwin, J. (Ed.) (1993) *Rediscovering childhood trauma.* Washington, DC: American Psychiatric Press.

Gordon, B. N., Ornstein, P. A., Nida, R. E., Follmer, A., Crenshaw, M. C., & Albert, G. (1993). Does the use of dolls facilitate children's memory of visits to the doctor? *Applied Cognitive Psychology,* **7,** 459–474.

Herman, J. L., & Schatzow, E. (1987). Recovery and verification of memories of childhood sexual trauma. *Psychanalytic Psychology,* **4,** 1–14.

Howe, M., Courage, M. L., & Peterson, C. (1994). How can I remember when "I" wasn't there: Long-term retention of traumatic experiences and the emergence of the cognitive self. *Consciousness and Cognition,* **3,** 327–355.

Hudson J. A. (1990). The emergence of autobiographical memory in mother–child conversations. In R. Fivush & J. A. Hudson (Eds.), *Knowing and remembering in young children* (pp. 116–196). New York: Cambridge Univ. Press.

Hudson, J., & Fivush, R. (1987). As time goes by: Sixth graders remember a kindergarten experience. *Emory Cognition Project Report No. 13,* Emory University, Atlanta.

Kail R. (1990). *The development of memory in children* (3rd ed.). New York: Freeman.

Kobasigawa A. (1974). Utilization of retrieval cues by children in recall. *Child Development,* **45,** 127–134.

Lepore, S., & Sesco, B. (in press). Distorting children's reports and interpretations of events through suggestion. *Journal of Applied Psychology.*

Liwag, M. D., & Stein, N. L. (1993, March). *The effects of retrieval instructions on children's memory for emotion episodes.* Paper presented at the Society for Research in Child Development Meetings, New Orleans, LA.

Loftus, E. F., Polonsky, S., & Fullilove, M. T. (1994). Memories of child sexual abuse: Remembering and repressing. *Psychology of Women Quarterly, 18,* 67–84.

Main, M., Kaplan, N., & Cassidy, J. (1985). Security in infancy, childhood, and adulthood: A move to the level of representation. *Monographs of the Society for Research in Child Development,* **50** (1–2), 66–104.

Nader, K., Pynoos, R., Fairbanks, L., & Frederick C. (1990). Children's PTSD reactions one year after a sniper attack at their school. *American Journal of Psychiatry, 147,* 1526–1530.

Nader, K., Stuber, M., & Pynoos, R. (1991). Posttraumatic stress reactions in preschool children with catastrophic illness: Assessment and needs. *Comprehensive Mental Health Care, 1,* 223–238.

Nelson, K. (1986). *Event memory.* Hillsdale, NJ: Erlbaum.

Nelson, K. A., (1993). The psychological and social origins of autobiographical memory. *Psychological Science, 4,* 7–14.

Ornstein, P. A., & Naus, M. J. (1985). Effects of knowledge base on children's memory strategies. In H. W. Reese (Ed.), *Advances in child development and behavior* (Vol. 19). New York: Academic Press.

Ornstein, P., Baker-Ward, L., Gordon, B., & Merritt, K. (1993). Children's memory for medical procedures. In N. Stein (Chair), *Children's memory for emotional events.* Symposium presented at the Society for Research in Child Development Meetings, New Orleans, LA.

Peters, D. P. (1989, April). Stress and arousal effects on the child eyewitness. In C. Brainerd (Chair), *Children's ability to remember witnessed events: Theoretical and applied perspectives.* Paper presented at the Society for Research in Child Development, Kansas City, MO.

Pillemer, D. B., & White, S. (1989). Childhood events recalled by children and adults. *Advances in Child Development and Behavior, 21,* 297–340.

Price, D. W. W., & Goodman, G. S. (1990). Visiting the wizard: Children's memory of a recurring event. *Child Development, 61,* 664–680.

Pynoos, R. (1992). *A model of post-traumatic stress disorder and memory in children.* Paper presented at the Developmental Psychobiology Research Group Conference, Estes Park, CO.

Pynoos, R., & Nader, K. (1988). Children memory and proximity to violence. *Journal of the American Academy of Child and Adolescent Psychiatry, 27,* 567–572.

Rudy, L., & Goodman, G. S. (1991). Effects of participation on children's reports: Implications for children's testimony. *Developmental Psychology, 27,* 1–26.

Saywitz, K., Goodman, G. S., Nicholas, E., & Moan, S. (1991). Children's memories of physical examinations involving genital touch: Implications for reports of child sexual abuse. *Journal of Consulting and Clinical Psychology, 59,* 682–691.

Schactel, E. (1947). On memory and childhood amnesia. *Psychiatry, 10,* 1–26.

Steward, M. S. (1993). Understanding children's memories of medical procedures: "He didn't touch me and it didn't hurt!" In C. A. Nelson (Ed.), *Memory and affect in development: The Minnesota Symposia on Child Psychology* (pp. 171–225). Hillsdale, NJ: Erlbaum.

Stuber, M. L., Nader, K., Yasuda, P., Pynoos, R. S., & Cohen S. (1991). Stress responses after pediatric bone marrow transplantation: Preliminary results of a prospective longitudinal study. *Journal of the American Academy of Child and Adolescent Psychiatry, 30,* 952–957.

Terr, L. C. (1988). What happens to early memories of trauma? A study of twenty children under age five at the time of documented traumatic events. *Child and Adolescent Psychiatry, 27,* 96–104.

Terr, L. C. (1991). Childhood traumas: An outline and overview. *American Journal of Psychiatry,* **148,** 10–20.

Tobey, A., & Goodman, G. S. (1992). Children's eyewitness memory: Effects of participation and forensic context. *Child Abuse and Neglect, 16,* 779–796.

Usher, J. A., & Neisser, J. (1993). Childhood amnesia and the beginnings of memory for early life events. *Journal of Experimental Psychology: General, 122,* 155–165.

Vandermaas, M. O., Hess, T. M., & Baker-Ward, L. (1993). Does anxiety affect children's reports of memory for a stressful event? *Journal of Applied Psychology, 7,* 109–128.

Warren-Leubecker, A. (1991). The influence of stress and arousal on the child witness. In J. Doris (Ed.), *The suggestibility of children's recollections.* Washington, DC: American Psychological Association.

Warren, A., & Swartwood, J. (1992). Developmental issues in flashbulb memory research: Children recall the Challenger event. In E. Winograd & U. Neisser (Eds.), *Affect and accuracy in recall* (pp. 95–120). New York: Cambridge Univ. Press.

Williams, L. (1993, October). *Recall of childhood trauma: A prospective study of women's memories of child sexual abuse.* Paper presented at the Annual Meeting of the American Society of Criminology. Phoenix, AZ.

Yuille, J. C., & Tollstrup, P. A. (1992). A model of diverse effects of emotion on eyewitness memory. In S. A. Christianson (Ed.), *The handbook of emotion and memory: Research and theory* (pp. 202–216). Hillsdale, NJ: Erlbaum.

# Amnesia, Partial Amnesia, and Delayed Recall among Adult Survivors of Childhood Trauma

Mary R. Harvey[1] and Judith Lewis Herman

*The Cambridge Hospital Department of Psychiatry, Harvard Medical School,*
*1493 Cambridge Street, Cambridge, Massachusetts 02139*

Clinical experience suggests that adult survivors of childhood trauma arrive at their memories in a number of ways, with varying degrees of associated distress and uncertainty and, in some cases, after memory lapses of varying duration and extent. Among those patients who enter psychotherapy as a result of early abuse, three general patterns of traumatic recall are identified: (1) relatively continuous and complete recall of childhood abuse experiences coupled with changing interpretations (delayed understanding) of these experiences, (2) partial amnesia for abuse events, accompanied by a mixture of delayed recall and delayed understanding, and (3) delayed recall following a period of profound and pervasive amnesia. These patterns are represented by three composite clinical vignettes. Variations among them suggest that the phenomena underlying traumatic recall are continuous not dichotomous. Future research into the nature of traumatic memory should be informed by clinical observation.

## INTRODUCTION

The past 20 years have witnessed a profound transformation in public and professional awareness of violence in the lives of women and children. Today, an ample literature documents the high prevalence of sexual assault in our society and the extensiveness of childhood physical and sexual abuse (Russell, 1984, 1986; Wyatt, 1985; Finkelhor et al., 1990; Sorenson et al., 1987; National Victims Center, 1992). Media attention has ensured widespread public awareness of these issues. Victim advocacy has realized important improvements in the professional treatment of victims, and feminist activism has helped to secure significant legal reform (Koss & Harvey, 1991; Harvey & Herman, 1992). Many states, for example, now allow victims of childhood trauma to file charges once they have achieved majority age (see, e.g., Washington, 1989; Lofft v. Lofft, 1989) or have acquired new memories or new understandings of abuse experiences located in the distant past (e.g., Riley v. Pressnell, 1991; Munsey v. Kellett, 1992).

It is in the changing forensic context of newly secured victim rights that aggressive challenges to victim credibility have received renewed attention among researchers, clinicians, defense attorneys, and the general public. Recently, in a few highly publicized court cases child abusers have been convicted of crimes or held liable for damages for abuses committed in the distant past (e.g., California

This article is reprinted by permission from *Consciousness and Cognition*, Volume 3, pp. 295–306 (1994).

[1] To whom reprint requests should be addressed.

v. Franklin; Commonwealth of Massachusetts v. Porter). The successful prosecution of these cases, and the possibility of new litigation, has prompted defense attorneys and some academic investigators to question the accuracy, authenticity, and forensic legitimacy of child abuse claims brought forward by adult complainants.

Of particular concern to these investigators is the phenomenon of delayed recall of traumatic childhood events following a period of full or partial amnesia. Loftus (1993a, 1993b), for example, has speculated that most if indeed not all delayed memories of childhood trauma are confabulations inculcated by the suggestive power of self-help literature and the leading questions of naive or unscrupulous psychotherapists. Ofshe and Watters (1993) claim that the phenomenon of repressed memory simply does not exist and that delayed recollections of childhood trauma are fictions resulting from intense pressures placed on vulnerable patients by practitioners whom they label "recovered memory therapists."

The confabulation hypothesis has several major flaws. First, and most importantly, it overlooks the evidence from documented cases in which the reports of adults who remembered childhood abuse after a period of amnesia have been independently confirmed by abundant evidence (Commonwealth of Massachusetts v. Porter, 1993). Second, it fails to explain how individuals might be induced to reconcile the contradiction between newly acquired but fictitious memories of childhood trauma with prior (and presumably more accurate) memories of happy family life. Although the power of therapist suggestion is regularly invoked by proponents of the confabulation hypothesis, there is no evidence to suggest that psychotherapists have the degree of power and influence that would be required to produce this effect. Indeed, there is no empirical evidence to suggest that psychotherapy is a factor at all in the majority of cases of delayed recall.

In the absence of convincing theory or systematic empirical evidence, those who advance the confabulation hypothesis rest their argument on the appeal of anecdotal reports. Loftus (1993a, 1993b), for example, cites a small number of high profile forensic cases to posit a virtual epidemic of false memories and false allegations, which she attributes in turn to widespread psychotherapeutic manipulation and an apparently hypnotic potency of the self-help book *Courage to Heal* (Bass & Davis, 1988). Whatever research may ultimately reveal about the accuracy of traumatic recall and the authenticity of adult memories of childhood trauma, these generalizations go far beyond the reach of available data and cast a chill on serious scientific dialogue.

In fact, aberrations in memory are central to the description and diagnosis of traumatic disorders. Symptoms diagnostic of post-traumatic stress disorder (PTSD) include, for example: intrusive recollections of traumatic events, nightmares and waking state flashbacks in which salient aspects of the traumatic event are reexperienced, reenactment sensations, and both amnesia and hypermnesia. Like other PTSD symptoms, these disturbances of memory may be apparent immediately following the traumatic event or "after long periods of apparent adjustment" (American Psychiatric Association, 1987).

Epidemiological and clinical studies have documented a high prevalence of PTSD among sexually abused children and among adult survivors of childhood sexual abuse (National Victims Center, 1992; Rowan & Foy, 1993). In addition, early, prolonged and repeated abuse and abuse by a primary caretaker have been associated with a long-lasting traumatic syndrome (Browne & Finkelhor, 1986; Briere, 1984; Herman, 1992). Among survivors of severe and protracted childhood sexual abuse, this syndrome has been found to include severe disturbances of memory and consciousness and complex dissociative reactions (Putnam, 1985, 1990; Putnam, Post, Giuroff, Silberman, & Barban, 1983; Briere & Runtz, 1988; Briere & Conte, 1993; Chu & Dill, 1990; Goodwin, 1989; Herman, 1992).

Criticisms of clinical research associating amnestic phenomena and delayed recall with childhood trauma focus on the largely retrospective nature of these studies and on their reliance on largely unverifiable self-reports of childhood histories by the patients whose symptoms are being described. Herman and Schatzow (1987) found, however, that among a group of women incest survivors, recently remembered histories of childhood sexual abuse were, in fact, independently verifiable. In a recent prospective study, Williams (1993) found that 38% of 129 women subjects evidenced varying degrees of amnesia for child sexual abuse incidents that had been documented 17 years earlier.

It is our impression that amnesia, partial amnesia, and delayed recall are relatively common factors in the clinical presentations of adult survivors of childhood trauma. The majority of these individuals do not enter psychotherapy solely or even primarily to acquire memories of an unremembered but suspected abuse history, however, but for help in understanding and managing the distress associated with memories already acquired. Some are hoping to contain a flood of newly intrusive and unwelcome remembrances; some are wanting to understand better the psychological impact of histories that are at least partially recalled; and some are wanting to give context, comprehensibility, and meaning to a bizarre and troubling assortment of relatively new and longer-standing remembrances. Virtually all bring with them into psychotherapy a combination of long-remembered and more recently recalled material.

The position taken in this paper is twofold: *first* that traumatic remembrance (including delayed recall) is not an all-or-none phenomenon, but a complex and continuous one; and, *second* that clinical observation is a reasonable starting point for scientific inquiry into the nature of traumatic memory. One aim of this paper is simply to describe the variations in traumatic recall that are frequently witnessed in clinical settings by ethical, observant, and reliable psychotherapists. Another is to counter an increasingly adversarial relationship between memory researchers who are relatively less familiar with clinical realities than they might be and clinicians who feel placed on the defensive by sweeping accusations of professional malfeasance. Toward these ends, this paper presents and discusses composite clinical vignettes drawn from adult survivors of childhood trauma currently being treated in our clinic.

## ADULT REMEMBRANCES OF CHILDHOOD TRAUMA:
## THREE CASE VIGNETTES

Each year the client population served by The Cambridge Hospital Victims of Violence (VOV) Program includes a number of adults (62 in 1993) who report at least one instance of sexual or physical abuse before age 18. Among these patients, three general patterns of traumatic remembrance can be identified: (1) relatively continuous and complete recall of childhood abuse experiences coupled with changing interpretations (delayed understanding) of these experiences, (2) partial amnesia for abuse events, accompanied by a mixture of delayed recall and delayed understanding, and (3) delayed recall following a period of profound and pervasive amnesia. These patterns are illustrated by clinical vignettes drawn from the intake interviews and clinical records of several patients.

### Vignette Number 1: Continuous Recall, Delayed Understanding

Carol B. is a 25-year-old single woman. She lives with two roommates in an apartment in Cambridge and is enrolled as a graduate student in a nearby university.

*Abuse history.* Carol's history includes a relatively benign childhood until age 11 when her parents divorced. From that time, her father showed little interest in her. When Carol was 13 her maternal uncle visited the family and for a short time became her primary adult companion. She remembers that she adored him and thought of him as her "best friend." Carol also recalls that her uncle began molesting her almost immediately. "At first, I didn't know what was going on. I really liked him. I couldn't believe he would hurt me. By the time I did get it, I felt responsible—like it was something I was doing." The abuse occurred as often as twice a week and escalated when she was 14 to include a single incident of vaginal intercourse. It ended shortly thereafter when her uncle moved away. Carol has seen him only intermittently since then. She never disclosed the abuse, and never really thought of it as abuse: "I just felt ashamed and relieved that he was gone."

*Continuity of recall/precipitants to delayed recall and delayed understanding.* At age 25, Carol reports that she "never forgot" her uncle's abuse, but that she did succeed in not thinking about it for many years. Recently, a number of events have caused her to recall and become increasingly preoccupied with the past. A few months ago, Carol ended a relationship with a man she had hoped to get closer to. Since then, she has wondered and worried about her seeming inability to tolerate sexual intimacy and closeness. Then, last month she learned from her mother that her uncle had returned to the area and was asking about her. Carol's mother wants her to attend a family reunion at which her uncle will be a guest of honor. Carol reports becoming "undone" by this news, feeling momentarily terrified and struggling to keep her distress to herself.

*Qualitative features of traumatic recall.* Carol's response to these events is shocking to her. She feels depressed, intensely anxious, is unable to concentrate, and has moments of "real rage." Her volatile emotional state and her preoccupation with memories of the abuse have caused Carol to review and rethink the past. Today, she labels the experience abuse and holds her uncle responsible. She wonders if the rape is implicated in her difficulties with intimacy and sexuality. She thinks about disclosing the abuse to her mother, but feels overwhelmed when she imagines doing so. She does not want to see her uncle, nor does she want to explain her reactions to her family.

*Therapy goals/memory assessments.* At this point, Carol is seeking psychotherapy to help her understand and repair the impact of the past on her current and future life. Her aims are to contain and stabilize her runaway emotions, to make new sense of the past, and to think through the issue of disclosure. At this point, Carol feels no need to uncover additional memories and no need to confirm the memories she has. She judges her memories of the past to be "reasonably complete" and generally accurate. "I may not be able to tell you the exact day and date, but I do know what grade I was in, where we were, and what I was wearing the day he raped me."

## Vignette Number 2: Partial Amnesia, Delayed Recall, and Delayed Understanding

Sarah G. is a 34-year-old woman currently separated from her husband of 11 years, a sporadically violent man with a long history (like herself) of polysubstance abuse. She is the mother of a 9-year-old daughter, Tracy. She and her daughter are living temporarily with a friend who is about to leave the area. Sarah has been sober for 11 months.

*Abuse history.* Sarah describes herself as someone who "always gets involved with the wrong guy." She reports a series of abusive relationships beginning in junior high, and a history of alcohol abuse beginning in early adolescence. Sarah remembers growing up in a "sometimes close, sometimes crazy and sometimes violent home" in which "all hell could break loose if mom and dad were drinking." Sarah has "always known" that she was sexually abused by her oldest brother. Recently, however, she has begun to think more about the abuse and has recalled "stuff I'd really forgotten about." The abuse began after Sarah's brother joined the army, on his first visit home. It occurred repeatedly thereafter, whenever he was home on leave. The abuse ended when Sarah was "12 or 13" and began menstruating. "There was never any explanation. It just stopped. It was like it had never happened."

*Continuity of recall/precipitants to delayed recall and delayed understanding.* Sarah's recollections of childhood are complex. She has relatively detailed recall for events up to age 8 or 9 but "real blank spaces after that." She also reports relatively complete recall from age 12 to age 15. Her memory after age 15 is compromised by her substance abuse but has improved with sobriety. And she has long-remembered aspects of her brother's abuse. Recently, however, Sarah learned that she was "only 9 years old" on her brother's first visit home. "Somehow, I thought I was older." Other details of the abuse had been forgotten, too. For example, Sarah remembers, now, that the abuse began on a night when her parents were drunk and fighting with one another. She was hiding in her room, frightened by the yelling and the violence. "He came into my room, held me, made me feel safe." On that night and other nights, her brother would first soothe and comfort her and then plead with her to "be nice to him, too." "Later, he would act like he was mad and it was my fault."

Sarah's memories appear to have been triggered by a series of events: First, when Sarah first left her marriage, she and her daughter stayed briefly with

Sarah's parents—reentering the home where the abuse took place. It was here that she learned from her mother how old she was when her brother joined the military. Second, Sarah's daughter recently had her ninth birthday, and "I suddenly saw how little 9 is." And, finally, Sarah hears in her husband's appeals for reconciliation "the same words, the same tone of voice" that her brother would use to cajole her into complying with his sexual demands.

*Qualitative features of traumatic recall.* Sarah's clinical presentation is complex. On the one hand, she is able to recall in great detail (but with little in the way of affect) much of the violence that characterized her marriage and other relationships. She'd thought she had fairly complete recall of her childhood, too, and believed that she remembered her brother's abuse "fairly well." Now, she realizes that in fact she had forgotten altogether when and how it began and that she "lost" parts of her childhood from age 8 or 9 to age 12. Her newer memories are accompanied by considerable distress: intrusive recollections, disrupted sleep, feelings of sadness and despair, low self-esteem, and, in her words, "shock." "How can you just forget stuff like this?"

*Therapy goals/memory assessments.* Sarah is less concerned with her memories of past abuse than she is with her history of involvement in abusive relationships and with the task of protecting herself, her daughter, and her sobriety in the future. As she recalls her brother's abuse and reexamines the often violent and alcoholic home in which the abuse occurred, she wants "to make it different for Tracy." Sarah is hoping that psychotherapy will help her maintain her own and Tracy's safety and acquire the self-confidence she requires. She believes that with sobriety, more memories of her childhood will emerge. Her goal is to be "ready to handle whatever comes up." She has not sought to confirm her memories but has learned from an older sister that her brother once "got in trouble" for molesting a cousin.

### Vignette Number 3: Profound Amnesia and Delayed Recall

Emily B. is a 45-year-old married woman. She and her husband recently relocated to the Boston area where she'd grown up. Emily has two siblings and an aging paternal aunt in this area. She was referred to psychotherapy by a local psychiatric emergency service, where she appeared in a state of confusion and despair following a reunion with her sister, whom she had not seen for many years.

*Abuse history.* Emily is the youngest of three children raised by their father and two paternal aunts following their mother's untimely death when Emily was 4 years old. The aunts were extraordinarily severe in their approach to punishment and discipline. Emily recalls that she and her siblings were frequently beaten with belts and "other objects," locked in closets, blindfolded for long periods of time, deprived of food, and subjected to verbal assaults and humiliation. Their father did not engage in this abuse, but he also did not protect them. At some point in her childhood—"maybe I was 10 or 11, but maybe I was younger than that"—Emily's father began molesting her. Once the abuse began, it escalated to include oral, anal, and vaginal penetration and by the time she was 13, it assumed violent and sadistic proportions. As far as Emily knows now, the abuse continued until she ran away at age "15 or 16."

*Continuity of recall/precipitants to delayed recall.* When Emily left home, she cut off all contact with her family. By the time she met and married her husband, she had "completely forgotten" the sexual abuse. "I never forgot the beatings, though." Among the major precipitants to Emily's remembrance of the sexual abuse are her return to the geographic area in which she was raised and her renewed contact with an older sister. It was while visiting this sister and hearing "one family horror story after another" that Emily began feeling extremely agitated and fearful. That night, she was awakened with terrifying dreams and for several days afterward was flooded with memories of her father's abuse. Since then, Emily has spent a great deal of time with her sister and has confirmed many of her new memories. She has learned that her sister and brother were also sexually abused by their father.

*Qualitative features of traumatic remembrance.* Emily's remembrance of the cruelty which she and her siblings endured at the hands of their paternal aunts is qualitatively different from her memories of sexual abuse by her father. The memories of physical abuse have long formed a part of Emily's autobiographical narrative. She can recall when it began, how she felt at the time, how the children tried to "stick together," and how determined she was "to get away." When she discusses this abuse, she does so with sadness, but also with distance. It is in the past. Her strongest feelings are for the memories of her mother's illness and death—these are events that ushered in the abuse that was to follow.

Emily's memories of sexual abuse are quite different. She feels no distance from those memories. She can suddenly feel frightened and overwhelmed. She has awakened from dreams to experience herself as a child again and her husband as the personification of her father. She can recall intricate details of the abuse ("like how he smelled and how he breathed") and yet cannot recall what led to what. She does remember now that as a child she would pretend to be asleep when her father entered her room. "I think I got good at it. I think I learned to believe it was a dream."

*Therapy goals/memory assessments.* Emily is currently overwhelmed by her memories. She is aware now of her extraordinary ability to "put things away," "to forget," and of the fact that these new memories are leaving her feeling "very young, very afraid." Emily's goals in therapy are "first of all to calm down," and later, "to try and make sense of things." She is unable to assess the completeness of her memories, is unsure about their accuracy, and at times doubts her own reality. She is unclear, still, about when and how her father's abuse began. Indeed, she is fearful that additional memories will simply cause her more distress, and she has no desire to seek additional confirmation of her memories. In fact, she tries hard, but without success, to avoid thinking about the past.

## DISCUSSION

The clinical materials from which these vignettes were compiled suggest that adult survivors of childhood trauma arrive at their remembrances in a number of

ways. They differ from one another on many dimensions, including the age at
which the remembered events first occurred, the frequency, duration, chronicity,
and degree of violence and violation which attended these events, the social or
ecological context in which the abuse occurred and in which protection was or
was not afforded, and in the recency, clarity, and confidence with which they are
able to recall the abuse. Most are able to confirm salient aspects of their histories
even though they are unable to recall other, perhaps equally salient, features of
those same histories.

*Vignette Number 1*

The patients represented by Vignette Number 1 report largely intact and continuous remembrance of their abuse experiences. Some, but not all, also report a
much delayed understanding of their early experiences: a belated awareness of
the abusive nature of the experience and a lifting not of the amnesia but of the
veil of denial and minimization that enabled them to preserve secrecy and illusion.
It appears that many patients who find themselves rethinking and reinterpreting
a long-remembered past do so as a result of specific developmental or relational
events.

*Vignette Number 2*

It is our impression that vignette number 2 is most characteristic of the adult
survivors of childhood trauma who are seen in our clinic. Among these patients,
the clinical presentation is mixed. It includes both newly recalled and continuously remembered events and a mixture of delayed recall and delayed understanding. The patients whose materials contributed to this composite generally reported partial amnesia for particular time periods, especially for periods
associated with the onset and escalation of abuse and for abuse experiences
located in early childhood. Contemporary precipitants to delayed recall also included developmental challenges and relational events. The content of newly
recalled material often led to a review and rethinking of the remembered past
and then ushered in new interpretations and delayed understanding of an abusive
past. Often, these patients reported that their revised beliefs caused as much
distress as their new memories.

*Vignette Number 3*

This vignette describes patients with the type of memory disturbance of concern to Loftus (1993a, 1993b). However, these patients do not conform in any
other way to Loftus' generalizations. None of the patients represented in Vignette
Number 3 had taken or anticipated taking legal action against an offender. All
were less interested in uncovering additional memories than in understanding
and containing the press of recently acquired memories. All reported severe and
repeated sexual and physical abuse, beginning in early childhood and continuing
into early adolescence. Many reported amnesia not only for the abuse that occurred, but also for whole eras of development (e.g., early or middle childhood)

and whole categories of experience (e.g., events inside the home or contacts with specific family members) as well. Most reported witnessing family violence as well, and many reported abuse by more than one perpetrator.

## False versus Genuine Memories of Abuse

From our vantage point, characterizations of "false" versus "true" memory fail to capture the complexity of traumatic remembrance that is regularly witnessed in clinical settings. Neither these vignettes nor the patients whose experiences contributed to them fit such descriptions. Instead, the most apt characterization of the adult survivor is a person who arrives at adulthood with some, but not all, memories of the abuse intact, and who at some point in time begins to confront and rethink the past, blending new memories with earlier ones, new assessments with alternative ones, gradually constructing a meaningful and largely verifiable personal history: a history that is patently "true" though never complete and never wholly accurate in all detail. The process of discovering one's history is not an all or none event, but rather unfolds in a relational and developmental context accompanied by marked emotional and symptomatic changes. The veracity of the history does not hang on the accurate and detailed recall of specific events. The development of a complete narrative often includes a search for confirmation of facts and verification in the remembrances of others; however, the timing and circumstances of this verification process are idiosyncratic and highly variable.

## Precipitants to Delayed Recall and Delayed Understanding

Clinical observation suggests that memories of childhood victimization—and reinterpretations of childhood events not originally understood as abusive—may resurface unexpectedly when lifecycle changes introduce new relational demands. The adult survivor may begin to recall a history of childhood trauma upon entering or ending an intimate relationship, for example. Memories may start to break through in the form of flashbacks or nightmares when the survivor gets involved in a sexual relationship, marries, or has a child. Delayed recall may occur when another victim of the same perpetrator discloses the abuse or when an aging perpetrator falls ill and expects his victim to care for him. It may be, of course, that virtually all remembrances are, in fact, instances of delayed recall and that delayed recall of traumatic events differs from normal memory not in its temporary absence from conscious awareness, but in the painful reexperiencing of the trauma itself and in the often bizarre and fragmentary nature of the memory.

## Psychotherapy with Adult Survivors of Childhood Trauma

The case vignettes presented here are illustrative not only of the type of traumatic remembering that is witnessed in clinical settings, but also of the kind of issues that typically prevail in clinical work with trauma survivors. Most patients who enter psychotherapy for help in dealing with a traumatic past do so because of what they do remember and not because of what they do not. Many enter psychotherapy after years of silence and secrecy, not after years of amnesia. They are hoping to better understand the impact of a long-remembered past. Others, like Carol in vignette 1, may find themselves newly preoccupied with long-remembered events and feel stunned by their extreme emotional reactions to new understandings of these events. They enter therapy for help in managing their distress, for assistance in absorbing and "metabolizing" their new understandings, and, sometimes, for help in resolving the issue of family disclosure. Still, others, like Sarah in vignette 2 and Emily in vignette 3 have acquired new memories that are deeply troubling. While these new memories may indeed become a focus of psychotherapy, psychotherapy is not the source of the memories. When clinicians work with trauma survivors who are experiencing distress as a result of traumatic remembrances, the work typically involves the containment of runaway affect and help with stabilization of functioning, not an archaeological search for more in the way of traumatic recall. Contrary to the portrait of clinical work with trauma survivors being promulgated by the popular press and the false memory literature, the aim of clinical exploration of the traumatic past is neither to uncover more and more horror, nor to assign blame and responsibility for adult life to others, but rather to help the adult survivor name and assign meaning and comprehensibility to the past, to facilitate the integration of traumatic remembrance into an ongoing personal narrative, and to help the patient grieve the past and be freed of it.

*Future Research*

Clinicians familiar with traumatic disorders emphasize the role of memory retrieval in a multidimensional recovery process and the danger inherent in premature or poorly paced traumatic recall (Herman, 1992; Lebowitz, Harvey, & Herman, 1993). To date, however, neither the phenomenon of delayed recall of traumatic memories nor specific approaches to memory work with trauma survivors have been subjected to systematic study. Required catalysts for these investigations are inquiries into the psychological mechanisms, biochemical mediators, and neurological substrata of delayed recall, on the one hand, and, on the other, conceptualizations of normal and traumatic memory that can facilitate collaborative inquiry by basic researcher and clinical investigator.

Three sets of issues raised by the phenomenon of delayed recall should be distinguished and considered separately. The first set of issues is *forensic* in nature and has less to do with what is "true" of a remembered past than with considerations of due process and the weight that ought be granted evidence brought forward as delayed recall. Should these memories be considered in the same manner as any other testimony? Ought they be supported by other forms of evidence? How should judges and jurors understand and make use of the research on confabulation, suggestion, and the fallibility of human memory?

The second set of issues focuses on the nature of *clinical* practice with adults who are reporting or wondering about an abusive past. What should psychotherapy with remembering adults look like? Should clinical practice with patients who have long-remembered histories differ substantially from practice with patients who report newly acquired memories of abuse? How ought the therapist respond to patient speculations about the past? What is leading? What is not? How often is psychotherapy the sole or even the primary source of delayed recall? How widespread is therapist manipulation of patient recall? How suggestible are trauma patients? Is verification of an abuse history clinically necessary? If so, why? If not, why not?

A final set of questions are central to *memory research.* These concern the role of strong emotion in the encoding, storage, and retrieval of emotionally laden material. How does traumatic memory differ from normal memory? Does the emotional arousal characteristic of traumatic exposure heighten the probability of a deeply engraved memory? Might it instead have a disorganizing effect and actually interfere with memory storage? If traumatic memories are indeed indelibly stored at the point of exposure, then why and how do they get lost? How and under what circumstances are they retrieved?

Clinical observation is a reasonable and valid starting point for the scientific exploration of these issues. An adequate theory of human memory cannot ignore or dismiss clinical observations. On the contrary, a science of memory must be able to account for the aberrations of memory and consciousness repeatedly witnessed by ethical, reliable, and observant clinicians. Similarly, effective treatment of these phenomena can and must be informed by basic research.

## ACKNOWLEDGMENTS

We thank Research Assistants Gemima Remy and Gabrielle Goodstein for their assistance in organizing clinical intake data and for technical assistance with this paper.

## REFERENCES

American Psychiatric Association (1987). *Diagnostic and statistical manual.* (Third Edition, Revised). Washington, DC: American Psychiatric Association.

Bass, E., & Davis, L. (1988). *The courage to heal.* New York: Harper & Row.

Briere, J. (1984). Long-term clinical correlates of childhood sexual victimization. *Annals of the NY Academy of Sciences,* **528,** 327–334.

Briere, J., & Conte, J. (1993). Self reported amnesia for abuse in adults molested as children. *Journal of Traumatic Stress,* **6,** 21–31.

Briere, J., & Runtz, M. (1993). Childhood sexual abuse: Long term sequelae and implications for psychological assessment. *Journal of Interpersonal Violence,* 8(3), 312–330.

Browne, A., & Finkelhor, D. (1986). Impact of child sexual abuse: A review of the research. *Psychological Bulletin,* **99,** 66–77.

Chu, J. A., & Dill, D. L. (1990). Dissociative symptoms in relation to childhood physical and sexual abuse. *American Journal of Psychiatry,* **147,** 887–892.

Commonwealth of Massachusetts v. Porter (1993).

Finkelhor, D. (1990). Early and long-term effects of child sexual abuse: An update. *Professional Psychology: Research and Practice,* **21,** 325–330.

Goodwin, J. (1989). *Sexual abuse: Incest victims and their families.* Chicago: Year Book Medical Publishers.

Harvey, M. R., & Herman, J. L. (1992). The trauma of sexual victimization: Feminist contributions to theory, research and practice. *PTSD Research Quarterly, 3*(3), 1–7.

Herman, J. L. (1981). *Father–daughter incest*. Cambridge: Harvard Univ. Press.

Herman, J. L. (1992). *Trauma and recovery*. New York, NY: Basic Books.

Herman, J. L., & Schatzow, E. (1987). Recovery and verification of memories of childhood sexual trauma. *Psychoanalytic Psychology, 4*(1), 1–14.

Koss, M. P., & Harvey, M. R. (1991). *The Rape Victim: Clinical and community interventions*. Newbury Park, CA: Sage Publications.

Lebowitz, L., Harvey, M., & Herman, J. L. (1993). A stage by dimension model of recovery from sexual trauma. *Journal of Interpersonal Violence, 8*(3), 378–391.

Lofft, K., v. Lofft, D. (1989). Complaint for Damages, Case No. 617151, Superior Court of the State of California for the County of San Diego.

Loftus, E. (1993a). Repressed memories of childhood trauma: Are they genuine? *Harvard Medical School Mental Health Letter, 9*(10).

Loftus, E. (1993b). The reality of repressed memories. *American Psychologist, 48*(5), 518–537.

Munsey v. Kellett, Middlesex (Massachusetts) Superior Court, Civil Action 91-5984 (1992).

National Victims Center (1992). *Rape in America: A report to the nation*. Washington, DC: National Victims Center.

Ofshe, R. J., & Watters, E. (1993). Making monsters. *Society, 30*, 4–16.

Putnam, F. W. (1985). Dissociation as a response to extreme trauma. In R. P. Kluft (Ed.), *Childhood antecedents of multiple personality disorder*. Washington, DC: American Psychiatric Press.

Putnam, F. (1990). Disturbances of ''self'' in victims of childhood sexual abuse. In R. P. Kluft (Ed.), *Incest-related syndromes of adult psychopathology*. Washington, DC: American Psychiatric Press.

Putnam, F. W., Post, R. M., Giuroff, J., Silberman, E. K., & Barban, L. (1983). 100 cases of multiple personality disorder. *American Psychiatric Association*, New Research Abstract No. 77. Washington, DC.

Riley v. Pressnell, 409 Mass. 239 (1991).

Rowan, A. B., & Foy, D. W. (1993). Post-traumatic stress disorder in child sexual abuse survivors: A literature review. *Journal of Traumatic Stress, 6*, 3–20.

Russell, D. E. H. (1986). *The secret trauma: Incest in the lives of girls and women*. New York, NY: Basic Books.

Russell, D. E. H. (1984). *Sexual exploitation: Rape, child sexual abuse, and workplace harassment*. Beverly Hills, CA: Sage Publications.

Sorenson, S. B., Stein, J. A., Siegel, J. M., Golding, J. M., & Burnam, M.A. (1987). The prevalence of adult sexual assault: The Los Angeles epidemiological catchment area project. *American Journal of Epidemiology, 126*, 1154–1164.

Spiegel, D., & Scheflin, A. W. (1994). Dissociated or fabricated? Psychiatric aspects of repressed memory in criminal and civil cases. *International Journal of Clinical and Experimental Hypnosis, XLII*, 411–432.

State of Washington (1989). Rev. Code Ann. Sec. 4 16.340 (1989 Suppl).

Williams, L. M. (1992). Adult memories of childhood abuse: Preliminary findings from a longitudinal study. *The Advisor (APSAC), 5*, 19–20.

Wyatt, G. E. (1985). The sexual abuse of Afro-American and white-American women in childhood. *Child abuse and neglect, 9*, 507–519.

# Comparing Amnesic and Nonamnesic Survivors of Childhood Sexual Abuse: A Longitudinal Study

CATHERINE CAMERON

*Behavioral Science Department, University of La Verne, La Verne, CA 91750*

This chapter presents findings from a nine-year longitudinal study of "amnesic" and "nonamnesic" women who entered therapy, prior to the recovered memory controversy, to confront memories of childhood sexual abuse. The goal of the study was to compare the experiences, over time, of these two memory samples. Extensive survey data, retrospective and concurrent (gathered in 1986, 1988, 1992, and 1995), provided self-report information. Repetition, in 1992, of certain questions from the first survey allowed objective comparison of symptom improvement for individuals and for groups. In this study, amnesia was considered a probable cause, effect, and moderating influence. It was hypothesized that a higher percentage of the (formerly) amnesic group would report severe sexual abuse, long-term consequences, and crisis reactions on remembering, and that a lower percentage would report improvement six years later.

## INTRODUCTION

The controversy over adult memories of childhood sexual abuse has raised important scientific and humanistic issues for experimental and clinical psychologists. Both groups are interested in human memory, yet pivotal topics such as amnesia to sexual abuse and the validity of delayed recall in adulthood lend themselves neither to cause-and-effect experiments nor to therapeutic investigation. If we are to move beyond case-by-case arguments and the anecdotal evidence that have defeated past discussion, substantive data are essential.

This chapter presents a 9-year longitudinal study of self-reported adult survivors[1] of childhood sexual abuse. They had entered therapy, in the early 1980s, with memories of child sexual abuse that were recently recovered by some but never forgotten by others. These people were surveyed in four successive periods to examine how the presence or absence of amnesia was associated with trauma and to determine its effects over time.

This study is particularly valuable because of its fortuitous timing. Most of the former amnesics, who were first surveyed in 1986, had recovered initial memories of sexual abuse between 1979 and 1985. The agents that critics now charge with implanting such memories—for example, "recovered memory therapy," self-help books, hypnosis, and "incest survivor groups"—were scarce until after the second survey in 1988. Moreover, 73% of the amnesics had recovered their

---

[1]Throughout this chapter, for simplicity of exposition, the terms "survivor," "abuser," and "sexual abuse" are used with the recognition that these are claims made by respondents. "Memory" and "amnesia" (anomalous memory loss) are conditions respondents reported of themselves.

first memories before they entered therapy, and 65% obtained external validation of their abuse.

The presentation of data in this chapter is organized around comparisons of two subsamples of survivors, women who had, and those who had not, been amnesic to childhood sexual abuse. In comparing these groups, six sequential research questions were posed. The study developed extensive self-report data, gathered retrospectively and concurrently over the 9-year period. It also provided a comprehensive, objective 6-year pre-post-comparison of survivors who had been amnesic with those who had always remembered their abuse.

The following six research questions are addressed in this chapter:

• Question I. Was the presence or absence of amnesia associated with reported severity of sexual abuse?
• Question II. What reported long-term consequences were associated with the presence or absence of amnesia during the interim years?
• Question III. What motivations to confront memories in adulthood were associated with the presence or absence of amnesia?
• Question IV. At the initial time of recall, were crisis reactions associated with (prior) presence or absence of amnesia?
• Question V. What characteristics of the continuing remembering process were associated with (prior) presence or absence of amnesia?
• Question VI. What personal changes, between the interim period and the third survey in 1992, were associated with the (prior) presence or absence of amnesia?

## THE RESEARCH CONTEXT

### Historical Setting

Researchers have been slow to recognize the prevalence and traumatic effects of sexual abuse. We need not look back a hundred years to Freud to demonstrate this. Alfred Kinsey's radical research in the middle of this century broke taboos to advance the understanding of human sexuality, but it trivialized the nature and gravity of sexual abuse.[2] Kinsey's broad surveys on the sexual behavior of adult males (Kinsey, Pomeroy, & Martin, 1948) and females (Kinsey, Pomeroy, Martin, & Gebhard, 1953) could have provided vital material on survivors of sexual abuse. Instead, relevant survey information was euphemistically classified as male "premarital intercourse" in the 1948 book, and under female "preadolescent sexual development" in the 1953 book. "Incest" was indexed only once in more than 1600 pages.

In interviews of 4441 females, the Kinsey researchers (Kinsey et al., 1953) found that 24% reported prepubertal "contacts" with adult males, 23% of whom were relatives. Although most experiences were reported to be verbal or exhibi-

---

[2]Maria Jean Arrigo, a doctoral candidate at Claremont Graduate School, provided me with this insight into Kinsey's work and that of other key references. These have strengthened this chapter in important ways. I am grateful for her wisdom and support.

tionistic (62%), and judged by the researchers to be "unlikely to do the child any appreciable harm" (p. 122), 80% of the girls had been frightened or upset. The authors found it difficult to understand why a child, "except for cultural conditioning, should be disturbed at having its genitalia touched, or . . . even more specific sexual contacts" (p. 121). They therefore concluded that it was societal "hysteria over sex offenders" and parental warnings that had frightened the girls, and perhaps even caused their later sexual maladjustment in womanhood (p. 121). The researchers omitted other troublesome findings. A large sample of prostitutes and female convicts revealed such a high proportion of serious childhood sexual abuse that they were dropped from the study (p. 22).

After Kinsey's publications, a quarter of a century passed before the writings of Kempe on the "battered child" set off a domino effect in which successive forms of abuse came before the public eye and into the purview of research. Physical abuse, child neglect, the battering and rape of women, and abuse of the elderly and the disabled all tumbled into public and professional awareness. The latest type of abuse to inspire research, as well as outrage, was incest, especially between parent and child (Herman, 1981; Meiselman, 1978).

## Study of Trauma

The study on which this chapter was based was designed in 1985 and continued longitudinally to 1995. It was particularly influenced by research and theory concerning symptoms of post-traumatic stress disorder (PTSD) among (a) veterans of warfare, (b) other traumatized populations, and (c) survivors of sexual abuse. The concept of PTSD provided an organizing principle for investigating three enigmas commonly associated with severe child sexual abuse. These are its lasting impact on the victim, amnesia and other memory decrements, and the delayed recovery of memories.

*From shell shock to PTSD.* Traumatic stress reactions during and following war have in past generations been reported under various labels. Today, "posttraumatic stress disorder" is the accepted term (American Psychiatric Association, 1994). PTSD has two phases, one characterized by numbness and the other by high arousal. Both may alternate rapidly during any given time period, but often the denial phase may prevail for decades, as in the lives of many Vietnam veterans (Horowitz, 1976), before florid symptoms erupt.

A growing number of systematic studies have reported amnesic syndromes (e.g., Putnam 1985), with up to 20% of veterans reporting amnesia for their combat experiences. Research over a 50-year period (from Sargant & Slater, 1941, to Goldberg, True, Eisen, & Henderson, 1990) has found similar percentages of soldiers and veterans with amnesic syndromes or PTSD. Statistics have varied from about 5% (with no exposure to combat) to three to nine times that percentage (as severity of combat exposure increased). Many of the traumatic situations that had evoked amnesia were historically documented.

*Other sources of trauma.* The study of trauma has not been limited to military populations, however. Amnesia, memory impairment, and dissociation can be immediate or long-term reactions to any major trauma (Koopman, Classen, Cardena, & Spiegel, 1995). During the decade 1985 to 1995, trauma researchers were increasingly reporting amnesic syndromes during peace as well as war (e.g., Putnam, 1985) among victims of torture and prisoners of war or politics (Sutker, Uddo, Brailey, & Allain, 1993), among victims of natural disaster, and among children (Eth & Pynoos, 1985), as well as in the general population (Ullman, 1995). Comparing various traumatized groups, Wilson, Smith, and Johnson (1985) reported war veterans as decidedly the most severely traumatized, with one surprising statistical exception. A small sample of "victims of rape, battering, and child abuse" (p. 167) had an equally severe rating on PTSD. For these researchers, symptoms that alternately blunt or dramatize the reactions of victims of trauma were considered natural responses to overwhelming stress. Shareable findings from these varied studies of the etiology and nature of PTSD have advanced the empirical and theoretical study of amnesia to sexual abuse as well (e.g., Cameron, 1994a; Elliott & Briere, 1995; Williams, 1994).

*Trauma in the home.* Studies of sexual abuse published around 1980 documented more clearly than ever before its historical reality (Rush, 1978), current prevalence (Finkelhor, 1979; Kempe, 1978), and long-term impact, especially if the abuse occurred in the home (Herman, 1981; Meiselman, 1978). In these early works, the loss and recovery of traumatic memories were everywhere assumed, but nowhere made the focus of study. Findings from these studies influenced the planning, focus, and thrust of the study presented in this chapter.

Gelinas (1983) linked incest to PTSD. She described the delayed outbreak of florid symptoms in adulthood as a "time bomb" that erupted after years of seeming normalcy. Briere and Runtz (1987) discussed "post–sexual-abuse trauma" as a variant of PTSD that features cognitive, emotional, and interpersonal effects. Finkelhor (1986) delineated four "traumagenic dynamics" in sexual abuse: traumatic sexualization, betrayal, powerlessness, and stigmatization. For Courtois (1992), memory loss and delayed recall were two sides of a coin, manifesting the denial-numbing phase of PTSD and the intrusive-arousing phase, respectively (p. 21). During the first phase, survivors avoid remembering, recognizing, or defining their abuse; during the second, its reality bombards them. Either phase may be interrupted by opposing symptoms. During amnesia, dulled emotions can explode in inappropriate ways, and during recall, new memories can be undermined by recurring denial.

Herman (1992) argued for a broader understanding of stress responses to trauma that should be viewed as "a spectrum of conditions rather than as a single disorder" (p. 119). For victims of prolonged and repeated trauma, she recommended the diagnosis "complex PTSD." Terr (1990) distinguished Type One trauma (a single shocking event) from Type Two trauma (repeated abuse over time). She noted that memories for Type One trauma were clearer and more complete. Cameron (1994a), comparing 72 sexual abuse survivors to Vietnam veterans with PTSD, pointed out surprising similarities (and differences) in their experience of trauma and its aftermath. In Europe, Ensink (1992) studied psychiatric symptoms—dissociation, hallucinations, self-injury, and suicidality—in 97 adult sexual abuse survivors, and van der Kolk (1987) and Bremner, Davis, Southwick, Krystal, and Charney (1994) documented lasting physiological brain changes in trauma victims that created their tenacious symptoms. Moreover, the longitudinal research of Trickett and Putnam (1995) verified hormonal changes in the bodies of adolescent survivors. These contributors have, separately and together, clarified the impact of sexual abuse by elaborating on the concept of PTSD. By what they included and what they omitted, they influenced the focus, planning, and coverage of the longitudinal study described in this chapter.

*Validation.* Recovered memories of many traumatic events (such as military battles and natural disasters) can be historically documented. Moreover, the prevalence of reported amnesia and of external verification of recovered memories is being recorded. Herman and Schatzow (1987) reported that 67% of their clinical sample of 57 women had experienced a period of amnesia to their abuse, and 75% were able to find external validation. In Briere and Conte (1989), 60% of the clinical sample had experienced a period of amnesia to their abuse. Feldman-Summers and Pope (1994), surveying therapists, found 24% reporting sexual or physical childhood abuse. Forty percent had experienced a period of amnesia to part or all of their abuse, and half of these reported corroboration. Williams (1995) based a prospective study on old hospital records of children who had been examined for documented sexual abuse. Nearly two decades later, 129 adults were interviewed as part of a "health study," and 16% of the respondents had "recovered memories" of their earlier verified abuse. These women had no more discrepencies, compared with hospital reports, than those always remembering. As for the study discussed in this chapter, 16 of 22 women (73%) experienced first memories *before* seeking a therapist. Thirteen of 20 amnesic women (65%) received one or more *external* validations of sexual abuse from another victim (9), from a perpetrator (7, usually after lengthy and adamant denial), or from relatives (5). Some had archival or physical evidence as well.

## METHOD

### Sample

The sample discussed in this chapter was composed of two groups of women[3] who were currently in therapy to deal with memories of childhood sexual abuse. The "amnesic" group reported having, until recently, no memory of their abuse for 15 to 54 years. Some had been aware of memory gaps, but they had assumed that this was normal. The "nonamnesic" group had had uninterrupted memory of their abuse since it occurred, but about half had been unaware of its meaning and its impact on their lives. Harvey and Herman (in this volume) also use the terms "amnesic and nonamnesic" for two of their clinical groups. Their descriptors "profound amnesia, delayed recall" and "continuous recall, delayed understanding" also apply to the groups in this study.

In this study, I contacted a number of licensed California therapists through professional networks who had one or more women survivors among their clients. Questionnaires were sent to cooperating therapists for distribution to cli-

[3]Today there is research on male survivors, but 10 years ago, few males were entering therapy to deal with childhood abuse.

ents (a) who had been, until recently, fully amnesic to their abuse for at least 15 years, or (b) who had never forgotten it. This procedure was intended to ensure that the questionnaires would go to women at both extremes on the memory continuum and that these respondents would have therapeutic support available. In 1986, speaking at a 4-day multidisciplinary conference on child sexual abuse, I described my study and the need for more participants. In response, therapists not known to me picked up questionnaires for their clients. Subjects from other states (15% of the total sample) were obtained this way, as well as a few more from California. In sum, 24 therapists, social workers, marriage counselors, psychologists, and psychiatrists enlisted 25 amnesic and 21 nonamnesic clients to participate in the study.[4] Most therapists provided one or two clients, none more than four.

In 1986, the 46 respondents filled out seven-page questionnaires in the first survey. Those who sent their names and contact information were personally interviewed. Six of the 46 never identified themselves, and others moved away and were unavailable for follow-up questionnaires and interviews in 1988 and 1992. This attrition was compensated for by the high response rate in these follow-up surveys, 74% of the *original* respondents participated in at least one of them. In 1992, a subset of questions was repeated and the individual responses of the 34 women were compared with their own responses to the same questions in 1986. This provided a robust measure of perceived change in their lives. A fourth survey, a semistructured telephone interview was also conducted (Cameron, 1995).

*Family background.* Almost all respondents in the study were Caucasian. Most came from Protestant homes (60%), with the rest from Catholic (16%), Jewish (7%), and nonreligious (12%) homes. For 78%, their parents' marriage was intact when they graduated from high school. Their father's occupation placed 58% of them in professional or white collar status (rather than blue collar) as children; but by 1986, "respondent occupation" placed 90% of the women in these categories. From a societal perspective, however, the amnesic women had had a "better" childhood environment than nonamnesics. More of their parents' marriages were still intact when the daughters finished high school (89% vs. 71%, nonsignificant), and more had been raised in professional or white collar homes (75% vs. 39%, $p < .01$).

*Personal demographics.* In 1986, half of the women in the study were between 30 and 40 years old. For the amnesic and nonamnesic samples, the means (40 vs. 37 years), medians (late thirties), and age ranges (25 to 65 vs. 25 to 56) were similar. One half of the respondents were married, and about a quarter each were divorced or had never married. On average, about 30 years had elapsed between first abuse and entering therapy to address the abuse. There were some minor variations: More amnesics were still in first marriages and none had divorced more than once.

---

[4] Fourteen other respondents were found to have partial amnesia (Cameron, 1994a, 1994b). However, for a clear contrast in this chapter, only amnesic and nonamnesic women are discussed.

*Instruments*

*Questionnaires.* The respondents provided extensive information on their abuse, its consequences during the interim period that followed childhood abuse, and the crisis of confronting the past in adulthood. Their memories of childhood abuse and of the following years of secrecy were retrospectively reported; information about the recovery process was gathered concurrently in 1986 and during the 9 years that followed. Pretesting of the survey had demonstrated that some survivors found it emotionally overwhelming to articulate their memories. For example, it was more difficult to write out, "My grandfather ejaculated in my mouth," than to check options on an abuser and abuse list. Therefore, most questions were presented in checklist format, with simple response options of Yes, Somewhat, and No. Space was also provided for elaboration or alternative answers. Twenty percent of the women wrote extensive additional information, taking many hours to answer the first seven-page questionnaire instead of the typical hour to hour and a half needed. The complex and dynamic data from the first survey prompted follow-up surveys to determine later developments in a longitudinal design. The second and third follow-up questionnaires were each four pages long, used a similar format, and required about an hour to fill out. The data reported in this chapter address only a subset of the questions from the first three questionnaires and interviews. The factors listed in Tables 1 to 3 are the specific issues probed. The 1995 phone interviews have provided updated information about each woman.

*Interviews.* Each respondent was interviewed after she had returned the completed questionnaire, retaining a carbon copy for her own records. This session took place at her convenience and at her choice of location. The semistructured interview typically lasted at least 2 hours, but 4 or 5 hours was not unusual. The interviews provided a clearer understanding of the meaning of the written responses and contributed greatly to the content of further surveys and to the interpretation of the data in this chapter. The task of the interview was primarily to clarify and enlarge upon the questionnaire responses.

## RESULTS

The presentation of results is organized around the six key questions posed in the introduction. Background research that helped to motivate each question is presented here as well. To address the issue of whether there was a difference between the amnesic and nonamnesic groups on each key question, specific relevant items were placed on questionnaire 1 in 1986. Each was responded to with a checklist offering three response options, Yes, Somewhat, and No. To record strong endorsement and to reduce possible response bias, only strong endorsement (Yes) was counted in the percentage response. Independent chi-square tests were used to analyze differences between the two groups. The significance level for all comparisons was $p < .05$.

*Question I. Was the Presence or Absence of Amnesia Associated with Reported Severity of Sexual Abuse?*

Women in therapy to deal with child sexual abuse have usually had a "severe" experience, according to Russell (1986). She identified three criteria as constituting severe sexual abuse: a parent abuser, penetration, and violence. These factors, and others defined as severe in Finkelhor's review of research (1986), were chosen as abuse variables in this study. It was hypothesized that a higher percentage of amnesics would report severe abuse than nonamnesics. Results are presented in Table 1. Occasionally data are missing (e.g., one amnesic woman had never learned her abuser's identity).

*Findings regarding seriousness of abuse.* It had been predicted that both groups of respondents would come from the serious end of the abuse spectrum. This proved to be so. Incest was the norm and single perpetrators and isolated events were unusual or rare. All of the women (except for two nonamnesics) had been sexually abused by at least one relative, and many amnesics (42%) and nonamnesics (29%) had also been victimized by nonrelated persons concurrently or sequentially. Fourteen respondents reported a single abuser over time. For all six amnesics and for two of the eight nonamnesics, it was the natural father. One respondent in each group reported a single event—rape by two or three teenagers when they were about 8 years old.

Furthermore, significantly more amnesics than nonamnesics reported sexual abuse that was considered severe by researchers. The abuse reported by the amnesic group began at a younger age than that of nonamnesics (mean age of 3.7 vs. 7.0 years). The mean duration of primary abuse was lengthy for both groups, sometimes providing time for abuse to escalate from toddlerhood to preteens, or even into adolescence. The amnesics were more than 2 times as likely as the nonamnesics to report sexual abuse by their natural mother [5] (33% vs. 14%) and more than 3 times as likely to report sexual abuse by their natural father (75% vs. 24%). More than 2 times as many amnesics as nonamnesics experienced sexual violence (50% vs. 19%), and almost 2 times as many had been penetrated in one or more ways at some time during the period of abuse (100% vs. 57%). The chance of amnesics experiencing fellatio (65% vs. 33%), the most common form of penetration used on very young victims (Kempe, 1978), was 2 times that of nonamnesic respondents. Moreover, amnesics were 3 times as likely to report that, during childhood, there was not even one adult they could rely on (48% vs. 14%).

*Question II. What Reported Long-Term Consequences Were Associated with the Presence or Absence of Amnesia during the Interim Years?*

Previous research on the impact of child sexual abuse minimized the long-term as well as the immediate consequences (Kinsey et al., 1953), but more

---

[5] Some respondents named their mother as an abuser in the absense of sexual contact (e.g., she arranged for the child to service a stepfather, watched them, and forced the child to observe adult sexual acts).

TABLE 1
Characteristics of the Sexual Abuse of Amnesic and Nonamnesic Women

| Characteristics | Amnesic (N = 24) | Nonamnesic (N = 21) | Sig. level |
|---|---|---|---|
| Mean age when first abused | 3.7 years | 7.0 years | *** |
| Mean duration of primary abuse | 5.7 years | 4.4 years | ns |
| Mean number of related abusers | 1.9 | 1.6 | ns |
| Father was an abuser | 75% | 24% | *** |
| Mother was an abuser | 33% | 14% | * |
| Stepfather was an abuser | 8% | 19% | ns |
| No childhood supporter | 48% | 14% | ** |
| Abused often or regularly | 67% | 60% | ns |
| One or more forms of penetration | 100% | 57% | *** |
| Fellatio | 65% | 33% | ** |
| Experienced sexual violence | 50% | 19% | * |

*Note.* One-tail $t$ tests or chi-square tests (occasional missing data). ns, not significant.
*$p$ <.05. **$p$ <.01. ***$p$ <.001.

recent research has confirmed the seriousness of its impact (Briere & Elliott, 1994; Ensink, 1992; Finkelhor, 1986; Russell, 1986; Wyatt, 1985). In this study, comparison of the amnesic and nonamnesic groups was made in four symptom categories: (a) negative self-perception, (b) maladaptive coping styles, (c) long-term somatic problems, and (d) PTSD symptoms. Because of the greater severity of their abuse, it was hypothesized that a higher percentage of amnesics than nonamnesics would report long-term consequences during the interim years in each symptom category.

*Findings regarding negative self-perceptions.* By the mid-1980s, negative self-perceptions were being used by all key researchers as one measure of the impact of sexual abuse (e.g., Finkelhor, 1986; Russell, 1986). Contrary to expectation, the data indicated that self-perception did not distinguish the two groups. Amnesic women did not report having had a more negative self-perception than the nonamnesic women during the interim years. Indeed, unusually high endorsement of most of these negative items created something of a ceiling effect. As can be seen from the data in Table 2, the 46 women saw themselves retrospectively as having been "people-pleasers" who felt that they were different from others and "never good enough." Something was "wrong" with them, and they had blamed their unhappiness on their own deficiencies.

*Findings regarding long-term coping styles.* Coping behaviors adopted by child victims may reduce psychic pain during the abuse period and during the interim period before help is sought, but these behaviors tend to generalize and become more elaborate over time (Briere & Elliott, 1994), becoming increasingly maladaptive. Because the amnesics had experienced especially severe abuse, it was hypothesized that they would report more use of each coping style, labeled effort, avoidance, and support-seeking, during the interim years than would nonamnesics. The results, however, did not reveal significant differences between

## TABLE 2

Percentage of Amnesic and Nonamnesic Women Who Reported Long-Term Consequences of Child Sexual Abuse during the Interim Period and Persistence of Consequences in 1992 (in Percent)

| Consequences | During interim period | | | Status in 1992 | | |
|---|---|---|---|---|---|---|
| | Amnesic (N = 25) | Nonamnesic (N = 21) | Sig. level | Amnesic (N = 18) | Nonamnesic (N = 16) | Sig. level |
| Self-perception | | | | | | |
| Unworthy/never good enough | 100 | 91 | ns | 11 ††† | 0 ††† | ns |
| Different from others | 88 | 76 | ns | 28 ††† | 13 †† | ns |
| Something wrong with me | 88 | 86 | ns | 22 ††† | 0 ††† | ns |
| To blame for my problems | 76 | 86 | ns | 0 ††† | 6 ††† | ns |
| Excessive need to please | 76 | 86 | ns | 6 ††† | 6 ††† | ns |
| Coping styles | | | | | | |
| *Effort* | | | | | | |
| Trying harder | 85 | 76 | ns | 17 ††† | 19 ††† | ns |
| Seeking approval | 84 | 81 | ns | 6 ††† | 13 ††† | ns |
| Keeping busy | 80 | 67 | ns | 39 † | 44 ns | ns |
| Hiding (facade) | 71 | 70 | ns | 12 ††† | 7 ††† | ns |
| *Escape* | | | | | | |
| Compulsive eating | 55 | 69 | ns | 50 ns | 54 ns | ns |
| Excess sleeping | 48 | 76 | ns | 6 †† | 27 †† | ns |
| Alcohol/drugs | 40 | 24 | ns | 0 †† | 0 † | ns |
| *Support* | | | | | | |
| Religion | 48 | 57 | ns | 44 ns | 67 ns | ns |
| Talking about feelings | 36 | 29 | ns | 72 † | 73 † | ns |
| Counseling (nonsexual) | 32 | 14 | ns | 50 ns | 53 †† | ns |
| Somatic symptoms | (n = 18) | (n = 16) | | | | |
| *Eating* | | | | | | |
| Bulimia | 13 | 6 | ns | — | — | |
| Anorexia nervosa | 6 | 19 | ns | — | — | |

| | | | | | | |
|---|---|---|---|---|---|---|
| *Gynecological* | | | | | | |
| Menstrual/premenstrual | 72 | ns | — | ns | 56 | — |
| Other female problem | 28 | ns | — | ns | 38 | — |
| Unexplained pelvic pain | 22 | ns | — | ns | 6 | — |
| *Head and jaw* | | | | | | |
| Migraine headache | 61 | ns | — | ns | 44 | — |
| Tight jaw | 50 | ns | — | ns | 44 | — |
| Teeth-grinding | 44 | ns | — | ns | 31 | — |
| *Respiratory* | | | | | | |
| Oversoft voice | 33 | ns | — | ns | 19 | — |
| Asthma | 17 | ns | — | ns | 19 | — |
| Allergies | 11 | ns | — | ns | 56 | — |
| *Miscellaneous* | | | | | | |
| Self-abuse | 50 | ns | — | ns | 44 | — |
| General unwellness | 44 | ns | — | ns | 38 | — |
| Accidents | 28 | ns | — | ns | 25 | — |
| PTSD Symptoms | | | | | | |
| *Avoiding/denial/numbing* | | | | | | |
| Numbed emotions | 72 | ns | 6 ††† | ns | 57 | 0 ††† |
| Depression (withdrawal) | 64 | ns | 22 †† | ns | 57 | 0 †† |
| Suicidal feelings | 52 | ns | 6 †† | ns | 38 | 0 †† |
| Sexual problems | 80 | ns | 33 †† | ns | 67 | 13 ††† |
| *Reexperiencing/arousal* | | | | | | |
| Flashbacks | 96~ | ns | 17 ††† | ns | 90~ | 0 ††† |
| Intrusive thoughts | 64~ | ns | 6 ††† | ns | 67~ | 13 † |
| Troubled sleep/nightmares | 52 | ns | 17 † | ns | 57 | 13 †† |

*Note.* "Yes" responses only (occasional missing data). ~These PTSD symptoms were measured *after* crisis of recall instead of during interim period. ns, not significant.

*p < .05. **p < .01. ***p < .001. One-tailed chi-square test, comparison *between* groups.
†p < .05. ††p < .01. †††p < .001. McNemar test, improvement *within* each group.

the two groups; both had coped with stress primarily through excessive effort (trying harder, seeking approval, and keeping busy) while hiding their distress behind a carefully maintained facade of normalcy. These results are presented in Table 2. The amnesics had a nonsignificant tendency to use more dangerous *escapes* (drugs or alcohol) than nonamnesics. Also, at some time during the interim years, between childhood abuse and its confrontation in adulthood, amnesics had been more likely to seek *support* from counselors for depression, relationship problems, and addictions, although not for sexual abuse.

*Findings regarding long-term somatic problems.* Researchers have found survivors of sexual abuse prone to somatic symptoms. Gelinas (1983) described such symptoms as "disguised representations" of sexual abuse, hiding the past from both counselor and counselee. In 1986, respondents were asked, in an open question, to specify any health problems that they had experienced during the interim years. On the basis of responses, a checklist of long-term health problems was designed and given to the women who remained in the sample in 1992. This group included 18 amnesics and 16 nonamnesics. Major items listed were eating, respiratory, and gynecological problems, and headache or jaw pain. In addition, respondents were asked about miscellaneous somatic symptoms—accidents, self-abuse, an oversoft voice, and general unwellness. Although it was hypothesized that a higher percentage of amnesics than nonamnesics would endorse somatic symptoms, there were no significant differences in percentages between the groups except for "allergies," for which the outcome was the opposite of that expected. Apparently, measures of the frequency, duration, and severity of the symptoms might have been more sensitive to group differences.

*Findings regarding PTSD symptoms.* Traumatic symptoms are quite common in survivors of child sexual abuse. Today, many researchers believe trauma symptoms to be a major and complex consequence of repeated incest (e.g., Briere & Runtz, 1987, J. Freyd, 1994, Herman, 1992, and van der Kolk, 1987). PTSD symptoms were included in checklists about respondents' health during the interim period. Although it was hypothesized that amnesics would report a higher percentage of PTSD symptoms than would nonamnesics, there were no significant differences between the two groups. Indeed, the most striking findings in Table 2, across four categories of consequences during the interim period and three dozen items, are (a) the high proportion of all respondents reporting problems, and (b) the absence of significant differences between the amnesic and nonamnesic groups.

*Summary.* Whether respondents had been amnesic or nonamnesic, during the interim years they had developed negative perceptions about self and life, maladaptive coping mechanisms, health problems, and symptoms of PTSD (chronic or in remission). The expectation that more amnesic women would report disabling symptoms in these four categories during the interim years between abuse and the crisis of recall received no support. Future research using precise measurement of the frequency, duration, and severity of symptoms may reveal differences not determined in this study.

*Question III. What Motivations to Confront Memories in Adulthood Were Associated with the Presence or Absence of Amnesia?*

Case studies of sex abuse survivors frequently mention cues that first trigger clients' memories of sexual abuse. The study presented in this chapter used a checklist to gain information on the subject. Respondents were asked to note which cues had induced them to confront, as adults, memories that they had been unaware of or had ignored for decades. It was hypothesized that a higher percentage of amnesics than nonamnesics would endorse such cues.

*Findings on motives to remember.* The list of general and specific factors that may have triggered the return of memories in this study is presented in Table 3.

TABLE 3

Percentage of Amnesic and Nonamnesic Women Who Reported Each Characteristic of Adult Recall: Motivation to Recall, Crisis Responses, and the Return of Memories

| Characteristics | Amnesic (N = 25) | Nonamnesic (N = 21) | Sig. level |
|---|---|---|---|
| Motivations to recall | | | |
| *General life context* | | | |
| Feeling safer | 68 | 24 | ** |
| Feeling overwhelmed | 21 | 42 | ns |
| *Specific cues* | | | |
| Abuse of someone close | 60 | 57 | ns |
| Similar setting/context | 42 | 38 | ns |
| Body contact | 35 | 24 | ns |
| Bad dreams | 33 | 19 | ns |
| Media information | 12 | 29 | ns |
| Crisis responses | | | |
| *Turbulent emotions* | 68 | 76 | ns |
| Horror | 67 | 24 | *** |
| Grief | 67 | 57 | ns |
| Guilt | 63 | 57 | ns |
| Anger | 58 | 81 | ns |
| Disillusionment | 57 | 29 | * |
| *Support required from:* | | | |
| Therapy | 92 | 67 | * |
| Any and all resources | 52 | 10 | *** |
| Talking about it | 50 | 71 | ns |
| Temporary hospitalization | 17 | 11 | ns |
| *Avoidance* | | | |
| Denial | 83 | 24 | *** |
| Suicidal ideation | 54 | 29 | * |
| Drugs/alcohol | 21 | 5 | ns |
| *Other* | | | |
| Agitation/exhaustion | 67 | 52 | ns |
| Relief, understanding | 63 | 57 | ns |
| Normal coping fails | 63 | 43 | ns |
| Sexual feelings change | 54 | 24 | * |

TABLE 3—*Continued*

| Characteristics | Amnesic (N = 25) | Nonamnesic (N = 21) | Sig. level |
|---|---|---|---|
| Return of memories | | | |
| *Premonitions* | | | |
| Uneasy, ominous feelings | 61 | 65 | ns |
| Sense of "moving away" | 58 | 45 | ns |
| Air seems close, stuffy | 33 | 35 | ns |
| *Memory modalities* | | | |
| Sensory components | 100 | 90 | ns |
| Visual | 84 | 65 | ns |
| Kinetic/visceral/touch | 64 | 30 | ** |
| Auditory | 52 | 45 | ns |
| Olfactory | 60 | 30 | * |
| Emotions | 76 | 70 | ns |
| Thoughts | 56 | 55 | ns |
| Dreams | 64 | 75 | ns |
| *Timing of memories* | | | |
| Came over many months | 68 | 55 | ns |
| Bits and pieces make sense | 72 | 45 | * |
| With gathering intensity | 52 | 15 | ** |
| In intermittent surges | 48 | 55 | ns |
| As whole memories | 8 | 30 | ns |

*Note.* "Yes" responses only (occasional missing data). ns, not significant.
*$p < .05$. **$p < .01$. ***$p < .001$. One-tailed chi-square test.

Comparisons were tested with chi-square tests. Amnesics were nearly 3 times as likely as nonamnesics (68% vs. 24%) to believe that they had remembered their sexual abuse at a "safe" time in their lives. Half as many amnesics as nonamnesics (21% vs. 42%) sought help because they were feeling overwhelmed. Feeling safer or feeling overwhelmed formed a general life context of the two groups and played a significant role in the readiness of amnesics and nonamnesics to confront the past. Within that context, specific cues (that did not distinguish between the groups) triggered recall.

*Question IV. At the Initial Time of Recall, Were Crisis Reactions Associated with (Prior) Presence or Absence of Amnesia?*

The strong reactions of survivors immediately after they breeched denial of their childhood abuse can be found throughout the clinical literature. However, systematic data have been needed. Most nonamnesics, never having discussed what they remembered, denied certain aspects and held a distorted view of the abuse, the abuser's motives, and who was responsible. It was hypothesized that a higher percentage of amnesics than nonamnesics would report crisis responses.

*Findings regarding crisis responses.* The relevent results in this study are presented in Table 3. In the first 2 weeks after the beginning of recall, crisis was experienced by many respondents. This was especially true of former amnesics.

They were almost 3 times as likely to experience the emotion of horror (67% vs. 24%) and nearly 2 times as many felt disillusioned (57% vs. 29%); they required greater support from therapy (92% vs. 67%) and depended far more than nonamnesics on any and all resources (52% vs. 10%). The amnesics were 3 times as likely to evidence avoidance through denial (83% vs. 24%) and about 2 times as likely to consider suicide (54% vs. 29%). Their suicidal ideation was current and urgent. Their sexual feelings were 2 times as likely to be disturbed (54% vs. 24%).

## Question V. What Characteristics of the Continuing Remembering Process Were Associated with (Prior) Presence or Absence of Amnesia?

Previous studies have not systematically examined the process of remembering traumatic events after the initial crisis of recall. Table 3 presents a list of factors that characterized for respondents the *continuing* remembering process. Because the formerly amnesic group had to process memories involving new information rather than reprocess more familiar material, it was hypothesized that a higher percentage of amnesics would check items in all three categories listed in Table 3—premonitions to flashbacks, memory modalities, and the timing involved in memory recovery.

*Findings regarding the continuing remembering process.* There was no difference between amnesic and nonamnesic respondents in reporting uncomfortable premonitions that eventually alerted them to impending flashbacks. However, the amnesics were 2 times as likely to report sensory "memories" of smell (60% vs. 30%) and touch (64% vs. 30%). The timing of reported memories also revealed differences. For both groups, memories tended to come over many months and in intermittent surges. However, more amnesics reported memories as bits and pieces (72% vs. 45%), gradually making sense, rather than as whole memories (8% vs. 30%). The returning memories of amnesics also featured increasing intensity of content and emotion (52% vs. 15%).

## Question VI. What Personal Changes, between the Interim Period and the Third Survey in 1992, Were Associated with the (Prior) Presence or Absence of Amnesia?

Although there is a significant amount of literature in the mental health field about "the healing process," there have been scant systematic data on outcome. To address the question of whether amnesia was related to personal change over time in the symptoms of survivors in the present study, checklist items for the same problem areas identified in 1986 as having troubled them over the interim years—self-perception, coping, somatic symptoms, and PTSD—were repeated in 1992. As before, yes responses only were tallied for each item and each woman was compared with herself over time. The results, presented in the fourth and fifth columns of Table 2, give the percentage of amnesics and nonamnesics who still had the problems that had troubled them during the interim years. Because of the more serious nature of the amnesics' abuse, it was hypothesized that there would be *less* improvement for them on these items than for nonamnesics. The McNemar test was used to analyze change for individuals *within* each group of respondents over time (comparing column 1 with column 4 and column 2 with column 5). One-tailed chi-square tests were used to analyze the difference in 1992 status *between* the two memory groups (column 6).[6]

*Findings regarding personal change.* During the interim period prior to 1986, a high percentage of women (in both groups) had formed highly *negative self concepts* on all five measures (see the first two columns of Table 2). By 1992, the yes responses of each group had dropped significantly across the board by 63 to 91% (see columns 3 and 4 of Table 2). However, the difference in improvement *between* the groups was not significant. *Coping style* was the second major variable to be followed over time. During the interim years prior to 1986, similar percentages of women in both groups had used coping styles that involved excessive personal effort, unhealthy escapes, inadequate support, or some combination of these. By 1992, each group's yes responses for coping through effort (trying harder and winning approval) and for escaping through excessive sleep and alcohol had dropped significantly, 24 to 78%. The *difference* in improvement *between* the groups on coping styles was nonsignificant, except that the nonamnesics' current use of therapy had more than doubled that of the interim years. One half of the women in each group were still in therapy, at least from time to time. The third major variable was the set of *somatic symptoms*. However, change is not shown in columns 4 and 5, as a checklist of somatic symptoms was first presented in 1992 and thus there were no earlier data to compare them with. It is of interest to note, however, that respondents reported their greatest improvement in the miscellaneous category—damage to the body through self-abuse, accidents, alcohol, and general poor health.

The fourth set of long-term problems was *PTSD symptoms*. During the interim years before 1986, fairly similar percentages of women in both groups had experienced PTSD symptoms, especially those listed under the avoiding-numbing phase (see the first two columns of Table 2). The crisis of recall brought florid symptoms of PTSD into ascendency. By 1992, as predicted, each group's yes responses to PTSD were significantly reduced (by 38 to 66% on avoiding symptoms, and by 35 to 90% on intrusive symptoms). Flashbacks, the most common symptom, had dropped more than any others (see columns 4 and 5 of Table 2). The difference in improvement *within* each group on PTSD symptoms was significant. The difference in improvement *between* the groups on PTSD symptoms was nonsignificant. As with previous comparisons under question VI, the high degree of change *within* each group created a ceiling effect on comparisons *between* them.

As a final note, omitting Somewhat responses from the tally of data may have

[6] In 1992, data were used only for respondents continuing from the original 1986 sample. However, findings probably also represent the original sample for three reasons: (a) The response to Questionnaire 3 was exceptionally high, with 92% of those still available (about three-quarters of each original subsample) participating. (b) The missing respondents were split between amnesics and nonamnesics—those who never identified themselves for follow-up (numbering 4 and 3), those who had moved (1 and 1), and those who chose not to respond (2 and 1) to the follow-up. (c) The differences in the 1986 data between the entire sample and those who later continued were slight.

minimized demand characteristics, but it also hid lingering traces of symptoms in 1992. Amnesics were more likely than nonamnesics to check Somewhat in 1992 rather than to change directly to No. Improvement was remarkable, but it was not complete.

## GENERALIZATIONS AND LIMITATIONS

The general hypothesis for this study was that a higher percentage of amnesics than nonamnesics would report the following: severe childhood sexual abuse, serious consequences over time, acute reactions in the crisis of recall, an intense remembering process, and greater difficulty in changing these patterns. It was found that a significantly higher percentage of amnesic than nonamnesic women had experienced severe child sexual abuse on most variables, crisis reactions upon recalling it, and intense involvement in the remembering process. However, the amnesic women did not report more negative consequences during the interim years, nor a significantly slower recovery process. Indeed, both groups acknowledged a high percentage of symptoms during the interim period between abuse and the crisis of recall, and both showed a high percentage drop in these symptoms 6 or more years later. These data on symptoms and the later reduction of these symptoms showed minor differences in the predicted direction, but further research is needed, as well as more precise measures of comparison. For example, measurement of the frequency, duration, and intensity of symptoms (during the interim years) and of their reduction (after memories are faced) may capture subtle differences and further illuminate the complexity of the relationship between the presence or absence of amnesia and other factors.

Other than being formerly amnesic or nonamnesic, the subjects were relatively homogeneous. They had all entered private therapy by 1985 to deal with childhood sexual abuse for the first time. In addition, they were demographically similar; they were typically middle class, educated, Caucasian, upwardly mobile women who had been raised in two-parent households. However, respondents undoubtedly differed from women who were either institutionalized or "unaffected" by their sexual abuse, and from persons who did not want, or could not afford, private therapy. Findings from this study should not be generalized to those other populations.

Interestingly, the *amnesic* women in this sample and their parents strongly resembled the accused parents and accusing daughters described by a research report in the False Memory Syndrome Foundation newsletter (P. Freyd, 1992). Most accused parents belonging to the FMSF were also in long marriages and held socioeconomic status and community respect. Most accusing adult children of FMSF members held similar status. When they claimed incestuous abuse, from a young age, their siblings seldom believed them. In this longitudinal study, the amnesics were somewhat more likely than nonamnesics to have been brought up by professional (as opposed to working-class) parents in enduring marriages, to have retained or achieved professional status, and to be currently in first marriages. However, in contrast to the FMSF report, in this sample, therapy had generally followed the return of memory (rather than vice versa), there was usually some external validation of abuse (rather than none), the women felt that their families had abandoned them (rather than the other way around), and, over time in therapy, they reported increasing strength and life satisfaction (rather than emotional deterioration) and none of them were suing their parents. Indeed, some respondents have become healing influences within their families and communities according to the most recent survey (Cameron, 1995).

## DISCUSSION

This chapter has presented a comparison of the reports made by two groups of women—(former) amnesics and nonamnesics—concerning their childhood sexual abuse, its consequences over time, the crisis of recall in adulthood, and the changes brought about in their lives. The following discussion features key issues important to the debate on recovered memories. These issues are, in order, the reported severity of sexual abuse, the documentation of amnesia, the seeming normality of the interim years, the context and cues (or suggestions) that evoke memories, the crisis precipitated by recall, the return of "lost" memories, and, finally, alleged improvement over time.

### Severe Sexual Abuse

One issue that creates a stumbling block in the debate about "recovered" memories is skepticism concerning the severity of the abuse remembered. However, researchers and mental health practitioners have found striking commonalities between two seemingly disparate groups (Cameron, 1994a; van der Kolk, 1987): war veterans, traumatized on battlefields, and survivors of severe child sexual abuse, traumatized in their homes. Decades after combat or abuse, both sought therapy, often with florid symptoms of PTSD. And for both groups, the severity of the original stressor was not only associated with a need for therapy, but with various levels of dissociative symptoms, including amnesia.

Increasingly, systematic studies have refined the understanding of what constitutes severity in sexual abuse. The most sophisticated measures used factor analysis to create a cumulative trauma score (e.g., Herman, Perry, & van der Kolk, 1989) for assessing the overall severity of abuse for each respondent. Researchers have reported that a high percentage of survivors in therapy had experienced "severe" abuse, such as that listed in Table 1 (e.g., Cameron, 1994a; Ensink, 1992; Herman & Schatzow, 1987). Ensink (1992) compared her findings with those of two other research studies using clinical samples (Frenken & van Stolk, 1987; Herman, Russell, & Trocki, 1986) and found all three in rather close agreement on the level of "severe" abuse. The data from this study (with memory groups pooled like the others) are italicized in the following comparison of findings for Ensink, Frenken, Herman, and *Cameron*. Most subjects were abused by father figures (67%, 69%, 75%, *60%*) starting before the age of 10 (69%, 48%, 32%, *89%*) and continuing 4 or more years (74%, 54%, N.A., *54%*). As children, many had experienced force (43%, 37%, 11%, *36%*) and penetration

(67%, 78%, N.A., *80%*). These four studies, from two continents, provide mutual affirmation that therapy-seeking survivors do report serious abuse. Moreover, among sexual abuse survivors in therapy, those *most* likely to report severe abuse were women who had developed amnesia to it.

Formerly amnesic women were also younger at first abuse. This has made "early memories" of sexual abuse another area of contention, but perhaps unnecessarily so. Terr (1994) suggested that children traumatized prior to language development tended to express implicit memories of abuse through their actions, attitudes, and emotions. When respondents in this study were asked in interviews when they thought their abuse started, they often based their answers on regressive flashbacks to fragmentary images, smells, emotions, or visceral pains that some called "body memories." It is understandable that cognitive psychologists, who would not use the term "memories" in the absence of a narrative and time line, may find "body memories" an unacceptable concept. Yet in regressive flashbacks, in which senses and emotions prevailed over thought, subjects *perceived* pressures and intrusions, images and smells, and desolate emotions.

### Documentation of Amnesia

Not only do therapy-seeking respondents report serious abuse, but among them, those who had experienced amnesia were the most likely to report it. Ensink (1992) and Herman and Schatzow (1987) also recorded periods of amnesia to childhood sexual abuse for their samples (29% and 67%, respectively), as did other researchers mentioned in the review of the literature. Briere and Conte (1989), studying 468 outpatients, all of whom reported sexual abuse, reported that 60% of them had been unable to remember the abuse for "a period of time" *prior* to adulthood. The study described in this chapter, however, departed from other research by searching out cases in which amnesia had been profound and had lasted well into adulthood. Making the presence or absence of amnesia (thus defined) the central variable in a longitudinal study produced additional understanding of abuse and its aftermath. A typical amnesic in this study had been subjected, through preschool and most of elementary school, to escalating sexual abuse at the hands of one or both natural parents. (Because most parental marriages were intact, few stepfathers were named as abusers.) Moreover, about one half (48%) of the amnesic respondents reported not having a single adult on whom they could depend for support.

Amnesics were asked their opinion on how the amnesia set in. Their answers yield subjective but intriguing data that can be categorized as follows: (a) automatic response to overwhelming assault (e.g., following violent rape), (b) involuntary response (e.g., with dissociation fragmenting the experience as it occurred so that it could not be experienced as a whole), (c) voluntary effort (e.g., the memory was rejected over time until it was no longer accessible), and (d) self-deception (e.g., idealization of the abuser). (These responses might be categorized by clinicians as physiological, dissociative, repressive, and intellectualized defenses, respectively.) Two other causes contributing to amnesia were implied by the women. First, they had lacked any schema for understanding sexual violation as young children. Second, their perceptions of what occurred were disconfirmed by the abuser, the family, and society. A quote from a former amnesic sums it up and echoes Jennifer Freyd's "betrayal-trauma theory" (1994):

> I was sure, deep down, that Dad was an honest, loving person. A kid really needs to believe in the parent caring for her. If you can't validate for yourself what's happening, you shut it out. If nothing makes sense, you blot out the conflict.

The amnesics apparently denied at the time what was happening to them, or, after it stopped, what had occurred. However, they did not lose semantic knowledge or procedural skills. It was personal memories that were missing. As adults, several respondents had looked back on a childhood devoid of personal biography. Others were aware of blank years. Some lost only moments in time ("I remembered that car ride, but not how it ended"). A few developed multiple personalities. But whatever form the amnesia took, it denied to explicit memory the particular moments or hours or years of sexual abuse. *Implicit* memory remained as a source of unexplained reactions and emotions ("I was so afraid to be on the earth"), inappropriate urges ("I unnerved boys by knowing more about sex than they did"), and alienation from self and others ("I didn't trust anyone, not even myself").

The nonamnesics, when asked why they had always remembered their abuse, gave answers that revealed certain differences in their childhood situation: (a) it was easier, with vigilence, to avoid a *non*-parental abuser; (b) the pervasive sexuality in some extended families involved frequent, but less intrusive, molestations that were relatively undisguised; and (c) several nonamnesics deliberately remembered in order to choose models *unlike* their abuser. In other words, nonamnesics did not deny the abusive events, but they distorted their meaning and impact.

*Interim Years*

One would expect severe consequences to follow severe abuse and therefore that amnesics should be more vulnerable than nonamnesics during the interim years. But this was not apparent in the findings. Asked whether or not they had experienced negative consequences during the interim period, the groups did not differ significantly in their self-perception, coping styles, somatic problems, or symptoms of PTSD. There are two alternative explanations. First, there really was *no* difference between them. Amnesia may have cushioned the impact of the interim period, making it less stressed than it might otherwise have been. Alternatively, there *was* a difference but it was not evident because (a) many women in both groups endorsed the items, creating a "ceiling effect," or (b) the frequency, duration, severity, and incapacitation of the symptoms (e.g., migraine headaches) were not part of the measure, making it less precise.[7]

Support for the second explanation can be found in other research (e.g., Finkelhor, 1986) in which the severity of a particular form of sexual abuse (e.g.,

---

[7]Differences stand out more clearly in Table 1 partly because questions were, by their nature, more factual and provided a wider range of answer options.

penetration) has been linked to long-term consequences. For example, Ensink (1992, p. 107) found a strong correlation between severity of sexual trauma and serious disturbances of consciousness, which, in turn, led to more likelihood of hospitalization.

It seems probable that, in this study, there were also real sample differences during the interim period that were not clearly revealed. Certainly, the nonamnesics, remembering abuse, experienced problems during adolescence that amnesics, in their ignorance, were spared. Examples include "It was still going on. I lied to my friends daily to cover it up," and "Before our wedding, I dreamed I was walking down the aisle, to my husband-to-be, dressed like a harlot. My father had said Joe would leave me if I told him."

Hard as the interim years were for both groups, however, they were probably more difficult for the amnesics. Several findings in this research support this position: Although the differences were not significant, somewhat higher percentages of amnesics endorsed most interim symptoms. This tendency was especially strong on key items. The amnesics were more likely to cope by putting excessive effort into their daily lives. They chose more serious escapes (alcohol, drugs) and a third of them were troubled enough during the interim years to seek counseling (for nonsexual problems), suggesting that they were more stressed. Gelinas (1983) called such early efforts to get counseling "disguised presentations" that caused a troubled person to seek help while hiding the underlying problem from both therapist and client. In addition, more of the amnesics experienced, during the interim years, symptoms of the denial phase of PTSD, including numbed emotions, sexual problems, and suicidal feelings.

Probably the most insidious long-term problem for both groups was cumulative developmental damage of the sort referred to in the old saying, "As the twig is bent, so grows the tree." The sexual abuse occurred during the most formative years of life. The particular developmental stage (or stages) at the time of trauma (Pynoos, 1994) molded the young child's views of self, other, and the world (Cameron, 1994a) in ways that became increasingly entrenched and maladaptive.

## Context, Cues, and Confronting the Past

Amnesics tended to remember their abuse at a "safer time" in their lives (68% vs. 24%), whereas nonamnesics focused in on their memories when they felt overwhelmed by life (21% vs. 42%; Table 3). What was meant by "a safer time"? Apparently, it was whatever had strengthened them—distance from the family of origin, death of the abuser, a supportive work and marriage environment, good friends, or earlier therapy (e.g., for addictions) that had expanded their repertoire of coping. What did being "overwhelmed by life" mean to the nonamnesics? Interviews revealed that they thought they were "over" the remembered abuse until an accumulation of problems made them recognize that they could run no longer. ("I zombied through the years until one day, everything fell in on me. I *had* to deal with the abuse.")

Within these differing life contexts, however, specific cues brought out the memories. It had been hypothesized that a higher percentage of amnesics than nonamnesics would cite cues because they had a greater need to recall. Yet the two groups responded similarly. Exposure to the abuse of someone close or to a similar setting or emotion was most likely to cue memories for both groups. ("When my niece was raped, I fell apart." "Our plane suddenly plunged hundreds of feet. Feeling helpless and utterly terrified, I flashed back to the torture.") There were other influences, such as nonabusive body contact. For some respondents, during intercourse with a loved partner, force was suddenly recalled. In nightmares of danger, family members, hiding behind closed doors, deserted the dreamer. Although most respondents checked two or more cues to memory, only 2 of 25 amnesics cited media influences and none cited a book. About three-quarters (73%) of the amnesics had their first memories prior to therapy and, by 1995, about two-thirds (65%) had obtained external validation of abuse that had started (on average) about 40 years earlier. Sometimes support came from a relative or another victim. However, recantation by a perpetrator, if any, usually issued from the perpetrator's deathbed (Cameron, 1994b). Lisa's case was an astounding exception. A decade ago, Lisa began to recover memories of sexual abuse by her brother and, several years later, by both parents. They became increasingly resentful of her "creating trouble" in their close-knit family, so Lisa left town. After lonely years away from everyone she knew, she telephoned home. She was astonished when both her parents confessed that they had indeed sexually abused her and were feeling deep remorse for the pain they had caused her. They were ready to help, in any way, to reconstruct her past in order for her to heal.

## Crisis of Recall

Many respondents had experienced the numbed existence common to chronic PTSD during the interim period. This may have protected them as children, but coping by avoidance becomes increasingly maladaptive in adulthood (according to this interpretation). The crisis of recall, disruptive as it was, swept aside entrenched perceptions of self and society and defensive ways of coping. The arousing-intrusive symptoms of PTSD, which had erupted occasionally during the interim period, now took priority over numbed emotions. The abuse issue could no longer be avoided, but facing it provided an opportunity to make healthier choices. Amnesic respondents had been unaware until the crisis of recall that they had experienced trauma as a child, that it had involved sexual abuse by a relative, and that it had affected their lives. Nonamnesic respondents had had to redefine remembered abuse and admit its effect on their lives. It was therefore expected that the amnesics faced greater distress in the crisis of recall.

In recognizing their own childhood abuse, the research respondents had developed new schemata for the role played by child sexual abuse in their lives. In the immediate aftermath, most women were in crisis. The two groups are generally similar (Table 3) except in terms of crisis reactions. The amnesics were especially disoriented. ("My world came off its axis, and I had no place to stand to put it back together.") They simultaneously faced knowledge of past trauma, recognition that someone close had betrayed them, and assessment of the cumulative impact on their lives. Their lives had been greatly different from what they had believed. More than half now felt suicidal—not, as before, "sometimes, over decades," but currently and urgently.

Although the nonamnesic women had always known the facts of their abuse, denial had obscured much of the truth about it. About one half had never defined what had happened to them as sex abuse. They had thought of it as normal, as punishment, or as some peculiarity in the abuser that they must endure. Suddenly, as adults, there was a profound shift in their understanding. They were shocked into redefining what had happened and recognizing its impact on their lives. Interestingly, 6 months later, half of the nonamnesics, who had *never* forgotten, found themselves denying facts they had always acknowledged and their suicidal feelings also rose. Members of both groups experienced painful, intrusive memories and turbulent emotions after years of numbed avoidance.

Recall brought realization to amnesics, for the first time, of their childhood sexual abuse. The shock was profound. "I felt as if I had been plugged into an electric circuit and inside me a thousand loose ends were misfiring." It was no longer possible to cover feelings with a smile; but this allowed the women to get in touch with sadness and anger and betrayal that they had long denied. Mood dependence cued in additional unhappy memories, so for a while, there was little beyond the intrusion of painful thoughts and memories. Both groups experienced the breakdown of denial and with it a major challenge to previous coping styles, which failed many of them (63% vs. 43%). Amnesics, recognizing incest and usually a parent as the abuser, experienced significantly more horror (67% vs. 24%) and disillusionment (57% vs. 29%) and an urgent temptation to suicide (54% vs. 29%). They plunged in and out of denial. In the crisis, amnesics sought support from any and all resources (52% vs. 10%). As indicated in Table 3, the nonamnesics were somewhat more aware of turbulent emotions in general and were willing to talk about them. In redefining what had happened and the behavior of the abuser, their most powerful emotion was anger.

*Return of Memories*

The remembering process, described on the basis of data gleaned from questionnaires and information from interviews, was especially intense for the amnesics. As indicated in Table 3, amnesics reported more proneness to flashbacks and that they tended to experience through their senses, through dissociation, and through regressive emotions. Memories that had started with fragmentary visual or tactile experiences expanded over many months and were augmented by overwhelming emotions and dismaying cognitions. These memories became sufficiently complete (although never fully) to alter their picture of childhood. The nonamnesics were generally affected somewhat less, but flashbacks and spontaneous memories forced them to bring their adult understanding to bear on the past. For them, reexamination of the past—sometimes sequentially, sometimes not—obliged them to use a different perspective. Their memories sometimes came as whole narratives to which they could now connect definition, emotion, and an understanding of how the abuse had affected them over the years.

The recovery of early childhood "memories of abuse" for both groups generally involved sensory and emotional experiences dissociated from other elements found in complete memories. Such fragments were not, in themselves, cognitive narratives with time, place, and meaning. (Terr, 1988, discusses early memories.) However, increasingly complex memories from later ages tended to enlarge on and support the themes of early fragments and to provide at least a Swiss cheese history of abuse. The most intense period of remembering occurred over many months as abusive events were reexperienced, processed, and then integrated into a more realistic understanding of childhood. No respondent claimed that she had recalled "everything." The women were likely to say that they had remembered "enough," or that they felt "emptied" or "at peace" inside. Flashbacks and intrusive thinking diminished, and attention turned increasingly, with the passage of time, from dealing with past negatives to strengthening positives in their lives.

## Improvement Over Time

Three-quarters of the original sample of amnesics and nonamnesics (93% of those still available) returned the 1992 questionnaires. Each woman's responses were compared objectively with her own answers 6 years earlier, which made it possible to measure reported change over time. Improvement was noted in the following areas: self-perception, means of coping, and PTSD symptoms. Improvement in somatic symptoms and psychosocial strengths was also rated (worse, same, better, much better) by the women themselves and this subjective material will be briefly noted.

*Change in self-perception.* Using a self-description checklist in 1986 (e.g., *Did* you feel "different from others"?), respondents had endorsed the negative self-perceptions, coping styles, and symptoms of PTSD that had characterized them during the interim years. When the same checklist items were repeated for 1992 (e.g., *Do* you feel "different from others"?), the proportion of both groups checking the unequivocal Yes (instead of Somewhat) to negative self-perceptions had dropped markedly (see columns of 4 and 5 of Table 2). The overall finding was that the women were feeling a great deal better about themselves, and they were more discriminating. For example, during the interviews, some reported that they were "different from others" but they now saw this as a positive, affirming their demonstrated capacity for growth. They also distinguished between the self-blame that had been so prevalent during the interim period (see the first two columns of Table 2) and the strong sense of responsibility for their lives today.

*Changed means of coping.* Wickramasekera (1994) suggested that remission of various stress-related symptoms comes with recovery of traumatic memory (p. 153). This shift signaled, for him, the transfer of source information from implicit to explicit memory. As respondents in this study established the source of their troubling symptoms in childhood trauma, there was a decline in long-standing problems of all kinds (see columns 4 and 5 of Table 2). There was a similar remission for the nonamnesic women as they redefined memories of abuse. Coping mechanisms that the women had clung to for decades had not changed overnight. However, the crisis precipitated by recall had been a watershed, forcing a major change in direction. The data in columns 4 and 5 of Table 2 suggest that respondents had radically reversed the coping priorities they had reported for the interim years (the first two columns). They no longer had to put such effort into living, pleasing others, and keeping overbusy. The old escapes (with the exception of compulsive eating) were being abandoned. They were open to support. Religion (or, as was emphasized in the interviews, a growing "spirituality") and strong relationships with others were important in their lives. Therapy (which had been the last choice for coping among respondents in earlier years) had been catapulted to first place for some time. By 1992, one half of the respondents in both groups were still in therapy (at least occasionally), and others saw it as an available resource. In the interview, several women mentioned that they were surprised that life had not become easier, but that they had instead grown stronger. The ordinary ups and downs seemed challenging, rather than overwhelming and, when serious difficulties arose, they were more patient with themselves and more compassionate of others. Another "surprise," stated with pleasure during interviews, was, "I *really* like myself!"

*Improvement in somatic symptoms.* Survivors of sexual abuse are prone to long-term somatic symptoms (Gelinas, 1983; Wickramasekera, 1994), and these respondents had been no exception. When they were asked about health-related problems during the interim years *before* they began to deal with their sexual abuse, they checked an average of 8 items from the original list of 22 symptoms. According to their self-reported progress, three-quarters of these earlier somatic complaints had improved or ceased to be a problem by 1992. (There were no significant differences between amnesics and nonamnesics.) Some problems, of course, had been eliminated even *before* the breakthrough of memories ("I stopped drinking and *then* I remembered"). Stress symptoms improved steadily ("My jaws relaxed and the awful migraines came to a stop"). Self-abuse had dropped sharply by the 1992 interview, as respondents reported "taking care of myself better."

*Improvement in PTSD symptoms.* Wickramasekera (1994) noted that reduction of involuntary physiological activity (such as certain PTSD symptoms) tended to follow the recovery of memory (p. 153). "Avoidance" symptoms had dominated *before* memories were faced and "intrusion" symptoms *after* (with some intermixing). Highly significant improvement was evident by 1992 in both these categories (see columns 4 and 5 of Table 2). Respondents, however, reported that they sometimes felt vulnerable in moderate threat situations that evoked feelings such as the fear and helplessness associated with their abuse. Among the examples were, "A mild earthquake reduces me to a terrified heap on the floor" and "If I plan to drive to another city in the morning, I wake up convinced that 'this is the day I die.' "

## A CONCLUDING ISSUE: TRAUMA, AMNESIA, AND VALIDATION

The literature reviewed in this chapter and findings from the longitudinal study support the conclusion that amnesia to psychic trauma is *not* a recent, rare, or unverified phenomenon. Nor is it reported only by survivors of sexual abuse. Knowledge of trauma in general has enhanced the study of specific trauma populations. Data on persons traumatized by war or natural disaster have informed the study of survivors traumatized within their family. Studies like the one presented here can stimulate research on trauma and memory among other populations, and this volume, taken as a whole, represents scientific cooperation in the study of trauma in various populations and under different circumstances, which builds a stronger science.

Similarly, clinicians and experimentalists can learn from each other's disciplines. During this longitudinal study, most of the women (including half of the nonamnesic group) recalled additional key information unavailable to them earlier. Furthermore, many formerly amnesic women recognized that "intrinsic" memories (a knowing beneath the not knowing) had influenced their lives. Although they had lacked conscious awareness of trauma for decades, their self-concept, relationships, behavior, attitudes, and emotions had been profoundly shaped by what they had experienced.

Apparently, throughout the continuum between amnesia and nonamnesia there run cords of both memory and forgetting that have yet to be unraveled, and layers of complexity that have yet to be explored.

Clinical and experimental psychologists have both studied memory, yet they have often ignored each other's special expertise. This longitudinal survey of amnesics suggests that there are areas for mutual rapprochement. Clinicians, finding that early childhood recollections are more sensory and emotional than cognitive and verbal, can help experimenters develop a broader conception of the multifaceted phenomenon we call memory. Experimenters studying context-, mood-, and state-dependent learning and cued recall can help clinicians understand the loss and triggering of traumatic memories. Both disciplines can be mutually enhanced by collaboration. The combined resources of researchers and mental health professionals, as well as government support and public awareness, will be required to find honest and humane answers to the individual and societal problems generated by sexual abuse. Particularly needed are creative research designs (such as some in this volume) that respect the breadth and depth of the topic, substantive and testable hypotheses, data that permit comparisons and establish connections, interpretations that are responsive to findings, and an open attitude that does not label memories as simply true or false but instead recognizes their complexity.

## ACKNOWLEDGMENTS

I want to thank my colleagues at the University of La Verne for their continuing support of this longterm research, and Dr. Kathy Pezdek and the psychology department at the Claremont Graduate School for their encouragement and provision of research space and computer facilities.

## REFERENCES

American Psychiatric Association (1994). *Diagnostic and statistical manual.* (4th ed., rev.). Washington, DC: American Psychiatric Association.

Bremner, J. D., Davis, M., Southwick, S. M., Krystal, J. H., & Charney, D. S. (1994). In R. S. Pynoos (Ed.), *Post-traumatic stress disorder: A clinical review* (pp. 65–98). Lutherville, MD: Sidran Press.

Briere, J. N., & Conte, J. (1989). *Amnesia in adults molested as children.* Paper presented at the annual meeting of the American Psychological Association, New Orleans, LA.

Briere, J. N., & Elliott, D. M. (1994). Immediate and long-term impact of child sexual abuse. *The Future of Children,* 4(2), 54–69.

Briere, J., & Runtz, M. (1987). Post-sexual abuse trauma. *Journal of Interpersonal Trauma,* 2(4), 367–379.

Cameron, C. (1994a). Veterans of a secret war: Survivors of childhood sexual trauma compared to Vietnam War veterans with PTSD. *Journal of Interpersonal Violence,* 9(1), 117–132.

Cameron, C. (1994b). Women confronting their abusers: Issues, decisions, and outcomes. *Journal of Child Sexual Abuse,* 3(1), 7–35.

Cameron, C. (1995). Data from the fourth longitudinal survey, currently under analysis.

Courtois, C. A. (1988). *Healing the incest wound.* New York: Norton Press.

Courtois, C. A. (1992). The memory retrieval process in incest survivor therapy. *Journal of Child Sexual Abuse,* 1(1), 15–31.

Elliott, D. M., & Briere, J. N. (1995). Post-traumatic stress associated with delayed recall of sexual abuse; A general population study. *Journal of Traumatic Stress,* 8(4), 629–647.

Ensink, B. J. (1992). *Confusing realities: A study of child sexual abuse and psychiatric symptoms.* Amsterdam: VU University Press.

Eth, S., & Pynoos, R. S. (Eds.). (1985). *Post-traumatic stress disorder in children.* Washington, DC: American Psychiatric Press.

Feldman-Summers, S., and Pope, K. S. (1994). The experience of "forgetting" childhood abuse: A national survey of psychologists. *Journal of Consulting and Clinical Psychology,* 62(3), 636–639.

Finkelhor, D. (1979). *Sexually victimized children.* New York: Free Press.

Finkelhor, D. (1986). *A sourcebook on child sexual abuse.* Beverly Hills, CA: Sage Publications.

Frenken, J., & van Stolk, B. (1987). *Hulpverleners en incestslachtoffers.* Deventer: Van Loghum Slaterus.

Freyd, J. (1994). Betrayal-trauma: Traumatic amnesia as an adaptive response to childhood abuse. *Ethics and Behavior,* 4, 307–329.

Freyd, P. (1992). False Memory Syndrome Foundation newsletter, April 1 and May 1.

Gelinas, D. (1983). Persisting negative effects of incest. *Psychiatry,* 46, 312–332.

Goldberg, J., True, W. R., Eisen, S. A., & Henderson, W. G. (1990). A twin study of the effects of the Vietnam War on post-traumatic stress disorder. *Journal of the American Medical Association,* 263, 1227–1232.

Herman, J. L. (1981). *Father-daughter incest.* Cambridge, MA: Harvard University Press.

Herman, J. L. (1992). *Trauma and recovery.* New York: Basic Books.

Herman, J. L.; Perry, C.; & van der Kolk, B. (1989). Childhood trauma in borderline personality disorder. *American Journal of Psychiatry* 146(4), 490–495.

Herman, J. L., Russell, D., & Trocki, K. (1986). Long-term effects of incestuous abuse in childhood. *American Journal of Psychiatry,* 143(10) 1293–1296.

Herman, J. L., & Schatzow, E. (1987). Recovery and verification of memories of childhood sexual trauma. *Psychoanalytic Psychology,* 4(1), 1–14.

Horowitz, M. J. (1976/1986). *Stress response syndromes.* New York: Jason Aronson.

Kempe, C. H. (1978). Sexual abuse, another hidden pediatric problem. *Pediatrics,* 62, 382–389.

Kinsey, A. C., Pomeroy, W. B., & Martin, C. E. (1948). *Sexual behavior in the human male.* Philadelphia: W. B. Saunders.

Kinsey, A. C., Pomeroy, W. B., Martin, C. E., & Gebhard, P. H. (1953). *Sexual behavior in the human female.* Philadelphia: W. B. Saunders.

van der Kolk, B. A. (1987). *Psychological trauma.* Washington, DC: American Psychiatric Press.

Koopman, C., Classen, C., Cardena, E., & Spiegel, D. (1995). When disaster strikes, acute distress disorder may follow. *Journal of Traumatic Stress,* **8**(1), 29–46.

Meiselman, K. C. (1978). *Incest.* San Francisco: Jossey-Bass.

Putnam, F. W. (1985). Dissociation as a response to extreme trauma. In R. Kluft (Ed.), *Childhood antecedents of multiple personality* (pp. 65–97). Washington, DC: American Psychiatric Association.

Pynoos, R. S. (1994). Traumatic stress and developmental psychopathology in children and adolescents. In R. S. Pynoos (Ed.), *Post-traumatic stress disorder: A clinical review* (pp. 65–98). Lutherville, MD: Sidran Press.

Rush, F. (1978). *The best kept secret.* Englewood Cliffs, NJ: Prentice Hall.

Russell, D. (1986). *The secret trauma: Incest in the lives of girls and women.* New York: Basic Books.

Sargant, W., & Slater, E. (1941). Amnesic syndromes of war. *Proceedings of the Royal Society of Medicine,* **34,** 757–764.

Sutker, P. B., Uddo, M., Brailey, K., & Allain, Jr., A. N. (1993). War-zone trauma and stress-related symptoms. *Journal of Social Issues,* **49**(4), 33–49.

Terr, L. (1988). What happens to the memories of early trauma? *Journal of the American Academy of Child and Adolescent Psychiatry,* **27,** 96–104.

Terr, L. (1990). *Too scared to cry.* New York: Harper & Row.

Terr, L. (1994). *Unchained memories.* New York: Basic Books.

Trickett, P., & Putnam, F. (1995). Impact of child sexual abuse on females: Toward a developmental psychobiological integration. *Psychological Science,* **4**(2), 81–87.

Ullman, S. E. (1995). Adult trauma survivors and post-traumatic stress sequelae: An analysis of reexperiencing, avoidance, and arousal criteria. *Journal of Traumatic Stress.* **8,** 179–188.

Wickramasekera, I. (1994). Somatic to psychological symptoms and information transfer from implicit to explicit memory. *Dissociation,* **7**(3), 153–166.

Williams, L. M. (1994). Recall of childhood trauma: A prospective study of women's memories of child sexual abuse. *Journal of Consulting and Clinical Psychology,* **62**(6), 1167–1176.

Williams, L. M. (1995). Recovered memories of abuse in women with documented child sexual victimization histories. *Journal of Traumatic Stress,* **8**(4), 649–673.

Wilson, J., Smith, W., & Johnson, S. (1985). A comparative analysis of PTSD among various survivor groups. In C. Figley (Ed.), *Trauma and its wake* (pp. 142–172). New York: Brunner/Mazel.

Wyatt, G. (1985). The sexual abuse of Afro-American and white-American women in childhood. *Child Abuse and Neglect,* **9,** 507–519.

# True Memories of Childhood Trauma:
# Flaws, Absences, and Returns

LENORE TERR

*University of California San Francisco, San Francisco, CA 94108*

This chapter examines what can be learned about flaws, absences, and returns of memory from clinical research studies of true, proven traumatic events from childhood. Timing and visual perceptual flaws in otherwise correct narratives were commonplace in studies of the Chowchilla school bus kidnapping victims. After the *Challenger* space shuttle disaster, 30% of randomly selected schoolchildren exhibited misunderstandings as to what had occurred. Adolescents tended to correct these mistakes, latency children did not. Absences of memory in proven traumas occur before the age of 28 to 36 months. Despite this infantile amnesia, post-traumatic symptoms form and linger, reflecting nonverbal memories. In a study of more than 100 young women who had been documented to have visited emergency rooms 17 years before for sexual abuses and attacks, Williams (1994) found that 38% could no longer remember these visits. In another study, Linton (1986) determined that of all her own adult life events (each documented), the negative ones were most likely to be forgotten. Accuracy of memory retrieval was studied by Herman and Shatzow (1987), who found that 70% of their patients were able to obtain confirmation of the events that they had remembered. Thus, true memories of documented events can be flawed or temporarily absent.

## INTRODUCTION

The clinical fields of psychiatry, psychology, social work, and counseling are currently in the midst of an enormous controversy called the false memory debate. Although this debate concerns adults—can they remember with accuracy those horrors inflicted on them in childhood which, for a while, were entirely out of mind?—the argument really has to do with children. Can a child come to remember things that never, ever happened? And can a child completely forget things that are so hideous that they might indeed have become the central theme of the child's life? Can such memories, once hidden, come back to plague the child now grown up? Do therapists implant traumatic memories into adults who suffered no childhood traumas whatsoever? And in fact, when the debate nears its farthest reaches, the question is asked, can psychotherapy be trusted at all?

These questions concern everyone in the psychotherapy professions. Yet few of us have turned to what we know are bona fide traumatic memories—"true memories," in other words—to glean some of the answers. Most of the public's attention around the memory controversy in the past few years has been paid to the few, singly occurring, sensational cases that hinge on the question of wholly untrue memories. Although studies have existed for years on the true, we have dwelled, instead, on the false. We have spent considerable recent television and print time, for example, on the young man named Steven Cook who retracted

*The Recovered Memory/False Memory Debate*
Copyright © 1994 by Academic Press, Inc.

his accusations against Chicago's Cardinal Bernardin, although he continued to insist that some church authority sexually abused him as a child (Woodward, 1994); on the Paul Ingram case in Olympia, Washington, a case in which a man confessed to sexually abusing his daughters and since then has tried in a number of ways to retract these confessions, claiming that they were entirely false memories (Wright, 1994); on the courtroom case in which a girl, based on repeated and extreme suggestion from her mother, falsely claimed that her therapists had tied her up and exposed her to the most disgusting and humiliating forms of sex (Terr, 1994); and on the Napa Valley, California, trial involving Holly Ramona, in which a jury held that Ramona's therapists had used improper techniques to deal with the then 19-year-old's returning memories of incest (Butler, 1994). These cases caught the public's attention and showed the possibilities of wholly false remembrances and of wholly implanted ideas. But they did not help the public to develop a general understanding of the false memory phenomena.

These cases were single anecdotal reports. Few large clinical studies came along to demonstrate how much wholly false or implanted memory was festering in the adult population at large. Yapko (1994) surveyed master's level mental health counselors about to take hypnosis workshops and reported that therapists were ignorant about their own powers to influence patients, particularly through hypnosis. The survey revealed that a number of therapists got hunches about incest or child sexual abuse which they then suggested to their patients until the patients accepted the idea. This contention was not well backed up in Yapko's surveys, however, because they did not reveal what anyone was actually doing within the therapeutic consulting rooms. It was not disclosed how many therapists and by what process these therapists were influencing their adult patients' memories.

We came closer to knowing some of this from a sample of 145 American and 57 British psychologists analyzed by Poole, Lindsay, Memon, and Bull (1995). Here, the data indicated that the surveyed therapists had often relied on symptom complexes to aid them in diagnosing childhood sexual abuse, and that 71% of them had used potentially suggestive techniques, such as hypnosis or dream interpretation, to help their clients recover memories. Poole et al. concluded that 25% of the therapists who had answered the questionnaires harbored beliefs and used therapeutic practices that would have influenced the relatively high rates of memory recovery that these same therapists reported. But this was still a somewhat small sample, with a 38% rate of return and an additional number of surveys discarded because the respondents had not seen what the investigators believed to be a sufficient number of women clients. To form more accurate conclusions on these issues, further studies are needed that combine neutrality, randomness, large numbers, and truthfulness from the research subjects. Monitoring real therapeutic sessions with real patients could provide valuable data, but this does not promise to be accomplished in the foreseeable future.

Much of the information we now have about false memories comes from research in the important, but nonclinical, fields of cognitive and developmental psychology. Rather than reviewing this literature, which although important, is not directly clinically applicable, I will take a different turn. I will review what we do know about true memories of trauma—about bona fide, historically true memories—and from this, I will try to inject some clarity into the false memory debate.

To help me take this perspective on "true" traumatic memory from childhood, I cite five studies: three of my own, plus studies by Herman and Shatzow (1987) and Williams (1994). I have examined the flaws, absences, returns of true memories from childhood. My thesis is that even when a trauma is historically true, it cannot be narrated with 99.44% purity. The human mental apparatus does not allow for total accuracy of recall. Perception and registration, storage, and retrieval of traumatic memory are all subject to interference. The surprise of traumatic events, the horror, the sadness, the confusion, the intensity, and the humiliation can interfere with human cognition and memory. Because terrible events are capable of creating so much feeling all at once, there is ample opportunity for a memory to become flawed (Terr et al. 1996) or even absent with time. However, this does not mean that these memories are basically untrue. As the romantic poet Gerard Manly Hopkins once declared in his fascination with "pied" things—with blotched, flecked, imperfect things—one may find that the true memories of true childhood traumas are equally fascinating, partly because they are so "pied." Their gists are almost always correct. True, I would say; however, people make fascinating mistakes around these gists.

## FLAWS IN TRUE MEMORIES

The flaws in true child memories of true traumas became evident to me when I went to Chowchilla in 1976. Twenty-six summer school children had been kidnapped on their bus on July 15th that year by three young, slim, white men. We knew who the children were because they were all registered in summer school, they were driven home every day on a certain bus, and they appeared at Santa Rita Prison some 28 hours after they had disappeared from the face of the earth on a hot Thursday afternoon. We also know what happened to them because there was an FBI investigation, a police investigation, and hundreds of newspaper accounts—it was the international news story of 1976—and there was a carefully conducted criminal trial in Alameda County, California. It was also evident that almost every one of these children had seen the kidnappers use a white van and a green van (and the police had taken these same white and green vans into custody). So when a kidnapped boy said that *he* saw a light blue van, his memory—in this one regard—was incorrect. Pied. Flawed. In other words, he was reporting true memory with false detail (Terr et al., 1996).

The Chowchilla children's memories of their terrors at the hands of their kidnappers were basically true. The gists of their stories corresponded well to each other (Terr, 1979). Even 4 to 5 years later, they could recall the stories central to their kidnapping (Terr, 1983a). They were stopped on a back road by a van seemingly in trouble. They all remembered that. Three stocking-masked people jumped into their school bus toting large guns. One took over the driving, another pointed a gun directly at them, and a third drove the seemingly disabled van away. When the schoolbus drove down into a slough, the children were herded one by one into two blackened vans, the one that had stopped them and a second one waiting there. The group was then driven about with nothing to see, nothing to eat, nothing to drink, no bathroom stops, nothing spoken to them, and only one or two breaks in their motion for 11 hours. Every child remembered that. They were then told, one by one, to get out, to answer some questions delivered by a masked man holding a flashlight under his chin, to give up a personal item, and to tell their names. That, too, they all remembered. Then they were ordered to go down into that "hole." They heard the sounds of rocks and dirt being shoveled above them. They then stayed in their hole, actually a buried moving-van trailer in a rock quarry, for 16 hours. When the ceiling of the hole began to collapse because one child had moved a stake holding it up, some boys climbed up to inspect the ceiling of their burial place. They thought perhaps they could pry open the top the way someone might open a sardine can if they were stuck inside. They remembered that, too. The two boys who dug were successful. In a few hours, each child, with the help of the bus driver, crawled out of an opening in the top of the van. The children remembered all of that.

So all of the victims, 26 children with the exception of one girl who had moved away without a forwarding address, remembered the gist of their experiences for me the first year and the fifth year after their kidnapping. This was a strikingly different event from anything that had ever happened to them before.It could be remembered with clarity and with fullness.

But there were flaws in these children's memories. An important type of flaw concerned timing. Some children were unable to get their durations or sequences quite right, especially about their symptoms but sometimes about the event itself (Terr, 1979, 1983a, 1983b, 1984). The kidnapping felt shorter than 28 hours to a few of them, and time was confused for a couple of others (Terr, 1983b). One older boy, a heroic digger, had become mixed up about whether it was dusk or dawn when he looked into the opening at the top of the van; yet, he had emerged into the broad daylight of a midsummer, California afternoon. Many children misplaced dreams, fears, and crank calls or statements made by other people after the kidnapping into positions prior to the kidnapping, making them, in effect, predictive (Terr, 1979, 1984). I termed this phenomenon "time skew." The children had psychologically needed the powers of prediction to regain what they felt to be totally lost control. But they had also sacrificed, in so doing, some accuracy of memory. True victims of a known and proven trauma, in other words, were beginning to report details of memory that were flawed—"false," in fact, as some of my colleagues would say.

Besides the memories of time, memories of visual perceptions were also becoming distorted by the Chowchilla victims (Terr, 1979, 1983a). Three children had hallucinated during the kidnapping experience. There were no women, older men, black people, or masterminds with peg legs arrested by the police; yet six children reported seeing these very people. Happily, three of the Chowchilla children spontaneously corrected their remembered misperceptions over the next 4 years. They may have read other accounts, watched TV, attended the kidnappers' trial, or had a good corrective conversation with someone. However, by the fourth and fifth years after the kidnapping, 13 children were still reporting missightings. When I added the three who had given up on theirs, I had a total of 16 out of 25 kidnapped children who had seen, heard, or construed the wrong impression of the kidnappers' looks (or in the case I have already mentioned, of the color of the kidnappers' van).

Flaws of true memory were also evident in a study conducted by my research team after the 1986 explosion of the U.S. space shuttle, *Challenger* (Terr et al., 1996). In this study, we were not looking at a direct traumatic event, but at a very distant event: we compared the memories of 153 children: those who were watching the shuttle from the Cape Canaveral viewing stands; randomly selected 8- and 15-year-olds from Concord, New Hampshire, schools (where Christa McAuliffe, the schoolteacher designated to teach from space, had taught); and randomly selected 8- and 15-year-olds from Porterville, California, where the children rode school busses to school and who were thus unaware of the explosion at the time it happened. Here again the gists of the children's memories corresponded acceptably to what we all had seen: the *Challenger* went up for a few seconds and then disappeared in a fiery ball that sent trailers over the Florida sky; NASA announced a malfunction; and the people on TV looked extremely sad. But there were mental mistakes here too. The first year that they were interviewed, 7% of 8-year-old children in this study misordered the sequences having to do with *Challenger*'s ill-fated flight. Misperceptions of what they had seen or heard were reported by 13% of the children in the East within the first few weeks of the explosion. Misunderstandings of what had actually happened were evidenced by about 30% of all children during those first few weeks. Later, the newspaper and TV campaign probably corrected many of the adolescent children's misunderstandings—only 8% of adolescents exhibited this type of memory mistake 14 months after the disaster. But in 1987, for the 9-year-olds, the media explanations did relatively little; by a year after *Challenger* exploded, 29% of them still reported a misunderstanding of what had happened, an almost identical number to the 30% who had originally misunderstood. Overall, about 30% of children either incorrectly saw or thought something connected with the *Challenger* disaster. Although a number of older children gave up these flawed segments of memory by a year afterward, the younger ones clung to their mistakes.

## ABSENCES OF TRUE MEMORIES (EARLY INFANTILE AMNESIAS)

At this point, I will turn to what can be learned about absences of memory from studies of true, documented traumas. In 1988, I reported on the memories of 20 children who were traumatized under the age of 5 and who came to my office with external verification—confessions, eyewitness reports, police reports, photographs—of their plights (Terr, 1988). This was a very small, preliminary study and it reflected how difficult it is to obtain a large number of very young trauma victims for a research series because parents hope that nothing serious has happened to their children's minds and often fail to bring their youngsters for evaluation. This study also demonstrates how hard it is to obtain convincing corroborations of these early traumas; from the original group of 32 children of this age who had been evaluated by the author, only 20 came with outside corroboration.

From this study of true, verified preschool trauma, some striking preliminary findings about memory emerged. Children who were under the approximate age of 28 to 36 months at the time of their traumas could not verbally remember the gist of their experiences. A girl might remember one moment in the sequence of events, remembering at age 11, for instance, having her face washed when she was 27 months old, when in fact the child had actually fallen face-first into the inboard motor of a boat and that most important part of her story, the gist on which everything else turned, was not available to consciousness. Or a kindergarten girl might remember a general feeling that at the age of 15 to 18 months there had been "grave danger" in a certain "lady's" house, when actually the "lady" and her husband, who had run a day care program, had taken pornographic pictures of this child which were confiscated by the authorities when an attempt was made to sell them. Because the child had a distinctive birthmark, it was easy to tell who she was even though 2½ years had elapsed before her parents ever learned anything about her trauma. Obviously, they could not have planted a story into their child's mind as they had known nothing about the offenses that had occurred. But the child herself could not remember the offenses either; the events themselves would have been the gist, yet her fragmentary verbal memory had to do only with a vague kind of danger.

Five children in this study, who were at or below 28 months when they were traumatized, did not have a single shard of verbal memory from that event. They had not been fully verbal at the time of their traumas and, therefore, had been incapable of forming permanent memory traces through the explicit, declarative memory system. Before the ability to speak in phrases is established, it is difficult, almost impossible, to form completely remembered narratives of experience.

This study of 20 children under the age of five with documented and corroborated experience demonstrates another point that applies to the false memory debate. Of the nine children traumatized at an age older than 36 months, each one of them could remember something of his or her trauma. But those three children who could remember only shards of their stories at this slightly older age were the same children who had suffered many traumatic events or a single, long-standing event. As traumas accumulate, it appeared that a child's memory becomes less complete. If, from this study, the four children at the borderline age (28 to 36 months) for verbal memory of trauma are added in, those two children who could remember nothing or only snippets of memory from their traumas were the same children who had experienced long-standing or repeated events. It appeared that prolonged or recurring traumatic events would be less fully remembered than a single, short traumatic event. This is an interesting counterintuitive finding, running in opposition to standard learning theory (Terr, 1991).

Does a young child's lack of memory for very early traumatic events correspond to a lack of post-traumatic symptoms? No. Most of the children with no verbal memory in this study of 20 verified preschool traumas did have symptoms, as I will shortly describe. The only factor linked to having no trauma-specific symptoms turned out to be harboring a false memory. One 25-month-old child in this study of 20 documented cases had not been exposed to the event that had traumatized three of her siblings. Because it was a family nightmare, she heard the story repeatedly from family members. She was included in this study of 20 children because I had documentation for her *not* having been at the location where the event had taken place. This child gave the only memory in this study that entirely reflected what others had told her. She suffered from no post-traumatic symptoms because she was not directly traumatized by the event.

It might be interesting to note at this juncture that 15 of the 20 children's primary caretakers were not immediately present at the time of these children's traumas. They could not later have told their youngsters a traumatic tale in full, detailed form. Of the five children whose primary caretakers were present at the time of the ordeals, one child reported a false memory and two reported very brief and non-gist-related shards. Only two children who had been with their parents, both over 28 months of age at the time of their traumas, reported full memories. It is unlikely, therefore, that the children in this particular sample of verified trauma victims were significantly influenced by their parents insofar as their verbal memories were concerned.

The symptoms most commonly observed in this group of 20 corroborated cases were post-traumatic play (16 children), personality change (9 children), and trauma-related fears (9 children). In this very young group, dreams were not a particularly important symptom; only four of the children could remember dreams with trauma-related content, and another four children were reported to have screamed at night with no observable dream content.

## ABSENCES OF TRUE MEMORIES (THE DEFENSES)

When a person is old enough to have processed his or her memories through the hippocampus, and a traumatic memory is absent or very spotty, one should consider the explanation that the psychological defenses may have interfered with memory. Defense, in fact, is the most likely explanation, I believe, for the counterintuitive, counter-learning theory finding in the children who forgot parts of their traumas when they were over the age of 28 months. Of the 13 children at or above the age of 28 months at the time of their traumas, one child was unable to produce any verbal memory and four other children could report only spots of memory. These snippets did not fully account for their terrible experiences. These five children had suffered prolonged or repeated traumas, experiences that, in my view, would have encouraged the development of defensive maneuvers (Terr, 1991). Mechanisms of defense are those operations used consciously or unconsciously to deal with conflicts, either entirely within the self or between the self and the external world. Defenses help to ward off intense anxiety. Those children who experienced prolonged or repeated traumas would have come to expect more trauma, and, thus, would have mustered up their defenses to hold their horrors in check. Of the eight children over 28 months of age who had remembered the whole story of their verified traumas, only one of them had been subjected to a prolonged event, a kidnapping for ransom. It was my opinion in evaluating him that this boy did not mentally defend himself at the time of his trauma in a way that would have blocked verbal memory.

Lord Byron put the problem of, what I would consider, mounting a defense against repeated or prolonged trauma into a letter that he wrote to John Murray from Venice, May 30, 1817 (Marchand, 1982). After describing a series of executions that he had witnessed, Byron said:

> The first turned me quite hot and thirsty, and made me shake so I could hardly hold the opera-glass (I was close, but was determined to see, as one should see everything, once, with attention); the second and third (which shows how dreadfully soon things grow indifferent), I am ashamed to say, had no effect on me as a horror, though I would have saved them if I could.

Children old enough to remember their traumas may defend themselves from prolonged or repeated terrors by putting their traumas out of mind, deliberately "suppressing" or unconsciously and undeliberately "repressing" them. Traumatized children may also dissociate, teaching themselves to self-hypnotize and to enter planes of consciousness in which they may even fail to take in and register full memories of their traumas. Children may split, creating good sides to themselves that know nothing about the awful experiences their cut off, bad selves know. They may even displace, concentrating deliberately on something similar but less cathected than the trauma, and, thus, make their memories slip away. I have found in my evaluations of adults who have lost parts or all of their memories of childhood traumas that all five of these defenses can work against memory (Terr, 1994). In addition to the defenses I have already mentioned, intellectualization, projective identification, passive into active, and denial in fantasy may also partially or totally block traumatic memories. In fact, in studying in depth two of the sexually abused Van Derbur sisters, now adults (one from her appearances on TV and the other from a long personal interview), I learned of seven defenses that could conceivably have protected the young girls in this family from the full knowledge of what their father had done to them (Terr, 1994). As Vaillant (1992) says in his book on the defenses, any of the defenses can be used to the purpose of blocking memory.

How do children accomplish their almost purposeful losses of traumatic memory? Rarely are they able to put what they actually did into words, but two boys did describe for me the ways in which they had removed themselves from traumatic scenes: One concentrated first at being at a picnic with his head in his mother's lap; then no picnic, but the lap; then no lap. The other boy concentrated upon taking himself to a planet where he could be invisible (Terr, 1991). Interestingly, most children—and adults for that matter—with true absence of part or all of a traumatic memory can offer no description of how they originally made their memories go away. The techniques, more than even the memories themselves, defy retrieval.

One interesting situation that arose in 1994 in California is, I think, a fascinating single-case example of a true absence of memory for a true documented trauma. A man named Henry Miller, age 22, had never felt quite right about his own family—always believing, but not remembering, that he had been born to someone other than the people who were raising him. When the Polly Klaas Foundation began advertising about their kidnapping investigations, Miller's niece phoned on his behalf to ask if anyone like him had ever been kidnapped as a child. After a week, the Foundation sent Miller and his niece a poster regarding a missing black boy from Inglewood, California, the section of Los Angeles that lies adjacent to the airport. A child had been kidnapped from an Inglewood park at age 4, well beyond the age at which most children would be capable of retaining full verbal memories. The face on the poster was Henry Miller's. His name had been Kevin Portis, the poster said. His case had been unsolved for 18 years.

Within weeks, the young man had a powerful reunion with his father and mother (Hardy, 1994). After that, he told people to call him Kevin and had his mother's name tattooed on his chest. The family was given a series of DNA tests by the police. The young man *is* Kevin Portis. He has been proven by DNA matching to belong to the two people whom he recently met. But Kevin Portis said he still did not remember his life with these people before the age of 4. Even meeting them did not restimulate his memories. Nor could he remember the events connected with his kidnapping from the Inglewood park. The lady who raised him as "Henry Miller" claimed that he was sold to her for $50. The case against her for the 18-year-old abduction or the child purchase was dropped for lack of evidence, according the Inglewood Police Department. But the amazing point of this story to professional bystanders is the fact that at an age when he should have had the capacity to remember something, Kevin Portis did not remember. This implies the defense of repression rather than the passive act of simple forgetting. True and indisputable trauma, being kidnapped or even sold to another individual, is too important to slip from a person's mind. I believe that the episode and its aftermath must have been actively banned from the young man's consciousness. With Portis, the defenses appeared to be alive and well.

Probably one of the most interesting recent large-scale studies of memory is the one in which absences of true memory were proven by documentation from 17 years before. Williams (1994) was part of a team that from April 1973 to June 1975 took extensive notes on the histories of girls, under age 12, who had come to a Boston hospital emergency room for examinations connected with rape or sexual abuse. Seventeen years later, in 1990 and 1991, Williams located more than a hundred of these girls, now grown up. On the pretext of a follow-up of old emergency room visits, she set out to determine how many women remembered, and what they remembered of their own abuses. Thirty-eight percent of Williams' sample had forgotten. Although the data on their actual emergency room visits were there for the investigators to read, the patients themselves could not remember. Of course, as with my study of trauma and early amnesia (Terr, 1988), the children who were the youngest at the time of the trauma (ages 1 to 3) were among the ones with the absent or spotty memories. But those who had been abused within their own families or by someone they knew also had poor memory for the abuse experiences. This, again, argues for the presence of psychological defenses. If one simply "forgets" the unimportant, why would one tend to forget the most important, that is, harm by those who were the closest of friends or family? One would have to employ silent, but active, psychological maneuvers—the defenses—to put such betrayals out of mind.

This same tendency to forget the most negative, highly charged emotional episodes was also reported by Linton (1986). Linton recorded her own true daily events and true memories over a number of years. She reported that the negatively charged events (nontraumatic) that had occurred in her life were the ones that were the most likely to be lost to her spontaneous and unprompted memory.

## RETURNS OF TRUE MEMORIES

Now we come to the part of this subject—the return of true memory—that probably is connected with the most controversy of all. How do true memories come back? And what do we as therapists do to force out a person's memories and distort them in the process? Ramona vs. Isabella and Rose, the 1994 Northern California case that I referred to at the beginning of this chapter, began a trend of putting therapists on the hot seat. Eventually, two practitioners and a hospital were fined $500,000 for using, what a Napa County jury found to be, improper techniques to assist young Holly Ramona, then age 19, to retrieve early memories of sexual abuse at the hands of her father (Butler, 1994). The American public became fascinated with this case because of the very obvious disintegration of a high-living, well-to-do wine country family. But the treating counselor and the treating psychiatrist, like Rosenkrantz and Gildenstern, suffered mightily at the edges of public awareness. The judge in this case instructed the jury that they did not have to decide whether or not Holly Ramona was abused or whether or not her memories were true. Shortly afterward, the foreman said on a television news show and in a newspaper quote, that the jury's verdict was intended to warn other therapists to doubt their patients' stories (Ness & Salter, 1994), and to go so far as to challenge their memories (*Dateline NBC,* May 17, 1994).

A study by Herman and Shatzow (1987) helps us with the issue of memory retrieval. Herman and Shatzow had worked therapeutically with 53 women, who, in the course of group therapies, had retrieved memories of childhood sexual abuse. The two clinicians suggested to each patient that she go out and find proof. It is well known that early abuse is difficult to confirm; it is a secret between two people. But occasionally, others suspect. Occasionally, others, too, have been abused by the same person, and the perpetrators—every once in a while—confess. Forty-eight of Herman and Shatzow's patients agreed to go out and look for proof. Seventy percent of them came back with outside corroboration by siblings, parents, a perpetrator who confessed, or some other evidence. There were 30% who could not get such external confirmations and 5 who did not try, but 70% found that somebody else had perceived their earlier ordeals. Corroboration is something worth having, and it is something worth asking patients to get.

Shortly before writing this chapter, I saw a woman in her mid-thirties who had been terrified of elevators since childhood and who often dissociated during the day, entering weird, out-of-touch trances. She had just recently retrieved a frightening memory of falling down a dark hole, the way Lewis Carroll's Alice had descended. Instead of landing in a meadow with Mad Hatters, White Rabbits, and Queens, this woman had landed onto a table where—she felt quite sure—a man had sexually assaulted her. She had been 3 or 4 years old, she said. The memory was fragmentary and phony-sounding. Descending through a black hole? Onto a table?

I asked for confirmation. "Do you still know anyone from when you were 3 or 4?"

"Yes," she said, "an old friend of our family's who lived nearby."

"Can you phone her, tell her what you've remembered, and ask if she knows anything?"

"I'll try."

The next week the woman had brightened considerably. "Guess what?" she said. "I called that person I knew when I was 3. She told me that the 'hole' part of my memory was easy. It was a neighbor man's laundry chute. He used to let us climb into it from his second-floor bathroom and then fall onto his workroom table in the basement. She has always remembered that."

"And what about the abuse?" I asked, amazed that 3- or 4-year-olds could emerge physically unscathed from repeated free falls from such a height.

"Well, my friend wasn't so sure about the abuse. She said he had never abused *her*," the woman replied. "But her sister always claimed that the very same man raped *her*."

That was confirmation enough for me. A second person, out of contact for years with my patient, claimed for years that she had experienced childhood assault at the hands of a man whose house and workbench were depicted in my own patient's fragmentary memory. Her black hole and her table were the keys— location memories are often associated with complete, partial, or temporary absence of trauma-related memories (Terr, 1990).

Obviously, from what I have written in this review of true memories of true, proven traumas, we need much more research on the nature of traumatic memory. Questions can eventually be answered by clinical, epidemiological, and prospective long-term developmental studies. I hope that 25 years after the Chowchilla kidnapping, I will go back and see how the victims view their own children and, just as important, how they remember. I hope to think up some new ways to challenge children—without hurting them—to repress, or perhaps to retrieve, certain kinds of old remembrances. These are difficult studies to conceptualize, but they are needed. Without scientific studies to back them up, childhood victims, who have always suffered, will suffer further.

I hope to have shown in this chapter that we know a great deal more about memory than we sometimes give ourselves credit for. True memory is a good starting point toward understanding the memory issue. Therapists will survive whatever attacks are made on them by those who do not trust the memories of childhood trauma. It is up to everyone, however, to see to it that the traumatized children survive, and that their remembrances are treated with compassion and respect.

# REFERENCES

Butler, K. (1994, June 26). House divided. *Los Angeles Times Magazine,* pp. 12–14, 16, 34, 36, 38.

Dateline NBC. (1994), May 17).

Hardy, C. C. (1994, January 2). Kidnap victim's own story. *San Francisco Examiner,* pp. B1, B3.

Herman, J. and Shatzow, E. (1987). Recovery and verification of memories of childhood sexual trauma. *Psychoanalytic Psychology, 4,* 1–14.

Linton, M. (1986). Ways of searching and the contents of memory. In D. C. Rubin (Ed.), *Autobiographical memory* (pp. 50–67). New York: Cambridge University Press.

Marchand, L. (Ed.) (1982). *Lord Byron: Selected letters and journals* (letter to John Murray). Cambridge, MA: Belknap Press.

Ness, C. & Salter, S. (1994, May 15). Therapists unsettled by memory verdict. *San Francisco Examiner,* p. A1.

Poole, D. A., Lindsay, D. S., Memon, A., & Bull, R. (1995). Psychotherapy and the recovery of memories of childhood sexual abuse: U.S. and British practitioners' opinions, practices, and experiences. *Journal of Consulting and Clinical Psychology, 63* (3), 426–437.

Terr, L. (1979). Children of Chowchilla: A study of psychic trauma. *Psychoanalytic Study of the Child, 34,* 547–623.

Terr, L. (1983a). Chowchilla revisited: The effects of psychic trauma four years after a schoolbus kidnapping. *American Journal of Psychiatry, 140,* 1543–1550.

Terr, L. (1983b). Time sense following psychic trauma; A clinical study of ten adults and twenty children. *American Journal of Orthopsychiatry, 53,* 244–261.

Terr, L. (1984). Time and trauma. *Psychoanalytic Study of the Child, 39,* 633–666.

Terr, L. (1988). What happens to early memories of trauma? *American Journal of Psychiatry, 27,* 96–104.

Terr, L. (1990). *Too scared to cry: Psychic trauma in childhood.* New York: Harper & Row.

Terr, L. (1991). Childhood traumas: An outline and overview. *American Journal of Psychiatry, 148,* 10–20.

Terr, L. (1994). *Unchained memories: True stories of traumatic memories, lost and found.* New York: Basic Books.

Terr, L., Bloch, D., Michel, B., Shi, H., Reinhart, J., & Matayer, S. A. (1996). Children's memories in the wake of *Challenger. American Journal of Psychiatry, 153:* 5.

Vaillant, G. (Ed.). (1992). *Ego mechanisms of defense: A guide for clinicians and researchers.* Washington, DC: American Psychiatric Press.

Williams, L. M. (1994). Recall of childhood trauma: A prospective study of women's memories of child sexual abuse. *Journal of Consulting and Clinical Psychology, 62* (6), 1167–1176.

Woodward, K. L. (1994, March 14). Was it real or memories? *Newsweek,* p. 54.

Wright, L. (1994). *Remembering satan.* New York: Alfred A. Knopf.

Yapko, M. D. (1994). *Suggestions of abuse: True and false memories of childhood sexual trauma.* New York: Simon & Schuster.

# Functional Retrograde Amnesia as a Model of Amnesia for Childhood Sexual Abuse

NEAL J. COHEN

*Amnesia Research Laboratory, Beckman Institute and Department of Psychology,
University of Illinois, Urbana, Illinois 61801*

The study of patients with functional retrograde amnesia, outside of the domain of sexual abuse, is offered as a potentially powerful way of exploring issues about claims of amnesia for, and recovered memories of, childhood sexual abuse. This chapter attempts to document that (a) functional amnesia does occur in response to certain instances of severe stress or psychological trauma; (b) at least in some forms of functional amnesia, recovery of memory invariably occurs; and (c) the nature of the memory deficit in some forms of functional retrograde amnesia has strong commonalities with memory deficits reported in many claims of amnesia for childhood sexual abuse. Finally, the chapter briefly outlines one way of viewing functional retrograde amnesia, namely, as an encapsulation of memory in which childhood sexual abuse seems like a plausible precipitating event for the development of amnesia.

## INTRODUCTION

In recent years there has been tremendous polarization of opinion on the veracity and implications of claims of recovery of repressed memory for childhood sexual abuse, and on the opposing claims about false memory syndrome. On the one hand, so many claims of recovered memory have made their way into the clinic, the courtroom, and the popular press that there have been changes in therapy strategies, legislation, and public perceptions about the frequency of sexual abuse of children in this country. On the other hand, there have also been enough apparent instances of false or illusory memory, and of recantations of claims of recovered memory, that many observers have become concerned about the suggestibility of patients and the distortability of memory.

When confronted with a claim of recovered memory, whether as a scientist, a clinician, an interested reader of the scientific or the popular literature, a juror in a legal case, or just a friend and neighbor, we are faced with the question of how to go about evaluating the claim. The extreme polarization of views, and the apparent documenting of believable cases on both sides of the recovered memory/false memory divide, make it difficult to know exactly how to proceed.

Some writers on this subject, including several writing in this volume, have endeavored to show that memory can suffer distortions and have attempted to use such demonstrations to warn of the potential of false memory of childhood sexual abuse. The work by Loftus, Ceci, and others discussed in various chapters in this volume reveals that illusory or false memories can indeed be induced under certain conditions, which raises very real concerns about the effect that

81

certain kinds of therapy strategies and interview approaches can have on memory reports.

Other writers on this subject, including some in this volume have attempted to document that recovered memories can be veridical, at least in some instances. This is, in many ways, a more difficult undertaking than the one directed at documenting false memory. To confirm recovery of repressed memory for childhood sexual abuse it is necessary to document that sexual abuse did occur, that repression of memory occurred (i.e., that there was a period of time when the individual could not recall the sexual abuse), and that the recovered memories of the abuse were in fact accurate. To get *first-hand evidence* of recovered memory, therefore, it would be necessary to track individuals from a time period when they cannot remember childhood abuse through a time period when they can recover memories of the abuse. Ideally, the transition from amnesia for the abuse event or events to recovered memory of the abuse event(s) would have occurred in the absence of any intervention strategies that might have induced the construction of false memories or false beliefs about childhood events. Then, some verification of the abuse and confirmation of the specific memories would have to be obtained from the perpetrator or a witness. This really is a tall order.

## AN ALTERNATIVE APPROACH

Perhaps there is a different approach in which one looks for analogous phenomena, outside of the domain of childhood sexual abuse, that might provide support for the possibility of recovered memory for some traumatic event. In this chapter, I argue that an analogous phenomenon does exist in the form of functional retrograde amnesia. Functional, or psychogenic, amnesia is a deficit in memory precipitated by psychological stressors rather than by structural brain damage, and usually entails loss of (or loss of access to) some domain of information that was acquired normally prior to the onset of amnesia (functional *retrograde* amnesia). It will be defined more fully below.

In the discussion of functional amnesia to follow, four main points will be made. First, functional retrograde amnesia *can* occur after (psychologically) traumatic events. This is a critical point, because some investigators, in making their case for the false memory side of the recovered memory/false memory debate, have not limited themselves to citing evidence for memory distortions and memory illusions, but have also attacked the notion of repressed memories. However, it must be pointed out that no matter how convincing the evidence for memory distortions and memory illusions might be, such evidence can only speak to the believability of claims of *recovery* of repressed memory for childhood sexual abuse. That evidence cannot speak to the logically prior issue of whether there can be (unrecovered) repressed memory for childhood sexual abuse. In this context, the existence of functional retrograde amnesia precipitated by severe stress or psychological trauma lends credence to the possibility of functional retrograde amnesia for childhood sexual abuse. It is worth considering that the phrase "repressed memory" is a loaded one, with a long history tied to the psychoanalytic tradition, and some of the disagreement with the notion of repressed memory for childhood sexual abuse may conceivably arise from disagreement with that psychoanalytic tradition. It seems wise, perhaps, to stick to the phrase "functional retrograde amnesia" for childhood sexual abuse. This chapter will argue that functional retrograde amnesia for childhood sexual abuse is perfectly plausible, quite apart from *any* consideration of whether such an amnesia can fully recover and whether "recovered memory" can be fully veridical.

Second, the phenomenology of functional amnesia also includes recovery of temporarily lost or inaccessible memories in at least one form of functional retrograde amnesia. The progression from amnesia to recovery in this form of functional amnesia will be discussed in the next section. However, the chapter will have little to say, on the whole, about recovery of memory, either in this form of functional retrograde amnesia or in amnesia for childhood sexual abuse. The chapter focuses on amnesia rather than on recovery.

Third, the nature of the memory deficit in a different form of functional retrograde amnesia, described in some detail later on, has strong commonalities to memory deficits reported in many of the claims of amnesia for childhood sexual abuse. Such commonalities begin to suggest that cases of functional retrograde amnesia from outside the domain of childhood sexual abuse might provide a good model for considering amnesia for childhood sexual abuse.

Finally, I outline one way of viewing functional retrograde amnesia, namely as an encapsulation of memory, in which childhood sexual abuse seems like a plausible precipitating event for the development of amnesia.

## FUNCTIONAL RETROGRADE AMNESIA

Perhaps the best way to define functional retrograde amnesia is by comparison with the memory impairments seen in the organic amnesias. That the amnesia is *functional,* or psychogenic, refers to the fact that it is caused or triggered by a severe psychological stressor, such as a psychologically traumatic event or set of events, rather than by physical insult to or structural change of the brain. The idea that the presence of severe psychological stress in the period immediately preceding the onset of amnesia could serve as the precipitating cause of the amnesia has guided work in this field from the earliest reports of functional amnesia (Abeles & Schilder, 1935; Kanzer, 1939; Stengel, 1941; Parfitt & Gall, 1944; Berrington, Liddell, & Foulds, 1956). Thus, unlike the organic amnesias, functional amnesias occur in the absence of any detectable structural brain damage.

That it is a *retrograde* amnesia refers to the impairment selectively affecting information that occurred prior to the onset of amnesia. Anterograde amnesia, by contrast, refers to impairment in acquiring new information since the onset of amnesia. Functional amnesias almost invariably are exclusively retrograde amnesias, with no clinically significant anterograde impairment, whereas the organic amnesias almost invariably include both anterograde and retrograde impairments (e.g., see Kopelman, 1987; Schacter & Kihlstrom, 1989).

Finally, functional retrograde amnesias typically recover over time, as we shall see, whereas the organic amnesias rarely do. This is not a defining feature, however. Some organic amnesias, such as in certain instances of closed head injury, or following a course of treatment of depression using bilateral electro-convulsive therapy (ECT), do recover. And some functional retrograde amnesias, such as the cases K and F described in a later section, do not recover. However, even the cases of functional amnesia that do not recover are distinguishable from the organic amnesias with regard to their defining characteristics: they are not caused by structural brain damage, they are associated with the presence of a severe psychological stressor, and their memory impairment is a selective retrograde amnesia.

Functional retrograde amnesias can take one of a number of different possible forms. One form is amnesia for the traumatic event itself. Someone who witnessed or just barely survived some horrific event may be unable subsequently to remember that event [for reviews, see Schacter & Kihlstrom, 1989; Kopelman, 1987; elsewhere, as in the DSM-IV, it is often discussed as a symptom of post-traumatic stress disorder (PTSD)]. Such an amnesia can be remarkably selective, preventing recall only of the traumatic event, with the rest of memory apparently unaffected. With the passage of time, if the amnesia does not resolve, a person with such an amnesia may well be unaware of the gap in memory in the conduct of everyday life, paralleling at least some claims of amnesia for childhood sexual abuse.

Perhaps the most widely known form of functional retrograde amnesia is an impairment of autobiographical memory. In such cases, the person suffers from amnesia for all information about self—who they are, where and with whom they live, and so forth. Occasionally, cases of this sort will appear in the local newspaper, with a picture and description of the individual, asking anyone with knowledge about the identity of the person to come forward. This amnesia can also be selective, often with little or no impairment of knowledge about the world or impairment in acquiring new memories (e.g., Schacter, Wang, Tulving, & Freeman, 1982; Christianson & Nilsson, 1989; Kopelman, Christensen, Puffett, & Stanhope, 1994). Perhaps most important to an attempt to apply functional amnesia to the recovered memory/false memory debate is the fact that this particular form of functional retrograde amnesia almost invariably recovers. The progression of this form of functional amnesia from impairment to recovery is the subject of the next section.

## Stages of Functional Retrograde Amnesia for Autobiographical Memory

Functional amnesia for autobiographical memory usually progresses through a series of stages: a fugue state, then awareness of amnesia, and finally recovery of memory. The first stage is a fugue state in which the person typically wanders around, sometimes for hours or days, with loss of autobiographical memory and any sense of personal identity. Next comes a stage in which there is an awareness of amnesia. The person becomes aware that she does not know who she is or how she came to be in her current location. Typically, such a person will at this point seek help, going to a hospital or a police station. Usually within a few days, particularly if family members appear on the scene, autobiographical memory starts to recover. Recovery of memory may begin in a fragmentary way, with recognition of some people but not others and recall of some but not other autobiographical information. Recovery of autobiographical memory is almost complete, except for whatever events occurred during the fugue state, for which there is invariably permanent amnesia.

One well-studied example of functional amnesia for autobiographical memory is the patient P.N., reported by Schacter et al. (1982). This patient apparently entered into a fugue state after the funeral of his grandfather, with whom he was very close, and ended up wandering around the city for days before becoming aware of his amnesia and asking for help. After 4 days during which he was unaware of his identity, his memory recovered completely while watching a scene involving a funeral procession in the TV miniseries Shogun. He was never able to reconstruct his activities during the fugue state, however.

With regard to what lessons this form of functional retrograde amnesia might offer to the recovered memory/false memory debate, the key point is that recovery of memories lost (or inaccessible) during a functional amnesia can and does occur. Although claims of amnesia for childhood sexual abuse rarely involve such an extensive loss of autobiographical memory, the fact that the amnesia resolves provides an existence proof of recovered memory.

## Temporally Specified Retrograde Amnesia

There is another, apparently more rare form of functional retrograde amnesia in which the memory deficit has a strong commonality with the nature of the deficit claimed in amnesia for childhood sexual abuse. Two cases are presented that exhibit a temporally specified, informationally general memory deficit: a retrograde amnesia specific to a particular time period. The two patients discussed here were studied in close collaboration with Molly Treadway and Michael McCloskey. They are reported in greater detail elsewhere (Treadway, McCloskey, Gordon, & Cohen, 1992).

Many of the claims of amnesia for childhood sexual abuse are about amnesia specific to a particular time period. A woman who comes to realize as an adult that she cannot remember details of her life between the ages of 6 and 10 that her siblings can recall, or cannot remember events that occurred during the period when her family lived on Oak Street, or remembers nearly nothing about the year when her stepfather worked the night shift and was home during the day while her mother was out working a day job, would seem to have a temporally specified retrograde amnesia.

Because the repressed memory/false memory debate has become so polarized (meriting books such as this one), it seemed important to be able to step outside the domain of childhood sexual abuse to document that temporally specified functional retrograde amnesias can actually occur. This form of functional amnesia may provide a particularly good model for understanding amnesia for childhood sexual abuse.

*Patient K*

At the time of onset of his amnesia in December, 1984, K was a 53-year-old man who was married and had two children, aged 15 and 17. One day, when they returned from shopping, his wife and children found him lying, unresponsive, on the kitchen floor of their home. He was clutching the heating element from the electric oven (which apparently he had been trying to repair) in his hand, which was twitching. When his family could not rouse him, they called for medical help. The paramedics who soon arrived on the scene also found him unresponsive and took him to the hospital.

The next morning, when K could communicate once again, it became apparent that he thought the year was 1945 rather than 1984, that he was 14 years old rather than 53, and that he was awakening in the hospital after having been hit in the head while playing baseball with his buddies on a nice summer day in August, 1945.

Intensive study of K over the next several years indicated that he had lost (or lost access to) all memories acquired between 1945 and 1984. This deficit was domain-general, affecting each of the following aspects of memory:

- memory for personal facts and events,
- world knowledge,
- skills, and
- personality and personal identity.

The deficit in each of these aspects of memory is documented in the following sections, with some illustrative examples. The conclusions that we drew about patient K's impaired and spared memory abilities are based on information amassed from dozens of hours of tape-recorded conversations with K; visits to his hometown and to where he lived in later years, involving interviews with family, former friends, classmates, and teachers; and inspection of medical records, school records, employment records, and town records.

*Personal facts and events.* When K "came to" in the hospital, he could not understand why his parents were not there to visit and to take care of him, although in fact his father was long deceased and his mother still lived in K's hometown, thousands of miles away. K could not recognize his wife and children, and, indeed, found it very strange that anyone could think that he, a 14-year-old, might have a wife and teenage children. When his wife took him back home from the hospital, he related to her and to their children as though they were nice people who were kind enough to take him into their home.

He could not remember any of his schooling nor any of his school friends after the seventh grade. Yet, his memory of his schooling before the summer of 1945, including his knowledge of classmates and teachers and of events in which they took part, was remarkably good—easily as good as that of anyone from among his former classmates and teachers who were interviewed.

K could not remember any of the jobs he had held in his life nor any of his co-workers. He could not remember any of the places where he had lived, nor any of the places that he had visited, since 1945. He did not recognize the places depicted in various photographs he had hanging on the walls of his home, even though the photographs were ones he had taken during family vacations.

Perhaps the starkest illustration of the temporally specific nature of his amnesia comes from the finding that although he had lived in or near his hometown through 1952, and had visited many times since then, including several times during the 1980s (because his mother still lived there), his memory of the town reflected the way the town had been in 1945. For example, when he was asked to make a map of Main Street and indicate for us all the businesses, restaurants, and so forth that were "currently" there, he drew it as it had been in 1945. His map only had businesses that were there in 1945, and only in the locations that they had actually occupied in 1945, despite the fact that by 1984 fully 89% of the businesses had changed.

*World knowledge.* K's knowledge of the world for the period before 1945 was intact, but he showed profound impairment for information from after that time. He did not use vocabulary that had come into the language after 1945 and was unaware of the meanings of the post-1945 words with which we probed him (e.g., computer-related terms or words referring to current musical or popular culture trends). His knowledge of public events and people was similarly affected. He could recount much information about the progress of World War II up until the summer of 1945, including, for example, the end of the war in Europe and the death of President Roosevelt. But K knew nothing at all about the end of the war in the Pacific, including anything at all about the dropping of atomic bombs on Japan early in August 1945, and did not remember anything about the Korean or Vietnam wars. His performance on two formal tests of memory for public events confirms these observations. On a four-choice recognition memory test of public events that occurred between 1940 and 1979 (Cohen & Squire, 1981), he performed well for the period before 1945 but was at chance for the period after 1945 (see Table 1). K performed similarly when tested with photographs of famous public events (Sagar, Cohen, Corkin, & Growdon, 1985): He had no difficulty identifying events from before 1945, such as Wendell Wilkie campaigning for President in 1940, but he could not identify famous scenes from after 1945, such as Jack Ruby shooting Lee Harvey Oswald in 1963.

TABLE 1

K's Performance on a Four-Choice Recognition Memory Test of Public Events for the Time Period 1940 to 1979

| Time period | Performance (%) |
|---|---|
| 1940–1945[a] | 75 |
| 1946–1979[b] | 24 |

[a]Prior to the time period for which K reports amnesia.

[b]During the time period for which K reports amnesia.

His knowledge of products and inventions that came into use after 1945 was negligible. He was amazed by the TV (and by its remote control) that he saw while still in the hospital. When his wife picked him up from the hospital and took him home in their (then new) 1984 Lincoln, he thought it was a space car; the last car he remembered seeing was his parents' 1939 Packard. He was apparently unable to use the various TVs, VCRs, and stereo systems that were much in evidence around his house, even though these were items that he had purchased and had set up in his home before the onset of amnesia.

K showed a sharp discontinuity in his knowledge of advertising slogans or campaigns that were run pre- versus post-1945. When presented with an advertising jingle or line and asked to fill in the particular product to which it referred, K performed well if the product and its campaign were from the pre-1945 period but performed at chance levels for products and advertising campaigns from after 1945.

*Skills.* K's impairment for information acquired after 1945 also extended to skills. The morning after his arrival at the hospital, when he was once again able to communicate, it became clear that his accent had changed to that of someone living in the part of the country where he grew up, and hence more similar to the way he must have sounded when he was younger, rather than the accent he exhibited throughout his adulthood. His handwriting also changed, consistent with that of a much less mature individual.

Furthermore, skills such as photography, tennis, and swimming, at which he had become accomplished by the time of onset of his amnesia, had become decidedly rudimentary. For example, whereas he swam well enough as an adult to have taught swimming at a local YMCA, when we took him swimming we found him to be relatively unskilled. And, whereas his competence in photography as an adult was documented by the photographs hanging on the walls of the family's home, when we took him to Baltimore's Inner Harbor to shoot pictures we found no evidence that he retained that level of skill.

*Personality and personal identity.* K literally thought himself to be 14 years old and acted like it. He had the mannerisms of a young and immature boy. For example, on more than one occasion we found him skipping across the street and, once, even sliding down the bannister of an escalator in an upscale shopping center. He frequently spoke about "having no one to play with" or about "having to go to the boys room," and frequently referred to people 20 to 30 years younger than he as "sir" or "ma'am." He was very uncomfortable about "girls" and believed that his two children (15 and 17 at the time of onset of his amnesia) were older than he was.

To occupy himself when he was back home from the hospital he played with trains and toy soldiers in the basement. So comfortable was he with such play items that he tried to buy toy soldiers *for us* once when he went shopping, and apparently would have bought them had his wife not intervened.

Early in his amnesia, K had a difficult time looking at himself in the mirror; he felt that he was a 14-year-old boy in a man's body and seemed surprised each time he saw himself in that body. He often fantasized that people looking at him could somehow know that he was really a 14-year-old boy. K was so convinced that he was 14 years old that he would sit on the stoop of his house as boys from the local middle school would go by on their way to the school yard, hoping that he would be invited to play baseball with them.

Particularly revealing were K's responses when asked to recount specific episodes from his life as probed with certain cue words. Whereas most people tend to report recent memories rather than more remote memories in response to these cues (Crovitz & Schiffman, 1974), K consistently remembered episodes from when he was in seventh or sixth grade, and, when asked to date these memories, he reported them as having occurred "a few months ago" or "last year."

*Discussion of K's amnesia.* K exhibited a profound functional retrograde amnesia, affecting memory in a temporally specific way. He lost and/or was unable to gain access to any memory acquired within the time period between 1945 and 1984. Despite the apparent "physical" triggering of the onset of his amnesia, the impairment is best understood as a functional amnesia, for the following reasons. First, the pattern of memory loss is reflective of a psychogenic rather than of an organic amnesia. The amnesia was selectively a retrograde impairment, without any clinically significant anterograde amnesia. Moreover, the impairment included skills along with other aspects of memory, thereby differing from the organic amnesias, in which there is impairment of declarative memory (memory for facts and events) while leaving procedural memory (memory supporting the acquisition and expression of skill) intact (see Cohen, 1984; Cohen & Eichenbaum, 1993).

Second, there was no evidence of K having sustained structural brain damage on electroencephalography (EEG), computerized tomography (CT), or magnetic resonance imaging (MRI) exams, nor on neurological examination. He did not have any burns on his hand nor any evidence of having had a heart attack from handling the electric oven. Whatever the consequences were of K's accident with the electric oven, no structural brain abnormalities were produced that were capable of causing his amnesia.

Third, there were severe psychological stressors in K's life at the time of the onset of amnesia that seem capable of precipitating his amnesia. Just prior to the onset of K's amnesia in 1984, he was under serious job-related and marital stress. He was receiving poor performance reports from work and was concerned about his job, and was also attempting to put together his own business venture at that time. The stress manifested itself in a nervous condition that included restricted breathing, chest pains, and speech difficulties. He was on disability leave from work as a result of these symptoms, believed by his doctors at the time to be of psychogenic origin, and was faced with having to return very soon to work when his amnesia occurred.

These aspects of K's impairment offer strong support for the conclusion that it is a functional retrograde amnesia. What is most compelling about K's impairment, particularly in the context of the recovered memory/false memory debate, is that it is a temporally specified amnesia—an amnesia for a specific time period. Insofar as this kind of amnesia resembles the claimed memory impairment for a specific period of childhood in some women who were apparently sexually abused as children, it raises the possibility that K's amnesia can serve as a model for exploring (some examples of) amnesia for childhood sexual abuse.

## Patient F

In 1976, at the age of 39, F suffered a ruptured aneurysm of the left carotid artery and became confused and incoherent. After 5 days in the hospital, she underwent surgery for repair of the aneurysm. When she recovered consciousness after the surgery, it became apparent that she thought it was 1960 and that she was 23 years old. Like K, she seemed to have lost (or lost access to) all memories for a period of years, in this case extending from 1960 to 1976. The deficit included all of the domains of memory affected in K, including memory for facts and personal events, world knowledge, skills, and personality and personal identity. Her deficits parallel K's closely.

When F regained consciousness, she believed that she had three children between the ages of 2 and 5 years old rather than four nearly grown children, the youngest of whom was 14. F did not recognize the youngest (fourth) of her children when the family came to the hospital. Also, F remembered the family having just moved into a new home, although actually they had lived there 16 years at the time of onset of her amnesia.

F's performance on the famous scenes test of memory for public events (Sagar et al., 1985), also administered to K (see preceding case study), shows clearly the selective memory loss for the period 1960 to 1976. For example, she recognized the planting of the flag by U.S. Marines at Iwo Jima (1944) and the famous newspaper headline "Dewey defeats Truman" (1948), both occurring in the period before 1960. She also recognized the royal wedding of Prince Charles and Lady Diana (1981) and Anwar Sadat's assassination (1980), both occurring in the period after 1976. Yet, she could not recognize Jack Ruby shooting Lee Harvey Oswald (1963) or Martin Luther King, Jr.'s assassination (1968) from the affected (1960 to 1976) time period. Her performance on that test is summarized in Table 2.

F also did not remember the products or technological advances that had oc-

TABLE 2

F's Performance on Famous Scenes Test of Memory for Public Events for Various Time Periods

| Time period | Performance (%) |
|---|---|
| Pre-1960[a] | 62 |
| 1960–1976[b] | 23 |
| Post–1976[a] | 60 |

[a]Outside of (prior to or after) the time period for which F reports amnesia.

[b]During the time period for which F reports amnesia.

curred since 1960, nor did she know how to use them, paralleling K's deficit for products and inventions after 1945. For example, the last car that F remembered owning was a 1956 Ford, rather than the family's new (at the time of onset of her amnesia) 1976 Grand Prix; and she did not know how to operate the family's dishwasher, acquired in the years after 1960.

She believed herself to be 23 years old and acted that way. In the aftermath of the onset of her amnesia, her taste in music changed to classic rock from Johnny Mathis, and her taste in clothes to jeans. By the time we interacted with F, in the mid to late 1980s, she treated her adult daughters as though they were her contemporaries rather than her children, behaving as though she was their age.

*Discussion of F's amnesia.* The temporally specified memory deficit seen in F should be considered a functional retrograde amnesia just as with K. First, F did not exhibit any clinically significant anterograde amnesia. Like K, F demonstrated the ability to acquire new information since the onset of amnesia, relearning much information from the affected time periods (although both patients reported that the information they were able to relearn had a book-learning quality to it and was never fully integrated into the rest of their knowledge of their own lives) as well as learning new information from the events of ongoing life.

Second, there was no evidence that structural insult to the brain *caused* the severe amnesia observed in F. Whereas there was no detectable structural brain damage in K, F did have brain damage as a result of her stroke. But it occurred in an area of the brain—left temporal lobe—that has never been reported to produce an amnesia of this type. Moreover, despite the difference between the two patients with regard to neurological status and to etiology of their amnesias, they have the same functional deficit, suggesting that the form of amnesia they exhibit is not tied to any common site of structural brain damage.

Third, F had in common with K the presence of severe stress in the period immediately preceding the onset of amnesia. At the time of onset of F's amnesia in 1976, she was faced with family discord concerning the discovery that one of her daughters, then an unmarried teenager, had just had an abortion. This may have been particularly salient and stressful to F because of the similarity of these circumstances to her own situation 14 years earlier when she gave birth to her fourth child (the one whom she did not remember after the onset of her amnesia), who, we believe, was the product of an extramarital affair with a married neighbor. These circumstances are described somewhat more fully in Treadway et al. (1992). The circumstances of K and F's lives immediately prior to amnesia onset suggest that severe stress is likely to be the precipitating cause supporting the interpretation of their memory deficit as being a functional amnesia.

## FUNCTIONAL RETROGRADE AMNESIA: A MODEL FOR AMNESIA FOR CHILDHOOD SEXUAL ABUSE?

These two cases provide an existence proof of a functional amnesia that can affect a specific, limited period of time—a deficit often claimed in cases of amnesia for childhood sexual abuse. Moreover, in considering how to conceptualize functional amnesia to account for this temporally specific form as well as for the other forms of functional amnesia previously discussed, we will discuss an idea about the *encapsulation of memory* that makes childhood sexual abuse appear to be a plausible precipitating cause of amnesia.

How *does* functional amnesia work? A reasonable place to start to answer this question is by thinking of functional amnesia as an adaptive mechanism that "protects" an individual from being reminded of some traumatic event or events. The question that is raised by such a view is how memories of the traumatic event(s) can be set off from other memories, such that the individual can have access to all those memories needed to lead a normal life while not permitting access to those specific memories that would cause pain and stress. The view I would like to advocate here is that severe stress or psychological trauma could cause a functional separation or encapsulation of some subset of memories that would prevent those memories from being accessed through the usual associative linkages.

The encapsulated subset of memories would need to share a particular categorical "tag" that would permit them to be kept separate from other memories. The category or subset of memories that would be encapsulated might vary greatly across individuals. In some cases, it might be limited to information about the traumatic event itself; in other cases, it might extend to include memories of all personal events and other aspects of autobiographical knowledge (that is, memory related to "self"); and in still other cases, it might be for particular life contexts.

In considering the functional amnesia exhibited by K and F, Treadway et al. (1992) argued:

> Memory may be organized around "life contexts" bounded by salient landmark events. Instead of viewing memory as one large, fully integrated set of associations, this hypothesis envisions coalitions or constellations of memories. Such constellations would be composed of memories that are tied more strongly to other memories sharing the same life context than to memories that share some other life context. On this view, landmark life events (e.g., moves from one city to another, job changes, marriage) may significantly alter life contexts and so may demarcate constellations of associated memories. (p. 403)

The landmark life events noted in the preceding extract are of the kind that most people experience. But individuals who end up with a functional amnesia seem to be exposed to landmark life events of a substantially more stressful and traumatic nature, which may well produce a more exaggerated pattern of functionally separated subsets of memories. Applying this idea to K and F, Treadway et al. (1992) speculated that the period from 1945 to 1984 for K and from 1960 to 1976 for F represented a very different, more negative, and more stressful life context than earlier periods in their lives, and that when faced with a very severe stressor (in 1984 for K and in 1976 for F) there was an adaptive "forgetting" of all those memories associated with the negative life context (see Treadway et al., 1992, for explication of and support for this interpretation).

What is interesting in the context of the recovered memory/false memory debate about this idea of encapsulation of memory is that it makes it plausible to consider childhood sexual abuse as a likely precipitator of functional amnesia. It is easy to imagine that a period of systematic, ongoing deprivations, violence, and/or sexual abuse might lead to an extreme exaggeration of the pattern of functionally separated subsets of memories described earlier. In such a case, rather than coalitions or constellations of memories being gradually formed that are relatively more strongly tied to one another than to other memories, a fully encapsulated subset of memories might be formed that is not tied at all to other memories. This seems particularly plausible in the case of repeated sexual abuse of a child by an adult. A situation in which a parent or stepparent is repeatedly abusing a child and, through threats or other inducements, convinces the child of the need for complete secrecy, would seem to be the ideal trigger for encapsulation of memory. Despite the ongoing abuse occurring to the child away from public view, the child needs to act normally around the parent or stepparent when in public situations. If it were possible to encapsulate the memories of the abuse such that they were not accessible except in the very specific context in which the abuse actually occurs, then the child might be able to cope with the abuse in a manner that appears outwardly normal and the child might even actually feel comfortable with that adult in most situations.

## CONCLUDING REMARKS

The idea of encapsulation of memory as a way of understanding functional amnesia, and the attempt to extend it to amnesia for childhood sexual abuse, should be considered highly speculative. Less speculative, however, is that the study of functional amnesia brings interesting and important questions to the recovered memory/false memory debate. Functional amnesia occurs in response to certain instances of severe stress or psychological trauma. Some forms of functional amnesia invariably include recovery of memory. These features of functional amnesia would seem to offer existence proofs that counter some of the arguments made on the false memory side of the debate. Furthermore, some forms of functional amnesia have memory deficits very similar to the deficits that are claimed in amnesia for childhood sexual abuse. Such similarities deserve further study. The study of functional retrograde amnesias outside the domain of sexual abuse provides a potentially powerful way to explore issues concerning the plausibility of claims of recovery of repressed memory for childhood sexual abuse.

Perhaps the way in which knowledge about functional retrograde amnesia can best contribute to the repressed memory/false memory debate is as something of a counterweight to the impact that studies of memory distortions have on this debate. That is, the recent work on distortions of memory outside of the domain of childhood sexual abuse, work that is well represented in other chapters in this book, has led many to favor the false memory side of this debate. The reasoning seems to be something like the following: If normal memory is so prone to distortion under certain leading (or misleading) instructional or interview conditions, how much credence can we pay to "memories" that were apparently "repressed" for years and were "recovered" only after many sessions with therapists who are determined to elicit such memories?

The data on memory distortions are compelling, and do give pause when contemplating the veridicality of anyone's memories, whether or not they are claimed memories of childhood sexual abuse. However, many commentators have made an unwarranted logical leap of also calling into question the whole idea of "repressed memory," casting doubt not only upon any claims of recovery of memories but also claims of amnesia. The work on functional amnesia discussed in this chapter, work that is likewise outside of the domain of childhood sexual abuse, can play an important role here. This work suggests that certain stressors *can* cause functional amnesia, rendering some memories inaccessible. Moreover, functional amnesias exist that resemble the pattern of loss of memory claimed in some cases of childhood sexual abuse. Finally, many functional amnesias *do* recover over time, permitting the re-emergence of access to previously inaccessible memories. These facts about memory and amnesia deserve time along with the facts about the distortability of memory in the recovered memory/ false memory debate.

## ACKNOWLEDGMENTS

I thank Molly Treadway and Michael McCloskey for their close collaboration in studying patients K and F over several years. This chapter benefited from discussions with Patricia Deldin, Susanne Crabtree, Jennifer Keller, Gregory Miller, Louise Fitzgerald, Bill Brewer, and Judy DeLoache about the implications of cases such as K and F for understanding amnesia for childhood sexual abuse, and from comments by Gregory Miller and Eli Vakil on an earlier version of this manuscript.

## REFERENCES

Abeles, M., & Schilder, P. (1935). Psychogenic loss of personal identity. *Archives of Neurology and Psychiatry, 34,* 587–604.

Berrington, W. P., Liddell, D. W., & Foulds, G. A. (1956). A reevaluation of the fugue. *Journal of Mental Science, 102,* 281–286.

Christianson, S.-A., & Nilsson, L.-G. (1989). Hysterical amnesia: A case of aversively motivated isolation of memory. In T. Archer & L.-G. Nilsson (Eds.), *Aversion, avoidance, and anxiety* (pp. 289–310). Hillsdale, NJ: Erlbaum.

Cohen, N. J. & Squire, L. R. (1981). Retrograde amnesia and remote memory impairment. *Neuropsychologia, 19,* 337–356.

Crovitz, H. F., & Schiffman, H. (1974). Frequency of episodic memories as a function of their age. *Bulletin of the Psychonomic Society, 4,* 517–518.

Kanzer, M. (1939). Amnesia: A statistical study. *American Journal of Psychiatry, 96,* 711–716.

Kopelman, M. D. (1987). Amnesia: Organic and psychogenic. *British Journal of Psychiatry, 150,* 428–442.

Kopelman, M. D., Christensen, H., Puffett, A., & Stanhope, N. (1994). The great escape: A neuropsychological study of psychogenic amnesia. *Neuropsychologia, 32,* 675–691.

Parfitt, D. N., & Gall, C. M. C. (1944). Psychogenic amnesia: The refusal to remember. *Journal of Mental Science, 90,* 511–531.

Sagar, H. J., Cohen, N. J., Corkin, S., & Growdon, J. (1985). Dissociations among processes in remote memory. *Annals of the New York Academy of Sciences, 444,* 533–535.

Schacter, D. L., & Kihlstrom, J. F. (1989). Functional amnesia. In F. Boller & J. Grafman (Eds.), *Handbook of neuropsychology* (Vol. 3, pp. 209–231). New York: Elsevier.

Schacter, D. L., Wang, P. L., Tulving, E., & Freeman, M. (1982). Functional retrograde amnesia: A quantitative case study. *Neuropsychologia, 20,* 523–532.

Stengel, E. (1941). On the aetiology of the fugue states. *Journal of Mental Science, 87,* 559–572.
Treadway, M., McCloskey, M., Gordon, B., & Cohen, N. J. (1992). Landmark life events and the organization of memory: Evidence from functional retrograde amnesia. In S.-A. Christianson (Ed.), *Handbook of emotion and memory* (pp. 389–410). Hillsdale, NJ: Erlbaum.

# II. THE DEVELOPMENT OF SELF AND AUTOBIOGRAPHICAL MEMORY

Autobiographical memory is our personal history. It is the special set of stories and memories that contains the chronicle of our existence. These memories are important for many reasons, but probably the most important is that they tell us who we are.

The articles in this section cover some of the questions frequently asked about autobiographical memory. The question of at what age was our earliest memory acquired is of enduring interest. We all want to know when we started to be who we are, and what started us on the way to being who we are. The topic of this book gives a special reason for interest in this question because the earliest age of a reportable memory would mark the earliest possible incident of abuse or sexual violation that a person could later recall. Also in line with the focus of this book is the question of whether traumatic events have the power to be recalled from an earlier age or with greater accuracy than more ordinary events. None of the authors in this section concludes that traumatic memories have an inherent advantage over nontraumatic memories in being remembered. On the other hand, these memories do not seem to be less reliable or more subject to elaboration and falsification than nontraumatic memories.

Contrasting hypotheses about the limit on earliest memories are proposed by Tessler and Nelson, and by Howe, Courage, and Peterson in this section. Howe et al. argue that the emergence of the cognitive self is required to provide the basis for maintenance of autobiographical memories. Infantile amnesia occurs for the oldest memories because they predate this organizing self and are therefore lost. Although Howe et al. recognize the importance of language in cognitive development, they maintain that language development is secondary to autobiographical memory. They acknowledge the difficulties in disentangling effects of emerging selfhood from effects of increasing language competence, but are able to point to evidence in their research that supports their hypothesis.

Tessler and Nelson argue that autobiographical memory is social in origin, that it has its origin in interactions between child and caretaker, and that, because language is essential to this interaction, the emergence of autobiographical memory depends on language. Maintenance of the autobiography over time also depends on language, because the narrative structure that knits remembered events into a personal history itself depends on language. Theirs is a position that qualifies autobiographical memory as something distinctly and uniquely human. It is also a position that relates qualities of personality and autobiographical memory to the linguistic and (undoubtedly more important) cultural group in which a child grows up. Evidence for their hypothesis, reported in this article, is found in their study of the interactions between children and their mothers in creating a narrative. For children aged 3.5 and 4.5 years, they found that the way mothers discussed events had a strong effect on the children's encoding and recall of the events. Although this is far from the only source of evidence for their approach, it has particular resonance with the topic of this book because it suggests that important childhood memories can be molded and influenced by the guidance of the caretaker.

Fivush, however, does not find a strong relationship between the mother's recall of an event known to parent and child and the child's independent recall of it. It is possible that the difference comes from the difference in the method used: Tessler and Nelson based their conclusions on observations of interaction between the mother and child when they experienced something new together; Fivush had them discuss an event from the past that may have been less subject to modification. It is possible that the mothers did not have the sort of influence on the children's memory in Fivush's study that they did in Tessler and Nelson's because in Fivush's the memories were already encoded. Whatever the ultimate resolution of the disagreement between these two sets of findings, the Fivush study does show that children's memories are not so easily modified that the child will abandon his or her version of the events when the mother's differs.

Stein suggests still another basis for children's memory: that memory is tightly connected with schemas related to goal-seeking behavior. These schemas are causally structured and provide coherence to the flow of information in the environment. Memories can be formed as early as a child can have event-structuring goals. This position holds that children can have enduring memories at a very young age if all of the conditions for causal coherence are met. The position also provides a basis for knowledge, experience, beliefs, and emotions to have an effect on memory. Stein's position also contradicts any argument that very early memories cannot be established because the child lacks the ability to encode events. It seems clear that the ability to encode rather complex episodes is present surprisingly early in development.

Stein's position is in strong contrast with Tessler and Nelson's, which is based on language and social interaction rather than perceptual integration. The two positions could be seen as opposite ends of the spectrum, representing diametrically opposed conceptions of intellectual development. The approach of Howe et al. is not incompatible with the conclusions Stein draws about the importance of perceptual coherence. However, Howe et al. could point out that although coherence may be a precondition for encoding an event in memory, the mere possibility of encoding does not ensure the incorporation of that memory into the personal autobiography, or even ensure remembering it as an isolated episode for an extended length of time. Tessler and Nelson could make the same rejoinder, namely, that the conditions for encoding that Stein outlines are just that, and more (use of language in their case) is needed for these memories to be woven into the personal autobiography.

Although these positions are in conflict at the theoretical level, they offer contrasting ways of approaching the same question and by their very opposition may provide the basis for converging and productive approaches.

# Making Memories: The Influence of Joint Encoding on Later Recall by Young Children

Minda Tessler[1] and Katherine Nelson

Department of Psychology, Lehman College, City University of New York, Bronx, New York 10468

The premise of this research is that autobiographical memory is essentially social in origin and that the social-interactive aspects of an experience influence the content and form of what is later recalled. Two studies are reported in which an ongoing event was observed in order to track the way present experience enters past memory. In the first study, the talk between 3½-year-old children and their mothers during a visit to a museum was analyzed. In a second study, the effects of maternal style on 4½-year-old children's encoding and later recall were examined. Strong effects of talk during the experience were found in both studies, confirming the hypothesis of a social-interactive effect on children's encoding and later recall of a situation shared with an adult. It is proposed that autobiographical memory development and language are inextricably bound together because of the role of linguistic input in adult–child construction of experience. Implications of this model for children's memory of traumatic events are discussed.

The question remains . . . as to how to establish in fact what recollection can tell us. How do we know what is being accomplished in recollection, the particular function it may be serving in ordering the past? *Data of ongoing experience are needed to serve as a baseline for casting retrospectively derived meaning into relief. It is through reading the "text" lying at the interaction of immediate experience and recollection that we are in a position to ascertain the interpretive work that is being accomplished.* (Freeman & Csikszentmihalyi, 1986, p. 170 [italics added])

The paradox inherent in autobiographical memory is that while, by definition, it pertains to recall of the past from the perspective of the present, the line of directionality in fact leads in both directions: Memory moves forward but is remembered backward.

From the earliest researches on autobiographical, or personal memory, however, the focus has been on only one direction, the retrospective: on what has been forgotten, or difficult to access, rather than on what became memorable and stayed memorable enough to become part of an individual's autobiographical memory.

Yet the question of how this formerly present is carried forward into the "future" to become the "past"—that is, how things *become* memorable—is a critical one for the study of autobiographical memory development and would seem to have strong implications for the matters under consideration in this issue. Shifting the perspective from retrospection *on* experience to present-tense con-

This article is reprinted by permission from *Consciousness and Cognition*, Volume 3, pp. 307–326 (1994).

[1] To whom correspondence and reprint requests should be addressed.

*The Recovered Memory/False Memory Debate*
Copyright © 1994 by Academic Press, Inc.
All rights of reproduction in any form reserved.

struction *of* experience, for instance, opens up for investigation questions such as the following: How important to one's recollection of a personal experience are the conditions of its encoding? What aspects of an event-in-progress, seen as a potential memory-in-progress, influence the event-as-remembered or memory as product? How open to influence is the encoding process during a socially shared experience, particularly one shared by a child and an adult?

Much evidence suggests that memory begins as an undifferentiated generic system (semantic memory, in Tulving's terms; see Nelson, 1993a, 1993b). Adults' questions and cues during and after an experience may be instrumental in breaking the generalized experience down into episodic and then a fully developed autobiographical memory system.

Language is an essential aspect of autobiographical memory, as is the narrative form that connects and relates remembered events in the form of a coherent life story. The narrative form constitutes a prime distinction between episodic memory in general and autobiographical memory as a specific system, while the self as a point of reference is an essential aspect differentiating between memory in general and autobiographical memory: the memory of what happened to the remembering "I" at a specific time, in a specific context, and evoking a specific affect.

Not every episodic memory becomes part of one's autobiographical memory, however. Many episodic memories either drop out or are remembered in the form, for instance, of knowledge *about,* rather than personal experience *of.* The ability to become part of the story-in-progress that we are always writing about ourselves is certainly one determinant of whether a particular event will be magnetized to the self in some way, related to other relevant memories, and thus retained over a long, perhaps life-long, period of time.

A general model of memory development in early childhood based on studies of parent–child talk about the past and spontaneous recounting monologues was outlined by Nelson (1993a, 1993b). In that model it is suggested that episodic memories first emerge from a generalized system and are retained for periods of time that depend upon opportunities for reexperiencing in part or recounting. Social recounting influences both the way in which memories are formulated and the length of the retention period. It is claimed that children learn to remember experience in specific ways—structuring their remembered experience according to the models presented by their social partners, particularly their mothers. The models exist in language, and it is in language that autobiographical memory becomes established. In this model it is the retention in accessible memory for extended periods of time that characterizes the autobiographical system. Other aspects of experience might be retained (although not as whole narratives) in the generic system of events as fragments of image memory, which Pillemer and White (1989) have suggested exists in parallel with the verbal memory system.

The proposal here is that autobiographical memory is essentially social in origin, developed through adult–child interactions in which children internalize a particular, "adult" way of encoding experience in the present and recalling it once the present has become the past. The "product" of this autobiographical memory process is thus seen as the result of a joint construction in the present of the experience later to become the memory, in interaction with joint reconstruction afterward. A dialogic process here described as "joint encoding" is postulated as playing a crucial role in the representation of a shared event by highlighting certain aspects and not others as it takes place.

Joint construction of the present and reconstruction of the past are set forth as the two aspects of the "learning" of autobiographical memory making and recall by young children. It is proposed that in this learning process, the representational operations involved in autobiographical memory and language as a representational system are inextricably bound together because of the role of language in adult–child social interaction, with the cognitive representation by an individual of a shared event seen as created across persons in the same way that discourse meanings are created.

Corsaro (1979) has described the socializing function of the language directed to children by adults in interactions that not only affect children's developing linguistic skills but, through their exposure of children to "adults' perspective on the normative social order," gradually bring the children's reality into line with that of the adults' (p. 389). The research presented here was designed to test the proposition that there is something in the way in which adults guide children through the events of their daily lives that leads to the conventionalization and acculturation of a process that subjectively may feel the most private and personal of all, while actually being continually shaped and modified to match that of the child's first culture—that of the family; it is further proposed that this process can be seen, in microcosm, in a close examination of everyday experiences shared by adults and their children.

## MEMORY IN A SOCIAL CONTEXT

Research following Neisser's 1978 challenge to examine the uses of memory in everyday life led to surprising new insights into the hitherto unacknowledged memory capabilities of even very young children. The early work of Nelson (Nelson & Gruendel, 1981; Nelson, 1986), for instance, showed striking abilities in young children to form unexpectedly complex cognitive representations of their social world. Research by Ratner (1980) and others documented the demands that children's social worlds, in the form of the adults around them, place on them to remember, and research into children's development of the ability to talk about the past (Eisenberg, 1985; Engel, 1986; Fivush & Hamond, 1990; Hudson, 1990) has illuminated the extensive help children receive from adults as they elicit, scaffold, and structure the earliest versions of such talk.

This research provides convincing evidence for an essentially social origin and explanation for autobiographical memory as a whole and has opened up new questions of particular relevance to this special issue. If, for instance, talk about the *past* can be seen as a socially "taught" and "learned" cultural genre, what might be the parallel social and cultural effects of the *present-tense* construction of the "data of ongoing experience" or memory-in-progress that will subsequently become the memory-as-told-to? Are memories born or made, and if made with another, how influential are adult contributions or interventions in children's encoding process during a shared experience?

By about 3 years of age, when the child's language facility is well established, much more explanatory and interpretive talk from adults to children takes place in the course of shared activities than in previous years. The hypothesis here is that the language used highlights certain aspects of a situation, making them more salient and hence more memorable. Children in turn may consciously or unconsciously use this language in reconstructing memories of the experience on their own. Language thus becomes both a stimulus to recall and an object of recall.

Supporting evidence for this hypothesis comes from Dudycha and Dudycha's (1933) findings that almost every one of their adult subjects' childhood memories dated from the period after language had been established and were memories of social-interactive situations and from Waldfogel's (1948) analysis showing an increase of early childhood memories parallel to an increase in language ability. These findings bear on several key aspects of autobiographical memory development in childhood: the essentially *shared* nature of young children's early experience and the development during this same time period of language as a shared representational system and as a primary medium for social interaction.

Studies of language and discourse development provide additional clues regarding the establishment of memory from talk in the present. Adults' use of questions with children, for instance, often serves to direct attention and thus has an implicit socializing function, informing the child in a nondirective way what the culture finds it appropriate to attend to. This function is critical, as Krauss (1980) has noted in another context: The crucial problem is not how to process information once given, "but how to decide what the information *is* in an immensely complex, confusing and subtle social environment." What adults are thus doing is "teaching" their children what information is considered salient, often through what Bruner (1983) describes as formats in which "*what should be processed from the context* has been prearranged by practice and ritualization." Sachs (1983) has characterized the adult strategy as one of using questions "to pull information from the child that he/she could not know how to supply" because of not finding the information relevant to attend to until taught to do so. Training in the conventions of discourse and training in the conventions of encoding coincide.

The proposal here is that all adult–child talk is also a form of memory talk or memory instruction. What has been referred to as joint encoding is understood as a form of on-line representation, or construction-of-memory talk, and the hypothesis is put forth that the "training" of attention and, later, of talk about the present and the past is not merely instruction in how to tell, but in how and what to notice, represent, and remember—how, in effect, to experience—with the result that the child's memory undergoes a process of increasing conventionalization.

This raises a question of direct relevance to the matters in focus in this issue. If children are learning what to remember and how to remember in autobiographical memory from their interaction with adults, the question inevitably arises as to whether such interactions might also in some cases serve to reinterpret an experience, or to introduce an element that might cause the child to reconstruct the experience in a different way, or even to mask the experience in such a way that its original meaning for the child is lost. Our research cannot directly answer these questions, but the evidence that we present here of the influence of social construction at the time of the experience, in addition to that previously documented of its influence at the time of recall, is surely relevant.

Two studies (Tessler, 1986, 1991) were carried out to investigate the way ongoing experience enters past memory. The first was a preliminary exploration of to what extent and by what devices adults frame and structure experience for young children and to what extent children internalize these frames in their representation and recall of a shared event. This study uncovered important individual differences in mothers' styles of discourse that were investigated systematically in the second study.

## STUDY 1. MUSEUM VISIT

Ten mothers and their 3- to 3½-year-old children were observed and audio tape recorded as they visited the American Museum of Natural History in New York City. All dyads followed the same route, viewing the same dioramas. Half the mothers were asked to interact with their children as they ordinarily would on such an occasion; the other half were asked merely to respond to their children's questions or comments but not to initiate or elaborate on this talk. Mother–child talk was transcribed and analyzed using a version of Wasserman and Solomon's Maternal Style Scale (1985).

The children were interviewed at home 1 week later. Mothers were not present for this interview. Children were asked to tell what they remembered of the visit, in an open-ended format, followed by a standard set of memory questions, which probed for recall of specific objects and scenes viewed in the museum displays. The most striking finding was that no child, in either group, showed any recall (in either free recall or response to probes) of objects that had been seen but not talked about. This finding confirmed the original hypothesis that talk itself between adults and children during an ongoing experience would have a structuring effect on children's experience of the event and would be internalized in their own representation and later recall.

Moreover, it appeared that at least at this age, there was a need for the attention to the object, and for the talk, to be mutual: There was no recall by children in either group of objects talked about by the mother only or by the child only. Of course, objects talked about varied between dyads, but in every case the sole objects recalled were those that had been the focus of joint conversation by mother and child.

Initially it had been expected that the presence or absence of maternal talk would account for any differences in recall between the two groups of children. However, the unexpected finding of within-group differences in recall suggested that the presence or absence of talk was not the only influence at work. A reexamination of the data revealed that there were differences between mothers in style of discourse that were not attributable to the different experimental conditions. Then the transcripts of the museum visit were coded for content and it was found that mothers differed not only in the amount of their talk, but also in their style of talk, even when the talk consisted only of responses to their children (see Appendix for coding scheme).

These representational behaviors seemed to be best defined in terms of Bruner's (1986) Narrative and Paradigmatic styles. The Narrative style is characterized by dynamic rather than static descriptives (e.g., *Describes Activity* rather than *Describes Category*); a high proportion of references to autobiographical recall; use of fantasy or verbal play; and generally more interpretive utterances relating to the objects being viewed, such as attributions of intentionality or feelings, variations on temporal sequencing, particularly in an interpretive or imaginative way (i.e., "What do you think he'll do next?"), and an emphasis generally on connecting and contextualizing.

The Paradigmatic style showed a high proportion of categorizing (e.g., *Describes Category*) and specifying (e.g., *Describes Properties, Same/Different, What Part of*?) utterances, and a greater number of references or questions directed to the child's knowledge base rather than to autobiographical recall. This was a style of representation in which the emphasis appeared to be on explanation and differentiation as ways of ordering experience.

The within-group differences among the children paralleled those among the mothers. Three children in the Talk group and one child in the No Talk group showed a higher frequency of Narrative-type utterances (specifically *Describe Activity, Temporal, Interpretation,* and *Autobiographical Recall*) than the other children; these children all had mothers who had been characterized as Narrative. On the other hand, two children in the Talk group had a higher number of *Describe Category* and *Knowledge Base* (Paradigmatic-type) references, as did four children in the No Talk group. These children all had mothers whose behaviors were characterized as Paradigmatic. The resulting $2 \times 2$ distribution of Paradigmatic or Narrative Mother by Paradigmatic or Narrative Child (6 P/P, 4 N/N, 0 P/N, 0 N/P) was significant at the $p < .05$ level by the Fisher Exact Test. These results implied that, regardless of experimental manipulations, children's discourse about the event mirrored that of their mothers' style.

Based on this analysis, it appeared that as early as age 3 years children are internalizing, and are able to use, quite different ways of encoding and talking about experience. Taken together, these findings seemed to indicate a twofold effect of present-tense talk on memory: on *whether* a particular aspect of an experience will be remembered and on *how* it will be remembered.

That different forms of social interaction appeared to have different effects on children's representation of an event was taken as preliminary evidence for the social nature of autobiographical memory development. The effects of such differences on children's development of the representational style in which their autobiographical memory would take form remained to be explored.

## STUDY 2. PICTURE-TAKING WALK

The aim of the second study was to observe and describe, first, the manner in which a shared experience was being jointly represented by mothers and their 4- to 4½-year-old children and then to determine whether the representational style influenced the children's later recall. The major experimental questions in this study were (a) Are maternal styles consistent across situations? (b) Does the representational style to which a child has the greatest exposure influence the development of the child's own representational style?

The specific focuses of the study were on (a) the styles in which mothers and children represented a shared experience; (b) reconstructive talk between the experimenter and the children 1 week later in the same or different representational style; and (c) the children's representational style 3 weeks later with a different inteviewer. Adult's style of talk (Narrative or Paradigmatic) and time of talk (during the encoding of the experience or during the reconstructive talk afterward) were the major independent variables. Mothers' styles were identified prior to the experience and recorded during the experience. The reconstructive talk was guided by the experimenter in either the mother's style or the alternative style.

*Subjects*

Forty-eight dyads consisting of mothers and their 4- to 4½-year-old children (mean age 4;4) participated in this study, recruited from preschools in Manhattan and through mothers' referrals as the study progressed. Only mothers and children whose first language was English were included. The sample included 24 males and 24 females. All the children were Caucasian and came primarily from middle- to upper-middle-class homes.

The mean age of the mothers was 38 years and their mean educational level was 17.5 years. Because the major hypothesis being tested was that children's exposure to a particular maternal representational style would influence the development of their own, only mothers who spent at least half a day with their children were included in the study.

This sample is obviously not a typical one, the mothers being generally older and more highly educated, and occupying more professional positions (thus with more flexible schedules) than we would expect to find in the general urban population. It does not appear that their special characteristics limit the generality of the findings of the study, given the variability within the group on the measures of importance here.

*Design*

The participants were first divided into two groups, each composed of 24 dyads, on the basis of maternal style characterized as Narrative or Paradigmatic. These groups were then subdivided by assigning children from each randomly to one of two treatment groups, resulting in four groups of 12 mother–child dyads each. The basic paradigm consisted of mothers doing the constructive talk during the experience, and the experimenter doing the reconstructive talk 1 week later, with four variations on this scheme.

The Narrative/Narrative (N/N) group was composed of children whose mothers used a Narrative style; these children received reconstructive talk in the form of cues and questions in the Narrative style. The Narrative/Paradigmatic (N/P) group also included children whose mothers used a Narrative style, but these children received reconstructive talk in the Paradigmatic style. The Paradigmatic/

Paradigmatic (P/P) group included children whose mothers used a Paradigmatic style and who received reconstructive talk in that style. The Paradigmatic/Narrative (P/N) group included children whose mothers were Paradigmatic and who received reconstructive talk in the Narrative style.

*Procedure*

The study was carried out in three sessions. Session 1 included a picturebook reading by mother and child in the home, designed to assess maternal style. This was determined by coding mothers' utterances according to the categories in Appendix A, classifying each mother as Narrative or Paradigmatic in terms of the proportion of these types of utterances overall. The picturebook reading was followed by a mother–child picture-taking session on three city streets not in their immediate neighborhood, to ensure unfamiliarity for the children. Mothers and children took 12 pictures of anything they wished. Their talk during this experience was tape recorded and transcribed, and the mother's and child's talk coded as to amount and proportion of Narrative and Paradigmatic constituents in their conversation, where each utterance was coded according to the type of information requested or provided (see Appendix).

In Session 2, a week later (Recall Session 1), the child was interviewed alone in an open-ended format to obtain free recall of the experience. Then the child constructed a picture booklet of his or her photographs with the experimenter and was engaged in Narrative or Paradigmatic talk with her. The experimenter showed each photograph to the child. The children in all four groups were asked "What's this a picture of?" (providing a measure of recognition). Next, the 12 children in the N/N group were presented with four Narrative questions or cues per picture, derived from aspects of the discourse code that were deemed most characteristic of the Narrative style: *Location, Temporal, Activity,* and *Interpretation.*

The 12 children in the N/P group received four paradigmatic questions or cues, derived from the aspects of the code deemed most characteristic of the Paradigmatic style: *Category, Knowledge Base, What Part of,* and *Specific Physical Properties.* Similarly, the 12 children in the P/P group received the four Paradigmatic cues per picture, and the 12 children in the P/N group received the four Narrative cues.

After each of the photographs had been viewed and talked about, the experimenter helped the child place the photographs in the inserts of the folder. The mother was asked not to talk about the experience with her child and to try to prevent others from doing so. The experimenter took the inserts and photographs back from the child with the excuse of making a special cover for them with the child's name on it. This session was tape recorded, transcribed, and coded as to the proportion of Narrative and Paradigmatic information in each child's response to the four cues.

Three weeks later (Recall Session 2), a different interviewer returned with the child's photographs and the special cover the child had been promised. The child's free recall of the photographs and the picture-taking walk was recorded in an open-ended interview first. The interviewer then explained that the pictures had become disarranged. While assisting the child in replacing them in the inserts, the interviewer first asked the child to identify the pictures (providing a recognition measure) and then presented every child, from every group, with all eight of the Narrative and Paradigmatic cues for each picture. This talk was also tape recorded, transcribed, and coded as to proportion of the Narrative and Paradigmatic responses by the children to the interviewer's cues.

*Reliability.* Twenty-five percent of the transcripts of the picturebook reading and the picture-taking walk, chosen randomly, were coded by an independent judge for Narrative and Paradigmatic discourse using the code in the Appendix. Intercoder agreement on the assignment of utterances to code category was 92% for the picture-taking reading and 89% for the picture-taking walk.

## Results and Discussion

*Consistency of style.* The correlation between the mothers' styles during the picturebook reading and during the picture-taking walk was $r = .83$. The two styles presented two distinctly different profiles. Mean scores on the original classification task were .69 for the Narrative mothers and .30 for the Paradigmatic mothers, based on the ratio $N/N + P$ (Total Narrative utterances/Narrative + Paradigmatic utterances). There was no overlap in these distributions (see Table 1). These results confirmed the existence of the two maternal styles observed in the earlier study and supported the hypothesis that the maternal style would be consistent across situations.

On the two tasks in which children were observed interacting with their mothers, the distribution of the children's scores (that is, the proportion of Narrative and Paradigmatic elements in their talk) very closely paralleled that of their mothers, with correlations between mother and child scores of .94 for the picture-book reading and .94 for the picture-taking walk. This finding supports the hypothesis that the children's representational style would reflect that of their mothers, which is most critical for the general hypothesis of a social-interactive influence on children's representation of autobiographical experience.

*Free recall and recognition, Recall Session 1.* Ten pictures for each child were used in the recall sessions to equate numbers of pictures across children, since occasional pictures were not interpretable. Of this total, children in the Narrative group recalled a mean of 4.25 pictures and children in the Paradigmatic group 3.0 ($t = 3.16$, $p = .003$). There were no significant differences in recognition scores, however (see Table 2).

TABLE 1
Proportion of Narrative Utterances in Each Task as a Function of Maternal Style

|  | Narrative group (N = 24) | Paradigmatic group (N = 24) |
| --- | --- | --- |
| Book reading | .69 | .30 |
| Picture taking | .58 | .19 |

*Note.* $N/N + P$, Proportion of narrative utterances.

TABLE 2
Children's Memory and Discourse Measures Study 2, Recall Session 1

| Free recall | | Narrative group | | Paradigmatic group |
|---|---|---|---|---|
| Pictures recalled | | 4.25 | | 3.0* |
| Pictures recognized | | 7.75 | | 7.12 |
| Cued recall | N/N (N = 12) | N/P (N = 12) | P/P (N = 12) | P/N (N = 12) |
| Mean IUs/picture | 16.8 | 14.1 | 9.7 | 8.7 |
| Proportion Narrative IU | .56 | .52 | .42 | .43 |

*Note.* IU, Information unit/proposition; N/N, Narrative maternal style, Narrative questions; N/P, Narrative maternal style, Paradigmatic questions; P/P, Paradigmatic maternal style, Paradigmatic questions; P/N, Paradigmatic maternal style, Narrative questions.

$*p < .003$.

In this study, as in the first one, no recall was shown by any child of something that had not been talked about. However, while in the previous study the talk had to have been engaged in by mother and child together, in Study 2 all that was necessary was for someone—either mother or child—to have encoded the object verbally. In fact, the vast majority of pictures, remembered or not, were at least labeled, but not all were the focus of conversation. (The degree to which pictures were differentially discussed in relation to subsequent memory has not yet been subjected to analysis).

For each picture, children responded to four questions in either the Narrative or Paradigmatic style, as detailed under Procedure. The number of information units provided per picture is shown in Table 2. Because the two groups (N/N and P/N and N/P and P/P) received different questions, separate one-way ANOVAS were run comparing responses of the maternal style subgroups on each different question type. These analyses indicated significant differences between the N and P maternal style groups in terms of IUs per picture at the $p < .01$ level or better for all question types except *Activity* $(P < .04)$ and *What part of* $(p < .06)$. The differences were in the direction expected, with Narrative children responding more to Narrative type cues and Paradigmatic children to the Paradigmatic type cues.

An unexpected result was that children not only showed the hypothesized preference for the style to which they were most accustomed, but also maintained this preference even in response to talk in opposite style, as shown in Table 2 in the proportion of Narrative-type utterances. All four groups maintained their original profiles no matter what the cue, responding to talk of either type mainly in their characteristic Narrative or Paradigmatic format or style. This pattern was confirmed on the second return visit (Recall Session 2) when the children were exposed to cues in both styles.

*Free recall and recognition: Recall session 2.* A 2 (Maternal Style) × 2 (Question Group) ANOVA was conducted on the recall data in Recall Session 2. Neither main effect was significant, nor was the interaction significant (See Table 3). There was also no main effect for Mother Style or Question Type for recognition scores, but there was a significant interaction between type of mother and type of question at Recall Session 1 ($F = 10.02$, $p < .003$), indicating that children who received questions at Time 1 in a style congruent with their mothers' (N/N and P/P) recognized more pictures at Recall Session 2 than noncongruent groups (see Table 3). Between-cell comparisons indicated that the difference between the P/P and the P/N groups were significant ($t = 2.87$, $p < .01$).

It will be recalled that in this session every child received all eight of the Narrative and Paradigmatic cues for each picture. Both the format and the content of the children's talk reflected their original style classifications. As shown in Table 3, there were no differences by Question Style at Time 2 on responses to questions at Time 3. Again a one-way ANOVA was run on each question type. Significant differences between Maternal Style groups at the $p < .01$ level of better were found for all question types except *What Part of* ($p < .02$) in the expected directions.

Furthermore, children's responses mirrored those of their mothers, regardless of question groups, as also shown in Table 3 in terms of proportion of Narrative utterances for children in each group.

*Style Differences.* It appeared that when faced with cues in the style different from the one they were accustomed to, children reformatted them, thereby turning the talk they were receiving in the present into the format they were used to receiving in the past. Presented with an *Interpretation* cue, Paradigmatic children often turned it into a *Knowledge Base* cue. For example, asked "What do you think's going on there?" they would focus in on a specific property of something in the picture and respond, "That's an _____." Similarly, Narrative children presented with a *Knowledge Base* cue such as "What do people do in a bank?" might reply with an *Autobiographical* ("My sister threw my piggy bank on the floor and it broke") or *Interpretation* reference ("That man [in the picture] is gonna rob the bank!")

What seemed to make this process of reformatting possible was the capacity of the children to use the same discourse categories in different ways, and in different combinations, in the service of different orientations. For instance, when Narrative children used *Specific Physical Properties* references, these often accompanied an *Autobiographical* ("That's [gargoyle] like the one on *our* building. I have the book about it") or *Interpretation* utterance ("That boy is going to

TABLE 3
Children's Memory and Discourse Measures Study 2 Recall Session

|                            | N/N  | N/P  | P/P  | P/N  |
|----------------------------|------|------|------|------|
| Mean pictures recalled     | 4.2  | 4.0  | 4.0  | 3.7  |
| Mean pictures recognized   | 9.0  | 8.2  | 9.2  | 7.5  |
| Mean IUs/picture           | 28.7 | 28.6 | 17.7 | 17.4 |
| Proportion Narrative IUs   | .54  | .55  | .41  | .40  |

school. See his book bag?'') In such usages, it appeared to be a personal or interpretive context, fairly global or holistic, that was the initial way in to understanding, with a calling forth of the individual attributes for purposes of making that understanding known. On the other hand, *Specific Physical Properties* references more often accompanied *Knowledge Base* and *Category* utterances for the Paradigmatic children, who seemed to build up from an accumulation of details a category or explanation for the object focused on: "See the yellow? It's a school bus."

The ways in which these representational styles embody not only differences in ways of talking but also differences in attentional orientations are apparent in the strong consistencies between children's talk during the recall sessions and their verbal interactions with their mothers during the picture book reading and picture-taking experience.

The orientation of the Paradigmatic mothers toward specification and distinctions gave their dialogues with their children a different flavor from those of the Narrative mothers and children. Of a picture in the book in which a woman is seen sitting on a chair, with one shoe off, when her child said, "Look, a lady!" one Paradigmatic mother replied, "Yes, what's she doing?" and went on to the next page when her child responded, "She's just sitting." Of that same picture, another child said, "Look at the lady sitting there." Her Narrative mother replied, "Yeah, how come she's just sitting there like that?" When her child responded, "Maybe she's tired" the mother answered: "Sure she is. Look at all she's bought!" and pointed to the overflowing shopping bags at the woman's feet.

In terms of the form of joint encoding that this talk embodies, one can find in the Narrative dialogues the same "combinational," descriptive, highly modified kind of talk in both the picture book reading and the picture taking:

C: I'm gonna take that lady!
M: The lady waiting for the bus?

Here the mother has provided an interpretive context and an elaboration for the child's representation of the lady.

In the following Paradigmatic example, another child wants to take a picture of a woman at a bus stop:

C: How about that lady? I wanna take a picture of that lady.
M: Well, let's go around the other side so you can get her front and not her back.

If we compare the talk here with that in the Narrative example of the same situation, the two different ways in which the scene was jointly encoded could eventuate in two different kinds of representation and recall: one of a woman-in-context, performing and recalling to memory an activity familiar to all city children—waiting for a bus; the other of a woman as an object-in-herself, decontextualized.

Bruner's (1986) original characterization of the Narrative and Paradigmatic modes of thought seems best to sum up the differences between these groups:

"The Narrative mode is concerned with action, intentionality, and situations unfolding in a temporal rather than timeless realm, subject to interpretation rather than logical verification procedures." The Paradigmatic mode, on the other hand, is based upon "categorization or conceptualization and the operations by which categories are established, instantiated, idealized, and related one to the other to form a system."

## GENERAL DISCUSSION

Nelson (1993a, 1993b) has proposed a general model of memory that could account for the emergence of an autobiographical memory system in the late preschool years, building on the availability in early childhood of both semantic and episodic memory and incorporating the narrative models of memory provided by adults who engage the child in memory recounting. In this model both personal and interpersonal contributions to remembering are required, and it is specifically through language that the child becomes cognizant of the social functions of shared memory constructions. Through such constructions the child may become aware of and reflect on the self as an independent actor in shared activities, and through this process build up a self-history, which is crucial to the emerging self-concept.

The findings from these studies support the proposed model by demonstrating the strong effects of talking about experiences at the time of the event, as well as the ways in which talk is organized at that time and at the time of recall. The strong effects of style of talk emphasize the important contributions of language to the child's construction of autobiographical recall. What might be the implications of such effects on long-term memory? We can only speculate, but the following propositions from the combined theory and the data seem relevant:

1. The emergence of autobiographical memory is dependent upon the more basic development of the ability to represent events in verbal form and to incorporate the verbal representations of others into one's own mental representation system. This development can be seen at about 3 to 4 years of age, which is when autobiographical memories begin to be established, as has been well documented in prior research (see Pillemer & White, 1989). Prior to this age language of extended discourse is not securely established, and construction of knowledge through discourse is not therefore feasible.

2. As demonstrated in these studies, the child's verbalized memory for an experience is strongly influenced in form and content by the way in which the event is talked about during the ongoing experience, as well as after the experience.

3. During the period when this linguistically based representational capacity is developing (3 to 4 years), verbal memory accounts of other people may be confused with the child's own memory to a greater extent than in later years, when source information is more firmly established (Foley & Johnson, 1985).

4. Children may yet retain information that is not accessible to the verbal account, as was evident in the study here where children of both style groups showed equally good recognition memory for pictures.

## A Self Among Others: Interpersonal Foundations of Autobiography

This model is formulated to explain memory development in the preschool years, emphasizing the importance of the co-construction of memories through social discourse. But of equal importance is the emerging construction of self through the establishment of a self-history. What we are proposing is a view of self-in-relation to others in which the child is simultaneously taken into and takes in the social world.

Howe and Courage (1993) have recently surveyed the literature on infantile amnesia and early episodic memory and have proposed a quite different view of the relation of self-concept and autobiographical memory. Specifically, they claim that self-concept emerges at about age 2 and that this enables the child to see herself as an actor in relation to others and thereby to begin to retain episodic memories, which in turn overcomes infantile amnesia.

We find several features of this explanation problematic. First, infantile amnesia does not disappear at age 2 as claimed. A century of research with children and adults has converged on age 3½ years as the average age of first memories retained in later life. But even then such memories are few, and significantly fewer than would be expected by the forgetting function that applies after the age of 5 (Wetzler & Sweeney, 1986).It is true that contemporary research has shown that children form episodic memories at least from the late infancy period and may retain them for many months, even years. But these early memories are not retained in the autobiographical system of later childhood and adulthood, and it is this discrepancy that poses the paradox of infantile amnesia.

The second issue is the development of language and its relation to memory. Howe and Courage emphasize the emergence of language between 18 months and 2 years, but at the same time they view requisite language skills (agent expressive, temporal locating) as dependent on the cognitive construction of self. Like many developmental psychologists, they do not distinguish the level of language skill attained by the 2-year-old from the level seen in the 4- or 5-year-old, which permits the construction of connected discourse about sequenced events. It is the latter skill that is crucial to the interpretation of others' representations of events, as well as the child's own representation of experience in verbal (narrative) form.

The third problem is the view of the self-concept that Howe and Courage espouse. Their concept seems to emerge full-blown from infancy in terms of self-recognition at the age of 18 to 22 months. Again, the level of self-knowledge displayed in mirror recognition is not distinguished from the level of self-knowledge apparent in the 4-year-old's personal narratives. Moreover, and most important, neither language skill nor self-concept is related in their model to the interpersonal world of other people. Not surprisingly this world also plays no part in their model of autobiographical memory.

In Howe and Courage's view, the child apparently exists alone in some otherwise unoccupied theoretical space. In contrast, real children in a real world are born not into a bare room, but into one that adults have furnished with labels, concepts, routines, and evaluations; they eagerly introduce the child into it, both as observing subject and observed object. Children do not create their world, no more than they create themselves. A child embedded in a social context, engaging from the first in social experiences, is at best coauthor but not sole author of her self. Interpersonal dramas of everyday life confront the young child, demanding that she make sense of who and where she is in the world, and thus contribute to the continuing construction of a coherent self.

In our view, the relation between autobiographical memory and a sense of self is a dynamic, interactive process in which self and memory organize, construct, and give meaning to each other in a way so intimate that we can truly say that we are what we remember and that our memories are ourselves (see also Fivush, 1988; Schank & Abelson, 1994). But our selves and our memories do not exist in a vacuum. As our work has shown, they enter into a social process in which language serves to organize and emphasize what it is important to remember and how. Thus the self concept develops as a self history emerges from the articulation of experience, first with others, eventually alone as well.

## Implications for Adult Memories of Childhood

The research reported here concerns experiences of everyday, untraumatic events. We have shown that the way adults construe those events, and convey that construal to children through language, affects how the event is remembered by the children. We cannot generalize from these neutral findings to the recovery of a memory of traumatic experience. But it is possible to assert that if children learn what and how to remember during situations shared with adults close to them, the interpretations that adults put on their experiences may determine what and even whether something is remembered in later life. It is not only a memory but an interpretation that is created in socially shared situations.

We may speculate that many factors may be important in the generalization of our findings to other situations. For example, an experience not talked about (such as a secretive sexual abuse episode) may not be recallable by the child. This is one possible reason for poor memory for some such incidents. The role of affect in the construction of a memory may compete with the construal of the adult. For example, anxieties and fears may be retained, often without clear targets, despite verbal reassurance from adults. But it might also be possible for the adult's verbal construction to impose a different affective interpretation on the event. A close relative, one whose styles of interpretation are familiar, may have a more enduring effect on one's memory than a stranger. Many issues of this kind are open to further investigation.

Our work has emphasized the close connection between social construction in language and the emergence and retention of autobiographical memories. What is the fate of experiences not talked about or those taking place before the child has the requisite degree of language mastery? Pillemer and White (1989) suggest that an image-based memory may coexist with the narrative memories that constitute the autobiographical system. This suggests that some memories may persist in an unorganized, free-floating way, becoming available at some later date for reinterpretation when, perhaps, a newly acquired cognitive category intersects with the memory fragment. Such fragments would not be ordinarily encountered because not organized into the basically verbal autobiographical system. The earliest memories of adults tend to be highly visual, but when interpreted or reinterpreted later in life may or may not be consistent with the original experience.

A point to be emphasized is that the experience does not need to be subsequently discussed to enter into a verbally based system. Socially shared experiences, as documented here, incorporate naturally occurring language into the representation of the event. Whether or not a child discusses an event—traumatic or nontraumatic—with anyone else afterward, we may assume that (some) talk during the event has become part of the representation of that event and is available thereafter as both cue to and object of recall. An ambiguous experience that does not easily fall into a familiar storyline may be especially subject to the adult's construal. For example, a favorite uncle's sexual handling characterized by him as an important secret for the two of them to keep, at an age when the child has no familiarity with that as a particular category of story into which she can fit the memory, may be easily distorted by the child in the direction of the adult's story. The age of the child is of crucial importance in determining whether the experience becomes part of an ongoing life narrative or remains isolated unless or until a later circumstance gives it a newly perceived significance.

In conclusion, the strong claim of our model and the research backing it is that autobiographical memory in childhood is social in origin and depends to a large degree upon the verbalized accounts of others, in particular on those of adults with whom the child shares social–emotional bonds, most obviously the parents. How experiences are formulated in the child's accessible autobiographical memory system is then strongly dependent on how they are formulated by adults who share the experience. The possibility of distorting memories within this kind of system is obvious, and the possibility that the influence could be used in ways detrimental to the child's emotional and mental well-being cannot be discounted. Beyond this we cannot speculate, but it seems premature to rule out entirely the dual possibilities of distortion on the one hand and, on the other, recovery of partial memories of experiences underlying—or separate from—the verbal accounts.

## APPENDIX A

Coding Scheme Used to Categorize Utterances of Mothers and Children During Museum Visit (Study 1) and Picture-Book Reading, Picture-Taking Walk and Children's Utterances During Recall Sessions 1 and 2 (Study 2).

| Type of Utterance* | Definition |
| --- | --- |
| *Describe Activity* | A depiction in basic, "surface" (as differentiated from interpretive) form of a behavior or occurrence taking place in view of mother and child. *Example:* "That lady *walking* down the street." |

APPENDIX A—*Continued*

| Type of Utterance* | Definition |
|---|---|
| *Aesthetic* | A depiction in aesthetic rather than informative terms. *Example:* "Those white jars are *beautiful*, aren't they?" |
| *Color* | Self-explanatory. *Example:* "Why don't you take that *red* car?" |
| *Location* | Reference to an actual place (*Example:* "Shall we go to the *park?*") or utterance locating the object or person in a visual context (*Example:* "Do you want me to stand *in front of* the gingko tree?") |
| *Temporal* | Reference to past, present or future. *Example:* "We're going to do that *tomorrow*." Also reference to sequence. *Example:* "We'll take that one *first,* and *then* we'll take that." |
| *Autobiographical* | A reference to something in the (usually shared) personal past; often a way of explaining by means of connecting the sight/activity/occurrence with something already experienced by the child. *Example:* "Where were we, not so long ago, when we saw something like this?" |
| *Affective* | Expression of an emotion or attitude toward the thing observed. *Example:* "I *love* those! They're my *favorite!*" |
| *Interpretation* | Utterance going beyond the basic information given about the feelings, intentions, possible future sequence of events or behaviors relating to the person or object being observed. *Example:* "She might be crying because she's afraid to cross the street alone." |
| *Theme* | Utterances (more than 2) establishing a leitmotiv that recurs throughout the experience. *Example:* "We're going to a *different neighborhood!* . . . Wow, this really is a *different neighborhood* . . . What do you think's *different* about this neighborhood from our neighborhood?" |
| *Describe Category* | Utterance labeling an object (or person), defining class it belong to. *Example:* "*What kind of store* is that? A *video store*, right!" |
| *Size* | Self-explanatory. *Example:* "You mean that *tall/big/little* . . . ?" |
| *Quantity* | May be a specific reference (*Example:* "Those *three* guys?") or interrogative (*Example:* "How many?") |

## APPENDIX A—*Continued*

| Type of Utterance* | Definition |
| --- | --- |
| *Knowledge Base* | As with *Autobiographical*, often used for purpose of explaining something in present situation by reference to something child already knows. Unlike *Autobiographical*, reference is to child's "semantic" knowledge rather than "episodic" experience. *Example:* "Sure you know that. Where do wolves live?" |
| *Specific Physical Properties* | Reference, often for purpose of focusing attention, to perceptual (rather than more content-laden informational) properties of object. *Example:* "See the fancy stuff—that's called molding—around the windows?" |
| *What Part Of* | Used in attempt at specification. *Example:* "What part of the car are you taking?" |
| *Another* | Often used in conjunction with *Category* in classification mode. *Example:* "Are you taking another car?" |
| *Same/Different* | Also used as form of classification. *Example:* "This is the same kind as that one." |
| *Which One* | Also used as specifier. *Example:* "Which one are you aiming at? This one or that one?" |

* May be in either declarative or interrogative form.

## APPENDIX B

Narrative and Paradigmatic Cues and Sample Responses by Children (Study 2)

### NARRATIVE CUES

| | |
| --- | --- |
| *Location* | *Where did you take this picture?* |
| *Temporal* | *When did you take it? (If child does not respond: Before this one or after this one? If the initial picture: Was this your first one?)* |
| *Activity* | *What's [he/she/they] doing?* |
| *Interpretation* | *What do you think's going on here?* |

### PARADIGMATIC CUES

| | |
| --- | --- |
| *Category* | *What kind of [store/truck/etc.] is that?* |
| *Knowledge Base* | *Do you know what people [buy/do/etc.] in a _____?* |
| *What Part Of* | *What part of that were you taking?* |
| *Specific Physical Properties* | *Wow! What do you think of that _____?* |

## ACKNOWLEDGMENTS

This article is based on research undertaken by the first author in partial fulfillment of the requirements for the degree of Doctor of Philosophy at the Graduate Center, City University of New York. Special thanks are due Odine Kleiner, for assistance in data collection; Mara Silgailis, for reliability coding; and Mary Brown Parlee, for helpful advice and feedback throughout the project.

## REFERENCES

Bruner, J. S. (1983). *Child's talk: Learning to use language.* New York: Norton.

Bruner, J. S. (1986). *Actual minds, possible worlds.* Cambridge MA: Harvard Univ. Press.

Corsaro, W. A. (1979). Sociolinguistic patterns in adult–child interaction. In E. Ochs & B. B. Schieffelin (Eds.), *Developmental pragmatics.* New York: Academic Press.

Dudycha, G. J., & Dudycha, M. M. (1933). Some factors and characteristics of childhood memories. *Child Development, 4,* 265–278.

Eisenberg, A. R. (1985). Learning to describe past experiences in conversation. *Discourse Processes, 8,* 177–204.

Engel, S. (1986). *Learning to reminisce: A developmental study of how young children talk about the past.* Unpublished Doctoral Dissertation, City University of New York Graduate Center.

Fivush, R. (1988). The functions of event memory: Some comments on Nelson and Barsalou. In U. Neisser & E. Winograd (Eds.), *Remembering reconsidered: Ecological and traditional approaches to the study of memory* (pp. 277–282). New York: Cambridge Univ. Press.

Fivush, R. (1993). Emotional content of parent–child conversations about the past. In C. A. Nelson (Ed.), *Memory and affect in development: The Minnesota Symposia on Child Psychology* (Vol. 26, pp. 39–77). Hillsdale, NJ: Erlbaum.

Fivush, R., & Hamond, N. R. (1990). Autobiographical memory across the preschool years: Toward reconceptualizing childhood amnesia. In R. Fivush & J. A. Hudson (Eds.), *Knowing and remembering in young children* (pp. 223–248). New York: Cambridge Univ. Press.

Freeman, M., & Csikszentmihalyi, M. (1986). Adolescence and its recollection: Toward an interpretive model of development. *Merrill-Palmer Quarterly, 32,* 167–185.

Howe, M. L., & Courage, M. L. (1993). On resolving the enigma of infantile amnesia. *Psychological Bulletin, 113,* 305–326.

Hudson, J. A. (1990). The emergence of autobiographical memory in mother–child conversation. In R. Fivush & J. A. Hudson (Eds.), *Knowing and remembering in young children* (pp. 166–196). New York: Cambridge Univ. Press.

Krauss, R. M. (1980). *Cognition and communication.* Paper presented at Society for Experimental Social Psychology Meeting, Stanford, CA.

Mead, G. H. (1934). *Mind, self, and society.* Chicago: Chicago Univ. Press.

Neisser, U. (1978). Memory: What are the important questions? In M. M. Gruneberg, P. E. Morris, & R. N. Sykes (Eds.), *Practical aspects of memory.* New York: Academic Press.

Nelson, K. (1986). *Event knowledge: Structure and function in development.* Hillsdale, NJ: Erlbaum.

Nelson, K. (1993a). The psychological and social origins of autobiographical memory. *Psychological Science, 4,* 1–8.

Nelson, K. (1993b). Towards a theory of the development of autobiographical memory. In A. Collins, M. Conway, S. Gathercole, & P. Morris (Eds.), *Theories of memory* (pp. 185–283). Hillsdale, NJ: Erlbaum.

Pillemer, D. B., & White, S. H. (1989). Childhood events recalled by children and adults. In H. W. Reese (Ed.), *Advances in child development and behavior* (vol. 21, pp. 297–340). New York: Academic Press.

Ratner, H. H. (1980). The role of social context in memory development. In M. Perlmutter (Ed.),

*Children's memory: New directions for child development* (Vol. 10, pp. 49–68). San Francisco: Jossey-Bass.

Rovee-Collier, C., & Hayne, H. (1987). Reactivation of infant memory: Implications for cognitive development. In H. W. Reese (Ed.), *Advances in child development and behavior* (Vol. 20, pp. 185–283). New York: Academic Press.

Sachs, J. (1983). Talking about the there and then: The emergence of displaced reference in parent–child discourse. In K. E. Nelson (Ed.), *Children's language* (Vol. 4, pp. 1–28). Hillsdale, NJ: Erlbaum.

Schank, R. C., & Abelson, R. P. (1994). Knowledge and memory: The real story. In R. S. Wyer, Jr., & T. Srull (Eds.), *Advances in social cognition* (Vol. 8). Hillsdale, NJ: Erlbaum.

Tessler, M. (1986). *Mother–child talk in a museum: The socialization of a memory*. Unpublished manuscript, City University of New York Graduate Center.

Tessler, M. (1991). *Making memories together: The influence of mother–child joint encoding on the development of autobiographical memory style*. Unpublished doctoral dissertation, City University of New York Graduate Center.

Waldfogel, S. (1948). The frequency and affective character of childhood memories. *Psychological Monographs, 62,* 1–39.

Wasserman, G. A., & Solomon, C. R. (1984). *Maternal Style Scale*. Department of Child Psychiatry, New York State Psychiatric Institute.

Wetzler, S. E., & Sweeney, J. A. (1986). Childhood amnesia: An empirical demonstration. In D. C. Rubin (Ed.), *Autobiographical memory* (pp. 191–201). New York: Cambridge Univ. Press.

# How Can I Remember When "I" Wasn't There: Long-Term Retention of Traumatic Experiences and Emergence of the Cognitive Self

Mark L. Howe,[1] Mary L. Courage, and Carole Peterson

*Department of Psychology, Memorial University of Newfoundland,*
*St. John's Newfoundland, Canada A1B 3X9*

In this article, we focus on two issues, namely, the nature and onset of very early personal memories, especially for traumatic events, and the role of stress in long-term retention. We begin by outlining a theory of early autobiographical memory, one whose unfolding is coincident with emergence of the cognitive self. It is argued that it is not until this self emerges that personal memories will remain viable over extended periods of time. We illustrate this with 25 cases of young children's long-term retention of early traumatic events involving emergency room treatment. On the basis of both qualitative (case profiles) and quantitative (analysis of covariance) analyses, we conclude that (a) very young children (under the age of 2 years) retain limited memories for events which they commonly express behaviorally, (b) coherent autobiographical memories are not constructed until the child develops a cognitive sense of self (on average, at 24 months of age), (c) autobiographical memories for traumatic events are essentially no different from those for nontraumatic events, (d) stress is only related to long-term retention inasmuch as it is one variable that serves to make an event unique, and (e) like nontraumatic events, traumatic memories lose peripheral details during the retention interval and retain the central components of the event. These results are discussed both in terms of their implications for theories of early autobiographical memory as well as the ways in which we might differentiate implanted (or false) memories and authentic memories for traumatic events.

When do our earliest memories of childhood begin? This question has perplexed humankind for over a century. Most of the research since the nineteenth century that bears on this question has fixed the age of our earliest memory at the third or fourth year of life (for a review, see Howe & Courage, 1993). More recently, some investigators have argued that we can recall memories from the earlier age of 2 years (Howe & Courage, 1993; Howes, Seigel, & Brown, 1993; Usher & Neisser, 1993).

If, as this latter scientific literature attests, our earliest memories of childhood start around the age of 2 years (see Loftus, 1993a, for some healthy scepticism about the prematurity of this age estimate), then why are there so many recent reports from the legal and therapeutic communities of memories being "recovered" from very early in life, in particular, before the age of 2? Indeed, a number

This article is reprinted by permission from *Consciousness and Cognition*, Volume 3, pp. 327–355 (1994).

[1] To whom correspondence and reprint requests should be addressed. E-mail: mhowe@kean.ucs.mun.ca.

of legal cases have involved testimony based on 25-year-old memories of alleged abuse that occurred during the first year of life. For example, highly detailed memories of father–daughter sexual abuse was reported in a case in Santa Clara County in California. The alleged abuse apparently started when the daughter was 6 months of age and continued until she was 18 (*Collier v. Collier,* 1991, cited in Loftus, 1993b). Similarly, a woman in her late 40s at the time of the trial accused her parent of sexual, emotional, and physical abuse from birth to 25 (cited in Loftus, 1993b). Still other cases involve more bizarre allegations. One daughter accused her father of incest, rape, and murder, claiming she had been abused from 3 months of age onward. She also claimed that he murdered three women, one of whom he cut up and put in a meat grinder while she watched (False Memory Syndrome Foundation Newsletter, 1993, p. 7). Considerably more bizarre claims concerning satanic rituals and abuse have arisen in a number of other cases, many of which have been publicized in the popular press (e.g., see Wright, 1993a, 1993b).

Perhaps such recollections are possible because of the strong emotional content of such memories.[2] Historically, a special status has often been accorded memories for traumatic experiences. For example, Freud (1905/1953) suggested that because infantile memories are weak, increases in an event's memorability can be brought about if the event is traumatic. Indeed, according to Freud, traumatic events, regardless of when they occur, can be retained permanently. Even in the more recent literature it has been suggested that our early memories are distinguished by their emotional content, although there is disagreement concerning whether such affect must necessarily be positive (e.g., Waldfogel, 1948), negative (e.g., Cowan & Davidson, 1984; Dudycha & Dudycha, 1941), or either (e.g., White & Pillemer, 1979).

Although strong emotional content was said to confer memorability, Freud (1905/1953) also speculated that traumatic memories might become distorted. Rather than remain in their pristine form, emotionally laden memories were thought to be extensively revised after the event by the unconscious. This process leads to systematic distortions of the content of event memory. Indeed, such traumatic memories might later appear in disguised forms with altered affect.

The most up to date scientific literature does not provide support for these speculations about affect and accuracy. In fact, most of this recent work has shown that not only are early memories accurate (particularly for central details), but they are also no more likely to be emotional in content than memories from

---

[2] Another recent example of the presumed importance of emotion in memory can be found in the so-called flashbulb memories. These are said to be highly detailed (almost photographic) memories of important personal or public events such as the death of John F. Kennedy or the Challenger disaster. In fact, the level of detail contained in these memories is said to be of such high resolution that they even contain perceptual details of the event. Although space does not permit a detailed discussion of this phenomenon here, suffice it to say that considerable controversy exists concerning the veridicality of these memories. In particular, although subjects who report these memories feel confident that these memories are accurate, attempts to corroborate the contents of flashbulb memories have typically failed (primarily for peripheral as opposed to central aspects of the event), leaving us with the conclusion that such recollections are no different than other memories for autobiographical events (also see Loftus & Kaufman, 1992; Neisser & Harsch, 1992).

other parts of the lifespan. For example, both Howes et al. (1993) and Usher and Neisser (1993) found that early childhood memories, even those back to a person's second year of life, were reasonably accurate (as confirmed by parents). Similarly, Terr (1988) found that memories of early childhood trauma (e.g., murder of a sibling or parent, sexual assault, and so on) were typically accurate (as confirmed by others who were also present during the traumatic event). Thus, it would seem that early childhood memories may not be as distorted as Freud (1905/1953), for example, would predict. Moreover, Howes et al. (1993) found that the recovered contents of early memories did not vary systematically as a function of whether the memories were emotionally positive, neutral, or negative.[3]

That many of these memories are accurate (at least for the central details of these events—see later discussion), and that emotion (positive or negative) may not be any more important in early recollections than in recollections from any other part of the lifespan, suggests that memories of early childhood might conform to the more general laws of retention and forgetting that govern most, if not all memories, including autobiographical ones. Recently, two of us (Howe & Courage, 1993) have proposed a theory of the onset of autobiographical memory, one that embraces these general laws about basic processes in memory and proposes that improvements in performance that lead to the offset of infantile amnesia are not due to changes in basic memory functioning per se. Rather, they reflect changes in other cognitive domains (in particular, the emergence of the "cognitive self") that, in turn, influence the way memory is organized, but not the fundamental properties that direct memory very early in life.

In the remainder of this article, we first outline our theory of the onset of autobiographical memory. We then outline some preliminary findings from an ongoing study of children's long-term recollections of documented traumatic events. We conclude by discussing some of the potential differences between memories from authentic traumatic events and those that have been implanted.

## AUTOBIOGRAPHICAL MEMORY AND THE EMERGENCE OF THE COGNITIVE SELF

Research conducted over the past decade has shown that infants (and fetuses) can process and retain information in memory for considerable periods of time. For example, newborn infants can recognize certain characteristics of a prose passage heard in the last trimester of their prenatal life (DeCasper & Spence, 1986). Moreover, Rovee-Collier and her colleagues have demonstrated long-term retention of an operant foot-kick response in infants between 2 and 6 months of age and have isolated a number of factors important in the development of long-term memory (e.g., see Rovee-Collier & Shyi, 1992). Further advances in infants' memory performance occur during the second half of the first postnatal year. These include a new proficiency in deferred imitation of novel action sequences witnessed (but not performed) by them 24 h earlier (Meltzoff, 1985, 1988a, 1988b,

---

[3] There was some evidence from their study, however, that memories that were originally emotional in nature were recalled as emotionally neutral in adulthood.

1990), as well as the ability to search for and retrieve hidden objects (see Willatts, 1990, for a review).

Development in the second year of life brings further sophistication in young children's memory accomplishments, at which time improvements in performance are likely due not to increases in memory mechanisms per se nor to maturation of underlying neurological structures (see Howe & Courage, 1993, for a discussion), but rather to a growing sophistication in related cognitive processes. For example, DeLoache and her colleagues found that 24- to 30-month-olds were better than 18- to 22-month-olds at using landmark cues, strategies such as rehearsal and memory monitoring and spatial categorization to aid the retrieval of hidden toys (DeLoache & Brown, 1983, 1984; DeLoache, Cassidy, & Brown, 1985; DeLoache & Todd, 1988). Finally, studies of young children's memories for both naturally occurring and contrived events that occurred during their infant and toddler years show that these are remembered and may endure for months or years (Bauer & Shore, 1987; Fivush, Gray, & Fromhoff, 1987; Fivush & Hammond, 1989; Myers, Clifton, & Clarkson, 1987; Perris & Myers, 1990; Perris, Myers, & Clifton, 1990; Sugar, 1992; Terr, 1988).

It is important to note, however, that while infants and very young children remember something of the events and experiences that have occurred in their past, exactly what it is that they recall is an empirical question. Somewhere between 2 and 3 years of age children begin to narrate about events in relation to themselves and it is clear that the events have been organized autobiographically in memory. If, however, their recognition (recall) of prior events is nonverbally expressed or limited to single words or simple motor responses (as was the case in some of the studies cited above), we cannot be sure that their behavior reflects anything more than conditioned responding cued by some aspect of the experimental situation or recollection based on (and limited to) the representation of a generalized learning experience in memory. This is not unimportant and attests to the enduring effects of early experience. However, the evidence that very young children remember certain aspects of their infant experiences should not obscure the fact that what they actually remembered was sometimes fragmentary.[4]

This caveat notwithstanding, by the time children are about 2 years of age the developmentally more advanced autobiographical memory (i.e., personal memories of specific events coded with respect to time and place) begins to appear. As noted above, we believe that the emergence of these personally coded memories does not follow from any structural or functional change in long-term memory per se but rather is the result of developments in other areas of cognitive functioning, in particular, the emergence of the self concept. Since autobiographical memory by definition is memory for information and events pertaining to the self, it is only with knowledge of one's self as an independent entity that experiences can be organized in memory as personal or autobiographical. In effect, we are

[4] Although it can be argued that much (if not all) of recall is based on reconstructing memories from fragments, it is not clear that these early fragments of experience are sufficient for reconstructive processes to regenerate the original event in memory.

claiming that the development of the self concept has a significant impact on the way in which memories are organized and that it is not until this development of the self occurs that we observe the emergence of autobiographical memory. Although we regard the development of the self as preeminent in the emergence of personal or autobiographical memory, we recognize that these developments do not occur in isolation from certain other cognitive, linguistic, and socioemotional changes which we will elaborate later.

## Development of the Self

Although speculation about the nature and function of the self has a long history, it remains a difficult concept to define precisely (see Damon & Hart, 1988, for a discussion). However, over the years theorists from diverse perspectives have agreed that neonates are probably unaware of their separateness from the environment and come to recognize this only following a gradual process of individuation (Bowlby, 1969; Freud, 1915/1959; James, 1892/1961; Mahler, Pine, & Bergman, 1975; Mead, 1934; Piaget, 1954). This view is also reflected in a recent special issue of *Developmental Review* (Vol. 11(3), 1991) devoted to the early development of self. Furthermore, there has generally been agreement that there exist at least two fundamental facets of the self, the "I," a subjective sense of the self as a thinker, knower, and causal agent, and the "me," an objective sense of the self with the unique and recognizable features and characteristics that comprise one's self concept. Although intuitively discriminable, these two aspects of the self are complexly related and their development is currently being investigated in both theoretical and empirical domains (Bullock & Lutkenhaus, 1990; Case, 1991; Cicchetti, 1991; Damon & Hart, 1988; Emde, Biringen, Clyman, & Oppenheim, 1991; Harter, 1983; Lewis, 1991; Lewis & Brooks-Gunn, 1979; Neisser, 1991; Pipp, Fischer, & Jennings, 1987).

The methodological challenge inherent in tracing the origin and development of the self in the preverbal infant has been resolved with elegant simplicity by researchers who have recorded the behavior of infants to their visual images in mirrors, on videotape, and in photographs. Before briefly reviewing this literature it should be noted that the development of self-recognition revealed by this approach is only one aspect of the self concept, one that is relatively easy to operationalize for research with infants. The self concept implies more than recognition of one's physical features and is a fundamental aspect of social cognitive development that continues to evolve throughout childhood and adolescence (see Damon & Hart, 1988, for a review).

Regardless, the primary research on the development of visual self-recognition has involved measurement of infants' reactions to their mirror images (Amsterdam, 1972; Berenthal & Fischer, 1978; Bullock & Lutkenhaus, 1990; Darwin, 1877; Dixon, 1957; Johnson, 1983; Lewis & Brooks-Gunn, 1979; Lewis, Brooks-Gunn, & Jaskir, 1985; Lewis, Sullivan, Stanger, & Weiss, 1989; Pipp et al., 1987; Preyer, 1893; Priel & DeSchonen, 1986; Schulman & Kaplowitz, 1977). Collectively, these studies indicate that from about 3 months of age infants are very attentive toward mirrors. They respond by smiling, bouncing, vocalizing, and reaching toward the image. Later, at about 9 months, they show awareness of the contingency cues provided by the tandem movement of the image with themselves and use these cues for play and imitation. They also reveal some knowledge of the reflective properties of mirrors and will turn around to locate objects and people that they see reflected. However, full self-recognition of the mirror image as their own is not manifest in most infants until they are about 18 months of age. At this time they first respond to a spot of rouge that has been covertly applied to their noses by touching their own noses rather than the mirror image, clearly indicating that they have a schema for their faces that does not include a red spot. Contiguous with mark-directed behavior, infants begin to show self-consciousness (shy smiling, gaze aversion, and self touching) when confronted with their images and by about 22 months of age will correctly label the image with their own name. While these coincident behaviors do not on their own provide evidence of self-recognition, their co-occurrence with mark-directed behavior toward the spot of rouge are consistent with the hypothesis that the infant now recognizes the mirror image as "me."

Subsequent research by Lewis and his colleagues has shown that in addition to these trends, there are also substantial individual differences in the developmental course of self recognition. For example, Lewis and Brooks-Gunn (1979) found that whereas some of their 15-month-olds showed mark-directed behavior to the red spot, others did not show self-recognition until the end of the second year. While these individual differences have not been fully examined, they are believed to be a function of both social interaction (e.g., quality of infant attachment) and cognitive developmental (e.g., intelligence) variables (Brooks-Gunn & Lewis, 1984; Hill & Tomlin, 1981; Lewis et al., 1985; Loveland, 1987; Mans, Cicchetti, & Sroufe, 1978; Spiker & Ricks, 1984).

To date, many additional issues concerning the emergence of the sense of self in both its subjective and objective aspects across infancy and childhood are unresolved (see Howe & Courage, 1993, for a discussion). What is clear to our thesis that a sense of self (albeit primitive) is fundamental to the development of autobiographical memory is that by 18 to 24 months the infant has a concept of him/herself that is sufficiently viable to serve as a referent around which personally experienced events can be organized in memory. In fact, the contributors to the recent special issue of *Developmental Review,* "Development of the Self" (1991) concur that a significant shift in one's sense of self occurs at about this time. Although the exact nature of this change has not been specified, it is clear that at this point the self achieves the "critical mass" necessary to serve as an organizer and regulator of experience (also see Emde et al., 1991). The fact that this time frame corresponds with the onset of autobiographical memory is, we believe, more than coincidental.

*The Role of Language Acquisition*

The concept of the self further evolves as children acquire language (e.g., Miller, Potts, Fung, Hoogstra, & Mintz, 1990), which enables them to think and talk about "I" and to elaborate their categorical knowledge of "me." These personal pronouns are the first that toddlers acquire at about 22 months of age, with "you" added to the repertoire about 2 months later (Brown, 1973; de Villiers & de Villiers, 1978). Correct use of these pronouns would seem to be a challenging task, one that requires an inversion of point of view. The young child must realize that he/she is "I" when speaking but "you" when spoken to and also that other people can be "I" and "you." Yet normal 2-year-olds rarely confuse these two (de Villiers & de Villiers, 1978; Reich, 1986). The facility with which toddlers acquire correct pronoun use probably reflects to some extent their awareness of themselves as both subject and object and their appreciation of the distinction between self and other. In contrast, children who are handicapped by blindness or autism have considerable difficulty with correct pronoun usage and continue to reverse them for several years (Dawson & McKissick, 1984; Fraiberg, 1977; Kanner, 1946; Neuman & Hill, 1978). It is interesting that the acquisition of correct pronoun use by blind children at about 4 to 5 years of age is contiguous with the onset of self-recognition as assessed by identification of their own voice on tape and by the beginning of imaginative play. Moreover, it is only when blind children acquire self-recognition and stable pronoun use that they begin to talk about past events (Fraiberg, 1977). On the other hand, autistic children who also persistently reverse pronouns do show mark-directed behavior on the rouge task. Thus, self-recognition may be a necessary but not a sufficient condition for stable pronoun use. Unfortunately, memory for events in these children has not been investigated.

The representation of the self in language is followed shortly by another important linguistic achievement—the use of markers which designate the past tense. Whereas toddlers between the ages of 1 and 2 years converse in one- or two-word utterances only about events that are in the present, 2-year-olds lengthen their verbalizations to include simple sentences, begin to add grammatical morphemes (e.g., -ing, -ed) to their repertoire, and start to talk about events in the past (Brown, 1973; de Villiers & de Villiers, 1978; Sachs, 1983). This shift from conversation restricted to "here and now" to that which includes "there and then" marks a significant transition in the development of language, one which provides an important vehicle for the narration of personal or autobiographical events. Initially, however, children's narratives are sparse and rely heavily on support from the listener to provide both structure and prompting, with the need for such "scaffolding" only gradually becoming less across the preschool years as children learn to converse easily and spontaneously about past events (Peterson, 1990; Sachs, 1983).

On the other hand, a number of writers have contended that narrative is much more than an outlet for autobiographical memory, arguing that the limitations in early language and conversational skills are at the heart of young children's apparent inability to relate personal events and indeed to formulate these events as such in memory. For example, Nelson and her colleagues (e.g., Fivush & Hamond, 1990; Hudson, 1990; Nelson, 1990, 1993), like Pillemer and White (1989), suggest that autobiographical memory evolves (and conversely infantile amnesia devolves) only through the linguistic sharing of memories with others. That is, as young children learn to converse about the past with adults, both the ability to narrate about events and the organization of these personal events in memory are facilitated. Furthermore, Nelson (1993) maintains that autobiographical memory is quite late to develop and is only complete in the late preschool years. It is our contention, however, that these important (language) developments are secondary to the primary ontological shift which is the development of a sense of self.[5]

In conclusion, a progression of significant developmental events takes place when infants are between 18 and 30 months of age which prepares them to talk about personally experienced events. First, at about 18 months of age infants learn to recognize their features in the mirror. This acquisition is followed several months later by a more advanced and abstract representation of the self reflected in their pronominal reference to the self as "I" and "me." Finally, the child learns to converse about immediate, then more distant past events in narrative, the language of autobiographical memory. Both narrative skill and autobiographical memory continue to develop in structure, organization, and content over the preschool years (Fivush & Hamond, 1990; McCabe & Peterson, 1991), but by then infantile amnesia has become a phenomenon of the past. While we believe that the emergence of the cognitive sense of self is logically prior to developments in language and that it is this sense of self that is the catalyst for the onset of autobiographical memory, we recognize that this remains an empirical question. However, although autobiographical memory does not require verbal competence for its expression and, indeed, can be communicated nonverbally (e.g., Eisenberg, 1985; Terr, 1988) it logically does require a sense of self, something which emerges gradually across the early months of life predating the use of language.

---

[5] Recently, Nelson (1993, in press) has attempted to restrict the meaning of the term "autobiographical memory," a change that has implications for its appearance, developmentally. Nelson argues that although such memories are considered to be a part of episodic memory, not all memories of events are necessarily autobiographical. For example, memories for events that are experienced repeatedly (i.e., five or more times; e.g., see Nelson, 1993, p. 11), in much the same form become script-like, lose their unique character, and ultimately become part of a generic event memory system. Alternatively, a particular event memory can attain autobiographical status if it is reinstated through the linguistic sharing of the memory with others. Consequently, autobiographical memory requires sophisticated language-based representational skills, ones that do not emerge until the late preschool years (Nelson, 1993, in press). Further, Nelson argues that the memories for events that toddlers and young preschoolers do retain are not, strictly speaking, autobiographical.

We do not disagree that language plays an important role, both in the development of the self concept and autobiographical memory. However, it is our contention that autobiographical memory is ushered in much earlier than the late preschool years and does not depend on sophisticated linguistic (representational) skills. Rather, it is our position that autobiographical memory coincides with the emergence of the cognitive self, an event that typically precedes the onset of language production. Moreover, we contend that the post-hoc and seemingly arbitrary assignment of memories to either a generic event memory, an episodic memory system, or an autobiographical memory subsystem is, at this time, not warranted by extant data. Further, until the nature of this decision mechanism is specified, tests of its role in determining whether events become classified as autobiographical cannot be carried out. For these reasons, as well as others that are beyond the scope of this article, we prefer to define a memory as autobiographical in the traditional sense; that is, that the memory for an event is organized with reference to the self and can be expressed either verbally or nonverbally. Clearly, however, a fair and comprehensive evaluation of these two positions must await the resolution of a number of thorny methodological and definitional issues.

## REMEMBERING TRAUMATIC EVENTS

According to our theory, children who have not acquired a sense of self will be unable to form reliable and accurate autobiographical memories. This is true regardless of the content of the potential memory, including whether the event itself involves positive or negative affect or is affectless. What this means is that, on average, autobiographical memories for any experience will not be formed until approximately the age of 2 years. As we have mentioned, this is not because young children are incapable of forming memories, but simply because a sense of self is necessary for these memories to be organized autobiographically.

Although our theory bestows no particular advantage to traumatic memories, such memories are worthy of investigation if for no other reason than their current prominence in the legal system and in the popular press. Although forensically relevant memories tend to be formed during times of high stress, at present, there is no definitive answer concerning the impact of stress on memory. For example, consistent with our position, studies have shown that emotional content is not a key factor in adult memories of early childhood (e.g., see Howes et al., 1993). Moreover, recent studies with children and adults show that stress sometimes enhances memory formation, sometimes results in poorer memory, or may have no effect (for recent reviews, see Christianson, 1992, and Goodman, Hirschman, Hepps, & Rudy, 1991).

Unfortunately, however, few, if any, of the studies that we have cited have approximated the levels of stress and trauma that are coincident with real sexual, physical, and emotional abuse. Ergo, many of these findings may not bear directly on the issue of stress and memory in real criminal events. There are, however, a handful of clinical studies that seem to show that high levels of stress, while not necessarily enhancing memory, do not interfere with it either. For example, Terr (1988) described a number of clinical cases in which individuals exposed to documented traumatic experiences in early childhood, such as a sibling's murder or their own rape, were able to recollect their experiences in detail. We are finding similar results with children who received hospital emergency room treatment for lacerations or broken bones. In this research, recall for both the trauma and the treatment as well as recognition memory for the hospital staff (using "mug-shots"), although declining over a 6-month interval, was still reliable, at least for central details. Consistent with our proposal, stable personal memories of this sort were available only for the children who, given their age, had a sense of self. For younger children whose sense of self was still emerging (again, as reflected by their age), only a fragmentary memory was available, one that was expressed behaviorally. The details of this study are provided next.

### Children's Memory for Trauma and Emergency Room Treatment

In order to more closely approximate the levels of stress and trauma experienced in childhood abuse, we decided to study children's memories for traumatic events that required emergency room treatment at a local children's hospital. We selected only those cases involving broken bones, lacerations requiring sutures, or anomalous injuries causing high levels of stress but were not the result of suspected child abuse. For the purposes of this article, we selected 25 children for whom data were available from both immediate and 6-month interviews. Of the 25 children, 5 (1 male, 4 females) had an average age of 18 months (range = 17–18 months), 5 (3 males, 2 females) had an average age of 30 months (range = 27–33 months), 5 (1 male, 4 females) had an average age of 36 months (range = 34–40 months), 5 (3 males, 2 females) had an average age of 48 months (range = 44–52 months), and 5 (2 males, 3 females) had an average age of 60 months (range = 56–66 months). All of the children were white and came from predominantly lower middle class homes.

Parents were approached in the emergency room by a researcher who asked for permission to visit them at their home at a later date (usually a few days following treatment) to discuss the accident and treatment. At that time, the researcher first interviewed the child and then the parents about the events surrounding the incident. Interviews consisted of a free-recall session followed by a standardized cued-recall segment. Free recall was used first in order to evaluate the child's spontaneous recollection of the events and cued recall second to elicit additional details from memory. The cued-recall segment consisted of two types of questions, open-ended questions (e.g., "Where were you when you got hurt?") and forced-choice questions requiring a yes–no response (e.g., "Did it hurt?"). In addition, the parents were asked to rate (on a 6-point scale) what their child's level of stress had been both at the time of the traumatic incident and again during the emergency room procedure. Finally, parents were asked not to rehearse the incident with the child over the ensuing 6-month retention interval. As well, when arrangements were made for the 6-month followup, parents were again reminded that it was the child's memory we were interested in and, therefore, were asked not to rehearse the event with the child.

Following approximately 6 months, the children were interviewed again using free recall first followed by cued recall. The cued-recall segment this time was based on the transcript of their earlier interview and that of their parents. In addition, the child was asked to select from a "lineup" of four photographs the emergency room staff member who treated them (e.g., in the case of a fracture, the x-ray technician, or in the case of a laceration, the attending physician). All of the interviews were tape recorded and subsequently transcribed for both memory and narrative analyses.[6] In what follows, we provide two levels of analysis of the data, one qualitative and the other quantitative. In terms of qualitative analyses, we begin by presenting specific case descriptions to illustrate typical protocols for children from each of the 5 age groups mentioned earlier. We included a protocol for a very young child (i.e., 18 months at the time of the incident), one for a slightly older child (i.e., 28 months at the time of the incident),

---

[6] For all of the analyses presented in this article, responses were coded as either central to event (e.g., what happened, how it happened, what treatment was adminstered) or peripheral to the event (e.g., what they were wearing, who took them for treatment, what they had done while waiting for emergency room treatment, who took them home, whether a "treat" had been given following treatment). Two raters scored 30% of the narratives with an acceptable interrater reliability of 90%. Any disagreements were resolved through discussion. The remaining narratives were scored by a single rater.

as well as more mature children (i.e., 40 months, 52 months, and 66 months at the time of the incident). The selection of these age ranges is obviously not haphazard but were chosen to illustrate memories of traumatic events for children prior to the onset of the cognitive self (Case 1), just after the onset of the cognitive self (Case 2), and children whose cognitive self was well established (Cases 3, 4, and 5).[7] In terms of quantitative analyses, we present an analysis of covariance (ANCOVA) of the different forms of recall using stress as the covariate.

*Qualitative Analyses*

*Case 1.* KB was an 18-month-old female who caught a fish bone in her throat. As she was preverbal at the time of the incident, only the parents were interviewed immediately. According to her parents, the bone became lodged in her throat while she was eating dinner. She did not seem distressed at the time but continued to cough and retch over the next few hours. Her father took her to the family physician who saw the bone in her throat following tongue depression but was unable to extract it. The child at this point was "hysterical" (given the highest rating of a 6 on the stress scale). The family physician referred them to the emergency department of the local children's hospital where the attending physician removed the bone quickly and skillfully (given a rating of 4.5 on the stress scale).

Seven months later, when KB was 25 months old and by now verbal, she was unable to verbally relate any of the details of the incident either in free or cued recall. However, she correctly identified the photo of the physician who removed the bone. Interestingly, her mother reported that since the incident KB refuses to eat fish and had become very upset when approached with a tongue depressor by another physician treating her for a sore throat.

This protocol is typical of the fragmentary memories in very young children that we discussed earlier in this article. We would argue that KB does have some memory of this traumatic event, although it is neither coherent nor does it appear to be autobiographical. Whereas KB's language skills were just beginning at the time of the second interview, it is clear that she could not express her memory of that event verbally. Equally clear, however, is the fact that her expression of memory for that event was tied to nonverbal indices. These included both visual recognition of the attending physician and the anecdotal changes in her behavior that were noted by her mother.

---

[7] Unfortunately, this report of the preliminary findings of our study on memory for traumatic events does not contain measures of the self. This is because when we conducted the initial interviews with the children it became apparent that they were still experiencing residual stress from the incident. Because we did not wish to exacerbate the situation by conducting numerous tests, wanting instead to minimize the extent of interventions during the interview process, we elected to omit direct measures of the cognitive self at this stage. Even if we had included such measures, they would be purely correlational and arguably weak. What is needed are more precise indexes of the early development of the self. For these reasons, and because narrative recall was the highest priority, measures of self-recognition were omitted and we, therefore, relied on mean age estimates of when the cognitive self emerges from previous studies cited earlier in this article.

*Case 2.* AB was a verbally fluent 28-month-old female child who sustained a dislocated elbow while having dinner with her family in a restaurant. At the initial interview she freely recalled the central details of the event; that is, that her sister had pulled hard on her arm and hurt it, that they had been in a restaurant at the time, and that she had been taken to the doctor who fixed it. Further cuing yielded the additional details that several other family members were present at the restaurant, that her father was not there as he had gone on a plane to a meeting, and that she had ordered chicken nuggets, fries, and bread. She also recalled that she had not gone to the hospital that day but went home after the meal. She added that her arm still hurt the next day and that she was driven to the hospital where she waited while sitting on her mother's lap. She reported that an x-ray was taken by a man, that it had hurt, but that she had not been given a needle. Her mother reported that she was not particularly distressed when the incident occurred, but became extremely upset when she was having the x-ray taken and had to be restrained (stress ratings were 2 and 6, respectively).

Six months later, she spontaneously recalled only the basic details that her sister had pulled her arm and hurt it. Cued recall yielded further information that she had been having dinner, the name of the specific hotel where they had been eating, the other family members who were present, that she had been hurt, cried, and driven to the hospital by her mother for an x-ray. Further, that she had seen a doctor, been "fixed with a camera," and given a popsicle. She did not recall that she had not gone to the hospital until the next day, nor could she identify a photo of the doctor who had treated her. In addition, this account of her experience at the hospital contained several intrusions from other minor accidents and another visit to the hospital that occurred in the 6-month interval.

In this case, verbal recall of the traumatic event declined between the initial and followup interviews. Interestingly, it was primarily the peripheral, not central, aspects of the event that were forgotten, a pattern of forgetting that is typical for the retention of many (nontraumatic) events. In addition, during open-ended cued recall, one new detail was introduced (the name of the hotel in which the incident occurred) and no errors of commission were noted.

*Case 3.* CE was a 40-month-old male child who fell against a heater at his daycare center and sustained a cut that required stitches. A few days after the accident, he freely recalled that he had fallen against a heater at his daycare center and cut his head, that it had hurt, and that he had been taken to the hospital and given two stitches. With cued recall he related further details that he had been playing with two other boys at the time of the accident and that they were pushing each other and throwing blocks. He reported that he had screamed for his mother and that the daycare personnel had come running to assist and used a cloth and bandaids to stop the blood. Next, his mother arrived and, as the family car was "broken," she had called a friend to come and drive them to the hospital where he had waited until his name was called and was given stitches by a doctor, the stitches hurt, and he cried. Finally, he had a coke and went back to his mother's office. All of his recollections were correct. Apparently he was only moderately upset when the incident occurred, but became hysterical at the hospital when he was restrained for stitching (stress ratings were 3 and 6, respectively).

After 6 months, he spontaneously related only that he had been throwing blocks, he was pushed by his friend, and had gone to the hospital where he was checked. When prompted with cued-recall questions he added that he had fallen and cut his head, it had hurt and bled, he cried and called for his mother and that the daycare staff had attended to him with a face cloth and bandaids. He further recalled that his mother had called a friend to drive them to the hospital (family car broken), that he had been given two stitches by a doctor, and that he had cried. He incorrectly recalled that his father had been present and that he had gone straight home following treatment at the hospital. No photo of the attending doctor was available for recognition.

Again, like Case 2, central details were available and were freely recalled following a 6-month interval. However, unlike Case 2, both correct and incorrect information was reported when cued-recall questions were posed. Importantly, incorrect cued recall was confined to peripheral, not central, details about the event.

*Case 4.* TU was a 52-month-old male who required stitches to the forehead following a fall in the kitchen of his home. During the immediate recall session, TU freely recollected the core of the event. That is, he recalled running around the kitchen, banging his head off a piece of furniture and blood "flying everywhere," and putting a cloth on his head and going to the hospital. During probed recall he added that his parents were not present, but his sitter, brother, and sister were all there, that it hurt, that he cried, that his sitter put the cloth on his head (but incorrectly thought the cloth was red and white when it was in fact blue), the drive to the hospital, having his blood pressure taken, being given a popsicle, and staying up late when he got home. Interestingly, although he correctly recalled crying when he received six stitches, he failed to recall getting a shot in the lacerated part of his forehead. The mother noted that during this latter procedure, TU was extremely stressed (a 6 on the stress scale) and had to be restrained. (During the accident itself, he was given a stress rating of 4.)

Following a 6-month interval, TU was able to freely recall that he had cut his forehead and went to the hospital. Interestingly, he added an unconfirmed detail that they had been playing "motorcycles" at the time the accident occurred. During cued recall he remembered that his sitter, sister, and brother were present, that he was driven to the hospital where he received 6 stitches, that the doctor was male, and that the laceration was bandaged following suturing. Although he remembered that he was crying after the incident, he again failed to recall that he received a needle in the lacerated part of his forehead. Finally, TU correctly identified the photograph of the attending physician.

As in the preceding two cases, verbal recall of the traumatic event declined over the 6-month interval. Curiously, TU failed to recall (both immediately and 6 months later) the most stressful (according to both his mother and his own reactions) part of the experience, namely, receiving a local anaesthetic injection in the lacerated part of the forehead. In addition, during both free and cued recall,

TU introduced false details. During free recall, he stated that he was "dead" following the incident and during cued recall he added that "they put me to sleep." As before, the errors that were made in recall tended to involve peripheral rather than central details (e.g., the color of the cloth).

*Case 5.* LK is a 66-month-old girl who was bitten by a dog. She freely recalled that on the previous Tuesday she had been running up a hill and had seen the neighbor's "rabbit" dog (a beagle) by the fence and when she reached out to pet him he had bitten her cheek. She also reported that she had cried and called for her mother and that the owner of the dog came and picked her up. She also recalled that her aunt, who was a nurse, was visiting and that she (LK) had wanted her to accompany them to the hospital. She reported that her mother had refused to allow this to happen and this had made her angry. She added that she had told her mother that she hated her and that she would move in with her aunt when they got back (this was confirmed by the mother).

Further details of the incident were elicited with cued recall. She remembered that she had intended to play with the dog, that the bite had left three holes in her cheek, that it hurt, bled, and that she had cried. She identified several people who were present at the time of the incident, noted that the owner had "got a fright" and had taken her inside to the bathroom and washed her face with a blue and white cloth, and that the owner's son had smacked the dog. When she had been cleaned up her mother arrived, at which time she and her friend who witnessed the attack were both still crying. She reported that she had held on tight to her aunt and that her mother had to "pry her loose" from her aunt to take her to the hospital. At the hospital, she didn't wait long, she had cuddled into her mother, a doctor had examined the cut, rubbed something on it, and applied tiny, skinny bandaids. Finally, they went home (her stress ratings were 6 and 2, respectively).

After 6 months, she freely recalled only the central details that she had been running up a hill and that a dog had bitten her. Cued recall yielded the additional details that she had been going to a friend's house to play and that when the dog bit her she covered her face with her hands and fell to the ground. She added that the owner's son had picked her up, looked at her face, and taken her into his house to be cleaned up. Her mother had been called and had driven her to the hospital in the family car. She again reported that she had wanted her aunt to accompany her and that her mother had opposed this. At the hospital, she recalled new details (not reported previously) that she had her blood pressure checked and that while waiting for the doctor she had looked at a story book. After the tiny, skinny bandaids were applied, they went home. She correctly identified the physician who had treated her at the hospital in a photo lineup.

Again, verbal recall of central details was fairly consistent across interviews, but recall of peripheral details declined over the 6 months. In addition, several new and correct details were elicited through cued recall during the 6-month interview. Finally, the report produced by this child was considerably more detailed than that of the younger children in this study. Moreover, it was not simply the sheer quantity of reported factual detail that was impressive in this case, but rather, the extent to which children of this age begin to introduce details concerning the emotional circumstances surrounding the event. That is, the child spent relatively more time than the younger children in this study mapping out the emotional status of the other participants (e.g., that the owner got a fright and that her friend was crying).

*Summary of qualitative findings.* Overall, it is clear that regardless of age (except for the 18-month-old), the amount of detail about traumatic events declines over time. More particularly, these declines are confined primarily to peripheral aspects of the event, with central features remaining essentially intact. This is consistent with what we know about forgetting in general and indicates that, at a fundamental level, the retention of traumatic events probably does not differ greatly from that of nontraumatic events. In addition, the children's accounts of the traumatic events were extremely accurate, both immediately and at 6 months, and few errors of commission were noted. When errors did occur, they were most often confined to peripheral aspects of the event. We turn now to the quantitative analyses, all of which confirm and extend the conclusions from our qualitative examination of the data.

## Quantitative Analyses

In order to investigate quantitative trends, the data from the immediate and 6-month narratives of 25 subjects were coded according to specificity of recall prompts used to elicit the information (free recall, open-ended cued recall, and forced-choice cued recall) and the centrality of the information recalled (central versus peripheral details—see footnote 6). Specifically, narratives were scored according to the following six categories: (1) free recall of central information (FR/C), (2) free recall of peripheral information (FR/P), (3) cued recall (open-ended) of central information (CROE/C), (4) cued recall (open-ended) of peripheral information (CROE/P), (5) cued recall (forced-choice) of central information (CRFC/C), and (6) cued recall (forced-choice) of peripheral information (CRFC/P).

Errors for each of the different categories were also scored. However, as noted earlier, very few errors of commission were made. As it turned out, the number of errors committed was so small that quantitative analyses were not feasible. Furthermore, a cursory appraisal of these errors revealed no reliable trends. In addition, because there were a number of instances in which photo lineups were not available at the 6-month interview (due to technical difficulties), there was insufficient photo recognition data for analysis. Finally, a composite stress score was computed and consisted of an average of each subject's different stress ratings.

In order to evaluate patterns of correct recall with the effects of stress controlled, an analysis of covariance (ANCOVA) was conducted. That is, we analyzed correct recall using a 5(age: 18 months vs 30 months vs 36 months vs 48 months vs 60 months) × 6(recall type: FR/C vs FR/P vs CROE/C vs CROE/P vs CRFC/C vs CRFC/P) × 2(test: immediate vs 6-month) ANCOVA where the first variable was between-subjects, the latter two variables were within-subject, and the covariate was the composite stress score. As it turned out, the covariate was not significant, $F(1,19) < 1$, $p < .94$. Consistent with a number of previous findings, varying levels of stress did not influence recall (e.g., Goodman, Bottoms, Schwartz-Kenney, & Rudy, 1991; L. Peterson, Moreno, & Harbeck-Weber, 1993).

Before reporting the main effects and interactions it is important to note that although the covariate was not significant at a global level, scores may still have been adjusted to control for the effects of stress on recall (the lack of significance simply means that these adjustments were not statistically reliable across the different conditions in the analysis). Although such adjustments may be minimal, we report the results of the ANCOVA as our concern is with differences in correct recall with the effects (small as they may be) of stress controlled. Second, because the sphericity test was significant ($p < .01$), the Geisser–Greenhouse adjustment (e.g., see Kirk, 1982) was used where relevant. Because the results were always identical, no further adjustments were necessary and it can be concluded that regardless of the circularity assumption, the outcomes are genuinely significant (see Hays, 1988, p. 525).

Three main effects were obtained: (a) a main effect for age, $F(4,19) = 33.98$, $p < .0001$, where Newman–Keuls ($p < .05$) analyses indicated that correct recall increased with age in the following manner, 18 months (adjusted $M = .16$) < 30 months (adjusted $M = 1.85$) = 36 months (adjusted $M = 2.65$) < 48 months (adjusted $M = 3.71$) < 60 months (adjusted $M = 5.22$); (b) a main effect for recall type, $F(5,100) = 25.50$, $p < .0001$, where free (adjusted $M = .91$) and forced-choice cued recall (adjusted $M = .43$) of peripheral details were significantly (Newman–Keuls post-hoc tests, $p < .05$) poorer than free (adjusted $M = 3.17$) and cued recall (both open-ended (adjusted $M = 4.54$) and forced-choice (adjusted $M = 2.77$)) of central details and open-ended cued recall of peripheral details (adjusted $M = 4.22$); and (c) a main effect for test, $F(1,20) = 62.31$, $p < .0001$, where recall on the immediate test (adjusted $M = 2.82$) was superior to that on the 6-month test (adjusted $M = 2.61$).

These main effects were modified by the presence of three first-order interactions, namely, an Age X Test interaction, $F(4,20) = 3.08$, $p < .04$, a Recall type X Test interaction, $F(5,100) = 4.79$, $p < .006$, and an Age X Recall type interaction, $F(20,100) = 8.11$, $p < .0001$. The Age X Test interaction is shown in Fig. 1. It is clear from this figure that amount recalled both immediately and at 6 months increased linearly with age. In addition, regardless of when the test occurred, age differences in amount recalled were significant (Newman–Keuls tests, $p < .01$) between 18 and 36, 30 and 48, and 36 and 60 months. The interaction can be attributed to the fact that whereas recall across consecutive age groups did not differ at the 6-month recall interval, they did differ significantly (Newman–Keuls tests, $p < .05$) between 18 and 30 months as well as between 48 and 60 months at the immediate recall interval.

The Recall type X Test interaction is shown in Fig. 2. There are several interesting features in this figure. To begin, this figure clearly illustrates the pattern of responding noted earlier in the main effect for recall type; that is, cued recall of the open-ended variety produced the most accurate responding (both central and peripheral details), followed by free recall and forced-choice cued recall of the

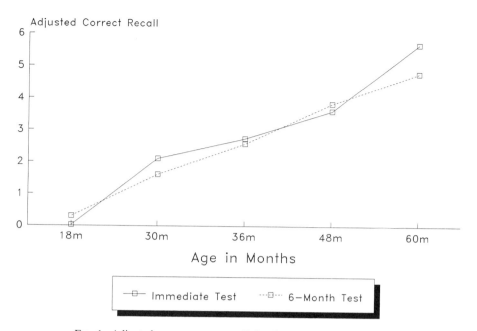

FIG. 1. Adjusted mean correct recall for the Age × Test interaction.

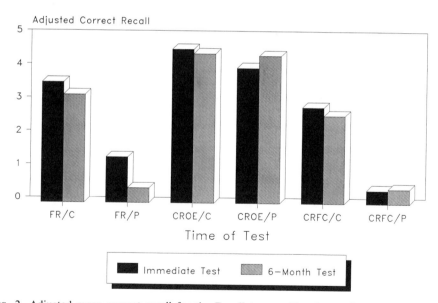

FIG. 2. Adjusted mean correct recall for the Recall type × Test interaction where FR/C, free recall, central information; FR/P, free recall, peripheral information; CROE/C, cued recall open-ended, central information; CROE/P, cued recall open-ended, peripheral information; CRFC/C, cued recall forced-choice, central information; and CRFC/P, cued recall forced-choice, peripheral information.

central details, and free recall and forced-choice cued recall of the peripheral details produced the lowest levels of accurate responding. Interestingly, there were two factors that contributed to the interaction. First, whereas no differences were observed for recall of peripheral details using free recall or open-ended cued recall on the immediate test of retention, these differences were significant (favoring open-ended cued recall) on the 6-month retention test (Newman–Keuls tests, $p < .01$). Second, the only reliable difference between immediate and 6-month retention occurred for free recall of peripheral details (poorer at 6-months than immediately; Newman–Keuls tests, $p < .05$). This latter finding (poorer free recall of peripheral details across lengthy retention intervals), as well as the generally poorer free recall of peripheral information, is consistent with any number of recent theories of long-term retention (for reviews, see chapters in Howe, Brainerd, & Reyna, 1992).

The Age X Recall type interaction is shown in Fig. 3. Despite the seeming complexity of this interaction, it is really quite straightforward. First, consider age effects in forced-choice cued recall. Here, there were no age differences for recall of peripheral information and only one age difference, that between 18 and 30 months favoring the 30-month-olds (Newman–Keuls tests, $p < .05$), for recall of central information. Second, consider age effects in open-ended free recall. Here, like the general pattern depicted in Fig. 1, recall of both central and peripheral information increased linearly with age, with age differences occurring between 18 and 36, 30 and 48, and 36 and 60 months (Newman–Keuls tests, $p < .05$). Finally, consider age effects in free recall. Here, recall increased almost linearly (except between 36 and 48 months) for central information. Like age

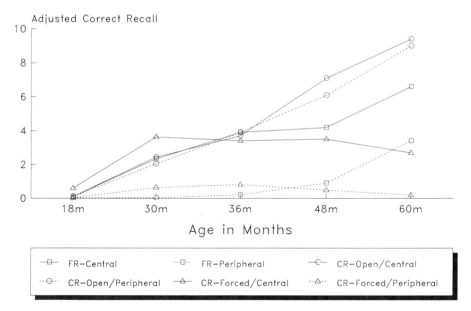

FIG. 3. Adjusted mean correct recall for the Age × Recall type interaction where FR, free recall; CR, cued recall; Open, open-ended; and Forced, forced-choice.

differences in cued recall, Newman–Keuls tests ($p < .05$) indicated that significant differences in free recall of central information was confined to nonconsecutive ages (i.e., between 18 and 36, 30 and 48, and 36 and 60 months). In contrast, free recall of peripheral information remained at or near floor until 60 months ($p < .05$).

*Summary of quantitative findings.* To summarize, these quantitative findings lead to a number of conclusions that compliment those observations made based on the more qualitative assessments. First, like other recent studies of the effects of stress and trauma on long-term retention (e.g., Goodman, Bottoms, Schwartz-Kenney, & Rudy, 1991; L. Peterson et al., 1993), degree of stress in the current study was unrelated to recall. Apparently, increased stress neither enhances nor diminishes long-term retention of traumatic events. Second, errors of commission were few, were unrelated to type of recall, and did not increase with the use of probes in open-ended cued recall. This pattern is important because it confirms other recent studies in which low commission error rates have been reported (e.g., Goodman, Bottoms, Schwartz-Kenney, & Rudy, 1991) and because it serves to dispel the common folk wisdom that the use of cues automatically leads to increases in the rate at which children fabricate information. Third, it is abundantly clear that, regardless of age or retention interval, open-ended cued-recall questions were the most reliable way of eliciting both central and peripheral information. This pattern is consistent with previous research on questioning techniques and underscores the importance of using open-ended questioning methods in which the probes presented are not misleading (e.g., Poole & White, 1991, 1993). Fourth, these findings also illustrate the relative ineffectiveness of forced-choice cued-recall methods of questioning, particularly in trying to elicit peripheral information. Fifth, although free recall of central information was quite robust across a 6-month retention interval, the same could not be said for free recall of peripheral information. Not only was peripheral information less likely than central information to be freely recalled regardless of time of test, but also significant declines in free-recall over the 6-month interval were confined to peripheral information. Finally, although verbal recall (regardless of type) increased linearly with age at both the immediate and 6-month retention intervals, the Age X Recall type interaction revealed that such developmental advantages were restricted to free recall of central information and open-ended cued recall of both central and peripheral information. Again, such findings are consistent with most theories of long-term retention of nontraumatic events.

## GENERAL DISCUSSION

The qualitative and quantitative results of this study provide a remarkably clear set of findings, ones that converge on several important conclusions. Although case studies are always difficult to interpret, being subject to numerous conjectures which frequently represent diametrically opposed theoretical predispositions, they can also represent a wealth of information due in large measure to their open-ended structure. Fortunately, in our particular case, we were able to augment our case presentations with quantitative analyses of narrative recall (or, alternatively, we might say that our quantitative analyses were augmented by our case illustrations). In any event, both sets of analyses provide convincing and convergent evidence that allow us to make a number of assertions about children's long-term memory for traumatic events. First, consistent with our theory concerning the emergence of autobiographical memory, very young children whose cognitive self was not well formed at the time of the incident (i.e., children under 24 months of age, on average; e.g., Case 1) failed to provide a coherent account of the traumatic event (using either free- or cued-recall techniques). Indeed, for KB, the memory that did exist 7 months following the incident (when she was 25 months old) tended to be incomplete and fragmentary. Moreover, this memory was expressed almost exclusively at a behavioral level even though she, like children of her age, had acquired some linguistic facility enabling her to talk about the past (e.g., see Peterson, 1990).

Obviously, we do not want to convey the impression that children whose sense of self is still emerging cannot form a memory for an event. As our first case so clearly illustrates, the event is represented in memory. However, although we can presume that such memories are not organized autobiographically, the precise nature of its structure remains an empirical question. As a first step toward understanding this representation, it is evident that the central details of the traumatic event were retained in memory, although they were expressed behaviorally. That is, KB could visually recognize the physician who removed the bone from her throat, developed an aversion to fish, and now resists the use of tongue depressors during routine throat examinations. Although these behavioral expressions of memory are impressive, they are not indicative of a well-integrated autobiographical memory. Rather, these behavioral indices are reminiscent of the fragments that are characteristic of immature memory for early (traumatic) experience (see our earlier discussion, Howe & Courage, 1993, and Howes et al., 1993).

It might be argued that what was really exemplified in our first case was a failure to use language to narrate memory for the traumatic event. Although such an interpretation cannot be completely ruled out in the absence of further empirical evidence, we contend that the root of this problem is not language per se but the absence of a cognitive self. This is because, first, KB did have language at the time of her second interview and, at least according to some norms, should be at least beginning to be able to talk about the past (e.g., Peterson, 1990). Second, we maintain that a sense of self is logically prior to autobiographical memory. As we have argued previously,

> Autobiographical memory, by definition, is memory for information and events pertaining to the self. Therefore, knowledge of the self as an independent entity with characteristics, thoughts, and actions that are separate and distinct from those of others is perhaps the minimum criterion for the existence of autobiographical memory. Without a clear recognition of an independent self, there can be no referent around which personally experienced events can be organized. Prior to articulation of the self, the infant will learn and remember, but these experiences cannot be recognized as specific events, coded with respect to time and place, that happened to a "me." (Howe & Courage, 1993, p. 306)

These points notwithstanding, we do not deny that the role language plays in autobiographical memory is important. The extent to which the emergence of the self and corresponding developments in language contribute to the growth of autobiographical memory remains open to empirical scrutiny (also see footnote 5). To this end, we will be following KB's (as well as a number of other subjects) memory in the future.

The second point we wish to make is that for older ("postself") children (Cases 2 through 5), memory for the central features of the traumatic experience remained intact over a 6-month interval. Most of what these children forgot tended to be details of a peripheral sort (e.g., color of the cloth used to stop the bleeding). These results were confirmed in our quantitative analyses in which the only significant decline in recall over the 6-month interval was free recall of peripheral details (see Fig. 2). These results are consistent with some of the literature on eyewitness memory, although there are some recent reports in which the claim is made that recall failures exist for central as well as peripheral details (for a review, see Ceci & Bruck, 1993). Despite this debate, from a pragmatic viewpoint it is important to know that memories for real-life traumatic events (at least for our subjects) retain the gist of those events over extended retention intervals.

Third, the finding that recall of peripheral details declined over the 6-month interval is consistent with patterns of "normal forgetting" that are typically observed in laboratory studies (for recent overviews, see Howe & Brainerd, 1989; Howe et al., 1992). That is, like normal forgetting, recollection of peripheral details of authentic traumatic events declines over time. This finding is consistent with our proposal that traumatic and autobiographical events enjoy no special status in long-term memory. That is, unlike what some theorists would have us believe (e.g., Freud, 1905/1953), these memories are not held in some secret repository that is immune to the ravages of normal forgetting. Rather, like all memories, early autobiographical memories and memories for traumatic events are subject to the same laws that govern the retention of memories in general.

Equally important, these results, like those from the laboratory studies, stand in contrast to the patterns of retention observed for so-called implanted memories. Studies in which implanted memories have been examined across repeated interviews have found that the amount "recalled" tends to increase across interviews (particularly details peripheral to the event, e.g., see Ceci, 1993). Although reminiscence (and reinstatement) effects can certainly account for some increases in recall across repeated interviews (e.g., see Howe, 1991; Howe, Courage, & Bryant-Brown, 1993), typically, net recall declines over time, indicating that forgetting exceeds reminiscence, particularly for peripheral details. These findings are similar to those reported by Goodman, Hirschman, Hepps, and Rudy (1991). In their study, children's recollections of stressful events declined over a 1-year interval and there was no reliable hypermnesia. Moreover, across all of the experiments reported in Goodman, Hirschman, Hepps, and Rudy (1991), the rate of children's forgetting was the same for stressful and nonstressful events. Thus, not only are certain (peripheral) details of these memories forgotten over time, but also, as we argued earlier, stressful memories are no better preserved than nonstressful ones.

Clearly, inasmuch as these as well as other data indicate that memory for stressful events "fades" over time, just like normal memories for nonstressful events, it would seem that such memories are not accorded any special status that protects them from normal forgetting. It would seem unlikely, therefore, that such memories could subsequently be recovered in pristine form. Rather, like any other memory trace, memories for traumatic events are susceptible to the same constructive, destructive, and reconstructive processes that occur routinely within the memory system.

That traumatic and nontraumatic memories appear to behave in much the same manner may have a number of implications for the current controversy about the reality of recovered, repressed memories. Our findings, like those of others (Goodman, Bottoms, Schwartz-Kenney, & Rudy, 1991; Goodman, Hirschman, Hepps, & Rudy, 1991; L. Peterson, Moreno, & Harbeck-Weber, 1993), provide no indication that amount of stress per se affects the memorability of traumatic events. Indeed, both our qualitative profiles (which revealed little impact of level of stress on recall)[8] and our quantitative analyses (particularly the absence of a significant effect of our covariate) indicated that levels of stress were unrelated to levels of recall. These findings are consistent with the testimonial evidence of victims of abuse (physical as well as sexual) in which corroborative evidence of the abuse was available. For example, in a recent series of convictions for both physical and sexual abuse of young boys in a local church-run orphanage (e.g., for a partial description of these incidents, see the Hughes Commission Report, 1991), it was obvious that many of the complainants in the case, who were now of adult age, were unable to recall many of the peripheral aspects of the abusive experience (e.g., whether an event occurred during Easter or summer vacation), but were able to recall central aspects of the abuse (e.g., who had committed the abuse and the type of instrument used in the abusive act). In fact, it was abundantly clear that, at least with respect to the core elements of these events, the victims were disturbed not because they forgot what happened to them, but because they were *unable* to forget what happened to them! Like the data from the current study, then, these observations substantiate the general position that although peripheral details tend to diminish with time from the memories of abuse victims, the central information about what happened to them remains available.

The above evidence is inconsistent with the notion that traumatic memories may be repressed and subsequently recovered. However, this apparent robustness of traumatic memories might be seen as evidence consistent with theories in which trauma, stress, or intensity of affect (see Slackman, Hudson, & Fivush, 1986) is said to enhance the memorability of events, inoculating them

---

[8] Recall that one of the children (Case 4) failed to recollect a memory for what appeared to be a highly stressful aspect of the treatment (a needle in the laceration) either immediately or after 6 months. Although this represents only a single memory in a single case, and although it is impossible to tell whether this subject formed a memory for this extremely stressful part of the treatment sequence and cannot, or was reluctant to, report it, or simply did not form the memory at all, it is perhaps significant because it may alert us to the possibility that extremely high levels of stress can have an impact on memory. Equally important, unlike traditional notions about repressed memories in which the entire memory is seconded to the "unconscious," this case illustrates the possibility that individuals can retain memories of most of the event and simply "elect" to suppress a single element.

against forgetting. How can we reconcile this with the frequent observation (both here and elsewhere, see earlier discussion) that rated levels of stress are unrelated to memorability? One possibility is that our rating scales are insensitive to the levels of trauma needed to enhance memory. For example, one of our mothers commented, when asked to rate their child's highest level of distress, "isn't there a 10 on this scale?" Although such measures are admittedly crude (e.g., it might be preferable to obtain more precise, convergent evidence from autonomic system measures, blood chemistry analyses, and so on), the failure to find a relationship between rated stress and recall across a number of recent investigations makes it seem unlikely that instrument insensitivity is the source of this observation.

Alternatively, failures to observe a relationship between stress and memory may be due to the classic third-variable problem in correlational analyses (e.g., see Howe, Rabinowitz, & Grant, 1993); that is, the (statistical) relationship between two measured variables may appear and disappear simply as a function of the influence of a third, unmeasured variable that is related to each of the measured variables. In the present case, a potential third variable that is related to both traumatic events and memorability is *uniqueness*. It is well known that uniqueness (frequently operationalized as distinctiveness) facilitates long-term retention of information (e.g., see Brainerd, Reyna, & Kneer, 1994; Hunt & McDaniel, 1993). Oftentimes the traumatic events that we experience are unique and may be more salient in memory because they stand out from our "script-like" memories for recurring, everyday events. To illustrate, consider the following example. For many of us, witnessing a serious car accident on our walk to work would be both unique and stressful. Indeed, it would not be unusual for us to remember that experience for a longer period of time than we would what we had for breakfast that day. However, similar memorability might occur if, instead of a car accident, we witnessed a car stopping and a clown jumping out and handing a bouquet of balloons to another passerby. This latter event is arguably equally unique but clearly does not have the same stress value associated with it. Thus, to the extent that trauma, stress, or intensity of affect make an experience unique, memorability may be enhanced. The point here is that because memorability is affected by the uniqueness of the event, variations of which do not map directly onto levels of stress, we should not expect stress and recall to be necessarily correlated.

Another important point concerning the similarities between traumatic and non-traumatic memories is that it may be possible to distinguish so-called implanted memories from those that are real by tracking memory performance across interview sessions. Although memories can undergo some reminiscence, details of real memories tend to "fade" over time leaving the kernel of the event as the most reliable component of the trace. Over repeated interviews, other details of such events may be retrieved from time to time, but the most consistent reporting will be for the gist of the event. To the extent that implanted memories have the tendency to "grow" with time, repeated interviews should result not only in the retelling of the gist of the event, but also in the "recovery" of numerous, more-or-less peripheral, details (those being the components that produce richly elaborated stories and lead to increments in recall). Thus, unlike the pattern observed in Fig. 2 in which free recall of peripheral details declined over the 6-month interval, implanted or false memories might actually exhibit an increase in free recall of peripheral details.

Finally, it is important to note that open-ended cued-recall questions were perhaps the best elicitors of recall, both immediately as well as at 6 months. This is consistent with the recommendations of other investigators concerning the types of questioning techniques that facilitate accurate recall (e.g., Poole & White, 1991, 1993). Furthermore, like the findings in other recent reports (e.g., Goodman, Bottoms, Schwartz-Kenney, & Rudy, 1991) the use of memory probes did not result in greater errors of commission. In fact, very few errors of commission were made in this study, and those that did occur were not systematically related to age, recall type, or time of test.

## CONCLUSION

We began this article by inquiring whether certain properties of trauma itself served to inoculate memories against forgetting, a claim that is frequently made in connection with cases of so-called "repressed" and later "recovered" memories. Although the theoretical viewpoints are many, extant research on the role of stress and memory is ambiguous on this topic. To be fair, however, it is not at all clear that the levels of stress and trauma documented in empirical studies approximate those found in real life cases of abuse. In order to more closely approximate these real life levels of stress, we examined young children's immediate and 6-month memories for traumatic events that involved emergency room treatment. What we found was that children whose sense of self was still emerging could not remember the traumatic event in a conscious, coherent fashion. It was only older ("postself") children who exhibited normal patterns of recollection. That is, central features of the traumatic incident, as well as the postevent treatment, were extremely well remembered both immediately and at 6-month recall, but the amount of peripheral information that was freely recalled declined over a 6-month retention interval. This pattern is consistent with laboratory-based studies of long-term retention.

From a theoretical standpoint, these results are consistent with our proposals about the role of the cognitive self in the offset of infantile amnesia and the onset of autobiographical memory. Specifically, the youngest of our children who was "preself" at the time of the incident (18 months) showed no coherent memory for the event 7 months later when she was 25 months old. Although children at this latter age are generally able to narrate about the past, KB was unable to do so about the traumatic event. Instead, she exhibited only visual recognition (of the attending physician) and some behavioral memories related to the trauma (e.g., avoidance of fish, dislike of tongue depressors).

As well, consistent with our proposals, older children's memories of traumatic events are no more likely to be inoculated against forgetting than memories for other events. That is, like the forgetting of nontraumatic events, memories for the features of the traumatic event decreased with time, with forgetting being confined primarily to peripheral, not central, details. With the sole exception of one child's memory for a single, highly stressful event (a needle in the lacerated area of his forehead, see footnote 8), it seems safe to conclude that traumatic memories are as reliable as any other memory and that, like any unique experience, they are more memorable than other, everyday events only to the extent that they are distinct from other episodes in memory.

In closing, we would once again like to underscore the difficulties inherent in constructing measures of the cognitive self that are independent of the emergence of productive language. Although we believe we have fashioned a reasonable case for the role of the cognitive self in establishing autobiographical memories, we are also aware that the database we have presented is preliminary and limited to 25 cases. However, we have conducted initial interviews with another 25 children (and/or their parents) between the ages of 12 and 60 months who were also treated for traumatic injuries. The pattern of findings for those children who have been reinterviewed 6 months later are consistent with those that we have reported in this article. With the development of more sensitive measures of the very early development of the cognitive self, we anticipate that our conclusions concerning the importance of the cognitive self for the emergence of autobiographical memory will be confirmed.

## ACKNOWLEDGMENTS

Preparation of this article was supported by Grants OGP0003334 (to Mark L. Howe), OGP0093057 (to Mary L. Courage), and OGP0000513 (to Carole Peterson) from the Natural Sciences and Engineering Research Council of Canada.

## REFERENCES

Amsterdam, B. (1972). Mirror self-image reactions before age two. *Developmental Psychobiology,* **5,** 297–305.

Bauer, P. J., & Shore, C. M. (1987). Making a memorable event: Effects of familiarity and organization on young children's recall of action sequences. *Cognitive Development,* **2,** 327–338.

Berenthal, B. I., & Fischer, K. W. (1978). Development of self-recognition in the infant. *Developmental Psychobiology,* **14,** 44–50.

Bowlby, J. (1969). *Attachment and loss* (Vol. 1). New York: Basic Books.

Brainerd, C. J., Reyna, V. F., & Kneer, R. (1994). *False-recognition reversal: When similarity is distinctive.* Manuscript submitted for publication.

Brooks-Gunn, J., & Lewis, M. (1984). The development of early visual self-recognition. *Developmental Review,* **4,** 215–239.

Brown, R. (1973). *A first language: The early stages.* Cambridge, MA: Harvard Univ. Press.

Bullock, M., & Lutkenhaus, P. (1990). Who am I? Self-understanding in toddlers. *Merrill-Palmer Quarterly,* **36,** 217–238.

Case, R. (1991). Stages in the development of the young child's first sense of self. *Developmental Review,* **11,** 210–230.

Ceci, S. J. (1993, August). *Cognitive and social factors in children's testimony.* Master lecture presented at the annual meeting of the American Psychological Association, Toronto, Canada.

Ceci, S. J., & Bruck, M. (1993). The suggestibility of the child witness: A historical review and synthesis. *Psychological Bulletin,* **113,** 403–439.

Christianson, S.-A. (1992). Emotional stress and eyewitness memory: A critial review. *Psychological Bulletin,* **112,** 284–309.

Cicchetti, D. (1991). Fractures in the crystal: Developmental psychopathology and the emergence of the self. *Developmental Review,* **11,** 271–287.

Cowan, N., & Davidson, G. (1984). Negative affect may preserve memory of childhood events. *Journal of Genetic Psychology,* **145,** 101–107.

Damon, W., & Hart, D. (1988). *Self-understanding in childhood and adolescence.* New York: Cambridge Univ. Press.

Darwin, C. R. (1877). An autobiographical sketch of an infant. *Mind,* **2,** 186–294.

Dawson, G., & McKissick, F. C. (1984). Self-recognition in autistic children. *Journal of Autism and Developmental Disorders,* **14,** 383–394.

DeCasper, A. J., & Spence, M. J. (1986). Prenatal maternal speech influences newborns' perception of speech sounds. *Infant Behavior and Development,* **9,** 133–150.

DeLoache, J. S., & Brown, A. L. (1983). Very young children's memory for the location of objects in a large-scale environment. *Child Development,* **54,** 888–897.

DeLoache, J. S., & Brown, A. L. (1984). Where do I go next? Intelligent searching by very young children. *Developmental Psychology,* **20,** 37–44.

DeLoache, J. S., Cassidy, D. J., & Brown, A. L. (1985). Precursors of mnemonic strategies in young children's memory. *Child Development,* **56,** 125–137.

DeLoache, J. S., & Todd, C. M. (1988). Young children's use of spatial categorization as a mnemonic strategy. *Journal of Experimental Child Psychology,* **46,** 1–20.

de Villiers, J. G., & de Villiers, P. A. (1978). *Language acquisition.* Cambridge, MA: Harvard Univ. Press.

Dixon, J. C. (1957). Development of self-recognition. *Journal of Genetic Psychology,* **91,** 251–256.

Dudycha, G. J., & Dudycha, M. M. (1941). Childhood memories: A review of the literature. *Psychological Bulletin,* **38,** 668–682.

Eisenberg, A. R. (1985). Learning to describe past experiences in conversation. *Discourse Processes,* **8,** 177–204.

Emde, R. N., Biringen, Z., Clyman, R. B., & Oppenheim, D. (1991). The moral self of infancy: Affective core and procedural knowledge. *Developmental Review,* **11,** 251–270.

False Memory Syndrome Newsletter (July 3, 1993). *Letters,* **2**(7), 7.

Fivush, R., Gray, J. T., & Fromoff, F. A. (1987). Two-year-olds talk about the past. *Cognitive Development,* **2,** 393–409.

Fivush, R., & Hamond, N. R. (1989). Time and again: Effects of repetition and retention interval on 2 year olds' event recall. *Journal of Experimental Child Psychology,* **47,** 259–273.

Fivush, R., & Hamond, N. R. (1990). Autobiographical memory across the preschool years: Toward reconceptualizing childhood amnesia. In R. Fivush & J. A. Hudson (Eds.), *Knowing and remembering in young children* (pp. 223–248). New York: Cambridge Univ. Press.

Fraiberg, S. (1977). *Insights from the blind.* New York: Basic Books.

Freud, S. (1905/1953). Three essays on the theory of sexuality. In J. Strachey (Ed. and Trans.), *The standard edition of the complete psychological works of Sigmund Freud* (Vol. 7, pp. 135–243). London: Hogarth Press.

Freud, S. (1915/1959). Instincts and their vicissitudes. In E. Jones (Ed.), *Collected papers of Sigmund Freud* (pp. 317–385). New York: Basic Books.

Goodman, G. S. (1991). Commentary: On stress and accuracy in research on children's testimony. In J. Doris (Ed.), *The suggestibility of children's recollections* (pp. 77–82). Washington, DC: American Psychological Association.

Goodman, G. S., Bottoms, B. L., Schwartz-Kenney, B. M., & Rudy, L. (1991). Children's testimony about a stressful event: Improving children's reports. *Journal of Narrative and Life History,* **1,** 69–99.

Goodman, G. S., Hirschman, J. E., Hepps, D., & Rudy, L. (1991). Children's memory for stressful events. *Merrill-Palmer Quarterly*, **37**, 109–158.

Hays, W. L. (1988). *Statistics* (4th ed.). New York: Holt, Rinehart, & Winston.

Hill, S. D., & Tomlin, C. (1981). Self-recognition in retarded children. *Child Development*, **52**, 145–150.

Howe, M. L. (1991). Misleading children's story recall: Forgetting and reminiscence of the facts. *Developmental Psychology*, **27**, 746–762.

Howe, M. L., & Brainerd, C. J. (1989). Development of children's long-term retention. *Developmental Review*, **9**, 301–340.

Howe, M. L., Brainerd, C. J., & Reyna, V. F. (Eds.)(1992). *Development of long-term retention*. New York: Springer-Verlag.

Howe, M. L., & Courage, M. L. (1993). On resolving the enigma of infantile amnesia. *Psychological Bulletin*, **113**, 305–326.

Howe, M. L., Courage, M. L., & Bryant-Brown, L. (1993). Reinstating preschoolers' memories. *Developmental Psychology*, **29**, 854–869.

Howe, M. L., Rabinowitz, F. M., & Grant, M. J. (1993). On measuring (in)dependence of cognitive processes. *Psychological Review*, **100**, 737–747.

Howes, M., Siegel, M., & Brown, F. (1993). Early childhood memories: Accuracy and affect. *Cognition*, **47**, 95–119.

Hudson, J. A. (1990). The emergence of autobiographical memory in mother-child conversation. In R. Fivush & J. A. Hudson (Eds.), *Knowing and remembering in young children* (pp. 166–196). New York: Cambridge Univ. Press.

Hughes Commission Report (1991). *Royal commission of inquiry into the response of the Newfoundland criminal justice system to complaints*. St. John's, Nfld.: The Commission.

Hunt, R. R., & McDaniel, M. A. (1993). The enigma of organization and distinctiveness. *Journal of Memory and Language*, **32**, 421–445.

James, W. (1892/1961). *Psychology: The briefer course*. New York: Harper.

Johnson, D. B. (1983). Self-recognition in infants. *Infant Behavior and Development*, **6**, 211–222.

Kanner, L. (1946). Irrelevant and metaphorical language in early infantile autism. *American Journal of Psychiatry*, **103**, 242–246.

Kirk, R. E. (1982). *Experimental design: Procedures for the behavioral sciences* (2nd ed.). Belmont, CA: Brooks/Cole.

Kopp, C. B., & Brownell, C. A. (Eds.)(1991). The development of the self: The first three years [Special issue]. *Developmental Review*, **11**(3).

Lewis, M. (1991). Ways of knowing: Objective self-awareness or consciousness. *Developmental Review*, **11**, 231–243.

Lewis, M., & Brooks-Gunn, J. (1979). *Social cognition and the acquisition of self*. New York: Plenum.

Lewis, M., Brooks-Gunn, J., & Jaskir, J. (1985). Individual differences in early visual self-recognition. *Developmental Psychology*, **21**, 1181–1187.

Lewis, M., Sullivan, M. W., Stanger, C., & Weiss, M. (1989). Self development and self-consciousness emotions. *Child Development*, **60**, 146–156.

Loftus, E. F. (1993a). Desperately seeking memories of the first few years of childhood: The reality of early memories. *Journal of Experimental Psychology: General*, **122**, 274–277.

Loftus, E. F. (1993b). The reality of repressed memories. *American Psychologist*, **48**, 518–537.

Loftus, E. F., & Kaufman, L. (1992). Why do traumatic experiences sometimes produce good memory (flashbulbs) and sometimes no memory (repression)? In E. Winograd & U. Neisser (Eds.), *Affect and accuracy in recall: Studies of "flashbulb" memories* (pp. 212–223). New York: Cambridge Univ. Press.

Mahler, M., Pine, F., & Bergman, A. (1975). *The psychological birth of the infant*. New York: Basic Books.

Mans, L., Cicchetti, D., & Sroufe, L. A. (1978). Mirror reaction of Down's syndrome infants and toddlers: Cognitive underpinnings of self recognition. *Child Development, 49,* 1247–1250.

McCabe, A., & Peterson, C. (Eds.)(1991). *Developing narrative structure.* Hillsdale, NJ: Erlbaum.

Mead, G. H. (1934). *Mind, self, and society.* Chicago: Univ. Chicago Press.

Meltzoff, A. N. (1985). Immediate and deferred imitation in fourteen- and twenty-four-month-old infants. *Child Development, 56,* 62–73.

Meltzoff, A. N. (1988a). Infant imitation after a 1-week delay: Long-term memory for novel acts and multiple stimuli. *Developmental Psychology, 24,* 470–476.

Meltzoff, A. N. (1988b). Infant imitation and memory: Nine-month-olds in immediate and deferred tests. *Child Development, 59,* 217–225.

Meltzoff, A. N. (1990). Towards a developmental cognitive science: The implications of cross-modal matching and imitation for the development of representation and memory in infancy. In A. Diamond (Ed.), *The development and neural bases of higher cognitive functions* (Vol. 608, pp. 1–29). New York: New York Academy of Sciences.

Miller, P. J., Potts, R., Fung, H., Hoogstra, L., & Mintz, J. (1990). Narrative practices and the social construction of self in childhood. *American Ethnologist, 17,* 292–311.

Myers, N. A., Clifton, R. K., & Clarkson, M. G. (1987). When they were very young: Almost-threes remember two years ago. *Infant Behavior and Development, 10,* 123–132.

Neisser, U. (1991). Two perceptually given aspects of the self and their development. *Developmental Review, 11,* 197–209.

Neisser, U., & Harsch, N. (1992). Phantom flashbulbs: False recollections of hearing the news about *Challenger.* In E. Winograd & U. Neisser (Eds.), *Affect and accuracy in recall: Studies of "flashbulb" memories* (pp. 9–31). New York: Cambridge Univ. Press.

Nelson, K. (1990). Remembering, forgetting, and childhood amnesia. In R. Fivush & J. A. Hudson (Eds.), *Knowing and remembering in young children* (pp. 301–316). New York: Cambridge Univ. Press.

Nelson, K. (1993). The psychological and social origins of autobiographical memory. *Psychological Science, 4,* 7–14.

Nelson, K. (in press). Explaining the emergence of autobiographical memory in early childhood. In A. Collins, M. Conway, & S. Gathercole (Eds.), *Theories of memory.* Hove, England: Erlbaum.

Neuman, C. J., & Hill, S. D. (1978). Self-recognition and stimulus preference in autistic children. *Developmental Psychobiology, 11,* 571–578.

Perris, E. E., & Myers, N. A. (1990, April). *Expressing memory for an infant event.* Poster presented at the International Conference on Infant Studies, Montreal, Canada.

Perris, E. E., Myers, N. A., & Clifton, R. K. (1990). Long-term memory for a single infancy experience. *Child Development, 61,* 1796–1807.

Peters, D. P. (1991). The influence of stress and arousal on the child witness. In J. Doris (Ed.), *The suggestibility of children's recollections* (pp. 60–76). Washington, DC: American Psychological Association.

Peterson, C. (1990). The who, when, and where of early narratives. *Journal of Child Language, 17,* 433–455.

Peterson, L., Moreno, A., & Harbeck-Weber, C. (1993). "And then it started bleeding": Children's and mothers' perceptions and recollections of daily injury events. *Journal of Clinical Child Psychology, 22,* 345–354.

Piaget, J. (1954). *The construction of reality in the child.* New York: Basic Books.

Pipp, S., Fischer, K., & Jennings, S. (1987). Acquisition of self- and mother-knowledge in infancy. *Developmental Psychology, 23,* 86–96.

Poole, D. A., & White, L. T. (1991). Effects of question repetition on the eyewitness testimony of children and adults. *Developmental Psychology, 27,* 975–986.

Poole, D. A., & White, L. T. (1993). Two years later: Effects of question repetition and retention interval on the eyewitness testimony of children and adults. *Developmental Psychology,* **29,** 844–853.

Preyer, W. (1893). *Mind of the child* (Vol. 2). New York: Appleton.

Priel, B., & DeSchonen, S. (1986). Self-recognition: A study of a population without mirrors. *Journal of Experimental Child Psychology,* **41,** 237–250.

Reich, P. A. (1986). *Language development.* Englewood Cliffs, NJ: Prentice–Hall.

Rovee-Collier, C., & Shyi, G. (1992). A functional and cognitive analysis of infant long-term retention. In M. L. Howe, C. J. Brainerd, & V. F. Reyna (Eds.), *Development of long-term retention* (pp. 3–55). New York: Springer-Verlag.

Sachs, J. (1983). Talking about the there and then: The emergence of displaced reference in parent–child discourse. In K. Nelson (Ed.), *Children's language* (Vol. 4, pp. 1–28). New York: Gardner Press.

Schulman, A., & Kaplowitz, C. (1977). Mirror image response during the first two years of life. *Developmental Psychobiology,* **10,** 133–142.

Slackman, E. A., Hudson, J. A., & Fivush, R. (1986). Actions, actors, links, and goals: The structure of children's event representations. In K. Nelson (Ed.), *Event knowledge* (pp. 47–69). Hillsdale, NJ: Erlbaum.

Spiker, D., & Ricks, M. (1984). Visual self-recognition in autistic children: Developmental relationships. *Child Development,* **55,** 214–225.

Sugar, M. (1992). Toddlers' traumatic memories. *Infant Mental Health Journal,* **13,** 245–251.

Terr, L. (1988). What happens to early memories of trauma? A study of twenty children under age five at the time of documented traumatic events. *Journal of the American Academy of Child and Adolescent Psychiatry,* **27,** 96–104.

Usher, J. A., & Neisser, U. (1993). Childhood amnesia and the beginnings of memory for four early life events. *Journal of Experimental Psychology: General,* **122,** 155–165.

Waldfogel, S. (1948). The frequency and affective character of childhood memories. *Psychological Monographs,* **62** (Whole No. 291).

White, S., & Pillemer, D. (1979). Childhood amnesia and the development of a socially accessible memory system. In J. F. Kihlstrom & F. J. Evans (Eds.), *Functional disorders of memory* (pp. 29–73). Hillsdale, NJ: Erlbaum.

Willatts, P. (1990). Development of problem-solving strategies in infancy. In D. F. Bjorklund (Ed.), *Children's strategies: Contemporary views of cognitive development* (pp. 23–66). Hillsdale, NJ: Erlbaum.

Wright, L. (1993a). Remembering satan—Part I. *The New Yorker, LXIX* (No. 13, May 17), 60–81.

Wright, L. (1993b). Remembering satan—Part II. *The New Yorker, LXIX* (No. 14, May 24), 54–76.

# Young Children's Event Recall: Are Memories Constructed through Discourse?

Robyn Fivush

*Department of Psychology, Emory University, Atlanta, Georgia 30322*

The ways in which event memories may be reconstructed or transformed through discussion with others is a critical question both for understanding basic memory processes and for issues concerning legal testimony. In this research, white middle-class preschool children were interviewed first by their mothers and then by a female experimenter about personally experienced events when they were 40, 46, 58, and 70 months of age. Analyses indicated that at all four time points children only incorporated about 9% of the information initially recounted by the mother into their independent recall of the event with the experimenter. Moreover, children only repeated about 20% of the information they themselves recalled across the two interviews. Additional analyses indicated that information mutually discussed by the mother and child was no more likely to be incorporated or repeated when recalling the event with the experimenter than information not mutually discussed. These results indicate that young children's personal memories are not so fragile that they easily incorporate information provided by another into their own recall. © 1994 Academic Press, Inc.

As adults, we have constructed a personal life history based on our past experiences (e.g., Bruner, 1987; Neisser & Fivush, in press). This history is a complex tapestry that includes many different kinds of events. Highly prominent are those personally experienced events that are culturally marked as personal transitions, such as graduations, weddings, and births. Also included are memories of events that are personally if not culturally significant, and obviously these events will be more idiosyncratic to the individual. Perhaps the most intriguing events that are integrated into our autobiographical life histories are those events for which we have no personal memories but have, nonetheless, become an important or defining part of who we are through the family and cultural stories we share with others. For example, many people begin their life narrative with the story of their own birth (Stone, 1988), although they clearly do not remember this experience.

In order to distinguish those events that we actually remember from those events that we only know about through others, we use various criteria such as vividness and clarity of detail (e.g., "I recall it in such clear detail, surely I must be remembering it."), social consensus (e.g., "Both my husband and I remember the same details about our trip to Paris, so it must have actually happened that way."), and logical relations to world knowledge ("Surely I cannot actually recall my own birth so it must be based on what I have been told."). However, as Ross and Buehler (in press) have argued in laying out these criteria, there are times when we can be misled about our own memories. For example, a personal memory which is quite vivid and detailed may be believed to be an accurate represen-

This article is reprinted by permission from *Consciousness and Cognition*, Volume 3, pp. 356–373 (1994).

tation of an actually experienced event, even in the face of contradictory evidence, exactly because the representation is so detailed.

Event memories which are based solely on personal experience and event memories based solely on others' accounts are really two ends on a continuum. The vast majority of the memories that comprise our life narratives are at least partly constructed in social discourse (Fivush, Haden, & Reese, in press; Nelson, 1993; Snow, 1990). Talking about our past experiences with others is a frequent and important part of everyday social interaction (Miller, in press), and intriguingly, this kind of reminiscing begins very early in development (Engel, 1986; Hudson, 1990; Sachs, 1983). As we reminisce with others, it may become difficult to determine what aspects of the event are remembered as experienced and what aspects of the event have been reconstructed and/or transformed through discourse. In most situations, this distinction may be unimportant. Autobiographical memories serve two major functions in daily interaction, to help define our self-concept (Brewer, 1986; Eder, in press; Fivush, 1988; Neisser, 1988) and to help create interpersonal connections (Fivush et al., in press; Neisser, 1988; Nelson, 1993). For these purposes, the ways in which we have constructed and reconstructed our memories in interaction with others may be more important than the veridicality of the representation. However, there are times when veridicality is ultimately important, as when personal memories are brought into the courtroom as testimony. In this situation, it becomes critical to determine whether the memory is veridical to the experience or has been changed as a result of discussing the event with others.

This question is embedded in much of the research on eyewitness testimony that has focused on children's and adult's susceptibility to suggestion (see, e.g., Ceci & Bruck, 1993, and Goodman & Bottoms, 1993, for reviews). In this literature, the issue of suggestibility of memory has been operationalized as the tendency of subjects to incorporate misleading or incorrect information provided by the experimenter into their own memory of an event. It has been clearly demonstrated that both children and adults are susceptible to various kinds of suggestion under certain conditions and that children, especially preschoolers, may be particularly susceptible to suggestion under a variety of experimental conditions.

That very young children's memories are especially vulnerable to misinformation has been largely accepted in the scientific and legal communities for several reasons. First, historically, young children's memories have been characterized as largely unorganized and fragmentary and therefore especially susceptible to suggestion (see Ceci, Toglia, & Ross, 1987, for a review). Second, research indicates that preschool children have more difficulty than older children and adults in monitoring the source of their memory information (Foley & Johnson, 1985; Gopnik & Graf, 1988). That is, preschool children often cannot distinguish whether they know something because they have actually experienced the event (e.g., I know there is candy in the blue box because I saw you put it in there). or have simply been told about it (e.g., I know there is candy in the blue box because you told me there was). Finally, there is widespread belief that very young chldren often confuse fantasy and reality (although the research seems to indicate that they do not, e.g., Wellman & Estes, 1986; but see also Harris,

Brown, Marriot, Whitall, & Harmen, 1991). These factors contribute to a conception of young children's memories as fragile, amorphous, and open to confusion and suggestion.

In contrast to this conception of early memory, there is a growing body of research demonstrating that even very young children can recall their past experiences accurately over extended periods of time (Fivush, Gray, & Fromhoff, 1987; Hamond & Fivush, 1990; Hudson, 1990; Nelson, 1988; Todd & Perlmutter, 1980; Sheingold & Tenney, 1982; see Fivush, 1993, for a review). In fact, 4-year-old children are able to recall accurately experiences that occurred more than 2 years in the past (Fivush & Hamond, 1990). One possible interpretation of these findings is that children are not actually recalling their experiences but rather are recalling what they have been told about these experiences. That is, children's memories are indeed fragile and open to suggestion; what young children recount when asked to recall a personally experienced event is information that has been "suggested" in discussions of the event with others. If this information is veridical then young children appear to have accurate memories; if this information is incorrect, then children appear vulnerable to suggestion. A critical question thus becomes the extent to which young children incorporate information recounted by others into their own independent recall of personally experienced events.

Research aimed directly at examining young children's susceptibility to suggestion cannot fully address this question for two reasons. First, this research has examined young children's incorporation of misinformation into their memories of an event without providing any baseline information about the ways in which children's memories are transformed in the normal course of discussing past experiences with others. That is, we must interpret young children's susceptibility to suggestion within an understanding of basic memory processes. Second, the majority of research on young children's susceptibility to suggestion has relied on children's correct and incorrect *recognition* after misleading information has been presented. Almost nothing is known about how information, whether correct or misleading, presented in the course of discussing an event with others may come to be incorporated into children's *recall* of that event. Thus, the major purpose of the present research was to examine whether children's recall of a personally experienced event will be transformed as a result of discussing that event with another person, in this case the mother who experienced the event with the child and who would therefore be viewed as an accurate source of information. Moreover, this question was examined longitudinally to determine whether children's tendency to incorporate information about an event provided by another changes across the preschool years.

To date, only two studies have addressed this question. Hudson (1990) asked mothers and their 2-year-old children to discuss four events once a week for 4 weeks. During a fifth visit, an experimenter queried the children about these four events yet again. Analyses revealed that very little of the information discussed during any one mother–child conversation was discussed again during a subsequent conversation. More relevant to the present discussion, when recalling the event with the experimenter, children recounted very little information that had been provided by the mother on any of the previous interviews. In a similar study, my colleagues and I (Fivush, Hamond, Harsch, Singer, & Wolf, 1991) found little tendency for young children to incorporate information provided by others into their own independent recall. We assessed 32- to 35-month-old children during two conversations 6 weeks apart about the same events under three conditions: (1) both conversations with their mother; (2) both conversations with the same female stranger; or (3) a first conversation with the mother and a second conversation with a female stranger. In all three conditions, only about 12% of the information that the adult had originally provided during the first conversation was incorporated into the child's recall during the second conversation. These results indicate that young children's memories are not completely open to suggestion and modulation by what others recall. Still, because these studies were exploratory, it is important to replicate these findings and extend them developmentally.

In the present study, then, based on the limited research conducted to date, we expected to see very little incorporation of information initially provided by the mother into children's subsequent recall of a personally experienced event. However, in this research, in contrast to the previous studies, we assessed children longitudinally at four points from age 3 to 6. Because developmental differences have not been examined before, no strong predictions were made; however, two developmental changes seemed possible. On one hand, as children grow older and become more mnemonically competent, we may see even less of a tendency to incorporate information initially provided by another into children's own recall. On the other hand, as children grow older and become more socialized into the activity of reminiscing (Fivush et al., in press; Nelson, 1993), the distinctions between one's own memory of an event and anothers' may actually become more blurred, and children may therefore show a greater tendency to incorporate information initially provided by another into their own recall. Finally, we also examined possible individual differences in children's tendency to incorporate information initially provided by another into their subsequent independent recall of events. Although most of the research of children's memory and susceptibility to suggestion has examined group differences, it is important to begin to examine individual differences for both theoretical and applied purposes.

## METHOD

### Subjects

As part of a larger longitudinal study of autobiographical memory and narrative development across the preschool years, families were visited in their homes at four time points: The first time point occurred within 2 weeks of the children's 40-month birthday, the subsequent time points occurred when the children were 46, 58, and 70 months old. Families were contacted through county birth records and were informed of our interest in children's memory development. Twenty-four white middle class families participated at various points in the study but only 19 families completed all four visits. Of these, 5 of the children were female first-born, 3 were female later born, 8 were male first-born, and 3 were male later born. All parents completed some college and 15 of the mothers worked 15 h or more outside the home. At each time point, children either received a book or a book gift certificate for their participation.

## Procedure

At each time point, families were visited in their home for four separate sessions scheduled at their convenience. Three female graduate student experimenters were responsible for data collection, and each family was always visited by the same experimenter. Only the two sessions relevant for the data presented here will be described.

*Mother–child memory interview.* At the beginning of this session, the experimenter informed the mother that we were interested in children's memories of their past experiences, and mothers were asked to discuss three novel past events that they and their child had experienced together. Out of earshot of the child, the experimenter helped the mother select three past events that spanned no more than a day and that did not involve going to a movie or show, as these events tend to elicit memory for the storyline rather than the child's own activities. Once the events were selected, the mother and child settled comfortably together with a tape recorder nearby, and the experimenter left the room. The mother was free to discuss the events in anyway she chose and for as long as she liked.

*Experimenter–child memory interview.* A few days after the mother–child interview, the experimenter returned to the home and queried the child about three novel past events. At each time point, one of the events that the experimenter asked the child to recall was one of the events that the mother had discussed with the child a few days before. During this interview, the experimenter asked only very general open-ended questions, such as "Tell me about the circus," "Tell me more," and "What else happened" or encouraged the child to continue with general comments, such as "That sounds like fun" and "Wow." Thus, in these interviews children were provided with no cues or guides as to what information should be recalled about the event under discussion, but were free to recount whatever information they selected.

Note that a different event was targeted at each of the four time points for each child. Although there was some variability in the events discussed, most conversations focused on family outings, such as trips to the zoo or the circus, holidays, such as Halloween and Easter, or visits with special friends or relatives. Most mother–child and experimenter–child conversations lasted approximately 30 min. All memory interviews were tape recorded and transcribed verbatim for coding and analysis.

## Data Reduction and Coding

All informational units recounted by mothers during the mother–child interviews and all informational units recounted by children during the mother–child and the experimenter–child interviews were counted. An informational unit was defined as each unique mention of a location (e.g., "We were at the *beach*."), a person (e.g., "*Billy* came with us."), an activity (e.g., "We *jumped*."), an object (e.g., "There were *seashells*."), or a descriptor (e.g., "They were *red*."). Obviously, many propositions included more than one unit of information; for example, "You and *your brother collected pretty seashells* on the *beach*" was coded as a person (your brother), an activity (collected), an object (seashells), a descriptor (pretty), and a location (on the beach), for a total of 5 units of information. Similarly, "We *ran* and *jumped* and *swung around* on the *playground*" was counted as 3 separate activities and 1 location for a total of 4 units of information (see Fivush et al., 1987, for details on this coding scheme). Two judges independently coded 25% of the mother–child and experimenter–child interviews at each time point and achieved 84% agreement on counting units of information. The remaining interviews were coded by one of the judges.

Once informational units were identified, it was possible to examine the content of children's independent recall of the target event with the experimenter. All information recounted by children to the experimenter was coded into one of three categories: (1) information initially recalled by the mother during the previous interview, i.e., *incorporated* information; (2) information that had been recalled by the child during the previous interview with the mother, i.e., *repeated* information; and (3) information not recounted by either the mother or the child during the previous interview, i.e., *new* information. Two judges independently coded 25% of the children's recall during the experimenter–child interviews at each time point into these three categories and achieved 90% agreement. The remaining interviews were coded by one of the judges.

Unfortunately, because they were provided with no specific cues or prompts, children, especially at the earlier time points, often did not recall any information about the event when queried by the experimenter. Because the major purpose of this set of analyses was to determine whether children incorporate information initially recounted by the mother into their own independent recall of an event, only those children who recalled at least 2 units of information with the experimenter were included. Moreover, because this was a longitudinal design, allowing us to examine the same children over time, only those children who recalled at least 2 units of information about the target event at all four time points were included in the analysis. This limited the sample to 9 mother–child pairs, 5 males and 4 females. Although the final sample was small, it allowed for a within subjects analysis of children's memories over time.

## RESULTS

The results are presented in three subsections. First, the amount of information recounted by mothers and children over time is presented. Second, children's recall with the experimenter is examined for evidence of incorporation of maternal information. Finally, in the third section, individual differences in children's tendency to incorporate maternal information are explored. All analyses were conducted at the $p < .05$ level of significance unless otherwise noted.

### Amount of Information Recounted

In order to evaluate children's tendency to incorporate information initially provided by the mother into their own independent recall, it is important to

TABLE 1
Mean Number of Units of Information (and Standard Deviations)
Recalled by Mothers and Children Over Time

| | Units of information | | |
| | Mother–child conversations | | Experimenter–child conversations |
| Time (months) | Mothers | Children | Children |
| --- | --- | --- | --- |
| 1 (40) | 14.4 (9.13) | 8.0 (3.87) | 11.4 (2.83) |
| 2 (46) | 17.3 (13.5) | 19.3 (10.60) | 14.4 (7.48) |
| 3 (58) | 23.6 (17.5) | 13.3 (8.61) | 12.6 (9.51) |
| 4 (70) | 18.2 (10.1) | 20.2 (11.37) | 18.1 (6.83) |
| Mean | 18.0 | 15.2 | 14.1 |

consider how much information mothers are providing overall and how much information children are recounting, both in discussion with their mothers and with the experimenter. Table 1 displays the mean number of informational units recounted by mothers and children at each interview over time.

*Mother's recall.* A one-way analysis of variance indicated no changes over time in amount of information provided by mothers. Although there appear to be differences, particularly at Time 3, there was also a great deal of variability among mothers, as indicated by the large standard deviations, and the group differences did not reach statistical significance.

*Children's recall.* Amount of information children recalled was analyzed in a 4(time point) by 2(conversational partner: mother versus experimenter) analysis of variance. Not surprisingly, children recalled more information over time, $F(3,24) = 3.40$. However, children recalled approximately the same amount of information in conversations with their mother and with the experimenter at all time points.

### Content of Children's Recall

The critical question, of course, is whether children recounted information in conversation with the experimenter that had initially been provided by the mother. In order to determine this, the proportion of information recounted by the mother on the initial interview that was subsequently recounted by the child was calculated for each child at each time point. That is, of all the information provided by the mother at each time point, how much was later recounted by the child with the experimenter at that time point? Thus, this was a measure of the proportion of information that the child incorporated from the mother. A similar proportion was calculated for information that the child repeated across the mother and experimenter interviews at each time point. That is, of all the information provided by the child on the initial interview, how much was again recalled with the experimenter? Table 2 displays the proportion of incorporated information, repeated information, and new information at each time point. Because these proportions add to 100, three separate one-way analyses of variance were

TABLE 2
Mean Proportion of Incorporated, Repeated, and New Information
(and Standard Deviations) Provided by Children Over Time

| Time (months) | Type of information | | |
|---|---|---|---|
| | Incorporated | Repeated | New |
| 1 (40) | .05 (.06) | .20 (.17) | .75 (.16) |
| 2 (46) | .13 (.10) | .21 (.20) | .63 (.20) |
| 3 (58) | .07 (.13) | .12 (.14) | .79 (.24) |
| 4 (70) | .11 (.10) | .27 (.20) | .65 (.10) |
| Mean | .09 | .20 | .71 |

conducted to determine whether these three sets of proportions changed over time.

As can be seen, the proportions of incorporated, repeated, and new information were stable over time. At all four time points, in conversation with the experimenter, children recalled about 9% of the information previously recounted by the mother, and they recalled about 20% of the information that they themselves had recounted on the previous interview. In contrast, the great majority of information children recounted with the experimenter was new and different information from that which had been recounted by either the mother or the child in the initial interview. Clearly, these results indicate little tendency to incorporate information provided by another into one's own recall of an event. They further suggest that preschool children are quite inconsistent in information they recount about an experienced event on different recall occasions. Children do not recall the same information again and again. It should be noted that, although accuracy of children's recall was not formally assessed, informally mothers confirmed almost all of the information that children recalled. Thus, children were recalling different but still accurate information about previously experienced events on different recall occasions.

While children did not incorporate much information provided by the mother into their own recall of an event, they do include some, and it may be instructive to take a closer look at exactly what information is incorporated. Is there some systematic reason why particular information is incorporated into children's subsequent recall? One possibility is that children incorporate that information in which they are more interested or involved for some reason. For example, Tessler and Nelson (this volume) report that information that is mutually discussed by mother and child as an event is occurring is more likely to be recalled later by the child than information which is mentioned by only the mother or even only by the child. Would we see similar effects in discussion of past events?

In order to answer this question, the mother–child interviews were examined for evidence of mutual elaboration of information. For example, when the mother asks, "Do you remember going to Seaworld and seeing Shamu" the child might elaborate on this information by responding, "Yeah, he was black and white."

On the other hand, the child might not elaborate on the mother's provision of information, either by simply confirming or denying the information, by not responding at all, or by changing the topic. Thus, all information recounted by the mother was first categorized as elaborated or not elaborated by the child. Then, all information children recalled during the interview with the experimenter was classified as incorporated from the mother's recount or not incorporated as described earlier. In this way, all information initially recounted by the mother was categorized into two orthogonal categories: elaborated or not elaborated by the child during the mother–child interview and incorporated or not incorporated by the child on the experimenter–child interview. For example, if the child elaborated on seeing Shamu at Seaworld when the mother mentioned it and then subsequently incorporated seeing Shamu when recalling the event with the experimenter, it was counted as incorporated information that was elaborated by the child. On the other hand, if the child had not elaborated on seeing Shamu in conversation with the mother but then recalled seeing Shamu with the experimenter, it was categorized as incorporated information that was not elaborated. Similarly, information provided by the mother that was not incorporated by the child (i.e., the child does not recall Shamu at all with the experimenter) was also coded as having been elaborated or not elaborated by the child during the mother–child interview.

Proportion of incorporated information that was elaborated was then calculated as the number of units of maternally provided information elaborated by the child that was subsequently recalled with the experimenter over the total number of mother's units of information that the child elaborated. Similarly, proportion of nonincorporated information that was elaborated was calculated as the number of units of maternally provided information that the child elaborated on and then did not recall with the experimenter over the total number of maternal units of information that was elaborated on. Thus, these proportions captured whether children were more or less likely to incorporate information that they had elaborated on over information that they had not elaborated on. These proportions are presented in Table 3. A 4(time point) by 2(incorporated or nonincorporated) analysis of variance was conducted to determine whether a higher proportion of incorporated information was elaborated on than nonincorporated information.

Two findings emerged from this analysis. First, in general, children elaborated on about 1/3 to 1/2 of the information recounted by mothers during the mother–child interview, indicating that children were engaged in these conversations and were responding to their mothers' comments. Second, children were no more likely to incorporate information that they had elaborated on when their mother provided it than information they had not elaborated on, and this pattern held over time. If anything, there was a slight tendency for children to elaborate on information that they subsequently did not incorporate into their own recall than to elaborate on information they did incorporate, $F(1,8) = 2.90$, $p = .12$. In general, then, it is not the case that children are more likely to incorporate information provided by another into their own independent recall if they expressed more interest in that information through elaboration than if they did not.

A similar question arises as to the information that children repeat across recall

TABLE 3

Mean Proportion of Information That Was Elaborated (and Standard Deviations)
for Each Type of Information Over Time

| Time (months) | Type of information | | | |
| --- | --- | --- | --- | --- |
| | Incorporated[a] | Nonincorporated[b] | Repeated[c] | Nonrepeated[d] |
| 1 (40) | .26 (.43) | .37 (.28) | .59 (.49) | .52 (.39) |
| 2 (46) | .46 (.47) | .59 (.24) | .51 (.42) | .53 (.23) |
| 3 (58) | .28 (.44) | .45 (.30) | .27 (.42) | .57 (.32) |
| 4 (70) | .39 (.49) | .48 (.25) | .81 (1.23) | .54 (.31) |
| Mean | .35 | .47 | .55 | .54 |

[a] Number of units of maternally provided information elaborated by the child and then recalled by the child with the experimenter over the total number of child elaborated units.

[b] Number of units of maternally provided information elaborated by the child and then not recalled by the child with the experimenter over the total number of child elaborated units.

[c] Number of units of child provided information elaborated by the mother and then recalled by the child with the experimenter over the total number of maternally elaborated units.

[d] Number of units of child provided information elaborated by the mother and then not recalled by the child with the experimenter over the total number of maternally elaborated units.

interviews. Given that with the experimenter, children recall about 20% of the information that they had recalled with their mother, are they more likely to repeat information across recall interviews that their mothers had elaborated on? In order to answer this question, a parallel analysis to the one above was computed. All of the information recounted by children during the mother–child interview was categorized as repeated or nonrepeated and elaborated on by the mother or not elaborated on by the mother, and proportion of repeated information elaborated on and not elaborated on was calculated (see Table 3 for means). Note that overall mothers elaborate on just over half of all information recounted by children, again indicating mutual engagement in the memory conversation. And again, a 4(time point) by 2(repeated or nonrepeated information) analysis of variance indicated that nonrepeated information was just as likely to be elaborated on as was repeated information at all four time points. So again, information which is more elaborately discussed by both conversational partners is no more likely to be recalled again by the child than information not so discussed.

This pattern of results indicates that information which is mutually discussed by mother and child is no more likely to be recalled by the child on a subsequent recall occasion than information not mutually discussed, and this pattern holds for both information incorporated from anothers' recount and information one repeatedly recalls oneself.

## Individual Differences

Although analyses examining children as a group indicated little incorporation of information initially provided by the mother, it seemed possible that there would be individual differences in this tendency. That is, some children may show little incorporation of information whereas other children may show more substantial amounts of incorporation. There may also be individual differences in children's tendency to repeat the same information they themselves recall across recall occasions. In order to explore possible individual differences, a series of correlational analyses were conducted examining relations among the variables at each time point as well as relations over time.

*Correlations at each time point.* A first question focused on possible relationships among the variables at each time point. For example, is it the case that children who recall more information in conversation with their mothers subsequently repeat a higher proportion of this information in conversation with the experimenter? Or is amount of information recounted by the mother related to the proportion of information children will subsequently incorporate into their own recall? Correlations were computed among all variables at each time point: (1) amount of information provided by the mother, (2) amount of information the child recalled with the mother, (3) amount of information the child recalled with the experimenter, (4) proportion of information the child incorporated from the mother, (5) proportion of information the child repeated from her own recall, (6) proportion of incorporated information that was elaborated, and (7) proportion of repeated information that was elaborated. None of the correlations reached significance at the first or the last time points. There were three significant correlations at Time 2: Amount of information recounted by mothers was negatively related to the proportion of information children incorporated, $r = -.68$, $p < .05$, and also negatively related to amount of incorporated information that was elaborated, $r = -72$, $p < .05$; in addition, the amount of information children repeated was positively related to the proportion of repeated information that was elaborated, $r = .76$, $p < .05$. There was only one significant correlation at Time 3, between the proportion of information that children incorporated and the proportion of information that children repeated, $r = .74$, $p < .05$. Although some of the significant correlations are suggestive, it must be noted that 49 correlations were computed among variables at each time point, and two to three correlations would be expected to be significant by chance alone. Moreover, any meaningful correlations among variables held at only one time point. Thus, there was little suggestion of patterns of relations among these variables indicating systematic individual differences.

*Correlations over time.* A second question focused on possible relations among the variables over time. More specifically, correlating the variables over time allows an examination of consistency of performance; do those children who recall more information at the first time point continue to recall more information over time? Similarly, do those children who incorporate more information than other children at the first time point continue to do so over time, and so on? Again, there was little indication of any systematic pattern over time. There were no significant correlations between any time points for amount of information mothers provided, for amount of information children recalled with their mothers or with the experimenter. There was a significant correlation between proportion of information children incorporated at the second time point and the proportion of information they incorporated at the last time point, $r = .67$, $p < .05$, but this correlation did not reach significance between Time 1 and Time 2, 3, or 4, or between Time 2 and Time 3 or Time 3 and Time 4. Similarly, there was a significant correlation between the proportion of information children repeated at Time 2 and the proportion of information they repeated at Time 4, $r = .69$, $p < .05$, but again, this relation did not reach significance in any other comparison between times. Finally, there was a significant correlation between the percentage of information that children incorporated that was elaborated between Time 2 and Time 4, $r = .71$, $p < .05$, but not between any other time points. Overall, then, there was little indication of consistency over time. In general, the correlational analyses do not suggest any systematic individual differences in the data. However, these data must be interpreted with extreme caution as the sample was quite small.

## DISCUSSION

Two major results emerged from this study. First, children showed little tendency to incorporate information initially provided by mothers into their subsequent independent recall of events. Only about 9% of all information recounted by mothers during mother–child conversations about past events was later incorporated into children's recall of those events with an experimenter in an open-ended interview, and this pattern held across the preschool years. Second, children were generally inconsistent in the information they recounted in conversations with their mother and conversations with the experimenter. Children repeated approximately 20% of the information they recalled with their mother during the subsequent interview with the experimenter.

Moreover information recurring in the experimenter–child interview was no more likely to be mutually discussed and elaborated during the mother–child interview than information that was not recounted again. Further analyses indicated few systematic individual differences among children either at any given point in time or over time in their tendency to incorporate information from another or repeat information they themselves recalled on a subsequent interview. These results have important implications both for a basic understanding of memory development and for thinking about the suggestibility of preschool children's memory.

First and foremost, these results confirm and extend previous findings (Fivush et al., 1991; Hudson, 1990) indicating that young children's memories are not simply a conglomeration of things they have been told. Young children's memories do not seem to be so fragile that they easily begin to "remember" aspects of events that others have recounted to them. Four additional points need to be addressed, however, in interpreting this basic finding. One, data were collected from only one previous conversation. It certainly seems possible that as an event is discussed over and over, children may come to incorporate information that another repeatedly recalls. However, it should be noted that the experimenter–child conversations took place just a few days after the mother–child conversations, and any information recounted by the mother would be expected to be the most easily activated or primed in the child's memory. And yet there was little evidence of incorporation under these conditions. While many theorists have postulated that memories may be reconstructed and transformed through discussion with others (e.g., Gergen, in press; Middleton & Edwards, 1990; Spence, 1982), these data suggest that such reconstruction may be a gradual process, particularly for young children. Charting such reconstructive changes developmentally both as a function of age and as a function of number and type of discussions is an important area for further research.

Second, it must be stressed that mothers did not recount any false information with their children, nor were mothers heavily invested in their children recalling these events in particular ways. Thus, many of the conditions existing when children are called on to give testimony did not hold in this study. In testimony situations, adults often have a stake in the child recalling certain aspects of an event in certain ways, and through the use of leading or suggestive questions repeated over and over may coerce the child into a particular recount. The data presented here do not speak to this issue directly, but they do demonstrate that the early memory system is not especially vulnerable; even young children have clear memories of personally experienced events and at least in the normal course of discussing these experiences with others, young children maintain their own account of what occurred. Thus data on young children's susceptibility to suggestion must be interpreted within a framework of relatively intact early event memories.

Third, it must be noted that although children showed little tendency to incorporate information recounted by others into their own recall of an event, 9% of the information children recounted to an experimenter was information initially recounted by the mother. While 9% is a statistically small amount, in legal situations even this could be disastrous. Of course, the incorporated information was accurate information about what occurred. It is possible that children may have recounted this information by themselves but in the course of the conversation, the mother mentioned it first. It may also be the case that the mothers' recount reminded children of information they were having difficulty retrieving, but once mentioned, children recognized the information as correct and subsequently recalled it. Again, additional research is needed to see if incorrect information would be incorporated into children's subsequent recall at the same rate as correct information.

Finally, we need to consider the kinds of events that children were asked to recall in this study. Although the majority of events were salient and novel experiences, such as a first plane ride or a special family outing, they were certainly not of the emotional magnitude and significance of events children are called on to recall in most testimony situations. While it is still not clear from the research whether, and if so, how high emotionality affects children's memories (see, e.g., Goodman, Rudy, Bottoms, & Aman, 1990; and Terr, 1988, versus Peters, 1991), it seems possible that events which evoke stronger emotions than the events studied here might be remembered differently. Moreover, most of the research examining this issue as applied to testimony has focused only on stress and has not examined other aspects of emotionality which may play a critical role in the way in which events are remembered (see Fivush & Kuebli, in press, for a discussion). On one hand, it is possible that high emotionality might lead to a weaker or more disorganized memory, thus rendering children more susceptible to incorporating other's accounts of what occurred. On the other hand, it may also be the case that highly emotional events may be of particular personal significance, and thus even less malleable than less emotional events (Liwag & Stein, 1993). Clearly, more research is needed which systematically examines the influences of emotionality on children's event memory.

Somewhat surprisingly, there was no evidence in this study that the limited information that was incorporated was special in some way. The fact that children were no more likely to incorporate information that they elaborated on than information not elaborated on seems to indicate that incorporated information was not more salient or interesting to children. This finding contrasts with recent findings reported by Tessler and Nelson (this volume) in which it is quite clear that information mutually discussed as an event is occurring is more likely to be recalled subsequently by children than information not so discussed. This discrepancy raises the interesting possibility that the way an event is discussed as it unfolds and the way it is discussed in retrospect may have different consequences for children's developing memories of the event. What gets encoded during the ongoing experience seems to be influenced by what is highlighted in mother–child conversation. But once the event is encoded, and children have a stable representation of what occurred, mother–child conversation does not seem to play a large role in what children remember over time. More specifically for issues of testimony, the present findings suggest that children are not more likely to incorporate information just because it is discussed in detail when reminiscing.

Perhaps more surprising than the limited incorporation of information from another was the high inconsistency in children's own recall across conversations. When children were asked to recall the same event with their mother and with the experimenter, they recalled almost completely different information. This pattern has also been found in previous research (Fivush et al., 1991; Fivush & Hamond, 1990; Fivush & Shukat, in press; Hudson, 1990). Moreover, although we did not systematically assess accuracy in this study, informally mothers confirmed almost all information recalled by children. And in studies with children in the same age range in which systematic assessment of accuracy was conducted, more than 90% of children's recall is confirmed as accurate (Fivush et al., 1987; Fivush et al., 1991; Hamond & Fivush, 1990). Thus children are recalling different but still accurate information each time they recount an event.

One possible explanation for this high level of inconsistency is that children in this study recalled events with the experimenter just a few days after they discussed the event with their mothers. Perhaps children believe they should not recall the same information and actively search their memories for new information to recount. There are at least two reasons why this possibility is unlikely. First, children were recalling the events with two different people on each occasion, so any rudimentary awareness that one should provide new and different information in order to hold the listener's attention would not be operating in this situation. Second, this finding replicates previous research finding high inconsistency of recall over several weeks delay (Fivush et al., 1991) and even several years (Fivush & Shukat, in press), as well as high inconsistency whether recalling events with the same conversational partner or with different conversational partners (Fivush et al., 1991; Hudson, 1990). While it is unclear at this point why preschoolers are so inconsistent in their event recall (see Fivush, 1993, for a discussion of this issue), it is quite clear that inconsistency cannot be taken as an index of either inaccuracy or susceptibility to suggestion.

A final issue concerns individual differences. Several researchers have argued that children may differ in their susceptibility to suggestion and studies have begun to investigate possible relations between suggestibility and various measures of personality such as temperament, attachment, and anxiety (Goodman, 1994; Ornstein et al., in press). This is an important and potentially fruitful direction for research. In this study, possible individual differences in children's tendency to incorporate information into their own recall was investigated, but because of the small sample size and the lack of independent measures of personality and temperament, analyses were limited to exploratory correlations, which revealed no systematic patterns of individual difference. Still, it should be stressed that research on individual differences in both basic memory abilities and susceptibility to suggestion are imperative.

In many ways, this study raises more questions than it answers. Its most important contribution is to call into question some widely held assumptions about the fragility and vulnerability of early memory. Clearly, a great deal of research has indicated that young children are susceptible to leading and suggestive questions, as are adults (Ceci & Bruck, 1993; Goodman & Bottoms, 1993). However, these findings must be placed in a larger perspective examining basic memory abilities and their development. Over the past decade it has become abundantly clear that even very young children retain accurate memories of personally experienced events over extended periods of time (Fivush, 1993; Fivush & Hudson, 1990). In order to integrate findings from these two related areas of research, we must begin to examine in detail the conditions under which children (and adults) tend to be misled and the conditions under which this is less likely. The results of the present study begin to lay out some of the parameters that must be considered. Most critical, young children do not quickly and easily incorporate information provided by another into their independent recall of an event. Thus the question for future research becomes under what conditions they may begin to do this. Until we understand how memories may and may not be reconstructed and transformed through the natural process of discussion and reminiscing, we cannot hope to understand how memories may be distorted, misled, or possibly even implanted.

## ACKNOWLEDGMENTS

This research was supported by a grant from the Spencer Foundation. Many people participated in various phases of this project. I would especially like to thank Catherine Haden, Elaine Reese, and Liza Dondonan for data collection, Laura Underwood and Marcella Eppen for transcription, Tami Palmer for data coding and analysis, and Catherine Haden and Janine Przybylinski for data analysis. I also appreciate comments by Catherine Haden and Janine Przybylinski on an earlier version of the manuscript.

# REFERENCES

Brewer, W. F. (1986). What is autobiographical memory? In D. C. Rubin (Ed.), *Autobiographical memory* (pp. 25–49). New York: Cambridge Univ. Press.

Bruner, J. (1987). Life as narrative. *Social Research,* **54,** 11–32.

Ceci, S. J., & Bruck, M. (1993). Suggestibility of the child witness: A historical review and synthesis. *Psychological Bulletin,* **113,** 403–439.

Ceci, S. J., Toglia, M. P., & Ross, D. F. (1987). *Children's eyewitness memory.* New York: Springer-Verlag.

Eder, R. (in press). Emotionality and narrative in the emergence of the self-concept. In U. Neisser & R. Fivush (Eds.), *The remembering self: Construction and accuracy in the self-narrative.* New York: Cambridge Univ. Press.

Engel, S. (1986). *Learning to reminisce: A developmental study of how young children talk about the past.* Unpublished doctoral dissertation, City University of New York.

Fivush, R. (1988). The functions of event memory: Some comments on Nelson and Barsalou. In U. Neisser & E. Winograd (Eds.), *Remembering reconsidered: Ecological and traditional approaches to memory* (pp. 277–282). New York: Cambridge Univ. Press.

Fivush, R. (1993). Developmental perspectives on autobiographical recall. In G. S. Goodman & B. L. Bottoms, (Eds.), *Child victims, child witnesses: Understanding and improving testimony* (pp. 1–24). New York: Guilford Press.

Fivush, R., Gray, J. T., & Fronhoff, F. A. (1987). Two year olds talk about the past. *Cognitive Development,* **2,** 393–410.

Fivush, R., Haden, C., & Reese, E. (in press). Remembering, recounting and reminiscing: The development of autobiographical memory in social context. In D. Rubin (Ed.), *Reconstructing our past: An overview of autobiographical memory.* New York: Cambridge Univ. Press.

Fivush, R., & Hamond, N. R. (1990). Autobiographical memory across the preschool years. In R. Fivush & J. A. Hudson (Eds.), *Knowing and remembering in young children* (pp. 223–248). New York: Cambridge Univ. Press.

Fivush, R., Hamond, N. R., Harsch, N., Singer, N., & Wolf, A. (1991). Content and consistency of young children's autobiographical recall, *Discourse Processes,* **14,** 373–388.

Fivush, R., & Hudson, J. A. (Eds.), *Knowing and remembering in young children.* New York: Cambridge Univ. Press.

Fivush, R., & Kuebli, J. (in press). Making everyday events emotional: The construal of emotion in parent–child conversations about the past. In N. Stein, P. O. Ornstein, B. Tversky, & C. Brainerd (Eds.), *Memory for everyday and emotional events.* Hillsdale, NJ: Erlbaum.

Fivush, R., & Shukat, J. (in press). Content, consistency and coherence of early autobiographical memory. In M. Zaragozza (Ed.), *Memory, suggestibility and eyewitness testimony in children and adults.* Thousand Oaks, CA: Sage Publications.

Foley, M. A., & Johnson, M. K. (1985). Confusion between memories for performed and imagined actions. *Child Development,* **56,** 1145–1155.

Gergen, K. J. (in press). Mind, text and society: Self-memory in social context. In U. Neisser & R. Fivush (Eds.), *The remembering self: Construction and accuracy in the life narrative.* New York: Cambridge Univ. Press.

Gopnik, A., & Graf, P. (1988). Knowing how you know: Young children's ability to identify and remember the sources of their beliefs. *Child Development,* **59,** 1366–1371.

Goodman, G. S. (1994). Trauma and children's memory. In N. L. Stein (Chair), *Emotion and Memory.* Symposium conducted at the International Society of Research on Emotion. Cambridge, England.

Goodman, G. S., & Bottoms, B. L. (1993). *Child victims, child witnesses: Understanding and improving testimony.* New York: Guilford Press.

Goodman, G. S., Rudy, L., Bottoms, B. L., & Aman, C. (1990). Children's concerns and memory: Issues of ecological validity in the study of children's eyewitness testimony. In R. Fivush &

J. A. Hudson (Eds.), *Knowing and remembering in young children* (pp. 249–284). New York: Cambridge Univ. Press.

Hamond, N. R., & Fivush, R. (1990). Memories of Mickey Mouse: Young children recount their trip to Disneyworld. *Cognitive Development,* **6,** 433–448.

Harris, P. L., Brown, E., Marriot, C., Whitall, S., & Harmer, S. (1991). Monsters, ghosts, and witches: Testing the limits of the fantasy–reality distinction in young children. *British Journal of Developmental Psychology,* **9,** 105–123.

Hudson, J. A. (1990). The emergence of autobiographic memory in mother–child conversations. In R. Fivush & J. A. Hudson (Eds.), *Knowing and remembering in young children* (pp. 166–196). New York: Cambridge Univ. Press.

Liwag, M. D., & Stein, N. L. (1993). *The effects of retrieval instructions on children's memory for emotion episodes.* Manuscript submitted for publication.

Middieton, D., & Edwards, D. (1990). Conversational remembering: A social psychological approach. In D. Middleton & D. Edwards (Eds.), *Collective remembering* (pp. 23–45). London: Sage Publications.

Miller, P. J. (in press). Narrative practices: Their role in socialization and self-construction. In U. Neisser & R. Fivush (Eds.), *The remembering self: Construction and accuracy in the life narrative.* New York: Cambridge Univ. Press.

Neisser, U. (1988). Five kinds of self-knowledge. *Philosophical Psychology,* **1,** 35–59.

Neisser, U., & Fivush, R. (Eds.) (in press). *The remembering self: Accuracy and construction in the life narrative.* New York: Cambridge Univ. Press.

Nelson, K. (1988). The ontogeny of memory for real world events. In U. Neisser & E. Winograd (Eds.), *Remembering reconsidered: Ecological and traditional approaches to memory* (pp. 277–282). New York: Cambridge Univ. Press.

Nelson, K. (1993). The psychological and social origins of autobiographical memory. *Psychological Science,* **1,** 1–8.

Ornstein, P. A., Shapiro, L. R., Clubb, P. A., Follmer, A., & Baker-Ward, L. (in press). The influence of prior knowledge on children's memory for salient memory experiences. In N. L. Stein, P. A. Ornstein, C. J. Brainerd, & B. Tversky (Eds.), *Memory for everyday and emotional events.* Hillsdale, NJ: Erlbaum.

Peters, D. P. (1991). The influence of stress and arousal on the child witness. In J. Doris (Ed.), *The suggestibility of children's recollections* (pp. 86–91). Washington, DC: American Psychological Association.

Ross, M., & Beuhler, R. (in press). Creative remembering. In U. Neisser & R. Fivush (Eds.), *The remembering self: Construction and accuracy in the life narrative.* New York: Cambridge Univ. Press.

Sachs, J. (1983). Talking about the there and then: The emergence of displaced reference in parent–child discourse. In K. Nelson (Ed.), *Children's language* (Vol. 4, pp. 1–28). Hillsdale, NJ: Erlbaum.

Sheingold, K., & Tenney, Y. J. (1982). Memory for a salient childhood event. In U. Neisser (Ed.), *Memory observed* (pp. 201–212). San Francisco: Freeman.

Snow, C. E. (1990). Building memories: The ontogeny of autobiographical memory. In D. Chicetti & M. Beeghly (Eds.), *The self in transition: Infancy to childhood* (pp. 213–242). Chicago: Univ. Chicago Press.

Stone, E. (1988). *Black sheep and kissing cousins: How our family stories shape us.* New York: Penguin Books.

Spence, D. P. (1982). *Narrative truth and historical truth.* New York: Norton.

Terr, L. C. (1988). What happens to early memory of trauma? A study of twenty children under age five at the time of documented traumatic events. *Journal of the American Academy of Child and Adolescent Psychiatry,* **27,** 96–104.

Tessler, M., & Nelson, K. (1994). Making memories: The influence of joint encoding on later recall by young children. *Consciousness and Cognition, 3,* 307–326.

Todd, C., & Perlmutter, M. (1980). Reality recalled by preschool children. In M. Perlmutter (Ed.), *New directions for child development, No 10: Children's memory* (pp. 69–86). San Francisco: Jossey-Bass.

Wellman, H., & Estes, D. (1986). Early understanding of mental entities: A reexamination of childhood realism. *Child Development, 57,* 910–923.

# Children's Memory for Emotional Events:
# Implications for Testimony

*University of Chicago, Chicago, IL 60637*

It is argued that memory for emotional events is regulated by mental schemas that focus attention on personally meaningful goals, the antecedent conditions that affect these goals, beliefs about the possibility of maintaining, attaining, removing, or avoiding conditions that facilitate or block important goals, the actions taken in the service of attaining these goals, and the outcomes that determine whether or not these goals are achieved. In this chapter, evidence is presented to show that even very young children use these causally structured mental schemas to monitor and appraise incoming information with respect to maintaining their goals and to carry out plans of action in the service of these goals. Young children attempt to talk about their emotional experiences as soon as they begin to utter two-word combinations, and they do so in a detailed organized fashion. Whether or not these representations are accurate depends on the organizational structure of the input, the amount of previous exposure and knowledge the children have about the event, and the ability to make causal inferences that connect one incoming event to another. To the extent that children encode a causal representation of incoming information, their memories remain stable over long periods of time. Instability results from a failure to organize and incorporate incoming information into a stable causal structure. The same principles of causal coherence account for adults' memories of emotional events. Future studies need to focus more on the encoding process and to describe the types of appraisals and causal inferences that occur as an event is encoded.

## INTRODUCTION

The goals of this chapter are to address issues central to understanding and remembering emotional events, especially those that pertain to eyewitness testimony. A recurring issue in current testimony debates focuses on the difficulties children under or around the age of 3 experience in understanding and remembering accurately what they have experienced (Bartsch & Wellman, 1995; Fivush & Hammond, 1990; Fivush, 1991; Fivush, this volume; Howe, Courage, & Peterson, this volume; Hudson, 1990). The prevailing belief is that children younger than 3 years have a great deal of difficulty encoding ongoing events with any degree of accuracy or intentional understanding, especially when other people's beliefs, goals, and behaviors (Bartsch & Wellman, 1995) are being evaluated.

A second related issue focuses on the claim that adults cannot remember events from the first 3 years of life in any significant detail (Nelson, 1990). This phenomenon is often referred to as infantile amnesia. Explanations regarding the inaccessibility of memories from very early childhood often focus on the fact that young children have yet to form stable or consistent belief structures that

*The Recovered Memory/False Memory Debate*
Copyright © 1996 by Academic Press, Inc.
All rights of reproduction in any form reserved.

hold up over time. It is the existence of specific belief structures that are thought to allow memories to become stable and then veridical (Holliday, 1995).

A third issue in the recovered memory/false memory debate concerns the reconstructive and (therefore) inaccurate nature of memory retrieval (Ceci, Huffman, Smith, & Loftus, this volume; Garry, Loftus, & Brown, 1994; Loftus, 1994; Neisser, 1982; Neisser & Harsch, 1992; Usher & Neisser, 1993). It has been argued that memory is reconstructive in nature and dependent on an interaction between already existing beliefs and attitudes and the nature and content of incoming information. It is often assumed that because of the reconstructive nature of memory, creating a stable memory representation is rare and at best difficult to achieve (Ceci et al., this volume; Garry et al., 1994; Neisser & Harsch, 1992).

Although situations exist in which both children and adults have been shown to have incomplete and inaccurate memories (see Stein, Wade, and Liwag, in press, for an analysis of the conditions under which autobiographical memories are accurate or inaccurate), just as many exist in which both young children and adults have detailed and accurate memories (see Bauer & Mandler, 1990; Goodman, Quas, Batterman-Faunce, Riddlesberger, & Kuhn, this volume; Mandler & McDonough, in press; Saywitz & Moan-Hardie, this volume; Stein & Levine, 1989; Stein, Wade, & Liwag, in press; Stein, Trabasso, & Liwag, 1994; Trabasso & Stein, in press). The problematic nature of memory in legal and courtroom situations has resulted in developmental and cognitive researchers overlooking critical facts about memory. The first is that the reconstructive nature of memory has no direct bearing on the accuracy and content of a memory representation. The second is that the amount of learning and skill development children undergo in the first 2 years of life is directly related to their ability to acquire detailed representations of the world that correspond to those of other people.

In all types of situations, children's successful adaptation depends on acquiring knowledge that overlaps with the knowledge of other people, especially those who care for them (Bloom & Capatides, 1987b; Dunn, 1988; Liwag & Stein, 1995; Rogoff & Mistry, 1990; Snow, 1990; Stein et al., 1994; Stern, 1985). The need for children and adults to interpret and respond to events in similar ways serves as a measure of the reality and validity of an event, as well as of the effectiveness of the instructional and enculturation process (Dunn & Brown, 1991; Rogoff & Mistry, 1990). The existence of common knowledge about the nature of an event is also critical in determining what will be the standard representation in testimony studies. If those who participate in an ongoing event cannot agree on a specific description of that event by referring to knowledge they share, then a standard cannot be set for measuring memory accuracy.

Commonality of knowledge between people comes from at least three sources: the specific properties and organizational structure of input during the experienced event, the similarities in prior knowledge and previous experience of the participants who appraise and interpret the event, and attempts to communicate, persuade, and instruct other people in the ways that an event should be perceived. In several studies (Liwag & Stein, 1995; Stein & Liwag, in press; Stein et al., 1994; Trabasso, Stein, Rodkin, Munger, & Baughn, 1992), we have illustrated that children's and parents' representations of a specific emotion episode include both similar and dissimilar dimensions before any detailed interchange occurs between the two. Similarities in their representations occur when both child and parent draw on common knowledge and experience to interpret an event, and when they have similar goals operating during the understanding process. The nature of the input they are interpreting is often highly structured and unambiguous in terms of its meaning.

Dissimilarities in representations occur when two people have access to different types of information during the interpretation of an event and when their goals are different during the encoding and interpretation of an event (Horton & Keysar, in press; Stein, Calicchia, & Bernas, 1995; Stein et al., 1994). The prototype of situations that result in two people encoding different representations is one in which two individuals are engaged in a dispute, one wants to compromise and the other wants to win. Memory for what the other person said during the dispute has been shown repeatedly to be highly inaccurate in these situations (Epstein, Pretzer, & Fleming, 1987; Noller, 1984; Stein, 1995).

Given the vehemence associated with the opposing stances on the accuracy and stability of emotional and traumatic memories (and the fact that a large number of studies support the claim that memory is both accurate and inaccurate), the conditions that produce accurate versus inaccurate memories need to be explored. In our overview of everyday and emotional memory literature (Stein, Ornstein, Tversky, & Brainerd, in press; Stein, Wade, and Liwag, in press), we have found that many researchers focus on the inaccuracies of memory without describing the accuracies, especially when young children are concerned. Here, an effort is made to show how suggestible memory is without illustrating how accurate it is. Thus, it is not surprising that investigators who focus only on inaccuracies reach very different conclusions about the nature and stability of memory than investigators who focus more on accuracies.

The position I take in this chapter is that children's memory, from a very early age, is quite similar to that of adults, especially when emotional memories are considered. Furthermore, very young children have the ability to retain "accurate" representations of incoming information just as adults do. My claims rest on the types of mental representations that both children and adults are thought to use to understand emotion-laden events (Frijda, 1987; Oatley & Johnson-Laird, 1987; Stein et al., 1994), the types of overt appraisals that both children and adults make when talking about emotional reactions (Stein & Levine, 1989; Stein & Liwag, in press; Stein et al., 1994), similarities in the organizational structure of the recall of emotional events (Stein & Levine, 1989), and similarities in the goals and planning structures that both children and adults generate when they react to an emotional event (Trabasso & Stein, in press; Trabasso & Ozyurek, 1995).

By the age of 8 to 12 months (Stenberg & Campos, 1990; Duncan & Farley, 1990; Willats, 1990), or earlier (Alessandri, Sullivan, & Lewis, 1990), the nonverbal precursors of children's verbal representations of emotional experience can be observed. Young children rapidly shift the focus of their attention when a novel stimulus is introduced into a situation, they attend to the novelty before expressing their emotion (Sroufe, 1979; Stenberg & Campos, 1990), they focus on the object or person who has directly blocked or facilitated their goals (Alessandri et al., 1990; Stenberg & Campos, 1990), they repeat or generate different plans of actions until they are able to attain a desired state, and they express their emotions as a direct function of the outcome of their actions.

When asked to construct a temporal sequence of events they have observed, 1-year-old children are able to reconstruct specific types of temporal sequences, and 16- to 20-month-old children are able to reproduce causal sequences of events, even after delays of 2 and 6 weeks (Bauer & Mandler, 1989, 1990; Bauer & Shore, 1987). Myers, Clifton, and Clarkson (1987) also report that one 33-month-old child, who returned to their lab after participating in a study between the ages of 6 weeks and 9 months, was able to recall verbally a picture of a whale that he had seen at 9 months of age. The memory of the whale was preserved despite the fact that the child had no word for "whale" at the time he saw the picture (see Mandler & McDonough, in press, for an extensive discussion of nonverbal memory in young children).

My belief is that young children's memory has been described as inadequate and qualitatively different from adults because of a deeply ingrained belief that the nature of brain development always imposes qualitative changes on the symbolic thinking processes of children (see Fischer, 1980, and Case, 1991, for stances supporting this belief). Qualitative differences in memory are often found, however, because researchers rely too heavily on an analysis of language and spontaneous conversations or on retrospective accounts of an event without obtaining a more detailed record of the on-line interpretation and encoded representation of an event (Bartsch & Wellman, 1995; Fivush, this volume; Howe et al., this volume). Observing children on-line as they attempt to understand an event, using systematic probe questions to elicit parts of the representation not included in spontaneous recall (Liwag & Stein, 1995; Stein & Levine, 1989), and observing nonverbal as well as verbal reconstructions of events (Mandler & McDonough, in press) are mandatory requirements for accurately describing memory representations.

When these measures are not included in a study, investigators often ignore overwhelming similarities in children's and adults' thinking that are discovered on further analysis. Many investigators have not heeded well or taken into consideration the mounting evidence (Donaldson, 1992; Chi, 1983; Mandler, 1983; Trabasso, Stein, & Johnson, 1981) that the development of children's memory is a direct function of their prior knowledge and that prior knowledge, not chronological age, accounts for the quality of a memory representation. Moreover, we have not considered or described in enough detail what Siegler (1991) refers to as the microgenetic process—the unfolding of the temporal or causal sequence inherent in a event—especially as the event is appraised, understood, and encoded.

We need to give more thought to how emotional events are understood (Eth & Pynoos, 1985; Stein, Trabasso, & Liwag, 1992, 1994; Stein, Folkman, Trabasso, & Christopher-Richards, 1995) and to models of the thinking process during the encoding of such events. We use words like suggestibility, instability, self knowledge, narrative, coherence, belief, and theory of mind, all of which are related to models of memory, but we rarely reference the systems or the structures of the mind that give rise to these constructs. To advance our understanding of these concepts, I discuss some of the thinking processes used to understand and remember emotional events.

It is my thesis, along with my co-workers (Stein & Liwag, in press; Stein et al., 1992, 1994), that the representation of emotional events is the foundational core of autobiographical memory and that even children younger than 24 months have many such representations. Moreover, children access and use these representations in their daily interactions (Duncan & Farley, 1990; Stern, 1992). When filmed records of children's talk and interactions are available, it is quite easy to discern those events that are emotionally meaningful to children and those events that children have ignored. Many studies, however, do not record or provide access to the record of the encoding process. Thus, it has been difficult to assess whether children are actually talking about events that were emotionally and personally meaningful to them and whether they attended to the unfolding of the stimulus event throughout the entire session.

How and when children attend to a stimulus event is critical, because children define what constitutes an emotional event, not a parent, teacher, or experimenter. A stimulus event, in and of itself, cannot be said to be emotionally significant just because a researcher or a parent thinks the event is emotional (Stein et al., 1994). Events acquire significance only through an appraisal and evaluation process by the experiencer of the event (Folkman & Stein, in press; Lazarus & Folkman, 1984; Stein & Levine, 1987). Before we can say whether children remember emotional events, we need to ensure that they in fact have responded to an event in an emotional way and that they characterize the event as emotional.

## The Nature of Emotional Events

We have focused on the study of emotional events for many reasons, one being that the experience of an emotion in response to an event always involves goals that are personally meaningful to the participant (Frijda, 1987; Lazarus & Folkman, 1984; Oatley & Johnson-Laird, 1987; Stein & Levine, 1987; Stein et al., 1992). Personal involvement, although sometimes debilitating, almost always ensures active processing of some aspect of the ongoing situation. The accuracy of a memory representation is not necessarily related to the content of the representation. Thus, when children and adults experience an emotion, they almost always recall the precipitating event that caused the emotion, the antecedent conditions that led up to the precipitating event, the reasons for experiencing a specific emotional response, thoughts and wishes that occurred at the time of the emotional event, and whether or not they were free to act in a way that was concordant with their wishes or desires (Stein & Levine, 1987, 1989).

Researchers who claim that adults have no access to memories before the age of 3 have rarely focused on memories that adults nominate as being emotional. As I previously noted, in most retrospective memory studies, the typical stimulus event is one in which researchers rather than participants have chosen the events. Few memory researchers have actually asked subjects to retrieve memories of their first 3 years and then have the participants define the events as emotional. For example, Usher and Neisser (1993) chose the birth of a sibling as an event that subjects had to recall. Although they may have assumed the event to be emotionally significant, they had no observational evidence that this event was emotional or even important to their subjects, nor did they attempt to elicit events that subjects defined as emotional.

From our recent studies on both children and adults (Levine & Stein, 1995; Liwag & Stein, 1995; Stein & Liwag, in press; Stein et al., 1994; Stein, Folkman, et al., 1995), we know that a large amount of variation occurs in the emotional evaluation of an event, even when participants experience an event that is thought to be emotional for "everyone," such as the loss of a relationship (Wortman & Silver, 1990). The type and intensity of the emotional response is regulated by the interpretation process, as is the encoding of the event.[1]

If subjects do appraise an event as emotional, their memories are almost always structured in a causally coherent fashion. Even 3-year-old children organize their memories according to causally organized principles. As an example, Trabasso, Stein, and Johnson (1981) gave 3-year-old children incomplete sentences such as: Billy was really angry. . . . Children were asked to complete the sentence by responding with the first thing that came to their mind. Almost all of the children generated responses that could be classified as events that initiated the emotional response (because his brother broke his favorite toy) or plans of action that were formulated in response to the emotion (so he decided to take his brother's favorite toy).

In one of our studies that focused on describing children's real-life emotional experiences, even 3-year-old children generated causally linked narratives in response to questions designed to elicit their memories for different kinds of emotional experiences (Levine & Stein, 1995). The degree of causal coherence in the narrative was a function of the specific emotion state being discussed. Fear and anger narratives were the most causally coherent, whereas happy and sad narratives, although causally organized, were looser in structure (e.g., each clause in a narrative did not have as many causal links to other clauses as they did in anger and fear narratives). The same results were found, however, in analyzing adult narratives of happiness and sadness as opposed to those of anger and fear (Stein & Levine, 1989).

In a second study (Liwag & Stein, 1995), we provided children with specific precipitating events reported by their parents as having caused an observable emotional reaction in their children. We asked the children to recall the events and, again, we found that children's narratives were almost always causally structured. The degree of elaboration and reporting varied as a function of the instructional strategies children used to recall their experience. If children en-

---

[1] Schank (1982) has accurately called the encoding process one of reminding, and he as well as many others have shown that memories cannot be formed without continual interpretation and inferencing (see Graesser, Singer, & Trabasso, 1994; Stein, Wade, & Liwag, in press).

acted the emotion episode as though it were occurring "right now," their reports were more detailed and more causally structured than if they recalled their memories without these instructions.

During this study, two of our young preschool children recalled rather traumatic events. One little boy recounted what he went through when he visited his father in the hospital. His narrative focused on his father dying of cancer and the fact that he had to spend long periods of time at the hospital with his mom, who alternated between crying, trying to take care of him, yelling at his older brother, and talking to his grandmother about how she was going to cope with his father not being around. A second little boy recounted the events that led up to the police coming to his house, his father being arrested, and his visit to see his father in the county jail. Not only were these narratives causally organized, but they also contained a large number of overt appraisals and evaluations of the remembered situations.

In appraising the remembered situation, children focused on what they liked and disliked, whether or not they thought the behaviors of other people were good or bad, positive and negative actions of other people, personality and mood state characteristics of other people, their expectations for what should have happened in the situation versus what really happened, what other people thought would happen, and what other people said would happen. The appraisals accounted for 20 to 25% of all clauses and were essential in adding coherence to the report of events that could be observed in an objective manner.

Other researchers (J. Folkman, personal communication; Merritt, Ornstein, & Spicker, 1994) also report that children's memories for emotional events, especially medical procedures, are quite detailed. When children's well-being and survival depends on their cooperation and understanding of specific procedures, they often achieve a good command of the exact nature of the procedure. In certain situations, having to undergo specific medical procedures becomes so frightening to children that their memories about the procedures and their reasons for their fears become very detailed and quite resistant to change. In fact, some cancer surgeons caring for these young children resort to creating therapy groups for their patients (J. Folkman, personal communication). After helping children to survive, pediatric surgeons find that the unfolding of the surgical events remain in children's memories for quite some time. These memories are often so vivid that they interfere with the encoding of new events, becoming intrusive in many activities a child performs (Eth & Pynoos, 1985; Terr, 1988). The traumatic impact of the surgical event causes children to repeatedly engage other people in conversation so that they can talk about the surgery until the nature of the event is better understood or until the child has a better plan to cope with the event (Stein et al., 1994).

If we look at children's talk and appraisals associated with real emotional or traumatic events, an analysis of the content and quality of their thinking provides a clear alternative to some of the conclusions from current eyewitness testimony studies. Many of the traumatic situations children reported resulted in *positive outcomes* (Stein & Liwag, in press) with regard to the children's physical and mental health. In these situations, adults were clearly the facilitators of children's survival and well-being, not evil and wrong-doing people who abused or took advantage of unsuspecting children.

These positively focused situations are important for two reasons. First, the tendency to deceive and lie, to produce biased accounts, and to acquiesce to parental or experimental authority is often not present. Thus, we can separate out what children remember versus what they say they remember because of external constraints. When children are presented with situations in which clear and present dangers exist in telling the truth, they will lie and become deceptive (den Bak & Ross, in press; Lewis & Saarni, 1993). Lying is not limited to older children. Three- to 5-year-old children do it very well, especially when they are attempting to get their siblings into trouble or to protect themselves.

The second advantage of using situations that end in positive outcomes is that subjects focus on ways in which they can maintain their positive state and prevent negative states from occurring (Stein et al., 1994). To accomplish this task, subjects frequently review and update their memories of past situations to try to get as accurate a representation of a past event as possible. Instead of their memories becoming more inaccurate over time, as the surface results of the Ceci et al. (this volume) study suggest, children's memories for real-life events become more accurate over time. One factor regulating the increase in accuracy is access to additional information that explains events in a causally related fashion.

Whether situations have positive or negative outcomes, however, is irrelevant to the broader theoretical goals: (a) to assess understanding and evaluation from the *child's* point of view during encoding; (b) to show whether a causal memory representation has been constructed during the understanding process; and (c) to predict, from the initial representation of an event, whether the representation will retain stability and resistance to change or whether it will undergo transformations. To achieve these aims, we created opportunities to collect appraisals and interpretations of an event as it unfolds (Stein, Bernas, Calicchia, & Wright, 1995; Trabasso & Stein, in press; Trabasso & Magliano, in press; Trabasso & Ozyurek, 1995). We first describe how an event is initially understood and encoded in terms of the causal structure and content of the event, and then we compare the on-line encoded representation to the retrospective representation.

Our findings suggest several things. First, we find that often the focal event has not been processed very deeply, has not been responded to emotionally, and has not been understood in an elaborated manner, even when we intended to provoke an emotion (Liwag & Stein, 1995; Trabasso & Stein, in press; Trabasso et al., 1992). Variability in the depth of encoding is present in both children's and adults' memories. Memory accuracy depends on the structure of the input, the subject's initial level and depth of understanding, and the ability to organize incoming information into a causally coherent representation (Stein & Trabasso, 1982a, 1985; Suh & Trabasso, 1993; Trabasso & Magliano, in press).

Second, the ability to interpret and understand the event during encoding is the more problematic element for us, not the retrievability or suggestibility of memory (Stein, Wade, & Liwag, in press; Trabasso & Stein, in press). Although much attention has focused on the suggestibility of memory, researchers have failed to explain why certain memories are suggestible and others are resistant to change. Ceci et al. (this volume) do show changes in memory through repeatedly talking about an event, but the most significant changes occur after the first representation. Few changes occur after this. Thus, a fair amount of stability in children's representations exists, and the representations appear to be resistant to further deterioration.

The issues of stability and change have been systematically addressed in the memory and discourse comprehension literature, especially in regard to narrative and everyday event comprehension (see Stein, Wade, & Liwag, in press, for a review). Studies have been done on factors that regulate the encoding, retrieval, and learning processes. Therefore, we turn our attention to issues that focus on understanding and remembering an emotional event.

## Understanding Emotional Events: The Use of Goal Appraisal Processes

Our model of emotional understanding assumes that the appraisals and evaluations made during attempts to understand the unfolding of an event control the flow of attention and the information that gets encoded. The types of appraisals people make are based on their prior knowledge, desires, preferences, and values that are activated in a given context. This assumption is not new. Bartlett (1932), who put forth the first concrete hypothesis about the reconstructive nature of memory, also believed that attitudes, desires, and prior knowledge structures continually guide, organize, and regulate how incoming information is incorporated into existing mental structures. Bartlett, however, did not tell us very much about the content and processes inherent in mental processes.

In a series of papers (Folkman & Stein, in press; Stein & Levine, 1987; Stein et al., 1992, 1994), we have described the content of these mental structures and processes used during understanding and representation of an emotional event. According to our theory, individuals are assumed to use a representational system that allows them to continually monitor subjective states and bodily reactions. The primary function of this system is to access knowledge that facilitates the evaluation of an event, action, object, or state with regard to its value (see also Mandler, 1984). This representational system includes information about states that are pleasurable and preferred, and states that are aversive and to be avoided. The system also contains information about the conditions that lead to specific goal states and information about the relative priority of goals in terms of the necessity for maintaining or avoiding certain states.

The existence of a value system is fundamental to emotional understanding and behavior (Lazarus & Folkman, 1984; Mandler, 1984; Stein & Levine, 1987) because the system alerts individuals to those situations that bring pleasure and pain. With such a system at work, two primary tendencies exist: the desire to attain or maintain a valued state and the desire to escape from or avoid an aversive state. A value system becomes operative primarily when an individual is in one particular state, imagines the existence of another state, and infers that the imagined end state will result in a more pleasurable outcome than the existing state. Plans of action are then enacted to attain or maintain valued goals. When goals succeed, positive emotional states are experienced. When goals are challenged or blocked, negative emotional states are experienced.

To evaluate the significance of an event with respect to the achievement or failure of valued goals, the following appraisals need to be made. First, the event in question must be perceived as personally significant such that the person believes that an important goal has been blocked, attained, or challenged by the occurrence of an event. Thus, emotional understanding is intimately connected to changes in the state of personally meaningful goals. We define a goal as a valued state that people either want to attain, maintain, avoid, or get out of (Stein & Glenn, 1979; Stein & Levine, 1987; Stein et al., 1994). Responding emotionally requires that a person be able to monitor the changes that occur in personally valued states.

Although monitoring the status of goals may require a set of complex cognitive processes, data from many different laboratories indicate that infants and very young children are quite skilled at carrying out these processes across almost any given context. Piaget (1981) proposed that infants have a built-in mechanism that enables them to repeat an action that results in goal success and a subsequent pleasurable emotion state. Thus, infants not only monitor goals but construct plans of action that result in the maintenance of their goals.

Monitoring a goal can be seen in the ability to track and attain physical objects, change body position, change the physiological state of one's body, and change the state of events in the world. Many different studies in the infancy literature (see Alessandri et al., 1990; Gergely, Nadasdy, Csibra, & Biro, in press; Haith, 1994; Reznick, 1994; Stenberg & Campos, 1990; von Hofsten, 1994; Willats, 1990) have established that infants form expectations and carry out goal-directed action quite early in life. Although researchers debate about the exact onset and meaning of goal-directed action, most document that goal-directed action is causally linked to emotional expression between the ages of 4 and 8 months. Alessandri et al. (1990; Lewis, Alessandri, & Sullivan, 1990) document the relationship between emotion and goal-directed action even earlier.

The second requirement for understanding the emotional significance of an event is the ability to access a prior representation of the focal event and to recognize that the current unfolding of the event is significantly different from what should have occurred.[2] As Haith (1994) argues, visual expectations are formed quite early in life, and the ability to habituate and dishabituate to an event cannot be achieved without forming some type of stable representation of an event. Sroufe (1979), however, explicitly shows that social expectations occur quite early in infancy, with laughter and smiling caused by a violation of infants' expectations. Duncan and Farley (1990) show that a good part of parent–child nonverbal interaction is parents and children developing and then violating expectations that are set by participation in conventional routines. Children under the age of 10 months and their parents repeatedly engage in many different

---

[2] Although the necessity to experience a violation of expectation with respect to feeling an emotion is debatable, almost every theory of emotional understanding requires either a violation of expectation or some novel element to be perceived during the encoding of a precipitating event.

"games," in which either the child or parent performs a violation of a well-known sequence of actions (convention), and then one or both experience an emotional reaction.

The third type of appraisal that must be made about an event, once a violation of expectation is perceived, concerns the possibility of reinstating a goal once it has failed, succeeded, or been challenged. Thus, not only does emotional understanding require the perception of a violation of expectation and a change in the status of a valued goal, but it also requires an assessment about the possibility of reinstating, maintaining, avoiding, or escaping from a particular state. In essence, these three appraisals are used to generate a working representation of an emotional event (Stein & Levine, 1987; Stein et al., 1992). The resulting mental representation of an emotional event includes the following dimensions:

1. recognition of the goals that shifted in status,
2. a specification of the event that caused the change in the status of a valued goal,
3. recognition that the change was unexpected,
4. an assessment of the consequences that will or have occurred because of the change in a goal's status,
5. an appraisal of whether or not the goal can be reinstated, maintained, or avoided,
6. accessing a plan to reinstate, maintain, revise, substitute, or abandon the current goal,
7. carrying out a plan of action, and
8. evaluating the results of action in terms of attaining goals.

Several studies from the early infancy literature (Alessandri et al., 1990; Meltzhoff, 1988; Willats, 1990) have illustrated that infants engage in detailed instrumental observation and action to reinstate states that are no longer present, and that their behavior is not random. The infants focus first on the object, event, or person who has caused an obstruction to their goal (Alessandri et al., 1990; Stenberg & Campos, 1990; Sroufe, 1979), they show a specific emotional expression, and then they act to change their current state and situation.

From detailed descriptions and assessments of intentional action sequences in infancy, we can explore the issues of whether infants have acquired enough knowledge to understand the conditions that facilitate or block their goals, and whether they are able to formulate specific plans of action (Trabasso & Stein, 1994) to achieve their goals. Infants' repeated engagement in goal-directed action, especially their attempts at reinstating important goals in the face of failure (Alessandri et al., 1990; Willats, 1990), strongly suggests that they use the same type of representational scheme of goal-directed action that adults use (Trabasso & Stein, 1994, in press).

Although we lack explicit evidence that very young children activate these types of mental schemas during everyday problem solving, a frequent mistake that developmental researchers make in thinking about the development of understanding and memory is to make the task of forming a goal-structured representation of an emotional event more difficult than it is. We as well as other investigators (Bloom & Capatides, 1987a, 1987b; Liwag & Stein, 1995; Stein & Liwag, in press; Stein & Levine, 1989; Wolf, 1990) have shown that as soon as children are able to talk about their emotions, they do so in a causal manner and include a majority of the eight categories of a goal-structured episode.[3]

In a study by Stein and Liwag (in press) in which children recounted events nominated by their parents as having caused emotional responses, a clear majority of the 3-year-old children recalled seven of the eight components of an emotional episode. The one component children frequently omitted was an explicit plan of action that would lead to overt action. Instead, children focused on the actual attempts they undertook to achieve their goals. Table 1 contains the complete narrative of one of our subjects who recounted what happened when he did not get an allowance from his mother.

This narrative illustrates the richness in the emotional memories children retrieve and the fact that the memory was organized around a valued goal the child wanted to achieve. This type of goal-directed organization was apparent in almost every single memory reported in this study, even memories recounted by very young 2½- to 3-year-old children. Although developmental differences were found in the overall length of the narratives, no significant differences were found in the unfolding of the emotion episode. If children remembered a particular event as having occurred, they could elaborate each part of the goal-directed episode.

Furthermore, children's narratives were filled with value-laden statements appraising the worth of people, objects, events, and actions. Children elaborated on their desires, beliefs about themselves and other people, and their beliefs about the harms and benefits they experienced during the unfolding of the emotional event. What was apparent in all of the children's recollections was the overwhelming predisposition to report what they liked and what they did not like about everything they experienced. Thus, our theory of emotional understanding with respect to describing the importance of maintaining valued goals was upheld.

The question for us with respect to the claim that autobiographical memory is dependent on the development of the "cognitive" self is whether researchers like Fivush (this volume) and Howe et al. (this volume) use the contents of children's appraisals and evaluations of themselves and situations to determine concepts of self versus other. To date, very simple measures are used to assess self knowledge, such as self-recognition in a mirror (Howe et al., this volume) and the use of "I" versus the names of other people (Huttenlocher, Smiley, & Charney, 1983). Our contention (Stein & Liwag, in press) is that self-recognition and pronominal references are not adequate indicators to assess children's knowledge

---

[3] We define an episode in terms of the causal unfolding of a goal–action–outcome sequence (Stein & Glenn, 1979; Stein & Trabasso, 1982b; Trabasso & Stein, 1994). We do not use episode in the same way that Tulving does in his attempt to distinguish between episodic and semantic memory. The episode is the basic higher order unit of an emotional representation and contains one goal-directed action sequence.

TABLE 1
Transcript of a Child's Anger Narrative from the Stein & Liwag (in press) Study

---

*Interviewer: Do you remember, just a little while ago, your mom said that she would give you an allowance if you cleaned your room.*
*Child's narrative:*
Well I was in my room,
and she said, if you clean up your room like your brother,
then I would, I will give you an allowance.
And it didn't happen.
Uh, well my brother got it
and I didn't.
And that made me feel mad.
Very mad.
Well, well one day when she was in her bed,
I said, give me allowance,
and she said no.
And I just, and she, and I just got her wallet,
looking for four dimes to get, buy some chips.
And I didn't find any.
And then I took her purse in to her, in my room
and I locked the door,
and I also emptied out all her money,
and I looked for four dimes,
and I didn't find any.
And then she got up and said,
I know what you're doing,
and open up the door right now.
And that's what she said.
*Interviewer: When this happened, what did you wish you could do?*
*Child:* I wished I could just, when my brother was asleep, I wished I could just uh, wake up and get his money.
*Interviewer: What did you do?*
*Child:* I really did nothing.

---

and awareness of themselves. Self knowledge, as well as knowledge about other people, is multidimensional, multimodal, and clearly evaluative. Much of the knowledge children have acquired about themselves and other people is nonverbal, quite detailed, and expressed only in certain situations. More detailed observations and procedures need to be implemented to describe the range of knowledge young children have acquired about themselves and their world.

One way of assessing this knowledge is to observe children during a task that requires comparisons between themselves and others (Stern, 1992) or to observe them performing actions in reference to themselves versus another person. Very young children will not perform actions that will result in pain for themselves. However, many will set up plans to perform these actions on another person, especially if the other is a sibling who has just made them angry (Dunn, 1988, 1993). Young children have also been observed to be very deceptive, especially when they want to engage in an activity that has been prohibited (den Bak & Ross, in press; Dunn, 1988). Both their verbal and nonverbal actions indicate that they are aware of other people's intentions, that they know that those intentions are different from their own, and that they know the other person will attempt to block their goal. These are the situations in which most deception occurs (Lewis & Saarni, 1993).

These observational findings clearly need more exploration, but they strongly suggest that young children engage in comparative processes that distinguish themselves from others in early infancy. The existing data also suggest that children remember quite well what works for them versus another child. The results from our own emotional memory studies (Levine & Stein, 1995) corroborate many of these findings. When 2½- to 4-year-old children were asked to recall real events that made their best friends or their siblings really happy, mad, sad, and afraid, they generated different scenarios for their friends than they did for themselves.

Children sometimes experienced difficulty in recalling events that made their friends "afraid" or "angry." In talking about their friends, children frequently reported that they had never seen their friend afraid or angry. In fact, one little boy got so exasperated with us for asking about an event that made his friend scared that he finally told us that he could not answer us because he did not live under his friend's skin! Many of the other children made the same type of comment by saying, "Well, I just don't play with her enough."

The most interesting finding in this study (Levine & Stein, 1995), however, was the comparison between children's memories for real events versus their accounts of events that *could make* their best friend or their closest sibling experience different emotions. Children often had difficulty generating real-life instances of their friends becoming scared or angry. They had little or no difficulty, however, in making up an entire scenario about an event that *could make* their friend angry or scared. The freedom to invent and use pretense allowed these young children the opportunity to activate relevant knowledge about both their friends and the process of emotional understanding. Many children were able to tell us in detail the reasons that their friend or sibling might experience either anger or fear. Table 2 illustrates a prototypic example of a 3-year-old girl's anger narrative about her friend, Rachel.

Our data are similar to those that Ceci et al. (this volume) report in reference to the ability of children to narrate about a nonevent. Our 3- to 5-year-old children not only had the capacity to talk about an event that had not happened, they also had the capacity to envision ways in which their friends would evaluate and emotionally react to such an event. The difference between our findings and those of Ceci et al., however, is that our subjects knew they had created a fictitious world for their friend. There was no slippage in children's judgments about whether or not their friend had experienced such an event. Similarly, we found that when children generated narratives about hypothetical situations in which they would be the ones who experienced specific emotional reactions, they were always aware of the fact that they were engaging in pretense and talking in the hypothetical.

One reason that children showed no confusion between real and hypothetical events was that they included conditions in their hypothetical narratives that

TABLE 2

A Three-Year-Old Child's Hypothetical Report about a Friend Getting Angry

---

*Experimenter: Pretend that Rachel's really, really mad.*
*What would make her feel that way?*
*Child?*
If somebody wouldn't let her talk.
They said "No!
Wait 'til I'm finished!"
and it was going to be until,
and they said
that they were going to talk until, until clean-up time.
*E: And that would make her mad, if someone didn't let her talk until clean-up time—*
*Child:*
MMMMM! (Shakes head vigorously with a yes)
And she would go like MMMMM!
"You never let me talk!"
*E: Well what would she be thinking about if someone wasn't going to let her talk?*
*Child:*
She would want to punch him,
but she wouldn't.
*E: She wouldn't? What would she do?*
*Child:*
She would tell the teachers.
Because it made
her feel bad.
*E: Because it made her feel bad, huh? And what would telling the teachers accomplish?*
*Child:*
The teachers would say,
"Take turns.
You could um, tell half of it,
and Rachel could tell half of what
she wants to say.
And you could tell half of it,
and she could tell half of it.
And you could tell half of it,
and she could tell half of it."
If they didn't let her
she could, I think she would tell the teachers that they keeped on doing it.
That's what I think she'd do,
that's what she always do, lah lah lah lah!
Just like my every, just like my every just like every of my friends.
*E: Oh really?*
*Child:*
All of my friends.
*E: All of your friends do that—*
*Child:*
All of my friends at my school do that—.
All the girl friends of mine, at least.
They tell the teachers!

---

they knew had not occurred in real life. They believed, however, that these hypothetical events could occur under the right set of circumstances. For example, the 3-year-old girl's narrative (Table 2) focused on a scenario about her friend Rachel. The narrator reported that Rachel would get mad if she had to wait a long time for a turn to talk. Our narrator knew that Rachel had difficulty waiting for her turn to talk in a group. The narrator had seen this happen several times, and she told us this in response to further probe questions after her initial narration. What she had *never* seen was Rachel not being given the floor when Rachel showed impatience. The narrator inferred that if Rachel were ever to be prevented from gaining the floor, she would show real anger.

The request to talk about emotional events predisposes children to focus on some novel dimension of a precipitating event. The fact that Rachel would not be given the floor in the hypothetical scenario was the event that would trigger her anger response. It would be a clear violation of expectation for Rachel. In our model (Stein & Levine, 1987; Stein et al., 1992), the violation of expectation associated with the unfolding of a precipitating event is the key element that triggers the emotional response and allows the event to be remembered quite accurately. When an event violates a set of prior expectations, it is tagged in memory as being different from what is already known. To incorporate the novel event into current memory structures, an explanation needs to be formulated to determine why the novel event occurred and the consequences associated with the event. By generating explanatory inferences about the causes and consequences of an unusual event, the event becomes more understandable and more predictable.

Constructing an explanatory framework for unexpected events, however, often takes effort and much reprocessing of specific aspects of the unusual event. Both children and adults will often access a memory representation repeatedly in their attempts to understand the nature of a real emotional event. Evidence for this reprocessing and reminding (Schank, 1982) came in our parental reports about the frequency with which parents had to talk to their children about emotional events, especially when their children experienced negative emotions. The fact that repeated processing is carried out in the service of understanding the nature of the emotional event often increases rather than decreases accuracy.

One dimension that helped children to keep their hypothetical representations separate from those that had actually occurred was that children knew that some of their hypothetical scenarios would be socially or morally unacceptable if the event were to occur, especially in the eyes of adults. Part of the glee children expressed in our study was due to the opportunity to think about circumstances that would present difficulties for their peers or siblings. The motives for revenge and making a peer uncomfortable, especially when that peer had caused past problems for the subject, was a consistent operating factor during the narrations of hypothetical circumstances.

### Accuracy of Emotional Memory: What Dimensions Control Veridicality

Given that young children can produce coherent representations of emotional situations, are their representations accurate in terms of some agreed on standard? What dimensions influence accuracy and what dimensions push a child to either transform incoming information or to transform an existing memory representation? Are children's memories subject to similar constraining and facilitating conditions when compared to adults?

Although the majority of studies in the eyewitness testimony area focus on the suggestibility of memory as the culprit in retaining accurate representations of events, our own work (Mandler & Stein, 1974; Stein & Mandler, 1975; Stein & Nezworski, 1978; Trabasso & Stein, in press; Trabasso & Magliano, in press) as well as the work of others (Bartlett, 1932; Mandler, 1983, 1984) strongly suggests that the majority of errors that occur in memory take place at the time of encoding. Either the relevant information was never encoded, or incoming information was appraised in such a way that the inference process caused serious transformations in the incoming information (e.g., deletions, additions, temporal inversions, incomplete integrations of information). As we and other researchers (Mandler, 1983, 1984; Schank, 1982; Schank & Abelson, 1977: Stein, Wade, and Liwag, in press; Trabasso & Magliano, in press) have pointed out, appraisals and inferences made during encoding give meaning to incoming information and become an integral part of the memory representation. We cannot construct a memory representation without making inferences about the incoming information, and the content of the inferences is a direct reflection of our prior knowledge about an event.

Several factors influence the accuracy of encoding, but four in particular stand out: (a) the goals of the subject, (b) the content and organizational structure of the input, (c) the content of the prior knowledge used to interpret incoming information, and (d) the number of causally relevant inferences made during the encoding process. The goals of the subject are critical because they control the focus of attention during an event. When two people are involved in an argument, their conversations are often heated and emotionally intense, with each party trying to best and compete with the other. Asked to recall an argument in which the outcome resulted in a standoff, the two disputants are rarely able to recall an accurate account of their interchange (Beck, 1988; Stein, 1995). In one of our recent negotiating studies (Stein, 1995), adolescents who won arguments were found to have the most inaccurate source and content memory compared with those who lost the argument or with those who compromised. Losers were found to have the most accurate overall memory, whereas compromisers had the most accurate memories of what was said, they just could not remember who said what.

I cite these findings because they underscore the role that strategic goal processes play during the encoding of information. When our subjects adopted the goals of winning an argument, they focused on two subgoals: attempting to invalidate each piece of information their opponent offered and countering with a reason as to why their own stance was better than their opponent's stance. The goal of winning biased attention and prevented winners from processing certain types of information. Winners did attend to the reasons that were offered for supporting the opposite position and the shortcomings of their own position. They transformed the meaning of their opponents' comments to include more damaging and hostile remarks than their opponent actually stated. Thus, arguing to win is one example of when errors in encoding are likely to occur. Conversely, arguing to discover the best course of action, independent of the original stance taken at the outset, is likely to result in a more accurate memory representation. More causal questions are asked during the negotiation, more comparisons are made between the two positions, and more attempts are made to determine the consequences of each position.

The amount of prior knowledge activated during encoding and the number and types of causal inferences made (Trabasso & Magliano, in press; Trabasso & Stein, in press; van den Broek, 1994) are two factors that have been continually associated with accuracy of memory in real world contexts, in academic contexts, and in studies of expertise across almost every domain (see van den Broek, 1994, for an extensive review of narrative comprehension and the importance of causal inferences). To the extent that incoming information corresponds to information already acquired, the memory representation tends to be highly accurate (Anderson, Spiro, & Montague, 1977; Mandler, 1983; Stein & Nezworski, 1978; Stein & Trabasso, 1982b; Trabasso, Secco, & van den Broek, 1984). To the extent that a causal structure can be imposed on incoming information, memory for incoming information will be very accurate. Thus, the organizational structure of an event is critical in determining whether or not an event will be remembered, and the ability to make causal inferences that link the events is also necessary.

These data strongly suggest that people have certain preferences in how they organize information for storage, and these preferences regulate the ways in which incoming information is remembered. Many different studies have now illustrated, from infancy through adulthood, that sequences of events that can be organized causally are better remembered than sequences that can be organized temporally. Thus, if people can make a causal inference to link one piece of incoming information to another, they are more likely to remember the two pieces of information than if they cannot (Mandler, 1983, 1984; Stein & Nezworski, 1978; Trabasso & Magliano, in press; Trabasso, Secco, & van den Broek, 1984).

When events as complex as everyday occurrences are considered, being able to create a causal chain of inferences that runs throughout the representation is critical to memory (Schank & Abelson, 1977; Stein & Trabasso, 1982b; Trabasso, Secco, & van den Broek, 1984; Trabasso & Stein, in press). Past studies have shown that if a causal chain can be established throughout the event sequence, then memory for the sequence will remain robust, even over long periods of time. What happens to the memory representation is that those events not on the causal chain appear in the first recall of information but do not surface in repeated recalls. Thus, if information is not causally relevant to the predominant topic or theme expressed throughout the event sequence, it will most likely be lost or not recalled (see Trabasso & Stein, in press, for an example of 4-year-old children's encoding and recall of event sequences).

With the exception of Ornstein's (Ornstein, Shapiro, Clubb, Follmer, & Baker-Ward, in press) research on children's understanding of medical procedures and exams, we have not seen eyewitness testimony researchers focus on the importance of the organizational structure of incoming information. Yet, the importance of causal schemas to interpret and remember incoming information has been known for quite some time (Ausubel, 1960; Bartlett, 1932; Mandler, 1967). The ease with which young children can remember everyday events and happenings will be directly related to the causal structure that can be inferred from the event sequence.

When emotional situations contain very familiar sequences, young children and adults have little difficulty remembering the actions and conversations of people. Children's and adults' memory for harmful acts is exceedingly good because the sequence of events that unfolds can be organized into a tight causal structure. A good example of a sequence that has tight causal structure would be one in which a perpetrator states his or her goal to do harm, tells the victims just how harm will befall them, and then carries out the specific plan of action that results in harm.

At other times, perpetrators rely on the unexpected, on deception, and on the creation of confusion for the victim. The presence of these dimensions put subjects at risk because certain types of occurrences are not expected and subjects often lack the prerequisite knowledge to interpret the incoming information. The unexpected is often experienced when a fire alarm goes off and people need to vacate a building rapidly. Similarly, people entering a bank and being held at gun point are at risk for remembering accurate details. Often, their vision is blocked by the people robbing a bank, they are pushed to the far side of a room with many different people surrounding them, or the noise and commotion of the robbery freezes and focuses their attention on a very small part of the event process.

In future research efforts, we need to explore in a more explicit manner whether the memory results of testimony studies can be explained by the types of causal processing carried out during the encoding process. We need more studies that assess what children know before encoding a specific type of event and then describe the types of interpretations that occur during the understanding process. We can then assess how prior knowledge and appraisals during encoding affected the accuracy of the memory representation. The types of strategic interventions that Saywitz and Moan-Hartie (this volume) have undertaken are essential for increasing our understanding of how children respond to and remember emotional situations. It is not the case that memory is always suggestible or changeable. Rather, it depends on how much people know before they experience a particular type of event, how they appraise and evaluate the event, and their ability to structure the incoming information into a causal sequence (Trabasso & Magliano, in press).

When the causal nature of a memory representation is considered, several hypotheses about the suggestibility of memory are not supported. The first hypothesis concerns the claim that repeated questioning increases the inaccuracy of a memory representation. The second concerns the ease with which an organized memory representation can be transformed. Although many studies focus on the ease with which a memory representation can be altered, just as many (see Stein, Wade, and Liwag, in press, for a review) show the resistance that both children and adults have in incorporating new information into current knowledge structures (Chinn & Brewer, 1993; Johnson & Siefert, in press; McNamara, Kintsch, Songer, & Kintsch, 1993). Having the same question repeated a number of times often solidifies and creates a more accurate representation (Fivush & Scwarzmueller, 1995; Poole & White, 1994; Stein & Glenn, 1979; Stein & Trabasso, 1982a). Thus, repeated questioning does not always result in inaccurate changes in a representation. Frequently, a tighter causal structure emerges (Stein & Glenn, 1979). The variables that predict the role that repeated questioning plays are the causal structure of incoming information, the content of the prior knowledge a subject already has, and whether or not a subject is able to interpret the incoming information in a causally meaningful manner (Stein & Trabasso, 1982b; Trabasso & Stein, in press; Trabasso & Magliano, in press).

## CONCLUSIONS

Several conclusions can be drawn from the preceding discussion about children's and adults memories for real-life emotional events. First and foremost, long before children reach the age of 3, they are able to encode information from their environment that conforms to the ways in which other people understand and remember the same information. They are not deficient in encoding skills. The probability of their being able to remember incoming information accurately, especially that which is the stuff of eyewitness testimony, is extremely high, given that they understood the nature of the event when it occurred and that they were able to organize the encoded information into a causal representation.

The role that highly structured input and causal inferences play in remembering are two dimensions that predict and account for both short- and long-term memory across almost every domain of interest (van den Broek, 1994). Although testimony researchers have shown that familiarity plays a role in remembering an event, it is not the familiarity of an event, per se, that leads to an accurate memory representation. Stein and Nezworski (1978) showed that event sequences that were arbitrarily organized and difficult to encode in a causal fashion could not be remembered, despite repeated presentations of the sequence. Thus, some sequences are inherently difficult to learn and remember because the incoming information cannot be organized into a coherent representation.

In line with these comments, we illustrated that the constructive process of remembering had no direct bearing on the accuracy of a memory representation. All memory representations result from constructive processes. The types of inferences and appraisals that are made during the understanding process determine the accuracy of the representation (Trabasso & Magliano, in press) and the stability of the representation.

We also illustrated the richness of 3- to 5-year-old children's narrative accounts of real-life emotional situations. We showed that the overwhelming majority of children recalled emotional events in a causally coherent manner and always included the same sets of dimension in their narratives. Specifically, children's narrations show that they organize emotional experience according to a goal-structured model of understanding. When recalling emotional memories, they talk about the event that precipitated their emotional response, who caused the precipitating event, whether or not the event violated their expectations, how the event changed the status of personally meaningful goals, what they wanted to do about the change in their goals, what they actually did, and the results of their actions.

The fact that children had such rich representations of emotional events before talking to their parents argues against the notion that they are learning everything about the event through talk or interaction with other people. Although children and adults both learn a great deal through conversing and observing other people, they also learn a great deal through personal problem solving, when no one else is present. The important point, however, is that even young children are able to construct detailed and stable representations of an event that contain both similarities and differences when compared to those of other people, such as their parents. When children are asked to talk about their representation of an event with their parent, no guarantee exists that children will accept what their parents tell them (den Bak & Ross, in press; Stein et al., 1994). Furthermore, children correct their parents representations of events, especially when parents attempt to tell how the children reacted and felt emotionally.

Thus, we argued for the importance of assessing prior knowledge and individual representations before putting together two people. Interactions between two individuals can promote learning from one another, but they can also promote disagreement and further entrenchment of a position. If children and adults each have a highly organized representation of an event before interacting, repeated interchanges with the other person does not necessarily alter either one of the representations. However, there are situations in which interaction can result in acquiring a more accurate representation of an event. We illustrated that in many emotional contexts, children and adults re-review how an event unfolded in order to better understand the nature and predictability of the event. This is especially true in medical situations in which children are subjected to invasive procedures that can be quite painful.

Finally, we urged that more consideration be given to building a model of the understanding process so that a priori predictions can be made about the accuracy and stability of memory. We now have an accumulated wealth of knowledge that memory can be both accurate and inaccurate, depending on the situation. A model of the understanding process would force us to consider just what inferences, appraisals, and prior knowledge affect both short- and long-term memory.

## ACKNOWLEDGMENTS

This research was funded in part by grants from the Smart Foundation on Early Learning to Nancy L. Stein and from the National Institute of Child Health and Human Development (Grant HD 25742 to Tom Trabasso and Nancy L. Stein), by a grant from the Spencer Foundation to Tom Trabasso, and by a grant from the National Institute of Mental Health (Grant MH44045) to Susan Folkman, Nancy Stein, and Tom Trabasso. I thank Bill Banks, Kathy Pezdek, Tom Trabasso, and Luminita Voinescu for helpful comments on an earlier draft of this manuscript.

## REFERENCES

Alessandri, S. M., Sullivan, M. W., & Lewis, M. (1990). Violation of expectancy and frustration in early infancy. *Developmental Psychology, 26*(5), 738–744.

Anderson, R. C, Spiro, R. J., & Montague. W. E. (1977). *Schooling and the acquisition of knowledge.* Hillsdale, NJ: Erlbaum.

Ausubel, D. (1960). The use of advance organizers in the learning and retention of meaningful material. *Journal of Educational Psychology, 51,* 267–272.

Bartlett, F. (1932). *Remembering. A study in experimental and social psychology.* Cambridge, UK: Cambridge University Press.

Bartsch, K., & Wellman, H. (1995). *Children talk about the mind.* Oxford: Oxford University Press.

Bauer, P., & Mandler, J. M. (1989). One thing follows another. Effects of temporal structure on 1- to 2-year olds' recall of events. *Developmental Psychology, 25,* 197–206.

Bauer, P., & Mandler, J. M. (1990). Remembering what happened next: Very young children's recall of event sequences. In R. Fivush & J. A. Hudson (Eds.), *Knowing and remembering in young children* (pp. 9–29). New York: Cambridge University Press.

Bauer, P., & Shore, C. M. (1987). Making a memorable event: The effects of familiarity and organization of young children's recall of action sequences. *Cognitive Development, 2,* 327–338.

Beck, A. T. (1988). *Love is not enough.* New York: Harper & Row.

Bloom, L., & Capatides, J. B. (1987a). Expression of affect and the emergence of language. *Child Development, 58,* 1513–1522.

Bloom, L., & Capatides, J. B. (1987b). Sources of meaning in the acquisition of complex syntax: The sample case of causality. *Journal of Experimental Child Psychology, 43,* 112–128.

Case, R. (1991). *The mind's staircase.* Hillsdale, NJ: Erlbaum.

Chi, M. (Ed.). (1983). *Trends in memory development research.* New York: Karger.

Chinn, C., & Brewer, W. F. (1993). The role of anomalous data in knowledge acquisition: A theoretical framework and implications for science instruction. *Review of Educational Research, 68*(1), 1–49.

Den Bak, I., & Ross, H. S. (in press). I'm telling! The content, context, and consequences of children's tattling on their siblings. *Social Development.*

Donaldson, M. (1992). *Human minds: An Exploration.* New York: Allen Lane, The Penguin Press.

Duncan, S., & Farley, A. (1990). Achieving parent–child coordination through convention: Fixed- and variable-sequence conventions. *Child Development, 61,* 742–753.

Dunn, J. (1988). *The beginnings of social understanding.* Cambridge, MA: Harvard University Press.

Dunn, J. (1993). *Young children's close relationships: Beyond attachment.* Newbury Park, CA: Sage Publications.

Dunn, J., & Brown, J. (1991). Relationships, talk about feelings, and the development of affect regulation in early childhood. In J. Garber & K. A. Dodge (Eds.), *The development of emotion regulation and dysregulation.* New York: Cambridge University Press.

Epstein, N., Pretzer, J. L., & Fleming, B. (1987). The role of cognitive appraisal in self-reports. *Behavior Therapy, 18,* 51–69.

Eth, S., & Pynoos, R. S. (1985). *Post-traumatic stress disorder in children.* Washington, DC: American Psychiatric Press.

Fischer, K. W. (1980). A theory of cognitive development. The control and construction of hierarchical skills. *Psychological Review, 87,* 477–531.

Fivush, R. (1991). The social construction of personal narratives. *Merrill Palmer Quarterly, 37,* 59–82.

Fivush, R., & Hammond, N. A. (1990). Autobiographical memory across the preschool years: Toward reconceptualizing childhood amnesia. In R. Fivush & J. A. Hudson (Eds.), *Knowing and remembering in young children* (pp. 223–248). New York: Cambridge University Press.

Fivush, R., & Schwarzmueller, A. (1995). Say it once again: Effects of repeated questions on children's event recall. *Journal of Traumatic Stress, 8*(4), 555–579.

Folkman, S., & Stein, N. L. (in press). A goal-process approach to analyzing narrative memories for AIDS-related stressful events. In N. L. Stein, P. A. Ornstein, B. Tversky, and C. Brainerd (Eds.), *Memory for everyday and emotional events*. Hillsdale, NJ: Erlbaum.

Frijda, N. H. (1987). Emotion, cognitive structure, and action tendency. *Cognition and Emotion*, **1**, 115–143.

Garry, M., Loftus, E. F., & Brown, S. W. (1994). Memory: A river runs through it. *Consciousness and Cognition*, **3**(3,4), 438–451.

Gergely, G., Nadasdy, Z., Csibra, G., & Biro, S. (in press). Taking the intentional stance at 12 months of age. *Cognition*.

Graesser, A. C., Singer, M. S., & Trabasso, T. (1994). Constructing inferences during narrative text comprehension. *Psychological Review*, **101**, 371–395.

Haith, M. M. (1994). Visual expectations as the first step toward the development of future-oriented processes. In M. M. Haith, J. B. Benson, R. J. Roberts, & B. F. Pennington (Eds.), *The development of future-oriented processes* pp. 11–38. Chicago: University of Chicago Press.

Holliday, L. (1995). *Children in the Holocaust and World War II: Their secret diaries*. New York: Pocket Books.

Horton, W. S., & Keysar, B. (in press). When do speakers take into account common ground? *Cognition*.

Hudson, J. (1990). The emergence of autobiographical memory in mother–child conversation. In R. Fivush & J. A. Hudson (Eds.), *Knowing and remembering in young children* (pp. 166–196). New York: Cambridge University Press.

Huttenlocher, J., Smiley, P., & Charney, R. (1983). Emergence of action categories in the child: Evidence from verb meanings. *Psychological Review*, **90**, 72–93.

Johnson, H. M., & Siefert, C. M. (in press). Sources of the continued influence effect: When misinformation in memory affects later inferences. *Journal of Experimental Psychology: Learning, Memory, and Cognition*.

Lazarus, R. S., & Folkman, S. (1984). *Stress, appraisal, and coping*. New York: Springer.

Levine, L., & Stein, N. L. (1995). *Young children's emotional memories of themselves and other children*. Unpublished manuscript, University of Chicago.

Lewis, M., Alessandri, S. M., & Sullivan, M. W. (1990). Violation of expectancy, loss of control, and anger expressions in young infants. *Developmental Psychology*, **26**(5), 745–751.

Lewis, M., & Saarni, C. (1993). *Lying and deception in everyday life*. New York: Guilford.

Liwag, M. D., & Stein, N. L. (1995). Children's memory for emotional events: The importance of emotion cue retrieval strategies. *Journal of Experimental Child Psychology*, **60**, 2–31.

Loftus, E. (1994). *The myth of repressed memory: False memories and allegations of sexual abuse*. New York: St Martin's.

McNamara, D. S., Kintsch, E., Songer, N. B., & Kintsch, W. (1993). *Text coherence, background knowledge, and levels of understanding in learning from text*. (Tech. Rep. No. 93-04). University of Colorado, Boulder, CO.

Mandler, G. (1967). Organization and memory. In K. W. Spence & J. T. Spence (Eds.), *The psychology of learning and motivation* (Vol. 1). New York: Academic Press.

Mandler, J. M. (1983). Representation. In J. H. Flavell & E. M. Markman (Eds.), *Cognitive development*. Vol. 3 of P. Mussen (Ed.), *Handbook of child psychology*. New York: Wiley.

Mandler, J. M. (1984). *Stories, scripts, and scenes: Aspects of schema theory*. Hillsdale, NJ: Erlbaum.

Mandler, J. M., & McDonough, L. (in press). Nonverbal recall. In N. L. Stein, P. A. Ornstein, B. Tversky, & C. Brainerd (Eds.), *Memory for everyday and emotional events*. Hillsdale, NJ: Erlbaum.

Mandler, J. M., & Stein, N. L. (1974). Recall and recognition of pictures by children as a function of organization and distractor similarity. *Journal of Experimental Psychology*, **102**(4), 657–669.

Meltzhoff, A. (1988). Infant imitation after a 1-week delay: Long-term memory for novel acts and multiple stimuli. *Developmental Psychology*, **24**, 470–486.

Merritt, K. A., Ornstein, P. A., & Spicker, B. (1994). Children's memory of a salient medical procedure: Implications for testimony. *Pediatrics*, **94**, 17–23.

Myers, N. A., Clifton, R. K., & Clarkson, M. G. (1987). When they were young: Almost threes remember two years ago. *Infant Behavior and Development*, **10**, 123–132.

Neisser, U. (1982). Snapshots or benchmarks? In U. Neisser (Ed.), *Memory observed* (pp. 43–48). San Francisco: W. H. Freeman.

Neisser, U., & Harsch, N. (1992). Phantom flashbulbs. False recollections of hearing the news about *Challenger*. In E. Winograd & U. Neisser (Eds.), *Affect and accuracy in recall: Studies of flashbulb memories* (pp. 9–31). New York: Cambridge University Press.

Nelson, K. (1990). Remembering, forgetting, and childhood amnesia. In R. Fivush & J. A. Hudson (Eds.), *Knowing and remembering in young children* (pp. 301–316). New York: Cambridge University Press.

Noller, P. (1984). *Nonverbal communication and marital interaction.* New York: Pergamon Press.

Oatley, K., & Johnson-Laird, P. (1987). Toward a cognitive theory of emotion. *Cognition and Emotion,* 1(1), 29–50.

Ornstein, P. A., Shapiro, L. R., Clubb, P. A., Follmer, A., & Baker-Ward, L. (in press). The influence of prior knowledge on children's memory for salient medical experiences. In N. L. Stein, P. A. Ornstein, B. Tversky, and C. Brainerd (Eds.), *Memory for everyday and emotional events.* Hillsdale, NJ: Erlbaum.

Piaget, J. (1981). *Intelligence and affectivity.* Palo Alto, CA: Annual Reviews.

Poole, D. A., & White, L. T. (1994). Tell me again and again: Stability and change in the repeated testimonies of children and adults. In M. Zaragosa, J. R. Graham, G. C. N. Hall, R. Hirshman, & Y. S. Ben-Porath (Eds.), *Memory and testimony in the child witness.* Thousand Oaks, CA: Sage, Inc.

Reznick, J. S. (1994). In search of infant expectation. In M. M. Haith, J. B. Benson, R. J. Roberts, & B. F. Pennington (Eds.), *The development of future-oriented processes.* Chicago. The University of Chicago Press.

Rogoff, B. & Mistry, J. (1990) The social and functional context of children's remembering. In R. Fivush & J. A. Hudson (Eds.), *Knowing and remembering in young children* (pp. 197–222) New York: Cambridge University Press.

Schank, R. (1982). *Dynamic memory.* New York: Cambridge University Press.

Schank, R., & Abelson, R. (1977). *Scripts, plans, goals, and understanding.* Hillsdale, NJ: Erlbaum.

Siegler, R. (1991). The microgenetic method. A direct means for studying cognitive development. *American Psychologist,* 46(6), 606–620.

Snow, C. E. (1990). Building memories. The ontogeny of autobiography. In D. Cicchetti and M. Beeghley (Eds.), *The self in transition: Infancy to childhood* (pp. 213–242). Chicago: University of Chicago Press.

Sroufe, A. (1979). Socioemotional development. In J. Osofsky (Ed.), *The handbook of infant development* (pp. 462–516). New York: Wiley.

Stein, N. L. (1995). *The role of outcome solutions in resolving and remembering arguments.* Paper presented at the Symposium on Conversation, Language Society of America, July, Albuquerque, NM.

Stein, N. L., Bernas, R., Calicchia, D., & Wright, A. (1995). Understanding and resolving arguments: The dynamics of negotiation. In B. Britton & A. G. Graesser (Eds.), *Models of understanding.* Hillsdale, NJ: Erlbaum.

Stein, N. L., Calicchia, D., & Bernas, R. (1995). *Understanding and resolving arguments: Do compromise instructions help?* Paper presented at the Symposium on Conversation, Linguistic Society of America, July, Albuquerque, NM.

Stein, N. L., Folkman, S., Trabasso, T., & Christopher-Richards, A. (1995). *The role of appraisal and goal processes in predicting psychological well-being in bereaved caregivers.* Paper presented at The Rashomon Conference, University of California, San Francisco.

Stein, N. L., & Glenn, C. G. (1979). An analysis of story comprehension in elementary school children. In R. O. Freedle (Ed.), *New directions in discourse processing* (Vol. 2, pp. 53–119). Norwood, NJ: Ablex.

Stein, N. L., & Levine, L. (1987). Thinking about feelings: The development and organization of emotional knowledge. In R. Snow & M. Farr (Eds.), *Aptitude, learning and instruction* (Vol. 3, pp. 165–197). Hillsdale, NJ: Erlbaum.

Stein, N. L., & Levine, L. (1989). The causal organization of emotion knowledge: A developmental study. *Cognition and Emotion,* 3(4), 343–378.

Stein, N. L., & Liwag, M. D. (in press). A goal-appraisal process approach to understanding and remembering emotional events. In P. van den Broek, P. Bauer, & T. Bourg (Eds.), *Developmental spans in event comprehension and representation.* Hillsdale, NJ: Erlbaum.

Stein, N. L., & Mandler, J. M. (1975). Development of detection and recognition of geometric and real figures. *Child Development,* **46,** 379–388.

Stein, N. L., & Nezworski, M. T. (1978). The effect of organization and instructional set on story memory. *Discourse Processes,* **1,** 177–193.

Stein, N. L., Ornstein, P. A., Tversky, B., and Brainerd, C. (Eds.). (in press). *Memory for everyday and emotional events.* Hillsdale, NJ: Erlbaum.

Stein, N. L., & Trabasso, T. (1982a). Children's understanding of stories: A basis for moral judgment and resolution. In C. J. Brainerd & M. Pressley (Eds.), *Verbal processes in children* (pp. 161–188). New York: Springer-Verlag.

Stein, N. L., & Trabasso, T. (1982b). What's in a story: An approach to comprehension and instruction. In R. Glaser (Ed.), *Advances in instructional psychology* (Vol. 2, pp. 213–267). Hillsdale, NJ: Erlbaum.

Stein, N. L., & Trabasso, T. (1985). The search after meaning: Comprehension and comprehension monitoring. In F. Morrison, C. Lord, & D. Keating (Eds.), *Advances in applied developmental psychology* (Vol. 2, pp. 33–57). New York: Academic Press.

Stein, N. L., Trabasso, T., & Liwag, M. D. (1992). The representation and organization of emotional experience. Unfolding the emotional episode. In M. Lewis & J. Haviland (Eds.), *Handbook of emotion* (pp. 279–300). New York: Guilford.

Stein, N. L., Trabasso, T., & Liwag, M. D. (1994). The Rashomon phenomenon: Personal frames and future-oriented appraisals in memory for emotional events. In M. Haith, J. B. Benson, R. J. Roberts, Jr., & B. F. Pennington. *The development of future-oriented processes.* Chicago: University of Chicago Press.

Stein, N. L., Wade, E., & Liwag, M. D. (in press). A theoretical approach to understanding and remembering emotional events. In N. L. Stein, P. A. Ornstein, B. Tversky, and C. Brainerd (Eds.), *Memory for everyday and emotional events.* Hillsdale, NJ: Erlbaum.

Stenberg, C. R., & Campos, J. J. (1990). The development of anger expression in infancy. In N. L. Stein, B. Leventhal, & T. Trabasso (Eds.), *Psychological and biological approaches to emotion.* Hillsdale, NJ: Erlbaum.

Stern, D. (1985). *The interpersonal world of the infant.* New York: Basic Books.

Stern, D. (1992). *Diary of a baby.* New York: Basic Books.

Suh, S., & Trabasso, T. (1993). Inferences during on-line processing: Converging evidence from discourse analysis, talk-aloud protocols, and recognition priming. *Journal of Memory and Language,* **32,** 279–301.

Terr, I. (1988). What happens to early memory of trauma? A study of 20 children under age 5 at the time of documented traumatic events. *Journal of the American Academy of Child and Adolescent Psychiatry,* **27,** 96–104.

Trabasso, T., & Magliano, J. P. (in press). How do children understand what they read and what can we do to help them? In M. Graves, P. van den Broek, & B. Taylor (Eds.), *The first R: A right of all children.* New York: Teachers College Press.

Trabasso, T., & Ozyurek, A. (1995). *Evaluation in narrative understanding.* Paper presented at the Symposium on Conversation, Linguistic Society of America, July, Albuquerque, NM.

Trabasso, T., Secco, T., & van den Broek, P. (1984). Causal cohesion and story coherence. In H. Mandl, N. L. Stein, & T. Trabasso (Eds.), *Learning and comprehension of text* (pp. 83–111). Hillsdale, NJ: Erlbaum.

Trabasso, T., & Stein, N. L. (1994). Using goal-plan knowledge to merge the past with the present and the future in narrating events on-line. In M. Haith, J. Benson, R. Roberts, & B. Pennington (Eds.), *The development of future-oriented processes* (pp. 323–349). Chicago: University of Chicago Press.

Trabasso, T., & Stein, N. L. (in press). Narrating, representing, and remembering event sequences. In P. van den Broek, P. Bauer, and T. Bourg (Eds.), *Developmental spans in event comprehension and representation.* Hillsdale, NJ: Erlbaum.

Trabasso, T., Stein, N. L., & Johnson, N. (1981). Children's knowledge of events: A causal analysis of story structure. *The Psychology of Learning and Motivation, 15,* 237–282.

Trabasso, T., Stein, N. L., Rodkin, P. C., Munger, G. P., & Baughn, C. (1992). Knowledge of goals and plans in the on-line narration of events, *Cognitive Development, 7,* 133–170.

Usher, J. A., & Neisser, U. (1993). Childhood amnesia and the beginnings of memory for four early life events. *Journal of Experimental Psychology: General, 122*(2), 155–165.

Van Den Broek, P. (1994). Comprehension and memory of narrative texts: Inferences and coherence. In M. A. Gernsbacher (Ed.), *Handbook of psycholinguistics.* (pp. 539–584). San Diego, CA: Academic Press.

Von Hofsten, C. (1994). Planning and perceiving what is going to happen next. In M. M. Haith, J. B. Benson, R. J. Roberts, & B. F. Pennington (Eds.), *The development of future-oriented processes.* Chicago: University of Chicago Press.

Willatts, P. (1990). The development of problem-solving strategies in infancy. In D. Bjorklund (Ed.), *Children's strategies: Contemporary views of cognitive development* (pp. 23–66). Hillsdale, NJ: Erlbaum.

Wolf, D. P. (1990). Being of several minds: Voices and versions of the self in early childhood. In D. Cicchetti & M. Beeghley (Eds.), *The self in transition: Infancy to childhood* (pp. 213–242). Chicago: University of Chicago Press.

Wortman, C. B., & Silver, R. C. (1990). Successful mastery of bereavement and widowhood. A life course perspective. In P. B. Baltes & M. M. Baltes (Eds.), *Successful aging.* New York: Cambridge University Press.

# III. CHILDHOOD MEMORY: DISTORTION AND SUGGESTIBILITY

In a 1993 *American Psychologist* article, Elizabeth Loftus proposed an alternative explanation to the clinical notions of "repression" and subsequent "recovery" of memory for traumatic events. She proposed that perhaps in many so-called repressed memory cases, the traumatic event never happened, which is why it was not remembered for so many years, and that the memory that appeared later in life was really a false memory that had been suggestively planted, most notably by a therapist. Loftus's explanation is a compelling one because of its parsimony. However, this explanation relies on a very strong notion of the construct of suggestibility. According to this view, a significant proportion of the population has come to believe that they had been sexually abused, often by a parent or stepparent, when in fact they had not, and this belief has resulted from their therapist's ability to plant suggestively such events in their memory.

Within the field of cognitive psychology there is a wealth of research over the past 20 years on the suggestibility of memory. In a typical study on suggestibility, participants first view a sequence of slides, a videotape, or a film of an event. After viewing this event, they read a narrative or are asked some questions that intentionally mislead them about the identity of a small set of target items viewed in the original event (the misled condition), or they do not receive the misleading information (the control condition). The principal result is that participants are more accurate recognizing the original target item in the control condition than in the misled condition; that is, they are misled by the postevent information presented in the narrative or questions.

In the early research in this area, recognition memory differences of 20 to 30% between the misled and control items were not unusual. However, subsequent research findings have forced a qualification of this conclusion; although the eyewitness suggestibility effect is real, the magnitude of the effect is highly variable. In a recent review of the research on eyewitness suggestibility, Lindsay (1993) argued:

> At present, we conclude that under some conditions MPT (misleading postevent information) can impair people's ability to remember what they witness and can lead them to believe that they witnessed things they did not, but that *neither of these effects is as large or robust as earlier research suggested* [italics added]. (p. 89)

Thus, the ability to mislead people regarding inconsequential events such as whether they saw a stop sign or a yield sign in a slide sequence, although statistically significant, does not appear to be robust. Furthermore, the extent to which such findings generalize to the implantation of whole events in memory has only recently been addressed.

Nonetheless, it seems clear that *some* recovered memories for childhood abuse are true and *some* are suggestively planted. The chapters in the third section of this volume begin to articulate the conditions under which memory is either vulnerable to or resistant to suggestibility. This is a critical issue for therapists, caseworkers, attorneys, and parents who are trying to sort out which memories are likely to be based on true events and which memories are more likely based on false events that were suggestively planted. This work carries on the tradition of the previous suggestibility research, but focuses on suggestively planting entire false events in memory, rather than simply suggestively changing an aspect of a true event in memory. This represents an important change from the earlier work in this area.

It is also worth noting at the outset that the research presented in this section does not involve real-world cases of traumatic events, and it would be an ethical violation to attempt to plant traumatic false events in memory. Nonetheless, this research is critical to the argument regarding the pervasiveness of suggestively planted false events in memory.

## REFERENCES

Lindsay, D. S. (1993). Eyewitness suggestibility. *Current Directions in Psychological Science, 2,* 86–89.

Loftus, E. F. (1993). The reality of repressed memories. *American Psychologist, 48,* 518–537.

# Memory for Childhood Events: How Suggestible Is It?

KATHY PEZDEK[1] AND CHANTAL ROE

*Center for Organizational and Behavioral Sciences,*
*The Claremont Graduate School, Claremont, California 91711*

The veracity of children's memory is frequently doubted because it is assumed that first, children's memory is generally not very good, and second, children and their memories are too vulnerable to suggestibility to be credible. In this article these two assumptions are evaluated and three experiments are presented that address constraints on the construct of suggestibility. In the first experiment, it is reported that memory for a more frequently occurring event is more resistant to suggestibility than is memory for an event experienced only once. This finding is especially relevant to memory for child abuse as it is common for perpetrators to frequently abuse the same child. In two additional experiments it is reported that it is relatively difficult to suggest to a child that something occurred when it did not. These results suggest that although memories for childhood events may be imperfect, they are not likely to be confabulated.

A great deal of attention has recently been focused on the veracity of children's memory. The specific context for this concern is the increase in the past two decades in the number of child abuse cases reported (Baker, 1992) and, in reaction, the debate about whether such claims are dependable. Whereas numerous researchers have reported that young children's memory is generally reliable and highly resistant to suggestibility (e.g., Berliner, 1985; Goodman, Rudy, Bottoms, & Aman, 1990; Jones & McGraw, 1987), others have described children as unreliable witnesses because they easily confuse fantasy with reality and are likely to incorporate information suggested by interviewers into their own memory (Feher, 1988; Gardner, 1989; Schuman, 1986).

The principal basis for doubting the veracity of childhood memories rests on two assumptions: first, that children's memory is not very good anyway and, second, that children and their memories are too vulnerable to suggestibility to be credible. This article focuses on evaluating both of these assumptions and presenting data that inform our understanding of some of the specific conditions under which memory is likely to be resistant to versus vulnerable to suggestibility. In the first portion of this article, literature regarding developmental differences in memory and suggestibility is reviewed. In the second portion of this article, three experiments are presented that address constraints on the construct of suggestibility.

This article is reprinted by permission from *Consciousness and Cognition,* Volume 3, pp. 374–387 (1994).

[1] To whom correspondence and reprint requests should be addressed.

## DEVELOPMENTAL DIFFERENCES IN MEMORY AND SUGGESTIBILITY

What do we know about the memory ability of children of various ages? Marked developmental differences have been reported in a range of traditional laboratory tests of memory. Generally, when children are asked to free recall an interaction with a stranger (Leippe, Romanczyk, & Manion, 1991), a story (Saywitz, 1987), or a list of words (Flavell, Beach, & Chinsky, 1966), there is a linear increase in the completeness of recall across the age span from preschool to early adolescence. Also, using stories (Paris & Upton, 1976) and pictures (Paris & Mahoney, 1974), 11-year-old children are more likely than 5-year-old children to make semantic inferences from information presented, and young children are generally less likely to use schemata for comprehension than are older children (Chi, 1978). However, although younger children free recall "less" than older children, their recall is *not less accurate;* that is, omission errors are more common with younger children but commission errors are generally rare and do not differ with age. This finding was most recently reported in a study by Goodman and Reed (1986) in which 3- and 6-year-old children played "Simon Says" with an adult male in a naturalistic setting. In contrast to results of *recall* tests, age differences in *recognition* memory are less pronounced (cf. Ceci, Ross, & Toglia, 1987; Jones, Swift, & Johnson, 1988; List, 1986; Nurcombe, 1986). Together these results suggest that if a child is asked direct questions about "what happened?" the content of their response is likely to be accurate but incomplete.

How do these developmental differences in memory relate to possible developmental differences in the suggestibility of memory? Although research on the suggestibility of children's memory can be traced back to the early twentieth century (cf. Binet, 1900), an increase in the number of studies on this topic has been noted, especially over the past 15 years. In this more recent work, a number of researchers, using a diverse set of methodological approaches with children of various ages, have reached quite mixed results. As this literature has been reviewed in detail elsewhere (cf. Ceci & Bruck, 1993; Cole & Loftus, 1987), the purpose of this discussion is simply to summarize these findings.

Whether age differences in the suggestibility of memory are observed depends on the age of the participants. As a general statement, few dispute the finding that "by the age of 10 or 11, children are no more vulnerable to suggestion than adults" (Cole & Loftus, 1987, p. 195). This conclusion follows from studies that have reported no difference in the suggestibility of memory between preadolescent children and adults with a wide range of tasks involving recall of a live confrontation (King & Yuille, 1987; Marin, Holmes, Guth, & Kovac, 1979), multiple-choice questions about a film clip (Cohen & Harnick, 1980), or answers to misleading questions about a cartoon slide sequence (Duncan, Whitney, & Kunen, 1982), a live lecture (Flin, Boon, Knox, & Bull, 1992), or an audiotape of a crime (Saywitz, 1987).

On the other hand, when *preschool children* have been compared to older children and adults, significant differences in the suggestibility of memory have been reliably reported. This conclusion follows from a review of 18 studies by Ceci and Bruck (1993) in which 15 of the 18 studies reported that preschoolers were more suggestible. Again, a wide range of tasks were employed across these 18 studies, many of which showed impressive ecological validity.

However, although this finding reflects the general developmental trend when the results of preschoolers are compared with those of older age groups, it is important to note that there are constraints on preschool children's vulnerability to suggestibility, and these are just beginning to be articulated. For example, Goodman et al. (1990) reported that 4- and 7-year-old children were strongly resistant to suggestibility regarding touching that did not occur and, in general, more resistant to suggestibility if they had participated in rather than simply observed activities involving playing with a clown. And Goodman, Aman, and Hirschman (1987) reported that 3- to 6-year-old children who visited an immunization clinic were more resistant to suggestion regarding the actions that occurred in the clinic and the nurse's appearance than to those regarding the characteristics of the room. These results are especially important given that in most cases that involve children's testimony, the actions of the perpetrator and their identity are more important than what the room looked like.

Together, these results suggest that in evaluating the reliability of memory of children of various ages, preadolescents should be considered as reliable as adults and no more vulnerable to suggestibility. On the other hand, although the recall of preschoolers is generally less complete but no less accurate than that of older children and adults, memory of preschool children is more vulnerable to potential sources of suggestibility. However, even so, there are constraints on the conditions under which adults and children of all ages are vulnerable to suggestibility. The program of research reported in this paper addresses some of the conditions under which memory is vulnerable to versus resistant to suggestibility.

## CONSTRAINTS ON THE CONSTRUCT OF SUGGESTIBILITY

In a typical study on suggestibility (Loftus, 1975; Loftus, Miller, & Burns, 1978; Pezdek, 1977), participants first view a sequence of slides, a videotape, or a film of an event. After viewing this event, they read a narrative or are asked some questions that intentionally mislead them about the identity of a small set of target items viewed in the original event (the misled condition), or they do not receive the misleading information (the control condition). The principal result is that participants are more accurate recognizing the original target item in the control condition than in the misled condition; that is, they are misled by the postevent information presented in the narrative or questions. Although the *eyewitness suggestibility effect* or *misinformation effect* is real and often robust, it does not occur under all conditions, and the size of the effect is highly variable (cf. Lindsay, 1993).

Two principles have been hypothesized to predict the probability that suggestibility will occur. The first principle is based on the hypothesis that suggestibility occurs because the test item is more likely to be matched with the falsely suggested information than the original information, although both are present in memory (Belli, 1989; Christiaansen & Ochalek, 1983; Lindsay & Johnson, 1987; McClockey & Zaragoza, 1985; Tversky & Tuchin, 1989). Accordingly, the probability of suggestibility depends on whether the retrieval conditions at the time of test bias one to use a strategy for accessing the original memory, in which case suggestibility would not occur, or a strategy for accessing the misleading memory, in which case suggestibility would occur.

In support of this view, Pezdek and Greene (1993) used the typical suggestibility paradigm but participants were tested with either a verbal recognition memory test (matching the verbal modality of the suggested item) or a visual recognition memory test (matching the pictorial modality of the original item). The typical suggestibility effect was obtained in the verbal test condition. However, with the visual recognition memory test the hit rates did not significantly differ between the control and misled conditions. Additional results supportive of this model of suggestibility were reported by Bekerian and Bowers (1983). Again, using the typical suggestibility paradigm, half of their subjects were presented with test items in a random order (i.e., the retrieval environment did not match the environment of the original memory) and half were presented test items in the order that matched the order seen during input. The suggestibility effect resulted in the random order but not in the matched order condition.

The second principle that specifies constraints on the suggestibility of memory is that of *trace strength theory* (cf. Brainerd, Reyna, Howe, & Kingma, 1990; Ceci et al., 1987; Howe, 1991; Pezdek & Roe, 1994). Trace strength theory specifies that stronger memories are more likely to resist suggestibility than weaker memories. Trace strength theory, for example, has been used to explain why younger children appear to be more vulnerable to suggestibility than older children (i.e., the strength of the original information in memory is weaker for younger children). Also, Lindberg (1991) demonstrated that children were less suggestible in domains in which they had greater knowledge (i.e., greater memory strength). However, in none of these studies has the strength of information in memory been directly varied for the purpose of measuring the effect on the vulnerability of the information to suggestibility. This is the focus of the study that follows.

### Memory and Suggestibility for Frequently Occurring Events

One of the principal assumptions examined in this paper is the view that memory for the sexual abuse is unreliable despite the fact that the abuse occurred frequently. A test of the suggestibility of memory as a function of the frequency of presentation of the original event was recently conducted in our laboratory (Pezdek & Roe, 1994). This issue is relevant to memory for traumatic events such as sexual abuse because perpetrators of sexual abuse often repeatedly abuse a child; sexual abuse is rarely an isolated event.

In this study, the typical suggestibility paradigm was used with the modification that in the presentation phase target items were presented either one or two times each. It has been demonstrated in previous studies (cf. Ebbinghaus, 1964, originally published 1885) that the strength of memory increases with the frequency of presentation. If stronger memories are more likely to resist suggestibility than weaker memories, then the difference in recognition memory between misled and control test items would be predicted to be greater under less memorable conditions (with frequency one) than under more memorable conditions (with frequency two). This predicted pattern of results would be reflected in a significant interaction of misled/control test item type with frequency.

*Method.* Sixty 4-year-old and 60 10-year-old children participated in a 2 (age) × 2 (frequency) × 2 (misled vs control condition) mixed design with age as the only between-subjects variable. They viewed two slide sequences, each 38 slides in length. Slides were presented for 3 s each. One sequence depicted a woman returning home from grocery shopping and performing various activities in the kitchen. The other sequence included a man working on a construction site performing various activities associated with building a house. In each sequence there were two target slides. In the kitchen sequence the two target slides were (a) a picture of the woman reaching up into an open cabinet and taking out a *plate* and (b) a picture of the woman reaching into a kitchen drawer and pulling out a *spoon.* In the construction sequence the two target slides were (a) a picture of the workman next to a pile of boards picking up a *hammer* and (b) a picture of the workman bending down to pick up a *brick.* Each child viewed all four target slides with two presented once each (one control and one misled) and two presented twice each (one control and one misled). Prior to viewing the slide sequences, the children were instructed to look at each picture carefully as they would be asked some questions afterward about what they had seen.

Following the presentation phase was a distractor task and then a postevent narrative was read. The narrative described the two slide sequences, summarizing the activities that were observed. A description of both target slides was included in each narrative. The misleading sentences suggested that the *plate* was a *bowl,* the *spoon* was a *fork,* the *hammer* was a *screwdriver,* and the *brick* was a *rock.* The control sentences were identical except that the generic phrase "something" was substituted for the name of each specific item (e.g., "The woman reached into the kitchen drawer and pulled out *something.*"). Following another brief distractor task, a recognition memory test was administered. The test was designed following suggestions of Tversky and Tuchin (1989). There were 12 test sentences each describing one of the four target slides. There were three versions of each of the four target items, each worded the same except that the key word referred to either (a) the item in the slide, (b) the item mentioned in the misleading condition of the narrative, or (c) a foil item. The foil items were *cup* for *plate, knife* for *spoon, paintbrush* for *hammer,* and *newspaper* for *brick.* The use of foil test items in addition to the slide and narrative test items allows an assessment of whether participants who were misled simply forgot the original slide item (in which case they would be equally likely to false alarm to the narrative and the foil test item) or whether they were more specifically misled to remember the item viewed in the slide as being that suggested in the narrative (in which case they would false alarm to the narrative test item but correctly reject the foil test item). As each sentence was read, each child responded "yes" or "no," indicating whether the sentence described *one of the pictures* they had viewed in the initial presentation phase.

*Results and Discussion.* The major predictions involve the participants' ability to discriminate between items they saw in the original slides and the corresponding items suggested in the narrative. Thus, the signal detection measure of $d'$ was computed. The $d'$ measure unconfounds response bias from memory sensitivity.

TABLE 1
Mean $d'$ Data in Each Condition for 4-Year-Old and
10-Year-Old Children in the Frequency Experiment

|  | Age 4 | Age 10 |
|---|---|---|
| Frequency 1 |  |  |
| Control | .28 | 1.52 |
| Misled | −.66 | −.57 |
| Frequency 2 |  |  |
| Control | .66 | 1.78 |
| Misled | .39 | .38 |

Because each subject responded to only one target item per each of the four conditions, the $d'$ values were based on the group hit and false alarm rates. These $d'$ data are presented in Table 1. These data follow the predicted pattern that the differences in $d'$ between the control and misled conditions were greater for frequency 1 than for frequency 2.

It was necessary to use nonparametric statistics to analyze the $d'$ data since each subject responded to only one target item per condition, with each response either correct (1) or incorrect (0). This analysis involved four steps. First, for each subject in each condition, a difference score was computed between his or her score on the target item (the item presented in the slide) and one minus their score on the suggested distractor item (the item that had been suggested in the narrative). These difference scores had values of −1, 0, or +1. Second, for each subject within each level of frequency, a difference score was calculated—the score in the control condition minus that in the misled condition. These difference scores, ranging from −2 to +2, provide an ordinal value for the extent to which each subject was misled at each level of frequency. Third, another difference score was calculated—the mean misled score for each subject in the frequency 1 condition minus that in the frequency 2 condition. A positive score indicates that a subject was misled more in the frequency 1 than frequency 2 condition; a negative score indicates that a subject was misled more in the frequency 2 than frequency 1 condition.

Finally, a sign test was computed to test if the number of positive difference scores between the frequency 1 and frequency 2 conditions differed significantly from what would be expected by chance. When computed across all 120 subjects in both age groups, the sign test revealed this outcome to be significant, $z = 2.076$, $p < .05$. For each age group separately, the binomial probability of the number of positive frequency 1 minus frequency 2 difference scores was significantly less than the $p < .05$ chance level (binomial $p = .03$ for 4-year-olds and binomial $p = .04$ for 10-year-olds). Thus, participants were more vulnerable to suggestibility in the frequency 1 than frequency 2 condition.

In addition, separate analyses of variance performed on the hit rate data (i.e., the probability of saying "yes" given that the item was from the originally presented slide) and false alarm rate data (i.e., the probability of saying "yes" given that the item was from the postevent narrative) yielded similar findings. Thus, the major result of this study, principally that subjects were more likely to be misled in the frequency 1 than frequency 2 condition, is not restricted to the pattern of hit rate or correct rejection rate data alone.

Finally, the average correct rejection rate for foil test items was quite high (.71 for 4-year-olds and .95 for 10-year-olds). This result confirms the findings of Tversky and Tuchin (1989) that the effect of the misleading information in the narrative is quite specific in that memory for the original item seen in the slide is not simply made less accessible in the misled condition, but more specifically, it is supplanted by the item suggested in the narrative.

Together, the results of this study support the *trace strength* hypothesis that stronger memories are more likely to resist suggestibility than weaker memories. These results are important because they articulate conditions under which children are likely to be reliable or unreliable eyewitnesses. For example, if a child is recalling an event that occurred several times to them, they would be expected to have more accurate memory for the event and be less vulnerable to suggestive influences such as biased interviewing procedures, compared to an event that occurred only a single time. This is especially important in child abuse cases because it is common for perpetrators to frequently abuse the same child. A child's memory for an incident that occurred frequently would be expected to be relatively reliable, even in the face of possibly suggestive interviewing. Although there are obvious differences between the procedure and materials in this study and those involved in real world cases of child abuse, nonetheless, this study speaks to the general memory processes that underlie suggestibility and memory.

### "Memory" for Events That Did Not Occur

Another principal assumption examined in this paper is the view that it is relatively easy to suggest to a child that something occurred when it did not. This assumption is at the heart of the claims that abuse did not occur but that the memories of abuse were suggestively planted by an overzealous police officer, social worker, or therapist who interviewed the child. To test this position, we recently conducted a study to examine how easy it is to suggest that something occurred when it did not. This study also addressed children's memory for being touched, a domain in which little research is available.

The large majority of the studies on the suggestibility effect involve a procedure in which something is observed (e.g., a stop sign), a different thing is later suggested (e.g., a yield sign), and the test probes what the participants remember having seen. In such studies, as was reported earlier in this article, developmental differences in the suggestibility of memory usually result between preschoolers versus older children and adults. On the basis of this research, there are those who conclude that preschool children are unfit to provide eyewitness testimony. More generally, these results have been taken to demonstrate that adults and children can easily be suggestively influenced to believe that certain things happened when in fact they did not. However, there is an important difference between the structure of this later generalization and the structure of the source experiments. Most of the suggestibility studies are structured such that event A is observed, event B is suggested, and memory is tested for A versus B. In the generalization claims, A is never observed, A is suggested, and memory is tested for A versus not A. There are significant differences between the structure of these two situations.

To examine the probability of suggestibility in these quite different circumstances, the present experiment compared suggestibility under three conditions:

- A is observed, B is suggested,
- A is not observed, A is suggested, versus
- A is observed, it is suggested that A was not observed;

compared with two control conditions,

- A is observed, nothing is suggested, and
- A is not observed, nothing is suggested.

By comparing the relative vulnerability to suggestibility among these conditions, additional constraints on the construct of suggestibility will be examined. More specifically, in this study, the relative difficulty of suggesting that something happened when it did not can be determined.

*Method.* Eighty 10-year-old children participated individually in one 25-min session. At one identifiable point in the session, the experimenter showed the child a picture of a rose projected on a screen and asked if they could see the rose clearly. At this point the experimenter, for about 2 s, put her hand on their hand (event A), put her hand on their shoulder (event B), or did not touch them at all. The suggestion phase occurred about 15 min later, after viewing a story told in a sequence of slides. At this point, each child was read a narrative that "reviewed" for them what had happened during the session. Regarding the target behavior, in the three experimental conditions, they were told that they had been touched in a different way (B was suggested if A had occurred or A was suggested if B had occurred), told that they had been touched (A or B) if they had not been touched, or told that they had not been touched if they had been touched (either A or B). In the two control conditions the narrative mentioned nothing about the touching incident. Across the three experimental conditions and two control conditions the type of touch, on the hand or on the shoulder, was counterbalanced across subjects so that each occurred in the observed and suggested position equally often.

Subsequently, the children were given a recognition test to assess their memory. The test included three questions:

1. When I showed you the picture of the rose and asked if you could see it, *did I touch you?*

2. When I showed you the picture of the rose and asked if you could see it, *did I put my hand on your shoulder?*

3. When I showed you the picture of the rose and asked if you could see it, *did I put my hand on your hand?*

The first general question was asked to assess the claim of Goodman and Clarke-Stewart (1991) that children often find general questions about touching unclear and that although using specifically worded questions may have a suggestive influence, children's responses to general nonspecific questions tend to be limited.

*Results and Discussion.* The major results involve the participants' ability to

TABLE 2
Mean $d'$ Data in Each Condition of the Hand–Shoulder and Nose–Cheek Touching Experiments

| | Hand–shoulder experiment | Nose–cheek experiment |
|---|---|---|
| Experimental conditions | | |
| 1. A occurs, B suggested | −1.18* | −.38* |
| 2. A occurs, not A suggested | .67 | .36 |
| 3. not A occurs, A suggested | 1.03 | 1.68* |
| Control Conditions | | |
| 4. A occurs, nothing suggested | 1.02 | 1.73[a] |
| 5. not A occurs, nothing suggested | 2.35 | 3.76 |

[a] In these conditions the $p$(hit) = 1.00 or the $p$(false alarm) = 0. Thus, it was necessary to compute an estimated $d'$ value using 15.5/16 for the hit rate and .5/16 for the false alarm rate.

* Experimental condition differs significantly from corresponding control condition at the $p < .05$ level.

discriminate between their response to the question regarding what really happened (touch on hand, touch on shoulder, or nothing) and their response to the question regarding the other type of touch that did not occur but was either suggested or not mentioned. Thus, the signal detection measure of $d'$ was used. These results were derived from participants' responses to questions 2 and 3 above. Because each subject responded to only one target item, the $d'$ values were based on the group hit and false alarm data. These $d'$ data are presented in the first column of Table 2 for each of the three experimental and two control conditions.

Nonparametric statistics were again used to analyze the $d'$ data since each subject responded to only one target item, with this response either correct (1) or incorrect (0). This analysis involved two steps. First, a difference score was computed for each subject between his or her score on the target item (the original touch condition) and one minus their score on the suggested distractor item (the suggested touch condition). These ordinal difference scores took on values of −1, 0, or +1. Second, three separate $\chi^2$ statistics were carried out to test if the frequency of −1, 0, and +1 scores differed between each of the three experimental groups and the corresponding control group for each.

First, consistent with previous research, the distribution of positive, negative, and zero difference scores differed significantly between experimental condition 1 and the corresponding control condition 4, $\chi^2$ (2) = 11.55, $p < .01$, with more higher difference scores and fewer lower difference scores in the control than in the experimental condition. However, the difference between experimental condition 2 and the corresponding control condition 4 ($\chi^2$ (2) = 1.11) and the difference between experimental condition 3 and the corresponding control condition 5 ($\chi^2$ (2) = 3.2) were nonsignificant. Thus, although we were able to suggestively influence participants to believe that a different event occurred other than the event that was experienced, we were not effective in suggesting that something occurred when it had not nor that nothing occurred when it had.

One potential criticism of this experiment is that the results might be limited to relatively innocuous touches such as a touch on the shoulder or on the hand—touches that perhaps are not very likely to be remembered anyway. To test this interpretation a second experiment was conducted in which two more unusual touches were used. This second experiment was identical to the first except that each of 80 10-year-olds was either touched on the nose or touched on the cheek for two seconds at a particular point in the experimental session. The results of this second experiment are presented in the second column of Table 2.

As anticipated, the mean $d'$ rates were higher in the second experiment than in the previous experiment; however, as can be seen in Table 2, the pattern of results in the second experiment was similar to that in the previous one. The difference in the distribution of difference scores between experimental condition 1 and control condition 4 was significant, $\chi^2 (2) = 6.83, p < .05$, with more higher difference scores and fewer lower difference scores in the control than in the experimental condition. This result replicates the findings with the classic suggestibility paradigm. The difference between experimental condition 2 and control condition 4 was not significant, $\chi^2 (2) = 3.39$. The difference between experimental condition 3 and control condition 5 approached significance, $\chi^2 (2) = 5.93, p < .06$. This difference is attributable to the fact that performance was so high in the control condition; all 16 subjects assigned to control condition 5 were correct in recognizing the target event compared to 11 of the 16 subjects in experimental condition 3. Thus, although experimental condition 3 differed significantly from its control condition 5, the large majority of the subjects in experimental condition 3 were correct in rejecting the suggested plant.

The similar pattern of results across these two experiments supports the generalizability of the results beyond simply innocuous touches. Consistent with the prior experiment, these results confirm that it is relatively easy to suggestively influence someone to believe that a different event occurred other than the event that was experienced. However, we were not reliably able to suggest that nothing occurred when it had, and although there was some qualified support for the ability to plant a memory for an event that had not occurred, the large majority of the participants were correct in rejecting a suggested plant. These results raise doubts about the claim that a significant number of children who had never been sexually abused, could, by the suggestion of a police officer, social worker, or therapist, come to believe that they had been abused, often repeatedly and often by a parent or teacher.

A final analysis was conducted to assess the accuracy of the 10-year-old participants answering the general question about touching that was always asked first (e.g., "When I showed you the picture of the rose and asked if you could see it, *did I touch you?*"). Averaged across both experiments, the level of accuracy answering the general questions was quite low, 50% correct averaged across the three experimental conditions and 63% correct averaged across the two control conditions. These rates do not differ from the 50% chance level. This finding confirms the claim of Goodman and Clarke-Stewart (1991) that although using specifically worded questions may have a suggestive influence, children's responses to general nonspecific questions tend to be limited.

The conditions of touching in these two experiments certainly do not approximate the type of physical contact that occurs in incidents of sexual abuse. However, the conditions of touching used in these experiments provide a more realistic condition for studying the suggestibility of abuse memories than those used in the classic suggestibility studies that have provided a basis for most of the claims about the suggestibility of memory for sexual abuse. In the classic studies, the suggestibility of, for example, people's memory for the appearance of a traffic sign in a briefly presented slide has been assessed (Loftus et al., 1978).

One of the few experimental demonstrations that an entire event can be suggestively planted in people's memory was reported by Loftus (1993). In this study, five acquaintances of the researchers were led to believe that they had been lost in a shopping mall when they were 5-years old. There are several reasons why these results would not be expected to generalize to the situation of having a therapist plant an illusory memory for incest. First, in the Loftus study the memory was planted by a sibling who, in reality, could have been there; there is some basis for concluding that they might remember what happened even if the participant did not. The assumption that a therapist who was not present in the client's past would be similarly likely to plant childhood memories is not convincing. Second, and most important, being lost while shopping is not such a remarkable implant. Children are often warned about the dangers of getting lost, have fears about getting lost, are commonly read classic tales about children who get lost (i.e., Hansel and Gretel; Snow White and the Seven Dwarfs; Pinocchio; Goldi Locks and the Three Bears), and, in fact, occasionally do get lost if only for a few frightening minutes. Therefore, it would be expected that most children have a preexisting schema for getting lost that would be accessed by the suggestion of a particular instance of getting lost in the Loftus demonstration. It is hardly likely that most children would have a preexisting schema for sexual abuse. That Loftus was sometimes able to plant memories for having been lost in a mall does not therefore mean that it is easy to plant memories for having been sexually molested.

## CONCLUSIONS

The findings presented suggest some of the constraints that exist on the construct of suggestibility. First, results were presented that showed that 4- and 10-year-old children were less vulnerable to suggestibility about more frequently presented information. These results suggest that if a child is recalling an event that occurred several times to them, their memory would be more accurate and less vulnerable to suggestive influences such as biased interview questions, compared to their memory for an event that occurred only once. Consequently, children who were repeatedly abused by the same perpetrator are more likely to have reliable memory for the abuse than those abused only once, regardless of whether potential sources of suggestibility intervened.

Second, although it is relatively easy to suggest that one event happened when a different but similar event really occurred, it is more difficult to suggest that an event happened when it really had not or that an event had not happened when it really had. Under some conditions it is certainly possible to plant memories for events that did not occur. Work in progress, for example, suggests that the probability of planting a memory increases with the number of times the planted item is suggested. This might explain how a child who is repeatedly exposed to suggestive interviewing might eventually come to remember the suggested information as real. However, given that in this study we were simply trying to suggest to a child that they had been touched on the hand or the shoulder, in one experiment, or on the nose or the cheek, in another experiment—and they were reluctant to comply with this suggestion when it had not occurred—it is difficult to imagine that a child could be misled to believe that they had been sexually abused, often by their parent or teacher, and often repeatedly over a prolonged period of time.

It is clear that the construct of suggestibility involves a complex set of cognitive processes that we are only beginning to understand. At this point, however, there is no empirical support for the view that childhood memories for frequently occurring events are generally unreliable or that it is easy to plant illusory memories for sexual abuse.

## ACKNOWLEDGMENTS

I am grateful to the Fletcher Jones Foundation for supporting the research presented herein. I am thankful to Maria Arrigo and Jennifer Freyd for their feedback and inspiration and to Ed Teyber for his support and patience.

## REFERENCES

Baker, R. A. (1992). *Hidden memories.* Buffalo, NY: Prometheus Books.

Bass, E., & Davis, L. (1988). *The courage to heal.* New York: Harper & Row.

Bekerian, D. A., & Bowers, J. M. (1983). Eyewitness testimony: Were we misled? *Journal of Experimental Psychology: Learning, Memory, & Cognition, 9,* 139–145.

Belli, R. F. (1989). Influences of misleading postevent information: Misinformation interference and acceptance. *Journal of Experimental Psychology: General, 118,* 72–85.

Berliner, L. (1985). The child and the criminal justice system. In A. W. Burgess (Ed.), *Rape and sexual assault* (pp. 199–208). New York: Garland Publishing.

Binet, A. (1900). *La suggestibilite.* Paris: Schleicher Freres.

Brainerd, C. J., Reyna, V. F., Howe, M. L., & Kingma, J. (1990). The development of forgetting and reminiscence. *Monographs of the Society for Research in Child Development, 55* (3–4, Serial No. 222).

Ceci, S. J., & Bruck, M. (1993). Suggestibility of the child witness: A historical review and synthesis. *Psychological Bulletin, 113,* 403–439.

Ceci, S. J., Ross, D., & Toglia, M. (1987). Age differences in suggestibility: Psychological implications. *Journal of Experimental Psychology: General, 117,* 38–49.

Chi, M. T. H. (1978). Knowledge structures and memory development. In R. S. Siegler (Ed.), *Children's thinking: What develops?* Hillsdale, NJ: Erlbaum.

Christiaansen, R. E., & Ochalek, K. (1983). Editing misleading information from memory: Evidence for the coexistence of original and post-event information. *Memory Cognition, 11,* 467–475.

Cohen, R. L., & Harnick, M. A. (1980). The susceptibility of child witnesses to suggestion. *Law and Human Behavior, 4,* 201–210.

Cole, C. B., & Loftus, E. F. (1987). The memory of children. In S. J. Ceci, M. Toglia, & D. Ross (Eds.), *Children's eyewitness memory* (pp. 178–208). New York: Springer-Verlag.

Duncan, E. M., Whitney, P., & Kunen, S. (1982). Integration of visual and verbal information in children's memories. *Child Development, 53,* 1215–1223.

Ebbinghaus, H. E. (1964). *Memory: A contribution to experimental psychology.* New York: Dover. (Original work published 1885)

Feher, T. (1988). The alleged molestation victim, the rules of evidence, and the Constitution: Should children really be seen and not heard? *American Journal of Criminal Law, 14,* 227.

Flavell, J. H., Beach, D. H., & Chinsky, J. M. (1966). Spontaneous verbal rehearsal in a memory task as a function of age. *Child Development, 37,* 283, 299.

Flin, R., Boon, J., Knox, A., & Bull, R. (1992). Children's memories following a five-month delay. *British Journal of Psychology, 83,* 323–336.

Gardner, R. (1989). *Sex abuse hysteria: Salem Witch Trials revisited.* Longwood, NJ: Creative Therapeutics Press.

Goodman, G. S., Aman, C., & Hirschman, J. (1987). Child sexual and physical abuse: Children's testimony. In S. J. Ceci, M. P. Toglia, & D. F. Ross (Eds.), *Children's eyewitness memory* (pp. 1–23). New York: Springer-Verlag.

Goodman, G. S., & Clarke-Stewart, A. (1991). Suggestibility in children's testimony: Implications for child sexual abuse investigations. In J. L. Doris (Ed.), *The suggestibility of children's recollections* (pp. 92–105). Washington, DC: American Psychological Association.

Goodman, G. S., & Reed, R. S. (1986). Age differences in eyewitness testimony. *Law and Human Behavior, 10,* 317–332.

Goodman, G. S., Rudy, L., Bottoms, B., & Aman, C. (1990). Children's concerns and memory: Issues of ecological validity in the study of children's eyewitness testimony. In R. Fivush & J. Hudson (Eds.), *Knowing and remembering in young children* (pp. 249–284). New York: Cambridge Univ. Press.

Howe, M. L. (1991). Misleading children's story recall: Forgetting and reminiscence of the facts. *Developmental Psychology, 27,* 746–762.

Jones, D., & McGraw, J. M. (1987). Reliable and fictitious accounts of sexual abuse in children. *Journal of Interpersonal Violence, 2,* 27–45.

Jones, D. C., Swift, D. J., & Johnson, M. (1988). Nondeliberate memory for a novelty event among preschoolers. *Developmental Psychology, 24,* 641–645.

King, M., & Yuille, J. (1987). Suggestibility and the child witness. In S. J. Ceci, M. Toglia,. & D. Ross (Eds.), *Children's eyewitness memory* (pp. 24–35). New York: Springer-Verlag.

Leippe, M. R., Romanczyk, A., & Manion, A. P. (1991). Eyewitness memory for a touching experience: Accuracy differences between child and adult witnesses. *Journal of Applied Psychology, 76,* 367–379.

Lindberg, M. (1991). A taxonomy of suggestibility and eyewitness memory: Age, memory process, and focus of analysis. In J. L. Doris (Ed.), *The suggestibility of children's recollections* (pp. 47–55). Washington, DC: American Psychological Association.

Lindsay, D. S. (1993). Eyewitness suggestibility. *Current directions in psychological science, 2,* 86–89.

Lindsay, D. S., & Johnson, M. K. (1987). Reality monitoring and suggestibility: Children's ability to discriminate among memories from different sources. In S. J. Ceci, M. P. Toglia, & D. F. Ross (Eds.), *Children's eyewitness memory* (pp. 92–121). New York: Springer-Verlag.

List, J. A. (1986). Age and schematic differences in the reliability of eyewitness testimony. *Developmental Psychology, 22,* 50–57.

Loftus, E. F. (1975). Leading questions and the eyewitness report. *Cognitive Psychology, 7,* 560–572.

Loftus, E. F. (1993). The reality of repressed memories. *American Psychologist, 48,* 518–537.

Loftus, E. F., Miller, D., & Burns, H. (1978). Semantic integration of verbal information into a visual memory. *Journal of Experimental Psychology: Human Learning and Memory, 4,* 19–31.

Marin, B. V., Holmes, D. L., Guth, M., & Kovac, P. (1979). The potential of children as eyewitnesses. *Law and Human Behavior, 3,* 295–305.

McCloskey, M., & Zaragoza, M. (1985). Misleading postevent information and memory for events: Arguments and evidence against the memory impairment hypothesis. *Journal of Experimental Psychology: General,* **114,** 1–16.

Nurcombe, B. (1986). The child as witness: Competency and credibility. *Journal of the American Academy of Child Psychiatry,* **25,** 473–480.

Paris, S. G., & Mahoney, G. J. (1974). Cognitive integration in children's memory for sentences and pictures. *Child Development,* **45,** 633–642.

Paris, S. G., & Upton, L. R. (1976). Children's memory for inferential relationships in prose. *Child Development,* **47,** 660–668.

Pezdek, K. (1977). Cross-modality semantic integration of sentence and picture memory. *Journal of Experimental Psychology: Human Learning and Memory,* **3,** 515–524.

Pezdek, K., & Greene, J. (1993). Testing eyewitness memory: Developing a measure that is more resistant to suggestibility. *Law and Human Behavior,* **17,** 361–369.

Pezdek, K., & Roe, C. (1994). The effect of memory trace strength on suggestibility. Unpublished Manuscript.

Saywitz, K. J. (1987). Children's testimony: Age-related patterns of memory errors. In S. J. Ceci, M. P. Toglia, & D. F. Ross (Eds.), *Children's eyewitness memory* (pp. 36–52). New York: Springer-Verlag.

Schuman, D. C. (1986). False allegations of physical and sexual abuse. *Bulletin of the American Academy of Psychiatry and the Law,* **14,** 5–21.

Tversky, B., & Tuchin, M. (1989). A reconciliation of the evidence on eyewitness testimony: Comments on McCloskey and Zaragoza. *Journal of Experimental Psychology,* **118,** 86–91.

# Contextual Influences on Children's Remembering

Peter A. Ornstein and Jennifer T. Myers

*University of North Carolina at Chapel Hill*

Because aspects of children's cognitive performance can be shown to vary markedly from context to context, it is difficult to make broad statements about cognitive development. In this chapter, we examine children's memory and suggestibility from the perspective of context specificity. We focus on memory for the details of salient, personally experienced events, in part because of its relevance for basic accounts of children's cognitive functioning, but also because of its relevance for understanding both the testimony of children and the efforts of adults to recover early memories. In our treatment of remembering, we examine two salient aspects of the context: the events being remembered and the conditions prevailing when memory is being assessed. We also emphasize the need to examine individual difference factors such as prior knowledge and coping style that influence both the deployment of attention as an event unfolds and the construction of a stable representation in memory.

## INTRODUCTION

Within the last decade, there has been a dramatic increase in research on children's memory and suggestibility (Goodman, 1984; Ceci & Bruck, 1993; Ceci, Toglia, & Ross, 1987; Doris, 1991; Ornstein, Gordon, & Baker-Ward, 1992). Much of this work has involved assessments of developmental changes in the completeness and accuracy of children's reports of the details of salient, personally experienced events, frequently over extended delay intervals. Because relatively little is known about children's long-term retention, recent studies contribute directly to our understanding of young children's memory and cognitive development. This research, however, is also of considerable applied relevance, especially with regard to children's testimony and adults' efforts to remember the details of early experiences. Indeed, knowledge of children's abilities to remember accurately and to resist suggestion is essential for understanding their abilities to provide evidence in legal proceedings. A developmental orientation, moreover, is essential to discussions of what adults can remember about their early experiences, as these memories are determined, in part, by the way these experiences were understood as they were taking place and by the stability of the resulting representation over time.

In this chapter, we discuss memory and suggestibility from the perspective of the context specificity that characterizes many aspects of young children's cognitive performance (Ornstein, 1991; Ornstein, Baker-Ward, & Naus, 1988). Estimates of children's cognitive skills can vary dramatically as a function of certain features of the context, and we focus here on the implications of variability. Most of our attention is directed to one salient aspect of context, namely, the nature and structure of the events that are being remembered. These events may be differentially understood as they are taking place, may vary in the degree to which they bring about the deployment of focal attention, may have contrasting courses of retention over time, and may vary in the extent to which they are susceptible to influence by misleading information. In addition, we discuss the profound influence of the contextual conditions prevailing as young children are questioned.

## CONTEXT SPECIFICITY

The context specificity of children's memory performance can be demonstrated readily in laboratory-based studies of developmental changes in the recall of sets of words, pictures, objects, and stories (see Folds, Footo, Guttentag, & Ornstein, 1990; Ornstein et al., 1988; Schneider & Pressley, 1989). Of course, at a general level, with increases in age children exhibit both better recall and more sophisticated use of strategies such as rehearsal and organization. These strategies, moreover, are thought to contribute to developmental changes in memory performance. However, even within the laboratory setting, our impressions of children's abilities vary markedly as a function of both the materials that are to be remembered and the prevailing assessment conditions.

Thus, for example, when third graders (in contrast to sixth graders) are presented with low-associated words and asked to form groups that will facilitate remembering, they do not base their sorting patterns on meaning. They readily do so, however, when presented with words that are highly associated members of taxonomic categories, and they are able to transfer such meaning-based sorting to low-associated items without additional training (Best & Ornstein, 1986). Similarly, although third graders do not typically engage in active rehearsal in which several to-be-remembered items are rehearsed together, they are nonetheless able to do so when provided with hints concerning strategy use, or when the information processing demands of the task are reduced (Guttentag, Ornstein, & Siemens, 1987; Ornstein, Medlin, Stone, & Naus, 1985). These demonstrations expose the difficulties that are inherent in characterizing the nature of children's mnemonic competence.

If context specificity is important in understanding children's recall of word lists and their deployment of strategies, how much more important must it be when we consider factors involved in remembering personally salient events from the "real world"? The experiences that children are often asked to remember in legal settings, as well as those that adults attempt to recover, differ substantially—in terms of personal meaning and level of arousal—from those typically used in laboratory studies of memory. In addition, these types of events vary markedly in terms of their structure and salience, as well as in the degree to which they are understood as they are experienced. Furthermore, the manner in which both children and adults may be questioned about these events can also vary substantially, with interview contexts ranging all the way from highly supportive to confrontational.

To illustrate these points, we first discuss several characteristics of to-be-remembered events and then examine features of the interview context. It should be noted at the outset, however, that these two factors may not be independent of each other. For example, memories of some types of experiences may be relatively stable across interview contexts, whereas those of other events may be quite labile and susceptible to suggestive forms of questioning, particularly as neutrally toned interviews turn into interrogations.

## Events to Be Remembered

Demonstrations of context specificity force us to consider seriously the possibility that our impressions of children's abilities to remember personal experiences over long time periods may vary markedly as a function of the events themselves. Consider, for example, how performance may vary as we move from relatively benign and familiar to more stressful and novel experiences. Events certainly vary in terms of (a) children's prior knowledge and, hence, understanding, (b) the degree of internal structure, (c) the level of arousal that is elicited, and (d) the strength of the underlying event representations that are established.

*Prior knowledge.* A considerable amount of research demonstrates that prior knowledge of the materials that are to be remembered influences all stages of cognitive processing, from the interpretation and encoding to the retrieval and reporting of information (Bjorklund, 1985; Chi & Ceci, 1987; Ornstein & Naus, 1985). These knowledge effects are powerful enough to bring about a reversal of the ubiquitous finding of improvement in performance as a function of age. Thus, for example, children who are chess experts are more adept at recalling the positions of chess pieces than are adults who are average players (Chi, 1978).

Knowledge is also important in terms of memory for events. In our laboratory, for example, we have examined the linkage between children's knowledge of physical examinations and medical routines on the one hand, and their memory for the details of a specific visit to the doctor, on the other hand. By pooling the responses of 5-year-olds to open-ended questions about what usually happens during a visit to the doctor, Clubb, Nida, Merritt, and Ornstein (1993) constructed composite knowledge scores for the features of the physical examination. We then reanalyzed the data of 5-year-olds from a previously reported study of memory for the details of a specific doctor visit (Baker-Ward, Gordon, Ornstein, Larus, & Clubb, 1993). The reanalysis basically involved moving from the individual subject to the particular feature of the checkup as the unit of analysis. In this way, we were able to derive memorability measures for the components of the physical examination that were comparable to the knowledge measures. The resulting analysis revealed that there was a strong linkage between children's general knowledge of the details of checkups and their recall of the components of a specific examination (Clubb et al., 1993; see also Ornstein, Shapiro, Clubb, Follmer, & Baker-Ward, in press).

*Structure of the event.* Events vary substantially in the extent to which they are internally structured or cohesive. Even infants are sensitive to event structure and show enhanced recall (in elicited imitation tasks) of actions that are causally or logically linked "relative to random actions" (e.g., Bauer, 1992; Bauer & Dow, 1994). In our research program, moreover, we have been able to contrast children's memory for the details of medical procedures that differ considerably in the degree to which the component features are integrated.

Although most of our work involves assessments of memory for routine well-child checkups, in which the features could be viewed as unordered and even unrelated, we have also explored recall of the details of an invasive radiological procedure (the voiding cystourethrogram, or VCUG) that is highly integrated and structured (Merritt, Ornstein, & Spicker, 1994). The structure of the VCUG is apparent when one considers that the component features are linked together in a series of enabling relations, for example, such that the bladder cannot be filled before the catheter is inserted, which cannot be done before the genital area is cleaned, and so on. In some respects, most notably in terms of providing information in response to open-ended probes, we observed enhanced recall for the features of the VCUG in comparison with that of the well-child checkup. Although a number of factors may contribute to the superior recall of the VCUG, it is possible that children were responding to the greater internal structure of the VCUG in contrast to the less clearly structured physical examination.

*Level of arousal.* Although there is a long history of research on the effects of stress on memory (see Christianson, 1992, for a review), little of this work has involved the recall of real-world events. Moreover, those studies that do explore children's memory for the details of stressful experiences have revealed that the linkage between stress and remembering is quite complex. Indeed, some researchers report a positive relation (Goodman, Hirschman, Hepps, & Rudy, 1991), whereas others report a negative one (Peters, 1991). Nonetheless, at present, there seems to be more support for a negative association between stress and remembering, that is, for higher levels of stress to be associated with lower amounts of recall (Peters, in press). An important caveat, however, is that the nature of the linkage itself may vary as a function of the way in which stress is conceptualized and measured (Ornstein, Merritt, & Baker-Ward, 1995).

Consider, for example, the enhanced recall of the features of the VCUG in comparison to the components of the more routine physical examination that was reported by Merritt et al. (1994). Although, the higher levels of open-ended recall observed in the VCUG study could have reflected the greater internal structure of this medical procedure in contrast to that of the routine checkup, there is also no doubt that the VCUG was much more stressful for the children than was the checkup. Thus, a comparison between these two events (see Ornstein et al., 1995) leads to the conclusion that there is a positive linkage between stress and remembering.

But there is more to the story, as different conclusions about stress and remembering emerge when we look within the VCUG event and ask about how individual variation in measured stress is related to comparable variation in remembering. The picture is quite complex, however, because the stress–remembering association depends on additional issues of measurement. Consistent with the emerging trend in the literature, a negative correlation is obtained between stress and remembering within the VCUG procedure itself, but this association is only observed when stress is measured behaviorally, that is, in terms of the ratings of radiological staff and the coding of trained observers. In contrast, when stress is measured physiologically, in terms of salivary cortisol production, there is no linkage between stress and remembering.

This bifurcation between physiological and behavioral indicators of stress forces a consideration of the psychological mediators of stress and coping. It is possible that children can be objectively stressed—and the VCUG procedure certainly involves putting children (and adults, for that matter) in a very difficult situation—and yet interpret the stress in different ways, with recall following from these differing interpretations. Consistent with this approach, it is necessary to replace global measures of stress with moment-to-moment indicators of stress as a to-be-remembered event unfolds, recognizing that an individual child may be stressed at one point in time but not at another. With such a research strategy, it will be possible to examine precisely how recall of the features of an event relates to the stress that was expressed when they were experienced. Such an approach will also permit a more fine-grained analysis of the qualitative differences in children's reactions to stress, as is discussed next.

*Strength of the event representation.* The interpretive processes that are set in motion as an event is experienced clearly influence the strength and organization of the representation in memory. An additional factor that affects the representation is the subject's experience with the event itself, operationalized in laboratory-like studies in terms of number of presentation trials. Other things being equal, increases in the number of presentations are associated with stronger event representations, which in turn are linked to enhanced long-term retention. In addition, it seems likely that the strength of the underlying representation is associated with resistance to suggestibility (Brainerd & Reyna, 1988).

From this perspective, susceptibility to the interfering effects of misleading postevent information should increase over time, as the strength of an underlying event representation fades. Pezdek and Roe's (this volume) report that children were less vulnerable to suggestion about information presented twice, as opposed to once, is consistent with this interpretation. Moreover, assuming that younger children's initial representations are both weaker and more likely to decay than those of older individuals, age differences in suggestibility would be expected (see Brainerd & Reyna, 1988; Ceci, Toglia, & Ross, 1988).

*Implications.* Although we certainly have not provided a taxonomy of events, it is clear nonetheless that events can vary markedly in terms of characteristics that may be associated with differences in remembering. Thus, certain events, in contrast with others, may be (a) better recalled initially, (b) more resistant to forgetting over time, and (c) more resistant to suggestion.

Concerning initial recall, for example, at the "broad event" level, children's open-ended recall of an integrated and aversive experience (the VCUG) is elevated in comparison with that observed after a routine physical examination (Merritt et al., 1994). Indeed, it is even possible that with aversive and arousing events such as the VCUG, age differences in performance are minimized. Even within the doctor visit event, however, some actions (e.g., receiving an injection, being given a prize) may be better remembered over time than other examination features (Ornstein et al., in press). Similarly, characteristics of retention and forgetting may also be driven by features of the event being remembered. Age differences in forgetting the details of the VCUG were not observed, and, in fact, levels of forgetting were minimal. And again, within-event exploration indicated that salient features of the doctor visit had very different (and elevated) retention functions than did other features (Ornstein et al., in press).

Furthermore, some events may be more resistant to suggestion than others. For example, Stein, Trabasso, and Liwag (1991) suggest that when children are asked to remember events that took place under salient conditions of emotional arousal (e.g., sadness, anger), and they have a commitment to a particular interpretation of those events, they may be quite resistant to suggestion. Thus, in contrast to the bulk of the literature that suggests greater suggestibility among young preschoolers, Stein and her colleagues have identified circumstances under which 3-year-olds can exhibit strong resistance to suggestion. Eisen, Goodman, and Qin (1995) also argue that there are conditions under which young children may be resistant to suggestion. In their preliminary study of children who were referred for evaluation because of suspected abuse, Eisen et al. found that preschoolers were more resistant to misleading suggestions when asked to talk about an invasive (presumably abuse-related) medical procedure than when questioned about a noninvasive event. Nonetheless, the younger children studied by Eisen et al. (1995) did make errors when asked misleading questions about the invasive procedure, and other data (e.g., Bruck, Ceci, Francoeur, & Rennick, 1995) indicate that preschoolers can be quite suggestible, even about actions that involve bodily contact.

## Assessment Context

Granted that our impressions of children's memory and suggestibility can vary as a function of the events that are being remembered, it is also the case that their reports can differ substantially across different assessment conditions (Ornstein, 1991; Ornstein, Larus, & Clubb, 1991). Interview contexts can vary markedly in terms of the supports for information retrieval that are provided, thus affecting the conclusions we reach as to the accuracy of children's memory. We turn now to a discussion of several contextual features that may influence memory performance.

*Metacognitive and social factors.* A number of factors have the potential to affect children's understanding of the interview process and hence the amount of accurate information that may be reported. Optimal performance clearly depends on the interviewer and the child having shared expectations about the nature of the interview process (Ornstein, 1991; Ornstein et al., 1991). Indeed, memory reports may vary as a function of the extent to which the child and the interviewer agree on just what it means to provide information about a previous experience or event.

For example, if a child assumes that an adult interviewer already has knowledge of the event under discussion, it is possible that he or she will not provide a full report (Ornstein, 1991). Similarly, as children may view their adult interviewers as authority figures, when they are questioned repeatedly, they may change their accounts. Indeed, if a child does not understand the purpose of being questioned repeatedly about a particular experience, he or she may assume that there was something "wrong" with the initial answer. Under these conditions, it becomes increasingly likely that children may be receptive to suggestions made (either explicitly or implicitly) by their interviewers.

*Cognitive factors and the type of questioning.* At a fundamental level, it is essential that interviewers exercise care in their use of language, matching what they say to the level of the child's understanding. It is also important to refrain from suggestive forms of questions, especially when young children are being asked about their previous experiences. Indeed, given reports that preschoolers are less resistant to suggestion than are older children and adults (Ceci & Bruck, 1993), a distorted impression of a child's memory will result from interviews that are not neutral in tone. It is recognized, of course, that a thorough assessment of memory for a particular event requires posing some questions about activities thought not to have been experienced. Nonetheless, for an interview to yield an uncontaminated account of what is remembered, it must be free from suggestive questions.

Another aspect of the assessment context concerns the level of specificity with which the child is probed. For example, there are clear age differences in the extent to which children can respond effectively to open-ended questions, perhaps reflecting corresponding differences in the use of language and in narrative skill (e.g., Baker-Ward et al., 1993). However, a different impression of children's memory abilities may be obtained by considering their performance with more specific, yes–no types of questions. Indeed, younger children's memory reports can be viewed as more complete when they are probed with yes–no as opposed to open-ended questions (Dale, Loftus, & Rathbun, 1978; Ornstein, Gordon, & Larus, 1992). However, from a variety of perspectives, reliance on yes–no questions is somewhat problematic. Not only can these probes be answered correctly 50% of the time simply by guessing, thus requiring the inclusion of lure items, but it is relatively easy for young children to fall into yes or no response sets (Geddie, Myers, & Ornstein, 1994).

*Setting.* The physical characteristics of the interview context can also affect what is remembered and, hence, our estimates of the competence of children (or adults, for that matter). Indeed, settings may vary considerably in the extent to which they contain environmental cues that enhance recall by reinstating the original context in which an event was experienced. In general, laboratory studies suggest that performance is facilitated when the interview context resembles the situation in which the event was experienced (Smith, Glenberg, & Bjork, 1978), particularly when aspects of the event have been integrated with the setting (Eich, 1985). Even adults' recall is improved when memory is tested in the situation in which the materials were presented initially (e.g., Godden & Baddeley, 1975). Conversely, of course, when attempting to remember painful experiences, it is possible that a return to the initial setting may elicit negative feelings that could interfere with memory performance. At a more general level, some interview situations may be more comfortable for young children than others, and it is possible that memory reports will vary with the level of comfort that is experienced (Ornstein, 1991).

*Timing of the assessment.* The scheduling of the interview is also an important consideration. Other things being equal, the completeness and the accuracy of an account will decrease as a function of time from the event in question. Indeed, both the passage of time and the experiences that intervene between the occurrence of an event and a subsequent interview can also affect the status of the underlying memory representation and memory reports. Of course, memory for an experience may be strengthened to the extent that the to-be-remembered event is discussed with others. At the same time, however, children's memories of a particular experience may be altered if information derived from adults or other sources results in a reinterpretation of the meaning of the event. Thus, as the child's memory representation is weakened as a function of time, it may be more susceptible to suggestive influences during the delay interval and in the interview setting (Brainerd & Ornstein, 1991; Albert & Ornstein, 1994). Accordingly, the longer the delay interval, the more problematic is the information provided in response to memory probes.

*Implications.* As there is not a great deal of research on contextual factors in interviews about personally experienced events (see Ornstein, 1991; Ornstein et al., 1991), this account of the assessment context can be viewed as somewhat speculative. Admittedly, our treatment of these issues represents a generalization from discussions of context specificity in laboratory settings (e.g., Folds et al., 1990). However, given the potential importance of contextual factors in assessments of memory for previous experiences, we feel that our generalization is warranted. Indeed, it is important to emphasize that different conclusions about what is remembered (and hence about the events in question) may result from variations in the contextual factors discussed previously. This fundamental linkage, moreover, is as relevant for researchers who are exploring the basic properties of children's long-term memory as it is for clinicians and lawyers who are attempting to make judgments about the accuracy of children's testimony. Furthermore, even though the discussion has focused on assessments of children's memory, parallel questions arise concerning the "interviewing" of adults in therapeutic settings when they are attempting to recover the details of experiences that took place in the distant past.

A final word is necessary about social pressure within the interview context. The assessments of both children and adults take place in social situations in which it is relatively easy for the interviewer to interject a personal point of view concerning the events under discussion. Although we can readily visualize children yielding to strong forms of pressure (Ceci & Bruck, 1993), it is possible that both children and adults may respond to more subtle pressures, even when interviews are free of explicitly misleading questioning. Moreover, it seems likely that the tendency to yield in response to such pressures will vary as a function of the nature of the events that are being discussed. Additional research is necessary to explore the conditions under which such effects are observed, as well as to examine the mnemonic consequences of giving in to pressures in an interview.

## General Implications

Because of the profound impact of context, it is difficult to make general state-ments concerning the mnemonic capabilities of children. Any such statement needs to be qualified by specific reference to the nature of the event and the characteristics of the assessment situation. It does seem likely, however, that performance would be enhanced when children are assessed in a supportive con-text for their memory of a cohesive to-be-remembered event about which they have a fair amount of relevant prior knowledge. Unfortunately, given the com-plexities of the stress–memory linkage, it is difficult to know how to factor stress and arousal into the equation. Most probably, knowledge and the expectations that it engenders affect the ongoing interpretation of an event as it unfolds, and these individualized interpretive processes in turn influence the degree of stress that is experienced. But additional work is required before statements of this sort can be made with any certainty, and, more generally, it is necessary to direct future research efforts to understanding the variability in children's mem-ory performance across contexts.

## TRANSFORMING THE NOMINAL STIMULUS INTO THE FUNCTIONAL STIMULUS

Any discussion of factors affecting the interpretation and understanding of events as they occur leads directly to the view that what would appear to be the same event from the perspective of a researcher or a medical professional may turn out to be a different experience for different subjects. This, in turn, brings us to an old distinction made by Underwood (1963) between nominal and func-tional stimuli. In the context of research on verbal learning, Underwood argued that the experimenter presents a stimulus, but the subject brings his or her inter-pretive processes to the task and constructs what serves as a functional stimu-lus. If this distinction was important in verbal learning, it is vital when we are dealing with memory for real-world, salient events.

To a considerable extent, different understandings of the same event may re-sult from the operation of many individual-difference factors that serve to trans-form the nominal stimulus into a functional one. Thus, temperament, coping style, reaction to stress, as well as variations in prior knowledge and understand-ing, are all likely to be involved in an individual child's deployment of attention during an event and in the interpretive processes that lead to the establishment of a representation. Consider, for example, the role played by temperament in the children's reports of the details of the VCUG (Merritt et al., 1994). In this study, certain dimensions of temperament, as assessed by a parent question-naire, the Temperament Assessment Battery for Children (Martin, 1988), are associated strongly with remembering. More specifically, approach/withdrawal ($rs \geq .69$) and adaptability ($rs \geq .52$) were correlated with open-ended and total recall, both initially and after a delay of 6 weeks.

Moreover, in a reanalysis of the data from two studies involving memory for stressful experiences—the VCUG (Merritt et al., 1994) and an emergency visit to a plastic surgeon (Baker-Ward, Burgwyn, Ornstein, & Gordon, 1995)—Ornstein et al. (1995) explored the different ways in which the children coped with the medical procedures. Within these two studies, for example, children who responded to stress by seeking explanatory information seemed to exhibit enhanced performance. For example, within the VCUG study, Ornstein, Merritt, and Baker-Ward observed an interesting correlation between the asking of questions during the procedure and the amount of information that was provided in delayed recall ($r = .43$). Moreover, in the plastic surgeon study, the asking of questions during the surgical procedure was associated with resistance to suggestibility ($r = .54$). In addition, children's tendencies to cry and to keep their eyes closed while receiving treatment were both correlated negatively with delayed open-ended recall ($rs \geq -.64$).

These analyses are consistent with the view that the provision of information during a difficult experience, stemming from the asking of questions, can lead to a richer and more elaborate representation in memory, which in turn can support remembering over time. They also suggest that imperfect attention may result in enough information getting into memory to support initial recall but that the resulting representations are insufficient for effective delayed recall performance. We are exploring the implications of these findings and of the emerging conceptualization that emphasizes the importance of on-line assessments of children's activities as events are unfolding. In this regard, our reanalyses are consistent with the implications of a recent investigation of children's contrasting reactions to a staged fire alarm. In this study, Stein and Boyce (1995) report that children who differ in physiological reactivity also differ markedly in terms of what they do when they experience an unexpected fire alarm and in the degree to which they are able to provide elaborative information about what happened during this stressful event. Collectively, this work underscores the importance of focusing seriously on the factors that are involved in the construction of a stable representation (i.e., the functional stimulus) that provides the basis for subsequent remembering.

## CONCLUSIONS

This account of memory leaves us with many problems and with many challenges. Given that performance varies as a function of the events being remembered and the conditions prevailing when memory is being assessed, it is difficult to make general statements about memory and its development. Indeed, any "diagnostic" conclusion about an individual's memory for a certain event must be referenced to the particular constellation of context variables in operation. This state of affairs is complicated further by the need to consider simultaneously the operation of individual-difference factors that seem to influence the establishment of a memory representation. To progress in our understanding, it seems essential to encourage systematic explorations of variability across contexts. Only in this way will we uncover the broad boundary conditions that we suspect will characterize our statements about memory and suggestibility.

## ACKNOWLEDGMENT

Preparation of this chapter was supported by Grant HD 32114 from the United States Public Health Service.

## REFERENCES

Albert, G., & Ornstein, P. A. (1994, April). The effects of intervening experiences on children's memory for a physical examination. In B. N. Gordon (Chair), *Young children's accounts of medical and dental examinations: Remembering and reporting personal experiences.* Conference on Human Development, Pittsburgh, PA.

Baker-Ward, L., Burgwyn, E. O., Ornstein, P. A., & Gordon, B. N. (1995, April). Children's reports of a minor medical emergency procedure. In G. S. Goodman & L. Baker-Ward (Chairs), *Children's memory for emotional and traumatic experiences.* Biennial Meeting of the Society for Research in Child Development, Indianapolis, IN.

Baker-Ward, L., Gordon, B. N., Ornstein, P. A., Larus, D. M., & Clubb, P. A. (1993). Young children's long-term retention of a pediatric examination. *Child Development, 64,* 1519–1533.

Bauer, P. J. (1992). Holding it all together: How enabling relations facilitate young children's event recall. *Cognitive Development, 7,* 1–28.

Bauer, P. J., & Dow, G. A. (1994). Episodic memory in 16- and 20-month-old children: Specifics are generalized but not forgotten. *Developmental Psychology, 30,* 403–417.

Best, D. L., & Ornstein, P. A. (1986). Children's generation and communication of mnemonic organizational strategies. *Developmental Psychology, 22,* 845–853.

Bjorklund, D. F. (1985). The role of conceptual knowledge in the development of organization in children's memory. In C. J. Brainerd & M. Pressley (Eds.), *Basic processes in memory development* (Vol. 5, pp. 79–123). Greenwich, CT: JAI Press.

Brainerd, C. J., & Ornstein, P. A. (1991). Children's memory for witnessed events: The developmental backdrop. In J. Doris (Ed.), *The suggestibility of children's recollections* (pp. 147–152). Washington, DC: American Psychological Association.

Brainerd, C. J., & Reyna, V. F. (1988). Memory loci of suggestibility development: Comment on Ceci, Ross, and Toglia (1987). *Journal of Experimental Psychology: General, 117,* 197–200.

Bruck, M., Ceci, S. J., Francoeur, E., & Rennick, A. (1995). Anatomically detailed dolls do not facilitate children's reports of a genital examination. *Journal of Experimental Psychology: Applied, 1,* 21–35.

Ceci, S. J., & Bruck, M. (1993). The suggestibility of the child witness. A historical review and synthesis. *Psychological Bulletin, 113,* 403–439.

Ceci, S. J., Toglia, M., & Ross, D. F. (Eds.). (1987). *Children's eyewitness memory.* New York: Springer-Verlag.

Ceci, S. J., Toglia, M., & Ross, D. F. (1988). On remembering . . . more or less. *Journal of Experimental Psychology: General, 118,* 250–262.

Chi, M. T. H. (1978). Knowledge structures and memory development. In R. S. Siegler (Ed.), *Children's thinking: What develops?* (pp. 73–96). Hillsdale, NJ: Erlbaum.

Chi, M. T. H., & Ceci, S. J. (1987). Content knowledge: Its role, representation, and restructuring in memory development. In H. W. Reese (Ed.), *Advances in child development and behavior* (Vol. 20, pp. 91–142). Orlando, FL: Academic Press.

Christianson, S.-A. (Ed.). (1992). *The handbook of emotion and memory: Research and theory.* Hillsdale, NJ: Erlbaum.

Clubb, P. A., Nida, R., Merritt, K., & Ornstein, P. A. (1993). Visiting the doctor: Children's knowledge and memory. *Cognitive Development, 8,* 361–372.

Dale, P. S., Loftus, E. F., & Rathbun, L. (1978). The influence of the form of the question on the eyewitness testimony of preschool children. *Journal of Psycholinguistic Research, 7,* 269–277.

Doris, J. (Ed.). (1991). *The suggestibility of children's recollections: Implications for eyewitness testimony.* Washington, DC: American Psychological Association.

Eich, E. (1985). Context, memory, and integrated item/context imagery. *Journal of Experimental Psychology: Learning, Memory, and Cognition, 11,* 764–770.

Eisen, M. L., Goodman, G. S., & Qin, J. (1995, May). The impact of dissociation, trauma, and stress arousal on memory and suggestibility in the assessment of abused and neglected children. In F. J. Morrison (Moderator), Invited symposium, *Children's memory: Implications for testimony.* Midwestern Psychological Association, Chicago, IL.

Folds, T. H., Footo, M., Guttentag, R. E., & Ornstein, P. A. (1990). When children mean to remember: Issues of context specificity, strategy effectiveness, and intentionality in the development of memory. In D. F. Bjorklund (Ed.), *Children's strategies* (pp. 67–91). Hillsdale, NJ: Erlbaum.

Geddie, L., Myers, J. T., & Ornstein, P. A. (1994, April). Children's memory of a physical examination: A comparison of recall and recognition assessment protocols. In B. N. Gordon (Chair), *Young children's accounts of medical and dental examinations: Remembering and reporting personal experiences.* Conference on Human Development, Pittsburgh, PA.

Godden, D. R., & Baddeley, A. D. (1975). Context-dependent memory in two natural environments: On land and underwater. *British Journal of Psychology, 66,* 325–331.

Goodman, G. S. (Ed.). (1984). The child witness. *Journal of Social Issues, 40*(2).

Goodman, G. S., Hirschman, J. E., Hepps, D., & Rudy, L. (1991). Children's memory for stressful events. *Merrill Palmer Quarterly, 37,* 109–158.

Guttentag, R. E., Ornstein, P. A., & Siemens, L. (1987). Children's spontaneous rehearsal: Transitions in strategy acquisition. *Cognitive Development, 2,* 307–326.

Martin, R. P. (1988). *Temperament assessment battery for children.* Brandon, VT: Clinical Psychology Publishing Company.

Merritt, K. A., Ornstein, P. A., & Spicker, B. (1994). Children's memory for a salient medical procedure: Implications for testimony. *Pediatrics, 94,* 17–23.

Ornstein, P. A. (1991). Commentary: Putting interviewing in context. In J. Doris (Ed.), *The suggestibility of children's recollections: Implications for eyewitness testimony* (pp. 147–152). Washington, DC: American Psychological Association.

Ornstein, P. A., Baker-Ward, L. E., & Naus, M. J. (1988). The development of mnemonic skill. In F. E. Weinert & M. Perlmutter (Eds.), *Memory development: Universal changes in individual differences* (pp. 31–50). Hillsdale, NJ: Erlbaum.

Ornstein, P. A., Gordon, B. N., & Baker-Ward, L. (1992). Children's memory for salient events: Implications for testimony. In M. L. Howe, C. J. Brainerd, & V. F. Reyna (Eds.), *Development of long-term retention* (pp. 135–158). New York: Springer-Verlag.

Ornstein, P. A., Gordon, B. N., & Larus, D. M. (1992). Children's memory for a personally experienced event: Implications for testimony. *Applied Cognitive Psychology, 6,* 49–60.

Ornstein, P. A., Larus, D. M., & Clubb, P. A. (1991). Understanding children's testimony: Implications of research on the development of memory. In R. Vasta (Ed.), *Annals of child development* (Vol. 8, pp. 145–176). London: Jessica Kingsley.

Ornstein, P. A., Medlin, R. G., Stone, B. P., & Naus, M. J. (1985). Retrieving for rehearsal: An analysis of active rehearsal in children's memory. *Developmental Psychology, 21,* 635–641.

Ornstein, P. A., Merritt, K. A., & Baker-Ward, L. (1995, July). Children's recollections of medical experiences: Exploring the linkage between stress and memory. In J. F. Parker (Chair), *Effects of stress and arousal upon children's memories.* Biennial meeting of the Society for Applied Research in Memory and Cognition, Vancouver.

Ornstein, P. A., & Naus, M. J. (1985). Effects of the knowledge base on children's memory strategies. In H. W. Reese (Ed.), *Advances in child development and behavior* (Vol. 19, 113–148). Orlando, FL: Academic Press.

Ornstein, P. A., Shapiro, L. R., Clubb, P. A., Follmer, A., & Baker-Ward, L. (in press). The influence of prior knowledge on children's memory for salient memory experiences. In N. L. Stein, P. A. Ornstein, B. Tversky, & C. J. Brainerd (Eds.), *Memory for everyday and emotional events.* Hillsdale, NJ: Erlbaum.

Peters, D. P. (1991). The influence of stress and arousal on the child witness. In J. L. Doris (Ed.), *The suggestibility of children's recollections: Implications for eyewitness testimony* (pp. 60–76). Washington, DC: American Psychological Association.

Peters, D. P. (in press). Stress, arousal, and children's eyewitness memory. In N. L. Stein, P. A.

Ornstein, B. Tversky, & C. J. Brainerd (Eds.), *Memory for everyday and emotional events.* Hillsdale, NJ: Erlbaum.

Schneider, W., & Pressley, M. (1989). *Memory development between 2 and 20.* New York: Springer-Verlag.

Smith, S. M., Glenberg, A., & Bjork, R. A. (1978). Environmental context and human memory. *Memory and Cognition,* **6,** 342–353.

Stein, N. L., & Boyce, W. T. (1995, April). The role of physiological reactivity in attending to, remembering, and responding to an emotional event. In G. S. Goodman & L. Baker-Ward (Chairs), *Children's memory for emotional and traumatic experiences.* Biennial Meeting of the Society for Research in Child Development, Indianapolis, IN.

Stein, N. L., Trabasso, T., & Liwag, M. (1991). *Children's and parents' memory for real life emotional events: Conditions for convergence or polarization.* Paper presented at the Biennial Meeting of the Society for Research in Child Development, Seattle, WA.

Underwood, B. J. (1963). Stimulus selection in verbal learning. In C. N. Cofer & B. S. Musgrave (Eds.), *Verbal behavior and learning: Problems and processes* (pp. 33–48). New York: McGraw-Hill.

# Repeatedly Thinking about a Non-event: Source Misattributions among Preschoolers

Stephen J. Ceci,[1] Mary Lyndia Crotteau Huffman, and Elliott Smith

*HDFS, Cornell University, Ithaca, New York 14853*

AND

Elizabeth F. Loftus

*University of Washington, Seattle, Washington 98195*

In this paper we review the factors alleged to be responsible for the creation of inaccurate reports among preschool-aged children, focusing on so-called "source misattribution errors." We present the first round of results from an ongoing program of research that suggests that source misattributions could be a powerful mechanism underlying children's false beliefs about having experienced fictitious events. Preliminary findings from this program of research indicate that all children of all ages are equally susceptible to making source misattributions. Data from a follow-up wave of data indicate that very young children may be disproportionately vulnerable to these kinds of errors when the procedure is changed slightly to create mental images more easily. This vulnerability leads younger preschoolers, on occasion, to claim that they actually experienced events that they only thought about. These preliminary findings are discussed in the context of the ongoing debate over the veracity and durability of delayed reports of early memories, repressed memories, dissociative states, and the validity risks posed by therapeutic techniques that entail repeated visually guided imagery inductions.

Recently, much has been written about the presumed suggestibility of children, especially very young children (Ceci & Bruck, 1993a, b). Although even adults are suggestible (e.g., Loftus, 1979), there appears to be a reliable age-related vulnerability to suggestive postevent questioning, with preschoolers disproportionately more vulnerable to these forms of suggestion than older children and adults (Ceci & Bruck, 1993a). This assertion may surprise some, as much confusion exists across studies in how suggestibility is defined and operationalized. As a result, it is easy to find scholars who express the view that there are no age-related differences in suggestibility or that any such differences are principally due to peripheral, unimportant details (e.g., whether a perpetrator wore a certain brand of sneakers when he robbed a store). Those expressing this view assert that young children are significantly less susceptible to erroneous suggestions about central actions or gist (e.g., whether a perpetrator touched a child who was

This article is reprinted by permission from *Consciousness and Cognition,* Volume 3, pp. 388–407 (1994).

[1] To whom correspondence and reprint requests should be addressed.

shopping when he robbed the store). Thus, some influential policymakers, such as the past president of Division 41 of APA and the APA Division of Children, Youth & Families, have opined that there is no real basis for assuming that children are any more suggestible than adults, except in cases concerning peripheral, unimportant details:

> There is now no real question that the law and many developmentalists were wrong in their assumption that children are highly vulnerable to suggestion, at least in regard to salient details. Although some developmentalists may be challenged to find developmental differences in suggestibility in increasingly arcane circumstances, as a practical matter who really cares whether 3-year-old children are more suggestible about peripheral details in events that they witnessed than are 4-year-old children? Perhaps the question has some significance for developmental theory, but surely it has little or no meaning for policy and practice in child protection and law. (Melton, 1992, p. 154)

Notwithstanding such claims, in a recent review Ceci and Bruck (1993a) reported that 83% of studies that have compared preschoolers with older children and adults have found increased levels of suggestibility among the preschoolers. Moreover, studies that have found increased susceptibility to suggestive questioning among preschoolers have not been confined to "arcane circumstances" or "peripheral details." Instead, they have included reports of bodily touching, emotional consequences of medical procedures, observations of simulated thefts, and anatomical doll interviews about genital touching (see Ceci, in press, for review). In short, there appears to be no useful purpose served by attempting to gainsay what is surely a scientifically robust conclusion, namely, that preschoolers present a special reliability risk if the postevent context has been riddled with repeated, erroneous suggestions. Young children's suggestibility proneness, while probably reduced for bodily events, is by no means nonexistent or negligible.

Having said the above, it is important for the sake of balance to also say that children, no matter how much more suggestible they are than adults, are nevertheless capable of recollecting large amounts of forensically accurate information when the adults who have access to them have not engaged in repeated erroneous suggestions. In many of the studies that have reported age-related differences in suggestibility, young children perform quite well—until and unless an interviewer persists in making repeated erroneous suggestions or subtly rewards the child for inaccurate answers. Short of this, the children do quite well.

Finally, age is a rather crude variable, masking important individual differences related to children's personality, intelligence, and family structure. Despite robust age-related normative trends, courts want to know whether a particular child in a particular setting is likely to be a reliability risk. To answer such questions, one must go beyond chronological age to examine the relevant contextual variables that might be operative. Specifically, it will be necessary in the future for those wanting to aid fact finders in examining how contextual factors (e.g., family structure, number of siblings, type of parenting style) moderate intellectual, personalogical, and motivational variables. Researchers are a long way from doing this at present.

## THE ROLE OF SOURCE MISATTRIBUTIONS

Although developmental differences in suggestibility seem to be well established, numerous attendant questions remain unresolved. These include such practically important matters as whether the magnitude of observed developmental differences is forensically relevant (and, if so, whether judges ought to give jurors cautionary instructions about young children's reliability risks), whether preschool children's greater suggestibility is memory-based (i.e., does suggestive questioning alter their memory trace for the event), or is their suggestibility socially based (e.g., are they more likely than older children and adults to defer the contents of their memories to their beliefs about what the interviewer wants them to report, e.g., Lindsay, Gonzalez, & Eso, in press; McCloskey & Zaragoza, 1985; Zaragoza, 1991; Zaragoza, Dahlgren, & Muensch, 1992).

The present paper is concerned with one of the conditions that has heretofore received only minimal attention in accounting for suggestibility among very young children, namely "source misattributions." Source misattributions refer to the difficulties that arise when one attempts to separate two or more sources of their memories, for example, an actual perception of some event versus an induction to imagine the event. A number of researchers have shown that preschool aged children find it more difficult to subsequently distinguish between actual and imagined self-generated acts, that is, between things that they merely imagined doing versus things that they actually did (Foley & Johnson, 1985; Foley, Santini, & Sopasakis, 1989). Even 9-year-olds have difficulty discriminating between acts they actually committed and those they merely imagined committing (Lindsay, & Johnson, 1987), as well as between acts of others they actually witnessed and those they only imagined that others performed. Recently, Lindsay and his colleagues (Lindsay et al., in press; Lindsay, Johnson, & Kwon, 1991) have extended this conclusion to argue that children are disproportionately more likely to confuse perceptually or semantically similar sources (e.g., acts performed by two different individuals who are similar in age). This work raises the possibility that children's source misattributions will occur when the two sources are similar and/or considered simultaneously. Therefore, by inducing even younger children to imagine what they might have seen or done, it is possible that false memories may be created.

In the past several years, attorneys have asked us to review the notes, audio tapes, and occasional videotapes of several hundred interviews with young children that were conducted by law enforcement, social work, and mental health professionals. The most frequent context for these interviews is the therapeutic session, since it is in therapy that important "disclosures" of sexual abuse are frequently made. Sometimes these disclosures come about after months or years of therapy, during which a child or adult has been encouraged to engage in visually guided imagery, self-empowerment training (e.g., reenacting alleged victimization scenes with victim and perpetrator dolls, and encouraging the child doll to dominate the perpetrator doll to regain control of presumed victimization feelings), symbol interpretation, hypnosis, and role playing (e.g., Fredrickson, 1992).

We decided to experiment with one of the techniques frequently used by therapists and social workers who interview preschool children, as evidenced by the tapes and transcripts that we have reviewed. The technique in question is a simple one, namely, the repeated encouragement of a young child by a therapist to think about a possible event that the therapist believes may have occurred sometime in the child's past, but is being denied or repressed by the child for a variety of reasons. Repeatedly encouraging a child to "think real hard" about an alleged event may create multiple sources of memories, some actually experienced and some only imagined, in the attempt at retrieval of nonexisting memories.

As indicated above, the source monitoring literature demonstrates that young children have greater difficulty separating memories of events that they actually experienced from those that they merely were asked to imagine enacting (Foley & Johnson, 1985; Lindsay et al., 1991). A number of researchers have shown that preschool aged children find it more difficult to engage in "realization judgments," that is, to distinguish between actual and imagired self-generated acts (things that they merely imagined doing themselves versus things that they actually did—Foley & Johnson, 1985; Foley, Santini, & Sopasakis, 1989). Even 9-year-olds have difficulty discriminating between acts they actually committed versus those that they merely imagined committing (Lindsay & Johnson, 1987), as well as between acts they actually witnessed and those they only imagined they witnessed.

Others have extended this conclusion to argue that children are disproportionately more likely to confuse perceptually or semantically similar sources (e.g., acts performed by two individuals who are similar in terms of age or gender) or acts performed by another person versus those they merely imagine that person to perform, since the source is the same individual in both cases (Lindsay et al., in press, 1991).

Before we describe how source misattributions might be involved in the production of inaccurate reports, and examine the developmental course of such misattributions, some historical background is useful.

## REPRESSED MEMORIES

Since the time of Hoffding (1891), it has been contended that stored information about life events fluctuates in its retrievability. The best known proponent of this early position was, of course, Freud (1938), who elevated repression to the center of the defensive organization, supplanting dissociation. Freud argued that memories about important societally conflictual events persist, repressed out of consciousness, or linger in a disguised form. For Freud (1905/1953, 1914/1963), successful therapy depended on the accessibility of these early events. He believed that autobiographical details were safely locked from consciousness but were accessible in the appropriate retrieval environment.

A great deal has been written about the validity of so-called "repressed memories," and Freud's own reversal of view about the presumed sexual fantasies of his 12 female clients has been singled out for criticism (Mason, 1984). Many scholars believe in the existence of latent memories that are inaccessible because of retrieval difficulties, including the classical Freudian notions of "blockading" due to frightening or sexual experiences (Briere & Conte, 1993; Fredrickson, 1992; Van Der Kolk & Van Der Hart, 1991; Williams, 1992). Other researchers, however, question the authenticity of such reports (e.g., Ofshe & Watters, 1993). For example, in a *Washington Post* story, Ulric Neisser, Ralph Haber, John Kihlstrom, and other well-known memory researchers expressed doubts about the authenticity of claims of repressed memories (Oldenberg, 1991). Recently, Loftus (1993) has argued that the evidence mounted by advocates of the repressed memory view is open to criticism and that the evidence for the repression of memories is either methodologically problematic or anecdotal, despite decades of effort.

Recently, the issue of repressed memories once again has come to the fore, this time not as a result of an academic debate over its underlying mechanism, but because of the alleged authenticity of plaintiffs' claims that they were the victims of childhood abuse that had been repressed or forgotten until adulthood. Courts in over 20 states have amended their statutes of limitation to permit plaintiffs to pursue repressed memory allegations starting from the time they become aware of their memory rather than the time of the alleged event.[2]

The best known repressed memory case involved Eileen Franklin-Lipsker, a housewife in Los Angeles. One day she looked up at her young daughter, Jessica, and noticed her hair. This momentary image triggered what was alleged to be a long repressed memory:

> The look in Jessica's eyes—her very blue eyes that were so much like Susie's—took Eileen back to a look of betrayal in the eyes of Susie Nason almost 20 years earlier. From then on, there were fragments. The first one she talked about to Kirk Barrett, her therapist, was the long silver ring. The ring was on Susie Nason's bloody hand and it was smashed. Then Eileen had an image of riding in a van, and then there was a mattress, and a lavender sweater. . . . The images were frightening. Little Susie Nason had been only 8 when she was murdered by an assailant who was never found. Eileen told Kirk Barrett that she couldn't believe that the images were coming into her mind and she didn't understand what they meant. It was 3 or 4 sessions later that her father was there—in her memory. As she eventually testified: "I remembered looking into Susie's eyes and I saw the silhouette of my father with his hands raised up above his head with a rock in them. . . . It was something that was completely, to my recollection, unknown to me, and it frightened me." (Edmiston, 1990, p. 229)

Franklin-Lipsker's revelation set in motion a series of statements that in turn set in motion a landmark case in which her father was tried and convicted of the 20-year-old murder of her girlhood friend (currently on appeal). During the past 3 years there have been many similar cases (Oldenberg, 1991), and it is now common to read about repressed memories dating back to toddlerhood. For example, in Albion New York an 8-year-old boy is currently claiming to have uncovered a memory of witnessing his father murder his mother with a baseball bat from when he was 23 months old.

---

[2] The analogy is made to medical malpractice case law where it has been firmly entrenched for many decades that patients are permitted to sue their doctors many years after being subjected to a medical procedure if they only discovered the connection between their suffering and the medical procedure in recent years. For example, if someone who had abdominal surgery a decade earlier never realized that the pain they experienced in recent years was due to a surgical sponge that had been inadvertently left in their stomach until an X-ray revealed this. Similarly, so-called survivors of childhood abuse are being permitted to sue their perpetrators upon "discovery" of their abuse memories in therapy.

Are these memories real or constructed? Does the memory system work the way that proponents of repressed memory maintain? As noted above, many believe that children and adults who testify about events from their distant past may be the victims of memory alteration resulting from repeated suggestions from therapists and others. If these "memories" are not real but have resulted from persistent, erroneous suggestions, then source misattributions could be the basis of *some* sexual abuse allegations, leading patients to have confidence in their vivid but inaccurate memories. As Rabinowitz (1990) has observed of the children from the infamous McMartin trial,

> . . . the worst thing about the long investigation and trial may be that, however unfounded the charges, the child witnesses grow up having internalized the belief that they have been the victims of hideous sexual abuse. (p. 63)

We have placed the words "repressed memory" in quotes because of the need for caution in accepting them as actual memories. Perhaps they *are* genuine memories, perhaps they are not. If the memories are not genuine, perhaps they are a product of suggestion. This hypothesis raises the question of whether it is even possible to inject an entire memory into the mind of someone for something that never happened. One recent study has shown that it is possible to inject an entire episode of being lost for an extended period of time into the mind of people (see Loftus & Coan, in press). However, no study of this type has been done with very young children.

Hence, the following study should be viewed as a "first pass," one that will undoubtedly require extension and replication by future researchers. But this study could be relevant to the debate over the validity of repressed memories by demonstrating one mechanism that can lead to vivid but false recollections, namely, source misattributions. While such a demonstration, if confirmed, would not rule out the validity of other types of delayed memory, it could elucidate some of the circumstances that can lead to false accounts.

## METHODS

*Subjects.* Children who were enrolled in two preschool programs in central New York served as subjects. No child attending these programs was excluded as long as parental agreement was obtained and the child had a sufficient understanding of English. Only one parent of nearly 125 declined to have their child participate, and only 8 children's language was deemed to be insufficient. The children came from a wide range of sociodemographic backgrounds, with approximately 40% the entire sample coming from professional families and 60% coming from blue collar and kindred occupations (with over half of this latter group receiving aid to families with dependent children at the time of the study). Approximately one-third of the sample was of African-American ancestry. The children were divided into two age groups: The young group ranged in age between 3 and 4 years and the older preschoolers were aged between 5 and 6 years. In total, 122 children began the study, with 96 of them completing a minimum of seven interviews by the end.

*Design.* Although the full design of this study is a 2 Ages at the time of the experiment (3–4 vs 5–6) × 2 Ages at the time of the actual events (1–2 months earlier vs 1 year earlier) × 2 time periods (initial interview vs terminal interview) × 3 Types of event (positive, neutral, negative), with the final three factors within-subjects, only part of this design will be discussed in this article. The reason for this is that the study is ongoing, with additional samples not scheduled to be completed until next year. At the time of writing, complete data on 96 children are available, and we shall confine all discussion to an analysis of this group of children. Of primary interest is age differences in the generation of true and false reports during the initial interview, and growth in false reports between the initial and terminal interviews. Future reports will consider the nature of events (positive, neutral, and negative) and the age of the child at the time of the original experience.

*Procedure.* Children's parents were interviewed to find out about events that transpired at various times in their children's lives (e.g., moving house, birth of younger siblings, vacation trips). Both affectively positive and negative events were elicited (e.g., surprise birthday parties, vacations to Disneyworld, injuries requiring stitches, deaths of pets). Parents were sent an information sheet explaining that the experimenters would present a list of events to their children and that the events on the list may or may not contain the actual events that the parents supplied. Events that did not come from parents were verified by them as never having occurred. In this wave of data, we focus on the children's reports of real events that occurred within the past 12 months and that were either negative or neutral participant activities (i.e., we do not report on real bystander activities nor on real events of any type that transpired more than 12 months earlier).

Children were interviewed individually and provided a list of both real (parent-supplied) and fictitious (experimenter-contrived) events. They were asked to judge which events on the list actually happened to them, emphasizing that some of the events did not happen to them. Lists contained two actual events provided by the child's parent, and these were very salient events. All lists also included two fictitious events that parents assured us had never happened to their children. One of these concerned getting one's hand caught in a mousetrap and having to go to the hospital to get it removed. The other involved going on a hot air balloon ride with their classmates. The interviewer held index cards on which the real and fictitious events were written and informed the child

> I am going to read some things that may have happened to you, and I want you to think real hard about each one of them that I am going to read. Try to remember if it really happened. We made this list up by talking to your mother and father to get them to tell us about things that really happened to you when you were younger, but not all of the things that I am going to read to you really happened.

Children were asked to try to recollect the events on 7–10 separate occasions, spaced on average approximately 7–10 days apart.[3] We suspected that simply

[3] Due to absences, unscheduled vacations, and occasional refusal to "play" with the interviewers, many of the children had weeks during which they were not interviewed at all. To ensure that children received the required number of interviews, they occasionally were given two interviews in a single week (Monday and Friday). This occurred, at most, twice for a given child.

asking preschoolers to think about the events so often might foster the conditions for fictitious "repressed memories." This work raises the possibility that misattributions of the sources of children's memories will occur when the two sources are similar or considered simultaneously. Therefore, by inducing even younger children to imagine what they might have seen or done, it is possible that false memories may be created.

Each occasion upon which a child falsely "recollects" an event in response to the interviewer's enjoinder to "think real hard if it happened" should serve to reinforce that event in memory. The last session (7th–10th) was always 10 weeks following the first session. At this time, a new interviewer asked the children for a free narrative about each of the real and imagined events. This interval was selected because research with adults' autobiographical memory shows that recognition of nonevents increases after a 3-month delay (Barclay & Wellman, 1986). During this final interview, children were asked to recall as much as they could about the events that were presented, including perceptual details such as location, clothing, utterances, and emotional expressions of others in the same context. They were also asked to rate their confidence for each detail as well as for the entire event, using a child-adapted rating scale. This final session was videotaped in order to collect data on adult judges' beliefs in the veracity of potentially misattributed memories, as well as to subject children's false reports to various techniques that have been touted as a means of discerning accurate and inaccurate reports (Raskin & Yuille, 1989). Many schemes for distinguishing between false and actual memories claim that they can be differentiated on the basis of internal consistency, perceptual details, unusualness of events, etc. (e.g., Schooler, Gerhard, & Loftus, 1986; Raskin & Yuille, 1989). Based on prior work with repeated erroneous suggestions, Ceci, Leichtman, and White (in press-a) have suggested that preschoolers' erroneous and accurate memories may not be distinguishable because repeated attempts to recollect false events may result in their incorporation into memory. In other words, perhaps false memories cannot be detected as false because the children, after repeatedly encouraged to imagine false events, have come to believe that they are accurately recalling real events. Therefore, they exhibit none of the signs of confabulation, tricking, or duping that characterize false reports by adults (Ceci et al., in press-a).

## RESULTS

The data in Table 1 are organized in terms of the first, third, fifth, and seventh sessions for both true and false assents. These data indicate the mean proportion of opportunities on which children assented to the false and true events. As can be seen, true events were nearly always recalled accurately, with little variation in all conditions. This is unsurprising since these were highly salient participatory events that had occurred during the past 12 months and probably received ample discussion and rehearsal in the children's homes.

While the findings for the true events were expected, this was not the case for the fictitious events. Our expectation that children would begin by denying that they remembered the fictitious events, but over time increasingly assent to them,

TABLE 1
Mean Proportion of True and False Assents as a Function
of Age and Session (SDs in Parentheses)

| | Sessions | | | |
|---|---|---|---|---|
| Age | 1 | 3 | 5 | 7 |
| | | False | | |
| Older | .25 | .33 | .37 | .32 |
| | (.31) | (.36) | (.39) | (.39) |
| Younger | .44 | .42 | .41 | .36 |
| | (.35) | (.38) | (.39) | (.34) |
| | | True | | |
| Older | .93 | .99 | .99 | .97 |
| | (.21) | (.08) | (.08) | (.12) |
| Younger | .93 | .92 | .93 | .85 |
| | (.21) | (.22) | (.21) | (.31) |

is not borne out, at least not overall (.34 false assent at 1st session vs .34 at 7th session).

But when the data are disaggregated by both ages, an interaction with sessions was apparent. Overall, twice as many younger children assented to false events at the initial interview than did older children (44% vs 25%). Interestingly, by the final (7th) interview approximately 3 months later, slightly fewer younger children were assenting (36%), whereas slightly more older children were now assenting (32%). Neither of these changes over time were significant.[4]

The above conclusions were confirmed in a series of repeated measures ANOVAs, with *Age* as a between-subject variable, and *Sessions* as a within-subjects variable. These analyses yielded a marginally significant *Age* × *Session* interaction, $F(3, 213) = 2.14, MS_e = .04, p = .097$. The interaction was the result of a 7% increase over sessions in false assents for older children, while younger children actually decreased in their false assents by 8% over sessions. Simple effects tests revealed that the difference between younger and older children's false assents at the time of the first interview was reliable, $F(1,71) = 6.04, MS_e = .11, p < .01$. In contrast, the difference between younger and older children's false assents at the time of the final interview was not significant ($F < 1$).

Thus, although older children are significantly more accurate than younger ones

[4] We ran these analyses different ways to see if the results would change if the length of time between first and final interview was held constant, as well as if the number of sessions was equated. When we used the 7th interview for all children, or the 10th week for all children (which for some children represented their 7th session, but for others only their 5th session), the findings were only slightly changed. The sole reliable difference was that younger children actually significantly declined in false assents between the first and final session ($M = .44$ vs .35, $F(1,71) = 4.25, p < .05$), whereas older children significantly increased in false assents ($M = .22$ vs .34, $F(1,71) = 4.07, p < .05$). With this single exception, the pattern of significant main effects and interactions were the same in both analyses. For ease of exposition, we have lumped together the 7th to 10th sessions, in view of the similar findings.

when all the false assent data are collapsed across all sessions, their advantage is relatively lessened over sessions so that by the final session there is no difference.

The ANOVAs do not tell the complete story, however. Specifically, they do not tell about the consistency of individual differences—that is, whether the same children who falsely assented during early sessions were still falsely assenting during later sessions. There is a modest degree of intraindividual variability, with only several children "flip-flopping" back and forth between assenting and not assenting. Stability coefficients that were computed on a third of the sample ranged between .62 and .87, for adjacent sessions. A conditional probability analysis calculated for the 1st, 2nd, 6th, and 7th sessions indicated that the likelihood of falsely assenting during session $n + 3$ was a function of the linear combination of assenting during sessions $n, n + 1$, and $n + 2$. In short, false assenting during later sessions was predictable from false assenting during previous sessions. The more prior false assents, the greater the likelihood of subsequent false assents. It was relatively rare to observe a child make a false assent for the first time at the final session.

Does flip-flopping back and forth between assent and denial imply anything about children's beliefs in their false claims? It may be that the children who flip-flopped possessed an uncertainty about the truth-value of their claims. But for those children who consistently assented over repeated sessions, we suspect that they believed their claims. We say this because some of the latter children clung tenaciously to their accounts, despite efforts by parents and strange interviewers to dissuade them. While we could not test this claim systematically, due to the approaching end of school year, we were able to reinterview some of the children who had consistently made false assents. We attempted to dissuade these children by first having their parents explain that the events were false and then having a strange interviewer attempt to get them to deny their assents. Despite this form of multilevel debriefing, these children resisted recanting in varying degrees. One boy, responding to his mother's assertion that his hand had never been caught in a mousetrap, told her "But it did happen. I remember it!" Another girl argued when her mother tried to disabuse her of her false assent, arguing that her mother wasn't at home when it happened; a third child insisted to his parents that he recalled this event happening when the family lived in their prior residence. He emphatically refused to accept their explanation that he had only imagined the false events.

## DISCUSSION

The results of this study demonstrate that while it is possible to mislead young children into claiming that they experienced nonevents, the frequency of doing so does not increase over time. Elsewhere, we have run a replication of this study, with an important modification: each week the interviewer informed the children that they had actually experienced the fictitious events and then asked them if they remembered having done so (Ceci, Loftus, Leichtman, & Bruck, in press). Under these conditions, there is a reliable increase in children's claims of having remembered the fictitious events over a 12-week period. By the penultimate (11th) interview, children's false assent rate had increased by over 80% from the rate at the first interview. At the final interview, the children were told that the individual who had been interviewing them during the prior 11 weeks had made lots of mistakes, including informing children that they had experienced events that they had not. Now when asked if they actually remembered experiencing fictitious events, nearly all of the children reduced their level of false assents, but the new rate was still more than 50% greater than their initial false assent rate. This indicates that very young children will increasingly assent to fictitious events over time, provided the procedure begins by informing them they had actually experienced the event. After a prolonged period of making such suggestions, the children are difficult to talk out of their "memories."

An examination of the children's final videotaped narratives in this follow-up study reveals richly detailed, but false, claims. At times, the children seem so convincing, inserting affect at the appropriate place, including low frequency details and spontaneous corrections. Although we were unable to examine increases in their vividness in the present study because videotapes of the initial interviews were often unavailable, in our replication study we videotaped all of the initial and final interviews. In this study there is some evidence that children's false reports increased in their vividness and amount of perceptual detail over time (i.e., increases over time in the mean length of descriptions, mean rated confidence on false assents, and the number of low frequency perceptual details provided by the child on false assents). There were no changes in the true event memories, with vividness measures increasing very little after the third interview.

As a test of our opinion that the children's final reports were highly credible, we selected five fictitious events that were reported by children during the final videotaped interview, along with five real events from the final interview, and showed them to 109 professionals in psychology, law enforcement, social work, and psychiatry to see if they could determine which events had actually been experienced by the children and which were fictitious.[5] (The psychologists were primarily clinicians and developmental psychologists.) We asked them to watch the videos, and rate their confidence on a 7-point scale that the event was actually experienced by the child (1, very confident that the child's narrative is essentially an account of an experienced event; 4, uncertainty about the accuracy of the child's narrative; 7, very confident that the child's narrative is essentially an

---

[5] In a separate study, transcriptions of 20 true and false reports from the same final interview were given to four experts who specialize in children's statement validity analysis. They were not informed of how many of the reports were true and false, but merely instructed to rate them using published CBCA criteria (Raskin & Esplin, 1991). These data are being analyzed at this time, but preliminary analyses by the second author, Crotteau, as part of her Master's thesis, indicate that CBCA was practically ineffective at distinguishing between accurate and inaccurate statements. It could be argued that the procedure is not a fair test of CBCA's discriminability because the statements were too short or because the interviewers did not adhere strictly to the recommended interviewing format (SVA), although they were conducted according to SVA recommended practices and none of the raters claimed that the statements were too brief for application of CBCA. We suspect that the reason CBCA was ineffective is because some of these children *appear* to have adopted false beliefs as a result of the repeated visualizations. Perhaps techniques such as CBCA fare better when the task is to detect overt lying rather than false beliefs.

account of a nonexperienced event). They were not told how many videos were true and false, only that some were of each type.

The results were as we expected: Professionals were fooled by the children's narratives: There were as many professionals who were reliably worse than chance at detecting which events were real as there were professionals who were at chance and above chance (overall $p = .62$, for two-tailed test, $\alpha = .025$ each tail).[6]

Ratings for each subject for each child's statement were used to construct a ROC curve. Hits and false alarms were tallied for each professional, summed across the events. Decision matrices were constructed for these aggregated data, with hits along the $y$ axis and false alarms along the $x$ axis (Banks, 1970), allowing a Receiver Operator Characteristics (ROC) curve to be plotted. The area under the curve ($A'$) was .529, corresponding to a $d'$ (discriminability) near zero (i.e., chance). This is persuasive evidence that these particular professionals were unable to reliably discriminate signals from noise in the determination of statements of children who have been persistently rehearsed and provided congruent stereotypes. We make no claim about the ability of professionals to discriminate signals from noise if children are consciously lying to protect loved ones, to gain rewards, or to avoid punishment; the present paradigm is not a lie detection study but a false belief one, and the children themselves appear to often believe the authenticity of their erroneous reports (see below).

The above findings are in accord with Horner, Guyer, and Kalter's (1993) recent finding that mental health specialists' predictions of the accuracy of sexual abuse cases was disturbingly unreliable, spanning the full range of estimated probabilities that a child was abused from 0 to 1.0. In the present study, there was slight confirmatory bias, resulting in a mean confidence rating of 2.88. Several professionals in the present study reported that they found it difficult to imagine any of the narratives being fabricated. They may be right—at least if by fabrication we mean "a conscious attempt to mislead a listener about the truth as one understands it" (Ceci & Bruck, 1993). We are of the opinion, although we cannot prove it in a scientifically adequate manner, that many of these children had come to believe what they were telling the interviewer. This is probably why they were so believable to the present professionals who watched them. They exhibited none of the tell-tale signs of duping, teasing, or tricking. They seemed sincere, their facial expressions and affect were appropriate, and their narratives were filled with the kind of low frequency details that make accounts seem plausible. Consider, for example, one 4-year-old's statement during the interview sessions. He is being asked if he remembered having his hand caught in a mousetrap and requiring hospital treatment:

> My brother Colin was trying to get Blowtorch (an action figure) from me, and I wouldn't let him take it from me, so he pushed me into the wood pile where the mousetrap was. And then my finger got caught in it. And then we went to the hospital, and my mommy, daddy,

[6] A static Bernouli sampling process specifies the likelihood of correctly judging a real claim ($p$) and the likelihood of achieving precisely $x$ correct in $N$ independent trials $= (N/x)\, p^x q^{N-x}$, where the probabilities for $x = 0$–10 correct guesses, $N = 10$ trials, and $p = .5$ and $q = .5$. A two-tailed test was preferred in view of our interest in the number of raters who performed above as well as below chance.

and Colin drove me there, to the hospital in our van, because it was far away. And the
doctor put a bandage on this finger (indicating).

As can be seen, this child supplies a plausible account, not simply yes/no
answers to suggestive questions. Such children can be very believable to raters
who are not told the ground truth about this experiment—individuals who are
merely shown these children's videotaped "disclosures" and asked to judge their
authenticity.

One further bit of evidence supports our impression that at least some of these
children had come to believe that they actually experienced the fictitious events.
When ABC's news program, *20-20,* heard about this study they requested to film
some of these children. We called some of these children's parents to ask if
they would bring their children back for a session with John Stossel, the *20-20*
interviewer. One parent came in with her 4-year-old son and reported to us that
her husband and she had thought that the experiment was over, and therefore
they explained to their son that the story about the mousetrap was fictitious and
had never happened. She said that her son initially refused to accept this debriefing, claiming that he remembered it happening when the family lived in their
former house. She and her husband explained that the story was just in his
imagination and that nothing like this ever happened. Two days later, when the
child came to do the *20-20* interview, John Stossel asked him if he ever got his
finger caught in a mousetrap and had to go to the hospital to get it off. The child's
mother was shocked at his reply. He stated that he remembered this happening,
and he proceeded to supply a richly detailed narrative. When Stossel challenged
him, reminding him that his mother had already explained that this never happened, the child protested that it really happened and refused to back down in
the face of inducements from the interviewer to recant.

While the above child's insistence in the validity of his inaccurate report, in
the presence of his mother, is not proof that he believed what he was saying
about this fictitious event, it does suggest that he was not duping us for any
obvious motive, given that the demand characteristics were all tilted against his
claiming that he remembered this.[7] We are currently pursuing this hypothesis
with a new set of experiments.

So, repeatedly thinking about a fictitious event appears to have led preschool
children to produce vivid, detailed reports that the present group of professionals

---

[7] As a result of this child's insistence, we asked eight other parents if we could reinterview their
children about the nonevents in the parent's presence. During these interviews, we asked the parent
to explain to their child that the nonevents never happened. Of these eight children, three did not
challenge the parent's debriefing in any way we could discern, three children protested mildly (e.g.,
asking "Are you sure, mommy?"), and two protested strongly, like the child interviewed by ABC
("It did so happen . . . you were not there when I got caught in the mousetrap . . . you were at work
that day"; "It happened but it was at our old house. Dad knows, you can ask him."). Finally, in a
follow-up experiment, the interviewer told children each time that they had experienced the false
events until the final interview, whereupon a new interviewer explained to the children that the
previous interviewer had gotten it wrong and told children they experienced events that they had
not. Interestingly, while children reduced their claims of having recalled false events when told this,
they did not return to baseline at the first interview.

were unable to discern from reports of actual events. While it is possible that professionals who are trained in lie detection methods such as CBCA (Raskin & Esplin, 1991; Devitt, Honts, & Peters, 1994) may perform better than these unselected professionals, this is conjecture awaiting empirical validation.

Recently, cognitivists have provided demonstrations of the various mechanisms that may induce adults to erroneously come to "remember" false events (Lindsay & Read, in press), including repeatedly thinking about events.

## REPRESSION, SUPPRESSION, FORGETTING, AND/OR CO-CONSTRUCTION?

In this concluding section, we shall comment briefly on the current debate over the validity of so-called repressed memories and the relevance of the work reported here for that debate. Several of us have been immersed in this debate for years, and others of us have been studying the pro and con positions as part of our role as members of the *APA Working Group on Investigation of Memories of Childhood Abuse* (APA Monitor, 1993). Here we shall confine our thoughts to two points, (1) the evidentiary basis of the pro and con positions and (2) the relevance of the present data to this debate.

*The canons of evidence.* One of the most surprising aspects of the present debate over the validity of adult recollections of childhood memories of abuse is the laxity of definitions that seem to be driving the pro and con positions. This can be seen by reviewing the most common evidence cited in support of the position that early abuse experiences can be repressed, only to resurface in therapy decades later. There are four longitudinal surveys of adults who allegedly experienced sexual assaults as infants and children (Briere & Conte, 1993; Herman & Schatzow, 1987; Loftus, Polansky, & Fullilove, 1994; Williams, 1992). Depending on which survey results you choose, the incidence of self-reported forgetting about early abuse-related experiences ranges from 19% (Loftus et al., 1994) to 26% (Herman and Schatzow (1987)[8] to 38% (Williams, 1992) to 59% (Briere & Conte, 1993) to 64% (if Herman and Schatzow's 28% of severe repression is combined with the 38% of moderate forgetting that also was observed in their study—as done by Briere and Conte). Thus, there is a very wide range of estimates of the prevalence of repression, and it is not easily narrowed by examining the differences in how each researcher defines sexual abuse (narrow vs broadly defined) or chooses their samples (two studies were composed mainly of middle class white female samples, namely, those of Briere and Conte, Herman and Schatzow, and the other two were comprised of predominantly inner city African-American women). Some but not all of the studies tend to associate memory lapses with an early onset of abuse, repetitive abuse, and the violent abuse. Adults who report abuse onset in early childhood are more likely to claim to have lost contact with the memory than adults whose abuse occurred during middle or later childhood. Moreover, memory of violent abuse is more likely to

---

[8] In the text of their report, Herman and Schatzow report that 28% of their subjects had severe repression but the actual number is 14 of 53, which comes to 26%.

be lost than memory of nonviolent abuse. And, finally, memory of repeated abuse is more likely to be lost than memory of isolated abuse.

Each of these studies is open to alternative explanations. The way that adult respondents interpret the critical abuse questions is of paramount importance, as is the interpretation researchers give to the responses. In the Briere and Conte survey, for instance, the wording of the critical question was as follows:

> During the period of time when the first forced sexual experience happened and your 18th birthday was there ever a time when you could not remember the forced sexual experience?

In the Loftus et al. study, the critical question, number 3, is worded:

> People differ in terms of how they remember their abuse. Which of the following experiences best characterizes your memory? 1) Some people have always remembered their abuse throughout their lives, even if they never talked about it. 2) Some people have remembered parts of their abuse their whole lives, while not remembering all of it. 3) Some people forget the abuse for a period of time, and only later have the memory return.

Some adults who were abused might have answered the Briere and Conte and Loftus et al. (No. 3) questions positively because they interpreted such questions to mean that there were long stretches of their life when they chose not to think about the abuse, due to its upsetting nature. Some crime victims report doing this; that is, following victimization they deliberately try to avoid thinking about their experience. Returning veterans frequently report that they engage in various forms of conscious blockading of combat memories. But there is little doubt that the vast majority of adult survivors of traumatic experiences can usually recall their frightful experiences if they are asked (e.g., "Do you remember being mugged in the parking lot when you worked at your former job?"; "Do you remember being in a concentration camp in Auschwitz as a young boy during the war?"). In fact, therapists who treat Viet Nam veterans report that the problem with post traumatic stress is not that the memories are repressed but that they cannot be forgotten; they frequently intrude into conscious awareness unexpectedly and/or in response to some auditory stimuli.

In the Loftus et al. survey, 81% of respondents report always having remembered part or all of their early abuse. But Loftus et al.'s third question is open to the alternative interpretation that some portion of 19% of respondents who claimed to have lost contact with their memory of abuse misunderstood the question to include nonrepressed memory lapses, e.g., long periods of time when they did not think about the abuse, even though they could have easily recalled it if asked to do so. To minimize such interpretive alternatives, a fourth question is needed such as *Was their ever a time when you would have said someone was crazy if they said that you had been abused as a child?* We suspect that if such a question were added to surveys, the number of respondents giving evidence of "repressed memory" would decline even further.

Another problem with assuming that an affirmative answer indicates that the abuse memory went underground, repressed into the unconscious, is that it is normal to forget experiences, both pleasant and traumatic ones. To be unable to retrieve an experience may not reveal repression, but merely ordinary forgetting processes. Thus, failure to recall early abuse experiences may be the result of normal memory decay and interference mechanisms, not fierce repression. To the extent that lost contact with memory reflects ordinary forgetting processes, as opposed to repression, we would expect that the memory, once rediscovered, would be an imperfect record of what had originally been experienced. That is, normal memory processes are highly constructive and susceptible to fading and shaping. So, when an adult purports to have uncovered an early abuse memory that is highly detailed, vivid, and coherent, memory experts are often skeptical. This is why it becomes more than a semantic distinction to decide whether the lost memory was the result of repression or ordinary forgetting; the latter would suggest that some highly vivid, detailed accounts of recovered memory are open to challenge.

The interpretative snarls go on. It is possible that many early abuse experiences were forgotten, not because of some fierce repression mechanism that blockaded the abusive experience from consciousness, nor because of ordinary forgetting processes, but rather because the event occurred prior to the offset of the infantile amnesia period. In other words, we expect the earliest experiences to be unrecallable—even pleasurable early experiences are unrecallable. The world of the 1- or 2-year-old may be beyond the ability of adults to resurrect. That adults who claim to have lost contact with experiences from the first couple years of their lives can suddenly do so in therapy or in a support groups raises doubts about the authenticity of their delayed "memories." While research still has a long way to go before it can claim to fully understand infantile amnesia, we do have a large corpus of scientific studies that suggest it is unlikely that as adults we can gain access to these earliest experiences in the form in which they were experienced and interpreted at the time by the infant. It is not clear that fondling or even fellatio are experienced by infants and young children as assaultive; they may at times be pleasurable or neutral, thus not carrying the psychic trauma needed for repression.

Of course, painful penetration is in a different class altogether. But even here it is not obvious that such experiences can be resurrected from the earliest years. Again, there is no evidence that circumcision, the insertion of anal suppositories, etc. are recallable from the first 2 years of life. Most adults cannot even recall painful medical procedures that occurred up to age 5 (e.g., tonsillectomy).

Interestingly, there is one study that we know of in which preschoolers were subjected to a highly aversive medical procedure called a "voiding cystourethrogram" or VCUG for short. The VCUG entails a stressful urinary tract catheterization, followed by filling the child's bladder with contrast fluid. This procedure is given for different reasons, including to check the reflex action of the urinary tract muscle. It is not only stressful, but also embarrassing, because after the child's bladder is filled to an extremely uncomfortable level, she is made to urinate on the examining table in front of the medical team. Films of children undergoing this procedure vividly demonstrate its aversiveness. Goodman and her colleagues have studied children who have been subjected to between one and six VCUGs, and they found that children who received repetitive VCUGs were no more likely to forget the details of their experiences than children who received only a single VCUG. In fact, repeated experience with this voiding procedure is, if anything, associated with superior recall (Goodman, 1993). While this does not prove that repetitive abuse is not more likely to be repressed, it does force us to ask what mechanism would lead to repression of illicit sexual abuse experiences but not to socially sanctioned genital probing. To say it is the socially sanctioned nature of the latter is to beg the question.

Thus, to whatever extent we as adults are capable of accurately recollecting memories of events that transpired during the first couple years of life, they are likely to be the product of family rehearsals during reunions and get-togethers; family members' retellings that become part of our oral history. We may remember getting car sick on the way to grandmother's house at age 3 or having an awful temper tantrum at the supermarket at age 2, not because we can gain access to the original encoding of these experiences, but because we heard accounts of them later in childhood and we mentally created images from these later retellings. The findings from the present study and the follow-up study briefly described here suggest that these mental images could take on a vividness that is easily mistaken for a veridical memory, much like the famous abduction anecdote that Jean Piaget thought he could "remember."

Finally, all of us forget experiences, positive and negative ones. It is physiologically impossible to maintain a conscious record of our complete past. We do not need to posit special repression or dissociative mechanisms to account for this type of forgetting.

If you add up these alternative interpretations, a reasonable reader of this literature could be persuaded that much—perhaps even most—of the reported inability of adults to recollect their abuse allegations at some point in their past is not the result of repression, at least not in its strong or "robust" form (Ofshe & Singer, 1993). Rather, most instances of forgetting early abuse experiences are due to ordinary forgetting (which would raise doubts about how authentic claims of veridicality and vividness are, since ordinary memories are not hermetically sealed and forgetting exacts a toll), infantile amnesia (which would preclude recalling accurately the earliest experiences, regardless whether they were positive or negative), or the way the respondent interpreted the question. Taken together, these considerations suggest that most so-called repressed memories may not have been repressed and later uncovered but were always accessible, although not dwelt on for long periods of time, or were forgotten for ordinary reasons or else were the result of false constructions.

Does this mean that repression is an invalid concept? Not at all. Even if we were to take the lowest incidence figure (19%) from the four studies (Loftus et al., 1994) and "discounted" it for the possibility of infantile amnesia (e.g., throwing out all claims of abuse that occurred during the first 2 years of life on the ground that they cannot be expected to have been recalled, thus including the failure to recall them as evidence that they were repressed inflates the prevalence of repression), ordinary forgetting, and so on, this might still leave a residual of cases that could not be dismissed as artifactual. We believe that the most prudent reading of this literature is that repression may occur, but not as frequently as any of the four studies indicate. We pointedly do not accept the higher rates that have been touted (i.e., over half of all abuse victims report having repressed their abuse at some time), because the demand characteristics associated with the recruitment methods are problematic (e.g., the respondents were members of "survivors of incest" support groups, who attended sessions with the aim of recovering memories; thus they are self-selected and cannot be used to extrapolate prevalence rates in the population of all abuse victims). While it is possible to criticize the lowest estimate of 19% on the assumption that some of the women (all participants in a drug rehabilitation program) who failed to report childhood abuse are still repressing the abuse memory, this would seem assume an answer to what ought to be the object of investigation.

Putting aside methodological issues in these four studies, there is a growing disillusionment in the adult cognitive literature with special mechanisms that have been invoked to validate of some of the more dramatic accounts of an alleged early abuse experience erupting into consciousness for the first time, replete with highly specific details (see Lindsay & Read, in press, for a good description of various cognitive mechanisms that might be responsible for memory errors). Such testimonials sound suspiciously similar to the claims by "flashbulb" researchers that have been rejected in favor of the view that even personally significant and surprising events are susceptible to the same constructive/schematic distortion processes as everyday memories:

> The point is that we appear to gain nothing by attributing these processes to special mechanisms. As stated earlier, it is impossible to reject that for some, somewhere a special neural memory mechanism permanently imprints details for certain events; it is just that as data accumulates, it does not appear this explanation is the best approach. (Wright, 1993, p. 136)

Elsewhere, we have reviewed the claim that highly stressful experiences are given privileged encoding (Ceci & Bruck, 1993), and we will not rehash that here, except to note that a fundamental difference of opinion exists among researchers regarding the role of affect in memory. Some believe that high levels of stress at the time of an event (e.g., a medical procedure) facilitates the events being remembered, while others claim the opposite (see debate between Goodman, 1991, and Peters, 1991). Interestingly, neither of these positions fits with the claim of some that trauma experiences are repressed.

## ACKNOWLEDGMENTS

Portions of this research were supported by a grant from the National Institute for Child Health and Human Development RO1 HD 25775, and NSF No. 1R01 MH50786-01.

## REFERENCES

APA Monitor (1993, November). APA panel is examining memories of child abuse, p. 44

Banks, W. (1970). Signal detection theory and memory. *Psychological Bulletin,* **74,** 81–99.

Briere, J., & Conte, J. (1993). Self-reported amnesia for abuse in adults molested as children. *Journal of Traumatic Stress,* **6,** 21–31.

Ceci, S. J. (in press). Cognitive and social factors in children's testimony. In B. Sales & G. Vandebos (Eds.) (1993). *Psychology and Law Master Lectures.* Washington, DC: APA Books.

Ceci, S. J., & Bruck, M. (1993b). Child witnesses: Translating research into policy. *SRCD Social Policy Report.* Vol. 7 (pp. 1–31).

Ceci, S. J., & Bruck, M. (1993a). The suggestibility of the child witness: A historical review and synthesis. *Psychological Bulletin,* **113**, 403–439.

Ceci, S. J., Leichtman, M., & White, T. (in press-a). Interviewing preschoolers. In D. P. Peters (Ed.), *The child witness in context: Cognitive, social, and legal perspectives.* Netherlands: Kluwer.

Ceci, S. J., Loftus, E. F., Leichtman, M. D., & Bruck, M. (in press-b). The role of source misattributions in the creation of false beliefs among preschoolers. *International Journal of Clinical and Experimental Hypnosis.*

Devitt, M., Honts, C., & Peters, D. (1994, March 12). Paper presented at the biennial meeting of the American Psychology/Law Society, Santa Fe.

Edmiston, S. (1990). A twenty-nine-year-old California woman charges her father with a 20-year-old murder. *Glamour,* **November,** 228–285.

Foley, M., & Johnson, M. (1985). Confusion between memories for performed and imagined actions. *Child Development,* **56**, 1145–1155.

Foley, M., Santini, C., & Sopasakis, M. (1989). Discriminating between memories: Evidence for children's spontaneous elaborations. *Journal of Experimental Child Psychology,* **48**, 146–169.

Fredrickson, R. (1992). *Repressed memories: A journey to recovery from sexual abuse.* New York: Simon & Schuster.

Freud, S. (1938). The psychopathology of everyday life. In A. Brill (Ed.), *The writings of Sigmund Freud.* NY: Modern Library (originally published 1914).

Freud, S. (1905/1953). Three essays on the theory of sexuality. In J. Strachey (Ed.), *The standard edition of the complete psychological works of Sigmund Freud* (Vol. 7), pp. 135–243). London: Hogarth Press (Originally published in 1905).

Freud, S. (1914/1963). *Instincts and their vicissitudes.* Collected papers. NY: Basic Books. (Originally published in 1915).

Goodman, G. S. (1993, August, 21). *Child victims, child witnesses.* Paper presented at the annual meeting of the American Psychological Association, Toronto.

Herman, J. L., & Schatzow, E. (1987). Recovery and verification of memories of childhood sexual trauma. *Psychoanalytic Psychology,* **4**, 1–14.

Hoffding, H. (1891). *Outlines of psychology.* NY: Macmillan.

Horner, T. H., Guyer, M. J., & Kalter, N. M. (1993). Clinical expertise and the assessment of child sexual abuse. *Journal of the Academy of Child and Adolescent Psychiatry,* **32**, 925–933.

Lindsay, D. S., Gonzalez, V., & Esso, K. (in press). Aware and unaware uses of postevent suggestions. In M. Zaragoza (Ed.), *Memory, suggestibility, and eyewitness testimony in children and adults.* Beverly Hills, CA: Sage.

Lindsay, D. S., & Johnson, M. K. (1987). Reality monitoring and suggestibility. In S. J. Ceci, M. Toglia, & D. Ross (Eds.), *Children's eyewitness memory.* (pp. 92–121). New York: Springer-Verlag.

Lindsay, D. S., Johnson, M., & Kwon, P. (1991). Developmental changes in memory source monitoring. *Journal of Experimental Child Psychology,* **52**, 297–318.

Lindsay, D. S., & Read, J. D. (in press). Psychotherapy and memories of childhood sexual abuse: A cognitive perspective. *Applied Cognitive Psychology.*

Loftus, E. F. (1979). Reactions to blatantly contradictory information. *Memory & Cognition,* **7**, 368–374.

Loftus, E. F. (1993). The reality of repressed memories. *American Psychologist,* **48**, 518–537.

Loftus, E. F., & Coan, D. (in press). The construction of childhood memories. In D. P. Peters (Ed.), *The child witness in context: Cognitive, social, and legal perspectives.* Netherlands: Kluwer.

Loftus, E. F., Polonsky, S., & Fullilove, M. T. (1994). Memories of childhood sexual abuse: Remembering and repressing. *Psychology of Women Quarterly.*

Mason, M. A. (1991). A judicial dilemma: Expert witness testimony in child sex abuse cases. *Psychiatry and Law,* **Winter–Fall,** 185–219.

McCloskey, M., & Zaragoza, M. (1985). Misleading postevent information and memory for events: Arguments and evidence against the memory impairment hypothesis. *Journal of Experimental Psychology: General,* **114,** 1–16.

McGough, L. (in press). *Fragile voices: The child witness in American courts.* New Haven, CT: Yale Univ. Press.

Melton, G. (1992). Children as partners for justice: Next steps for developmentalists. *Monographs of the Society for Research in Child Development,* **57**(Serial No. 229), 153–159.

Moll, A. (1913). *The sexual life of the child.* New York: Macmillan.

Ofshe, R., & Watters, E. (1993, March/April). Making monsters. *Society,* 4–16.

Ofshe, R. J., & Singer, M. T. (1993). *Recovered memory therapies and robust repression: A collective error.* Unpublished Manuscript, University of California, Berkeley.

Oldenberg, D. (1991). Dark memories: Adults confront their childhood abuse. *Washington Post.* **June 20,** D5.

Rabinowitz, D. (1990). From the mouths of babes to a jail cell: Child abuse and the abuse of justice. *Harper's Magazine,* **May,** 52–63.

Raskin, D. C., & Esplin, P. W. (1991). Statement validity analysis: Interview procedures and content analysis of children's statements of sexual abuse. *Behavioral Assessment,* **13,** 265–291.

Raskin, D. C., & Yuille, J. (1989). Problems in evaluating interviews of children in sexual abuse cases. In S. J. Ceci, M. P. Toglia, & Ross, D. F. (Eds.), *Adults' perceptions of children's testimony* (pp. 184–207). New York: Springer-Verlag.

Schooler, J., Gerhard, J., & Loftus, E. F. (1986). Qualities of the unreal. *Journal of Experimental Psychology: Learning, Memory, and Cognition,* **12,** 171–181.

Sherman, S. J., Cialdini, R. B., Schwartzman, D. F., & Reynolds, K. D. (1985). Imagining can heighten or lower the perceived likelihood of contracting a disease. *Personality and Social Psychology Bulletin,* **11,** 118–127.

Van Der Kolk, B. A., & Van Der Hart, O. (1991). The intrusive past: The flexibility of memory and the engraving of trauma. *American Imago,* **48,** 425–454.

Williams, L. M. (1992). Adult memories of childhood abuse: Preliminary findings from a longitudinal study. *APSAC Advisor,* **5,** 19–21.

Wright, D. B. (1993). Recall of the Hillsborough disaster over time: Systematic biases of 'flashbulb' memories. *Applied Cognitive Psychology,* **7,** 129–138.

Zaragoza, M. (1991). Preschool children's susceptibility to memory impairment. In J. L. Doris (Ed.), *The suggestibility of children's recollections* (pp. 27–39). Washington, DC: American Psychological Association.

Zaragoza, M., Dahlgren, D., & Muench, J. (1992). The role of memory impairment in children's suggestibility. In M. L. Howe, C. J. Brainerd, & V. F. Reyna (Eds.), *Development of long term retention* (pp. 184–216). New York: Springer-Verlag.

# Reducing the Potential for Distortion of Childhood Memories

Karen J. Saywitz[1] and Susan Moan-Hardie

*Department of Psychiatry, UCLA School of Medicine, Harbor/UCLA Medical Center,
1000 West Carson Street, Torrance, California 90509*

In the present research, two studies test the efficacy of an innovative procedure designed to reduce distortion and enhance communication of accurate childhood memories. One hundred two 7-year-olds participated in a staged activity and were randomly assigned to one of two treatment conditions (Intervention or Control). Two weeks later, half of the children participated in the innovative procedure designed to increase resistance to misleading questions by addressing sociolinguistic and socioemotional factors thought to promote acquiescence to misinformation. The other half of the children participated in control sessions and were given motivating instructions to do their best. Then, memory for the staged activity was tested in an interview with an unfamiliar authority figure. The results of both studies suggest that the children who participated in the innovative procedure made significantly fewer errors in response to misleading questions than children in the control groups, hence diminishing acquiescence. This was accomplished without generating additional errors on the other question types. These findings are interpreted as a promising first step toward reducing the potential for distortion in the recall of childhood memories. Implications for adult recall of childhood trauma are discussed.

Recent discussion of "forgotten" memories of childhood trauma is often cast in extremes. Such memories are viewed either as the fabrications of overzealous therapists and overly compliant patients or as veridical accounts of experiences from the distant past, repressed to avoid psychological pain. Yet, there is ample evidence that the recall of childhood trauma is a complex, multiply determined phenomenon that defies easy dichotomies or simple models. Retrospective studies of earthquake victims (e.g., Miller, Kraus, Tatevosyan, & Kamenchenko, 1993), combat veterans (e.g., Bremner, Southwick, Brett, Fontana, Rosenheck, & Charney, 1992), clinical psychologists (Feldman-Summers & Pope, 1994), emergency room patients (Williams, in press), and patients in psychotherapy (Briere & Conte, 1993; Loftus, Polonsky, & Fullilove, 1994) suggest that memories of childhood trauma take many forms. In this literature, substantial proportions of individuals report continuous memory of childhood trauma throughout their lives; memory loss for some but not all aspects of the trauma, with later recovery and corroboration; or temporary memory loss for the entire event.

Also reported in the clinical literature are memories that appear to be distortions of verifiable experiences. For example, Terr (1988) reported that long after being kidnapped and buried in a bus, children recalled the event but with distor-

[1] To whom reprint requests should be addressed.

This article is reprinted by permission from *Consciousness and Cognition*, Volume 3, pp. 408–425 (1994).

tions regarding, for example, the color of the bus and the sequence of events. Additionally, some researchers have concluded that individuals can construct false memories in response to the demand characteristics of the retrieval context (Loftus, 1993). For example, patients may redefine other painful childhood experiences as single perpetrator abuse for the sake of conceptual economy, protective idealization of the actual perpetrators, or in response to a therapist's presuppositions.

In short, the clinical literature provides many plausible hypotheses for the experimenter to consider. Some of these are more amenable to empirical study than others. Prospective, longitudinal studies are difficult undertakings due to the unpredictable nature of traumatic events and researchers' inabilities to record the event for later comparison to the subject's memory. Investigators cannot manipulate trauma in a systematic, rigorous manner for obvious ethical reasons. Analog laboratory studies are controlled and systematic, but rarely simulate key factors. Typically, these are studies of recall for stories, videos, or benign events that do not involve the overwhelming emotion that defines a traumatic memory and which, theoretically, is the catalyst for the amnesia. The subjects are "normals" who differ dramatically from genuine trauma victims in motivational, emotional, social, and cognitive characteristics. Many clinical hypotheses have yet to be subjected to scientific scrutiny. Hence, the extant experimental literature provides only fragments of understanding.

To date, the bulk of analog research has focused on individuals' susceptibility to suggestion. In the limited contexts studied, results indicate that memories of both children and adults can be distorted through suggestive questioning. Distortion is not inevitable and resistance can be steadfast; however, the potential for distortion exists. Perhaps it can be reduced. Minimizing the potential for distortion has clear benefits in the forensic and therapeutic context—fewer false allegations and greater recall of genuine abuse promote both justice and recovery. Beyond these practical implications, greater understanding may be achieved by examining factors that raise or lower the potential for distortion, in contrast to focusing exclusively on the veracity of childhood memories, a strategy that polarizes the debate and fails to address the complexities inherent in the process of reconstructing the past.

Available studies indicate that there are multiple pathways to distortion. Mnemonic, social, linguistic, contextual, and emotional determinants have been proposed (Ceci, Ross, & Toglia, 1987; Goodman, Bottoms, Schwartz-Kenney, & Rudy, 1991; Loftus & Davies, 1984; McClosky & Zaragoza, 1985; Saywitz, Goodman, Nicholas, & Moan, 1991; Saywitz & Nathanson, 1993; Zaragoza, 1987). Some determinants may be impossible to modify at the time of recall, such as the strength of the original memory (Warren, Hulse-Trotter, & Tubbs, 1991). However, distortion that arises out of the social, emotional, and linguistic interchange during retrieval might be comparatively more malleable. In this article, we describe two studies of children's recall that test the efficacy of an innovative intervention designed to reduce distortion by increasing resistance to misleading information. The intervention strives to modify metacognitive knowledge of social, emotional, and linguistic factors salient in the therapeutic and forensic context. It is a modest proposal, given the multiply determined nature of memory performance in everyday life.

## PREVIOUS EFFORTS TO REDUCE SUGGESTIBILITY

Notwithstanding the need for interviewers to minimize suggestive techniques, such an approach is unlikely to be a sufficient solution to the problem, especially when children are involved. Although children's spontaneous narratives of past events are generally accurate, they are also quite incomplete and loosely organized. Additional information is forthcoming in response to specific follow-up questions. Not all of it is accurate. Most of the information is elicited piecemeal in response to questions that tend to drive the organization of the material (Fivush & Hudson, 1990). Given children's limited knowledge of the investigative process and the limited number of retrieval strategies at their disposal, young children are somewhat dependent on adults for direction to search memories systematically and exhaustively. Hence, children are often unresponsive to completely open-ended and nonleading questions (e.g., "Is there anything you want to tell me?" "No"), necessitating somewhat specific and mildly leading questions to focus on the topic at hand (e.g., "What did you do after school Wednesday?") or to broach topics they would prefer to avoid, a common childhood strategy for coping with stress (Cramer, 1991), or to help children recognize forensic relevance (e.g., "Did he say anything to you? What did he say?"). Moreover, some determinants of suggestibility are extralinguistic factors inherent to the interaction between the respondent and the questioner that cannot be modified by rephrasing the question into a nonleading form, such as the power differential between a child and an adult (Ceci et al., 1987).

Two previous laboratory studies have shown reductions in the suggestibility effect. In one study, researchers reduced the status differential between questioner and witness. When 7-year-olds, instead of adults, presented misleading questions to preschoolers, the suggestibility effect was decreased, although not eliminated (Ceci et al., 1987). The results highlight the power of social factors in determining suggestibility even though using other children as interviewers would not be a practical method of reducing the potential for distortion. In a second study, children were warned that questions may be tricky and were instructed to tell only what they really remembered. A very small increase in resistance to misleading questions was induced by this warning (Warren et al., 1991). Although encouraging, both of these studies involved story recall, not memory for real world events in which children participate. Also, children's perceptions of the interviewer's knowledge of the story were not always controlled.

A third laboratory study failed to achieve a reduction in the suggestibility effect. The intervention was based on the fact that adult subjects made fewer false identifications when given the explicit option of saying "I don't know" (Warnick & Saunders, 1980). Before questioning children about a previously staged event, Moston (1987) gave them permission to admit lack of knowledge. The instruction was based on two assumptions about children's sociolinguistic expectations of the interview context. First, children may expect adults to view their lack of knowledge unfavorably, regardless of accuracy. Second, children are unaware of their response choices and thus expect that all questions require a substantive response. Other studies have indicated that children have a tendency to try to answer incomprehensible (Saywitz & Snyder, 1991, 1993) and bizarre, unanswerable (Hughes & Grieves, 1980) questions, especially when researchers imply that "I don't know" is not an acceptable response.

Moston found that the children given permission to say "I don't know" used this response more frequently than a control group, but this trend was not associated with fewer errors on misleading questions. He hypothesized that the children may not have fully understood his instructions, misinterpreting the instruction to mean that they should say "I don't know" whenever the memory was not immediately at hand and failing to apply the necessary energy and motivation to retrieval. Another viable explanation is that instructions alone are insufficient to guarantee use of the new response option when resisting adult suggestion. Metacognitive knowledge aids recall performance but develops gradually. Studies of metamemory and retrieval strategy training suggest that merely exposing children to a new response option is often ineffective unless it is accompanied by metacognitive knowledge about strategy utility, for example, information about the value of the strategy for improving their performance (e.g., Lodico, Ghatala, Levin, Pressley, & Bell, 1983). Children need to learn to recognize situations that call for the strategy and to practice how to apply the strategy in a given situation in order to improve memory performance (See Schneider & Pressley, 1989, for review and discussion). According to Schneider and Pressley (1989) the application of appropriate strategies to appropriate situations initially requires much conscious effort but, with experience, becomes more automatic and habitual (e.g., driving a car). Practice is likely to be an essential component of strategy maintenance for young children.

Another reason suggestibility was not lowered in Moston's study could be that social, motivational, and emotional factors, not addressed by the "I don't know" instruction, underlie the children's concerns that adults will react negatively if children challenge adults' suggestions. Children might overvalue compliance in the forensic context because it is so highly valued in their everyday life. Changing children's perceptions in this regard may be difficult because, by and large, their perceptions are accurate. In their limited experience, noncompliance is typically met with disapproval or disciplinary action. Instructions alone may be insufficient to alter children's expectations of such consequences. Children may need practical experience with an adult in a given situation who reinforces rather than shows displeasure when they challenge the adult's presuppositions. From this experience, children can expand their knowledge of acceptable responses and probable reactions in a given context. For generalization to potentially intimidating settings, like police stations, such extra efforts might be imperative to reduce the potential for distortion.

## RATIONALE FOR THE PRESENT INTERVENTION

Like playing a game without knowing all the rules, participants who are unfamiliar with the requirements, procedures, and practices of the mental health or legal systems are likely to find themselves at a disadvantage. Children not only lack substantive knowledge of the legal system (Saywitz, 1989), but also often possess limited knowledge of the task at hand, the context, their communication partner, and their own abilities, especially in complex and unfamiliar situations (Dickson, 1981; Flavell & Wellman, 1977). The result may be misperceptions that inhibit resistance and foster acquiescence to suggestive questions.

Children bring to the interview a set of expectations and beliefs about the rules for sociolinguistic and socioemotional interaction derived from their own experiences in everyday conversation (Irwin, 1982). Children may fail to appreciate that adults in the clinical or forensic context are operating under quite a different set of principles. First, listeners assume that speakers' utterances are sincere, germane, reliable, and intelligible (Grice, 1975). Adults learn to anticipate certain exceptions to these rules. However, studies suggest that until 9 to 13 years of age, children are gradually developing an appreciation for the conditions that violate these postulates of conversation (e.g., Demorest, Meyer, Phelps, Gardner, & Winner, 1984). Second, children perceive adults to be trustworthy and cooperative, if not supportive, conversational partners who seek to clarify rather than confuse (Garvey, 1984). For example, children may expect a degree of sincerity that is not always present in the adversarial process because they possess insufficient perspective-taking skills, inadequate knowledge of the context, and incomplete understanding of the speaker's intent. Children may assume that adults would not be purposefully deceptive conversational partners. This is not an unreasonable assumption given the typically supportive role of parents and teachers in conversation. Third, children tend to consider adults to be highly credible sources of information, and more credible than children (e.g., Ackerman, 1983). Such expectations could promote suggestibility because children assume that adults rarely make mistakes and that an adult interviewer knows more than the child about what happened, overestimating adults' knowledge of the event.

Fourth, many authors have speculated that children acquiesce to leading questions in order to please adults, to avoid adult anger, or to protect self-image from humiliation. Such socioemotional explanations seem plausible given children's limited perspective-taking skills, relatively egocentric viewpoint, and their limited knowledge of the interviewer's motivation, the purpose of questioning, or the forensic relevance of their responses. Theories of "motivated remembering" have highlighted the significance of expectations, beliefs, self-efficacy, and coping strategies for memory performance (Paris, 1988). Within this framework, people's expectations regarding interviewer reaction (anger, retribution) and their perceptions of self-efficacy (insecurity, grandiosity), their coping patterns (denial, avoidance, hypervigilance, mastery), and their emotions (ambivalence, fear) can affect the retrieval process.

To examine whether children harbored misperceptions about the task of testimony and specifically about the questioner's intentions and reactions, Saywitz and Nathanson (1992) interviewed 80 7- to 8-year-olds regarding their impressions of an interviewer after they participated in mock testimony in two different settings about a past school activity. Half of the children were questioned in a small private room and half in a courtroom with a simulated trial environment. All were asked the same set of questions by the same male law student trained to maintain the same professional demeanor in both settings. When questioned later about their experience giving testimony, many children expected that the adult already knew the answers to the questions, even though he was not present at the event under investigation. Children frequently expressed concern about protecting their self-image. They worried that the interviewer would think they were stupid if they conceded lack of knowledge after admitting that they had been present at the event. Findings such as these suggested that children can possess a number of expectations about task demands and adult behavior that could facilitate acquiescence rather than resistance to misleading questions.

To address this problem, we developed an intervention to increase children's awareness of the (a) task demands (e.g., difficulty level and suggestiveness of questions, adults' expectations and intentions), (b) appropriate response options (e.g., acceptability of "I don't know" or "I don't remember" responses), and (c) probable response consequences (e.g., adults' reactions in the forensic and therapeutic context).

To increase children's awareness of the task, we warned children that questions might be misleading and to tell only what they really remembered, that is, that adults might put their guesses into the questions, but that since the adult was not present at the event under investigation, he or she could not know what really happened. To highlight the speaker's expectations, and to disabuse children of the notion that they are required to provide a concrete answer to every question, the researcher warned children that some of the questions might be difficult and some might be easy and that the interviewer did not expect them to know all the answers.

To increase awareness of response options, we went beyond giving permission to say "I don't know" by adding simple drawings to concretize and visualize response choices considered acceptable in the interview context: admitting lack of memory (e.g., picture of someone scratching his head), admitting lack of knowledge (e.g., picture of someone shrugging his shoulders), or telling the answer when they knew the answer (e.g., picture of someone smiling).

To address misperceptions regarding response consequences in the forensic context, based on socioemotional pressures to comply, we sought to modify expectations about adult's reactions to children's responses. Reasons why individuals might choose to acquiesce in some situations were discussed and validated, including avoidance of adult disapproval, embarrassment, and peer rejection. Then, unanticipated negative consequences for acquiescence were highlighted. The cost of error was discussed, including that the wrong person would be punished. Children were told the interviewer was interested in the most accurate memory possible, not efforts to please the adult. We also taught children to use self-statements during the interview to promote confidence and assertiveness (e.g., "I knew there would be questions like this. I can do it. I'll tell him he's wrong.").

To promote maintenance and generalization, children practiced answering leading questions about a previously viewed videotape. Challenging adult supposition and admitting lack of knowledge were met with praise for bravery, thoughtfulness, and honesty. The efficacy of this intervention package was tested in two experiments described below.

## EXPERIMENT I

### Method

*Subjects*

Fifty-five second graders ($M$ = 93.2 months; 34 males, 21 females) from public schools in southern California participated in this study. Children were randomly assigned to one of two treatment conditions: (A) Training group—instructions and strategy training to resist misleading questions ($n$ = 28) or (B) Control group—motivating instructions to do their best ($n$ = 27). Treatment groups did not differ on distributions of gender, age, verbal fluency (as measured by standard scores on the *Peabody Picture Vocabulary Test—Revised*), social desirability (as measured by a modified version of the *Crandall Social Desirability Scale,* Crandall, Crandall, & Katkovsky, 1965), or socioeconomic status (as measured by the method described in Stevens & Cho, 1985).

*Procedure*

All of the children participated in a staged classroom event. Two weeks later, they participated in individual training or placebo sessions and were then interviewed about the classroom event with a standardized questionnaire comprising misleading, correctly leading, and specific questions.

*Staged event.* A 30-min classroom event was designed to simulate many of the elements of events about which children may testify (e.g., bodily touch). It was complex, with four distinct episodes, and rich in detail and action, which would later demand recall of a high calibre. It was emotionally compelling in that it implicated the children in a disagreement during a staged disruption and provided a distraction that could confuse the children later during demands upon them to reconstruct what had happened. To the extent that it stimulates demands typically made upon child witnesses, it is ecologically valid. It is bound to fall short because of the necessity to spare children harm or stress for experimental purposes. Careful attention was given to ensuring that children's memories were compared to the actual staging in which they participated instead of the script of what was supposed to have occurred. Variations across stagings are inevitable so each staging was videotaped for later comparison to the children's memories.

Two professional actors, hired to play student teachers, taught a history lesson, a craft activity, and a folk dance about Mexico. Midway through the craft activity, a confederate teacher entered, accusing the teacher of taking his materials without asking. She had already distributed the materials (e.g., markers) to the children who then became participants in the disagreement and its need for resolution. Some of the children hid the materials under their desks while the adults argued. When the disagreement was resolved, some children applauded. These actions indicated their emotional involvement in the event and its outcome.

*Treatment sessions.* RESISTANCE TRAINING. First, children in the training group listened to a story about a child who acquiesced to leading questions (i.e., who went along with the suggestions of people who put their guesses into questions).

Children discussed reasons why story characters did not disagree with question-
ers or resist suggestive questions (e.g., avoiding anger or disapproval). Unanticipated, negative consequences of acquiescence were highlighted in the story.
Eventually, the character learned the benefits of telling the truth even in the face
of suggestive questions by authority figures.

After discussing reasons why children might want to go along with a suggestive
question, children were given a rationale (high costs of error in the story) for
using an alternative response option (resistance). Then they were taught a new
response strategy that involved (1) stopping and thinking before answering (e.g.,
"Don't hurry into a wrong answer."); (2) mentally replaying the event and comparing one's own memory to the guess embedded in the question; (3) telling the
answer if they knew the answer and answering "I don't know" or "I don't
remember" if they did not; (4) using self statements to promote the confidence
needed to defy the questioner's implications and assert one's own response (e.g.,
"I knew there would be questions like this. I can do it." "I won't go along. I'll
tell her she's wrong.") as well as to inhibit inappropriate responses like guessing
(e.g., "I won't hurry into a wrong answer.").

The children watched a videotape provided by the Children's Television Workshop (CTW). Then they practiced the new response strategy, answering leading
and specific questions about the tape. The trainer gave specific feedback to every
response. Four cards containing schematic drawings representing the four acceptable response options (Yes, No, I don't know, I don't remember) were placed
on the table in front of the child prior to questioning. Before the questions about
the video began, sample questions were asked to give the children practice pointing to the cards to indicate an answer. The cards acted as reminders of the
acceptable response options in this setting.

During practice questioning children were instructed that they may not know
all the answers and were reminded that when adults are not present at events they
could not have firsthand knowledge of what occurred. They were also warned that
some questions might be easy but some might be hard and to be on guard against
adults putting their guesses into the questions. They were warned to tell only
what they really remembered and not to guess, but to tell the answer when they
knew the answer. The trainer explained her own expectations and intent by saying
that she did not expect children to have an answer for every question. She also
explained that in the interview situation, adults are more interested in the truth
than in efforts to please them. The children returned the next day for a 15-min
review session and were reinstructed to use the new response strategy in the
upcoming interview with a college professor.

CONTROL SESSIONS. The control group spent the same amount of time with the
same research assistants engaged in similar activities. They were asked the same
practice questions about the same CTW vignette, but without discussion, modeling, or feedback. Instead, they were given motivating instructions to do their best
and try hard. They also returned for a 15-min review session and were reinstructed to do their best in the upcoming interview with a college professor.

*Memory interview*. The children were individually interviewed about the classroom event by an unfamiliar adult who posed as the college professor of the

"student" teachers. She said that she needed the children's reports to grade her students. This was done to heighten task meaningfulness and promote ecological validity in terms of perceived consequences for error. The questions represented a range of social and linguistic pressure to acquiesce to the interrogator's suggestion. At one end of the continuum were highly suggestive questions that clearly indicated a preferred response (e.g., "The man who wanted his markers pushed the history teacher, didn't he?" and, "Isn't it true the dance teacher wore a scarf during the dance?"). Some leading questions suggested inaccurate information, referred to in this study as misleading questions (18). Others suggested information that was true of the event, referred to in this study was correctly leading questions (10). The remainder of the questions were referred to as specific questions (28). These questions included specific information but did not contain the added linguistic forms that press for acquiescence (e.g., "Did the history teacher tell you about Mexico?"). In some contexts, these questions would also be construed as leading; however, in this study they are differentiated from the highly suggestive, strongly worded questions we refer to as leading.

Suggestibility was measured by the proportion of incorrect responses to misleading questions. Correctly leading and specific questions were included to measure unintended effects on question types other than the target questions (i.e., misleading). Yes and no responses within each type of question were balanced to avoid response bias. Also, an effort was made to balance the number of questions concerning main ideas and peripheral details within each question type.

## Results and Discussion

In order to examine the efficacy of the experimental intervention, three 2 (treatment condition) by 2 (gender) MANOVAs were conducted. Proportions correct, incorrect, and don't know/remember on misleading, correctly leading, and specific questions were entered as dependent variables. Table 1 presents the means and significance tests on responses by treatment condition and question type.[2] To examine whether suggestibility effects were reduced, the proportion of errors on each question type was entered into the first MANOVA. The results revealed a main effect of intervention, $F(3, 49) = 3.37, p < .01$, with children in the training group producing significantly fewer errors than the control group. Univariate tests on each question type suggested that children in the training group produced significantly fewer errors on misleading questions ($M = .39$) than the control group ($M = .53$), indicating that they "resisted" the suggestions more often. Errors on correctly leading and specific questions were not affected by treatment conditions. Hence the intervention was successful in reducing false responses to misleading questions without generating additional errors on other question types.

When the proportion "I don't know/I don't remember" responses was entered into the second MANOVA, there was a significant main effect of intervention, $F(3, 49) = 3.72, p < .02$. Univariate tests on each question type revealed that

---

[2] Gender effects are reported elsewhere (Saywitz, Moan-Hardie, & Lamphear, 1991). Unless otherwise stated, interactions were not significant.

TABLE 1

Mean Proportion Correct, Incorrect, and "Don't Know/Remember" by Treatment Condition

| | Treatment condition | | |
| Responses | Training (n = 28) | Control (n = 27) | F |
|---|---|---|---|
| Misleading | | | |
| Correct | 0.45 | 0.42 | 0.25 |
| Incorrect | 0.39 | 0.53 | 8.36** |
| Don't know/remember | 0.15 | 0.05 | 8.86** |
| Correctly leading | | | |
| Correct | 0.73 | 0.82 | 7.09** |
| Incorrect | 0.18 | 0.15 | 1.39 |
| Don't know/remember | 0.09 | 0.03 | 5.25* |
| Specific | | | |
| Correct | 0.56 | 0.62 | 5.21* |
| Incorrect | 0.31 | 0.34 | 0.69 |
| Don't know/remember | 0.13 | 0.03 | 11.39** |

* $p < .05$.
** $p < .01$.

children in the training group responded more frequently with "I don't know or I don't remember" than the control group on all types of questions. This result is not surprising given that the intervention encouraged children to admit lack of knowledge or memory rather than acquiesce to suggestive questions or to guess.

When the proportion of correct responses was entered into the third MANOVA, again there was a main effect of treatment condition, $F(3, 49) = 3.53$, $p < .01$. Univariate tests on each question type revealed that treatment groups did not differ on proportion of correct responses to misleading questions. However, children participating in the experimental intervention produced fewer correct responses than the control group on correctly leading and specific questions. Thus, the intervention had the unintended effect of lowering correct responses to nontarget question types. The children may have developed an overly cautious response set and overgeneralized the "I don't know/remember" strategies at the expense of correct responses.

These data could be interpreted as a promising first step toward reducing the potential for distortion in the recall of childhood memories. In this study, 7-year-olds did learn to resist misleading questions. The benefit of the training was a 26% decline in percentage of error on misleading questions in comparison to a control group,[3] without generating additional error on any question type. The training effects are unlikely to be due purely to memory improvement. The memory improvement hypothesis predicts a significant difference between training conditions on specific questions, with the training group producing less error and more correct responses. This pattern did not emerge.

[3] Decline in percentage of error calculated as .53 − .39/.53.

In the present study, error on misleading questions was reduced but not eliminated. The effect size was modest (omega squared = .17). This is not surprising if suggestibility is multiply determined and many determinants are difficult to modify in real cases. Overgeneralization of the "I don't know" strategy at the expense of correct responses to specific questions demonstrates the need for rigorous testing of interventions used with child witnesses. Unintended side effects must be identified and eliminated. Hence, a second experiment was conducted to attempt to replicate the benefits of intervention with a new sample and to eliminate adverse effects on correct responses (Moan-Hardie, 1991).

## EXPERIMENT II

### Method

*Subjects*

Forty-seven second graders ($M$ = 89.77 months; 25 girls and 22 boys) from public elementary classrooms in southern California participated. Children were assigned randomly to one of two treatment conditions (Training, $n$ = 24; Control, $n$ = 23). Again, preliminary analyses showed that treatment groups did not differ on distributions of gender, age, verbal fluency, social desirability, or socioeconomic status as measured by instruments described in Experiment I.

*Procedure*

All of the children participated in the same staged event described in Experiment I. Two weeks later, each child accompanied a research assistant to a private room at their school. The assistant questioned the children about the staged event with a 36-item pretest described below. Next, half of the children received the experimental intervention described in Experiment I with three modifications described below. The other half participated in control sessions similar to those described in Experiment I. Immediately afterward, all children were interviewed about the classroom event with a 47-item post-test as described below.

*Pretest.* The design of Experiment I was modified to include a baseline suggestibility measure to determine preintervention levels of suggestibility that might account for group differences. At the beginning of the treatment session, subjects were individually asked 36 questions (17 misleading, 6 correctly leading, and 13 specific) about the staged event. Hence, the retention interval between the staged event and the baseline suggestibility measure was comparable to the interval between the event and the postintervention memory interview. None of the pretest questions were repeated on the post-test. The questions were chosen from an item analysis of the questions in Experiment I so that the pretest and post-test would be of comparable difficulty.

*Treatment sessions.* Experiment II made three modifications in the previous intervention in an attempt to increase the resistance effects and eliminate the presumed negative effects of intervention on correct responses. First, the children were trained in small, mixed-gender groups of three to four children rather than individually. Peer assistance, role modeling, and reinforcement, possible in small groups, has been shown to be helpful for children's learning (Bandura, 1984; Tharp & Gallimore, 1988). Also, small group training might provide peer support and increase self-confidence.

Second, the children who received training were also told that the interviewer did not believe that "children your age can tell what they remember very well." Saywitz (1989) found that child witnesses held the naive view that they would be believed by adults in the forensic context. If child witnesses are prepared for *potential* disbelief on the part of an interrogating adult, in conjunction with the intervention, they might be more self-confident and, thus, better able to resist the adult's misleading suggestion.

Third, greater emphasis was placed on encouraging children to provide a substantive response whenever possible. Less emphasis was placed on admitting lack of knowledge. That is, there was more opportunity and reinforcement for "telling the answer when you know the answer" in an effort to eliminate reduction in correct responses associated with the intervention in Experiment I.

The control sessions were the same as in Experiment I except that they were conducted in a group setting. The trainer did not make the disbelief statement to the control group.

*Memory interview.* As in Experiment I, children were interviewed by a confederate college professor. The memory post-test consisted of 47 questions (23 misleading, 9 correctly leading, and 15 specific). Again, yes and no responses were balanced to avoid response bias.

## Results and Discussion

Preliminary analyses of pretest scores were conducted to determine whether the treatment groups were comparable on proportion correct, incorrect, and "don't know/remember" responses for each question type prior to intervention. Results suggest that the two groups were comparable at pretest on these variables. Table 2 presents the pre- and post-test mean response scores by treatment condition and question type.

In order to examine the efficacy of the modified intervention, three 2 (treatment condition) by 2 (gender) MANOVAs were conducted.[4] The differences between pretest and post-test on proportion correct, incorrect, and "don't know/remember" responses were entered in these analyses as dependent variables. That is, the MANOVAs were conducted on the difference scores. Table 2 also displays the significance tests on difference scores by treatment condition and question type.

To examine whether suggestibility effects were reduced, the difference between proportion of errors on pretest and proportion of errors on post-test was entered into the first MANOVA. The results revealed a main effect of intervention, $F(3, 41) = 3.45$, $p < .02$. Univariate tests on each question type revealed that children in the training group achieved a significantly greater decline in incorrect responses to misleading questions from pretest to post-test ($M = -.26$) than the control group ($M = -.10$). These results indicate that the intervention was successful

---

[4] There were no significant effects of gender and no significant interactions.

TABLE 2
Pre- and Post-Test Mean Response Scores by Treatment Condition[a]

| | Treatment condition | | | | |
|---|---|---|---|---|---|
| | Training (n = 24) | | Control (n = 23) | | F |
| | Pre-test | Post-test | Pre-test | Post-test | |
| Misleading | | | | | |
| Correct | .29 (.15) | .41 (.15) | .35 (.13) | .43 (.17) | .47 |
| Incorrect | .69 (.15) | .43 (.18) | .62 (.14) | .52 (.17) | 9.52** |
| Don't Know | .02 (.05) | .16 (.17) | .03 (.07) | .05 (.07) | 12.90*** |
| Correctly Leading | | | | | |
| Correct | .96 (.09) | .74 (.18) | .91 (.13) | .78 (.17) | 3.03 |
| Incorrect | .04 (.09) | .17 (.15) | .06 (.06) | .20 (.15) | .03 |
| Don't Know | .01 (.03) | .10 (.17) | .03 (.08) | .02 (.06) | 7.51** |
| Specific | | | | | |
| Correct | .52 (.11) | .51 (.16) | .52 (.10) | .52 (.17) | .02 |
| Incorrect | .47 (.11) | .31 (.13) | .46 (.10) | .41 (.16) | 5.63* |
| Don't Know | .02 (.04) | .18 (.18) | .02 (.04) | .07 (.09) | 7.35** |

[a] Standard deviations are in parentheses.
* $p < .05$.
** $p < .01$.
*** $p < .001$.

in reducing children's acquiescence, and thus their errors on misleading questions. The children in the training group also achieved a significantly greater decline from pretest to post-test on incorrect responses to specific questions ($M = -.16$) than the control group ($M = -.04$). This represents an added benefit of the intervention that did not emerge in Experiment I. The training appears to have helped children reduce error on specific questions as well as misleading questions.

When the difference scores for "I don't know/remember" responses were analyzed, there was a significant main effect of intervention, $F(3, 41) = 4.27$, $p < .01$. Univariate tests on each question type revealed that children in the training group responded more frequently with "I don't know or I don't remember" than the control group on all types of questions. (See Table 2.) That is, the children in the training group achieved a greater increase from pretest to post-test of "I don't know or I don't remember" responses than the control group for all question types (misleading questions: $M_T = .14$, $M_C = .02$; correctly leading questions: $M_T = .09$, $M_C = -.01$; and specific questions: $M_T = .16$, $M_C = .05$). Hence, the pattern of "I don't know/remember" responding was similar to that of Experiment I.

When the difference scores for correct responses were entered into the analysis, the intervention effect was not significant $F(3, 41) = 1.02$, $p = .39$. In other words, in contrast to Experiment I, the modified intervention did not have the effect of lowering correct responses to any question types. Although correct responses for the children in the training group did not increase, the modifications made for this training program appeared to at least maintain preintervention levels of accuracy. Moreover, strength of the original memory will limit potential for assertion of correct responses.

In summary, the findings of this study were similar to those of Experiment I; reduced acquiescence and increased resistance to misleading questions, with the exception that in this study it was accomplished without adversely affecting correct responses to other types of questions. We also found an added benefit of reduced errors on specific questions.

## GENERAL DISCUSSION

These two studies begin to explore whether suggestibility is responsive to intervention. In the experimental setting it was. Reducing the potential for memory distortion outside the laboratory, without jeopardizing accuracy, could carry implications of significant import. Ultimately, the result could be fewer false allegations pursued, higher numbers of genuine perpetrators brought to justice, and greater numbers of children protected from maltreatment. The effectiveness of the intervention tested in the present research expands current conceptualizations by further highlighting the role of metacognitive knowledge as well as sociolinguistic and socioemotional factors in recalling and communicating past experience.

An impediment to interpretation of these findings is the fact that we cannot "unpackage" the intervention to determine the efficacy of individual components. Since certain determinants of suggestibility may be more readily modified than others, studies that independently vary specific training components will be worthwhile. Still, Moston (1987) has already demonstrated that merely giving permission to say "I don't know" is not effective with children. We added practice, feedback, and reinforcement for admitting lack of knowledge. We acknowledged and validated socioemotional reasons for acquiescence and highlighted the unintended adverse effects of compliance. We strove to increase children's awareness of interview task demands, response options, and response consequences unique to the forensic context. However, we did not directly assess whether children's expectations changed. Another fruitful area for further research could be a series of studies that directly assesses developmental differences in expectations about sociolinguistic interaction in the forensic context and the degree to which individual beliefs are modifiable.

### Implications for Adult Memories of Childhood Trauma

The studies presented above may provide insights into some of the underlying processes affecting adults as they attempt to reconstruct early life experiences after the passage of substantial periods of time. Some of the same socioemotional and sociolinguistic factors might facilitate or minimize distortion of adult recall. The potential for distortion may be particularly high in situations where there is a marked power differential like that between interrogator and child, therapist and patient, experimenter and subject, or parent and maltreated child. For example,

Zaragoza (1987) hypothesized that social pressures were responsible for adult acquiescence to misleading information in research studies. She speculated that acquiescence might be due to adult subjects' wishes to be viewed favorably by the experimenter. She also suggested that adults may trust the information provided by the experimenter more than their own memory. These concerns are not unlike those of the children in our studies. Also, therapists report that some adults, by virtue of their status as patients seeking help from the "expert" therapist, possess a childlike expectation that the therapist knows more and will be critical of failures to recall, suggesting these patients may require reassurance of nonomniscience no less than the children in our studies (Ferenczi, 1955).

A social–motivational model of memory suggests that beliefs, values, expectancies, incentives, and coping patterns can be important determinants of memory performance for people of all ages (Paris, 1988). This model is well suited to understanding the potential for distortion of childhood experience through suggestibility and repression. According to a social–motivational model of memory, efforts to cope with anxiety or to protect self-image can alter the selection and employment of retrieval strategies. For example, we can speculate that an individual might select an ineffective, but well practiced, low-risk response strategy (e.g., acquiescence, avoidance) instead of one that is more likely to result in detailed memories. This might occur because the more effective strategy requires higher levels of energy and motivation, and it carries greater risk of adverse consequences. This might be especially true of trauma victims. Sequelae of genuine trauma such as the symptoms of depression (i.e., anhedonia, indifference, fatigue, psychomotor retardation, and feelings of hopelessness or worthlessness) might predispose an individual toward the selection of certain response strategies, for example, those requiring low energy, little motivation, and little risk of failure or humiliation.

Narrowly focusing research on the veracity of childhood memories limits our ability to understand the full range of mechanisms that underlie the reconstruction of childhood experience. An additional focus on intervention effectiveness, especially social, motivational, and emotional influences that potentiate or lessen distortion, is one avenue for expanding knowledge that may ultimately prove useful in both forensic and clinical contexts. There have been a few previous efforts to warn adults about the possibility of future misinformation. These warnings have met with limited success (Christianson & Ochalek, 1983; Greene, Flynn, & Loftus, 1982; Warren et al., 1991; Warnick & Sanders, 1980). Although promising, they fail to address social, emotional, and motivational factors that are particularly salient in the forensic and therapeutic context.

In the forensic context, the potential harm to unfairly charged individuals demands that professionals exercise caution to maximize accurate communication of childhood memories. In the clinical context, an obligation to alleviate the suffering of genuinely traumatized individuals requires interventions that are effective in uncovering etiologies for current symptomatology. In the academic context, a complete understanding of memory outside the laboratory requires that models of eyewitness memory be expanded to encompass the sociolinguistic and socioemotional factors salient in real world interactions. Continued research on intervention effectiveness may bring us closer to the goals of justice, recovery, and new knowledge.

## ACKNOWLEDGMENTS

This research was supported by a grant from the National Center on Child Abuse and Neglect, U.S. Department of Health and Human Services. We are indebted to the parents, teachers, and students of the Redondo Beach and Torrance School Districts. We thank Dr. Vivian Lamphear for her ingenuity and guidance; she was instrumental in the design and data collection of Experiment I. For research assistance we thank Brenda Burke, Mike Espinoza, Kathy Lawrence, Maria Bucmaniuk, Sharon Esop, Marjorie-Graham Howard, Todd Westra, Eric Hoe, and Steve Bensen. Appreciation is extended to Patricia Savich, Ronald Gallimore, and Deborah Stipek for their suggestions. We thank Richard Romanoff for his insightful comments on an earlier draft of the manuscript. Appreciation also is extended to the Children's Television Workshop for lending its creativity and videotaped vignettes.

## REFERENCES

Ackerman, B. (1983). Speaker bias in children's evaluation of the external consistency of statements. *Journal of Experimental Child Psychology, 35,* 111–127.

Bandura, A. (1984). *Social foundations of thought and action: A social cognitive theory.* Englewood Cliffs, NJ: Prentice-Hall.

Bremner, J. D., Southwick, S., Brett, E., Fontana, A., Rosenheck, R., & Charney, D. (1992). Dissociation and posttraumatic stress disorder in Vietnam combat veterans. *American Journal of Psychiatry, 149*(3), 328–332.

Briere, J., & Conte, J. (1993). Self-reported amnesia for abuse in adults molested as children. *Journal of Traumatic Stress, 6*(1), 21–31.

Ceci, S. J., Bronfenbrenner, U., & Baker, J. G. (1988). Memory in context: The case of prospective remembering. In F. E. Weinert & M. Perlmutter (Eds.), *Universal changes and individual differences* (pp. 243–256). Hillsdale, NJ: Erlbaum.

Ceci, S. J., Ross, D., & Toglia, M. (1987). Age differences in suggestibility: Narrowing the uncertainties. In S. Ceci, M. Toglia, & D. Ross (Eds.), *Children's eyewitness memory.* (pp. 79–91). NY: Springer-Verlag.

Christianson, R. E., & Ochalek, K. (1983). Editing misleading information from memory: Evidence for the coexistence of original and postevent information. *Memory & Cognition, 11*(5), 467–475.

Cramer, P. (1991). *The development of defense mechanisms: Theory, research, and assessment.* New York: Springer-Verlag.

Crandall, V. C., Crandall, V. J., & Katkovsky, W. (1965). A children's social desirability questionnaire. *Journal of Consulting Psychology, 29,* 27–37.

Demorest, A., Meyer, C., Phelps, E., Gardner, H., & Winner, E. (1984). Words speak louder than actions: Understanding deliberately false remarks. *Child Development, 55,* 1527–1534.

Dickson, W. (Ed.) (1981). *Children's oral communication skills.* New York: Academic Press.

Feldman-Summers, S., & Pope, K. S. (1994). The experience of "forgetting" childhood abuse: A national survey of psychologists. *Journal of Consulting and Clinical Psychology, 62*(3).

Ferenczi, S. (1955). *Problems and methods of psycho-analysis.* New York: Basic Books.

Fivush, R., & Hudson, J. A. (Eds.) (1990). *Knowing and remembering in young children.* Cambridge: Cambridge Univ. Press.

Flavell, J. H., & Wellman, H. M. (1977). Metamemory. In R. V. Kail & J. W. Hagen (Eds.), *Perspectives on the development of memory and cognition* (pp. 3–34). Hillsdale, NJ: Erlbaum.

Garvey, C. (1984). *Children's talk.* Cambridge, MA: Harvard Univ. Press.

Goodman, G., Bottoms, B., Schwartz-Kenny, B., & Rudy, L. (1991). Children's memory for a stressful event: Improving children's reports. *Journal of Narrative and Life History, 1,* 69–99.

Greene, E., Flynn, M. S., & Loftus, E. F. (1982). Inducing resistance to misleading information. *Journal of Verbal Learning and Verbal Behavior, 21,* 207–219.

Grice, H. (1975). Logic and conversation. In R. Cole & J. Morgan (Eds.), *Syntax and semantics: Speech Acts.* New York: Academic Press.

Hughes, M., & Grieve, R. (1980). On asking children bizarre questions. *First Language, 1,* 149–160.

Irwin, J. (1982). *Pragmatics: The role in language development.* La Verne, CA: Fox Point Publishing.

Lodico, M., Ghatala, E., Levin, J., Pressley, M., & Bell, J. (1983). The effects of strategy-monitoring on children's selection of effective memory strategies. *Journal of Experimental Psychology, 35,* 263–277.

Loftus, E. (1993). The reality of repressed memories. *American Psychologist,* 518–537.

Loftus, E., & Davies, G. (1984). Distortions in the memory of children. *Journal of Social Issues, 40,* 51–68.

Loftus, E., Polonsky, S., & Fullilove, M. T. (1994). Memories of childhood sexual abuse: Remembering and repressing. *Psychology of Women Quarterly, 18,* 67–84.

McClosky, M., & Zaragoza, M. (1985). Misleading postevent information and memory for events: Arguments and evidence against memory impairment hypotheses. *Journal of Experimental Psychology: General, 114,* 1–16.

Miller, T. W., Kraus, R. F., Tatevosyan, A. S., & Kamenchenko, P. (1993). Post-traumatic stress disorder in children and adolescents of the Armenian earthquake. *Child Psychiatry and Human Development, 24*(2), 115–123.

Moan-Hardie, S. (1991). *Reducing suggestibility in children's eyewitness testimony: A training program to improve children's competence to resist misleading questions and aid retrieval.* Doctoral dissertation submitted to the University of California, Los Angeles.

Moston, S. (1987). The suggestibility of children in interview studies. *First Language, 7,* 67–78.

Paris, S. (1988). Motivated remembering. In F. Weinert & M. Perlmutter (Eds.), *Memory development: Universal changes and individual differences* (pp. 221–242). Hillsdale, NJ: Erlbaum.

Saywitz, K. (1989). Children's conceptions of the legal system: Court is a place to play basketball. In S. Ceci, M. Toglia, & D. Ross (Eds.), *Perspectives on children's testimony* (pp. 131–157). New York: Springer-Verlag.

Saywitz, K., Goodman, G., Nicholas, E., & Moan, S. (1991). Children's memories of a physical examination involving genital touch: Implications for reports of child sexual abuse. *Journal of Consulting and Clinical Psychology, 59*(5), 682–691.

Saywitz, K., Moan-Hardie, S., & Lamphear, V. (1991, August). *The effect of preparation on children's resistance to misleading questions.* Paper presented at the annual convention of the American Psychological Association, San Francisco, CA.

Saywitz, K., & Nathanson, R. (1992, August). Effects of environment on children's testimony and perceived stress. *In* B. Bottoms & M. Levine (Chairs), *Actual and perceived competency of child witnesses.* Symposium conducted at the annual convention of The American Psychological Association, Washington, DC.

Saywitz, K., & Nathanson, R. (1993). Children's testimony and their perceptions of stress in and out of the courtroom. *International Journal of Child Abuse and Neglect, 17,* 613–622.

Saywitz, K., & Snyder, L. (1991, April). *Preparing child witnesses: The efficacy of comprehension monitoring training.* Paper presented at the biennial convention of the Society for Research on Child Development, Seattle, WA.

Saywitz, K., & Snyder, L. (1993). Improving children's testimony with preparation. In G. Goodman & B. Bottoms (Eds.), *Child Victims, Child Witnesses* (pp. 117–146). New York: Guilford Press.

Schneider, W., & Pressley, M. (1989). *Memory development between 2 and 20.* New York: Springer-Verlag.

Stevens, G., & Cho, J. H. (1985). Socio-economic indexes and the new 1980 Census Occupational Classification Scheme. *Journal of Social Science Research, 14,* 142–168.

Terr L. (1988). What happens to early memories of trauma? A study of twenty children under age five at the time of documented traumatic events. *Journal of the American Academy of Child and Adolescent Psychiatry, 27*, 96–104.

Tharp, R., & Gallimore, R. (1988). *Rousing minds to life: Teaching, learning, and schooling in social context.* Cambridge: Cambridge Univ. Press.

Warnick, D. H., & Sanders, G. S. (1980). Why do eyewitnesses make so many mistakes? *Journal of Applied Social Psychology, 10*(4), 362–366.

Warren, A., Hulse-Trotter, K., & Tubbs, E. (1991). Inducing resistance to suggestibility in children. *Law and Human Behavior, 15*(3), 273–285.

Williams, L. (in press). Amnesia for childhood trauma: A prospective study of women's memories of child sexual abuse. *Journal of Consulting and Clinical Psychology.*

Zaragoza, M. S. (1987). Memory, suggestibility, and eyewitness testimony in children and adults. In S. Ceci, M. Toglia, & D. Ross (Eds.), *Children's eyewitness memory* (pp. 53–78). New York: Springer-Verlag.

# IV. REPRESSED MEMORY AND RECOVERED MEMORY

This section contains chapters that go to the central issues of whether memories of traumatic events can be lost and regained, whether they can exert psychological influences even though they are not remembered, whether and in what ways they may be distorted or modified by suggestion, and more. As it turns out, the seemingly simple issue of whether childhood memories of sexual abuse can be recovered after years of being unavailable opens up a host of questions. At every turn in thinking about the issue we find more assumptions that must be examined, and then more that turn up in the examination. What began as a seemingly straightforward exploration turns out to be a journey on a long and twisting path through a dense, and sometimes dangerous, jungle.

Consider first the recovery of memories. Many questions surround the circumstances of recovery. Often, researchers look for "pure" cases of recovery that did not occur under a therapist's care to guard against the charge that the memory was fabricated through an unintentional collusion between client and therapist. However, this appropriate scientific caution should not be overgeneralized; just because a memory was exhumed with the assistance of a therapist, we should not conclude that it is false. It is possible that most such memories could not be retrieved without the help of a professional. Despite recent earnest attempts (see sections I and III, and this section, for original reports and reviews of such research) to test the validity of recovered memories, we still do not have the data needed to estimate the proportion of accurate and inaccurate recovered memories from within versus outside of therapy. It is possible that memories recovered on the therapist's couch are more often valid than those arising from amateur work. We simply do not know; and in our ignorance, we are operating on the basis of unfounded conclusions.

Another question pertains to the nature of forgetting and the theoretical assumptions that are needed to support the conclusion that forgotten material can be recovered intact. If forgetting took place simply by decay of the trace, then there would be nothing to recover from a lost memory. Such a simplistic view can be discarded, because we do forget and then recall things. In the broadest sense we have "recovered" memory every time we recall the name of an old acquaintance we had forgotten, a long-lost song from summer camp, and so on. However, once we admit more complex theories of memory, we find that the retrieval process involves reconstruction, and the idea becomes dubious that a memory can emerge entirely undamaged from its hiding place and bear an accurate image of the forgotten event.

Still on the topic of forgetting is the whole question of repression. It is widely assumed that Freud, who invented the concept, meant it to be a defense mechanism that automatically exiled forbidden thoughts from awareness. Repressed thoughts were then to cause much trouble, rattling the bars of their dungeons in the unconscious. Therapeutically guided retrieval of childhood memories of sexual abuse and other violations would release the unfortunate victim from neurotic torment. As Toglia points out in a delicious triple irony, none of these assumptions about childhood sexual abuse is quite true to Freud. Furthermore, as Kihlstrom and others point out, memories can be blocked from access to awareness by processes that do not invoke any of the intellectual baggage of the concept of repression. Nevertheless, Freudian psychoanalysis is the prototypical recovered memory therapy, and his theoretical creations are surely the ancestors of the whole family of recovered memory approaches. Descendants of his ideas live on as unexamined assumptions, both in support of "memory therapy" and in opposition to concepts of possible recovery of memories.

The nine contributions in this section represent attempts to cut through the thicket of issues in this area, all "seeking the core" as Schooler aptly puts it. To this end, the authors look for a clear path to the truth and a clear path, as well, to appropriate clinical practices. The first four chapters are by researchers who have investigated basic issues in the controversy and who are experts in the field. The next three chapters are by distinguished clinical practitioners and authors who were members of the American Psychological Association's Working Group on Investigation of Memories of Childhood Abuse. The final two selections are the products of committees convened to investigate these issues for their professional societies and to make recommendations for clinical practice. The first of these is from the committee of the American Psychological Association on which our contributors served. The second is the report of the Working Party of the British Psychological Society.

Lindsay puts the controversy in historical and political context, and shows how some positions in the debate derive from prior, often unacknowledged, convictions. The tenacity of opinions and ferocity of debate in some cases may derive from these convictions, which are not directly addressed in the debate and hence have no chance of being examined and resolved through it.

Schooler shows how both sides have taken positions that are unrealistically extreme and thoughtfully marks off a sensible middle ground. He is able to see both sides clearly, and his chapter should be recommended as an antidote to dogmatism on either side.

Kihlstrom critically reviews the assumptions behind the central thesis of recovered memory therapy, which he terms the "trauma-memory argument," and finds it needing empirical support in every aspect. He also exposes the methodological weaknesses of the four studies that have been cited as supporting claims of accuracy of recovered memories. In the course of discussion, he comments on the rather surprising acceptance of hypnosis as a tool to recover memories, when there is evidence that it does not enhance accuracy of recall (Lindsay makes a similar point). Any future research on the validity of recovered memory must carefully observe the points that Kihlstrom makes.

Toglia points out that much of the debate may be fueled by differences in the approaches taken by experimental and clinical psychologists. The clinician typically has a patient who at this moment is in a crisis and needs help. There is no time to wait for the research to culminate in solid findings and professional recommendations. The only evidence of veracity of a report may be the clarity of the image or personal conviction the patient claims. Toglia makes several recommendations, both theoretical and empirical, for approaching the problems through research.

Alpert, Brown, and Courtois represent different approaches to recovered memory from the point of view of clinical practice. Alpert develops the contrast between memory researchers and clinicians. She justifies many of the criticized clinical procedures and points to areas of agreement with experimentalists and areas in which the criticism of clinicians is not supported. Her support of the Report of the British Psychological Society Working Party on Recovered Memories (reprinted at the end of this section) is in marked contrast with Kihlstrom's criticism and should be instructive as to how far apart the two sides can be.

Brown joins Lindsay in pointing out the powerful and often ignored political and social dimensions of the issue. Her account of the sociology of the debate is lucid and to the point. She asks what would happen if one side or the other "won." In some minds, if recovered childhood memory for sexual abuse is acknowledged, a radical feminist, antifamily agenda is endorsed; for others, if it is rejected, the poor victims would be victimized again. These are just two extreme positions, but no such positions have a place guiding science or clinical practice, and Brown's clear vision of these factors should help us recognize them and keep them separate and balanced.

Courtois ends the contributions in this section with what we consider to be extremely wise recommendations to therapists who are forced to face these issues. They are consistent with the classic Hippocratic injunction "First, do no harm." Harm can come as easily from the zealous recovery of memories as from refusal to recognize them. In Courtois's approach, recovery of memory is a secondary issue. "Memory work" is not the mode of therapy. The first priority is to establish stability and to attempt to restore normal functioning. The function of memory is to help rebuild the self and restore normal relations. We hope that her recommendations will be considered by all who may have to deal with clients of this type—and that includes virtually anyone working in a therapeutic psychological setting.

Finally, the two reports of association committees differ in their completeness. The report of the American Psychological Association is not complete as we write this, and we have reprinted only their brief Interim Report. The British Psychological Society Working Party prepared an in-depth analysis of the issues. Although much of what is known about memory, traumatic memory, and the possibility of accurate recovered memory is incorporated in this report, the reader should refer to the critique of this report in Kihlstrom's chapter for a stricter interpretation of some of the evidence on which it is based.

# Contextualizing and Clarifying Criticisms of Memory Work in Psychotherapy

D. Stephen Lindsay

*University of Victoria, Victoria, British Columbia V8W 242, Canada*

This article aims to reduce the polarization that has characterized discussion of memory work in psychotherapy. First, the article attempts to help critics of memory work understand the cultural and historical context in which their arguments have been received by practitioners and victim advocates: There are good reasons why attacks on memory work have been viewed with suspicion. Second, the article tries to convince practitioners and victim advocates that there nonetheless are legitimate grounds for concern about some forms of memory work. The goal here is to persuade practitioners whose work includes a focus on childhood trauma to be cautious in their use of memory recovery techniques, without undermining support for survivors of childhood sexual abuse.

In the past 2 years, a number of critics have charged that memory recovery techniques used in some approaches to psychotherapy can lead nonabused clients to develop illusory memories or false beliefs of childhood sexual abuse (CSA) (e.g., Coleman, 1992; Gardner, 1992; Lindsay & Read, 1994; Loftus, 1993; Ofshe & Watters, 1993; Read & Lindsay, 1994; Wakefield & Underwager, 1992; Yapko, 1993). Clients who experience recovery of memories of CSA in psychotherapy typically suffer a good deal in the process and sometimes accuse and/or break off relations with their families (and, in a small percentage of cases, take legal action against accused family members). Therefore, the claim that memory work in psychotherapy can produce illusory memories of CSA amounts to a very serious charge of malpractice.

Some practitioners and victim advocates have reacted sceptically to the claim that memories of CSA that arise in psychotherapy may be illusory. In addition to challenging the empirical bases of this claim, some defenders of memory work have characterized the criticisms as denial and backlash against our culture's dawning awareness of and support for victims of sexual abuse (e.g., Berliner & Williams, 1994; Olio, 1994).

The prevalence of concern about this issue is attested to in many forms: it has figured prominently in the popular media, numerous articles on the topic have appeared in professional journals, the American Psychiatric Association (1993) and the American Medical Association (1994) have released public statements on the issue (1993), the American Psychological Association and the British Psychological Society have empanelled groups of experts to produce policy statements, and a number of regional, national, and international meetings have been con-

This article is reprinted by permission from *Consciousness and Cognition,* Volume 3, pp. 426–437 (1994).

vened to discuss the issue. There is a large advocacy group for accused parents (the False Memory Syndrome Foundation), and a smaller support group for former clients who have retracted such accusations. In the courts, there have been cases of clients suing family members over abuse said to have occurred decades earlier, former clients suing therapists for allegedly implanting memories, and, most recently, accused parents suing therapists for allegedly implanting memories in their adult children.

To date, discussion of this issue has been emotionally charged and polarized. My aim is to reduce that polarization. First, I hope to help critics of memory work understand and appreciate the cultural and historical context in which their arguments have been received by practitioners and victim advocates. My central thesis in this regard is that there are good reasons why attacks on memory work have been viewed with suspicion and scepticism. Second, I hope to convince child and victim advocates and, especially, mental health care practitioners, that there nonetheless are legitimate grounds for concern about some forms of memory work in therapy. My goal here is to convince practitioners whose work includes a focus on childhood trauma to be cautious in their use of memory recovery techniques. I have attempted to make this argument in a way that does not undermine support for survivors of childhood sexual abuse.

## CULTURAL CONTEXT

The current controversy regarding recovered memories of CSA can only be understood in its broader cultural context. Simply put, that context is thousands of years of a male-dominated culture that typically turned a blind eye to sexual and physical abuse of children and women (e.g., Brownmiller, 1975; Finkelhor, 1979; Tong, 1984). Until relatively recently, acts that would now be considered crimes (e.g., abducting women, wife beating, child beating) were considered to be a man's private business. For example, the word "rape" comes from the ancient Roman term, raptus, which "was not a public crime but rather a private wrong against the man who had legal power over the woman or property violently seized by the raptor" (Brundage, 1993, p. 63). Similarly, until quite recently U.S. courts upheld the "right" of husbands physically to "chastise" (i.e., beat) their wives (Brownmiller, 1975). This view of patriarchal proprietorship, and the secrecy of incestuous child abuse, makes it difficult to estimate the prevalance of CSA throughout the history of Western society, but there are many reasons to believe that sexual abuse of children has long been part of our culture.

Public awareness of and concern about childhood sexual abuse has flared up in earlier times (e.g., according to Goodman, 1984, turn-of-the-century research on children's eyewitness testimony was sparked, in large part, by legal cases of alleged CSA; see also Finkelhor, 1979). Freud's publication of the seduction theory (1964/1897), in which he argued that sexual experiences in early childhood lay at the heart of his patients' neuroses, is another example. But just as Freud (1964/1899) quickly rejected the belief that his clients had been sexually abused (arguing instead that he had uncovered their fantasies of incestuous sex, thereby providing a rationale for viewing reports of CSA as psychodynamic wish fulfilment) (Masson, 1984), Western culture has typically shied away from the reality of CSA.

The past two decades have seen a more concerted and long-lasting movement toward acknowledging the reality of CSA and protecting and supporting its victims. Credit for this important and ongoing work is due largely to women working in numerous domains (grass-roots movements, shelters, social work, politics, mental health care, nursing, etc.). Researchers in the area of CSA were themselves stunned, in the early and mid-1970s, by their findings on the prevalence of CSA (e.g., Williams, 1994). Even when CSA is quite narrowly defined (e.g., vaginal penetration before age 16 years), and even when estimates are based on retrospective self-report studies (which likely underestimate prevalence because of respondents who have forgotten or choose not to report CSA), the best evidence reveals that there are millions of survivors of such abuse in North America (e.g., Russell, 1986). It is also well-established that CSA is associated with long-lasting psychological harm in adulthood (e.g., Beitchman, Zucker, Hood, daCosta, & Cassavia, 1992). Thus CSA is an enormous and important problem.

Sexual abuse does not stop in childhood. It was long normative for wives to submit to unwanted sex with their husbands, and today acquaintance rape of various forms is a huge problem. Although different studies have yielded widely varying prevalance estimates, all of the studies show shockingly high rates of violent physical and sexual assaults against women (Bourque, 1989). Male violence makes many parts of North American society dangerous for women, and legal prosecution of such assailants continues to be enormously difficult.

Efforts to protect and support victims of abuse and to prosecute perpetrators have recently begun to bear fruit, but progress toward this end has been slow and difficult (e.g., Brownmiller, 1975; Hechler, 1988). For example, there are currently 35 states in the United States in which it is legally impossible to charge a man with raping his wife, because no law proscribes this act. The U.S. Justice Department's Bureau of Justice Statistics recently reported that girls under 18 years of age are the victims of more than half of the rapes reported to police, even though there is an inverse relationship between youth of victim and likelihood of police report. Our courts have long been biased against child witnesses, and although there has been substantial (and hard-won) progress on this front in the last decade or so, it is still difficult to prosecute perpetrators. Books on our culture's response to the sexual victimization of women and children (e.g., Brownmiller, 1975; Hechler, 1988; Tong, 1984) document a sordid history of denial, minimalization, and victim-blaming—a history that we have not yet escaped.

## CLINICAL CONTEXT

Part of the zeitgeist of the late 1970s and early 1980s was a growing sensitivity among many mental health care providers to CSA. In the 1980s several publications reported case studies in which clients remembered or rediscovered instances of CSA in the course of therapy (e.g., Courtois, 1988; Ellenson, 1985; Gelinas, 1983; Olio, 1989). The authors argued that memories of CSA are often repressed during childhood because of their traumatic, inescapable, and secret nature. They also argued that repressed memories of CSA often reveal themselves in the form of adulthood psychological or physical symptoms and that dealing with such memories is an important part of the therapeutic process. Given that incestuous abuse often occurs early in childhood and is often kept secret, it is not unreasonable to argue that some adult survivors of abuse would not remember the abuse, and given that CSA is associated with adulthood psychopathology, it is not unreasonable to argue that CSA might play a role in the psychological problems of clients who do not remember the abuse. Finally, given that several well-established traditions in psychotherapy focus on childhood trauma as the source of adulthood psychopathology and prescribe "working through" memories of childhood trauma as a means of healing, it is not surprising that some therapists would encourage clients suspected of abuse to attempt to remember CSA.

These reasonable and understandable ideas led to the development and promulgation of therapeutic approaches, techniques, and ancillary practices aimed at helping clients recover suspected repressed memories (e.g., Bass & Davis, 1988; Blume, 1990; Claridge, 1992; Courtois, 1991, 1992; Dolan, 1990; Ellenson, 1986; Engel, 1989; Frederickson, 1992; Maltz, 1990; Olio, 1989). Of course, the purpose of such "memory work" was to help clients heal, and proponents of these approaches reported case studies in which clients painfully recovered and worked through memories of incestuous childhood abuse, ultimately emerging as more empowered human beings. There is no reason to doubt that these techniques can enable people to recover accurate but long-forgotten memories of childhood traumas. Unfortunately, as explained below, there are many reasons to believe that these same techniques can also enable nonabused clients to develop compelling but illusory memories and firmly held but false beliefs about CSA.

## CLARIFYING THE CONCERNS

Given our cultural context—centuries of secret abuse, followed by a hard-won and ongoing effort to acknowledge the reality of CSA and to begin to provide support for its victims—it is easy to appreciate why many mental health practitioners and victim advocates have been sceptical of claims that allegations of CSA that emerge in therapy may be illusory. The reality of CSA has long been denied or minimized in our culture, and this is likely to appear to be just another example.

The polarization has not been reduced by the confrontational tone used by some critics of memory work in psychotherapy. And the media, with their proclivity for simplified soundbites, have not helped matters. Furthermore, it is very likely that emotional denial and political backlash have fed into criticisms of memory work. Nonetheless, there are legitimate grounds for concern about some forms of memory work in psychotherapy. The issues are complex and multifaceted, and the discussion below only touches briefly on some of them. A more detailed discussion of these and related ideas is presented in Lindsay and Read (1994).

### 1. What Kinds of Memory Work Are Critics Criticizing?

Criticisms of memory work in psychotherapy have nothing to do with survivors of CSA who have always remembered their abuse, nor with those who spontaneously remember abuse. Furthermore, critics of memory work in psychotherapy do not claim that all or even most memories of CSA recovered in therapy are false. Finally, they do not suggest that practitioners should never broach the subject of CSA or that a few probing questions about CSA are likely to lead clients to create illusory memories.

Concern has focused on approaches to therapy that combine several techniques and ancillary practices in a prolonged program oriented toward helping clients recover suspected repressed memories. The practices include (a) telling clients who report no history of CSA that their symptoms are indicative of repressed memories of CSA, that many survivors do not remember their abuse, and that psychological healing depends upon recovering memories of abuse; (b) using memory recovery techniques such as hypnosis, age regression, guided imagery, sodium amytal, and instructions to work at remembering CSA (e.g., giving free rein to the imagination, stream-of-consciousness journalling, use of family photographs as retrieval cues, etc., with the aim of remembering childhood traumas); (c) interpreting dreams and physical symptoms as memories of CSA; (d) recommending that clients who do not remember abuse join survivors' groups and/or read popular books on remembering CSA; and (e) uniformly endorsing all reports related to abuse as accurate memories, and countering clients' expressions of doubt. Again, criticism has focused on therapies that combine several of these practices in a prolonged search for memories.

## 2. What Evidence Supports Criticism of This Kind of Memory Work?

Cognitive and social psychology offer a wealth of evidence documenting that techniques similar to those listed above can lead people to experience illusory memories and/or false beliefs. For example, research on eyewitness suggestibility demonstrates that people are often highly confident in illusory memories that are the products of suggestions and that they often believe they are remembering things they witnessed when they remember things that were merely suggested to them (see review by Lindsay, 1994). Importantly, reports based on suggestions often cannot be discriminated from reports based on accurate memories. The following factors have been shown to increase people's susceptibility to misleading suggestions about past events: perceived authority of the source of suggestions; repetition of suggestions; delay between the to-be-remembered event and the attempt to remember; perceived plausibility of suggestions; factors that enhance imagery of suggestions (e.g., hypnosis, imagery instructions, sodium amytal); and factors that lower response criteria (e.g., hypnosis, sodium amytal, instructions to guess). All of these factors are characteristic of the kinds of memory work about which concerns have been raised.

Social psychological research demonstrates that a person's beliefs and expectations can greatly influence other people's behavior (e.g., Ceci, Leichtman, & White, in press; Rosenthal & Jacobson, 1968; Snyder, Tanke, & Berschied, 1977). Moreover, people are often unaware of their influence on others and often fail to appreciate the extent to which their behavior is influenced by others (e.g., Bowers, 1984). Thus therapists' and clients' retrospective introspections about the extent to which the client's reconstructions of childhood traumas were influenced by the beliefs and expectations of the therapist (and by other sources of suggestion) should be viewed with some caution.

Research on the reliability of diagnoses and clinical judgments raises grave doubts about psychotherapists' ability to detect clients with repressed memories of abuse (e.g., Dawes, 1994). Even highly trained therapists often disagree about the appropriate diagnoses for particular clients, even when working with well-defined diagnostic categories (e.g., Di Nardo, Moras, Barlow, Rapee, & Brown, 1993; Herron, Schultz, & Welt, 1992). There is no diagnostic category for repressed memories of CSA in the DSM-III-R (although some practitioners rather paradoxically recommend use of the post-traumatic stress disorder diagnosis for categorizing clients suspected of repressed memories—e.g., Olio, 1989). The best available evidence indicates that CSA is associated with a panoply of psychological problems in adulthood, but to date no well-defined post-CSA-syndrome has been identified (Beitchman et al., 1992). Thus clinical judgments regarding repressed memories of CSA are almost certainly even less reliable than clinical diagnoses. Furthermore, even if one accepted the claims of proponents of abuse-focused memory work regarding the base rates of CSA and of complete amnesia of CSA (e.g., that 33% of women are survivors and that 50% of these have no conscious memory of the abuse), and even if one assumed that diagnostic accuracy among such therapists is extraordinarily high, the likelihood that diagnoses of repressed memories would be erroneous is surprisingly high (e.g., with these base rates and 90% diagnostic accuracy, and assuming symmetry between positive and negative diagnoses, 33% of positive diagnoses would be wrong).

Finally, several well-established cognitive biases may lead practitioners to overestimate the accuracy of their diagnoses and clinical judgments (e.g., illusory correlation, as in Chapman & Chapman, 1967; Dawes, 1989; Dowling & Graham, 1976; and the representativeness heuristic, as in Tversky & Kahneman, 1974). Because practitioners rarely have the opportunity to compare their clients to control groups and only sometimes have the opportunity to learn of other practitioners' independent diagnoses and clinical judgments regarding particular clients, it is likely often difficult to detect incorrect diagnoses or to get valid feedback about the accurcy of clinical judgments. These considerations contribute to the great challenge of providing good psychotherapy, and no doubt most practitioners are well aware of them. Unfortunately, awareness of such biases may not be sufficient to allow one to escape them, and they may nonetheless contribute to inflated impressions about the accuracy of one's diagnoses and clinical judgments.

In summary, research demonstrates that (a) procedures similar to those used in some forms of memory work can lead people to experience compelling illusory memories, (b) people are often unaware of the extent to which they influence others and of the extent to which they are influenced by others, (c) it is almost certainly difficult reliably to detect clients with nonreported histories of CSA, and (d) normal human decision biases may lead practitioners to have inflated views of the accuracy of their diagnoses and clinical judgments. These cognitive and social processes may both (a) lead clients doing extensive memory work to create illusory memories or beliefs of CSA and (b) lead practitioners to hold undue confidence in the accuracy of their diagnoses and clinical judgments, thereby making it difficult to convince those who use memory recovery techniques of their potential risks.

### 3. Can Studies of Illusory Memories Be Generalized to Therapy?

Some defenders of memory work in psychotherapy have argued that research on suggestibility and illusory memories cannot be generalized to therapy situations and memories of CSA. They argue that although suggestions lead to false memories of peripheral details in trivial laboratory studies, they cannot lead to false memories of traumatic autobiographical experiences. Five years ago this argument might have carried considerable weight, but a number of recent studies have shown that misleading suggestions can indeed give rise to illusory memories of dramatic (if not traumatic) autobiographical events and, moreover, that the same factors important in laboratory studies of suggestibility appear to be important when suggestions concern memorable real-life experiences (Bruck, Ceci, Francouer, & Barr, in press; Ceci et al., in press; Ceci, Loftus, Crotteau, & Smith, 1994; Hyman, Billings, Husband, Husband, & Smith, 1993; Loftus & Coan, in press; Oates & Shrimpton, 1991; Ornstein, Gordon, & Baker-Ward, 1992; Poole & Lindsay, in press). Existing evidence indicates that it is easier to create false memories of peripheral details in a trivial event than to create false memories of dramatic autobiographical experiences: A single passing suggestion about a detail in a slide show can lead many subjects falsely to report having seen the suggested detail in the slide show, but longer delays and more powerful suggestions are required to implant false memories of a scary childhood experience. But if the suggestibility manipulations are sufficiently strong, some subjects do experience illusory memories of autobiographical events. It is worth emphasizing that the suggestibility manipulations in all of these studies are trivially weak compared to those used in the kinds of memory work about which concerns have been raised.

In my view, there is little room for doubt that highly suggestive forms of memory work in psychotherapy (i.e., approaches that include several of the factors listed in the previous section) run a substantial risk of leading some nonabused clients to create illusory memories or false beliefs about CSA. To argue otherwise (e.g., on the basis that there has been no definitive laboratory study in which illusory memories of CSA have been shown to be caused by such techniques) would be akin to arguing that just because a drug causes blindness in lab animals there is no reason to be concerned about its use with humans. There is room for debate about the riskiness of particular techniques or combinations of techniques and need for further research on this question, but there is compelling evidence justifying concern about the multifaceted approaches advocated in popular books and in scholarly books and articles on recovering memories of CSA.

### 4. Do Therapists Actually Use Such Techniques?

Some defenders of memory work in psychotherapy have argued that few if any psychotherapists actually use the kinds of techniques and ancillary practices about which concerns have been raised. Reported use of such multifaceted attempts to foment memory recovery appear in numerous books and articles (e.g., Bass & Davis, 1988; Claridge, 1992; Courtois, 1988; Olio, 1989), and court transcripts document that at least some therapists do use such techniques (Loftus, 1994). Moreover, recent surveys of therapists in the United States and United Kingdom indicated that a substantial minority of highly trained therapists reported constellations of beliefs and practices that are consistent with the concerns raised above (Poole, Lindsay, Memon, & Bull, 1994; Smith, 1991; Yapko, 1994).

The results of Poole et al.'s (1994) survey make it clear that the majority of doctoral psychotherapists do not have a single-minded focus on clients' memories of CSA. On the contrary, most indicated that CSA was an issue with few if any of their adult female clients. This is consonant with the fact that many critics of extreme forms of memory work in psychotherapy are themselves clinical psychologists or psychiatrists (e.g., Cohler, in press; Ganaway, 1991; Haaken & Schlaps, 1991; Yapko, 1993). Yet the publication record shows that approaches to therapy that focus on helping clients recover suspected memories of CSA have been widely publicized in recent years, and the surveys indicate that a substantial minority of highly trained therapists have incorporated this focus. For example, Poole et al. (1994) found, in three independent national samples (two of United States doctoral psychotherapists and one of British registered clinical psychologists) that 25% of the respondents reported a constellation of beliefs and practices that raise concerns about the suggestiveness of their approaches to memory work in therapy. The return rates for these surveys were around 40%, suggesting that something between 9 and 25% of the population fit Poole et al.'s criteria for potentially risky, "memory focused" therapies (depending on the extent to which memory-focused practitioners self-selected themselves as respondents). Given that there are hundreds of thousands of people practicing psychotherapy with various qualifications and under various auspices, with each therapist working with scores of clients every year, these results suggest that very large numbers of clients have been exposed to potentially risky memory recovery techniques. Thus even if the techniques are only rarely misapplied to nonabused clients, and even if they only rarely lead such clients to create illusory memories or false beliefs, the number of clients harmed in this way would be large.

## 5. But I Don't Use Suggestive Techniques

There is both empirical and anecdotal evidence that indicates that trauma-focused therapists may not apprehend the potentially suggestive nature of the memory recovery techniques they use in psychotherapy. As mentioned above, social psychological research indicates that people often fail to appreciate the extent to which they influence others. More specifically, there is evidence that interviewers often ask suggestive and leading questions even when they are explicitly trying to avoid doing so (e.g., Ceci et al., in press). Yapko (1994) found that 19% of the 860 psychotherapists surveyed indicated that they knew of cases in which clients had developed trauma memories that the therapist believed were false memories suggested by other therapists, but very few thought that their own therapies had such effects. Similarly, in Poole et al.'s surveys of highly trained therapists, 91% reported that they believed that illusory memories of CSA are possible, but 90% indicated that few or none of their own clients had developed illusory memories in therapy, regardless of the memory recovery techniques used. Many of Poole et al.'s respondents reported use of memory recovery techniques that cognitive psychologists consider risky (e.g., hypnosis and dream interpretation) but also wrote comments such as "I don't use suggestive techniques").

Insensitivity to the potential suggestiveness of memory recovery techniques was nicely illustrated by a Ph.D. therapist at a recent symposium on this topic, who reported using "Ericksonian" hypnosis to help a client who wanted to remember suspected CSA to do so. This therapist clearly believed that because he did not specifically suggest memories of abuse while the client was hypnotized, the hypnotic procedure was a risk-free means of retrieving accurate memories. The day before, Nick Spanos (1994a; see also Spanos, 1994b) had reported research demonstrating that undergraduates who were told before hypnosis that being hypnotized would enable them to remember past lives were quite likely to do so and that prehypnotic suggestions about the nature of past lives (e.g., that people in the past were often sexually abused as children) had pronounced effects on the kinds of past lives subjects remembered. This anecdote illustrates the potential gap between practitioners' perceptions and research evidence concerning the riskiness of particular memory recovery techniques and underscores the importance (and the difficulty) of sharing research on human memory with practitioners whose work includes a focus on recovering memories of childhood traumas.

## 6. Why Has There Been So Much Focus on Criticizing Memory Work?

Childhood sexual abuse is a more important problem than risky memory work in psychotherapy. There are many times more victims of CSA, and CSA has a much longer history. Why, then, has there been so much focus on criticisms of memory work in psychotherapy? Part of that focus may correctly be ascribed to denial and backlash, but there are several other reasons for criticizing risky memory work. First, although the number of victims of therapy-induced illusory memories or false beliefs is small compared to the number of victims of CSA, there are good grounds to believe that substantial numbers of clients and families have been gravely harmed by these approaches. Second, whereas CSA is not a direct consequence of the practice of psychology, illusory memories of CSA caused by risky memory recovery techniques are. Thus I feel a professional responsibility as a psychologist to educate my practitioner colleagues about the potential risks of these techniques. Third, whereas stopping CSA has proved to be an extremely difficult problem, avoiding therapy-induced illusory memories of CSA should be relatively easy. After all, these approaches to therapy have only been popular for a few years, and they have been used with the aim of helping clients. As practitioners learn more about the risks of these techniques, they will become more cautious in their use of them. Happily, there is evidence that this transition is under way (Poole et al., 1994). Ultimately, we must strive toward a balanced approach that is sensitive and responsive to survivors of abuse but does not put nonabused clients at risk of creating illusory memories or false beliefs of childhood sexual abuse.

## REFERENCES

American Medical Association (1994, June 16). Report of the Council on Scientific Affairs: Memories of childhood abuse. CSA Report 5-A-94.

American Psychiatric Association (1993, December 22). *APA issues statements on memories of sexual abuse, gun control, television violence.* New Release No. 93-58.

Bass, E., & Davis, L. (1988). *The courage to heal: A guide for women survivors of child sexual abuse.* New York: Harper & Row.

Beitchman, J. H., Zucker, K. J., Hood, J. E., daCosta, G. A., & Cassavia, E. (1992). A review of the long-term effects of child sexual abuse. *Child Abuse & Neglect, 16,* 101–118.

Berliner, L., & Williams, L. (1994). Memories of childhood sexual abuse: A response to Lindsay and Read. *Applied Cognitive Psychology, 8,* 379–388.

Blume, E. S. (1990). *Secret survivors: Uncovering incest and its aftereffects in women.* New York: Ballantine.

Bourque, L. B. (1989). *Defining rape.* Durham, NC: Duke Univ. Press.

Bowers, K. S. (1984). On being unconsciously influenced and informed. In K. S. Bowers & D. Meichenbaum (Eds.), *The unconscious reconsidered* (pp. 227–273). New York: Wiley.

Brownmiller, S. (1975). *Against our will: Men, women, and rape.* New York: Simon & Schuster.

Bruck, M., Ceci, S. J., Francouer, E., & Barr, R. (in press). "I hardly cried when I got my shot!" Influencing children's reports about a visit to their pediatrician. *Child Development.*

Brundage, J. A. (1993). *Sex, law and marriage in the Middle Ages.* Brookfield, VT: Voriorum.

Ceci, S. J., Leichtman, M., & White, T. (in press). Interviewing pre-schoolers: Remembrance of things planted. In D. P. Peters (Ed.), *The child witness: Cognitive, social, and legal issues.* The Netherlands: Kluwer.

Ceci, S. J., Loftus, E. F., Crotteau, M. L., & Smith, E. (1994). Repeatedly thinking about a non-event: Source misattributions among preschoolers. *Consciousness and Cognition, 3,* 388–407.

Chapman, L. M., & Chapman, J. P. (1967). Genesis of popular but erroneous psychodiagnostic observations. *Journal of Abnormal Psychology, 72,* 193–204.

Claridge, K. (1992). Reconstructing memories of abuse: A theory-based approach. *Psychotherapy, 29,* 243–252.

Cohler, B. J. (1994). Memory recovery and the use of the past: A commentary on Lindsay and Read from psychoanalytic perspectives. *Applied Cognitive Psychology, 8,* 365–378.

Coleman, L. (1992). Creating "memories" of sexual abuse. *Issues in Child Abuse Accusations, 4,* 169–176.

Courtois, C. A. (1988). *Healing the incest wound: Adult survivors in therapy.* New York: Norton.

Courtois, C. A. (1991). Theory, sequencing, and strategy in treating adult survivors. *New Directions For Mental Health Services, 51*(Fall).

Courtois, C. A. (1992). The memory retrieval process in incest survivor therapy. *Journal of Child Sexual Abuse, 1,* 15–32.

Dawes, R. M. (1989). Experience and the validity of clinical judgment: The illusory correlation. *Behavioral Sciences and the Law, 7,* 457–467.

Dawes, R. M. (1994). *The house of cards.* Toronto: Maxwell Macmillan Canada.

Di Nardo, P. A., Moras, K., Barlow, D. H., Rapee, R. M., & Brown, T. A. (1993). Reliability of DSM-III-R anxiety disorders categories: Using the anxiety disorders interview schedule-revised. *Archives of General Psychiatry, 50,* 251–256.

Dolan, Y. M. (1990). *Resolving sexual abuse: Solution-focused therapy and Ericksonian hypnosis for adult survivors.* New York: Norton.

Dowling, J. F., & Graham, J. R. (1976). Illusory correlation and the MMPI. *Journal of Personality Assessment,* **40,** 531–538.

Ellenson, G. S. (1985). Detecting a history of incest: A predictive syndrome. Social Casework: *The Journal of Contemporary Social Work,* **66,** 525–532.

Ellenson, G. S. (1986). Disturbances of perception in adult female incest survivors. Social Casework: *The Journal of Contemporary Social Work,* **67,** 149–159.

Engel, B. (1989). *The right to innocence: Healing the trauma of childhood sexual abuse.* New York: Ballantine (Ivy Books).

Finkelhor, D. (1979). *Sexually victimized children.* New York: Free Press.

Frederickson, R. (1992). *Repressed memories: A journey to recovery from sexual abuse.* New York: Simon & Schuster.

Freud, S. (1962a). Screen memories. In J. Strachey (Ed. and Trans.), *The standard edition of the complete psychological works of Sigmund Freud* (Vol. 3, pp. 303–322). Toronto: Clark, Irwin and Co. (Original work published 1899)

Freud, S. (1962b). The aetiology of hysteria. In J. Strachey (Ed. and Trans.), *The standard edition of the complete psychological works of Sigmund Freud* (Vol. 3, pp. 191–221). Toronto: Clark, Irwin and Co. (Original work published 1896)

Ganaway, G. K. (1991, August). *Alternative hypotheses regarding satanic ritual abuse memories.* Paper presented at 99th Annual Convention of the American Psychological Association, San Francisco, CA.

Gardner, R. A. (1992). Belated realization of child sex abuse by an adult. *Issues in Child Abuse Accusations,* **4,** 177–195.

Gelinas, D. (1983). The persisting negative effects of incest. *Psychiatry,* **46,** 313–332.

Goodman, G. S. (1984). Children's testimony in historical perspective. *Journal of Social Issues,* **40,** 9–32.

Haaken, J., & Schlaps, A. (1991). Incest resolution therapy and the objectification of sexual abuse. *Psychotherapy,* **28,** 39–47.

Hechler, D. (1988). *The battle and the backlash: The child sexual abuse war.* Toronto: Lexington Books.

Herron, W. G., Schultz, C. L., & Welt, A. G. (1992). A comparison of 16 systems to diagnose schizophrenia. *Journal of Clinical Psychology,* **48,** 711–721.

Hyman, I. E., Jr., Billings, F. J., Husband, S. G., Husband, T. W., & Smith, D. B. (1993, Nov.). *Memories and false memories of childhood experiences.* Poster presented at the annual meeting of the Psychonomic Society, Washington, DC.

Lindsay, D. S. (1994). Memory source monitoring and eyewitness testimony. In D. F. Ross, J. D. Read, & M. P. Toglia (Eds.), *Adult eyewitness testimony: Current trends and developments* (pp. 27–55). New York: Cambridge Univ. Press.

Lindsay, D. S., & Read, J. D. (1994). Psychotherapy and memories of childhood sexual abuse: A cognitive perspective. *Applied Cognitive Psychology,* **8,** 281–338.

Loftus, E. F. (1993). The reality of repressed memories. *American Psychologist,* **48,** 518–537.

Loftus, E. F., (1994). Therapeutic recollection of childhood abuse: When a memory may not be a memory. *The Champion,* **18**(2), 5–10.

Loftus, E. F., & Coan, D. (in press). The construction of childhood memories. In D. Peters (Ed.), *The child witness in context: Cognitive, social and legal perspectives.* New York: Kluwer.

Maltz, W. (1990). Adult survivors of incest: How to help them overcome the trauma. *Medical Aspects of Human Sexuality,* December, 42–47.

Masson, J. M. (1984). *The assault on truth: Freud's suppression of the seduction theory.* New York: Farrar, Straus, Giroux.

Oates, K., & Shrimpton, S. (1991). Children's memories for stressful and nonstressful events. *Medicine, Science, and the Law,* **31,** 4–10.

Ofshe, R. J., & Watters, E. (1993). Masking monsters. *Society,* **30,** 4–16.

Olio, K. A. (1989). Memory retrieval in the treatment of adult survivors of sexual abuse. *Transactional Analysis Journal,* **19,** 93–100.

Olio, K. A. (1994). Truth in memory. *American Psychologist,* **49,** 442–443.

Ornstein, P. A., Gordon, B. N., & Baker-Ward, L. (1992). Children's memory for salient events: Implications for testimony. In M. Howe, C. Brainerd, & V. Reyna (Eds.), *Development of long-term retention.* New York: Springer-Verlag.

Poole, D. A., & Lindsay, D. S. (in press). Interviewing preschoolers: Effects of nonsuggestive techniques, parental coaching and leading questions on reports of nonexperienced events. *Journal of Experimental Child Psychology.*

Poole, D. A., Lindsay, D. S., Memon, A., & Bull, R. (1994). *Psychotherapy and the recovery of memories of childhood sexual abuse: U.S. and British Practitioners' Opinions, Practices, and Experiences.* Manuscript submitted for publication.

Read, J. D., & Lindsay, D. S. (1994). Moving toward a middle ground on the "false memory debate:" Reply to commentaries on Lindsay and Read. *Applied Cognitive Psychology,* **8,** 407–435.

Rosenthal, R., & Jacobson, L. (1968). *Pygmalion in the classroom.* New York: Holt, Rinehart, & Winston.

Russell, D. (1986). *The secret trauma: Incest in the lives of girls and women.* New York: Basic Books.

Smith, S. (1991). *Survey of 38 therapists specializing in sexual abuse recovery.* Unpublished Masters thesis, Ottawa University, Phoenix, AZ.

Snyder, M., Tanke, E. D., & Berschied, E. (1977). Social perception and interpersonal behavior: On the self-fulfilling nature of social stereotypes. *Journal of Personality and Social Psychology,* **31,** 64–67.

Spanos, N. P. (1994a, May). *Is hypnosis a reliable tool for retrieving memories?* Paper presented at the Simon Fraser University symposium on Memories of Sexual Abuse, Vancouver, B.C., Canada.

Spanos, N. P. (1994b). Multiple identity enactments and multiple personality disorder: A sociocognitive perspective. *Psychological Bulletin,* **116,** 143–165.

Tong, R. (1984). *Women, sex, and the law.* Totawa, NJ: Rowman & Allanheld.

Tversky, A, & Kahneman, D. (1974). Judgments under uncertainty: Heuristics and biases. *Science,* **185,** 1124–1131.

Wakefield, H., Underwager, R. (1992). Recovered memories of alleged sexual abuse: Lawsuits against parents. *Behavioral Sciences and the Law,* **10,** 483–507.

Williams, L. (1994). *Public forum: Memories of childhood sexual abuse.* Paper presented at the Simon Fraser University symposium on Memories of Sexual Abuse, Vancouver, B.C., Canada.

Yapko, M. (1993). The seductions of memory. *Networker,* Sept/Oct, 31–37.

Yapko, M. (1994). Suggestibility and repressed memories of abuse: A survey of Psychotherapists' beliefs. *American Journal of Clinical Hypnosis* **36,** 163–171.

# Seeking the Core: The Issues and Evidence Surrounding Recovered Accounts of Sexual Trauma

Jonathan W. Schooler

*635 Learning Research and Development Center, University of Pittsburgh, Pittsburgh, Pennsylvania 15260*

This review identifies some of the many layers that surround and potentially obscure the emotionally charged topic of recovered accounts of childhood abuse. Consideration of the, admittedly often indirect, evidence provides suggestive support for many of the components of both recovered and fabricated memories of abuse. With respect to recovered memories the available evidence suggests that: (1) although the prior accessibility of a memory may be difficult to determine, recovered memory reports can sometimes be corroborated with respect to their correspondence to actual abuse; (2) although individuals often retain memory for trauma, there is evidence for fluctuations in the accessibility of traumatic experiences, particularly for situations that are extremely difficult to talk about; (3) there are compelling mechanisms available to account for both the decreases and the subsequent increases in accessibility of traumatic memories that could lead to recovered memory reports. With respect to fabricated memories the available evidence suggests that: (1) people are highly capable of fabricating vivid recollections that can be confused with reality; (2) once fabricated, there seems to be no limit to the preposterous false memories that some individuals are capable of accepting particularly when in the presence of a persuasive individual in a position of authority. Although future research is needed to provide more direct evidence for the above claims, at present readers are urged to consider the strong likelihood that both recovered and fabricated memories correspond to real phenomena.

Forming conclusions about the issues surrounding recovered accounts of sexual abuse is much like peeling an onion: the removal of each layer leaves another to reckon with, and it seems as if one could continue the process indefinitely without revealing a final incontrovertible core. The many levels and complexities of the issue, together with its great emotional weight, have combined to polarize the field. Some vehemently assert that the recovery of long forgotten episodes of sexual abuse should generally be considered valid (e.g., Herman & Schatzow, 1987; Williams, in press), while others suggest that such accounts should be viewed with marked skepticism (e.g., Loftus, 1993; Ofshe, 1992). Although we can hope for a time when the unpeeling of this issue leads to a solid core of evidence, at present it is not even entirely clear what such a "core" of evidence would have to look like. Consequently, individuals unsatisfied with the conclusions revealed at any one layer may reasonably argue that we have not yet gotten to the bottom of the question. While we may never be able to agree about what evidence lies below, we can nevertheless make headway by attempting to classify

This article is reprinted by permission from *Consciousness and Cognition*, Volume 3, pp. 452–469 (1994).

and keep track of the layers that have been exposed. Indeed, some (although certainly not all) of the disagreements may result from disparities between the level of analysis at which individuals are considering the issue. In an effort to bring some clarity to the issue I will attempt to demarcate some of the layers that I have encountered in weighing the evidence on this complex and emotional topic.

## THE NATURE OF EVIDENCE

Both sides of the debate frequently argue that there is little or no direct evidence for the claims of the opposing view. For example, in a recent US News and World Report interview, Ofshe, a major advocate of the notion that recovered accounts of trauma are likely to be the product of suggestion, observed, "No one has ever shown that the memory of repeated abuses can be uncontrollably and completely stripped from a person's consciousness" (quoted by Horn, 1993, p. 55). On the other side, Harvey and Herrman (this volume), who emphasize the veridicality of recovered memories, assert that "there is no evidence to suggest that psychotherapists have the degree of power and influence that would be required to produce this [fabricated memories] effect" (p. 4). In considering claims of "no evidence" it may be useful to distinguish between two different possible meanings of the phrase. The absence of evidence for a claim may result from the failure of appropriately designed research to reveal the phenomenon in question. This type of a positive failure can be a compelling argument that the concept in question is either invalid or at least in need of revision. Alternatively, the absence of evidence can result because no research has been able to directly address the question, one way or the other. In this latter case, a lack of evidence should not necessarily be used as an argument against the concept.

In the absence of direct research, we must be cautious in drawing conclusions of "no evidence," just as we would be cautious to use an untested drug simply because there is no direct evidence that it might be harmful. Rather, we should consider the converging implications of the available indirect sources of evidence. While such evidence may not provide the proof of direct experimental demonstration, the confluence of indirect sources of evidence can be informative. Exactly how we use such indirect sources of evidence, however, again returns us to the level at which we are addressing the question. Different decisions require different degrees of evidence. If we are concerned about the use of a procedure that may have possible ill effects, then we would be well advised to consider all sources of indirect evidence. Such reasoning is involved in using the indirect evidence of animal studies as the basis for decisions regarding the safety of products for humans. Legal decisions require far greater degrees of evidence but even there the amount of evidence depends on the type of case: a preponderance of evidence is necessary for civil suits whereas beyond a reasonable doubt is required for criminal cases. A similar argument can be made in considering the evidence on recovered and fabricated memories of abuse. The amount of evidence necessary to inform a treatment decision may be markedly less than that required to convict an individual of child abuse. Perhaps, some of the heat of this debate has been due to the difference between the criteria for evidence required for different types of judgments. Thus, in reviewing the literature it may be helpful to refrain from making absolute judgments on the topic and instead attempt to assess the degree of evidence associated with each issue.

As the title of this special volume reveals, the issues of recovered and fabricated memories of abuse is often made out to be an either/or debate. Nevertheless, it is quite possible that some recovered memory reports may reflect real trauma while others may be merely the product of suggestion. In short, there are two distinct questions at issue, can memories be recovered and can memories be suggested. Both draw on distinct bodies of evidence, and both deserve separate consideration. In an effort to keep these two issues as distinct as possible, I will first review the issues surrounding recovered memories and then turn to memory fabrication.

## RECOVERED MEMORY REPORTS

The issue of reports of recovered memories of long forgotten traumatic events subsumes many difficult layers. For example, it begs the question of what mechanisms might be involved. Discussions of recovered memories often vacillate between considering the evidence for psychodynamic repression mechanisms versus the evidence that individuals can have recovery experiences in which they retrieve memories of trauma that they do not recall being aware of. While the mechanisms underlying reports of recovered memories of traumatic events is of great interest, the issue of mechanism can and should be differentiated from the question of whether this class of experience occurs at all. Even when we try to limit the question to whether individuals can recover memories for trauma we can run into difficulties because of the issue of what it means to "recover" a memory. An individual who reports recovering a memory for trauma is really indicating two sentiments that: (1) abuse occurred and (2) there was a period of time in which the memory was not accessible.

### Memory for the Abuse

Considerations of individuals' memory for abuse again require a distinction between memory for the occurrence versus the details of the abuse. While certain details of an abuse event may be critical, for example, in making determination between whether an adult was fondling a child or simply cleaning her, in many other cases the full specifics are really secondary. In short, one can have a valid memory for an abuse occurrence, that is, that an impropriety occurred, without necessarily maintaining a flawless recollection of that abuse.

### The Prior Unavailability of the Memory

A central component of the memory recovery experience is the report that prior to recovery, the memory was unavailable. However, this issue itself breaks down into multiple levels. At one extreme is the possibility that an individual might claim unavailability when in fact they are fully aware that their memory had been intact. Such strategic enactment has been suggested as an explanation for alleged memory lapses and other symptoms reported with multiple personality disorder (e.g., Spanos, 1989). At the other extreme is the possibility that the individual had a period in which they were completely incapable of recalling the event. Between these two extremes is a full continuum of possible prior memory states. As Tulving and Pearlstone (1966) observed many years ago, available memories require the appropriate retrieval conditions in order to be accessed. This distinction highlights the fact that a prolonged period in which a memory was not accessed does not necessarily indicate that memory was not available, it may simply reflect the previous absence of appropriate retrieval conditions. Thus, the retrospective determination that a memory was unavailable requires remembering instances in which one was exposed to the appropriate retrieval conditions yet nevertheless failed to recall the memory. Otherwise, such assessments must be based on the rather dubious task of estimating what one *would* have remembered had the appropriate retrieval conditions occurred.

To make matters worse, there is substantial evidence from other domains documenting the marked difficulty of reconstructing a prior knowledge state from the vantage of a new state. For example, individuals who are told facts about a topic tend to misremember that they previously knew those facts, even when independent evidence suggests that they did not (Fishoff, 1982). Similarly, individuals whose attitude changes as a result of persuasion tend to misremember their prior attitude as being consistent with their newly acquired one (Bem, 1972). Admittedly, these studies illustrate memory errors of *minimizing* differences between present and past knowledge states whereas recovered memory errors may involve *exaggerating* such differences. Nevertheless, at another level, both types of errors could reflect the well-documented tendency to maintain consistency (e.g., Festinger, 1980). Accordingly, individuals who have recovered memory experiences may misconstrue their prior knowledge state as being more different than it actually was, thereby maintaining the consistency of their attitude toward that knowledge (i.e., My memories of abuse must have been unavailable, because otherwise I would have been as upset then as I am now).

Because of the many layers associated with the issue of recovery, it may be helpful to begin to review the evidence with a rudimentary question: Can reported recoveries of abuse correspond to real incidents? This bare bones question leaves out many important questions including: the mechanism of the recovery, the completeness of the recollection, and the actual prior unavailability of the memory. However, it addresses an issue that is of tantamount importance to individuals who believe that they have had recovered memory experiences, whether their recollection of abuse may have some bearing in reality.

## Corroborating the Abuse Associated with Recovered Memory Reports

In reviewing the evidence documenting the abuse implicated in recovered memory reports, one observation seems clear: There simply is not a lot of research on which to base conclusions one way or the other. Some might argue that the absence of documentation reflects the absence of a phenomenon. However, because of the sensitivity of the issue, the difficulties of corroboration, and the dearth of systematic investigation, the relative lack of corroborated evidence for the contents of recovered memory reports may reflect nothing more than an absence of research. Indeed, given the current state of the field, it is not at all clear that we could reasonably expect greater evidence of corroborated recovered memory reports even if such reports commonly reflected actual experiences. As a case in point, until recently we had little idea of the frequency of childhood abuse simply because systematic investigation had not been conducted. Furthermore, consideration of the little direct evidence that does exist is at least consistent with the notion that recovered memory reports can correspond to actual abuse. Thus, while the existing corroboration for recovered memory reports may be scant, it is nevertheless sufficiently compelling to support the strong likelihood that such reports can correspond to actual incidences of abuse.

Herman and Schatzow (1987) describe the only published systematic effort to corroborate the memories of a sample of patients who reported recovered accounts of childhood trauma. Of 53 patients participating in group therapy for childhood abuse, they found that 64% reported severe or moderate forgetting of childhood abuse and 74% claimed to have what the authors viewed as strong corroboration (e.g., pornographic photos, diaries, confessions from the perpetrator). While this study provides suggestive evidence in support of memory recoveries, it is not as well documented as it might be. For example, the authors do not provide an independent analysis of the group of greatest interest, the 26% who reported completely forgetting the incident. On the basis of the published manuscript it could be speculated that the corroborated memories were limited to the 74% of the patient population who had full or partial recall. However, in a personal communication Herman (June 1994) indicated that there was no relationship in this study between patients' reports of forgetting and their likelihood of providing corroborating evidence. It is also conceivable that individuals who reported complete forgetting may have made up their evidence of corroboration. However, if we make the reasonable assumption that there was no widespread and deliberate attempt to mislead, then this study provides at least suggestive evidence that recovered memory reports can correspond to actual instances of abuse.

In addition to the Herman and Schatzow (1987) study, there are also a number of published cases of recovered memories of abuse for which there was corroborating evidence associating the alleged abuser with other instances of abuse (see Commonwealth of Massachusetts v Porter, 1993; Horn, 1993). Here I briefly review a new case for which I was personally able to acquire some indirect corroborative evidence. This case was introduced to me by ND, a clinical psychology faculty member and productive researcher at a major state university who had treated the individual in question JR for a totally unrelated problem, approximately 9 years before his recovered memory report. Subsequent to the treatment, ND and JR became good friends, and ND was thus privy to the unfolding of JR's recovered memory report and subsequent corroboration efforts. In a telephone interview, JR described how, at the age of 30, he had experienced marked agitation while watching a movie in which the main character grapples with memories of sexual molestation. Several hours after the movie while lying in bed, JR remembered an incident in which his parish priest had sexually molested him on a camping trip when he was 11 years old. Subsequently, JR reported recovering additional memories of abuse that he estimates spanned over the next several years.

There are multiple sources of indirect corroboration of this case. First, there is JR's description of his attempts to corroborate the abuse. According to JR, upon confrontation, the priest acknowledged the molestation and tried to assuage JR by indicating that he had sought treatment for sexually abusive clergy following an incident with another individual. Three of JR's brothers also indicated that they had been approached by the priest. In addition to JR's report of corroboration, there is also indirect corroborating accounts of other individuals. Although ND only learned of the events of this case indirectly, he maintained regular contact with JR throughout this ordeal. Thus, ND can at a minimum corroborate the temporal order in which the reported corroborating events took place. ND also knows JR quite well and it is therefore of some interest that ND strongly discounts the possibility that JR could have invented all of the corroborating evidence that he reported in their numerous conversations. In addition, subsequent to JR's memory recovery and attempted law suit, another individual reported that he too had been sexually approached by the priest. In a separate telephone interview, this individual described how at age 18 he went to the priest for counseling about homosexuality, whereupon the priest made sexual advances toward him. This individual indicated that he had maintained an intact memory for the priest's sexual improprieties but had been reluctant to disclose the memory due to his embarrassment.

There are a number of observations worth extracting from the above case. First, the evidence was indirect; i.e., there were no actual witnesses or direct physical evidence of the reported abuse. Thus this case does not speak to the precision of individuals' memories of abuse. Furthermore, there was no independent verification of JR's memory gap prior to the report of recovery, so we cannot determine to what degree the memories were previously unavailable.[1] While there are aspects of this case that cannot be validated, other elements strongly suggest that it did correspond to actual incidents of abuse. First, it involved a recovery that occurred outside the context of therapy, thereby reducing the likelihood that it was the product of a therapist's suggestion. Second, there was another individual who indicated that he had been involved in abusive behavior by the alleged perpetrator. While this corroborating report was elicited after the initial recovered memory, and was therefore potentially vulnerable to suggestion, it is worth noting that it was produced by an individual who claimed never to have forgotten the abusive incident. Even skeptics of recovered memories are reluctant to question the memories of an individual who "suffered silently her whole life with memories of abuse" (Loftus, 1994, p. 443). Thus, taken together

[1] It might be noted that although ND never discussed sex abuse with JR, they did discuss many intimate aspects of JR's life which ND believes were on par with the embarrassment one might feel at being sexually involved with a priest. The fact that ND discussed these other events but not his memories with the priest, leads ND, at least, to believe that JR was truly unaware of possessing the memories of abuse.

with other published cases, the present case provides converging evidence that recovered memory reports can, at least sometimes, be corroborated to the degree that they can implicate individuals who are prone to engage in abusive behaviors.

## Additional Aspects of the Question of Recovery

So far I have only argued for the most bare bones claim that some reports of recovered memories seem likely to have some correspondence to actual incidents of abuse. In paring the question down to this basic issue, I sloughed off many important layers. I now return to consider three of these other aspects of the recovered memory experience: (1) Do individuals actually forget memory for trauma? (2) Can memory for trauma fluctuate in availability? (3) What mechanisms might lead to the forgetting and recovery of trauma?

*Evidence that individuals can actually forget trauma.* Much of the research examining the incidence of forgetting childhood abuse has involved the retrospective reports of patients currently seeking treatment for sexual abuse (e.g., Briere & Conte, 1993; Gold, Hughes, & Hohnecker, 1994; Herman & Schatzow, 1987; Loftus, Polonsky, & Fullilove, 1994). Aside from the potential difficulties in corroborating the abuse and determining how patients interpreted the question used to elicit their reports (see Ceci, Crotteau, Smith, & Loftus, this issue), such studies are constrained by the intrinsic difficulties associated with (1) distinguishing a prolonged period in which a memory was not accessed from the claim that a memory was actually unavailable during that period and (2) assessing a prior knowledge state from the vantage of an altered knowledge state (see earlier discussion). Given the problems inherent in retrospective claims of unavailability, we should be cautious in using patients' retrospective reports as a source for conclusions about the actual prior state of their memories. Rather, the primary value of patients' retrospective analyses is documenting the frequency with which victims of sexual abuse patients *believe* that their memories were previously unavailable.

A more direct method of documenting actual forgetting of trauma is to identify individuals on the basis of their experience of trauma and then query them to determine whether they currently remember it. This approach can thereby document forgetting while it is still intact. Along these lines, Williams (in press) identified women who had been taken to a sex abuse clinic as children 17 years earlier. Of the 129 women who were interviewed in the study, 38% did not recall the abuse for which they had been treated. Williams conducted a variety of analyses to rule out explanations other than forgetting. For example, contrary to the suggestion that these results might reflect a failure to disclose abuse, she found that patients who failed to recall the abuse were just as likely to reveal other intimate facts as individuals who recalled the abuse. Against the suggestion that these results were due to infantile amnesia, Williams found that nearly one-third of those abused between the ages of 7 and 10 and over one-quarter of those abused between 11 and 12 reported no recollection of the abuse. Although Williams' study takes important steps towards documenting forgetting of incidents of sexual trauma, it does have some limitations. First, the study only addresses memory for individual instances of abuse and does not bear on the more general claim that individuals can forget repeated episodes of abuse. Second, many (68%) of the individuals who did not recall the particular incident for which they were treated, nevertheless recalled other sexual assaults. It is thus possible that some of these individuals may have confused their recollections of abuse rather than totally forgetting them. However, even when individuals who recalled other instances of abuse are removed, there still remains 12% of this population who reported that they were never sexually abused, when in fact they had been treated for such abuse. It would be nice to know the demographics (e.g., age distribution) of this particular subset of Williams' population. Nevertheless, at a minimum Williams' study suggests that individuals can forget individual episodes of abuse and at least some may forget that they were the victims of abuse altogether.

Another potential difficulty for the claim, implied by Williams' study, that forgetting of childhood sexual traumas can be common is the frequent demonstration that children typically maintain intact memories for a variety of nonsexual traumatic experiences including kidnapping (Terr, 1979), sniper attack (Pynoos & Nader, 1989), lightning strike (Dollinger, 1985); emergency room treatments (Howe, Courage, & Peterson, this volume), and even urinary tract catheterization (Goodman et al., this volume). One important consideration in assessing the implications of reports of children's intact memories for trauma is that these studies involve children's rather than adults' memories for childhood trauma. It is therefore quite possible, indeed likely, that greater forgetting would occur with further passage of time. It is also worth noting that there may be important differences between the traumatic events mentioned above and sexual abuse. The above traumas corresponded to single events that could be discussed with others and which would not entail profound degrees of embarrassment. The one exception to this generalization is the Goodman et al. study, involving urinary tract catheterization which at least hints at the possibility that some of these factors may be important. In many respects Goodman et al.'s study comes the closest to approximating the trauma associated with sexual abuse. The procedure was painful and embarrassing (entailing genital penetration and public urination), and at least some parents were reluctant to talk about the procedure with their children. If there is some validity to the notion of forgetting the childhood sexual abuse, then given the similarities between the procedure involved in Goodman et al.'s study and sexual abuse, one would expect to see greater hints of precursors to forgetting of trauma in this study then the other studies. And in fact, there are such hints. For one, a few children (the authors do not give the precise number) out of a sample of 46 denied that they experienced the medical test altogether. Although it is not possible to determine the reason for these denials, this is certainly the type of precursor to actual forgetting that one might expect. Second, Goodman et al. found that a number of factors that seem likely to be associated with sexual abuse were predictive of poor memory performance in their study. Specifically, embarrassment, lack of discussion of the procedure with parents, and PTSD symptoms were all negatively correlated with memory performance. If we extrapolate the trends observed in Goodman et al.'s studies to adult recollection of childhood sexual abuse in which the delay is much greater, the embarrassment potentially more pronounced, the discussion of the trauma typically a nonoccurrence (with secrecy frequently insured by threats of violence), and the incidence of PTSD symptoms frequent (Terr, 1991), then it is not unreasonable to expect that some individuals might in fact forget the abuse.

Examination of adult memory for nonsexual trauma also provides somewhat of a mixed picture, but one that is again not inconsistent with the possibility that individuals can forget memory for trauma. A number of studies have documented general memory disturbances with adults following a variety of nonsexual traumatic events including tornado (Madakasira & O'Brien, 1987), fire (McFarlane, 1988), airplane crash (Sloan, 1988), and the Hyatt regency disaster (Wilkinson, 1983). Unfortunately, these studies do not specify the precise nature of the memory deficits. Thus, while such studies suggest a general relationship between traumatic experience and forgetting, they cannot be used to provide direct evidence for specific forgetting of traumatic experiences. Although more scant, there have been a number of reports of specific forgetting of traumatic experiences, particularly wartime experiences (e.g., van Devanter, 1985; Parson, 1988; Silver & Kelly, 1985; Wilson, 1988). The reported forgetting of wartime memories is of particular relevance to the claim of forgetting of sexual abuse because of certain similarities between these two types of trauma. Specifically, in both cases individuals may have been involved in activities that they are especially reluctant to discuss. Indeed, many of the reported instances of forgetting of wartime trauma involved particularly troubling events such as the killing of women or children (Parson, 1988; Silver & Kelly, 1985; Wilson, 1988).

The suggestion that reported forgetting of trauma may be particularly associated with events involving embarrassment or shame (cf. Lewis, 1990) leads readily to the possibility that such reports do not entail forgetting at all but rather reflect an unwillingness to disclose the events in question. As mentioned already, there is some evidence arguing against a failure-to-disclose explanation for traumatic forgetting, e.g., Williams (in press) finding that predisposition to disclose intimate information was not associated with forgetting. However, even if we grant the possibility that an unwillingness to disclose may sometimes be involved in reports of forgetting, there is still good reason to believe that individuals may go for periods in which the traumatic event is relatively less accessible and then becomes much more so.

*Fluctuations in the accessibility of trauma.* The notion of fluctuation in access to traumatic events is strongly suggested by veterans' delayed reactivations of traumatic experiences. Reactivation of traumatic experiences can occur after durations in which individuals experience relatively few symptoms (Christenson, Walker, Ross, & Maltbie, 1981; Defazio, Rustin, & Diamond, 1975; Grinker, 1945; McGee, 1984, Williams, 1983). For example, Christenson et al. describe the case of Mr. A which they characterize as a typical example of a delayed reactivation of traumatic conflict. Following a brief treatment for "nerves" after World War II, Mr. A experienced a long period of good adjustment. Then, one day while working in an emergency room, he was asked to clean up a 9-year-old boy whom he did not know was already dead. The discovery that the boy was dead horrified Mr. A and was immediately followed by the onset of anxiety, depression, and nightmares about his wartime experiences. Mr. A was admitted to a hospital where he revealed the following information that he had not discussed for 35 years. Apparently, during a particularly traumatic period in the war, Mr. A had shot a 10-year-old boy who had been suspected of being wired as a human bomb. Although the above report did not make any claims with regard to whether Mr. A ever completely forgot about this incident, it clearly suggests that the traumatic and troubling experience became much more accessible following the triggering event.

There are a number of important observations that may be gleaned from consideration of veterans' delayed reactivation episodes. First, while we cannot know the precision of their memories, the fact that these individuals were involved in wartime events supports the strong likelihood that the reactivations are associated with some type of actual traumatic activity. At a minimum, veterans' reactivation episodes illustrate a situation in which individual experience increased accessibility to the fact that they were previously exposed to actual trauma. Thus, such experiences provide a useful comparison to reports of recovered memories of sexual abuse, for which the participation in actual trauma is less clear. And when we make the comparison the similarities are striking. First, as the above example illustrates, both delayed veteran reactivations and childhood sexual abuse can correspond to particularly troubling events for which the individual would understandably feel embarrassed or ashamed. Second, in both cases individuals can go for periods in which they do not discuss the event nor show direct evidence of being troubled by it. Third, in both cases a triggering event that shared some similarity with the alleged traumatic event (e.g., seeing a dead child, watching a movie about sex abuse) produces an onrush of emotion associated with the reported traumatic event. Fourth, after the triggering event, the individual begins discussing the traumatic experience. The striking parallels between recovered memory reports and veterans' delayed reactivations suggest that recovered accounts of sexual abuse may result from increased access to the fact that one was previously exposed to trauma. With this in mind, I now turn to a discussion of what mechanisms might drive such a process.

*Mechanisms of recovered memory reports.* In considering the mechanisms that might lead to recovered memory experiences it may be useful to consider what processes might produce the various attributes of both delayed veteran reactivations (cf. McGee, 1984) and recovered memories outlined above. First, the fact that these experiences correspond to situations that may cause embarrassment or shame suggests that individuals may be reluctant to talk about these experiences. Considerable research suggests that talking about life experiences helps to integrate those experiences into one's life narrative, thereby increasing its potential accessibility (Nelson, 1993). The absence of such discussion may thus reduce the accessibility of these experiences (Johnson, 1988b; Tessler & Nelson, this volume). In addition, embarrassment/shame may particularly predispose individuals to actively avoid (suppress) thinking about these experiences which may result in their temporarily reduced accessibility (Kihlstrom & Hoyt, 1990). Other mechanisms, including general forgetting as well as processes more specific to trauma such as dissociation (Speigel & Cardena, 1991), physiological processes (Southwick, Krystal, Morgan, Andrew, & Johnson, 1993), and perhaps even repression (Erdleyi, 1990), might also contribute to the decreased accessibility of the traumatic memory. As a result of this decreased accessibility, individuals may go for sometime without showing obvious extrinsic evidence of possessing the memory. However, when a situation is encountered that shares some fundamental similarity with the original traumatic experience, with respect to either context (Tulving & Thompson, 1973) or affective/physiological state (Clark & Teasdale, 1982; Goodwin, Powell, Brenner, Hoine, & Stern, 1969), the accessibility of the traumatic memory may increase along with its associated powerful emotions. Therapy situations may also increase accessibility of traumatic memories by eliciting emotional states corresponding to the trauma or by inducing relevant associative chaining that helps to cue the memory (Bower, 1990). Once access to the memory is increased, to the degree that suppression processes were involved in the initial reduction in accessibility to the memory, rebound effects may be experienced in which there is a flooding of the previously suppressed thoughts (Wegner, 1994). The resulting prevalence of thoughts about the trauma may powerfully contrast with the prior relative absence of such thoughts. From the perspective of this current flooding of thoughts about the trauma, the previous relatively reduced accessibility of the memory may be construed as a complete unavailability. The above account provides a highly feasible characterization of the recovered memory process without having to draw on the notion that traumatic memories are ever completely unavailable. This is not to say that traumatic memories may not be completely unavailable for some period of time, but merely that we do not need to postulate such a memory state in order to account for sincere reports of recovered memory experiences corresponding to actual incidents of trauma. At a very minimum, we cannot argue against the possibility of recovered memory experiences on the basis that there is no existing way to explain them.

## FABRICATED MEMORIES

The suggestion that recovered memory experiences can be associated with the increased accessibility to memories of actual abuse should not preclude the likelihood that recovered accounts of abuse might also be generated in response to suggestion. As with recovered memories, at present it is difficult to provide incontrovertible direct evidence for the premise of fabricated memories of abuse. Nevertheless, consideration of the indirect evidence at hand strongly supports the contention that recollections of abuse can result from suggestion.[2] In assessing the question of fabricated memories it may be useful to consider three questions: (1) Can suggestion lead to the production of image/impressions that are sufficiently vivid to enable them to be confused with reality? (2) If such image/impressions were produced in regard to childhood abuse, could individuals be persuaded to believe in them? (3) Is there any case evidence suggesting that individuals may

---

[2] The difference in the relative amount of discussion dedicated here to recovered and fabricated memories should not be taken as a reflection of the degree of evidence for these two constructs. It simply reflects the greater complexity of issues surrounding the topic of recovered memories and the pre-existence of an excellent review of the evidence for fabricated memories by Loftus (1993).

have been persuaded to believe in false memories of abuse? I discuss each of these questions in turn.

### Confusing Suggestions with Reality

There have now been innumerable demonstrations that individuals can come to vividly remember things that they never in fact experienced. This evidence comes from many different research traditions. Neurocognitive evidence of individuals with frontal lobe damage indicates that patients can readily fabricate and believe elaborate memories that are confabulated in order to tie together the real bits of memory that they retrieve (e.g., Moscovitch, 1989). Research on reality monitoring has shown that individuals can confuse self-generated thoughts with perceived thoughts, such that they remember experiencing stimuli that they in fact only imagined (e.g., Johnson, 1988a; Johnson & Raye, 1981). Research on the effects of postevent information has demonstrated that people can integrate the contents of misleading suggestions into their memories (for a brief review see Garry, Loftus, & Brown, this volume). The resulting memories can be held with as much confidence as real memories (Loftus, Donders, Hoffman, & Schooler, 1989b), can be described in marked detail (Schooler, Clark, & Loftus, 1988; Schooler, Gerhard, & Loftus, 1986), and are as likely as real memories to be maintained in the face of contradictory information (Loftus, Korf, & Schooler, 1989a).

One criticism about applying the research on both reality monitoring and misleading postevent suggestion to the present topic is that these research traditions frequently involve details about events rather than events themselves (e.g., Pezdek, this volume). However, all of the above lines of research have demonstrated that individuals can be lead to misrecollect entire events that never happened. The neurocognitive evidence reveals remarkably detailed and complex confabulations of entire events. Research in reality monitoring has shown that people can come to remember having had dreams that were in fact only told to them by others (Johnson, Kahan, & Raye, 1984). Research on the effects of misleading postevent suggestion has demonstrated that individuals can, as a result of suggestion, come to remember entire events such as being lost in a shopping mall (Loftus & Coan, in press) or getting one's finger caught in a mouse trap (Ceci et al., this volume, Ceci, Loftus, Leichtman, & Bruck, in press). These fabricated accounts of entire events can also be described in great detail and maintained in the face of contradiction (Ceci et al., this volume). In short it seems that the mind is quite capable of remembering vivid accounts of things that never actually happened.

### Accepting False Accounts of Abuse

If the mind is capable of producing vivid accounts of events that never in fact took place, then there is no principled reason why such accounts could not be fabricated with respect to childhood abuse. What is of question is whether, once generated, individuals could come to believe that such events actually occurred. There could be some scenarios that are simply too inconceivable to be confused with reality, no matter how vividly they were produced in one's mind.

In considering whether individuals can be persuaded to believe in fabricated memories of abuse, it is important to remember the many painful lessons, ranging from Nazi era Germany to Milgram's (1963) classic studies of obedience, demonstrating the remarkable degree to which individuals can be lead to accept preposterous suggestions when they are exposed to persuasive individuals in positions of authority. Thus, in assessing the possibility of fabricated memories of abuse, we must be ever vigilant not to make the same mistake we have made time and time before: underestimating just how persuadable people can be. There is, in fact, every reason to believe that people's propensity for persuasion extends to accepting memories for the seemingly preposterous. As a poignant example, in response to suggestions by leaders of religious groups, individuals have been known to report recovering memories of having been visited or abducted by space aliens (Persinger, 1992). Furthermore, both recovered accounts of sexual abuse and alien abduction can be: (1) elicited following the suggestions of the leader of a group, (2) "remembered" suddenly, (3) associated with a reduction of anxiety and panic attacks, and (4) accompanied by subsequent recollections of additional "memories" (Persinger, 1992). If individuals can recover (presumably false) childhood memories of being abducted or visited by space aliens then certainly they should be capable of falsely remembering being abused as a child. Moreover, the striking parallels (with respect to both the suggestion and the recovery) between the situations surrounding at least some recovered accounts of sexual abuse and alien abductions suggest that similar dysfunctional mechanisms might be involved in the fabrication of both types of memories.

## Retractions of Recovered Memories

If individuals could be persuaded to believe in memories of abuse that did not in fact occur, then one would expect that at least sometimes people would realize that they had been misled and retract their accounts. While such retractions would not necessarily prove that the memories were fabricated, they would at least be consistent with such a view. In a recent edited volume, Goldstein and Farmer (1993) provide a number of examples of such retractors including the account of Pasley (1993), who sought treatment for bulimia. Pasley's therapist told her that bulimia was commonly caused by sexual abuse and suggested that she had been abused. Following repeated suggestions by her therapist, often while under hypnosis, Pasley began having bizarre dreams and flashbacks including group sexual abuse and being sexually abused by animals. All of which Pasley's therapist insisted really happened. After 4 years in therapy, Pasley came to the conclusion that these alleged memories were in fact fictitious, the product of her imagination's collaboration with her therapist's suggestion.

One can of course interpret the above case in a manner that does not implicate the therapist's suggestions. Pasley could have reforgotten the memories or simply found it more palatable to reframe them as suggestions. However, there are compelling reasons to suspect that suggestions may have played a role. First, the recovery did not occur spontaneously, as in the cases described earlier, but only following the suggestion of a therapist that the reported symptoms were a likely product of sexual abuse. Second, the recovery occurred during hypnosis which is known to increase individuals' susceptibility to misleading memory suggestions (e.g., Putnam, 1979) (suggestibility is, after all, one of the hallmarks of the hypnotic state). Third, despite all of her therapy, Pasley ultimately concluded that her memories had no basis. In fact, her belief in the falseness of her memories was sufficient to convince a jury that her memories had been planted and to award her a six-figure settlement on that basis.

Pasley's case is not an isolated instance but rather reflects the sentiment of a growing number of individuals who have become disenfranchised with their recovered memories of abuse. It is of course possible that such retractions merely reflect individuals returning to denial stage (e.g., Gleaves, 1994). However, there is a certain irony to believing individuals when they recover memories but disbelieving them when they recant such memories (or vice versa for that matter). The fact that individuals can shift between believing and disbelieving in their recovered memories demonstrates the fundamental ontological uncertainty of such memories. It thus seems most appropriate that we be extremely cautious in assessing individuals' claims regarding either the veracity or the falseness of their recovered memories.

## CONCLUSION

In sum, although the available evidence remains primarily indirect, there is nevertheless a reasonable foundation for the existence of both recovered and fabricated memories. Even a skeptical view about the frequency with which one or the other of these phenomena actually occurs should be tempered by the importance of their probable existence. For example, even if the forgetting/recovery is an extremely rare reaction to trauma, given current estimates of the incidence of childhood sexual abuse (e.g., some studies estimate as many as one in three women, e.g., McCann, Sakheim, & Abrahamson, 1988), the absolute frequency of recovered memories could still be quite substantial. Similarly, even if fabricated memories only occur in highly suggestive circumstances, the documented, and perhaps even frequent, use of hypnosis, truth serum, and persistent suggestion by practitioners convinced that such abuse must have occurred (cf. Loftus, 1993) implies that whatever it takes to create a fabricated memory of abuse is likely to be occurring.

While there is certainly great controversy surrounding the topic of recovered accounts of sexual abuse, there is one point on which everyone is likely to agree: more research is needed. In closing it may be helpful to briefly identify some of the research topics that the present analysis suggests are worthy of pursuit. With respect to recovered memories two general lines of research seem especially important. First, extensive and thorough research is warranted to determine just how often the sexual abuse associated with recovered memory reports can be corroborated. Second, longitudinal assessments of documented victims of various types of traumas may help to identify the specific situations, personality factors, and mechanisms that may mediate forgetting, remembering, and fluctuations in access to memories for trauma. (It should be noted of course that repeated interviewing of individuals regarding their trauma is likely to have an impact on their memories.) With respect to the issue of fabricated memories of trauma, extensive surveys of therapy practices are needed (cf. Poole, Lindsay, Memon, & Bull, 1995) to assess the frequency with which individuals may be subjected to therapeutic techniques that risk introducing fabricated memories. It would be especially interesting to know the relationship between the use of suggestive therapeutic techniques and the relative likelihoods of both the occurrence and the possibility of corroborating recovered memory reports. If the recovered memory reports elicited in suggestive therapy situations are more common and less readily corroborated than those elicited by less suggestive practices, this would provide rather compelling evidence that suggestion may create memories of abuse.

The above research would clearly help to clarify some of the difficult issues that surround recovered accounts of childhood abuse. However, in the mean time we must rely on the evidence at hand. Although it is conceivable that in the unrevealed layers lies a core of definitive evidence in favor of one or the other extreme positions, at present it seems appropriate that we take the probable existence of both recovered and fabricated memories very seriously.

## ACKNOWLEDGMENTS

The writing of this paper was supported by a grant to the author from the National Institute of Mental Health. I thank Marte Fallshore, Steve Fiore, Elizabeth Loftus, Joe Melcher, Tonya Schooler, and Carmi Schooler for comments on earlier drafts.

## REFERENCES

Bem, D. J. (1972). Self-perception theory. In L. Berkowitz (Ed.), *Advances in experimental social psychology*. New York: Academic Press.

Bower, G. H. (1990). Awareness, the unconscious, and repression: An experimental psychologist's perspective. In J. L. Singer (Ed.), *Repression and dissociation*. Chicago: Univ. of Chicago Press.

Briere, J., & Conte, J. (1993). Self-reported amnesia for abuse in adults molested as children. *Journal of Traumatic Stress*, **6**(1), 21–31.

Ceci, S. J., Crotteau, M. L., Smith, E., & Loftus, E. F. (1994). Repeatedly thinking about a nonevent: Source misattributions among preschoolers. *Consciousness and Cognition*, **3**, 388–407.

Ceci, S. J., Loftus, E. F., Leichtman, M. D., & Bruck, M. (In press). The role of source misattributions in the creation of false beliefs among preschoolers. *International Journal of Clinical and Experimental Hypnosis*.

Christenson, R. M., Walker, J. I., Ross, D. R., & Maltbie, A. (1981). Reactivation of traumatic conflicts. *American Journal of Psychiatry*, **138**, 984–985.

Clark, D. M., & Teasdale, J. D. (1982). Diurnal variation in clinical depression and accessibility of memories of positive and negative experiences. *Journal of Abnormal Psychology*, **91**, 87–95.

Commonwealth of Massachusetts v Porter. (1993).

Defazio, V., Rustin, S., & Diamond, A. (1975). Symptom development in Vietnam era veterans. *American Journal Orthopsychiatry*, **45**, 158–163.

Dollinger, S. J. (1985). Lightning-strike disaster among children. *British Journal of Medical Psychology*, **58**, 375–383.

Erdleyi, M. H. (1990). Repression, reconstruction, and defense: History and integration of the psychoanalytic and experimental frameworks. In J. L. Singer (Ed.), *Repression and dissociation*. Chicago: Univ. of Chicago Press.

Festinger, L. (1980). Looking backward. In L. Festinger (Ed.), *Retrospections on social psychology.* New York: Oxford Univ. Press.

Fischoff, B. (1982). For those condemned to study the past: Heuristics and biases in hindsight. In D. Kahneman, P. Slovic, & A. Tversky (Eds.), *Judgment under uncertainty: Heuristics and biases* (pp. 335–351). New York: Cambridge Univ. Press.

Gleaves, D. H. (1994). On "the reality of repressed memories." *American Psychologist,* **49,** 441–442.

Gold, S. N., Hughes, D., & Hohnecker, L. (1994). Degrees of repression of sexual abuse memories. *American Psychologist,* **49,** 441–442.

Goodman, G. S., Quas, J. A., Batterman-Fauce, J. M., Riddlesberger, M., & Kuhn, J. (1994). Predictors of accurate and inaccurate memories of traumatic events experienced in childhood. *Consciousness and Cognition,* **3,** 269–294.

Goodwin, D. W., Powell, B., Bremer, D., Hoine, H., & Stern, J. (1969). Alcohol and recall: State dependent effects in man. *Science,* **163,** 1358–1360.

Goldstein E., & Farmer, K. (Eds.) (1993). *True stories of false memories* (pp. 347–365). Boca Raton, FL: Sirs Publishing.

Grinker, R. R. (1945). Psychiatric disorders in combat crews overseas and returnees. *Medical Clinic of North America,* **29,** 729–739.

Harvey, M. R., & Herman, J. L. (1994). Amnesia, partial amnesia and delayed recall among adult survivors of childhood trauma. *Consciousness and Cognition,* **3,** 295–306.

Herman, J. L., & Schatzow, E. (1987). Recovery and verification of memories of childhood sexual trauma. *Psychoanalytic Psychology,* **4,** 1–14.

Horn, M. (1993, 11/29/93). Memories lost and found. *U S News & World Report,* 53–63.

Howe, M. L., Courage, M. L., & Peterson, C. (1994). How can I remember when "I" wasn't there: Long-term retention of traumatic experiences and emergence of the cognitive self. *Consciousness and Cognition,* **3,** 327–355.

Johnson, M. K. (1988a). Discriminating the origin of information. In T. F. Oltmanns & B. A. Maher (Eds.), *Delusional beliefs: Interdisciplinary perspectives* (pp. 34–65). New York: Wiley.

Johnson, M. K. (1988b). Reality monitoring: An experimental phenomenological approach. *Journal of Experimental Psychology: General,* **117,** 390–394.

Johnson, M. K., Kahan, T. L., & Raye, C. L. (1984). Dreams and reality monitoring. *Journal of Experimental Psychology: General,* **113,** 329–344.

Johnson, M. K., & Raye, C. L. (1981). Reality monitoring. *Psychological Review,* **88,** 67–85.

Kihlstrom, J. F., & Hoyt, I. P. (1990). Repression, dissociation and hypnosis. In J. L. Singer (Eds.), *Repression and dissociation* Chicago: Univ. of Chicago Press.

Lewis, H. B. (1990). Shame, repression, field dependence, and psychopathology. In J. L. Singer (Eds.), *Repression and dissociation.* Chicago: Univ. of Chicago Press.

Loftus, E. F. (1993). The reality of repressed memories. *American Psychologist,* **48,** 518–537.

Loftus, E. F. (1994). The repressed memory controversy. *American Psychologist,* **49,** 443–445.

Loftus, E. F., & Coan, D. (In press). The construction of childhood memories. In D. P. Peters (Eds.), *The child witness in context: Cognitive, social, and legal perspectives.* The Netherlands: Kluwer.

Loftus, E. F., Korf, N., & Schooler, J. W. (1989a). Misguided memories: Sincere distortions of reality. In J. Yuille (Ed.), *Credibility assessment: A theoretical and research perspective* (pp. 155–174), Boston: Kluer.

Loftus, E. F., Donders, K., Hoffman, H. G., & Schooler, J. W. (1989b). Creating new memories that are quickly accessed and confidently held. *Memory and Cognition,* **17,** 607–116.

Loftus, E. F., Polonsky, S., & Fullilove, M. T. (1994). Memories of childhood sexual abuse: Remembering and repressing. *Psychology of Women Quarterly.*

Loftus, E. F., Garry, M., & Brown, S. W. (1994). Memory: A river runs through it. *Consciousness and Cognition,* **3,** 438–451.

Madakasira, S., & O'Brien, K. (1987). Acute posttraumatic stress disorder in victims of a natural disaster. *Journal of Nervous and Mental Disease, 175,* 286–290.

McCann, I. L., Sakheim, D. K., & Abrahamson, D. J. (1988). Trauma and victimization: A model of psychological adaptation. *The Counseling Psychologist, 16,* 531–594.

McFarlane, A. C. (1988). The longitudinal course of posttraumatic morbidity. *Journal of Nervous and Mental Disease, 176,* 30–39.

McFarlane, A. C. (1986). Posttraumatic morbidity of a disaster. *Journal of Nervous and Mental Disease, 174,* 4–14.

McGee, R. (1984). Flashbacks and memory phenomena. *Journal of Nervous and Mental Disease, 172,* 273–278.

Milgram, S. (1963). Behavioral study of obedience. *Journal of Abnormal and Social Psychology, 67,* 371–378.

Moscovitch, M. (1989). Confabulation and the frontal systems: Strategic versus associative retrieval in neuropsychological theories of memory. In H. L. Roediger III and F. I. M. Craik (Eds.), *Varieties of memory and consciousness.* Hillsdale, NJ: Erlbaum.

Nelson, K. (1993). The psychological and social origins of autobiographical memory. *Psychological Science, 4,* 1–8.

Ofshe, R. J. (1992). Inadvertent hypnosis during interrogation: False confession due to dissociative state; mis-identified multiple personality and the satanic cult hypothesis. *International Journal of Clinical and Experimental Hypnosis, XL,* 125–156.

Parson, E. R. (1988). Post-traumatic self disorders. In J. P. Wilson, Z. Harel, & B. Kahana (Eds.), *Human adaptation to extreme stress: From the holocaust to Vietnam.* New York: Plenum.

Pasley, L. E. (1993). Misplaced trust. In E. Goldstein & K. Farmer (Eds.), True stories of false memories (pp. 347–365). Boca Raton, FL: Sirs Publishing.

Persinger, M. A. (1992). Neuropsychological profiles of adults who report "Sudden remembering" of early childhood memories: Implications for claims of sex abuse and alien visitation/abduction experiences. *Perceptual and Motor Skills, 75,* 259–266.

Pezdek, K., & Roe, C. (1994). Memory for Childhood Events: How suggestible is it? *Consciousness and Cognition, 3,* 374–387.

Poole, D. A., Lindsay, D. S., Memon, A., & Bull, R. (1995). Psychotherapy and the recovery of memories of childhood sexual abuse: U.S. and British practitioners' opinions, practices, and experiences. *Journal of Consulting & Clinical Psychology, 3,* 426–437.

Putnam, B. (1979). Hypnosis and distortion in eyewitness memory. *International Journal of Clinical and Experimental Hypnosis, 4,* 437–448.

Pynoos, R. S., & Nader, K. (1989). Children's memory and and proximity to violence. *Journal of the American Academy of Child and Adolescent Psychiatry, 28,* 236–241.

Schooler, J. W., Gerhard, D., & Loftus, E. F. (1986). Qualities of the unreal. *Journal of Experimental Psychology: Learning, Memory, and Cognition, 12,* 171–181.

Schooler, J. W., Clark, C. A., & Loftus, E. F. (1988). Knowing when memory is real. In M. Gruneberg, P. Morris, & R. N. Sykes (Eds.), *Practical aspects of memory* (pp. 83–88). New York: Wiley.

Silver, S. M., & Kelly, W. E. (1985). Hypnotherapy of post-traumatic stress disorder in combat veterans from WW II and Vietnam. In W. E. Kelly (Ed.), *Post-traumatic stress disorder and the war veteran patient.* New York: Brunner/Mazel.

Sloan, P. (1988). Post-traumatic stress in survivors of an airplane crash landing: A clinical and exploratory research intervention. *Journal of Traumatic Stress, 1,* 211–299.

Southwick, S., Krystal, S. M., Morgan, J. H., Andrew, C., & Johnson, D. (1993). Abnormal noradrenergic function in posttraumatic stress disorder. *Archives of General Psychiatry, 50,*(4), 266–274.

Spanos, N. P. (1989). Hypnosis, demonic possession, and multiple personality: Strategic enactments and disavowals of responsibility for actions. In C. E. Ward (Eds.), *Altered states of consciousness and mental health* (pp. 96–124). Newbury Park, CA: Sage.

Spiegel, D., & Cardena, E. (1991). Disintegrated experience: The dissociative disorders revisited. *Journal of Abnormal Psychology,* **100,** 366–378.

Terr, L. C. (1979). Children of Chowchilla: A study of psychic trauma. In A. J. Solnit, R. Eissler, M. Freud, M. Kriss, & P. B. Neubauer (Eds.), *The psychoanalytic study of the child* (pp. 1543–1550). New Haven: Yale Univ. Press.

Terr. L. C. (1991). Childhood traumas: An outline and overview. *American Journal of Psychiatry,* **1,** 10–20.

Tessler, M., & Nelson, K. (1994). Making memories: The influence of joint encoding on later recall by young children. *Consciousness and Cognition,* **3,** 307–326.

Tulving, E., & Thompson, D. M. (1973). Encoding specificity and retrieval processes in episodic memory. *Journal of Experimental Psychology: Learning, Memory, and Cognition,* **8,** 336–342.

Tulving, E., & Pearlstone, Z. (1966). Availability versus accessibility of information in memory for words. *Journal of Verbal Learning and Verbal Behavior,* **5,** 381–391.

van Devanter, L. M. (1985). The unknown warriors: Implications of the experiences of women in Vietnam. In W. E. Kelly (Eds.), *Post-traumatic stress disorder and the war veteran patient.* New York: Brunner/Mazel.

Wegner, D. M. (1994). Ironic processes of mental control. *Psychological Review,* **101,** 34–52.

Wilkinson, C. B. (1993). Aftermath of a disaster: The collapse of the Hyatt Regency Hotel skywalks. *American Journal of Psychiatry,* **40,** 1134–1139.

Williams, C. C. (1983). The mental foxhole: The Vietnam Veteran's Search for Meaning. *American Journal of Orthopsychiatry,* **53.**

Williams, L. M. (In press). Recall of childhood trauma: A prospective study of women's memories of child sexual abuse. *Journal of Consulting and Clinical Psychology.*

Wilson, J. P. (1988). Treating the Vietnam Veteran. In F. M. Ochberg (Ed.), *Post-traumatic therapy and victims of violence.* New York: Brunner/Mazel.

# The Trauma-Memory Argument and Recovered Memory Therapy

JOHN F. KIHLSTROM

*Yale University*

The trauma-memory argument proposes that memories of childhood trauma can affect adult behavior outside awareness, and that such unconscious memories can return to awareness even after long delays—a situation which recovered memory therapy is intended to foster. Unfortunately, both the argument and the therapy are based on case reports of unknown representativeness and on clinical studies which are methodologically flawed or which do not consider alternative explanations. Of particular concern is the general lack of independent verification of the ostensibly forgotten memories. The trauma-memory argument is plausible, in at least some respects, given what we know about the processes of remembering and forgetting; but considerably more empirical research is needed before it can serve as a basis for scientifically sound clinical practice.

## INTRODUCTION

Why would adult memory researchers contradict the clinical findings and some research findings that adult women who were sexually abused as children may have memory problems and often remember the abuse during therapy? Certainly personal biases, such as distrust of therapists, desire to support male perpetrators, denial that "nice" men can molest children, enjoyment of the recognition provided by groups that rally around men who are allegedly falsely accused, prior experience with one or more unfounded (not untrue but unprovably legally) cases, and need to stand by a previously expressed position, may figure into such motivation. (Lenore A. Walker, 1994, p. 85)

An increasing number of researchers, clinicians, and members of the public at large have become interested in two related propositions: (a) that memories of childhood incest, sexual abuse, and other trauma can affect adult personality outside awareness; and (b) that such unconscious memories can return to awareness, even after long delays. This *trauma-memory argument* (e.g., Bass & Davis, 1988; Frederickson, 1992; Herman, 1992; Terr, 1994) typically begins with a child who has been the victim of trauma such as incest or sexual abuse. Under certain circumstances, it is argued, the child defensively invokes a mental process such as repression or dissociation, which in turn results in an amnesia for the trauma. Nevertheless, representations of the trauma have been encoded in memory; these representations persist and affect subsequent experience, thought, and action in the form of intrusive images, bodily feelings, repetitive dreams, and other mental and behavioral symptoms. The presence of these symptoms, then, is taken as a sign that a traumatic event occurred, and a traumatic memory for that event exists. At some later time, this unconscious memory may be recovered spontaneously in response to certain cues in the environment, or it may be exhumed by means of certain therapeutic techniques such as

297

guided interviews, hypnosis, and barbiturate sedation.[1] Exhumation of the original traumatic memory is an important step in the recovery process; in cases in
which the memory cannot be verified, its essential accuracy is demonstrated by
its explanatory value in the context of the person's presenting symptoms and
overall life history.

Acceptance of the trauma-memory argument has led to the development and
promotion of a set of treatment techniques known as *recovered memory therapy*.
This term covers a wide variety of therapeutic techniques which share three
assumptions: (a) the patient's current symptoms are caused by past traumatic
experiences, (b) memories of these events have been lost to conscious recollection, and (c) restoration of conscious recollection (or at least acknowledgment
that the trauma occurred) is essential to the successful treatment of the patient's
symptoms. Psychoanalysis is a prime example of recovered memory therapy:
for contemporary examples of the technique in action, see the cases of Miss
F. T. (reanalyzed by Prozan, 1992) and Penelope (analyzed by Prozan, 1993).
The counseling and therapeutic techniques advocated by Bass and Davis (1988,
1992) and by Frederickson (1992) are other examples.

It should be understood that recovered memory therapy rarely advertises itself
as such, although perusal of the telephone book in almost any large American
city will reveal large numbers of therapists offering hypnosis, journaling, guided
imagery, and other techniques, including past-life regression, intended to recover forgotten memories of trauma, abuse, and neglect—which, in turn, are
assumed to lie at the bottom of the client's problems. Some therapists simply
assume that their patients' memories, however they are recovered, are true,
without any attempt to seek collaboration. Other therapists set aside the issue
of factual accuracy, adopting the solipsistic stance that the memories are *true
for him or her*. Still others refrain from doubt or criticism in an attempt to create
a supportive and accepting therapeutic environment. In any case, recovered
memory therapists risk losing the ability to distinguish among what is true (or
even plausible) in their patients' memories, what is unknowable, and what is
fantasy.

In the final analysis, recovered memory therapy is best considered as a class
of therapies which accept the general terms of the trauma-memory argument and
therefore focus on the patient's memories of the past—however they are recovered. At one end is psychoanalysis, which in its classic form makes all three of
the preceding assumptions. Other therapies may make only some of them. Some
psychotherapies do not make any of these assumptions, and they do not qualify
as recovered memory therapies. For example, outside the continuum entirely
are insight therapies and exposure therapies that do not make reference to mem-

---

[1] The phrase *exhumed memory* was coined by Paul Buttenweiser (1993). In my view, it perfectly
captures the process by which ostensibly forgotten events are ostensibly discovered in the course
of therapy or self-help; I also prefer it because it is neutral with respect to the mechanism (e.g.,
repression or dissociation) ostensibly responsible for the ostensible forgetting. The metaphor is particularly apt: in paleontology, sometimes you get an *Australopithecus* skull, sometimes Piltdown
man.

ories of abuse, or use such memories in any formal way, and which do not make *a priori* theoretical assumptions about the historical causes of present symptoms. Recovered memory therapy is not the name of a particular therapeutic technique; it is a label for a class of therapies. Like all categories, its boundaries are somewhat fuzzy, but there are some clear exemplars, and maybe even a definite prototype, of recovered memory therapy.

## THOSE WHO CANNOT REMEMBER THE PAST ARE CONDEMNED TO REPEAT IT

If all of this seems familiar, it is because it *is* familiar. It is the same argument that Freud made about hysteria, abreaction, and catharsis 100 years ago as he began to promote psychoanalysis as a technique of psychotherapy (e.g., Breuer & Freud, 1893–1895/1955). It is an interesting argument, but there is one problem with it. Although we can agree that the exploitation and mistreatment of children, including incest and other forms of sexual abuse, is a major social problem, the scientific evidence supporting the rest of the trauma-memory argument was scant 100 years ago (Schimek, 1987; see also Esterson, 1993; Macmillan, 1991), and the situation has not really changed 100 years later (Baker, 1992; Kihlstrom, 1994b, 1995b; Lindsay & Read, 1994, 1995; Loftus, 1993; Loftus & Ketcham, 1994; Pendergrast, 1995; Ofshe & Waters, 1994; Yapko, 1994).

For the most part, evidence for the trauma-memory argument comes in the form of clinical case reports, similar to Freud's, in which a person, typically an adult receiving counseling or psychotherapy, recovers long-forgotten memories of abuse, trauma, deprivation, and neglect. Such anecdotes are often vivid and sometimes compelling, but we are all too familiar with the limitations of cases as evidence. Observations are likely to be nonsystematic and even biased. Data can be condensed or elaborated during the collection process. Interpretation can be confused with reporting. Hypotheses cannot be tested, and causal inferences cannot be made. Most important, we have no idea how representative a particular case, or series of cases, is—or how much we can generalize from them to the population at large. These problems are compounded when, as in a recent paper by Harvey and Herman (1994), the report presents *composite* cases: composites may be useful literary devices, and they help disguise the identities of individual patients, but they should not be confused with scientific evidence.

There is, of course, a considerable body of clinical research implicating childhood trauma, including incest and sexual abuse, in adult psychopathology. For example, Herman, Perry, and van der Kolk (1989) found a high incidence of incest and sexual abuse in a group of women with borderline personality disorder. There are many similar studies, especially in the domain of eating disorders and dissociative disorders (for a review, see Spiegel & Cardeña, 1993). Unfortunately, all of these studies are based on retrospective self-reports, raising the possibility that the patients' memories may be biased by their current clinical state (not to mention the biases of the interviewer); moreover, the claims of incest and sexual abuse are rarely corroborated by independent evidence. What we need are prospective studies of the adult outcomes of victims of confirmed child abuse. Even if such studies yield positive results, however, we need to separate the effects of the abuse as such from the confounding effects of the patient's social identification, including self-identification, as a victim of abuse. The context in which abuse occurs may be as important as the fact of abuse itself, or more so. More to the point, validation of the trauma-memory argument and recovered memory therapy requires separate evaluations of the effects of abuse which is remembered and of abuse for which the victim is amnesic.

With respect to the question of amnesia for childhood trauma, the evidence is even more scanty, and even more ambiguous, if only because some of the mechanisms that could be responsible for forgetting are in no way pathological. Four studies apparently exhaust the modern literature on this subject: each of them suffers from methodological problems relating to the manner in which trauma and amnesia are documented.

## The Herman and Schatzow (1987) Study

Perhaps the most commonly cited contemporary study of trauma and memory, by Herman and Schatzow (1987), was based on 53 participants in a therapy group for incest survivors. Of these, 14 patients had severe amnesia for their abuse: they strongly suspected that they had been abused, but could not remember it clearly. As part of the therapeutic process, the patients were offered the opportunity to gather evidence that would corroborate their memories, or suspicions, of abuse. Herman and Schatzow reported that such efforts were successful for 39 of the cases, or 74%. In interpreting this finding, however, it is important to recall that 39 of the group members had little or no amnesia to begin with. It would not be surprising if individuals who always remembered their abuse were able to validate their memories of it. The important questions are (a) whether any of the 14 patients who were amnesic for their abuse when they entered therapy subsequently recovered memories of abuse, in or out of therapy; and (b) whether any of these patients were able to verify those memories of abuse.

On these critical questions, the Herman and Schatzow (1987) study is silent. Although Herman and Schatzow (1987) provide information about the source of collaboration, they fail to report the relationship between the extent of memory and the quality of the corroboration obtained. All we know is that 14 patients had severe amnesia for their abuse, and that 14 patients were unable to obtain direct corroboration of their beliefs or suspicions that they had been abused. Nevertheless, Herman and Harvey (1993) cited this study as "directly addressing whether these adult memories [e.g., of abuse] can be verified," and as suggesting "that delayed recall of sexual abuse is as verifiable as any other form of disclosure" (p. 5).

Even if some of the initially amnesic patients did succeed in obtaining putative evidence of abuse, it is important to indicate what the nature of that corroboration was. Of the four cases offered in evidence by Herman and Schatzow (1987), Andrea (Case Example 1) had no memory problem; she confronted her father, who essentially confirmed her memories. Bernadette (Case Example 2) had some memories of abuse at the beginning of therapy and recovered additional memories during treatment; her memories were confirmed by her mother. Claudia (Case Example 3) recovered memories of abuse by her brother and found physical evidence of his behavior among his belongings after he died. Doris (Case Example 4) had a dense childhood amnesia at the beginning of treatment and experienced a flood of recovered memories during therapy; however, her corroborating evidence, which consisted of a question about her father posed by her sister, was indirect and highly inferential. On the other hand, it turns out that these cases, like those cited by Harvey and Herman (1994), are composites—that is to say, worthless as scientific evidence.

Setting the matter of corroboration aside, Herman and Schatzow (1987) further reported that their amnesic patients reported an average age of onset for the abuse of 4 to 5 years of age, whereas the nonamnesic patients reported onsets at about 8 to 11 years of age. They concluded that "massive repression appeared to be the main defensive resource available to patients who were abused early in childhood" (p. 9). But of course there are other possibilities. For example, the authors failed to consider the impact of infantile and childhood amnesia arising from physiological, cognitive, and environmental changes occurring normally over the course of early development.[2] Moreover, there is another alternative: lacking actual memories for abuse, but believing that they were incest survivors and knowing something of the concept of repressed memory, these patients may have *assumed* that their abuse occurred during that period early in childhood when their memories were poorest. Thus, the dating of their abuse may be based on attributional processes, and not on fact retrieval.

*The Briere and Conte (1993) Study*

Similar problems attend the work of Briere and Conte (1993), another commonly cited study claiming to provide evidence of repression for childhood sexual abuse. This research involved 468 patients with self-reported histories of sexual abuse. These individuals, who were mostly women, were recruited by their therapists and asked to complete a survey, on which appeared the following question: "During the period of time between when the first forced sexual experience happened and your eighteenth birthday was there ever a time when you could not remember the forced sexual experience?" Almost 60% of these patients reported that they had not remembered their abuse at some point in time after it had occurred.[3] Unfortunately, Briere and Conte (1993) provide no corroboration for the episodes remembered by the clients, nor do they offer any analysis of the nature of the forgetting reported.

By far the strongest predictor of amnesia (out of 40 variables entered into a

---

[2] Infantile amnesia covers the first 18 to 24 months of life and is commonly attributed to the lack of language ability; childhood amnesia covers the subsequent period up to about 5 to 7 years of age and is commonly attributed to poor encoding. For reviews of memory in infants and children, see Fivush and Hudson (1990).

[3] Because of a typographical error, this figure is mistakenly cited as 69% in Kihlstrom (1995c, p. 65).

discriminant function analysis) was the age of the patient at the time the abuse began: patients who had been amnesic for their abuse claimed they had been molested earlier than those who had not experienced amnesia. Again, it is important to note that the molestations were self-reported and not independently corroborated. Furthermore, no distinction was made between repression and ordinary forgetting due to infantile and childhood amnesia and other benign factors. For Briere and Conte (1993), as for Herman and Schatzow (1987), many of the ostensibly amnesic patients may have inferred that they were molested as children, perhaps on the basis of their current problems, and then attributed their molestation to a period in their lives covered by normal infantile and childhood amnesia.

Interestingly, Briere and Conte (1993) found that patients reporting a period of amnesia for the abuse obtained higher scores on the SCL-90, an instrument commonly used to assess the severity of psychiatric symptoms. This is the only evidence that connects memory failure to the severity of the individual's symptoms. However, because the reports of abuse were uncorroborated and the nature of the forgetting unknown, the meaning of this evidence is unclear.

### The Loftus, Polonsky, and Fullilove (1994) Study

A survey reported by Loftus, Polonsky, and Fullilove (1994) presents similar problems. In this study, 105 women in a substance abuse treatment program completed a face-to-face interview about life stressors. A total of 57 (54%) of the clients reported that they had experienced some form of sexual abuse during childhood. When they were asked about their memory for the abuse, 36 (63%) of these clients reported that they had always remembered the abuse, 6 (10.5%) said that they remembered parts of the abuse but forgot other parts, and 10 (17.5%) said that they had forgotten the abuse entirely for a time and the memory returned later; the remaining 5 clients did not respond to this question. Interestingly, clients who reported onetime partial or total forgetting rated their current memories as less clear and detailed than those who reported that they always remembered; and clients who reported total forgetting rated their affect at the time of the abuse as less intense than those in the other two groups. In terms of the characteristics of the abuse itself, however, those who forgot their abuse apparently did not differ significantly from those remembered it.

Loftus et al. (1994) correctly point out that not every instance of forgetting, not even every instance of forgetting trauma such as abuse, counts as evidence of repression. There are many reasons why a person might forget unpleasant experiences and then remember them later. In any event, as with the previous two studies, no corroboration was available for the abuse reported by the clients surveyed; and no information is available that would permit independent evaluation of the reports that memories of abuse were lost and subsequently recovered. Loftus et al. (1994) attempted to compare the incidence of amnesia in their study with that found by Herman and Schatzow (1987) and Briere and Conte (1993), but differences in sampling methods across the two studies, not to mention the failure of each of the three studies to corroborate the abuse, makes any such comparison difficult.

*The Williams (1994) Study*

With respect to the issue of corroboration, something of an advance was attempted by Williams (1994a), who followed up a group of 129 women who had been treated for sexual abuse as children some 17 years earlier.[4] Under the cover of a routine interview ostensibly concerning the medical care they had received as children, these subjects were asked questions about childhood sexual victimization. A total of 38% of the informants failed to report the incident of abuse which had brought them to the hospital as children, although most (68%) of these did acknowledge other experiences of abuse. A small minority of the sample, 12%, failed to report that they had ever been abused in childhood.

Although Williams (1994a) framed her findings in terms of repression, there is no reason to conclude that her informants' reporting failures were due to repression or dissociation, as opposed to benign processes. For example, the highest rates of reporting failure occurred in women who had been abused before 7 years of age: perhaps these events were covered by normal infantile or childhood amnesia. Alternatively, the index admission to the hospital—the only evidence against which the clients' reports were evaluated—may simply have been lost through normal forgetting. Nor, frankly, is there any compelling reason to conclude that the subjects' behavior reflected memory failure at all. There are any number of reasons why individuals who remembered their childhood abuse perfectly well might decline to disclose it to an unfamiliar interviewer (Della Femina, Yeager, & Lewis, 1990).

The Williams (1994a) study is an important advance because it allows for the independent confirmation of self-reports of childhood trauma; but like its predecessors, it does not provide enough evidence to permit the conclusion that amnesia for victimization experiences is common, nor does it provide any evidence that these experiences, or amnesia for them, are associated with pathological adult outcomes. Better methodology is required to distinguish between patients who do not recall actual abuse and those who do not report it; and among the former, between memory failures that reflect repression, dissociation, and other pathological processes and those mechanisms of forgetting that are benign.

## AMNESIA AND FORGETTING, MEMORY AND BELIEF

Issues pertaining to corroboration and the distinction between remembering abuse and believing that one was abused should not be dismissed lightly. Whenever a claim is made about what a person remembers and what he or she has forgotten, this claim can only be evaluated against some objective record of what happened in the past. There are huge epistemological differences among the possibilities: explicitly remembering that one was abused, believing that one was abused even though one does not remember it, reconstructing memories around such a belief, and reinterpreting as abuse an event that was not perceived as

---

[4]For other critiques of this study, see Lindsay and Read (1994), Pope and Hudson (1995), and Loftus, Garry, and Feldman (1994); for responses to the critique, see Berliner and Williams (1994) and Williams (1994b).

abuse when it occurred. These distinctions are not commonly made by advocates of the trauma-memory argument and recovered memory therapy, and they are only some of the possibilities.

Equally important, and equally uncommon, are other distinctions that apply to cases in which an individual fails to remember a documented episode of abuse. As in many of the cases discussed by Della Femina et al. (1990), the failure may be one of disclosure rather than of memory. But setting this possibility aside, even genuine failures of memory are not all of the same kind. Some experiences may have been lost to the normal forgetting that occurs with the passage of time. Others may have been covered by infantile and childhood amnesia. In neither case is there any reason to think that the forgotten episode has any untoward effect on adult behavior and adjustment; and in neither case is there any reason to think that therapeutic exhumation of such memories is possible, or, even if it were possible, to think that dredging them up would have any positive effect on therapeutic outcome.

Another possibility that is commonly ignored is that individual episodes of abuse have been assimilated to a generic (or semantic) memory of abuse, with the details of individual episodes forgotten. In this respect, Terr (1991) has distinguished between two types of trauma. Type I trauma consists of "unanticipated single events" (p. 14), and Type II trauma consists of "long-standing or repeated exposure to extreme external events" (p. 15). Terr (1991) notes that Type I traumas are typically remembered well, whereas Type II traumas are typically remembered poorly. Terr further attributes the memory failures in Type II trauma to such coping mechanisms as denial (in the psychodynamic sense), psychic numbing, repression, and dissociation (1991, p. 15). However, the memory failure observed in Type II trauma may be no different from the ordinary forgetting observed in normal adults, who may know that they attended third grade, for example, but have difficulty remembering particular events that occurred during the school year. There is no reason to think that such forgetting is reversible, or that reversal, even if it were possible, is therapeutically advantageous. Nor, in the case of generic memories of documented abuse, is there any reason to think that the person's inability to recall individual episodes has anything to do with any adjustment difficulties he or she may be experiencing.

Of course, some cases of forgetting may represent genuine functional amnesias produced by repression, dissociation, or some other pathological process (for reviews, see Schacter & Kihlstrom, 1989; Kihlstrom & Schacter, 1995). These should also not be dismissed out of hand. Although more than a half-century of research has failed to produce compelling laboratory evidence of repression (for reviews, see Pope & Hudson, 1995; Singer, 1990), experimentally produced dissociative amnesias, in the form of posthypnotic amnesia (Kihlstrom, 1985) and state-dependent memory (Overton, 1984)—including mood-dependent memory (Eich, 1995)—strongly indicate that it is indeed possible to disrupt, and then restore, conscious access to available memories. However, it should be understood that the laboratory research is as convincing as it is because there is independent evidence of the events which are to be remembered. Without such independent corroboration, clinical evidence for dissociative amnesia must remain ambiguous.

## COMMENTS ON THE REPORT OF THE BRITISH PSYCHOLOGICAL SOCIETY WORKING PARTY ON RECOVERED MEMORIES

Over the past few years, a number of professional associations have taken critical positions on the trauma-memory argument and recovered memory therapy (American Medical Association, 1994; American Psychiatric Association, 1993; Australian Psychological Society, 1994).[5] In their statements, each of these organizations noted that recovered memory therapy rests on a weak scientific base, warned of the problem of uncorroborated and false memories, and urged caution in dealing with patients' memories and beliefs about childhood sexual abuse. By contrast, the British Psychological Society (BPS; 1995) issued a report that seemed to take a more lenient attitude toward these problems. Among other conclusions, the report agreed that memories of psychological trauma could be lost and then recovered, even after a long period of forgetting; that instances of memory recovery were reported by therapists who were aware of the problems of suggestion; that clear, detailed recovered memories were likely to be broadly accurate; and that there was no evidence of widespread creation of false memories of childhood sexual abuse in the United Kingdom (nevertheless, the report ended with a number of guidelines for therapists intended to reduce if not eliminate the false memory problem).

Although the BPS Working Party attempted to grapple with the issues of trauma and memory in an evenhanded way, and reached many conclusions with which one can agree, their report has also drawn some criticism (Lindsay, 1995; Weiskrantz, 1995a, 1995b).[6] For example, the Working Party erred when it wrote (1995, p. 3) that the ground of the debate over recovered memories has shifted from the possibility of therapy-induced false beliefs to the question of the prevalence of such beliefs. For most scientific critics of the trauma-memory argument and recovered memory therapy, the issue has never been either the existence or the prevalence of false memories. Because the memories in question are typically not subject to objective verification, we will never know how many such memories are accurate and how many are inaccurate or false outright. The primary question of interest concerns the scientific validity of the trauma-memory argument and the scientific status of recovered memory therapy. Both the argument and the therapy, although intuitively appealing and well-intentioned (especially by those who have read their Freud and taken him to heart), rest on very shaky scientific ground. There is virtually no evidence supporting the claims on which recovered memory therapy is based and considerable evidence going against these claims.

---

[5]At the time this chapter was written, a report by the American Psychological Association Working Group on Investigation of Memories of Childhood Abuse had not yet been released. However, an interim report (American Psychological Association, 1994) concluded that although most victims of childhood sexual abuse remember all or part of what happened to them, it is possible for memories of such events to be forgotten and then later recovered; furthermore, the working group concluded that pseudomemories of abuse were possible, but that the processes underlying accurate and inaccurate recollections of childhood abuse were largely unknown.

[6]The remainder of this section is an elaboration, with permission of the editor, of material that first appeared in *The Therapist,* the journal of the European Therapy Studies Institute (Kihlstrom, 1995a).

Relatedly, the Working Party created something of a straw person with its depiction of extreme critics (unnamed) who maintain that recovered memories are impossible in principle and that all therapists lead patients into recovering memories of abuse (1995, p. 6). In fact, most critics of recovered memory therapy, including myself, are quite willing to concede the possibility of recovered memories; we just do not find the available evidence for the phenomenon remotely convincing. And although there clearly exists a subset of therapists who are predisposed to elicit recovered memories from their patients, nobody has claimed that all, or even most, therapists fall in this category.

Similarly, the Working Party erred in criticizing (1995, p. 6) those who, in turn, criticize the illogical and inflammatory statements contained in such popular self-help books as *The Courage to Heal* (Bass & Davis, 1988). This book, and others like it, has been enormously influential on both popular culture and therapeutic practice, and its empirical, logical, and rhetorical defects deserve wide advertisement so that therapists and practitioners will not continue to be misled by its errors and exaggerations (Kihlstrom, 1994b).

The conclusion of the Working Party that, with certain exceptions, the source of our memories is accurately attributed (1995, p. 10) was misleading for the simple reason that the exceptions noted by the Working Party include the typical therapeutic situation in which recovered memory occurs. Whether by self-help books such as *The Courage to Heal* or by therapists who base their practices on theories of "memory work," patients are encouraged to think about, and focus on, possible instances of past abuse, and to imagine situations in which such abuse might have occurred. These exercises effectively constitute rehearsal opportunities of just the sort that the Working Party (correctly) concludes lead to errors in source attribution. To be concrete, the available research (reviewed by Johnson, Hashtroudi, & Lindsay, 1993) suggests that the possibility of source misattributions is increased whenever the following typical characteristics of recovered memory therapy are present:

- the patient is seeking an explanation for his or her current troubles and the therapist is inclined to find it in the patient's childhood;
- the patient's past is unknown or uncertain;
- the therapist believes, and implies, that the patient's presenting complaints are the symptoms of abuse;
- the concept of repression or dissociation is offered as a convenient explanation for why the patient has no memory of abuse;
- trauma and abuse are broadly defined, so that ambiguous memories may be interpreted as evidence of trauma and abuse;
- imagination and other techniques of memory work (Frederickson, 1992) are used as routes to remembering;
- inference, supposition, and belief substitute for actual recollection;
- narrative truth is preferred to historical truth, or at least is considered satisfactory for therapeutic purposes (Spence, 1982, 1994);
- the therapist believes that his or her obligation is to support the beliefs of the patient, regardless of whether they are accurate.

The Working Party repeated the claim that repeated or extended abuse is more likely to be subject to amnesia (1995, p. 13) without critically analyzing the empirical basis for this claim. In fact, as discussed earlier, this claim rests on unsystematic clinical observations, anecdotally reported (e.g., Terr, 1994). The Working Party did properly suggest that individual episodes of such abuse might be assimilated into a generic memory in which the details of particular episodes are forgotten (1995, p. 9), but it should have emphasized that this form of forgetting has nothing to do with trauma per se, is not indicative of repression, dissociation, or any other pathological process, has no causal relation to the later development of clinical symptoms, and is unlikely to be reversed by any form of memory-enhancement technique, whether biological or psychological. Therefore, the fact that individual episodes of repeated or extended abuse are forgotten—if indeed this is the case—may have absolutely no therapeutic significance.

The Working Party noted that forgetting of trauma is often reported, but it failed to emphasize that this forgetting is rarely verified (1995, p. 13). That is to say, it is rarely clear whether the patient has forgotten the episode, merely failed to disclose it, or even that the episode in question occurred at all. And, as noted earlier, even in the case of verified amnesia it is not clear whether the forgetting is a product of normal or pathological processes. More important, it is often unclear whether the event in question actually occurred.

The Working Party believes that there is little danger that a few suggestive questions from therapists will lead patients to construct false memories of the past (1995, p. 15). It is somewhat ironic that the Working Party quotes Lindsay and Read (1994) in support of this conclusion, because Lindsay himself emerged as a critic of the Working Party's report (Lindsay, 1995).

Actually, the Working Party quoted Lindsay and Read (1994) out of context, and consequently distorted their meaning. Here is the passage as quoted by the BPS (1995, p. 15):

> There is little reason to fear that a few suggestive questions will lead psychotherapy clients to conjure up vivid and compelling illusory memories of childhood sexual abuse.

And here is the full passage from Lindsay & Read (1994, p. 294):

> There is little reason to fear that a few suggestive questions will lead psychotherapy clients to conjure up vivid and compelling illusory memories of childhood sexual abuse. However, as described above, the techniques some authorities advocate for recovering repressed memories of childhood sexual abuse are vastly more powerful than the laboratory procedures, and there is good reason to be concerned about the possibility that they sometimes lead to the creation of illusory memories.

It is apparent that Lindsay and Read (1994) were quite concerned about the very possibility that the Working Party dismissed.

If all we had to worry about were "a few suggestive questions," there might, indeed, be little cause for concern. But this is not the actual situation presented. Many therapists, including doctoral-level clinical psychologists, apparently believe, in the absence of convincing scientific evidence, that a history of abuse, especially abuse covered by amnesia, is causally associated with a wide variety of clinical symptoms. In many cases, these beliefs are explicitly communicated to patients early in therapy and are readily incorporated into the patient's system of beliefs and expectations as he or she works through his or her problems.

Moreover, of course, therapeutic encounters do not occur in a vacuum. Rather, therapy transpires in a cultural context that is increasingly permeated by unwarranted beliefs about the prevalence of abuse, traumatic amnesia, the clinical consequences of both abuse and amnesia, and the efficacy of recovered memory therapy. Within this sociocultural milieu, even a few probing questions and suggestive remarks by an authoritative figure such as a therapist may be sufficient to inculcate a belief on the part of a patient that he or she was abused, and start the patient on the road toward the "recovery" of false memories. Even a totally neutral therapist cannot prevent these cultural influences. For this reason, it is no comfort to discover, as the Working Party did, that a large portion of recovered memories first appear outside a formal therapeutic context.

The danger of false recollection is underscored by the Working Party's discovery that 9 out of 10 therapists surveyed believe that recovered memories are sometimes or usually essentially accurate (Andrews et al., 1995; for a critique, see Weiskrantz, 1995b).[7] Precisely because most recovered memories are not subject to independent corroboration, such beliefs on the part of therapists are completely unwarranted. Thus, we are returned to the essential issue in recovered memory therapy: the trauma-memory argument and recovered memory therapy are not supported by the available scientific evidence.

## INTUITIVE APPEAL AND SCIENTIFIC EVIDENCE

The trauma-memory argument derives its power from the social problem of child abuse and from the vivid case histories presented by its proponents. In some respects, it also gains some plausibility from scientific research on memory (Kihlstrom, 1995b). For example, studies of cued recall, recognition, and hypermnesia show that it is possible for people to remember at one point events that had been forgotten earlier (Kihlstrom & Barnhardt, 1993). Similarly, research on hypnosis shows that people can block conscious access to particular memories and regain access sometime later; and that in the meantime, the unconscious memories can have implicit effects on the person's experience, thought, and action (Kihlstrom, 1985).

In the final analysis, however, the available base of scientific evidence, especially direct evidence from clinical studies of the victims of trauma, is simply too weak to support global assertions about trauma and memory, amnesia and recovery, and related issues. As much as we sympathize with those who exhume memories of trauma, and the therapists and counselors who seek to help them, there is nothing in the available evidence that would permit us to have any confidence in any exhumed memory in the absence of independent confirmation, or

---

[7] Out of a sample of 202 certified psychotherapists from the United States and the United Kingdom responding to a recent survey, 25% engaged in psychotherapy focusing on memories of child sexual abuse, and 71% reported using hypnosis, dream work, body work, and other techniques to help their patients remember such episodes (Poole, Lindsay, Memon, & Bull, 1995).

to have any confidence that there are causal links between trauma, amnesia and psychopathology.[8] To demur in this way is not to "cast a chill on serious scientific dialogue" (Harvey & Herman, 1994, p. 296), or participate in a backlash against adult survivors of child sexual abuse (Bass & Davis, 1994, p. 475; Harvey & Herman, 1993) or against the gains rightly achieved by the women's movement, or to choose denial over accuracy (Walker, 1994, p. 85). On the contrary, it is to hold clinical theory and practice up to established standards of scientific knowledge.

## ACKNOWLEDGMENTS

This chapter is an expanded version of an invited commentary that initially appeared in a special issue of *Consciousness and Cognition* devoted to "The Recovery of Lost Childhood Memories for Traumatic Events" (Kihlstrom, 1995c). The point of view represented in this chapter is based on research supported by Grant MH-35856 from the National Institute of Mental Health. For more extensive coverage of these issues, see Kihlstrom (1994a, 1994b, 1995b). I thank Lawrence Couture, Jennifer Dorfman, Elizabeth Glisky, Martha Glisky, Victor Shames, Michael Valdiserri, and Susan Valdiserri for their comments during the preparation of this chapter.

## REFERENCES

American Medical Association. (1994). *Memories of childhood abuse* (Council of Scientific Affairs Report No. 5-A-94). Washington, DC: Author.

American Psychiatric Association. (1993). *Statement on memories of sexual abuse*. Washington, DC: Author.

American Psychological Association. (1994). *Interim report of the Working Group on Investigation of Memories of Childhood Abuse*. Washington, DC: Author.

Andrews, B., Morton, J., Bekerian, D. A., Brewin, C. R., Davies, G. M., & Mollon, P. (1995). The recovery of memories in clinical practice: Experiences and beliefs of British Psychological Society practitioners. *The Psychologist, 8*, 209–214.

Australian Psychological Society. (1994). *Guidelines relating to the reporting of recovered memories*. Sydney: Author.

Baker, R. A. (1992). *Hidden memories: Voices and visions from within*. Buffalo, NY: Prometheus Press.

Bass, E., & Davis, L. (1994). *The courage to heal: A guide for women survivors of child sexual abuse* (3rd ed.). New York: Harper & Row. (Originally published 1988; rev. ed., 1992)

Berliner, L., & Williams, L. M. (1994). Memories of child sexual abuse: A response to Lindsay and Read. *Applied Cognitive Psychology, 8*, 379–388.

Breuer, J., & Freud, S. (1955). *Studies on hysteria*. In J. Strachey (Ed.), *The standard edition of the complete psychological works of Sigmund Freud* (Vol. 2). London: Hogarth Press. (Originally published 1893–1895).

Briere, J., & Conte, J. (1993). Self-reported amnesia for abuse in adults molested as children. *Journal of Traumatic Stress, 6*, 21–31.

British Psychological Society. (1995). *Recovered memories: The report of the Working Party of the British Psychological Society*. Leicester, UK: Author.

Buttenweiser, P. (1993, August 1.) The exhumed memory [Book review of *Once upon a time: A*

---

[8]The exception to this conclusion is post-traumatic stress disorder, which is related to previous trauma by definition. I thank David Gleaves for pointing this out. Nevertheless, and somewhat paradoxically, it is important to recognize that the difficulties in operationalizing *trauma*—that is, whether it can, or even should, be objectively defined—call even this truism into question.

*true story of memory, murder, and the law* by H. N. MacLean] (pp. 9–10). *New York Times Book Review.*

Della Femina, D., Yeager, C. A., & Lewis, D. O. (1990). Child abuse: Adolescent records vs. adult recall. *Child Abuse and Neglect,* **14,** 227–231.

Eich, E. (1995). Searching for mood-dependent memory. *Psychological Science,* **6,** 67–75.

Esterson, A. (1993). *Seductive mirage: An exploration of the work of Sigmund Freud.* New York: Open Court.

Fivush, R., & Hudson, J. A. (Eds.). (1990). *Knowing and remembering in young children.* New York: Cambridge University Press.

Frederickson, R. (1992). *Repressed memories: A journey to recovery from sexual abuse.* New York: Simon & Schuster.

Harvey, M. R., & Herman, J. L. (1994). Amnesia, partial amnesia, and delayed recall among adult survivors of childhood trauma. *Consciousness and Cognition,* **3,** 295–306.

Herman, J. L. (1992). *Trauma and recovery.* New York: Basic Books.

Herman, J. L., & Harvey, M. R. (1993, April). The false memory debate: Social science or social backlash? *Harvard Mental Health Letter,* pp. 4–6.

Herman, J. L., Perry, J. C., & van der Kolk, B. A. (1989). Childhood trauma in borderline personality disorder. *American Journal of Psychiatry,* **146,** 140–145.

Herman, J. L., & Schatzow, E. (1987). Recovery and verification of memories of childhood sexual trauma. *Psychoanalytic Psychology* **4,** 1–14.

Johnson, M. K., Hashtroudi, S., & Lindsay, D. S. (1993). Source monitoring. *Psychological Bulletin,* **114,** 3–28.

Kihlstrom, J. F. (1985). Posthypnotic amnesia and the dissociation of memory. In G. H. Bower (Ed.), *The psychology of learning and motivation* (Vol. 19, pp. 131–178). New York: Academic Press.

Kihlstrom, J. F. (1994a). Delayed recall and the principles of memory. *International Journal of Clinical and Experimental Hypnosis,* **4,** 357–345.

Kihlstrom, J. F. (1994b). Exhumed memory. In S. J. Lynn & N. P. Spanos (Eds.), *Truth in memory* (in press). New York: Guilford.

Kihlstrom, J. F. (1995a). Recovered memories: British Psychological Society "misleading" [Letter to the editor]. *The Therapist,* **2**(4), 45–46.

Kihlstrom, J. F. (1995b). Suffering from reminiscences: Exhumed memory, implicit memory, and the return of the repressed. In M. A. Conway (Ed.), *Recovered memories and false memories* (in press). Oxford: Oxford University Press.

Kihlstrom, J. F. (1995c). The trauma-memory argument. *Consciousness and Cognition,* **4,** 63–67.

Kihlstrom, J. F., & Barnhardt, T. M. (1993). The self-regulation of memory, for better and for worse, with and without hypnosis. In D. M. Wegner & J. W. Pennebaker (Eds.), *Handbook of mental control* (pp. 88–125). Englewood Cliffs, NJ: Prentice Hall.

Kihlstrom, J. F., & Schacter, D. L. (1995). Functional disorders of autobiographical memory. In A. Baddeley, B. A. Wilson, & F. Watts (Eds.), *Handbook of memory disorders* (pp. 337–364). London: Wiley.

Lindsay, D. S. (1995). "Unsubstantiated claims" from the British Psychological Society [Letter to the editor]. *The Therapist,* **2**(4), 45.

Lindsay, D. S., & Read, J. D. (1994). Psychotherapy and memories of childhood sexual abuse: A cognitive perspective. *Applied Cognitive Psychology,* **8,** 281–338.

Lindsay, D. S., & Read, J. D. (1995). "Memory work" and recovered memories of childhood sexual abuse: Scientific evidence and public, professional, and personal issues. *Psychology, Public Policy, and the Law,* **1,** 846–908.

Loftus, E. (1993). The reality of repressed memories. *American Psychologist,* **48,** 518–537.

Loftus, E. F., Garry, M., & Feldman, J. (1994). Forgetting sexual trauma: What does it mean when 38% forget? *Journal of Consulting and Clinical Psychology,* **62,** 1177–1181.

Loftus, E., & Ketcham, K. (1994). *The myth of repressed memory: False memories and allegations of sexual abuse.* New York: St. Martin's Press.

Loftus, E. F., Polonsky, S., & Fullilove, M. T. (1994). Memories of childhood sexual abuse: Remembering and repressing. *Psychology of Women Quarterly,* **18,** 67–84.

Macmillan, M. (1991). *Freud evaluated: The completed arc* (Advances in Psychology, No. 75). Amsterdam: North-Holland.

Ofshe, R., & Watters, E. (1994). *Making monsters: False memories, psychotherapy, and sexual hysteria.* New York: Scribner's.

Overton, D. A. (1984). State-dependent learning and drug discriminations. In L. L. Iverson, S. D. Iverson, & S. H. Snyder (Eds.), *Handbook of psychopharmacology* (Vol. 18, pp. 59–127). New York: Plenum.

Pendergrast, M. (1995). *Victims of memory: Incest accusations and shattered lives.* Hinesberg, VT: Upper Access Press.

Poole, D. A., Lindsay, D. S., Memon, A., & Bull, R. (1995). Psychotherapy and the recovery of memoires of childhood sexual abuse: U.S. and British practitioners' beliefs, practices, and experiences. *Journal of Consulting and Clinical Psychology, 63,* 426–437.

Pope, H. G., & Hudson, J. I. (1995). Can individuals "repress" memories of childhood sexual abuse? An examination of the evidence. *Psychiatric Annals, 25,* 715–719.

Prozan, C. K. (1992). *Feminist psychoanalytic psychotherapy.* Northvale, NJ: Jason Aronson.

Prozan, C. K. (1993). *The technique of feminist psychoanalytic psychotherapy.* Northvale, NJ: Jason Aronson.

Schacter, D. L., & Kihlstrom, J. F. (1989). Functional amnesia. In F. Boller & J. Graffman (Eds.), *Handbook of neuropsychology* (Vol. 3, pp. 209–231). Amsterdam: Elsevier.

Schimek, J. G. (1987). Fact and fantasy in the seduction theory: A historical review. *Journal of the American Psychoanalytic Association, 35,* 937–965.

Singer, J. L. (Ed.). (1990). *Repression and dissociation: Implications for personality theory, psychopathology, and health.* Chicago: University of Chicago Press.

Spence, D. P. (1982). *Narrative truth and historical truth.* New York: Norton.

Spence, D. P. (1994). Narrative truth and putative child abuse. *International Journal of Clinical and Experimental Hypnosis, 42,* 289–303.

Spiegel, D., & Cardeña, E. (1993). Disintegrated experience: The dissociative disorders revisited. *Journal of Abnormal Psychology, 100,* 366–378.

Terr, L. (1991). Childhood traumas: An outline and overview. *American Journal of Psychiatry, 148,* 10–20.

Terr, L. (1994). *Unchained memories: True stories of traumatic memories, lost and found.* New York: Basic Books.

Walker, L. E. A. (1994). *Abused women and survivor therapy: A practical guide for the psychotherapist.* Washington, DC: American Psychological Association.

Weiskrantz, L. (1995a). Comments on the report of the working party of the British Psychological Society on "recovered memories." *The Therapist, 2*(4), 5–8.

Weiskrantz, L. (1995b). Commentary. *The Psychologist, 8,* 507–508.

Williams, L. M. (1994a). Recall of childhood trauma: A prospective study of women's memories of child sexual abuse. *Journal of Consulting and Clinical Psychology, 62,* 1167–1176.

Williams, L. M. (1994b). What does it mean to forget child abuse? A reply to Loftus, Garry, and Feldman (1994). *Journal of Consulting and Clinical Psychology, 62,* 1182–1186.

Yapko, M. D. (1994). *Suggestions of abuse: True and false memories of childhood sexual trauma.* New York: Simon & Schuster.

# Recovered Memories: Lost and Found?

MICHAEL P. TOGLIA

*State University of New York at Cortland*

The concept of repressed memory may be of limited usefulness in the current debate on the authenticity of recovered memories. The controversy concerning reclaimed memories can be chracterized generally as an escalating skirmish between researchers and practitioners, and it is now being argued in the courts as well. Although one might think that validating so-called "repressed memories" would be a common goal, the camps are virtually diametrically opposed on this issue. Researchers have embraced a scientific approach to determining whether a memory is genuine, whereas therapists typically have accepted repressed memories as real or believed that narrative truth is the most important reality. However, given the difficulty in distinguishing true memories from false memories, it is recommended that research on childhood memory be redirected, with the hope that refocusing experimentation so that it draws on both the cognitive literature on memory and forgetting and the clinical literature on trauma can be one avenue for curbing the acrimonious nature of the debate.

The controversy on the authenticity of repressed memories is now raging out of control, fueled by the recent increase of "recovered memories" of child sexual abuse during psychotherapy. In fact, as of 1994, in excess of 10,000 adults in the United States had made claims of recovered childhood memories of sexual victimization (Hochman, 1994). In Freud's (1920, 1933) development of psychoanalysis, a major component was his theory of repression. As there is no simple, agreed on definition of the term repression (Erdelyi, 1990), it conveys a multiplicity of meanings and thus broad clinical application. Aside from the fact that empirical support for a theory of repression is weak at best, the theory has currently become the basis for authenticating buried memories of child sexual abuse that are exhumed during therapeutic sessions. Indeed, these "memories" frequently become the focus of therapy even though a patient may have sought professional help for other complaints such as depression, personality problems, or eating disorders.

The irony of this is threefold: Freud never established that sexual trauma during childhood caused pathology in adulthood; he realized that not all recovered memories were true; and he speculated that psychoanalytic probing may have been the genesis of some memories. In fact, after initially arguing for the reality of repressed memories of childhood sexual abuse, he came to believe that many of these recollections were really patient's repressed fantasies of incest (Bonaparte, Freud, & Kris, 1954; cf. Gay, 1988). Although I do not concur with Freud's position on incestuous fantasies, my point is that Freudian theory has been distorted and misrepresented by many psychotherapists who accept without question the concept of repression of traumatic memories of early childhood

*The Recovered Memory/False Memory Debate*

experiences. Such blind faith not only runs contrary to clinical evidence (cf. Loftus, 1993) but is also challenged by a century of research, dating back to Ebbinghaus, devoted to understanding memorial processes and the mechanisms that trigger forgetting.

Erdelyi and Goldberg (1979) have argued that Freud's views on repression have been misunderstood to even a greater extent than I have indicated. They noted that memory theorists and clinicians alike have tended to ignore Freud's original conception of repression as conceivably an intentional, deliberate act and have focused almost exclusively on the notion that repression is a defense mechanism that unconsciously allows painful or dangerous memories to be banished out of awareness. Given the difficulties with the term repression just outlined, and its oft accompanying and questionable assumption that posits the existence of unconscious memories, I believe "repressed memories" is a misnomer. In line with arguments advanced by Ceci and Loftus (1994), I suggest that "recovered memories" is a more accurate term that is less likely to connote unconscious processes. In addition, the notion of recovery is more consistent with regaining access to true memories that may have been lost for a variety of reasons that typify normal forms of forgetting, such as decay, retroactive interference, and infantile amnesia.

## SUGGESTIBILITY AND MEMORY DISTORTIONS

The suggestibility of memory and its impact on forms of forgetting has become a central issue for those advocating an experimental approach to the repressed/recovered memory debate (cf. Lindsay & Read, 1994). To understand why, it is necessary to outline briefly the general conclusions of the research on memory and susceptibility to suggestion. During the last 20 years, a considerable body of data, compiled mainly with a paradigm in which misleading postevent information is presented, has revealed that adults are vulnerable to suggestive and leading questions (Belli, 1989; Loftus, Miller, & Burns, 1978; Ross, Read, & Toglia, 1994). Compared with control groups, adults presented with misinformation frequently show impaired memory for original events, a finding called the *misinformation effect*. Similarly, a more recent burst of experimental activity with children has demonstrated that they also are vulnerable to suggestion. Memory impairment is particularly evident for preschoolers, as they show a greater misinformation effect than older children and adults (Ceci, Ross, & Toglia, 1987; Toglia, Ross, Ceci, & Hembrooke, 1992).

The suggestibility of children is the result of a variety of cognitive and social factors, many of which have been described in other chapters in this volume (see also Ceci & Bruck, 1993b; Toglia et al., 1992). Research on children's memory in general (Brainerd & Ornstein, 1991) clearly indicates that young children use less sophisticated encoding strategies that result in weaker memory traces than older subjects. With the storage of weak, fragmentary memories, it is not surprising that preschoolers are especially suggestible and are prone to making source misattributions (cf. Ceci, Crotteau, Smith, & Loftus, this volume) and to depending on reconstructive processes. Deficits in memory can be compounded by social influences, such as the use of leading questions, the repeating of questions, and the prestige of the interviewer (Ceci et al., 1987). Although there is some data to the contrary (Toglia et al., 1992), young children tend to view adults as authority figures who would not deceive them. In this vein, child witnesses may depend on their parents and adult interviewers to aid them in reconstructing memories where gaps exist. This view is consistent with the social–interactive effects on children's encoding and retrieval of an event that were reported by Fivush (this volume) and Tessler and Nelson (this volume).

Sometimes the gaps in memory are more like craters. For instance, both Fivush, in the context of novel autobiographical episodes, and Goodman, Quas, Batterman-Faunce, Riddlesberger, and Kuhn (this volume), regarding a uretheral catheterization medical procedure, have reported that some children provide little or no relevant information about a target event when subsequently interviewed. Similarly, sometimes clients early in therapy say they do not remember anything about an event being probed by the therapist. Although "not knowing" should be taken seriously (Saywitz & Moan-Hardie, this volume), sometimes children are not believed or a therapist equates lack of knowledge with denial. The result is often an invitation to probe memory in ways that are conducive to suggestibility. In this regard, the conditions under which children are interviewed or adults are questioned during therapy are not unlike those found in suggestibility experiments.

The ease with which the misinformation effect can be obtained in the laboratory is highlighted by the fact that the retention intervals in such studies are not years but often only about 30 minutes or a few days, and typically not longer than 2 weeks. In countless studies involving an examination of memory performance over retention intervals, very often, although not always, there is a decline in retention of specific items or event details. Thus, forgetting, in terms of errors of omission (as well as in terms of intrusions or errors of commission), is a well-established phenomenon that occurs even when there is no attempt to tamper with memory. Given the basic laws of memory, one would expect "recovered memories" to be just as fragile as other memories, and perhaps more so given the passage of many years. But even if "lost" memories can be retrieved at some point in time, we are still left with the concern that some traces of childhood experiences are based upon faulty encoding. One might argue that fragility and poor encoding appear to fly in the face of the highly detailed and vivid nature of most recovered memories of abuse. In this vein, Howe, Courage, and Peterson (this volume) confirmed that real memories typically become less elaborate with the passage of time. The implication, of course, is that "repressed events" that are recounted more elaborately over time may very well be founded on fallacies.

However, because some memories of true events may be reported in an elaborated manner, accompanied by an aura of confidence, distinguishing true from false recollections will be a complicated task. This conclusion is supported by the work of Loftus and Pickrell (1995) and Ceci (1993) showing that false memories for stress-related events are often "recollected" with great clarity and detail. Thus, the vividness of a report and the expression of confidence cannot be relied on to identify true memories. Recent laboratory experiments addressing false memories for more benign episodes also dramatically demonstrate the confusability of true and false memories (Read, 1996; Roediger & McDermott, 1995). In fact, Roediger and McDermott remind us that evidence of false memories generated in the context of learning linguistic materials is not new and is actually quite common in the memory literature (e.g., Bransford & Franks, 1971; Sulin & Dooling, 1974; Underwood, 1965).

## FALSE MEMORY STUDIES AND THEIR RELEVANCE TO THE DEBATE

In an extension of this literature, Roediger and McDermott demonstrated how effortless it was to get subjects to recall verbal events that never occurred in a simple list learning paradigm credited to Deese (1959). They presented subjects with a series of short, 12-item lists of words such that for any given list all stimuli were associated with a critical nonpresented word. For instance, "chair" was a nonpresented item corresponding to a list that contained the words *table, legs,* and *seat,* and "sleep" was the critical nonpresented word associated with a list that included *bed, rest,* and *awake,* and so on. In two experiments, they found that critical nonstudied items such as "chair" appeared as intrusion errors in recall about 50% of the time, and such nonpresented words were even more likely to be falsely recognized, as false alarm rates exceeded 80% and were nearly as high as hit rates. Furthermore, the critical lures were recognized with high confidence that rivaled subjects' convictions regarding the words actually presented. In addition, in their second experiment, Roediger and McDermott employed the remember/know judgment procedure (Tulving, 1985) and found that subjects generally claimed to remember encoding the critical nonpresented items. They concluded that, in general, all remembering draws on constructive processes.

More recently, my colleagues and I (Toglia, Neuschatz, Goodwin, & Lyon 1995) used a subset of the lists employed by Roediger and McDermott to examine the bases for the reconstructive processes that produced the false memory effects observed. Because Roediger and McDermott read their subjects intentional memory instructions, we reasoned that their subjects probably engaged in some form of semantic processing. Accordingly, we manipulated the depth of processing with the expectation that nonsemantic processing would reduce the percentage of false memories. Subjects studied and recalled six lists, with immediate recall after each list, as in Roediger and McDermott's work. In the semantic condition, participants rated each item for its pleasantness, whereas nonsemantic processors were asked to determine whether or not each word contained the letter *a.* A level of processing effect was observed, as participants in the semantic condition correctly recalled 77.4% of the words versus only 66.2% by those who performed the shallow processing task. Our prediction concerning the critical items was supported by the data, as nonpresented items were falsely recalled at a rate of 58% in the semantic group, significantly surpassing the still rather high 44% intrusion rate in the nonsemantic group.

In a second study, we examined how list organization might contribute to the creation of false memories. To this end, we selected five of the lists used in our first study to produce one long list of 60 words. These items were either blocked by theme (e.g., all the "chair" words were presented consecutively, followed by each of the 12 words for the "sleep" theme, and so forth) or presented in a random order that tended to disguise the thematic nature of the list. After studying one of these types of lists under intentional memory instructions, subjects were administered a free recall test and then they rated each word in their protocols for the degree of confidence that a word had appeared on the study list. The pattern of results paralleled those found in the levels of processing experiment in that correct recall performance in the blocked condition was better, as expected, than that in the random presentation condition, but blocking produced more false memories (54%) than the random exposure format (35%). In addition, regardless of encoding condition, subjects were extremely confident of their recall of both studied and nonstudied critical items. On a 3-point scale, actual items were assigned an average confidence rating of 2.81, whereas the critical theme-consistent words received a mean rating of 2.49.

Thus, there are conditions that promote encoding of and access to thematic information, resulting in better memory for actually experienced material but at the expense of increased levels of false memories. Themes provide a basis for reconstruction and the potential for intrusion of false information. In the context of therapy, the introduction and discussion of abusive themes may lead a patient to report some false details even when some form of abuse trauma (e.g., verbal assaults, spankings) actually occurred. In cases in which a patient's presented symptoms prompt a therapist to suggest abuse when such trauma did not happen, molestation themes may not seem plausible at first, and patients who are eventually swayed frequently resist these suggestions early in treatment. However, if such themes are revisited session after session, consistent with research reviewed by Ceci (1993) and Ceci and Bruck (1993b), susceptibility to suggestion is likely to increase, with a concomitant rise in plausibility that translates into some clients coming to believe the false diagnosis that they were abused in childhood (but see Ceci et al., this volume, for an example of no increase in suggestibility). The pressure to believe may be intensified if the patient is told, or reads in self-help books, that accepting the suggested "memories" is vital to the healing process (cf. Bass & Davis, 1988). Instantiating such a belief is even more likely when misleading themes are presented in conjunction with "memory work" techniques that have been questioned as being highly suggestive and likely to facilitate the construction of false memories (Lindsay & Read, 1994; Loftus & Ketcham, 1994). These techniques include guided imagery, sexualized dream interpretation, journal writing, trauma-focused group therapy with other "survivors," and the use of sodium amaytal. Hypnosis is also sometimes part of memory work, in spite of the fact that a review of the literature on the effects of hypnosis (Kihlstrom, 1985) reveals little support for the notion that hypnosis yields increases in memory.

The constructive nature of memory is sufficient to create recollections that are essentially entirely false. Loftus (1993) and Loftus and Ketcham (1994) have argued that most "repressed" memories are of this untrue genre. Lindsay and

Read (1994) agree, while also noting that some patients may recover true memories of childhood sexual molestation during nonsuggestive therapy sessions. Arguing from a psychiatric perspective, Terr (1994) offers a thoughtful analysis of "true stories of traumatic memories" in her book *Unchained Memories*. Although these stories may in large part be "true," it is legitimate to inquire how much of these accounts are in fact just "stories." Terr realizes that some reports are simply what she labels a "wholly false memory," as in the case she discusses of Lua Greene, who falsely claimed that she had been molested by two mental health professionals. Terr defines a wholly false memory as "a full remembrance constructed out of nothing." I am inclined to believe, as alluded to earlier, that there are in fact bases for these constructions, such as invoking prior knowledge (themes/schemata), suggestive interviewing of witnesses, or the inappropriate use of memory recovery techniques. It is difficult to determine how many "recovered" memories are wholly false. More likely, a reclaimed memory may be believed even though it is largely false because it is supported by several slivers of truth. Thus, many recovered memories are not entirely fallacious in the sense described by Terr (1994). Similarly, the presence of constructive threads in the fabric of accurate memories suggests that the existence of what I will term "wholly true memories" is rare. To the extent that memories are blurred along the accuracy dimension, perhaps we should accept that in many situations one's account of an event will contain both true and false details. Obviously, this blurring further complicates the task of authenticating recovered memories and translates into a search for aspects of a reported recollection that point to whether or not it is *essentially* genuine.

Genuineness may also be related to the circumstances surrounding an experience. For instance, perhaps more elaborate and distinctive memories are a consequence of the degree of stress associated with an incident. This becomes relevant when one considers that in most studies of forgetting and suggestibility, subjects have not been exposed to traumatic events. However, memory for stressful experiences has not been ignored, as exemplified by research reported by Howe et al. (this volume) and Goodman et al. (this volume). Howe and his colleagues demonstrated that children as old as 5 who were treated at an emergency room showed forgetting over a 6-month interval. They concluded that autobiographical memory should be the same for traumatic and nontraumatic events. Goodman and her associates studied children aged 3 to 10 years old for their memory of a painful VCUG procedure. They found retention of a traumatic event was impaired by misleading questions and that the younger children were more suggestible. These results are consonant with those typically found in investigations involving nonstressful events. Although further research concerning the relationship between memory and stress is advised, the available evidence would seem to support the belief that traumatic memories should not be elevated to a special or privileged class. A similar caution was issued by McCloskey, Wible, and Cohen (1988) when they questioned the assumption that flashbulb memories (many of which involve a traumatic/emotional component) are unusually accurate and highly resistant to forgetting. They concluded that like other recollections, flashbulb memories are vulnerable to reconstructive errors and can be explained "in terms of ordinary memory mechanisms."

Implicit in the previous discussion of traumatic experiences is the assumption that the experiences were true. In two experiments, Pezdek and Roe (this volume) reported that it was relatively difficult for people to come to believe that they had experienced something that never occurred. However, other investigators have shown that there is considerable evidence that false memories can be implanted, although such implantation may sometimes be difficult. Not only is it possible, it is somewhat remarkable that researchers can plant seeds that blossom into elaborate false memories for both benign events, such as a birthday party at age 5 or attending a wedding at age 6 (Hyman, Husband, & Billings, 1995), and traumatic experiences such as getting lost in a shopping mall (Loftus & Pickrell, 1995), hurting your finger in a mousetrap (Ceci, 1993), and being touched inappropriately by a pediatrician during a physical examination (Ceci & Bruck, 1993a).

This last example is particularly relevant to the contention that it is possible to manufacture false memories of childhood sexual abuse. Does this mean that virtually any memory can be planted? Probably not. In this vein, establishing boundary conditions for the appearance and strength of false memories has already surfaced as an empirical issue. Pezdek (1995) reported a test of the "discrepancy theory of suggestibility" that predicts that suggestively planted memories are more likely for familiar events that are consistent with a person's life experiences. In this regard, Pezdek found that some subjects falsely "remembered" being lost in a mall about 10 years ago, but none of them recalled receiving a nonexistent rectal enema.

## FUTURE DIRECTIONS: THE ROLE OF THEORY IN A RESEARCH AGENDA

It is important to note that the skepticism expressed in this chapter does not imply that recovered memories are nonexistent. In the laboratory, the phenomenon of hypermnesia (see Payne, 1987, for a review), that after one study trial, memory can improve over time and repeated tests, is a clear testament that memory recovery is possible. More significantly, there are instances of recovered memories of child abuse that are known to be authentic because there was corroboration provided by other victims or witnesses, or by a confession by the suspected perpetrator (see Herman & Schatzow, 1987). It should be clear from the chapters in this book that validating repressed/recovered memories of sexual abuse (or other traumatic experiences for that matter) will not be easy. In fact, Goodman et al. (this volume) indicate that perhaps researchers should not tackle this task. They suggest that investigators might do well to examine the accuracy of children's memories and then longitudinally determine which memories are forgotten in adulthood. Several questions follow from this approach. If accurate and inaccurate aspects of previous stressful events are forgotten, how likely is it that they can be later retrieved? Whether access results in fragmentary or detailed memories is another interesting question. Whatever path future research takes, it will be critical to select events in the field or in the laboratory that score high on the ecological validity meter, thus permitting applications in therapeutic and forensic settings.

The designing of new studies must take into account our knowledge of memorial models and mechanisms as well as factors relevant to clinical trauma. In this way, cognitive science and clinical science both contribute to meaningful resolutions and assuage the bitterness presently characterizing the recovered memory debate. In time, we may marshal sufficient evidence to disambiguate truth from confabulation with a reasonable degree of certainty. The research agenda I envision has the potential not only to yield practical implications but also to promote theoretical advances in understanding memory and forgetting. Both of these outcomes can be facilitated by the current theoretical wisdom concerning the impairment of memories and the construction of false memories. I offer the following as examples of theory-based approaches.

In his discussion of episodic memory, Tulving (1983) argued that recollective experience for an event tends to change over time. Although such changes are sometimes a result of changes at the time of testing, in other instances, the modification of engrams may be responsible as a result of "recoding" processes that operate some time after encoding. Concerning recovered memories and their special status hypothesized by some practitioners, to what extent might they be protected from recoding? And if they are not sheltered, how vulnerable are they to the incorporation of false details that could be attributed to suggestive questioning?

Another promising approach is fuzzy trace theory, which has been mapped out in an extensive series of papers by Reyna and Brainerd and colleagues (e.g., Reyna & Brainerd, 1990, 1992; Reyna & Kiernan, 1994). This theory proposes that during the encoding of an event a learner develops in parallel both verbatim and gist memory traces. Immediate retention of studied material should favor the consulting of verbatim traces, although gist traces could also be examined. With delays, however, reduced access to verbatim representations tends to ensure that memorial reconstructions of actual events will be based almost entirely on gist memory records, resulting in the standard observation of forgetting across retention intervals. Once again, if true recovered memories are somehow insulated from distortion caused by the passage of time, then consulting an at least partially intact verbatim trace may be possible and may allow for a fairly detailed recollection. Errors in memory will emanate from gist representations of those episodes. This seems particularly clear when considering the source of false memories, inasmuch as, strictly speaking, verbatim traces should not exist for fictitious information. Events that involve general propositions should accommodate the encoding of thematic/schematic information that would produce gist representations for recalling theme-consistent details. As argued earlier, many false memories are in fact congruent with extracted themes.

Advances in neuropsychology are already contributing to our understanding of how the brain might create a false memory. For instance, Moscovitch (1996) reports that patients with brain injuries to the frontal lobe are prone to confabulations that expose deficits in source memory. In line with an observation made earlier, the confabulations do not seem to be "wholly false" in the sense that a patient latches onto a few fragments of real memories for which the sources have been lost and then fuses these with general knowledge to spin a reconstruction. Such source amnesia also seems to be a key to explaining how recovered memories could be faulty. It should come as no surprise that the source of an event experienced long ago could be forgotten. Once this happens, it is possible to confuse a suggested event with an actual event. Such confusions have been frequently shown in source monitoring studies (Lindsay, 1994).

Thus, it will be essential to discover what kinds of memories are most likely to be confused, manufactured, or both. Nevertheless, overall, research strongly points to the reality of false memories and progress is being made regarding what memorial processes and mechanisms might be responsible for their creation. It is not always obvious, however, whether or not a specific recovered memory is essentially accurate. For this reason, and the serious consequences of dismissing true traumatic memories, delayed recall of alarming events should be taken seriously. This attitude is more likely to be adopted, however, if clinical practitioners use nonsuggestive probing to minimize the chance of patients generating illusory memories.

## REFERENCES

Bass, E., & Davis, L. (1988). *The courage to heal: A guide for women survivors of child sexual abuse.* New York: Harper & Row.

Belli, R. F. (1989). Influences of postevent information: Misinformation interference and acceptance. *Journal of Experimental Psychology: General, 118,* 72–85.

Bonaparte, M., Freud, A., & Kris, E. (Eds.). (1954). *The origins of psychoanalysis* (Eric Mosbacher & James Strachey, Trans.). New York: Basic Books.

Brainerd, C. J., & Ornstein, P. A. (1991). Children's memories for witnessed events: The developmental backdrop. In J. L. Doris (Ed.), *The suggestibility of children's recollections* (pp. 10–20). Washington, DC: American Psychological Association.

Bransford, J. D., & Franks, J. J. (1971). The abstraction of linguistic ideas. *Cognitive Psychology, 2,* 331–350.

Ceci, S. J. (1993). *Cognitive and social factors in children's testimony.* Masters Lecture presented at the meeting of the American Psychological Association, Toronto.

Ceci, S. J., & Bruck, M. (1993a). The child witness: Translating research into policy. *SRCD Social Policy Report, 7,* 1–30.

Ceci, S. J., & Bruck, M. (1993b). Suggestibility of the child witness: A historical review and synthesis. *Psychological Bulletin, 113,* 403–439.

Ceci, S. J., & Loftus, E. F. (1994). "Memory work": A royal road to false memories? *Applied Cognitive Psychology, 8,* 351–364.

Ceci, S. J., Ross, D. F., & Toglia, M. P. (1987). Suggestibility of children's memory: Psycholegal implications. *Journal of Experimental Psychology: General, 117,* 38–49.

Deese, J. (1959). On the prediction of occurrence of particular verbal intrusions in immediate recall. *Journal of Experimental Psychology, 58,* 17–22.

Erdelyi, M. J. (1990). Repression, reconstruction, and defense: History and integration of the psychoanalytic and experimental frameworks. In J. L. Singer (Ed.), *Repression and dissociation* (pp. 1–31). Chicago: University of Chicago Press.

Erdelyi, M. H., & Goldberg, B. (1979). Let's not sweep repression under the rug: Toward a cognitive psychology of repression. In J. F. Kihlstrom & F. J. Evans (Eds.), *Functional disorders of memory.* Hillsdale, NJ: Erlbaum.

Freud, S. (1966). *A general introduction to psychoanalysis* (rev. ed.: Joan Riviere, Trans.). New York: Washington Square Press. (Original work published 1920)

Freud, S. (1993). *New introductory lectures on psychoanalysis,* New York: W. W. Norton.

Gay, P. (1988). *Freud: A life for our time..* New York: W. W. Norton.

Herman, J. L., & Schatzow, E. (1987). Recovery and verification of memories of childhood sexual trauma. *Psychoanalytic Psychology,* **4,** 1–14.

Hochman, J. (1994). Buried memories challenge the law. *The National Law Journal,* **16,** 17–18.

Hyman, Jr., I. E., Husband, T. H., & Billings, F. J. (1995). False memories of childhood experiences. *Applied Cognitive Psychology,* **9,** 181–197.

Kihlstrom, J. (1985). Hypnosis. *Annual Review of Psychology,* **36,** 385–418.

Lindsay, D. S. (1994). Memory source monitoring and eyewitness testimony. In D. F. Ross, J. D. Read, & M. P. Toglia (Eds.), *Adult eyewitness testimony: Current trends and developments* (pp. 27–55). New York: Cambridge University Press.

Lindsay, D. S., & Read J. D. (1994). Psychotherapy and memories of childhood sexual abuse: A cognitive perspective. *Applied Cognitive Psychology,* **8,** 281–338.

Loftus, E. F. (1993). The reality of repressed memories. *American Psychologist,* **48,** 518–537.

Loftus, E. F., & Ketcham, K. (1994). *The myth of repressed memory.* New York: St. Martin's Press.

Loftus, E. F., Miller, D. G., & Burns, H. J. (1978). Semantic integration of verbal information into visual memory. *Journal of Experimental Psychology: Human learning and memory,* **4,** 19–31.

Loftus, E. F., & Pickrell, J. E. (1995). The formation of false memories. *Psychiatric Annals,* **25,** 720–725.

McCloskey, M., Wible, C. G., & Cohen, N. J. (1988). Is there a special flashbulb memory mechanism? *Journal of Experimental Psychology: General,* **114,** 171–181.

Moscovitch, M. (1996). Confabulation. In D. L. Schacter, J. T. Coyle, G. D. Fischbach, M. M. Mesulam, & L. E. Sullivan (Eds.), *Memory Distortion.* (pp. 226–251). Cambridge, MA: Harvard University Press.

Payne, D. G. (1987). Hypermnesia and reminiscence in recall: A historical and empirical review. *Psychological Bulletin,* **101,** 5–27.

Pezdek, K. (1995, November). *What types of false childhood memories are not likely to be suggestively planted?* Paper presented at the Meeting of the Psychonomic Society, Los Angeles.

Read, J. D. (1996). From a passing thought to a false memory in 2 minutes: Confusing real and illusory events. *Psychonomic Bulletin & Review,* **3,** 105–111.

Reyna, V. F., & Brainerd, C. J. (1990). Fuzzy processing in transitivity development. *Annals of Operations Research,* **23,** 37–63.

Reyna, V. F., & Brainerd, C. J. (1992). A fuzzy-trace theory of reasoning and remembering: Paradoxes, patterns, and parallelism. In A. Healy, S. Kossyln, R. Shiffrin (Eds.), *From learning processes to cognitive processes: Essays in honor of William K. Estes* (Vol. 2, pp. 235–259). Hillsdale, NJ: Erlbaum.

Reyna, V. F., & Kiernan, B. (1994). Development of gist versus verbatim memory in sentence recognition: Effects of lexical familiarity, semantic content, encoding instructions, and retention interval. *Developmental Psychology,* **30,** 178–191.

Roediger, H. L., & McDermott, K. B. (1995). Creating false memories: Remembering words not presented in lists. *Journal of Experimental Psychology: Learning, Memory, and Cognition,* **21,** 803–814.

Ross, D. F., Read, J. D., & Toglia, M. P. (1994). *Adult eyewitness testimony: Current trends and developments.* New York: Cambridge University Press.

Sulin, R. A., & Dooling, D. J. (1974). Intrusion of a traumatic idea in retention of prose. *Journal of Experimental Psychology,* **103,** 255–262.

Terr, L. (1994). *Unchained memories.* New York: Basic Books.

Toglia, M. P., Neuschatz, J. S., Goodwin, K. A., & Lyon, M. L. (1995). *Thematic abstraction and the creation of false memories.* Paper presented at the meeting of the Society for Applied Research in Memory and Cognition, Vancouver, BC.

Toglia, M. P., Ross, D. F., Ceci, S. J., & Hembrooke, H. (1992). The suggestibility of children's memory: A social-psychological and cognitive interpretation. In M. L. Howe, C. J. Brainerd, &

V. F. Reyna (Eds.), *Development of long-term retention.* (pp. 217–241). New York: Springer-Verlag.

Tulving, E. (1983). *Elements of episodic memory.* New York: Oxford University Press.

Tulving, E. (1985). Memory and consciousness. *Canadian Psychologist, 26,* 1–12.

Underwood, B. J. (1965). False recognition produced by implicit verbal responses. *Journal of Experimental Psychology, 70,* 122–129.

# Professional Practice, Psychological Science, and the Recovered Memory Debate*

JUDITH L. ALPERT

*New York University*

The position of some memory researchers who are critical of mental health professionals is presented along with that of clinicians about patients who enter treatment with no or partial memories of child sexual abuse and who develop a fuller abuse story as treatment progresses. Some of the points developed in this chapter include: (a) that memory is complex and its accuracy may be affected by a number of factors; (b) that there is no reliable evidence that a plethora of therapists engage in the creation of false memories of child sexual abuse with their adult patients; and (c) the conviction that mental health professionals "know" what actually happened to the patient would be a welcome comfort given all the doubt that takes place within treatment. Implications for forensic activity, clinical practice, and research are also derived.

## INTRODUCTION

Two bodies of literature have relevance to our understanding of delayed memories of childhood abuse. One is the scientific memory research; the other is the scholarly literature on trauma and child sexual abuse. The areas of literature have been developed by professionals who have been trained differently and who work differently. In general, those engaged in scientific memory research are cognitive psychologists who conduct psychological research on memory and who may also teach in this area. Although cognitive psychologists have been trained in such areas as experimental methods, psychometrics, and statistical analysis, they have no clinical training or experience. In general, those engaged in the scholarly literature on trauma and child sexual abuse are practitioners or scientist-practitioners who treat victims of trauma and who may also be engaged in the scientific study and research of traumatology. Until recently, the experimental writings have been published in journals and books that are not oriented to clinicians. Similarly, the more clinical writings have been published in journals and books that are not oriented to memory scientists. Consequently, there has been little consolidation. What has been incorporated from one literature to the other has often been misinformation. Although this schism does not do justice to the existence of some heterogeneity, it is telling.

I am a scientist-practitioner and a practicing psychoanalyst. My perspective is that both clinicians and researchers should be informed about each other's many contributions to the issue of recalled memories of childhood sexual abuse. Parallel work by memory and trauma experts does not contribute to science, practice, or the people we serve. What is needed is a trauma-focused clinical paradigm that attends to the reconstructive nature of memory as well as a memory research paradigm that applies to traumatic events and their possible impact on memory, as put forth by Alpert, Brown, and Courtois (in press). It is my hope that such cross-fertilization of scholarship will facilitate research, theory, and practice, and that, ultimately, all of psychology will advance.

## THE STORY

I will tell a story. It is the notable story that Herman (1992) detailed in *Trauma and Recovery*. She examines the history of the ways in which mental health professionals and others have misunderstood, denounced, and sometimes understood victims of post-traumatic disorders. She notes the similarity among responses to various traumas, such as wife battering and combat experiences. She points out that victims have been responded to differently in different historical times. She illustrates how the standard personal responses to psychological trauma (denial, repression, and dissociation) also exist on the social level.

As Herman elucidates, throughout the history of the field there has been disagreement about whether persons with post-traumatic stress disorder—victims of combat, incest, wife battering, and other disasters—are entitled to care and concern or deserving of contempt and ridicule, whether they have truly agonized or not, and whether their life stories are reliable, credible, and real, or imagined, fabricated, and false. Throughout history, those who have been victims of post-traumatic stress disorder, such as victims of childhood sexual abuse, have been misunderstood and doubted by the general populace and have been provided with inadequate and improper care by the mental health professionals. Furthermore, this story of abuse of trauma victims begins with the inception of mental health treatment. Thus, it is a tale of villains, disbelievers, accusers, victims, scapegoats, charges, and blame. The doctor characters consist of Charcot, Janet, Freud, Breuer, military psychiatrists, and other mental health professionals. The doctor characters *do* or *do not* make unwarranted inferences, *do* or *do not* implant atrocious scenes into the memory of patients, and *do* or *do not* impose an elaborate form of mind management.

The tale also consists of hysterical women, war veterans, rape victims, battered women, sexually abused children, and adults who were sexually abused as children. These characters play conflicting roles during different historical times and even within any one historical time, depending on who is telling the story. They are cast, on the one hand, as crazy, defective, liars, constitutionally inferior, malingerers, cowards, moral invalids, suggestible, irrational, or vengeful, and, on the other hand, as human or noble. They are regarded with contempt and disdain or with dignity and respect, and are attended to with shame, threats, punishment, court martial, electric shock, rap groups, and consciousness-raising groups, or with humane treatment based on psychodynamic principles.

Unfortunately, the complex issues raised about the nature of human beings and our society are not conveyed by these groupings. These dichotomies ignore the following:

- the enormous learning from human behavior that can be used as a touchstone to consider the destructive impulses and forces of negativity that exist in human beings;
  - the matter of social and antisocial behavior;
  - the assertion that he to whom evil is done may do evil in return, and he to whom good is done may do good in return;
  - the understanding of the nature of the traumatized individual, that is, that some of the traumatized traumatize others; and
  - the need for socialization by humane and good treatment and a just and protective society.

Herman's tale recounts that (a) there is a history of polemics on how to regard and treat patients with post-traumatic conditions; (b) there is a long-term controversy as to whether the stories of these patients are authentic, credible, and real, or erroneous and the products of imagination, vicious fabrication, or construction; (c) there is a history of contention as to whether mental health professionals construct something new or participate in reconstructing something old; and (d) the investigations of trauma have been influenced by the political, intellectual, and social environment and have flourished in association with political movements.

## THE CONTEMPORARY STORY

In this chapter, I further develop the story; that is, I tell the contemporary story. Contemporary characters in this tale include academic researchers who, for the most part, study memory for normal events in experimental laboratories with volunteer subjects. They play disbelieving and, in some cases, accusatory roles. As I tell this story, I discuss some of the work of memory scientists. At least some memory scientists fervently promulgate the view that the abuser is now the therapist who pursues buried memories and that patients develop false memories of abuse as a direct result of this search and the use of such techniques as direct suggestion, guided visualization, hypnotic age regression, sexualized dream interpretation, sodium amytal, and body memory analysis. Although there are no laboratory studies of memory suggestibility in psychotherapy, this is nevertheless believed. These memory scientists seem to imply that the victims are no longer the ones who are molested but rather the ones who are falsely accused.

### Memory Scientists

Memory and trauma experts seem to agree on a number of points. I mention some here, based on the interim report of members of the American Psychological Association's Working Group on Investigation of Memories of Childhood Abuse (this volume). Some points of agreement are that

1. child sexual abuse is a complex and pervasive problem in America that has historically gone unacknowledged;

2. most people who were sexually abused as children remember all or part of what happened to them;

3. it is possible for memories of abuse that have been forgotten for a long time to be remembered, and similarly it is possible to construct pseudomemories for events that never occurred; and

4. mechanisms for either of these occurrences are not well understood.

Furthermore, memory and trauma experts agree that memories for events and the actual events may not be isomorphic. Memories of trauma can correspond to the central events of traumatic experiences. Memories can also reproduce the traumatic experience in homomorphic terms. In addition, in general, they agree that some people, especially young children, are suggestible, although they can recall material that is forensically appropriate (see review by Ceci & Bruck, 1993). Furthermore, they agree that certain events may be more difficult to change, such as those that are personally salient, that are central as opposed to peripheral, and that are experienced as opposed to observed. Also, certain events may be easier to believe, such as those that are positive and plausible. Although common, sexual abuse is not a plausible event to many people. Also, memory and trauma scientists and scholars seem to agree that both psychotherapy and research vary enormously and that both can be poorly conducted. These are some areas of agreement.

There are also some significant points of disagreement. A contemporary story that is being promulgated by some of the more vocal memory scientists is that psychotherapists pursue buried memories and that patients develop false memories of abuse as a direct result of this search, with the concomitant utilization of such techniques as sodium amytal, direct suggestion, guided visualization hypnotic age regression, sexualized dream interpretation and body memory analysis. This search for buried memories is not promoted by professional programs in psychology or by the mainstream professional literature on treatment of adult survivors (e.g., Briere, 1989; Courtois, 1988; Herman, 1992; Jehu, 1988; Kluft, 1990). There is no training program or mainstream literature that presents memory retrieval to the exclusion of other therapeutic tasks as the treatment goal, or that promulgates the utilization of techniques that are suggestive. Nor is there support for this position from laboratory studies of memory suggestibility in psychotherapy. Although suggestibility effects could theoretically occur in therapy, it does not follow that they indeed do.

In general, some memory scientists hold that a considerable number of therapists, believing that it is customary for people to have repressed sexual abuse memories, delve for such memories in patients who enter treatment without abuse recollections. From a reading of the study by Poole, Lindsay, Memon, and Bull (1995), one cannot assert that a significant number of therapists are misapplying therapeutic strategies. Although 29 to 34% of clinicians report that they are using hypnosis, for example, use and abuse cannot be equated. It is not that hypnosis is intrinsically misleading. The important issue concerns how hypnotic techniques are used. Those therapists who follow the recommendations put forward by the American Society of Clinical Hypnosis for the use of hypnosis with memory are maintaining the highest standards of therapeutic work, as Hammond (1995) indicates. As another example, dream interpretation is a well-established component of psychodynamic psychotherapy. The detailing of the injurious story and the integrating of the traumatic memories with their associated affects is not the same as pursuing buried memories. However, we need to remember that dreams serve many functions, as I indicate elsewhere (Alpert, 1995a). Sometimes they serve to tell exactly what happened. Sometimes, for the dreamer, they exist to obscure exactly what happened. Dreams can replicate the central events of traumatic experiences. Dreams can also reproduce the traumatic experiences in metamorphic terms. Dreams can be isomorphic. Sometimes they are homomorphic. Usually we do not know which occurs when. Transformations do scramble, reverse, omit, and add. Interpretation of dreams is a very complex business. The therapist should promote exploration while acknowledging that they (therapist or patient) may never know for sure whether the dream replicates the actual trauma.

Furthermore, there are studies (e.g., Poole et al., 1995; Waltz, 1994; Yapko, 1994) that support the finding that, in those therapy cases in which abuse is reported or suspected, most therapists do not have as their main focus the retrieval of memories. Yapko found that some therapists held inaccurate beliefs about the nature of memory, memory retrieval, and hypnosis, and he held that these beliefs could lead to suggestive practices in therapy. However, there is a difference between what is plausible (beliefs *possibly* resulting in suggestive practices) and what actually occurs (beliefs *actually* resulting in suggestive practices).

Memories sometimes return in treatment, and this finding is consistent with Bower's (1981) theory of state-dependent memory. This theory posits a connection between affect and content, and indicates that memory recall is strengthened by mood congruity. Therapy can induce a state that is similar to that which took place during the traumatic event, and this induced state, in turn, can result in recall. The return of memories in treatment can thus be explained. However, what has been found (Elliot, 1994) is that therapy is the least likely trigger for the return of memory, whereas the media is the most commonly reported stimulus for memory retrieval. What is the basis, then, for this contemporary story of therapists pursuing buried memories and misapplying therapeutic techniques or using questionable ones?

Results from laboratory studies on suggestibility with traumatized children or adults are applied to psychotherapy. The studies on children and suggestibility are designed with the intent to mislead children. Children are repeatedly asked questions by interviewers who presuppose the truth of the suggested material, and the children, in turn, are required to elaborate. The results of these studies cannot be generalized to all children who report sexual abuse or to adults who remember abuse experiences from childhood.

Much of the data in the laboratory studies with adults concern word lists, pictures, or stories that do not parallel the real-life traumatic experience of sexual abuse. As indicated elsewhere (Alpert, Brown, & Courtois, in press), recalling such items as nonexistent broken glass and tape recorders, or stop signs as yield signs, is different from remembering fictional, recurrent scenes of father–daughter incest and developing associated post-traumatic symptomatology. As I indicate later, memory for trauma and memory for normal events may perform differently. In contrast to memory for normal events, emotional memories have been described as being detailed, accurate, and not prone to error (Christianson, 1992). It is unfortunate that few memory scientists have studied trauma. Furthermore, it is unfortunate that when it has been studied, it has been defined in a way that could be conceptualized as nontrauma or less significant trauma. Witnessing other people's disasters, for example, is less traumatic than personally experiencing them. Seeing and hearing the space shuttle *Challenger* explode on television and talking about the event is very different from experiencing violation to one's body by a caregiver and being silenced about it.

It is important that research focus on the truly traumatic. As Christianson (1992) indicates in his review, emotional events are remembered differently from neutral or ordinary events. It appears that memory for trauma may be different from memory for normal events, as I indicate elsewhere (Alpert, 1995b). The limited research discussed here exemplifies a large body of findings that point to significant differences. For example, one interpretation of some memory literature is that encoding is influenced by prior knowledge to understand and to interpret the experience. From this it follows that a child would not remember if the child did not have some prior knowledge which would provide a foundation to remember. However, this reasoning does not attend to the fact that prior knowledge is also composed of affect and sensory experiences, and children clearly have the ability to retain these types of memories. In fact, recent research supports that there can be accurate verbal and cognitive retrieval for experiences encoded prior to the onset of speech (Hewitt, 1994; Terr, 1988, 1989). Memory of abuse may be encoded without language to articulate it or without a full understanding of the significance of the event. Memory for nontraumatic events may be encoded differently from memory for traumatic events and may be experienced in sensorimotor or somatosensory ways (Fisler, Vardi, & van der Kolk, 1994; Saporta & van der Kolk, 1992; van der Kolk, 1988; van der Kolk & van der Hart, 1991). Memory for the traumatic may occur nonverbally by means of startle responses, flashbacks, obsessions, compulsions, reenactments, and dreams. Noncognitive expressions of abuse memory are relevant for an understanding of memory for the nontraumatic. It appears that at least some vocal memory researchers discount the noncognitive and focus almost exclusively on cognitive aspects of memory.

A second example concerns the amount of exposure to an event. The research on normal memory suggests that the amount of exposure to a particular event and, specifically, the length of exposure and the number of repetitions have the potential to strengthen traces in memory and, therefore, they may be more readily retrieved (Crowder, 1976). When the focus is on traumatic memory, research findings seem to differ. The trauma literature indicates that memory of repeated abuse may be less likely to be retrieved. Terr (1991), for example, conceptualizes two types of childhood trauma. Type I trauma involves single-blow traumas, such as a disaster, and is associated with full, detailed memories, "omens," and misperceptions. Type II trauma involves variable, multiple, or long-standing traumas, common in incest, and is associated with denial and numbing, self-hypnosis and dissociation, and rage. These two types of trauma correspond to what is referred to within the psychoanalytic literature as discrete shock trauma and prolonged strain or cumulative trauma, respectively. The finding that children who experience single-blow traumas tend to present with full, detailed and etched-in memories, whereas those who experience long-standing or repeated trauma do not, contrasts with the research on normal memory cited earlier.

A third example involves memory over time. According to the memory research, passage of time is associated with increased difficulty in recall. In contrast, according to the trauma literature, unavailable, traumatic, repeated abuse memories may vacillate, may return over time, or may be constant (Herman, 1992; van der Kolk, 1984, 1987). The return of these memories may differ from the return of memories for normal events. Flashbacks and extreme responses to stimuli that would not elicit such responses from most individuals are often associated with the return of these types of memories (Horowitz, 1986; van der Kolk, 1987). These flashbacks and extreme responses are presently perceived to be the result of dissociated affect and trauma information (Spiegel & Cardena, 1991). This brief comparison of a few general findings from the two literatures illustrates that memory for trauma may be different from normal memory. Another possibility, however, is that they may be similar in, as yet, unexplicated ways.

Earlier I mentioned that the schism into two camps (the practitioners or scientist-practioners who treat victims of trauma versus the memory scientists) does not do justice to the existence of some heterogeneity. For example, there is a large body of research that points to the relative accuracy of memory (e.g., Christianson, 1984; Heuer & Reisberg, 1990; Reisberg, Heuer, McLean, & O'Shaughnessy, 1988; Yuille & Cutshall, 1986). Also, there are some memory scientists whose work supports the view that children seldom or never make up false stories of abuse, even when questioned in a way that pulls for false reports (Goodman & Aman, 1990; Rudy, Goodman, Nicholas, & Moan, 1991). These studies support the notion that children are not highly suggestible in cases involving trauma and that they have better memory when there is interpersonal support at or around the time of the traumatic event.

Among the studies that most approximate the trauma of sexual abuse are those by Goodman and her associates (e.g., Goodman & Aman, 1990; Goodman, Hirschman, Hepps, & Rudy, 1991; Goodman & Reed, 1986; Goodman, Quas, Batterman-Faunce, Riddlesberger, & Khuh, this volume; Goodman, Rudy, Bottoms, & Aman, 1990; Rudy et al., 1991; Saywitz, Goodman, Nicholas, & Moan, 1991). In the study in this volume by Goodman, Quas, Batterman-Fance, Riddlesberger, and Khuh, children were subjected to a painful and embarrassing procedure involving genital penetration and public urination, urinary tract catheterization. This study points to the *forgetting* of trauma. A few children out of the sample of 46 denied that they experienced the medical test. Also, such factors as embarrassment, lack of discussion of the procedure with parents, and post-traumatic stress disorder (PTSD) symptoms were predictive of poor memory performance in their study. These three factors are associated with sexual abuse.

In another study (Saywitz et al., 1991), 72 five- and seven-year old girls underwent a standardized medical checkup. For one half of the children, the checkup included a vaginal and anal examination (genital condition). For the other half, there was a scoliosis examination (nongenital condition). Children's memories were evaluated by means of free recall, anatomically detailed dolls, prop demonstration, and direct and misleading questions. It was found that the majority of children in the genital condition revealed vaginal and anal contact *only when asked directly about it*. Errors regarding vaginal and anal touch in response to direct questions were predominantly due to omissions. That is, some children in the genital condition, when asked directly, denied vaginal and anal contact. Children in the nongenital condition never falsely reported genital touch in free recall or doll demonstration. Furthermore, with direct questioning, the false report rate was rare. Thus, they found that young children only tell their "true genital touching" story when specifically asked and that those who were not touched were able to say so.

A document developed by a group of memory scientists and practitioners of the British Psychological Society (reprinted in this volume) is, in general, consistent with many of the points I develop here. Some of the points included in the report are (a) memories may be recovered within or independent of therapy, (b) memory recovery is reported by highly experienced and well-qualified therapists who are well aware of the dangers of inappropriate suggestion and interpretation, (c) there is no reliable evidence that the creation of false memories by therapists is a wide-spread phenomenon, and (d) there is evidence for incorrect memories but much less evidence for the creation of false memories. Thus, *not all memory scientists* see things the same way and *not all laboratory studies on memory* indicate the inaccuracy of memory. Memory can be strong and functionally accurate. Memory can also be quite malleable. We need to learn more about those conditions that make it more likely to be open to error and those that keep it secure. One study, for example, designed specifically to examine the conditions under which memories are or are not likely to be suggestively planted (Pezdek, 1995) found that false memories are more likely to be planted if they involve familiar events rather than unfamiliar events. More research such as this is encouraged. Also, we need to learn more about whether factors related to the vulnerability of memory parallel those existing within the traumatic experience of child sexual abuse.

I have discussed the contemporary story promulgated by some vocal memory researchers. Another and quite different story could have been written: *Abusers* cause their *victims* to develop *false memories* of *nonabuse*. They do so by using such techniques as direct suggestion, guided visualization, interpretation, and threats. An example is the perpetrator–father telling the child he was abusing to go back to sleep and that it was all a dream. He thus created a false memory. The child–victim develops this false memory of nonabuse and believes that it was all a dream. Later, she might develop post-traumatic symptomatology. She would be confused by these symptoms. She might present with other symptoms and diagnoses. The flashbacks, nightmares, and intrusive images would be bewildering. She might suspect sexual abuse but be quick to deny. The media might implant the false memory of nonabuse as well.

There is another story I heard recently. It is the story of a woman whose adult sister alleged father–daughter incest following recovery of abuse memories. The woman went with her father to a "therapist" of his choosing. The "therapist" used the session to inform her that her sister had "false memory syndrome" and that she should not allow her sister to press charges. The woman later learned that this "therapist" had also been accused of father–daughter incest. Furthermore, her sister's abuse was later validated by a brother. What is interesting about these two stories is that they could both be described as false memories and both be supported by the same results from the same suggestibility studies.

There are problems with applying the research on memory suggestibility to the case of sexual abuse, as I have indicated. The literature offers little support for either these stories of *false memory of nonabuse* or for the earlier story of *false memory of abuse*. However, if the memory literature is used to support one of the positions, it could be applied to the other as well. If the literature is used to support one story rather than the other, the issue of bias, interpretation, and selective application must be raised.

In sum, the literature on memory suggestibility offers little support for the story that is being circulated, the story that patients develop false memories of abuse as a direct result of therapists dredging, implanting, and creating. The story holds a great deal more complexity. There is inadequate support for the statement that a patient's memory may have changed; it is possible, for example, that patients who tell a different story in response to suggestion may be giving a compliant report in response to social factors. Their reporting of an event may have changed while their memory may have remained constant. There is no research that indicates that most mental health professionals working with adults who assert child sexual abuse do treatment that is suggestive and that almost exclusively focuses on memory retrieval, with little attention to other therapeutic aims. As of this writing, there are no laboratory studies of memory suggestibility in psychotherapy by memory scientists. Unfortunately, this undeveloped body of research is being used prematurely in the courtroom for purposes of defending alleged abuse perpetrators and prosecuting therapists alleged to have used suggestion.

It is not surprising that there are problems with ecological validity. Memory science has only become an applied science in the last 20 years, and, until recently, the focus has been on eyewitness reports of crimes. The application of laboratory research to the issue of delayed memory of childhood trauma is a new development. It is more likely to thrive if there is cross-fertilization of scholarship.

## The Psychoanalytic Clinician and Reconstruction

I turn now to another character in this contemporary story: the clinician. Up to now, the story I have told focuses on the role of memory scientists. They have been telling us what the clinician does. However, we cannot learn about what clinicians do from the writings of memory scientists. Although they will not tell the full story, the writings of clinicians need to be considered. Some mainstream literature that points to how clinicians work with sexual abuse victims is that by Briere (1989, 1992), Courtois (1988), Herman (1992), Kluft (1990), McCann and Pearlman (1990), and Wilson and Raphael (1993). In general, this literature indicates that therapists must use their training in neutrality, observation, and analysis in working with patients who report delayed memory, and that therapists should not suggest abuse to explain symptoms nor fail to explore abuse when warranted.

Another clinical literature that has received relatively little attention within the general memory discourse is that on psychoanalysis. Psychoanalysts continue to grapple with the question: Can, and, if so, how does, the analyst know truth and reality? The discussion that is ongoing within psychoanalysis speaks to the intricacy of the issues and the acknowledgment of uncertainty surrounding the nature of mind and memory and the topic of therapeutic action. This wrestling with the integrity of the clinical process is ongoing among mental health professionals of varying theoretical orientations. I tell the psychoanalytic story because it has not received much attention in the broader discourse on delayed memory. It is also a story in which I am presently most immersed. Let me be clear and state my position at the outset. I am not implying that the work of all psychoanalysts or all mental health professionals is privileged, justified, and above condemnation. Rather, what I am saying is that it is highly unlikely that most are engaged in therapeutic action that could be considered capricious, careless, or coercive. There are bad and poorly trained therapists. Similarly, there are bad and poorly trained researchers.

The word *reconstruction* should have its place in this story. Although it is seldom mentioned in this debate, it is central to the discourse. The technique of reconstruction is a foundation of clinical psychoanalysis. In reconstruction, fragments from the patient's past are joined into a cohesive life story that makes sense in the present. Freud held that an analyst should place before the patient, in a timely manner, an event that the patient does not remember but the analyst presumes to have occurred. He held that an inaccurate reconstruction was harmless because the patient would reject it. His reconstructions were quite specific and included such details as what took place, when, where, and with whom. Freud's task was complex. Believing that later events may retrogressively influence the significance of earlier events, he had the difficult task of determining the patient's relative age at the time of the event. For example, although it did not hold psychic significance until it was reactivated in a dream 4 years later when he was experiencing the oedipal conflict, Freud (1919) inferred that the Wolf-man observed the primal scene at 18 months. It seems as if some memory scientists are assuming that Freud's paradigmatic reconstructions are still operative today.

Reconstruction took on new meaning as time progressed. Whereas Freud believed that reconstructions of what actually happened was possible, the ego psychologists viewed the recovery of actual memories and reconstructions of discrete events as outdated aspirations. The ego psychologists were interested in the present experience of the past rather than in reconstructing what actually happened. Instead of focusing on the event itself, they focused on the immediate and subsequent thought processes and feelings that were elaborations of the event. Thus, they focused on that which did not exist at the time of the event.

Over time, there has been substantial reconceptualization and a steady shift away from the belief that a veridical account of the past can be reconstructed. Many different theoretical and sociocultural developments have converged to result in a deemphasis of the actual historical reality of past events. This is the time of radical deconstruction.

Rather than scientific objectivism, one contemporary hermeneutic trend emphasizes the role of narrative. The ego psychological approach to reconstruction leads naturally to the subjectivist, relativist positions of Spence (1982, 1993) and Schafer (1992) which point to the inaccessibility and irrelevance of historical truth. Clinical material is regarded as dependent on the observer, and reconstructed stories that are epistemologically consistent and clinically useful are thought to be not necessarily veridical. Reality is constructed by means of a theoretical perspective. A story that is told is but one of many versions that could be told and is only one version of the truth. In yet another hermeneutic trend (Hoffman, 1991), the analyst's personal involvement is included within the constructivist position. The term "social constructivism" incorporates both the role of the immediate analytic interaction, involving participation and reciprocal, interpersonal influence in the historical reconstruction as well as the construction of a clouded reality. Within social constructivism there is recognition that neither the analyst nor the patient has access to reality and that their individual and collective understanding is in process. Thus, current analytic thinking that takes into account constructivism, perspectivism, or narration acknowledges visions or versions of reality and the impossibility of knowing historical truth.

Even contemporary classical theorists (e.g., Blum, 1994) indicate that reconstructions are only approximations, as are all interpretive interventions. Contemporary classical proponents of reconstruction attempt to reconstruct the actual experience, the psychic trauma, the developmental phase disturbance, the sequence, and the sequelae. They view reconstruction as a process that is continually revised as analysis deepens.

When we move to a relational analytic paradigm within a constructivist model, there is a repudiation of historical truth in preference for intersubjective truth. Within this paradigm, there is a belief that reconstruction is impossible and the work is more appropriately called *construction*. Some relational psychoanalysts (e.g., Davies & Frawley, 1994) focus on the reenactment in the transference-countertransference work. Their sense of reconstruction, a word that is generally not used, is that whatever happens now, as evidenced within the transference, probably happened then. Memory is played out in transference phenomena. Relational analysts work collaboratively with the patient to encounter anew feelings from the past and to resolve these feelings. They are not concerned with the absolute truth of the life story, and seem to hold that one should not assume truth. The focus is less on the recovery of memories and more on the reintegration of those repudiated memories into a modified life story. The reliving and resolving, however, are different from the recovery of repressed memories.

There is no assumption that the revised stories represent a true reality. The concepts of ambiguity, interaction, construction, and co-construction are recognized. Neither the analyst nor the patient may know for sure whether the abuse event took place. The analyst's responsibility is to enable an atmosphere of inquiry, offer support, and maintain neutrality while recognizing that the judge for memories, personal history, and narrative is the patient.

The challenge for some analysts (e.g., Grand, 1995; Slavin, 1993) becomes how to rescue reconstruction within the relational paradigm. Grand would like to retain the egalitarian treatment model of social constructivism without negating the significance and accessibility of historical truth. Implicit here are the beliefs that reality is not entirely mutually constructed, that truth is not merely narrative, and that confusion and uncertainty can coexist with knowing something. There are times when we think we do know; there are times when the evidence is simply that substantial and convincing. The challenge for contemporary psychoanalysts who work within this theoretical frame of relational co-constructed reality in the analytic dyad is to find a way to acknowledge that there are some things that we do know and that not all historical accounts are equally valid, coherent, telling, or plausible.

The story that I have related contrasts sharply with the simplistic story of the impulsive, thoughtless therapist who pursues buried memories. As Harris (1995) writes,

> To counter the caricaturing of all therapists as destructive agents with primitive tools to divide and destroy families and persons, it is always important to assert the modest but terrifying goal of psychoanalytic work: the relief of suffering the development of the courage not to act but to bear loss that is irredeemable. In the treatment of abused patients, the losses can be particularly terrible: lost time, lost opportunities, above all lost innocence. (p. 15)

Thus, contemporary psychoanalysts, across orientations, are incorporating a therapeutic action paradigm in which there is recognition that experience is constructed and, at least within some of these paradigms, that the analyst is inescapably and intricately involved in a manner that influences the structure of understanding by means of narratives and the patient–self experiences. The belief that we *can* know would bring welcome relief from all of the doubt that takes place within the analytic context. Although occasionally the evidence is substantial and convincing, in those cases in which there is not memory, it is difficult to know.

## CONCLUSION

We need to keep in mind that victimizers have something to gain by distorting, disavowing, and misrepresenting. It is difficult to distinguish perpetrators from normal men and regular fathers. Our impulse may be to believe the victimizers. We do not want to believe that human beings could do such terrible things to children. We do not want to believe that debauchery survives. Also, victimizers can be very convincing. They may even have convinced themselves. It may be that they have disowned and dissociated from their abusing selves, and that they truly believe that they have not committed acts of abuse. We need to keep all of this in mind. At the same time, we also must keep in mind that the alleged victimizers may, in fact, be nonvictimizers. It is a difficult tightrope that we walk.

There are numerous themes in this story. One theme is that memory is very complex and that a memory's accuracy may be affected by a number of factors. Another theme is that there is no reliable evidence that a plethora of therapists engage in the creation of false memories of child sexual abuse with their adult patients. Another theme is that there is often doubt within the analytic context. To "truly know" would be a welcome comfort. This is a theme which I elaborate elsewhere (Alpert, 1995c).

In addition to these themes, there are the themes of *bias* and *politics*. The standard research situation is packed with occasions for bias. The occasion starts when a researcher decides what to study and opens more broadly when he or she makes decisions about how to study it. The opportunity for bias is opened even wider when the researcher attempts to interpret. As I have illustrated, the same data could be applied to support either false memory of nonabuse or false memory of abuse. The occasion for bias is wider still when the researcher decides when and where and for what purpose to present the research. Unfortunately, the undeveloped body of memory research is being used prematurely in the courtroom in defending alleged abuse perpetrators and in prosecuting therapists alleged to have used suggestion.

The story of reckless and suggestive therapists is diverting us from the real victims of child sexual abuse. What can we do to put the focus back on the child who has been victimized and on the adult who remembers in whatever way he or she does? Memory scientists and clinicians need to engage in joint inquiry and to work to develop (a) research on real traumatic memory that has ecological validity and helps to identify those conditions under which individuals would be more suggestible, and (b) research on real traumatic memory that would help us to understand the processes of forgetting and retrieving of trauma. Memory scientists and clinicians need to place some developed scientific material on the topics of trauma and memory processes into the standard curriculum of all students in psychology. Therapists need to be knowledgeable about the risks of improper suggestion and interpretation. Memory researchers need to be knowledgeable about human traumatization; it must not be minimized. Forensic psychologists need to specify limitations with respect to ecological validity and generalizability. Sometimes, research is so far afield that it is best left off-field. Lastly, the scapegoating of therapists should cease. It is poor judgment to think that delayed incest memories can be explained away by pointing to bad therapy. Rather than focus our revulsion on therapy, we need to face the overshadowed issue, which is that many children in this society are abused.

## REFERENCES

Alpert, J. L. (1995a). Dreams, trauma, and clinical observation: Comments on C. Brooks Brenneis's article. *Psychoanalytic Psychology, 12*(2), 325–328.

Alpert, J. L. (1995b). Trauma, dissociation, and clinical study as a responsible beginning. *Cognition and Consciousness,* **4,** 1–5.

Alpert, J. L. (1995c). Criteria: Signposts toward the sexual abuse hypothesis. In J. L. Alpert (Ed.), *Sexual abuse recalled: Treating trauma in the era of the recovered memory debate.* Northvale, N.J.: Aronson.

Alpert, J. L., Brown, L. S., & Courtois, C. A. (in press). *Symptomatic clients and memories of childhood abuse: What the trauma and child sexual abuse literature tells us.* In J. L. Alpert, L. S. Brown, S. Ceci, C. A. Courtois, E. Loftus, and P. A. Ornstein (Eds.), *Interim Report of the Working Group on Investigation of Memories of Childhood Abuse.* Washington, DC: American Psychological Association.

*Blum, H. P. (1994). Reconstruction in psychoanalysis: Childhood revisited and recreated.* Madison, CT: International Universities Press.

Bower, G. H. (1981). Mood and memory. *American Psychologist,* **36,** 129–148.

Briere, J. (1989). *Therapy for adults molested as children.* New York: Springer.

Briere, J. N. (1992). *Child abuse trauma: Theory and treatment of the lasting effects.* Newbury Park, CA: Sage.

Ceci, S. J., & Bruck, M. (1993). Suggestibility of the child witness: A historical review and synthesis. *Psychological Bulletin,* **113**(3), 403–439.

Christianson, S.-A. (1984). The relationship between induced emotional arousal and amnesia. *Scandinavian Journal of Psychology,* **25,** 147–160.

Christianson, S.-A. (1992). Emotional stress and eyewitness memory. *Psychological Bulletin,* **112** (2), 284–309.

Courtois, C. A. (1988). *Healing the incest wound: Adult survivors in therapy.* New York: W. W. Norton.

Crowder, R. G. (1976). *Principles of learning and memory.* Hillsdale, NJ: Erlbaum.

Davies, J. M., & Frawley, M. G. (1994). *Treating the adult survivor of childhood sexual abuse: A psychoanalytic perspective.* New York: Basic Books.

Elliott, D. M. (1994, November). Trauma and dissociated memory: Prevalence across events. In L. Berliner (Chair), *Delayed trauma memories: Victim experiences and clinical practice.* Paper presented at the annual meeting of the International Society of Traumatic Stress Studies, Chicago, IL.

Fisler, R. E., Vardi, D. J., & van der Kolk, B. A. (1994). Nontraumatic autobiographical memories in trauma survivors: A preliminary study. Poster presented at the Harvard Medical School, Cambridge, MA.

Freud, S. (1919). From the history of an infantile neurosis. *Standard edition of the complete psychological works of Sigmund Freud* (Vol. 17, pp. 7–12). London: Hogarth Press.

Goodman, G. S., & Aman, C. (1990). Children's use of anatomically detailed dolls to recount an event. *Child Development,* **61,** 1859–1871.

Goodman, G. S., Hirschman, J. E., Hepps, D., & Rudy, L. (1991). Children's memory for stressful events. *Merrill-Palmer Quarterly,* **37,** 109–158.

Goodman, G. S., & Reed, R. S. (1986). Age differences in eyewitness testimony. *Law and Human Behavior,* **19,** 317–332.

Goodman, G. S., Rudy, L., Bottoms, B. L., & Aman, C. (1990). Children's concerns and memory: Issues of ecological validity in the study of children's eyewitness testimony. In R. Fivush & J. Hudson (Eds.), *Knowing and remembering in young children* (pp. 249–284). New York: Cambridge University Press.

Grand, S. (1995). Incest and the intersubjective politics of knowing history. In J. L. Alpert (Ed.), *Sexual abuse recalled: Treating trauma in the era of the recovered memory debate.* Northvale, NJ: Aronson.

Hammond, C. (1995). Hypnosis, false memories, and guidelines for using hypnosis with potential victims of abuse. In J. L. Alpert (Ed.), *Sexual abuse recalled: Perspectives for clinicians.* Northvale, NJ: Aronson.

Harris, A. (1995). *False memory; false memory syndrome; "false memory syndrome"; the so-called false memory syndrome?* Paper presented at the White Institute Conference on Delayed Memories, New York City.

Herman, J. L. (1992). *Trauma and recovery.* New York: Basic Books.

Heuer, F., & Reisberg, D. (1992). Emotion, arousal, and memory for detail. In S. A. Christianson (Ed.), *The handbook of emotion and memory,* pp. 151–506. Hillsdale, NJ: Erlbaum.

Hewitt, S. A. (1994). Preverbal sexual abuse: What two children report in later years. *Child Abuse and Neglect,* 18(10), 821–826.

Hoffman, I. Z. (1991). Discussion: Toward a social-constructivist view of the psychoanalytic situation, *Psychoanalytic Dialogues: A Journal of Relational Perspectives,* 1(1), 74–105.

Horowitz, M. (1986). *Stress response syndromes.* New York: Jason Aaronson.

Jehu, D. (1988). *Beyond sexual abuse: Therapy with women who were childhood victims.* New York: Wiley.

Kluft, R. P. (1990). Incest and subsequent revictimization. In R. P. Kluft (Ed.), *Incest-related syndromes of adult psychopathology* (pp. 263–288). Washington, DC: American Psychiatric Press.

McCann, I. L., & Pearlman, L. A. (1990). *Psychological trauma and the adult survivor.* New York: Brunner/Mazel.

Pezdek, K. (1995, November). *What types of false childhood memories are not likely to be suggestively planted?* Paper presented at the Meeting of the Psychonomic Society, Los Angeles.

Poole, D. A., Lindsay, D. S., Memon, A., & Bull, R. (1995). Psychotherapy and the recovery of memories of childhood sexual abuse: U.S. and British Practitioners opinions, practices, and experiences. *Journal of Consulting and Clinical Psychology,* 63(3), 426–437.

Reisberg, D., Heuer, F., McLean, J., & O'Shaugnessy, M. (1988). The quantity, not quality, of affect predicts memory vividness. *Bulletin of the Psychonomic Society,* 26, 100–103.

Rudy, L., Goodman, G. S., Nicholas, E., & Moan, S. (1991). Effects of participation on children's reports: Implications for children's testimony. *Developmental Psychology,* 27, 1–26.

Saporta, J. A., & van der Kolk, B. A. (1992). Psychobiological consequences of severe trauma. In M. Basogh (Ed.), *Torture and its consequences* (pp. 151–181). New York, Cambridge University Press.

Saywitz, K. J., Goodman, G. S., Nichols, E., & Moan, S. F. (1991). Children's memories of a physical examination involving genital touch: Implications for reports of child sexual abuse. *Journal of Consulting and Clinical Psychology,* 59(5), 682–691.

Schafer, R. (1992). *Retelling a life: Narration and dialogue in psychoanalysis.* New York: Basic Books.

Slavin, J. (1993, August). *The poisoning of desire: Memory, fantasy, dissociation, and agency in sexual abuse.* Discussion presented at the annual meeting of the American Psychological Association, Toronto.

Spence, D. (1982). *Narrative truth and historical truth: Meaning and interpretation in psychoanalysis.* New York: Norton.

Spence, D. 1993. The hermeneutic turn: Soft, science or loyal opposition? *Psychoanalytic Dialogues,* 3(1), 1–11.

Spiegel, D., & Cardena, E. (1991). Disintegrated experience: the dissociative disorders revisited. *Journal of Abnormal Psychology,* 100 (3), 366–378.

Terr, L. (1988). What happens to the early memories of trauma? A study of twenty children under age five at the time of documented traumatic events. *American Journal of Child and Adolescent Psychiatry,* 27 96–104.

Terr, L. (1989). Treating psychic trauma in children: A preliminary discussion. *Journal of Traumatic Stress,* 2(1), 3–20.

Terr, L. (1991). Childhood traumas: An outline and overview. *American Journal of Psychiatry,* 148(1), 10–20.

van der kolk, B. A. (1984). *Post-traumatic stress disorder: Psychological and biological sequelae.* Washington, DC: American Psychiatric Press.

van der Kolk, B. A. (1987). *Psychological trauma.* Washington, DC: American Psychiatric Press.

van der Kolk, B. A. (1988). The trauma spectrum: The interaction of biological and social events in the genesis of the trauma response. *Journal of Traumatic Stress,* 1, 273–290.

van der Kolk, B. A., & van der Hart, O. (1991). The intrusive past: The flexibility of memory and the engraving of trauma. *American Image,* 48, 425–454.

Waltz, J. (1994, November). Treatment and memory recall. In L. Berliner (Chair), *Delayed trauma memories: Victim experiences and clinical practice.* Symposium conducted at the annual meeting of the International Society for Traumatic Stress Studies, Chicago, IL.

Wilson, J. P., & Raphael, B. (Eds.). (1993). *International handbook of traumatic stress syndromes.* New York: Plenum.

Yapko, M. D. (1994). Suggestibility and repressed memories of abuse: A survey of psychotherapists' beliefs. *American Journal of Clinical Hypnosis, 36*(3), 163–171.

Yuille, J. C., & Cutshall, J. L. (1986). A case study of eyewitness memory of a crime. *Journal of Applied Psychology, 71*(2), 291–301.

# On the Construction of Truth and Falsity:
# Whose Memory, Whose History

LAURA S. BROWN

*Independent Practice, Seattle, WA, and Department of Psychology, University of Washington*

This chapter addresses the general as well as professional politics that underlie the current debate on memories for childhood abuse. Two levels of the debate are defined. The first level is that of science as commonly understood in the cognitive and behavioral sciences. The second level of the debate addresses the issue of who owns and defines the history of family and childhood experience. Starting from the notion that "history is written by the winners," this chapter explores the questions of what it would mean to win this debate and how "winning" writes or rewrites the historical narrative of our culture. I argue that an examination of the texts generated by this debate, using a sociology of knowledge analysis, reveals that the control over history is at least as important as the scientific realities. Implications of this formulation of the problem for the future directions of both science and practice are discussed.

## INTRODUCTION

When the debate over the reality of recovered memories first began to rage at my door in 1992, I found myself going back to the words of the Israeli essayist and politician, Yael Dayan. "Memory is not history," she wrote. Three years into this debate, with little more certain and much more strife in the interval, I find these words to be more compelling than ever. For it seems that this debate has two levels, both of which are worthy of our attention as psychologists, be we non-clinical researchers, non-research clinicians, or some hybrid of both. The first level is that of science; what do we know, how do we know it, can we test our hypotheses, verify or falsify them, or generalize our findings beyond the confines of an experiment? This is the level of the debate most directly addressed by the writings in this collection that report investigations into how children remember. The second level of the debate, one only implied but equally compelling to me, has to do with who owns and defines the history of childhood and families. The cliché is that "history is written by the winners." What would it mean to win this debate? How does such "winning" write or rewrite the historical narrative of our culture? In examining the texts generated by both the recovery movement and the false memory movement, it is apparent to me that the control over history is at least as important, if not more so, than the scientific realities. Consequently, in my comments here, I will attempt to respond both to the science that the researchers have generated and to the question of historical narrative and the direction that this consideration takes us in the future. My perspective reflects the questioning inherent in our sociology of knowledge and the larger discourse regarding control and ascription of authority.

*The Recovered Memory/False Memory Debate*

## WHAT DOES SCIENCE SAY?

First, what does the research reported here tell me? I am a clinician who works with adult survivors of a variety of forms of trauma, ranging from combat to childhood physical and sexual abuse. In that capacity, I have been the witness to countless experiences of individuals who believed that they were gaining access to memories of painful events that had previously been unavailable to them consciously. As a psychologist trained in the scientist-practitioner tradition, I found myself intrigued by and curious about what I was observing. I was also, especially at first, skeptical of what I saw and heard. I can recall speaking with a colleague, late in the 1970s, about what I was observing, and commenting that I found it hard to credit that a trauma could be forgotten. But clients often uncovered corroboration—diary entries from childhood, the reports of friends and relatives, photos and tapes sent home from Viet Nam, all kinds of materials that led me to a stance that much of what I saw and heard had its basis in reality. This growing body of clinical observation was bolstered by what I heard from colleagues and read in the scholarly literature—that as we began to ask questions about the possibility of violence in peoples' lives and to admit our willingness to hear such stories, it then became possible for people to know and speak about what they had previously not known or appeared to forget.

However, I remained curious about how and why this could happen. Another interesting piece of data about why there was so little information available to answer my questions emerged at a social gathering in the early 1990s consisting of approximately 20 therapists and one well-known memory researcher. Our hostess had been the treating therapist of the woman who had fought for the change in Washington State law to allow delayed discovery lawsuits for people who, like this client, came to knowledge of their abuse only as adults, through delayed recall. The therapists present, myself among them, asked the memory researcher why she did not study this thing we were seeing in our therapy offices. We, the therapists, wanted to comprehend this phenomenon, and were disappointed that our researcher colleague seemed to be able to shed little light on the matter. It seemed as if the scientists of memory had not been very interested in the strange things that happened to the memories of people who had been traumatized. The data necessary to answer my question were, it seemed, simply not there.

Consequently, the research described in this volume was a valuable addition to my continued search for understanding of the science surrounding the experience of delayed recall of trauma. I found my review of these articles both informative and frustrating. The informative aspect arises in part from the sheer volume and inventiveness of the attempts made by these researchers to understand how children can remember, forget, and be misled in their memories. I was also informed by the immense degree of variability in the theories proposed for what has been found, as well as by the different emphases and interpretations used in discussing sometimes identical sorts of findings. There does not appear to be a convergence of thought, but rather differently developing schools, each attending with different degrees of emphasis to sometimes quite separate sets of underlying knowledge claims. The more that is known about memory, the more possible explanations appear to emerge for its vagaries; are we seeing an information-processing phenomenon, a social/interpersonal one, or an expression of the development of self?

As an example of this dynamic tension among theories, Tessler and Nelson (this volume) argue strongly for the notion that self and memory cannot be disconnected, that the two are jointly socially constructed within the social and interpersonal matrix of the child's emotional environment. Howe, Courage, and Peterson (this volume) rebut this argument, urging us to see "self" as primary, and the capacity to construct an autobiographical memory narrative arising only after there exists a self about whom to tell the story. Clearly, as might be true in any field of scientific endeavor that is relatively young, no one clear picture has emerged; no "truth" is known or can be assumed as self-evident. This is reassuring and confusing at the same time. No one can say what "the memory research" tells us without referring to the differences in this discourse; but the science currently available does not appear to offer any certain explanations, only ways for us to ask the next set of questions.

Not surprisingly, the one constant is that for children as well as for adults memory can and does vary in degree of accuracy. Children's memories for all kinds of events, from banal to painful, can be distorted by adult intervention *some of the time,* in *some social/emotional contexts,* with *some* types of misleading suggestions. But *sometimes,* it would appear, that almost nothing and no one will induce a child to recall that which never happened. At other times, children appear to be relatively easily persuaded of the reality of non-events. In some instances, strong affect appears to be an asset to the process of retention and recall. In other circumstances, it does not. Children are not a unitary phenomenon, even with age held constant; the child/social/familial context matrix may be as or more important in how and what is recalled, and what can be distorted, than any other factors in the memory equation.

In fact, the variability in the nature of findings across research groups has led to another set of questions for me as a reader. The presence of confirmatory bias in research is a question little raised, but relevant in this context. It appears that those researchers (e.g., Ceci and his colleagues, Loftus and her colleagues) who are most firmly convinced of the malleability of memory achieve results that support their findings. Other researchers, apparently less convinced of this proposition (e.g., Pezdek and her colleagues, Goodman and her colleagues) achieve findings that are more tentative and equivocal. To what degree are we observing a Rosenthal effect at work on the research process? Scientists who are more certain of the power of suggestion seem also to be more willing to generalize from their findings regarding the suggestibility of children to the possible suggestibility of adults as regards the creation of fabricated "recollections" of childhood sexual abuse (Ceci, Huffman, Smith, & Loftus, this volume), whereas those who find suggestion less compelling as a source of distortion also seem less convinced that there are clear parallels between suggestibility of children in a laboratory setting and that of adult psychotherapy clients.

But what, if anything, does this research tell me and other clinicians working with adults who allege that they recall being abused sexually, physically, emotionally, even ritually as children about the possible accuracy of those recollections? To what degree do these studies of children's memory possess sufficient ecological validity to allow for the sort of conclusions made in the article by Ceci et al. (This volume) that the research on childhood memory and its suggestibility casts important doubt on adult reports of recovery of memories of such childhood abuse, implying that most of these reports represent confabulations induced by therapists, reading of self-help books, and watching the likes of Oprah?

My answer—not very much. That is, the relationship between children who are suggestible when purposely misled and adults' suggestibility in response to therapeutic inquiries into the possible presence of sexual abuse appears strikingly unclear. The phenomena that can affect how well a child recalls an event give us insufficient information with which to assess the credibility of *adult* reports of delayed recall, aside from setting the boundary conditions for the age at which autobiographical memory commences (although even that, on close reading, appears to be still in dispute). The proposition that the one sort of suggestion is equivalent to the other, that reading in a book that "if you believe you were abused you probably were" carries the same meaning to an adult as is conveyed by a child being told by an adult "remember the time you got your finger caught in a mousetrap" seems to beg credulity, much less any clear empirical or theoretical underpinnings. As a number of these authors note to their credit, even recent research on attempts to implant confabulated memories of childhood (Hyman, Husband, & Billings, 1995; Loftus & Coan, in press) suffers from this sort of problem, inhibiting generalizability. As Pezdek and Roe note in this volume, it is a good deal easier to believe your older brother when he tells you that you were lost in the mall, because, after all, he was probably there, and being lost while out shopping with one's parents is an extremely common event in the life of the post-World War II North American, than it is to believe a therapist, no matter how powerful, who is insisting that you were sexually abused by a beloved family member.

In contrast, the therapist can never assert having witnessed the event; and in my experience observing people who are dealing with the question of whether they were abused, most people would rather consider themselves utterly insane than to believe that their father/grandfather/favorite priest sexually assaulted them, even when subsequent corroborating evidence is incontrovertible, for example, uncoerced confessions by a perpetrator or the presence of co-victims (Fitzpatrick, 1994). Further, the results of Pezdek (1995) indicate that it is quite difficult to suggest to people that something unusual and shameful (in her study, receiving a rectal enema as a child) happened to them, even when the person doing the suggesting alleges that they were present and observed the suggested event.

I have no doubt that it is possible, given the necessary conditions, for the implantation of a pseudomemory, or more likely, the *belief* in a pseudo-event as a memory, to occur in the context of therapy, because I have also observed this phenomenon. In my role as a forensic psychologist, I testified in 1988 in a case of psychotherapeutic malpractice in which such false beliefs were temporarily induced in a patient by an out-of-control therapist. This case was full of complexities; a client with a possible underlying and untreated psychotic disorder, group chanting sessions in which the therapist repeatedly recited lurid tales of ritualized abuse, sexual contact between therapist and client, and a cultlike atmosphere surrounding the entire treatment process. The research reported here does little to illuminate the question of how this creation of pseudobeliefs might have happened, which is an aspect of my frustration with these findings. The complexities of the therapy situation in which suggestions of abuse can take hold—for instance, varying levels of client suggestibility (see D. Brown, 1995, for a discussion of this issue), varying degrees of therapist suggestiveness, the presence or absence of peer pressure, the underlying psychopathology of the client, the client's own belief systems about what is possible in the world—are not well addressed by the research reported here. There are some hints about which children remember their painful experiences best and which children are more likely to report the pseudomemory suggested by the researcher, but this does not shed enough light on the clinical reality of what happens when therapeutic malpractice does take place.

We also know very little from these findings about the people who actively resist suggestions by a therapist. In a second case in which I served as a forensic expert, for example, a powerful therapist made repeated suggestions to his client that she had been sexually abused by her father. Although she gave in to many of his other suggestions (specifically, that she participate in sexual contact with the therapist as a condition of her recovery), she resisted this suggestion no matter how often it was made, and no matter how much that resistance was interpreted by the therapist as a sign of illness. This case also involved large group experiences, cultlike involvement between the therapist and various clients, and some underlying client psychopathology. Why did this woman resist suggestion and the first woman succumb?

This complexity raises questions about the findings reported by Lindsay (this volume; see also Poole, Lindsay, Menon, & Bull, 1995) regarding possible risky "memory work" procedures used by therapists. Lindsay argues that his findings regarding therapists' willingness to endorse the use of certain procedures that may be suggestive and their apparent ignorance about the suggestive potential of those procedures imply that the risk of creation of pseudomemories of childhood sexual abuse is quite high. Lindsay, however, argues from one position on the spectrum of understanding memory and suggestibility, and fails, in my opinion, to take into account the complex variables that I have previously described. He also assumes that what is created in those instances is a pseudo*memory,* an assertion for which we have no empirical evidence, rather than a false belief. But Lindsay does not ask other, equally important questions, such as what appears helpful to clients in the reduction of symptoms? in the containment of distress? and to what degree do manifestly helpful therapeutic strategies overlap with his categories of suggestive and risky ones? And are there some clients for whom all the suggestive techniques in the world will make no difference, whereas there are others who, no matter how hard the therapist strives to be

neutral, will experience suggestion? Bibliotherapy, for example, has been a modality suggested for the empowerment of clients for many years, with the notion
that offering clients written information might dilute the power of the therapist.
Yet one such reader (Butler, 1994) alleged that simply by reading one popular
self-help book about childhood sexual abuse she was induced to have an entire
complex network of "memories" of a history of abuse that she later believed to
be false. The question in this instance is not simply, can reading *The Courage
to Heal*'s noninfamous statement that "if you believe you were abused, you
were" induce beliefs in a nonexistent history of abuse, but also, who is likely to
believe such an assertion when the currently available data (Pezdek, in press)
suggest that this is a very difficult sort of false memory to implant?

Writing on the topic of therapy with people who report delayed recall of
trauma, Pope and myself (Pope & Brown, in press) have argued that a major
premise underlying the possibility of our comprehension of this phenomenon is
that the issues in this area are not well addressed by attempts to choose between
clinical and scientific approaches, or between the artificially created categories
of "true" and "false" memories of trauma. In our extensive review of both scientific and clinical literature, we were able to find no convincing evidence that a
forced-choice dichotomy is accurate or that it necessarily leads to more valid
and useful conclusions. We have also argued that science and practice in this
area must not proceed in ignorance of each other but must adequately inform
one another if either is to claim intellectual integrity; neither can be considered
without the other, or as being more important than the other. This resonates
with Schooler's (this volume) conclusion that at present, we are not in a position
to engage in this sort of description of other people's realities as completely true
or false. Daniel Brown (1995) has suggested that although many clinicians have
little familiarity with research on memory, few researchers in the field of memory are familiar with the parameters of trauma or with what happens in psychotherapy. His comment appears to be born out by some of the discussions ap-
pended to the research findings in this book.

## FUTURE DIRECTIONS FOR INTERPRETING THE HISTORICAL NARRATIVE

This research does open some other doors by suggesting models for understanding how memories of repeated interpersonal victimization in childhood are
lost, in whole or in part, to conscious cognitive recall. We know, from the many
life stories of survivors of such abuse, that directions from the perpetrator about
remembering or forgetting the event are not uncommon. How do these attempts
to distort memory at the time of the event affect later recall? Many persons who
have always had some recollection of their abuse experience have a fragmentary
or incomplete picture of what has happened to them (Briere, 1989; Courtois,
1988; Harvey, in press; Harvey & Herman, this volume); an implication of some
of the studies reported here is that certain interpersonal conditions inherent in
childhood sexual abuse (e.g., isolation, secrecy, absence of opportunity to discuss the experience) are parallel to those shown in some of these studies to
affect the quality of children's remembering (Fivush, this volume; Goodman,

Quas, Batterman-Faunce, Riddlesberger, & Kuhn, this volume; Tessler & Nelson, this volume).

We also know that some of the factors that Goodman et al. indicate may affect quality of recall of a painful event are also factors in the lives of some sexually abused children. If Dad is sexually abusing you and Mom is drunk, depressed, distant, or otherwise unavailable, what does this mean for the quality and reliability of recall? Could a faint memory trace be retained under these circumstances that is then enhanced sufficiently to lead to a long-delayed reporting of an event under the changed conditions of adult life? It may be the case that a change in an amnestic survivor's social milieu may create the sort of boundary conditions for memory retrieval that Goodman's research suggests are important.

This hypothesis is supported by extensive clinical case reports. Many people who have experience delayed recall describe how the recall process appeared to be triggered by otherwise unrelated life circumstances. These were events that changed the meaning of the social environment either to one of greater safety, or to one of renewed conditions of danger. The findings presented here provide hints about the directions that future researchers might take in the study of currently sexually abused children; that is, to what degree do perpetrators of childhood sexual abuse account, through their instructions, manipulations, and intentional attempts to distort, for some or all of the difficulties with memory retrieval experienced by some adult survivors? To what degree does the social context surrounding sexual or other kinds of childhood abuse affect later memories of those events? These notions are, for the clinician who has watched hundreds of memories emerge unasked and unsought, tantalizing and deserving of further study. Jennifer Freyd's model (1995, in press) of Betrayal Trauma begins to blend the findings of cognitive memory research with a clear recognition of the actual parameters of childhood abuse. This model provides us with a paradigm of how such research might be directed by explicitly attending to the interaction of social cognitions, evolutionary considerations, and the capacity to retain, know, and recall the experience of sexual abuse by a caregiver.

A final consideration for research echoes the comments of Harvey and Herman (this volume) regarding the necessity for researchers and commentators in the field of adult recovered memory to pay closer attention to what actually occurs in therapy with the population of adult trauma survivors. Much of the current public thrashing of therapists (Ofshe & Watters, 1993) has been based largely on reference to self-help books or to reports made by third parties who were never present at the scene of the alleged suggestive psychotherapy. As scientists or scientist/practitioners, we should be careful about giving any credence to "scholarly" materials that rely solely or primarily on analyses of popular press sources or on the accounts of third parties, in this case almost always an accused parent with a clear investment in how therapy is portrayed. In fact, we have no direct empirical studies of what happens in therapy; oddly, researchers such as Lindsay (this volume) seem content to rely on the memories and metamemories of therapists about what was done in treatment and never question how reliable those accounts might be.

That sort of careful attention to what does happen in therapy, relying on direct observation (rather than on reports of angered third parties such as accused caregivers), would in many instances reveal precisely that which is stated by Harvey and Herman. Therapy with survivors does *not* commonly consist of an archeological expedition in search of the Holy Grail of memory. The available documentation on the experience of remembering sexual abuse indicates that memories of childhood abuse, whether always present or delayed, are experienced by most people as intrusive. When they emerge, no matter how long their absence, they are frequently overpowering, painful, and the target of avoidance attempts that range from compulsive consumption to self-harm and even suicide (Briere, 1989; Courtois, 1988; Kluft, 1990). The ethical and competent therapist is too focused on aiding containment and self-care for their clients to be especially interested in trolling for that which will only make life more frightening. That same therapist would be vastly aided in working with her or his clients were the research on memory of childhood trauma to give us better answers that would help us and our clients to understand the how and why of their powerful, painful subjective experience. At this point in the development of our science, it would appear that we still do not have the answers to the questions that my therapist colleagues and I offered to our researcher colleague at that seemingly long-ago party: what accounts for the phenomenon of delayed recall of trauma? and how can we know what is real and what is not?

## OWNERSHIP OF HISTORY AND THE POLITICS OF MEMORY

But even were the science as complete and definite as we might wish, or even if it were possible for us to understand the biological, social, and psychological factors that might lead a person to "un-know" a traumatic experience then later know of it inescapably, we would still be faced with the question of history and its meanings. What happens if one or another version of reality about delayed recall of childhood sexual abuse "wins" in the public discourse?

As Herman has noted (1992), the study and recognition of trauma, even very public trauma, is an inherently political act. To call an experience traumatic gives it a particular meaning. To deny an experience, or to minimize its frequency while admitting to its reality, is also political. To define a trauma as occurring primarily within certain segments of a society is also a political act.

An interesting example can be found in the treatment of Vietnam-related combat trauma. In the mid-1970s, when I interned in the Veteran's Administration system, it was still forbidden to identify service in Vietnam as traumatic; therefore, the veterans who had been traumatized there and who developed post-traumatic psychological problems had their trauma denied and were diagnosed as having underlying pathologies. In large part because of the political work of mental health professionals who had served in Vietnam, and who knew that such service was potentially traumatic, the picture has reversed 180 degrees in two decades. In the process, the hidden trauma survivors of earlier wars are being uncovered and treated; as we are coming to understand that even service in a "good war" can be traumatic. The redefinition of combat service, no matter how popular the war, as a possible traumatic stressor for any combatant, has both emerged from a changed social discourse (in which war *per se* is no longer necessarily seen as a positive or heroic thing) and has itself changed the social discourse.

The topic of childhood sexual abuse is more radioactively charged than war might ever be. Masson (1984) notes that the reality of abuse of children, both physical and sexual, has emerged repeatedly into the consciousness of Western cultures, and just as repeatedly has been thrust back into the depths of unknowing. Thus, one common discourse on childhood sexual abuse has been that it is taboo and therefore does not occur (at which point I am reminded of the Hebrew school teacher who commented, as our class of adolescents giggled its way through the sexual restrictions of the Leviticus holiness code, that the reason that so many things are forbidden in Jewish law is that human beings have been known to do all of them). Or the discourse is constructed so as to locate the problem outside of the family. This is the familiar "stranger-danger" image of the child molester lurking in the bushes or attempting to lure children into his car with offerings of sweets. A variation of this theme is to admit that sexual abuse of children can happen in families—but only in certain kinds of families. Commonly, this is either implicitly or explicitly defined as families who are marginal to the culture: families of color, poor families, immigrant families, the "Other."

This aspect of the discourse that "incest happens, but not in *our* lovely family" can be seen in its purest form in the writings of the False Memory Syndrome Foundation (FMSF). In their earliest newsletters, this organization emphasized how utterly middle-class and "normal" their members, people accused of sexual abuse and the spouses of the accused, are. Research was conducted to demonstrate that these were families that ate together, took vacations together, had highly educated parents, and went to church or synagogue. One description extolled the attractiveness and vigor of FMSF members. The message here was implicit: "nice" families, "good" families are not families where sexual abuse of children occurs; thus, the allegations made by the adult offspring of these attractive people must be false. Ironically, what little study has been made of the comparative validity of childhood memories finds that parents, not their adult offspring, tend to distort; and that those distortions are in the direction of a more positive picture than warranted by external data sources, which tend to refute parental recall and corroborate that of the remembering adult (Brewin, Andrews, & Gotlib, 1993).

In the past two decades, an attempt has been made to rewrite this discourse regarding the sexual abuse of children; in effect, to take the political step of changing history, both personal and societal. Second-wave North American feminisms began to create the forum for victims of violence and betrayal in families and in intimate relationships to tell their stories and to make it known that for many people, even white, middle-class people, family was not only unhappy, it was also dangerous. When, in 1978, Sandra Butler's *Conspiracy of Silence* and

Louise Armstrong's *Kiss Daddy Goodnight* appeared with their first-person accounts of incest across the spectrum of families, the process of rewriting the history of the family was set into motion.

As feminist family therapist Deborah Luepnitz later observed (1988), the North American family, viewed through a feminist lens, is rarely a safe place for children, no matter how middle-class, mainstream, or conventional. The uncovering of incest by feminist activists and therapists fueled this argument, as it called for change in the structure of families toward greater equity of a sort theorized to reduce the risk of harm to those in the family.

It is not surprising that some of the anger of FMSF writers has fallen on feminists and feminism (P. Freyd, 1993, 1994; Underwager & Wakefield, 1994). Their concerns are, at a deep level, accurate. Feminist analysis is in fact attempting to rewrite history, the general history of the family, the classist and racist narratives of the North American family, and the history of sexual abuse in the family in particular. The willingness of feminists in the mental health professions and behavioral sciences to identify incest as a source of distress and as an aspect of cultural oppressive norms in families has clearly played a central role in punctuating incest as a common problem.

The appeals to "science" issued by FMSF, and the gathering about themselves of an advisory board that includes many eminent researchers, appear to be another attempt to undo rewriting; in this case, the analyses of sociologists and philosophers of science who argue against the wholesale hegemony of logical positivist epistemologies (Bleier, 1988; Harding, 1986; Keller, 1985) and who, interestingly, find scientific psychology to be one of the last bastions of this epistemic method, even when contrasted with the physical sciences. FMSF contrasts "science," which is supposed to be pure and objective, with the allegedly biased views of feminists, identified as the only participants in the discourse to hold a political agenda. It then argues that science tells us that repressed memory is a myth and scientifically unsupportable.

Ironically, as a review of the science reported in this volume indicates, there is no infallible thing called "science of memory" that speaks with one voice to the question of whether and how recall of childhood sexual abuse can be delayed or false beliefs implanted. Science seems to tell us that there is not enough that we know yet about what might lead to what we observe clinically; science, truly, is keeping its mind and its bets open. Yet the statements of FMSF board members (Dawes, 1994; Loftus & Ketcham, 1994; Ofshe & Watters, 1993) would, if taken at face value, lead to the conclusion that there is a unified voice of the "science of memory," and that attempts to "rewrite history" by using any other source of information about delayed recall of childhood abuse represent cultlike "True Believer" behaviors (Loftus & Ketcham, 1994) that endanger the well-being of, as it turns out, families. The privileging of the well-being of the family over the well-being of an adult who remembers sexual abuse and those who support her or him in that process is, as it emerges, a consistent theme of much of the writing of the FMSF and its most prolific board members.

There is also a politic about the value or danger of psychotherapy expressed in this debate. As a therapist with her own serious reservations about this profession (L. S. Brown, 1994) who has spent her career working to stop abusive psychotherapies and to develop therapeutic methodologies that reduce power imbalances between client and therapist, I find myself resonating to calls for an end to potentially suggestive or coercive psychotherapeutic practices. Yet again, there is a subtext in the discourse that I find chilling. In this case, the metamessage is that "safe" and "good" therapy is not conducted by those therapists who are young, female, or themselves survivors of childhood sexual abuse, and certainly not by those with an erstwhile political agenda such as feminist therapists. As the available data on dangerous therapy is that it is overwhelmingly conducted by older, traditionally trained male practitioners (see Pope, 1994, for a review of this literature), what is the meaning of finding this group of more risky therapists being asserted in the current discourse as the safest practitioners?

I would argue, consequently, that the debate over memory for childhood abuse and the possibility of the creation of pseudomemories in psychotherapy is as much about politics as it ever will be about science. The politic is that of how we write the experience of children in families, as well as what kinds of data behavioral scientists and mental health professionals will admit to our discourses as valid sources of information, over what shall constitute our cultural and professional "history." It would appear that the stakes for winning or losing control over our collective histories are very high, to judge by the intensity of the debate and the ad hominem turn that it takes in newsletters, conferences, and email discussions.

Thus, in closing, I would encourage the researchers among us to be aware of the influence on their work of the politics of the discourse, as it is abundantly clear that clinicians have already done so (Enns, McNeilly, Corkery, & Gilbert, 1994; Herman, 1992; Harvey & Herman, this volume). How a question is asked, what questions are asked, how variables are defined, how results are interpreted, and even how the abstract is written are not simply scientific decisions. They represent a politic regarding science, mental health practice, and, ultimately, the social construction of the family in North American cultures. As an example, it is a political choice to interpolate into a study of how children might develop pseudomemories, a discussion of whether sexual abuse is always traumatic to children (Ceci, Huffman, Smith, & Loftus, this volume; Ornstein, Ceci, & Loftus, in press). This is not, as some would argue, simply an empirical inquiry; rather, it writes an entirely political subtext regarding the negative consequences of sexual abuse that could be used to support the argument that sexual abuse by a family member is potentially inconsequential and thus not a reason for, as an example, denying custody to the perpetrator of the abuse (Gardner, 1993).

Most importantly, however, it continues to be necessary to carry on the search for understanding what is being observed and what has for many years been seen in thousands of therapy offices: the adult struggling with emergent, fragmentary, overpowering, dissociated images of sexual abuse in childhood. If we comprehend this phenomenon, we will also comprehend other things about the workings of our minds in response to complex events that carry multiple meanings. If such study helps us to comprehend more precisely the abuses and exploitation of power in psychotherapy so that we can incorporate that knowledge into what is already known and make this process even safer and more effective, it will have added value. The bumblebee, whose flight was once deemed scientifically impossible, flew for millennia before the mechanisms of its flight were scientifically comprehended. So too does delayed recall of trauma deserve our further study, because (or perhaps especially) to illumine it and finally have clear scientific comprehension of its underlying mechanisms will lead to further challenges to our mythologies of happy families and childhoods, and to better comprehension of the workings of memory and the mind.

## REFERENCES

Armstrong, L. (1978). *Kiss daddy goodnight: A speakout on incest*. New York: Pocket Books.

Bleier, R. (1988). A decade of feminist critiques in the natural sciences. *Signs: Journal of Women in Culture and Society, 14,* 186–195.

Brewin, C. R., Andrews, B., & Gotlib, I. A. (1993). Psychopathology and early experience: A reappraisal of retrospective reports. *Psychological Bulletin, 113,* 82–98.

Briere, J. (1989). *Therapy for adults molested as children*. New York: Springer.

Brown, D. (1995). Pseudomemories: The standard of science and the standard of care in trauma treatment. *American Journal of Clinical Hypnosis, 37,* 1–24.

Brown, L. S. (1994). *Subversive dialogues: Theory in feminist therapy*. New York: Basic Books.

Butler, K. (1994). Caught in the cross-fire. *Family Therapy Networker, 19,* 24–34.

Butler, S. (1978). *Conspiracy of silence: The trauma of incest*. San Francisco: New Glide Publications.

Courtois, C. (1988). *Healing the incest wound: Adults survivors in therapy*. New York: W. W. Norton.

Dawes, R. M. (1994). *House of cards: Psychology and psychotherapy built on myth*. New York: Free Press.

Enns, C. Z., McNeilly, C., Corkery, J., & Gilbert, M. (1994). The debate about delayed memories of child sexual abuse: A feminist perspective. *The Counseling Psychologist, 23,* 181–279.

Fitzpatrick, F. (1994). Isolation and silence: A male survivor speaks out about clergy abuse. *Moving Forward, 3,* 4–8.

Freyd, J. (1995). Betrayal-trauma; Traumatic amnesia as an adaptive response to childhood abuse. *Ethics and Behavior, 4,* 307–329.

Freyd, J. (in press). *Betrayal trauma theory*. Harvard University Press.

Freyd, P. (1993). Editorial. *FMS Foundation Newsletter, 2*(7), 1–3.

Freyd, P. (1994). Editorial. *FMS Foundation Newsletter, 3*(6), 1–3.

Gardner, R. A. (1993). A theory about the variety of human sexual behavior. *Issues in Child Abuse Accusations, 5,* 105.

Harding, S. (1986). The instability of analytical categories of feminist theory. *Signs: Journal of Women in Culture and Society, 11,* 645–664.

Harvey, M. R. (in press). An ecological view of psychological trauma and trauma recovery. *Journal of Traumatic Stress*.

Herman, J. L. (1992). *Trauma and recovery*. New York: Basic Books.

Hyman, I. E., Jr., Husband, T. H., & Billings, F. J. (1995). False memories of childhood experiences. *Applied Cognitive Psychology, 9,* 181–197.

Keller, E. F. (1985). *Reflections on gender and science*. New Haven: Yale University Press.

Kluft, R. (Ed.). (1990). *Incest-related syndromes of adult psychopathology*. Washington, DC: American Psychiatric Press.

Loftus, E. F., & Coan, D. (in press). The construction of childhood memories. In D. Peters (Ed.), *The child witness in context: Cognitive, social, and legal perspectives*. New York: Kluwer.

Loftus, E. F., & Ketcham, K. (1994). *The myth of repressed memory*. New York: St. Martins Press.

Luepnitz, D. A. (1988). *The family interpreted*. New York: Basic Books.

Masson, J. M. (1984). *The assault on truth: Freud's suppression of the seduction theory*. New York: Farrar, Straus, & Giroux.

Ofshe, R., & Watters, E. (1993). Making monsters. *Society, 30,* 4–16.

Ornstein, P. A., Ceci, S. H. & Loftus, E. F. (in press). The science of memory and the practice of psychotherapy. In J. Alpert, L. S. Brown, S. J. Ceci, C. A. Courtois, E. F. Loftus, & P. A. Ornstein, *Final report of the working group on investigation of memories of childhood abuse*. Washington, DC: American Psychological Association.

Pezdek, K. (1995, November). What types of false childhood memories are not likely to be suggestively implanted. Paper presented at the meeting of the Psychonomic Society, Los Angeles.

Poole, D. A., Lindsay, D. S., Memom, A., & Bull, R. (1995). Psychotherapy and the recovery of memories of childhood sexual abuse: U.S. and British practitioners' opinions, practices and experiences. *Journal of Consulting and Clinical Psychology, 63,* 426–437.

Pope, K. S. (1994). *Sexual involvement with therapists: Patient assessment, subsequent therapy, forensics*. Washington, DC: American Psychological Association.

Pope, K. S., & Brown, L. S. (in press). *Recovered Memories of Abuse: Assessment, therapy, forensics*. Washington, DC: American Psychological Association.

Underwager, R., & Wakefield, H. (1994). *Return of the furies: An investigation into recovered memory therapy*. Chicago: Open Court.

# Informed Clinical Practice and the Delayed Memory Controversy

CHRISTINE A. COURTOIS

*Psychologist, Private Practice*
*Clinical Director*
*THE CENTER: Post-Traumatic and Dissociative Disorder Program*
*Psychiatric Institute of Washington, Washington, DC*

Therapists face many difficult challenges in treating patients who disclose a history of abuse, especially if the disclosure involves memories that were absent for a period of time and then return. A major controversy has erupted concerning the validity of previously repressed memories for past abuse. Therapists have been criticized for believing that these memories accurately represent real events and for using techniques that are overly suggestive of an abuse history. Whether the criticisms are founded or not, they have changed the practice environment quite significantly. To practice responsibly and to attend to risk management issues, therapists must be informed about the parameters of the controversy, must be knowledgeable about both human memory processes and traumatic stress response, and must stay abreast of the newly emerging research on both topics. They must incorporate this information into clinical practice and develop a standard of care for the treatment of this population. This chapter provides an overview of recent developments in the treatment of adults reporting childhood abuse and offers general guidelines for informed practice.

## INTRODUCTION

The contemporary study of incest and other forms of child sexual abuse began in the mid-1970s. Researchers investigated prevalence and occurrence patterns as well as initial and long-term aftereffects (Browne & Finkelhor, 1986; Burgess, Groth, Holmstrom, & Sgroi, 1978; Finkelhor, 1979, 1984; Herman, 1981; Meiselman, 1978; Russell, 1983, 1986). The aggregate data identified sexual abuse as a serious interpersonal stressor with high potential to traumatize the victim both at the time of its occurrence and across the life span. These research findings spurred the development of new treatment methods for abused children and formerly abused adults that emphasized the abuse as an important, although not exclusive focus of treatment (Briere, 1989; Courtois, 1988; Friedrich, 1990; James, 1989; McCann & Pearlman, 1990; Sgroi, 1982). This perspective was in marked contrast to other therapeutic orientations that dismissed or minimized reports of abuse (whether by children or by adults) as either unimportant or as wishes or fantasies on the part of the child (Rush, 1980).

Over the past decade, as a result of new social awareness and discourse about sexual abuse, ever increasing numbers of adults reporting a past history of abuse have sought therapy for its effects. Some of these individuals reported continuous and intact memory for the abuse (whether they had previously disclosed it or not), whereas others reported variable memory accessibility over the years. Still others reported the emergence of memories of abuse after years of no previ-

*The Recovered Memory/False Memory Debate*
Copyright © 1996 by Academic Press, Inc.
All rights of reproduction in any form reserved.

ous awareness, sometimes in the course of therapy (Briere, 1989; Courtois, 1988; McCann & Pearlman, 1990). Delayed or even repressed memory for abuse was understood by many therapists to be caused by the dynamics of shame, secrecy, and silencing surrounding abuse and to be consistent with the amnesia patterns found in post-traumatic conditions. Delayed reporting in therapy was also believed to be consistent with much of what happens in the course of psychotherapy as patients engage in analysis of conscious and unconscious emotional material and as they struggle with issues of shame that often limit disclosure.

In recent years, a major controversy has developed concerning delayed and/ or repressed memories of sexual abuse especially in those cases in which memory was previously absent, the abuse was identified in the course of ongoing therapy, and the therapy involved the use of techniques deemed to be suggestive. Critics (many of whom are academics who specialize in the study of human memory, along with some clinicians, and parents who allege that they have been falsely accused of abuse) have charged that some therapists are naive and uninformed about the operation of memory and have used techniques (wittingly or unwittingly) that run the risk of creating or implanting false memories of abuse in suggestible clients who enter therapy for other life difficulties. They have also charged that some therapists have a simplistic understanding of sexual abuse and its consequences, have been overzealous in seeking out or suggesting abuse as the cause of their patients' difficulties, and have too readily accepted narrative accounts as historical reality (Lindsay & Read, 1994; Loftus, 1993; Loftus & Ketchum, 1994; Yapko, 1993).

No doubt, some of the points made by the critics are valid. It is likely that some therapists have practiced substandard therapy, have exceeded the available knowledge base in their work, have used techniques that have an unacceptable degree of risk, or have misconstrued narrative accounts as historical truth. Although these issues may be in evidence in professionally trained therapists, they are confounded by the fact that many untrained and unlicensed individuals legally call themselves therapists and provide a variety of services and practices. Some claim to specialize in treatment for sexual abuse aftereffects and there is reason to believe that some of the difficulties described by the critics are the result of their problematic practice conducted without adequate training or oversight.

It is also clear, however, that some of the critiques are overstated and have been discrediting to the work of well-trained and ethical therapists and the legitimacy of real abuse victims, especially those who have not retained continuous memory. Some have been challenged as exaggerated and inaccurate, extending well beyond the available data (D. Brown, 1995), and as polemic rather than constructive and collaborative (Courtois, 1995a, 1995b). One major line of rebuttal has been with ecological validity: To what degree is memory research undertaken in a laboratory setting on nontraumatized subjects applicable to traumatized individuals? Is memory for traumatic experiences somehow different from memory for less emotional events? Have memory researchers incorporated the available data on memory in traumatized individuals into their formulations about memory? (Alpert, Brown, & Courtois, 1996). Additionally, can nonclinicians fairly assess and critique psychotherapeutic practice or should they restrict themselves to making recommendations about factors that increase or lower the risk of suggestion or distortion?

Memory researchers and therapists come from two very different professional traditions and orientations. Memory researchers (experimental/cognitive psychologists, by and large) have no clinical training or experience, whereas therapists (some of whom conduct research in the scientist/practitioner model) and trauma researchers who do not practice have had little exposure to memory research until just recently. Care must therefore be taken not to overextend data from one area of expertise to the other without regard for these differences. As a first step, clinicians who treat traumatized patients and academics who study memory must become informed about each others' fields and must take great pains to communicate with each other and to undertake collaborative work. At this point in time ". . . a trauma-focused clinical paradigm that does not attend to the reconstructive nature of and suggestibility of memory is incomplete, as is a memory research paradigm that does not attend to the possible impact of personally experienced trauma on memory" (Alpert et al., 1996).

It is critically important that the controversy not eradicate advances in the treatment of adults reporting a sexual abuse history. If this were to happen, an emerging field of study with great promise for cross-fertilization between memory and trauma researchers and practicing therapists would be curtailed rather than developed. Most significantly, abuse survivors could potentially be returned to the position of being silenced rather than assisted (Rush, 1980). Instead, an opportunity exists to articulate guidelines for informed practice and for an emerging standard of care for the treatment of adults traumatized through past child abuse that takes into account scientific information about the effects of abuse and traumatization and about memory processes.

This chapter traces the major developments of this treatment focus, some of which set the stage for the current controversy. The chapter also identifies important parameters associated with informed practice and presents the evolving standard of care for the treatment of this population.

## DEVELOPMENT OF THERAPY FOR PAST CHILD SEXUAL ABUSE

The treatment of adults with a history of child sexual abuse is a relatively recent specialty in clinical practice. Here, we review some of the historical highpoints in the development of this clinical focus to place the contemporary delayed memory controversy in context.

### Study of Child Sexual Abuse

Incest and other forms of sexual abuse have been studied sporadically since the 1920s (Courtois, 1988; Rush, 1980), although the findings were not applied to the development of a specific treatment method. The main impetus for the contemporary study of sexual abuse occurred in the late 1960s with the simultaneous emergence of two social movements: the human rights movement (encompassing attention to civil rights and women's issues) and the Vietnam War and its aftermath. The women's movement focused on the influence of gender on the life experience of women. In addition to general patterns of discrimination, sexual assault (by strangers, acquaintances, and most scandalously by family members) and domestic violence surfaced as shockingly common but largely unacknowledged occurrences in the lives of girls and women. Early intervention efforts were made at the "grass roots" level, undertaken mostly by lay or paraprofessional volunteers whose efforts were best exemplified by rape crisis centers and battered women's shelters. Professional involvement took place more slowly: women's issues (much less such taboo topics as sexual assault and battering) were not viewed as legitimate areas of academic investigation or mental health intervention. These traditional positions gradually yielded to the impact and momentum of the human rights activities of the era.

Beginning in the mid-1970s, studies of child sexual abuse were undertaken to document its prevalence, patterns of occurrence, and initial and long-term impact, and to develop intervention methods. Studies of contemporaneous abuse of children and past abuse reported retrospectively by adults were conducted (Browne & Finkelhor, 1986; Burgess et al., 1978; Butler, 1978; Finkelhor, 1979; Herman, 1981; Meiselman, 1978; Russell, 1983, 1986). Findings from these and other studies documented a high rate of acquaintance and incestuous abuse (involving related and quasirelated individuals) occurring in the context of other forms of domestic abuse and dysfunction, including physical violence, emotional abuse and neglect, parental alcoholism, and so on.

As a consequence of the newly emerging data, an upgrading of child protective services was given priority. Reporting, intervention, investigation methods, and legal procedures were developed for situations of ongoing abuse. Treatment efforts were undertaken that were directed at all involved parties (Burgess et al., 1978; Sgroi, 1982). In cases of incest, treatment of all family members was recommended in an attempt to achieve the goals of abuse cessation and family reunification. Despite research documentation of high levels of distress among previously abused adults, treatment for this population was deemed less urgent and given less priority; nevertheless, preliminary writings on treatment strategies began to appear (Butler, 1978; Courtois & Watts, 1982; Herman, 1981; Meiselman, 1978).

*Study of War Trauma and Post-Traumatic Stress Disorder*

During the same period, the study of veterans returning from Vietnam was beginning. Findings from these studies brought renewed attention to the traumatic consequences of war and resulted in the development and inclusion of formalized diagnostic nomenclature for post-traumatic reactions, post-traumatic stress disorder (PTSD) in the *Diagnostic and Statistical Manual III* (*DSM;* American Psychiatric Association, 1980). This diagnosis codified many of the earlier observations about the post-traumatic response in veterans of World Wars I and II, and the Korean War (Herman, 1992b; van der Kolk, 1984, 1987).

Although some modifications have been made to the PTSD diagnosis in later editions of the *DSM* (American Psychiatric Association, 1987, 1994), its basic formulation remains. In response to the experiencing or witnessing of an inescapable traumatic stressor of sufficient intensity to overwhelm a victim's coping mechanisms, the human post-traumatic response involves an alternation between two phases of reaction. The first encompasses the reexperiencing and recollection of traumatic material and the second the deliberate avoidance or suppression of thoughts, feelings, or conversations about the trauma (van der Kolk, 1984, 1987). Persistent symptoms of anxiety and physical hyperarousal not present before the trauma are also hallmarks of this diagnosis. Three forms of PTSD have been identified: (a) acute—of 6 months' duration or less; (b) chronic—persistent and of greater than 6 months' duration; and/or (c) delayed—developing after a period of time during which the individual was asymptomatic. A new post-traumatic diagnosis, acute stress disorder, was included in the recently published *DSM IV* (American Psychiatric Association, 1994). Its essential feature is the development of characteristic anxiety, dissociation, and other symptoms within 1 month after exposure to an extreme traumatic stressor, lasting for at least 2 days to 4 weeks. If not resolved during that time period, the diagnosis is changed, most often to full-blown PTSD.

Throughout the 1980s, the diagnosis of PTSD began to be applied to many traumatized populations besides war veterans. Data accumulated to support the conclusion that the human trauma response, like the human stress response identified by Selye (1976), has a common pattern of occurrence, irrespective of the type of traumatic stressor (McCann & Pearlman, 1990; van der Kolk, 1984, 1987). Moreover, the possible role of trauma in the development of later mental health distress was identified. The traditional view of psychopathology as predominantly intrapsychic was challenged by the newly emerging data. Many researchers and clinicians suggested the need to take traumatization into account as a major and often unacknowledged externally derived etiological factor in later distress (Figley, 1985; van der Kolk, 1984, 1987). Some researchers described a victim-to-patient process (Rieker & Carmen, 1986), leading others to speculate about a new diagnostic classification system that was trauma-based or, alternatively, a hierarchy of post-traumatic reactions and disorders (Herman, 1992a, 1992b; Ross, 1989).

A field of study, referred to as traumatology or traumatic stress studies, and a professional organization, the International Society for Traumatic Stress Studies (ISTSS), originated during this time period. War trauma provided the group's initial focus—the earliest members of the ISTSS were primarily researchers in U.S. Veterans Affairs (VA) hospitals and laboratories and academics who had trained in the VA. Since then, the field of traumatology has rapidly expanded in scope. It is now a cross-cultural field of study encompassing all forms of traumatization. Two main types of trauma are now identified, those due to (a) natural, accidental, or technological circumstances (e.g., hurricanes, floods, transportation accidents, disasters such as Chernobyl), and (b) human influence (e.g., war, torture, sexual and physical assault, domestic violence).

As the field of traumatology has expanded and become more sophisticated, data have accumulated to suggest that responses to these two types of trauma differ. Post-traumatic responses have been found to be more complicated when the trauma is human-induced rather than accidental. With this type of traumatization, the victim must struggle with the issue of being intentionally harmed by another human being. Within the category of human-induced victimization, other variables have been associated with a more complex or profound post-traumatic reaction. These include situations that are chronic and escalating in seriousness over time, entrapping, forceful or violent, involve a high degree of interpersonal conflict and ambivalence (this is normally the case when the victimizer is an acquaintance or a relative, especially when victim and victimizer have ongoing contact and an ongoing relationship), and/or occur during childhood. Trauma of this type is prototypic of various forms of domestic violence including spousal battering and child abuse and of situations of wartime captivity (Herman, 1992a, 1992b).

With traumatization of this sort, victims often manifest many of the symptoms of standard PTSD; however, a different and additional set of symptoms that reflect developmental damage to the personality structure and to the patient's ability to relate to others has also been identified. These developmental symptoms include: impaired ability to modulate emotions; self-destructive and impulsive behaviors; dissociative symptoms; somatic complaints; feelings of ineffectiveness, shame, despair, hopelessness or of being permanently damaged; the loss of previously sustaining beliefs and meaning in the world; hostility and aggression; social withdrawal; feeling constantly threatened; impaired relationships with others; and a change from the patient's previous personality characteristics and functioning (American Psychiatric Association, 1994, p. 425). A new diagnosis encompassing this formulation and which is labeled as either complex PTSD (Herman, 1992a, 1992b) or disorder of extreme stress, not otherwise specified (DESNOS) was proposed and field tested but not included in the most recent edition of the *DSM*. It is now under consideration for future inclusion (Green, 1995).

The study of trauma and the determination of the diagnostic criteria for PTSD have been mostly the domain of medicine (psychiatry) and the mental health professions. By and large, cognitive psychologists and memory researchers have had little contact with these developments despite the fact that memory disturbance—the inability to recall an important aspect of the trauma (amnesia) and recurrent and intrusive distressing recollections of the event (hypermnesia)—has been a hallmark of the diagnosis from its inception.

*Study of Dissociation*

Concurrent with the study of traumatization and partially spurred by it, psychological dissociation has received renewed scientific interest in the last two decades. It was first studied in the late 1890s when it was identified as a defense mechanism used to ward off the effects of trauma (Breuer & Freud, 1893–1895/ 1955; Janet, 1889). It was later eclipsed, as Freud's revised psychoanalytic theory which emphasized repression rather than dissociation achieved widespread acceptance. Today, dissociation is again the subject of scientific inquiry, not only by clinicians but also by cognitive psychologists, after Hilgard's neodissociation theory of divided consciousness (Hilgard, 1986) revived attention in Janet's work.

Dissociation is increasingly accepted as a quite common and adaptive response to traumatization; indeed, some traumatologists and diagnosticians believe that post-traumatic responses are inherently dissociative because of the alternation between intrusion and suppression of aspects of the trauma. (At this writing, however, PTSD is formally categorized within the anxiety disorders in the *DSM*, and the dissociative disorders constitute a separate category, as discussed next.) It is not unusual for an individual who has been severely traumatized to be diagnosed with PTSD and a dissociative disorder. This is especially likely when the trauma was violent or coercive, repetitive and chronic, conflict-laden, physically intrusive, occurring in childhood, or entrapping. Trauma of this sort is pathognomic of incest and other forms of ongoing abuse; furthermore, it is the type of trauma discussed previously that is likely related to complex variants of PTSD.

The specific category of dissociative disorders was first included in the *DSM-III* (American Psychiatric Association, 1980), although these disorders had previously been listed in *DSM I* and *II* under the categories of psychoneurotic disorders and neuroses, respectively; all emanated from the early descriptions of hysteria, particularly those of Charcot and Janet (Kihlstrom, 1994). As currently defined, "The essential feature of the Dissociative Disorders is a disruption in the usually integrated functions of consciousness, **memory,** identity, or perception of the environment. The disturbance may be sudden or gradual, transient or chronic" (American Psychiatric Association, 1994, p. 477) (consistent with different onset and duration patterns associated with PTSD, discussed earlier). Dissociative amnesia, one of the five identified dissociative disorders "is characterized by an **inability to recall** important personal information, **usually of a traumatic or stressful nature,** that is too extensive to be explained by ordinary forgetfulness" (p. 477; emphasis added).

In the past decade, the study of dissociation has been spurred by the development of psychometric instruments and clinical guidelines for its assessment (Carlson & Armstrong, 1994; Steinberg, 1995). A growing body of research now indicates a connection between a history of trauma, especially severe and ongoing trauma in childhood, and dissociative disorders in adulthood.

## Development of Theory and Treatment Strategies

These three lines of research, (a) child sexual abuse and its initial and long-term effects, (b) trauma and post-traumatic responses, and (c) dissociation and its relation to trauma, especially trauma in childhood, independently and collectively made theoretical contributions to a new understanding of the effects of child abuse. They led to the development of theory and research-based treatment strategies and formulations for post-traumatic therapy in general (Brown & Fromm, 1988; Figley, 1985; Herman, 1992b; McCann & Pearlman, 1990; Ochberg, 1988; van der Kolk, 1984, 1987), and more specifically for adults sexually abused as children (Briere, 1989, 1991, 1992; Courtois, 1988; Davies & Frawley, 1993; Gil, 1988; Herman, 1981; Jehu, 1988; Kluft, 1990; Meiselman, 1978, 1990) and/or patients diagnosed with dissociative post-traumatic conditions, especially multiple personality disorder (Braun, 1986; Kluft, 1985; Kluft & Fine, 1993; Putnam, 1989; Ross, 1989). Many similarities in approach can be found across the work of these clinicians. This body of work can thus be used to provide a preliminary consensus regarding the treatment of this population as well as a foundation for the evolving standard of care. At present, few outcome studies of this treatment model are available. Future efforts must be directed toward the scientific study of the efficacy of this model.

## INFORMED PRACTICE: THE EVOLVING STANDARD OF CARE

The standard of care as discussed here is consistent with the general definition offered in a recent article by Brown (1995) as "evolving professional peer definitions of a standard established by expert testimony, by authoritative clinical-scientific literature, and also by regulatory and ethics guidelines. The standard of care for trauma treatment is defined by the evolving literature on diagnosis, as defined by *DSM-IV*, and on trauma treatment written by trauma experts" (p. 16). Therapists working with the population of traumatized and possibly traumatized patients have a responsibility to stay as informed as possible about treatment recommendations from both trauma and memory experts and to take these into consideration in their work. In particular, the therapist must pay careful attention to social influence and risk factors that might lead to false beliefs, reports, and memories, and closely monitor his or her own beliefs and countertransference as they might translate to problematic strategies and techniques.

The strategies recommended for the treatment of the long-term effects of sexual abuse by the authors listed in the previous section differ from more generic therapy by virtue of their post-traumatic perspective (Ochberg, 1988). They emphasize the significance of traumatic circumstances in general and childhood trauma in particular in the etiology of the patient's distress. Much of what is later considered maladaptive and even pathological may have originated as the child's attempts to cope with ongoing abuse and lack of protection. Therapeutic gain is achieved by normalizing rather than pathologizing these responses and by educating the patient as a preliminary step in the change process. Of particular importance is the treatment of the patient's developmental disturbances and every day life difficulties. These initially take precedence over the trauma.

It is assumed that the majority of patients seeking treatment for the aftereffects of sexual abuse will retain full or partial memory for the abuse and that a small minority will have totally absent memory (American Psychological Association, 1994); however, it is also assumed that partial or fragmentary memory is normal in traumatized individuals and that the material may emerge in response to cues or triggers in the environment, in the treatment, or in both (Elliott & Briere, 1994).

*Phase-Oriented and Sequenced Treatment*

At present, a strong consensus is evident among these trauma experts concerning the general format of treatment for post-traumatic conditions (Herman, 1992b). As opposed to a treatment strategy that is oriented solely to the trauma and to a full remembering or reexperiencing of the trauma (commonly identified as abreaction), the model is oriented toward what Kepner (1995) has labeled "healing tasks" that are worked on in a sequenced and a hierarchical fashion. When and if the trauma is treated directly, it is only undertaken when the patient has achieved enough stability, skills, and ego strength (or mastered enough healing tasks) to be able to manage and tolerate the strong emotions likely to be generated. McCann and Pearlman (1990) labeled this progressive process as "self work before memory/trauma work."

The consensus model supports phase-oriented, sequenced, and paced treatment. Each phase has its own clear treatment objectives and the overall treatment strategy emphasizes functional capacity and symptom resolution modulated or titrated according to the psychological capabilities of the client. Although the model is presented here in a linear form, in practice, it is often more like a spiral, looping back on itself and repeatedly reworking in more depth and sophistication issues initially addressed during the crucial first phase (Courtois, 1991; Herman, 1992b; Kepner, 1995). Although some authors have developed a model with more than three phases, all of the models available thus far can be collapsed into the following three general phases.

*1. Stabilization with an emphasis on daily functioning and self-management of symptoms.* In this phase, emphasis is placed on the patient's safety, stability, personality functioning, and functioning in the world. In many ways, the tasks and issues that make up the work of this phase resemble those of non-trauma-oriented therapy; yet they differ quite substantially and are compounded as a result of post-traumatic influence. For example, this phase encompasses the development of a therapeutic relationship, a more or less straightforward process with a nontraumatized patient. With a patient who is traumatized and who perceives the therapist as a stand-in for other untrustworthy and abusive authority figures, and/or who perceives herself as totally unworthy of attention or positive regard, it may pose a daunting challenge.

Many therapeutic issues are encompassed in this phase, and these issues rarely unfold in a straightforward way. Jehu (1988) has noted that some issues need therapeutic attention and resolution before deeper issues emerge. Obviously, this phase begins with assessment and preliminary treatment planning that includes establishing treatment parameters and informed consent. Other typical issues undertaken in this phase include the development of coping skills, ego defenses, self-capacities, and self-protection strategies; the stabilization of mood disturbances and personality issues; the management of intrusive/reexperiencing and numbing symptoms associated with PTSD and dissociative disorders; the development of relationship skills leading to the creation of a support system outside of therapy; and the resolution of current life crises and difficulties, the most common of which often include abusive relationships and other forms of revictimization, addictions and compulsions, eating disorders, suicidality, and self-injury.

In this model, the client is continuously focused on the need for safety as well as on symptom stabilization and management *before* addressing trauma. Any work with traumatic material in this phase is cognitive and educational in format, directed toward actively teaching the patient about the process and aftermath of traumatization and about the management of post-traumatic symptoms. It also communicates the structure and rationale of the treatment model: traumatic material is not addressed haphazardly, but rather in a prepared manner when the patient has developed enough ego strength, life stability, and emotional capacity to face it. The structure, in and of itself, works against an ambiguous and open-ended treatment that creates conditions of dependence, retraumatization, and decompensation, or against those conditions that are suggestive or conducive to memory elaboration.

Obviously, this phase may take a great deal of time and effort, depending on the range and severity of the patient's needs. Some patients choose to stop treatment at this point, having already done a considerable amount of work that resulted in improvement in their functioning and life situation. Others may discontinue because they lack the personal, motivational, or financial resources to proceed. In either case, the patient is ideally healthier and has more personal and interpersonal resources than when therapy began.

*2. Systematic and titrated uncovering of the trauma.* This phase is also organized according to the needs and defenses of the patient. The patient is gradually assisted to face and integrate the traumatic material along with its associated emotions at a pace that is safe and manageable. Patients are not encouraged to do this work to foster regressive dependency or to get stuck in a morass of more and more serious trauma, and certainly not to create traumatic memories; rather, the purpose is to allow a personal understanding or narrative to develop and to allow the expression of associated emotion. In this phase, the patient grieves both the occurrence and the consequences of the abuse; these usually include significant personal betrayals and losses and the experiencing of intense emotional pain. It is in this phase that "things get worse before they get better," but getting worse is clearly in the interest of getting better, not in getting permanently stuck.

*3. Reconsolidation and reconnection.* This phase involves continued work on self-development, relations with others, and major life decisions, some of which might be associated with the trauma. Attention continues to be given to personality issues and emotional development, mood disturbances, personal safety, self-care, and personal boundary management. Hopefully, the patient has achieved a new level of development and maturity beyond the limitations imposed by post-traumatic responses and adaptations. These, in turn, lead to other changes. Relationships may require reassessment, rebalancing, direct therapeutic intervention, or termination. Relational work occurs in the context of the family of origin, work relationships, friendships, intimate relationships, sexual functioning, and childrearing. Although many of the issues addressed here may have been worked on previously, their complete resolution might only be possible in this later part of treatment, enabled by the trauma work of the previous phase.

## Therapy Issues Pertaining to Memory

According to D. Brown (1995),

> Most trauma experts agree that classic abreaction and the use of memory recovery techniques as a *main* focus of treatment are contraindicated. This is not to say that memory recovery doesn't have a proper place within phase-oriented treatment, but only after stabilization. Uncovering is usually conducted primarily with free-recall uncovering strategies along with coping-enhancement and affect-regulatory methods that help establish the emotional state through which memories come forth in a way that minimizes leading. While memory recovery is not always indicated, it is often indicated. Outcome research has shown that exposure to traumatic memories is associated with treatment gain in behavioral treatment of PTSD . . . and in the psychodynamic treatment of severe dissociative disorders. (p. 16)

Throughout the course of the treatment, the therapist must "walk a fine line" to be neutrally supportive of the patient, especially when the patient is confused and when clear memory of past abuse is not available. The therapist must be careful not to prematurely suggest or to dismiss abuse in the patient's background and must carefully manage risk factors that would encourage the production of false beliefs or reports during the course of therapy (American Psychological Association, 1994; Courtois, 1995a; Hammond et al., 1994).

It is recommended that treatment begin with a personality assessment and a broad-based psychosocial assessment that includes neutrally phrased questions about family functioning, any sexual contacts as a child with family members or other adults or children, and other childhood or family trauma. Any disclosure of abuse (at this or any other time in the treatment) should be documented in detail to provide a base line of information initially *reported by the patient*. The assessment should also include attention to beliefs the patient might hold about the possibility of past abuse and delayed or repressed memories, and any sources of influence or social compliance (e.g., a TV talk show, reading, participation in a support or self-help group).

The therapist should correct any misinformation that the patient communicates about memory processes and should provide information about how the therapy is to proceed, especially as concerns memory-related material. This information can be conveyed in writing as well as verbally. Specifically, the patient should be educated about the reconstructive nature of memory and that he or she will be encouraged to explore and analyze memories that emerge during the course of therapy to arrive at a personal understanding of their meaning. It should be made explicit that it is the patient's and not the therapist's responsibility to determine his or her personal narrative, and furthermore that the therapist cannot provide confirmation or disconfirmation of memories of abuse when outside evidence or corroboration is absent. What the therapist can do is prepare the patient to tolerate ambiguity and uncertainty and to provide a safe and supportive environment in which to explore.

The therapist must pay particular attention to issues of relational style, boundary management, and transference and countertransference in this treatment. A therapeutic style that is nonauthoritarian and collaborative with the patient is to be recommended. The therapy must be philosophically oriented toward personally empowering the patient to counter the powerlessness associated with victimization. The therapist's insistence on shared responsibility for the therapy discourages overdependence on the part of the patient. Additionally, a responsive and flexible therapeutic style invites engagment by the patient who, in all likelihood, is very mistrustful of authority figures and may have difficulty developing a therapeutic alliance.

Even though the therapist is nonauthoritarian in style, the therapy must be set up with clearly defined and communicated boundaries and limitations. Abused individuals experienced interpersonal inconsistency and blurred relationships and boundaries in their upbringing (often to the extreme in the most severe abuse) and frequently play these out in their therapy (Briere, 1989; Courtois, 1988; Davies & Frawley, 1994). The therapist must establish a "treatment frame" of operating guidelines for the therapy to provide an atmosphere of predictability, reliability, and safety for the patient. It is advisable that the therapist inform the patient at the outset about these operating guidelines. The most common treatment issues to be addressed include assessment and collaborative treatment planning; confidentiality and its limits; safety and dangerousness to self or others and duty to protect; therapist availability in times of crisis and outside of standard office hours; fees, payment, and insurance issues; record-keeping; adjunctive evaluations and consultations; the inadvisability of any dual relationship between therapist and patient; approaches to possible medication and hospitalization; use of any specialized technique and the need for informed consent (e.g., hypnosis, eye movement desensitization reprocessing); and, explicit agreements regarding no unplanned disclosure, confrontation, or legal action against an alleged perpetrator or anyone else without prior discussion, assessment, or preparation in therapy.

Transference and countertransference issues are crucial to monitor in this treatment. Chronically traumatized individuals are challenging to work with. They place heavy relational demands on others, often have post-traumatic personality disorders and disturbances, and present very difficult traumatic material to react to, and thus present major therapeutic challenges (Briere, 1989; Courtois, 1988; Lindy & Wilson, 1994; Pearlman & Saakvitne, 1995). Chu (1988) called these challenges "treatment traps" and indicated that without appropriate management by the therapist they would ultimately sabotage a treatment effort. The three most common types of countertransference reactions that lead to therapist error with this population are overinvolvement, leading to overreponsibility or rescuing efforts on the part of the therapist; avoidance, leading to disengagment from both the patient and the traumatic material; and anger, leading to some sort of retraumatiation, exploitation, or disengagement.

Unfortunately, few clinical training programs have provided specialized training for working with this population. This gap in professional training is certainly part of what has contributed to the current treatment controversy, as therapists have struggled to provide services without having received adequate preparation and supervision. It is also part of what makes ongoing continuing education—through workshops, reading, and supervision—essential for the therapist working with this population.

It is obviously of critical importance that therapists monitor their countertransference with the intent of using it therapeutically rather than enacting it with the patient. It is therefore also highly recommended that therapists have sources of outside consultation when working with this population so that they are not creating a closed system that is more conducive to suggestion and patterns of secrecy and reinforcement. Consultation also provides a venue for ventilation, perspective, and support outside of the context of the treatment relationship.

Finally, it is suggested that the therapist adopt a scientific attitude regarding treatment in general and traumatic recall in particular and teach the patient to do the same (D. Brown, 1995). As discussed previously, the therapist should be open to new sources of information on these issues and should actively seek out emerging literature on the topic as well as continuing education opportunities. The therapist should strive to avoid premature closure of issues and encourage a stance of careful and open evaluation and the consideration of alternate or competing hypotheses over time. As discussed by Liebowitz, Harvey, and Herman (1993), the main therapeutic achievement is for the patient to gain authority over both life experience and personal functioning. This is achieved not through repeated high-intensity abreactive experiences that often result in less rather than more emotional control or from a "hunt for the missing memories and the unremembered trauma." Rather, it occurs as a result of careful consideration and through cognitive and emotional resolution and mastery so that the patient is no longer in the throes of out-of-control intrusive recollections and emotional numbing responses.

## CONCLUSION

Informed treatment and the evolving standard of care for abused and possibly abused individuals posits a therapy that is sequenced, paced and titrated, and directed toward stabilization and the resolution of major symptomatology, sometimes achieved through direct work with traumatic content. The therapist who works within the parameters of this standard, and who recognizes that delayed memories and false memories or beliefs about past abuse are both possible, is best able to provide a rational and balanced therapeutic approach to these issues. Although some of the criticisms about this therapy are speculative and overgeneralized, some are clearly useful. The most pertinent of these suggestions should be incorporated into the emerging standard for post-traumatic therapy. This debate provides an opportunity for the integration of information from two diverse fields to achieve a scientifically derived theoretical and therapeutic model.

# REFERENCES

Alpert, J., Brown, L., & Courtois, C. (1996). *Symptomatic clients and memories of childhood abuse: What the trauma and child sexual abuse literature tells us.* (p. 17). Washington, DC: American Psychological Association.

American Psychiatric Association. (1980). *Diagnostic and statistical manual of mental disorders* (3rd ed.). Washington, DC: Author.

American Psychiatric Association. (1987). *Diagnostic and statistical manual of mental disorders* (3rd ed., rev. ed.). Washington, DC: Author.

American Psychiatric Association. (1994). *Diagnostic and statistical manual of mental disorders* (4th ed.).

American Psychological Association. (1994). *Interim report of the working group on investigation of memories of childhood abuse.* Washington, DC: Author.

Braun, B. G. (Ed.). (1986). *Treatment of multiple personality disorder.* Washington, DC: American Psychiatric Press.

Breuer, J., & Freud, S. (1955). *Studies on hysteria.* In J. Strachey (Ed. and Trans.), *The standard edition of the complete psychological works of Sigmund Freud* (Vol. 2). London: Hogarth Press. (Original work published 1893–1895)

Briere, J. (1989). *Therapy for adults molested as children.* New York: Springer.

Briere, J. (Ed.). (1991). *Treating child victims of child sexual abuse.* San Francisco: Jossey-Bass.

Briere, J. (1992). *Child abuse trauma: Theory and treatment of the lasting effects.* Newbury Park, CA: Sage.

Brown, D. (1995). Pseudomemories: The standard of science and the standard of care in trauma treatment. *American Journal of Clinical Hypnosis, 37,* 1–24.

Brown, D. P., & Fromm, E. (1986). *Hypnotherapy and hypnoanalysis.* Hillsdale, NJ: Erlbaum.

Browne, A., & Finkelhor, D. (1986). Impact of child sexual abuse: A review of the research. *Psychological Bulletin, 99,* 66–77.

Burgess, A. W., Groth, A. N., Homstrom, L. L., & Sgroi, S. M. (1978). *Sexual assault of children and adolescents.* Lexington, MA: Lexington Books.

Butler, S. (1978). *Conspiracy of silence: The trauma of incest.* New York: Bantam Books.

Carlson, E., & Armstrong, J. (1994). The diagnosis and assessment of dissociative disorders. In Lynn, S. J., & Rhue, J. W. (Eds.). *Dissociation: Clinical and theoretical perspectives.* New York: Guilford.

Chu, J. (1988). Ten traps in the treatment of trauma survivors. *Dissociation, 1,* 24–32.

Courtois, C. A. (1988). *Healing the incest wound: Adult survivors in therapy.* New York: W. W. Norton.

Courtois, C. A. (1991). Theory, sequencing, and strategy in treating adult survivors. In J. Briere (Ed.), *Treating victims of child sexual abuse* (pp. 47–60). San Francisco: Jossey-Bass.

Courtois, C. A. (1995a). Recovery memory/false memory polarities: Balance and collaboration needed. *Consciousness and Cognition, 4,* 133–134.

Courtois, C. A. (1995b). Scientist-practitioners and the delayed memory controversy: Scientific standards and the need for collaboration. *The Counseling Psychologist, 23,* 294–299.

Courtois, C. A., & Watts, D. L. (1982). Counseling adult women who experienced incest in childhood or adolescence. *Personnel and Guidance Journal, 60,* 275–279.

Davies, J. M., & Frawley, M. G. (1994). *Treating the adult survivor of childhood sexual abuse: A psychoanalytic perspective.* New York: Basic Books.

Elliott, D. M., & Briere, J. (1994, November). *Post-traumatic stress associated with delayed recall of sexual abuse: A general population study.* Paper presented at the annual meeting of the International Society for Traumatic Stress Studies, Chicago, IL.

Figley, C. (Ed.). (1985). *Trauma and its wake.* New York: Brunner/Mazel.

Finkelhor, D. (1979). *Sexually victimized children.* New York: Free Press.

Finkelhor, D. (1984). *Child sexual abuse: New theory and research.* New York: Free Press.

Friedrich, W. N. (1990). *Psychotherapy of sexually abused children and their families.* New York: W. W. Norton.

Gil, E. (1988). *Treatment of adult survivors of childhood abuse.* Walnut Creek, CA: Launch Press.

Green, B. L. (1995). Introduction to special issues on traumatic memory research. *Journal of Traumatic Stress*, **8**, 501–505.

Hammond, D. C. et al. (1994). *Clinical hypnosis and memory: Guidelines for clinicians and for forensic hypnosis*. American Society for Clinical Hypnosis Press.

Herman, J. L. (1981). *Father–daughter incest*. Cambridge, MA: Harvard University Press.

Herman, J. L. (1992a). *Trauma and recovery*. New York: Basic Books.

Herman, J. L. (1992b). Sequelae of prolonged and repeated trauma: Evidence for a complex post-traumatic syndrome (DESNOS). In J. R. Davidson & E. B. Foa (Eds.), *Post-traumatic stress disorder: DSM-IV and beyond* (pp. 213–228). Washington, DC: American Psychiatric Press.

Hilgard, E. R. (1986). *Divided consciousness: Multiple controls in human thought and action* (rev. ed.). New York: Wiley-Interscience. (Original work published 1977)

James, B. (1989). *Treating traumatized children: New insights and creative interventions*. Lexington, MA: Lexington Books.

Janet, P. (1889). *L'automatisme psychologique*. Paris: Alcan.

Jehu, D. (1988). *Beyond sexual abuse: Therapy with women who were childhood victims*. New York: Wiley.

Kepner, J. I. (1995). *Healing tasks: Psychotherapy with adult survivors of childhood abuse*. San Francisco: Jossey-Bass.

Kihlstrom, J. (1994). One hundred years of hysteria. In S. J. Lynn & J. W. Rhue (Eds.). *Dissociation: Clinical and theoretical perspectives*. New York: Guilford.

Kluft, R. P. (1985). *Childhood antecedents of multiple personality*. Washington, DC: American Psychiatric Press.

Kluft, R. P. (Ed.). (1990). *Incest-related syndromes of adult psychopathy*. Washington, DC: American Psychiatric Press.

Kluft, R. P., & Fine, C. G. (Eds.). (1993). *Clinical perspectives on multiple personality disorder*. Washington, DC: American Psychiatric Press.

Liebowitz, L., Harvey, M., & Herman, J. (1993). A stage-by-dimension model of recovery from sexual trauma. *Journal of Interpersonal violence*, **8**, 378–392.

Lindsay, D. S., & Read, J. D. (1994). Psychotherapy and memories of childhood abuse: A cognitive perspective. *Applied Cognitive Psychology* **8**, 281–338.

Lindy, J., & Wilson, J. (Eds.). (1994). *Countertransference in the Treatment of PTSD*. New York: Guilford.

Loftus, E. F. (1993). The reality of repressed memories. *American Psychologist*, **48**, 518–537.

Loftus, E., & Ketcham, K. (1994). *The myth of repressed memory: False memories and allegations of abuse*. New York: St. Martin's Press.

Lynn, S. J. & Rhue, J. W. (Eds.). (1994). *Dissociation: Clinical and theoretical perspectives*. New York: Guilford.

McCann, I. L., & Pearlman, L. A. (1990). *Psychological trauma and the adult survivor*. New York: Brunner/Mazel.

Meiselman, K. C. (1978). *Incest: A psycholological study of cause and effects with treatment recommendations*. San Francisco: Jossey-Bass.

Meiselman, K. C. (1990). *Resolving the trauma of incest*. San Francisco: Jossey-Bass.

Ochberg, F. M. (Ed.). (1988). *Post-traumatic therapy and victims of violence*. New York: Brunner/Mazel.

Pearlman, L., & Saakvitne, K. (1995). *Trauma and the therapist*. New York: W. W. Norton.

Putnam, F. (1989). *Diagnosis and treatment of multiple personality disorder*. New York: Guilford.

Rieker, P., & Carmen, E. (1986). The victim-to-patient process: The disconfirmation and transformation of abuse. *American Journal of Orthopsychiatry*, **56**, 360–370.

Ross, C. A. (1989). *Multiple personality disorder: Diagnosis, clinical features, and treatment*. New York: Wiley.

Russell, D. E. H. (1983). The incidence and prevalence of intrafamilial and extra-familial sexual abuse of female children. *Child Abuse and Neglect*, 7, 133–146.

Russell, D. E. H. (1986). *The secret trauma: Incest in the lives of girls and women*. New York: Basic Books.

Rush, F. (1980) *The best kept secret: Sexual abuse of children*. New York: McGraw-Hill.

Selye, H. (1976). *Stress in health and disease*. Boston: Butterworth.

Sgroi, S. M. (1982). *Handbook of clinical intervention in child sexual abuse*. Lexington, MA: Lexington Books.

Steinberg, M. (1995). *Handbook for the assessment of dissociation: A clinical guide*. Washington, DC: American Psychiatric Association.

van der Kolk, B. A. (1984). *Post-traumatic stress disorder: Psychological and biological sequelae*. Washington, DC: American Psychiatric Press.

van der Kolk, B. A. (1987). *Psychological trauma*. Washington, DC: American Psychiatric Press.

Yapko, M. D. (1993). Suggestibility and repressed memories of abuse: A survey of psychotherapists' beliefs. *American Journal of Clinical Hypnosis, 36,* 163–171.

# Interim Report of the Working Group on Investigation of Memories of Childhood Abuse

AMERICAN PSYCHOLOGICAL ASSOCIATION

## INTRODUCTION

The Working Group on Investigation of Memories of Childhood Abuse is concerned with the many issues that have come to surround the topic of memories of childhood abuse and the anguish that many individuals have experienced. The American Psychological Association is in a unique position to ensure that scientific knowledge and professional expertise inform future discourse on these issues.

To this end, the APA Council of Representatives voted, in February 1993, to establish a working group to review current scientific literature and identify future research and training needs regarding the evaluation of memories of childhood abuse. Members of the working group were named by the Board for the Advancement of Psychology in the Public Interest, in close consultation with the Boards of Professional and Scientific Affairs in March 1993.

The working group held its first meeting on August 7 and 8, 1993. Following the work plan established at the first meeting, members of the group presented and discussed preliminary data from reviews of the literatures on child sexual abuse, memory, and trauma at a second meeting on December 18 and 19, 1993. The group continued to discuss the various literatures at its third meeting, June 17–19, 1994, and determined the format for its final report. The final report will be composed of reviews of the trauma and the memory literatures. Each review will be followed by accompanying commentary and authorial responses. The final report will be presented to the Council of Representatives in February 1995.

At this point in its deliberations, the working group offers a set of interim conclusions and an identification of the issues that will be discussed in the final report in order to begin to address the concerns of the public and the profession as rapidly as is responsibly possible.

## INTERIM CONCLUSIONS

The key points of agreement among members of the Working Group on Investigation of Memories of Childhood Abuse are

- Controversies regarding adult recollections should not be allowed to obscure the fact that child sexual abuse is a complex and pervasive problem in America that has historically gone unacknowledged.
- Most people who were sexually abused as children remember all or part of what happened to them.

371

• It is possible for memories of abuse that have been forgotten for a long time to be remembered. The mechanism, or mechanisms, by which such delayed recall occurs is not currently well understood.

• It is also possible to construct convincing pseudomemories for events that never occurred. The mechanism, or mechanisms, by which these pseudomemories occurs is not currently well understood.

• There are gaps in our knowledge about the processes that lead to accurate and inaccurate recollections of childhood abuse.

## CONTENTS OF FINAL REPORT

In its forthcoming report, the working group will identify specific gaps in our knowledge and suggest research directions that may lead to a better understanding of mechanisms associated with accurate or inaccurate recollections. The working group will address research questions raised by clinical experience, as well as the application of clinical process research and treatment outcome validity studies to clinical practice issues.

The final report will also explore the ways current data may inform legal testimony, forensic evaluations, therapeutic strategies and professional training. It will also look at the relationship between basic research, field research, and clinical experience.

## APA WORKING GROUP ON THE INVESTIGATION OF MEMORIES OF CHILDHOOD ABUSE

Judith L. Alpert, Ph.D. (Co-Chair), New York University (212) 691-6587.
Peter A. Ornstein, Ph.D. (Co-Chair), University of North Carolina, Chapel Hill (919) 962-4138
Laura S. Brown, Ph.D. Seattle, Washington (206) 633-2405
Stephen J. Ceci, Ph.D. Cornell University (607) 255-0828
Christine A. Courtois, Ph.D., Washington, DC (202) 955–5652
Elizabeth F. Loftus, Ph.D., University of Washington (206) 543-7184

# Recovered Memories

## THE REPORT OF THE WORKING PARTY OF THE BRITISH PSYCHOLOGICAL SOCIETY

## EXECUTIVE SUMMARY

The working party was charged with reporting on the scientific evidence relevant to the current debate concerning recovered memories of trauma and with commenting on the issues surrounding this topic. We have reviewed the scientific literature, carried out a survey of relevant members of The British Psychological Society (BPS), and scrutinized the records of the British False Memory Society. On this basis, we came to the following conclusions:

• Complete or partial memory loss is a frequently reported consequence of experiencing certain kinds of psychological traumas including childhood sexual abuse. These memories are sometimes fully or partially recovered after a gap of many years.

• Memories may be recovered within or independent of therapy. Memory recovery is reported by highly experienced and well-qualified therapists who are well aware of the dangers of inappropriate suggestion and interpretation.

• In general, the clarity and detail of event memories depends on a number of factors, including the age at which the event occurred. Although clear memories are likely to be broadly accurate, they may contain significant errors. It seems likely that recovered memories have the same properties.

• Sustained pressure or persuasion by an authority figure could lead to the retrieval or elaboration of "memories" of events that never actually happened. The possibility of therapists creating in their clients false memories of having been sexually abused in childhood warrants careful consideration, and guidelines for therapists are suggested here to minimize the risk of this happening. There is no reliable evidence at present that this is a widespread phenomenon in the United Kingdom.

• In a recent review of the literature on recovered memories, Lindsay and Read (1994) commented that "the ground for debate has shifted from the question of the possibility of therapy-induced false beliefs to the question of the prevalence of therapy-induced false beliefs." We agree with this comment but add to it that the ground for debate has also shifted from the question of the possibility of recovery of memory from total amnesia to the question of the prevalence of recovery of memory from total amnesia.

## INTRODUCTION

This report sets out to investigate the scientific evidence surrounding the phenomenon of *recovered memories*[1] in which adults come to report memories of childhood events, having previously been in a state of total amnesia for those events. The members of the Working Party started their deliberations from a variety of standpoints. In the process of writing the report, we achieved consensus.

The cases that have evoked the most public interest are those in which the memories are recovered by clients in therapy, and those memories are of extended, traumatic sexual abuse. The amnesia could take the form that at the start of therapy, when the clients were giving their life history, they would not be aware of having been abused as a child. The client would report not having had such a memory for some period of time previously, usually several years. One claim is that such memories bear a reasonable approximation to the historical truth. The counterclaim is that amnesia and memory recovery of this kind are impossible and that the memories are manufactured in therapy.

Our first aim is to consider the scientific information that is relevant to the question of recovered memories of child sexual abuse. Our second aim is that of providing guidelines for clinical practice in the light of such information.

We do not question the existence of child sexual abuse (CSA) as a serious social and individual problem with long lasting effects. Very large numbers of children, boys and girls, have been and are being sexually abused, many of them by their parents. Estimates of frequency in the adult population vary with the sample and the definition of abuse. The minimum rate for women, reported in representative community samples, is 6% for CSA involving physical contact, but some estimates are several times larger. We are not directly concerned here with children who come forward to tell, or with adults who have known about abuse all their lives and only recently felt able to tell.

In some cases of public interest, the memories are reported in the course of therapy which employs *memory recovery techniques*[2] and the accused parents have denied the accusations. In the United States, an organization called the False Memory Syndrome (FMS) Foundation was formed in 1992 as a parents' support group. In the United Kingdom, an equivalent organization, Adult Children Accusing Parents (ACAP), was formed in 1993; this was renamed the British False Memory (FM) Society. The position of the parents' associations is that the recovered memories have been implanted by therapists who believe that a

---

[1]The term *recovered memories* should not be taken to imply that the content necessarily refers to actual events, as would be required by usages of the term *memory,* whereby, as a matter of definition, one cannot "remember" what never occurred. Our options are to place "memory," "remember," and other terms in scare quotes or to use some extended phrase such as "reported recovered memories." We have preferred to use *memory* unadorned in an unrestrictive sense.

[2]*Memory recovery techniques* include: hypnosis, especially hypnotic regression, in which the hypnotized client is asked to imagine themself as a child; journaling, where the client keeps a journal to prompt and record recollections of the past; guided imagery; guided meditation; and use of so-called truth drugs.

wide variety of psychological problems—depression, eating disorders, sexual dysfunction, low self esteem or difficulty maintaining a relationship, suicidal or self-destructive thoughts—invariably indicate sexual abuse in childhood.

In the United States, one problem is that a therapist is legally required to report any allegation of sexual abuse, however long ago, however tentative, whether they believe the allegation or not. Professionals not reporting such information are liable to criminal prosecution. This leads to the early involvement of the criminal justice system.

As a consequence, the structure of the public debate, particularly in the United States, has led to people taking extreme positions. One such extreme position is to argue that recovered memories are in principle impossible, and that therefore those of the particular accuser must be impossible. Equally, attacks on the principle of repression, adduced by some to be the major mechanism in amnesia prior to recovered memories, are carried out to invalidate the explanation and turn all recovered memories into false ones. Another extreme argument is to say that if some recovered memories are unbelievable, then all must be. Examples given include that of focusing on clear recovered memories of being transported to past lives or to alien space ships, or recovering memories of having been abused in the first year of life or even in the womb. Next, quotations are taken from one side of the debate and treated as though they were typical of all statements from that side. Thus, the following quotation from a leading survivors' text, which most people would see as illogical and inflammatory, is used against the whole survivors' movement: *"If you think you were abused and your life shows the symptoms, then you were" (Bass & Davies, 1988, p. 22).*

On the other hand, some therapists and many members of the survivors' movement believe that the discovery that some recovered memories can be substantiated means that all recovered memories could be substantiated. Further, the claims that a proportion of known survivors of CSA suffer from particular ailments (e.g., depression, eating disorders) has led to the claim that all people suffering from these disorders must have suffered CSA, whether they remember it or not. The allegation that the FMS Foundation or the British FM Society could possibly function as a refuge for perpetrators who joined the society for protection (possibilities readily admitted by the founders of the respective societies) is argued to weaken the position of these societies. All of these extreme positions are clearly untenable from a logical, a scientific, or a forensic point of view.

In the course of the debate raging in the United States, a number of claims have been made concerning the properties of human memory. We intend to review the available evidence. The issues which we address from the scientific literature are as follows:

- How accurate is our memory under normal circumstances?
- To what extent can we be sure of the source of our memories?
- What special properties do early memories have?
- What can we say about repression and other mechanisms of forgetting?
- Is it possible to have false beliefs about the past?

- What are the effects on memory of hypnotic techniques?
- Is there a relationship between false confessions and false memories?

In following our enquiries, we have examined the records of the British False Memory Society to get some idea of the characteristics of accusers and the nature of their accusations. In addition we have carried out a survey of relevant members of The British Psychological Society to investigate the extent of recovered memories in clinical practice and to get some preliminary indication of prevailing views about their validity.

In terms of therapy, we will not aim at any evaluation (e.g., did the process have the desired effects on the condition?) but, rather, concentrate on the propriety and reliability of particular memory recovery techniques. From this basis we can then look at the application to recovered memories.

Note that we cannot, in any case, pass any judgment on any particular instances of recovered memory. These are forensic matters rather than scientific, and, as such, are beyond the scope of our enquiry.

*A Framework for Memory*

One view of human memory is that it is like a videotape machine:

- it faithfully records, as if on film, every perception experienced by the witness,
- it permanently stores such recorded perceptions in the brain at a subconscious level, and
- the brain accurately "replays" them in their original form.

We will see that this picture is greatly mistaken.

To facilitate the task of understanding what follows, we present one kind of simplified framework for the operation of our autobiographical memory system.

The framework represents the most important operations that take place during registering and retrieval of memories. First, we consider the setting up of the original memory, as represented schematically in *Fig. 1*. When an event takes place, information from the senses is captured and the resulting representation is interpreted in the light of our previous experience. It is this interpretation that we are aware of. Some aspects of the representation and the interpretation are stored in memory. *Figure 2* represents an idealised view of the processes of remembering. Retrieval itself can be consciously driven or unconscious and automatic. In the latter case you might be reminded of some event involuntarily, or knowledge may be sought to help interpret the current scene. In either case, the retrieval process would start with an appropriate retrieval cue which is used to locate a particular memory record. The retrieved information will undergo some processing prior to awareness. This could include the incorporation of general knowledge or material from another record. When we are aware of our memory we might produce a narrative concerning it. After the remembering, information will be stored again, as a record of the remembering. Thus, next time you go through the cycle and recall the event, you might be recalling the

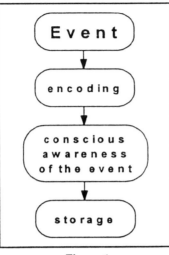

Figure 1

original, or you might be recalling the previous time you recalled. This framework is rather idealized and simplified. We will see the picture complicate in the following sections.

## EVIDENCE FOR CLAIMS

*How Accurate Is Our Memory under Normal Circumstances?*

Not every detail of our experience of an event is stored in memory. When the record of an event is retrieved, then, it will be incomplete and might need elaborating before it is intelligible to our consciousness. This would be carried out

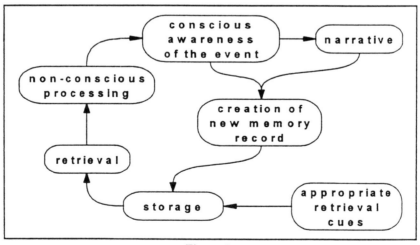

Figure 2

through the nonconscious processes referred to in *Fig. 2*. What we are conscious of is a mixture of reproduction and reconstruction. Reconstructive memory is characterized by the conflation of different events, the filling out of detail and importation of information, an extreme example being when entire events are confabulated.

Factors that influence the degree of reconstruction include:

- the personal significance of the event,
- its emotive content,
- the amount of time elapsed between when the event occurs and when it is remembered,
- the reasons why the person is remembering the event, and
- the circumstances of recall.

Events that are personally highly significant evoke deep beliefs, attitudes and emotional reactions, and may lead to a narrowing of attention. As a consequence, memories for peripheral details of such events may be more vulnerable to reconstructive error. Central details are likely to be remembered better but may still be in error. Research in autobiographical memory has demonstrated that people can sometimes dramatically misremember aspects of highly significant events, with these fictions being regarded as "fact." Importantly, this can occur without any conscious awareness on the part of the person. On the other hand, even minor details from highly significant events can be reproduced with little distortion. An analysis of the statements of 27 of the survivors of the Marchioness disaster produced 86 minor factual claims (such as who was where at different phases of the incident), which were in principle verifiable. Of these, 74 were verified in other statements. There was only one anomalous pair of claims.

Repeated events lead to a schematic, generalized representation which is used as a framework for recall of these events. As a result, individual events are liable to become confused. Thus, John Dean, Nixon's aide at the time of Watergate, claimed that he had a verbatim memory. His testimony, when compared with the tapes that Nixon made of White House conversations, showed that he generally got the gist correct, but often moved specific conversations from one time to another or combined two or more incidents into a new imagined one.

*Summary*. Normal event memory is largely accurate but may contain distortions and elaborations.

## To What Extent Can We Be Sure of the Source of Our Memories?

One of the strongest criteria for being certain an event has happened to us is that we are able to anchor it in time and place. Being able to do this enables us to link the event with our personal history. If an imagined event easily fits the mental record of our daily lives, then it would be difficult to distinguish from a real event.

Experimental research suggests that under most circumstances people can successfully distinguish events that happened from events that were imagined. However, if there is extensive rehearsal of an imagined event, the person can begin to believe that the event actually happened. The memory can become highly detailed and "vivid" to the person. Additionally, erroneous information given to the person after an event has been experienced can come to alter the memory for the event. The research demonstrating such breakdowns in reality monitoring has been primarily conducted with adults.

There are many experiments showing that recall for an event can be altered in matters of detail by suggestion or leading questions. The evidence suggests that such change often reflects factors such as compliance with the researcher's expectations, rather than genuine alterations in memory. Accordingly, people's suggestibility can be significantly reduced if they can be persuaded to pay more attention to locating the source of their memories.

*Summary.* With certain exceptions, such as when there has been extensive rehearsal of an imagined event, the source of our memories is generally perceived accurately.

### How Reliable Is Recall of Early Events?

It is sometimes claimed that there are circumstances in which recall of an early event is exact. Such claims cannot be upheld.

A recent experiment on recall of events that are known to have taken place early in life is by Usher and Neisser (1993). They targeted university students known to have experienced the birth of a sibling, hospitalization, the death of a family member, or moving house when they were between the ages of 1 and 5. Birth of a sibling was best remembered, although three quarters of the subjects who had experienced this between 1 and 2 years old remembered nothing of the event, the other quarter answered about half the questions they were asked about times, places, visits to the hospital, and so on. Mothers largely confirmed details of the memories. No one could recall anything at all of a house move that took place during the second year of life.

From this study we may conclude that for some people, some events occurring in the second year could be registered in memory in a form that is partially recoverable in adulthood. However, it is also possible that these successfully corroborated memories were not the original memories laid down at the time of the events, but, rather, at least partially manufactured through family stories with the aid of photos or other memorabilia concerning the event. Other studies, obtaining similar results, are less open to this objection, however.

In Usher and Neisser's experiment, memory performance increased steadily with age at occurrence for all events. For events occurring at 5 years, an average of about half the questions were being answered. The decrease in memory as the events become earlier represents the phenomenon of infantile amnesia which Freud had noted and accounted for by the concept of repression (e.g., Freud, 1933/1973, pp. 58–59). However, a number of recent accounts of infantile amnesia do not require the concept of repression. Rather they rely on normal cognitive or social mechanisms and imply that memory is in some way organized differently during the first 4 years of life from the way it is organized later. The consequence of this is that early memories either cannot be accessed or do not exist in an accessible form. Infantile amnesia becomes a natural consequence of the development of the memory system.

Within this framework, then, we can see how abuse which takes place before the age of 4 or thereabouts and does not continue beyond that age might not be retrievable in adulthood in a narrative form. Even if a memory that had been created in the first few years were retrievable, there is an additional problem that it would not be in a form that the individual could fully make sense of. An example of this is given by Terr (1991):

> Three and a half years after experiencing a series of traumatic events, a five-year-old child was discovered (through pornographic photographs confiscated by U.S. Customs agents) to have been sexually misused in a day-care home between the ages of 15 and 18 months. The girl's parents did not dare to speak to her about what they had learned from the investigators. They, in retrospect, realized that she had been sketching hundreds of nude adults beginning from the time when she had first begun to draw.
>
> While playing in my office, this child told me that a baby she had just drawn was "all naked" and "a bad girl." Unknowingly, she had just depicted herself. Despite the fact that the little girl's only verbal memory of the events was "I think there was grave danger at a lady—MaryBeth's—house," her volumes of drawings represented strongly visualized elements that she had retained and had needed to recreate from these very early, nonverbal experiences. (p. 12)

We have no reason to suppose that a very early memory, previously not recalled and intentionally recovered by an adult would be any more intelligible. It would remain fragmentary. This is not to say that, as an adult, we could not interpret these fragments. What might happen is that the adult would create a frame of reference within which the fragments could be fitted, and a new memory would be created with all the imported material from the story frame. The existence of the fragments, including affect and imagery, could make the newly created narrative seem real, even though the actual source of the fragments remained undiscovered.

There is no doubt that children can learn and remember from the earliest months of life, but such "memories" are implicit rather than explicit: they are reflected in behavior but remain beyond awareness and so cannot be expressed verbally. Thus, Myers, Clifton, and Clarkson (1987) traced a group of children now aged around 3 who had taken part in research on their hearing when aged between 6 and 40 weeks. These children were re-tested in the same room using the same equipment as previously and their behavior compared to controls who had not taken part in the earlier experiments. Results showed that the experienced children played more, and looked longer at the sound sources like the rattle and drum, than did the controls. However, only one child showed any awareness of having been in the room before.

*Summary.* Nothing can be recalled accurately from before the first birthday and little from before the second. Poor memory from before the fourth birthday is normal.

### What Can We Say about Repression and Other Mechanisms of Forgetting?

The literature is highly inconsistent in the use of the term *repressed memory*. Most discussions of repression focus on the hypothesized active inhibition of previously clear conscious memories for events, whether as a result of a conscious or an unconscious process. In our framework, this is equivalent to a blockage between retrieval and awareness. This mechanism has been used as an explanatory principle for recovered memories and the reality of such a mechanism has been the focus of attack by proponents of false memories. However, there are a number of alternative mechanisms for not remembering, which correspond to interruptions at different points in the processing in *Fig. 1 and 2:*

• The memory has never been consciously available because of "blacking out" at the time. The existence of "blacking out" in the course of some types of trauma is relatively well documented, although this has not generally been suggested in the case of childhood abuse and in any case memories from the period of "blacking out" are not thought to be ever recovered.

• The memory is not part of a person's habitual belief about themselves, that is, the person does not routinely think "I am a person who has experienced X." The memory would not be retrieved or would be excluded at the point of nonconscious processing in *Fig. 2.*

• The memory has come to mind in whole or in part (flashbacks, fragments, etc.) but was labeled or interpreted as something different.

• The memory has not come to mind because the person has never encountered the relevant retrieval cues.

• Event memory has been compartmentalized (*dissociated* is a term often used) so that certain events are only recalled when the individual is in a particular state of mind. The individual's state of mind would determine the nature of the retrieval cues that were formed and hence influence the success or failure of the retrieval attempt. In extreme instances, this condition may have the label multiple personality disorder or dissociative identity disorder, in which different "personalities" are amnesic to each other's experiences.

Trauma has a variety of effects. Sargant (1967) reports that during World War II there were many cases of what he called acute hysterical losses of memory. After Dunkirk, 150 of the first thousand admissions to his care were diagnosed that way. The treatment was to inject sodium amytal which brought the memory back, often accompanied by overwhelming emotional release and a reliving of the forgotten experiences. It has recently been argued that repeated or extended severe trauma or abuse is more likely to lead to extreme amnesia than single episodes. This is one of a number of possible reasons for the discrepancy between Sargant's data and the data from the Marchioness survivors already referred to.

In common with victims of some other forms of trauma, survivors of childhood abuse may sometimes experience periods when trauma-related memories intrude into consciousness and they routinely report attempts to avoid or block out these memories. There is also experimental evidence with normal subjects in support of active inhibitory processes in memory. Work on "directed forgetting" indicates that prior instructions to forget certain items renders those items more difficult to recall, although not to recognize. What is not clear is whether this deliberate process of blocking out specific memories can lead to a more general memory loss. The majority of the evidence cited in favor of this type of repressive process comes from clinical case studies. In a number of studies, surveys of sexual abuse survivors report between one third and two thirds having periods of time when they totally or partially forgot the abuse. Only one study made explicit the distinction between total and partial forgetting, reporting a rate of 19% total amnesia. Two studies addressed the issue of the corroboration of the abuse but neither looked separately at cases in which complete amnesia had been reported. This issue and the issue of the process of recovery of memories are in need of further enquiry.

*Summary.* Forgetting of certain kinds of trauma is often reported, although the nature of the mechanism or mechanisms involved remains unclear.

## Is It Possible to Have False Beliefs about the Past?

First of all, we wish to make a distinction between false memories (where the event never happened) and incorrect memories (where the event happened but the details are wrong). Because event memories are often fragmentary, there will always be a tendency to pad them out in order to make them coherent. The extent of this is not readily detectible by the individual, as there is an unstable relationship between confidence and accuracy. An entirely false memory is quite a different matter.

The morning after the *Challenger* space shuttle disaster, Neisser and Harsch (1993) had freshman students write down what they had been doing at the time they heard the news. Three years later, the students were asked again to recall the circumstances, particularly where they had been, what they had been doing, and who told them. It is not surprising that 11 out of the 44 subjects got zero correct—they incorrectly remembered how they heard the news, where they had been, who they had been with and what they had been doing at the time; it is surprising that three of them rated themselves as absolutely certain of every aspect of their recall. When they were shown what they had written 3 years previously, some subjects argued that they must have been wrong previously (24 hours after the event) because they were so certain that they were correct now. One thing that all the subjects had in common is that they recalled an event which was characterized as hearing about the disaster. None of them denied the fact that they had heard about the event nor did any claim complete forgetting of all detail.

More serious would be remembering an event that had not taken place. This would be an instance of a false memory. There are one or two preliminary, research-based examples of adults who have been persuaded that particular things have happened to them. For example, Loftus reports that certain adults and adolescents can be made to believe that they had been lost when young in a particular shopping mall, and they proceed to invent details of the fictitious event. We can think of this in terms of a memory record being created from material in the interview in such a way that the contents appear to be from a real event. Some people appear to be more susceptible than others to suggestion and people under hypnosis are particularly vulnerable to suggestion both that false things did happen and that real things did not happen. Authority figures would be more likely to influence memory. Much of the attack from the false memory organizations is on therapists who strongly suggest to their clients that they have suffered CSA. However, it is also the case that people traumatized as children are more suggestible as well as susceptible to hypnosis.

There are a number of reports of individual cases of apparent false beliefs being created, often after extended directed therapy. These issues are complex and are more forensic than scientific matters. However, overall, we agree with Lindsay and Read (1994) in a recent comprehensive review:

> There is little reason to fear that a few suggestive questions will lead psychotherapy clients to conjure up vivid and compelling illusory memories of childhood sexual abuse. (p. 294)

*Summary.* Although there is a great deal of evidence for incorrect memories, there is currently much less evidence on the creation of false memories.

### What Are the Effects on Memory of Hypnotic Techniques?

It is popularly believed that hypnosis can be used to help people to recall events or other material which had hitherto eluded them. In particular, the use of hypnosis has been common in criminal cases. It has sometimes been used in conjunction with age regression in cases where it has been claimed that memories have been recovered.

Hypnotic memory enhancement is based on the belief that human memory faithfully records every perception, permanently stores such recorded perceptions, and accurately "replays" them in their original form when the witness is placed under hypnosis and asked to remember them. None of these suppositions are correct, and experimental attempts to demonstrate improvements in memory as a result of hypnosis have failed even on highly susceptible subjects. Most studies also conclude that hypnosis increases the suggestibility of subjects to information suggested by the hypnotist.

There are one or two quite spectacular examples of the successful use of hypnosis in criminal cases. The problem is that there are innumerable failures. The successes, then, could be due not directly to the hypnosis, but indirectly to a factor such as increased relaxation. Where the possibility of objective verification has been present, it has been shown that recall under hypnosis is very insecure. In effect, under hypnosis, the individual's ability to track the source of individual bits of information is greatly impaired.

Hypnotic age regression is often used with the objective of encouraging individuals to relive past events that are unavailable for recall. The problem is that the relived episodes incorporate incorrect information. This was demonstrated in an experimental investigation of age regression conducted by O'Connell, Shor, and Orne (1970). Subjects were required to try to recall names of their school classmates. They recalled more under hypnosis but they also tended to confabulate more. In checking the descriptions produced by the subjects, the experimenters discovered that some of the individuals described had not been members of the subject's class.

Nash (1987) carried out a survey of 60 years of empirical study on investigations of whether there is reinstatement of childhood psychological or physiological faculties during hypnotic age regression. Of those studies that met minimum standards for experimental control, none showed any reliable memory effects.

There are legal cautions against the use of evidence obtained through hypnosis. In the 1980s a number of American states ruled that evidence acquired from a witness who has undergone hypnosis could not be admitted in court. In a recent UK criminal case, R v. Browning, an appeal was allowed in which a key witness had undergone hypnosis prior to giving testimony. Reputable organizations such as the British Society of Experimental and Clinical Hypnosis have firm guidelines on the use of hypnosis, which warn against using it as a means of memory retrieval.

It is known that hypnosis can be used to induce amnesia. Routinely, hypnotized subjects are given posthypnotic suggestions ("when the bell rings you will scratch your ear") and are told to forget the suggestion itself. Under certain circumstances they will recall the suggestion when back under hypnosis. This state resembles the clinical condition of dissociation. People working with known child sexual offenders report that some abusers describe using techniques similar to hypnotic control during abuse. It would seem possible, then, that some abused children, at least, could be described as having posthypnotic amnesia.

*Summary.* Hypnosis makes memory more confident and less reliable. It can also be used to create amnesia for events.

### Are False Memories like False Confessions?

There are numerous documented examples of innocent persons confessing to crimes they could not have conceivably committed, sometimes accompanied by otherwise convincing detail. Is there a parallel here with "false memories"? The answer seems to be if there is any parallel, it is a very imperfect one.

First, according to Gudjonsson (1992), many confessions are coerced, that is, the individual is encouraged to make confession through threats or inducements offered by the interrogator; they make a confession to escape from the situation they find themselves in. There is no suggestion that they actually believe themselves guilty of the crime to which they confess. Perhaps a closer parallel is the voluntary confession: suspects on occasion will come to believe that they must have committed a crime despite their initial denials. Such voluntary confessions are frequently the result of a long period of interrogation when accusations are repeatedly put to the suspect that they are guilty. Such individuals may confess under the belief that they must have been responsible, even though they were unaware of the event.[3]

However, even with voluntary confessions the analogy with "false memory" is very inexact. Both groups will show belief in their stories and display often quite convincing details. Both may arise from prolonged interviewing in which certain themes are repeated over and over again. However, apparent memories

---

[3] An example of this was Carole Richardson's "confession" of involvement in the Guildford bombings in which she eventually concluded she must have been present but so far under the influence of drink and drugs as not to recollect the events clearly.

of abusive incidents from childhood can occur quite spontaneously, usually trig-gered by some outside event or agency quite independent of any ongoing ther-apy. Moreover, false confessions are quickly abandoned in the face of contradic-tory evidence—Carole Richardson rapidly came to the conclusion that the events she had described could not have happened—whereas "false memories" are persistent and survive repeated denials by others of the reality of the events victims describe.

*Summary.* There are a number of significant differences between false confes-sions and false (recovered) memories which preclude generalizing from one to the other.

## OUR OWN ENQUIRIES

Public debate has focused on issues imported from the American experience:

* recovered memories occur during extended therapy,
* the therapists concerned have strong *a priori* beliefs concerning CSA,
* memories are recovered from impossibly early ages, and
* accusers always recover memories from total amnesia.

We have carried out some preliminary enquiries to test the likely extension of these issues to the United Kingdom.

### The Society's Recovered Memories Survey

One of the issues in the national and international debate concerns the inci-dence of recovered memories and related phenomena among well-trained prac-titioners. We decided to obtain some preliminary answers by circulating BPS-accredited practitioners with a one-page survey. This study will be reported in detail elsewhere and the results presented here should be regarded as prelimi-nary. We had answers from 810 Chartered Psychologists who see non-psychotic adult clients.[4]

More than 90% have seen clients in the last year who report CSA. We asked particularly about clients who reported recovering memories from complete am-nesia. About a third of our respondents said that they had had clients recovering such memories before they had any therapy. More than one in five have at least one client in the last year who recovered a memory of CSA and nearly a third (a total of 225) have clients recovering memories of a traumatic experience other than CSA. Over one half of the responders have had at some time clients recov-ering memories of some kind.

Recovered memories are seen as sometimes or usually "essentially accurate" by 9 out of 10 of our group. A negligible number of our sample believed that

[4]This was defined as follows: "we are interested in adult clients (over 18) with non-psychotic disorders—i.e., excluding schizophrenic, manic-depressive, or organic disorders. These clients could be using or attending mental health services or being seen for mental health reasons in primary care or private practice."

recovered memories were always accurate. Two thirds of our respondents thought that false memories were possible, and more than one in seven believed that their own clients had experienced false memories.

*Summary.* There are high levels of belief among qualified psychologists in the essential accuracy of recovered memories of child sexual abuse. These beliefs appear to be fueled by the high levels of experience of recovered memories both for CSA and for non-CSA traumatic events. The nondoctrinaire nature of these beliefs is indicated by the high level of acceptance of the possibility of false memories.

## *Summary of Investigation of the Records of the British False Memory Society*

Considering the nature of the claims concerning children accusing parents in the United States, we wished to determine whether a similar state of affairs existed in Britain. The British False Memory Society had 250 enquiries at the end of 1993 according to its director. A record had been completed for 200 of these cases. The rest involved individuals who had given no information about themselves, but who had requested information about the society. In the time available to us, over two visits during November 1993, we managed to examine all but 19 of the 200 cases ($n = 181$). The information in the case records was inconsistent and varied. About half of those we examined were very brief, sketchy, and unsystematically recorded notes from telephone enquiries revealing very little of the actual circumstances. The remaining 54% (97/181) contained

| | BRITISH RECORDS ($n = 97$) | U.S. SURVEY ($n = 284$) |
|---|---|---|
| Age of accusing child | | |
| Under 30 | 47% | 33% |
| 30 or over | 46% | 62% |
| Not known | 7% | 5% |
| Age (years) when alleged abuse began | | |
| 0–2 | | 26% |
| 0–5 | 27% | 66% |
| 6–12 | 20% | 11% |
| 13 + | 6% | 1% |
| Not known | 47% | 21% |
| Age (years) when alleged abuse ended | | |
| 0–5 | 5% | 8% |
| 6–12 | 10% | 27% |
| 13 + | 6% | 24% |
| Not known | 78% | 41% |
| Allegations of satanic/ritual abuse (Open-ended question) | 6% | 11% |
| (Closed question) | | 18% |
| Accusing child had hypno/regression therapy | 21% | 31% |

sufficient information to enable us to extract some crude statistics and it is estimated that about a third of the records contained other supporting material, most
usually in the form of letters from the accuser.

In contrast to the British FM Society, the False Memory Syndrome Foundation in the United States, founded in March 1992, had received several thousand
enquiries by January 1994 according to its newsletter. At the time of writing
there had been no report of any external or internal examination of FMS Foundation records, and it is not known what proportion of the contacts are genuine
or pertain specifically to accusations of sexual abuse involving recovered memories. However, 487 callers were mailed questionnaires in 1992 asking for details
of family background and the adult life of the accusing child. There were 284
respondents. A report of the FMS Foundation's survey was produced in summer
1993 by the director of the FMS foundation. Findings from the British records
are compared here with the results of this survey, wherever the same information is available from the two sources. It should be borne in mind, however, that
both open and closed questions were asked of the accused in the FMSF survey,
whereas the data we had available came from unsolicited information provided
by the accused (67%) or someone closely related to the accused (33%), with
supporting material from accusers in approximately one third of the records.

One major difference in the information collected concerns the recovery of
repressed memories. Close examination of the 97 British FMS records with sufficient information revealed that in only just under half was there explicit mention of memory recovery from total amnesia. If all the records we examined are
considered this proportion is reduced to a quarter (47/181). The FMS Foundation
state in the report of their survey that all accusations "are based on recovered
'repressed' memories." They give no information about how this has been documented or the nature of recovery, that is, from total or partial amnesia, although
18% of the accused could not say how many years (within a 10-year range) the
accuser's memory had been repressed.

*Summary.* There is not a lot of evidence that accusers fit a single profile.
From the British records, at least, there is no good evidence that accusers have
invariably recovered memories from total amnesia. Further documentation of
the phenomenon is needed by the False Memory societies in order to obtain a
more reliable picture. It appears that only in a small minority of instances do the
accusations concern abuse that ended before the age of 5.

## CLINICAL ISSUES

*Characteristics of Verified Abuse in Adulthood*

Among the claims of the FMS Foundation are that the adult children who are
now making accusations of abuse had happy and problem-free childhoods. No
evidence has been offered by them in support of this claim, and it is contradicted
by the Foundation's own data, which indicate a high rate of alcohol and drug
problems in the families. It should perhaps be noted that, in general, parents
consistently rate their children as happier and better adjusted than the children

rate themselves, and rate the quality of family relationships as higher than they are rated by the children. Certainly it would be surprising if independent assessment of a group of sexually abused children did not reveal more dysfunction than in a control group. The kinds of dysfunction empirically associated with CSA in children are sexualized behavior, behavior and learning problems at school, depression and suicidal ideation, low self-esteem, sleep disturbance, withdrawal, anxiety, and running away. With the exception of sexualized behavior, however, all these symptoms occur in dysfunctional families and are not specific to CSA. It is possible that CSA may also lead to inhibited sexual behavior and to delay in forming sexual relationships with peers. Recently, a number of studies have examined the additional contribution made by CSA over and above general family problems. The general conclusion is that although CSA is embedded in general family problems, it makes an additional contribution to mental health outcome.

## Long-Term Effects of Childhood Trauma

Most of the research in this area has focused on sexual abuse in childhood (CSA) with a limited literature on childhood physical abuse (CPA). The age at which childhood ends is usually defined as between 15 and 17.

Greater long-term harm is associated with more severe abuse, particularly abuse involving a father or stepfather, penetration, or use of force or violence. Considering only evidence from representative community studies, with one exception, all studies investigating depression in adult life as an outcome for CSA have demonstrated significant results. In addition, about half these studies have shown anxiety to be more common in CSA survivors. By way of illustration, in one study of more than 1500 women (Stein, Golding, Siegel, Burnam, & Sorenson, 1988), lifetime prevalence of anxiety disorders was 37% in CSA survivors compared with 14% with no CSA. Rates for lifetime depression were 22% and 6% respectively.

Eating disorders have also been investigated in relation to childhood trauma, but with conflicting results. Most of the work has been done on clinical populations. In the main, it appears that bulimic behavior may be more highly associated with a history of CSA than anorexia. More representative studies are needed, although those that exist show CSA to be a risk factor for eating disorders. Andrews, Valentine, and Valentine (1995) show a cohort effect: older women with CSA or CPA are more likely to be chronically or recurrently depressed, whereas younger women with such a history are more likely to have bulimic symptoms.

Studies of clinical populations show raised rates of trauma of between 90% and 50% of patients reporting a major physical or sexual assault at some time in their lives. Furthermore, a number of studies have shown that patients with such histories have more severe symptoms, borderline diagnoses, and more suicidal symptoms than other patients. Three clinical studies of multiple personality disordered patients in particular have shown rates of between 75% and 90% for CSA, and 50% and 82% for CPA.

In conclusion, the examples we give indicate that CSA substantially increases the risk of a variety of mental health problems in later life, but it does not invariably lead to such problems. Factors such as severity of the abuse, quality of early and later support, and biological vulnerability may all influence outcome. Similarly, CSA cannot explain all psychopathology and is not the only traumatic experience related to increased risk of disorders such as depression, anxiety, and bulimia. Physical and emotional abuse, and other abusive and stressful experiences throughout the life course have been shown to be independent risk factors for these disorders (e.g., Mullen, Martin, Anderson, Romans, & Herbison, 1993; Andrews, 1995).

## Issues in Clinical Practice

Although experimental evidence for repression and other forms of not knowing about trauma is scant, many clinicians report that forgetting of childhood trauma is common among clients with mental health problems. In our own survey, about half the respondents had clients who had at some time recovered memories of CSA. In the last 10 years or so, the recognition of childhood trauma of sexual abuse has become commonplace among mental health professionals. Many clients with severe mental health problems appear to have experienced disturbed and abusive childhoods. One problem with respect to recovered memories is assessing the likelihood of abuse given a presenting symptom.

We are agreed that it is important for both clinical and ethical reasons to avoid distorting the client's view of their background, particularly through suggestion; this would be a false solution for the client and could lead to considerable distress within the client's family. Moreover it is important not to form premature conclusions about the truth status of a recovered memory. The therapist should be genuinely neutral about this, helping the client to think about what his or her experiences might have been but without imposing the therapist's own conclusions. This involves considerable tolerance of uncertainty and reflects a very difficult discipline required on the part of the therapist. The therapist should help the client to consider a range of possibilities—that the material may be literally true, may be metaphorically true, or may derive from fantasy or dream imagery. Illustrations of metaphorical truth might be, for example, imagery of rape that represents experiences with a father whose behavior was intrusive but not literally sexual. Imagery of the murder of a baby could represent a memory that is literally true or might metaphorically represent a baby part of the self having been "murdered." The therapist him or herself cannot know the truth.

## Guidelines for Therapists

The following guidelines are intended to apply to a range of psychological therapies.

1. It may be necessary clinically for the therapist to be open to the emergence of memories of trauma that are not immediately available to the client's consciousness.

2. It is important for the therapist to be alert to the dangers of suggestion.

3. Although it is important always to take the client seriously, the therapist should avoid drawing premature conclusions about the truth of a recovered memory.

4. The therapist needs to tolerate uncertainty and ambiguity regarding the client's early experience.

5. Although it may be part of the therapists' work to help their clients to think about their early experiences, they should avoid imposing their own conclusions about what took place in childhood.

6. The therapist should be alert to a range of possibilities, for example, that a recovered memory may be literally true, metaphorically true, or may derive from fantasy or dream material.

7. If the role of the professional is to obtain evidence that is reliable in forensic terms, they need to restrict themselves to procedures that enhance reliability (e.g., use of the cognitive interview and avoidance of hypnosis or suggestion and leading questions).

8. CSA should not be diagnosed on the basis of presenting symptoms, such as eating disorder, alone—there is a high probability of false positives, as there are other possible explanations for psychological problems.

## OVERALL CONCLUSIONS

• Normal event memory is largely accurate but may contain distortions and elaborations.

• With certain exceptions, such as when there has been extensive rehearsal of an imagined event, the source of our memories is generally perceived accurately.

• Nothing can be recalled accurately from before the first birthday and little from before the second. Poor memory from before the fourth birthday is normal.

• Forgetting of certain kinds of trauma is often reported, although the nature of the mechanism or mechanisms involved remains unclear.

• Although there is a great deal of evidence for incorrect memories, there is currently much less evidence on the creation of false memories.

• Hypnosis makes memory more confident and less reliable. It can also be used to create amnesia for events.

• There are a number of significant differences between false confessions and false (recovered) memories which preclude generalizing from one to the other.

• There are high levels of belief in the essential accuracy of recovered memories of child sexual abuse among qualified psychologists. These beliefs appear to be fueled by the high levels of experience of recovered memories both for CSA and for non-CSA traumatic events. The nondoctrinaire nature of these beliefs is indicated by the high level of acceptance of the possibility of false memories.

• There is not a lot of evidence that accusers fit a single profile. From the British records, at least, there is no good evidence that accusers have invariably recovered memories from total amnesia. Further documentation of the phenomenon is needed by the False Memory societies in order to obtain a more reliable picture. It appears that only in a small minority of instances do the accusations concern abuse that ended before the age of 5.

• Guidelines can be laid down for good practice in therapy.

## RECOMMENDATIONS

1. We recommend that the Society use all means available to ensure that Chartered Psychologists who carry out therapy do so in accordance with our guidelines.

2. We recommend that BPS-approved training courses in psychological therapies should include appropriate information concerning the properties of human memory.

3. We recommend that the Royal Colleges of Psychiatrists, Nursing and General Practice, and the psychotherapy training organizations affiliated to the United Kingdom Council for Psychotherapy and the British Confederation of Psychotherapists should initiate action equivalent to (1) and (2) above.

4. We recommend that the Department of Health, Medical Research Council, and Economic and Social Research Council give increased priority to research in the areas covered in this report, particularly to those that integrate cognitive and clinical approaches. Examples include naturalistic studies of recovered memory, basic research on inhibitory processes of memory, and beliefs and practices in psychotherapy.

5. We recommend that the Department of Health take our findings into consideration in their review of NHS psychotherapy services, in relation to the quality of psychotherapy services and training.

6. We recommend that the Society and the Department of Health bring appropriate parts of our report to the attention of the general public to enable therapy clients to evaluate the conceptual and scientific basis of alternative therapies.

## ACKNOWLEDGMENTS

The British Psychological Society would like to thank and acknowledge the contributions of the authors of this report. The authors are John Morton—MRC Cognitive Development Unit, London (Chair), Bernice Andrews—Royal Holloway University of London, Debra Bekerian—MRC Applied Psychology Unit, Cambridge, Chris Brewin—Royal Holloway University of London, Graham Davies—Leicester University, and Phil Mollon—Dept of Psychiatry, Lister Hospital, Stevenage.

## REFERENCES

American Psychiatric Association. (1994). *Diagnostic and statistical manual of mental disorders (4th ed.) (DSM-IV)*. Washington, DC: Author.

Andrews, B. (1995). Bodily shame as a mediator between abusive experiences and depression. *Journal of Abnormal Psychology, 104*, 277–285.

Andrews, B., Valentine, E. R., & Valentine, J. D. (1995). Depression and eating disorders following abuse in childhood in two generations of women. *British Journal of Clinical Psychology, 34*, 37–52.

Bass, E., & Davies, L. (1988). *The courage to heal: A Guide for women survivors of child sexual abuse*. New York: Harper & Row.

Freud, S. (1933/1973). *Introductory lectures on psychoanalysis*. The Pelican Freud Library, Vol. 1. Harmondsworth: Penguin.

Gudjonsson, G. H. (1992). *The psychology of interrogations, confessions and testimony*. Chichester: Wiley.

Lindsay, D. S., & Read, J. D. (1994). Incest resolution psychotherapy and memories of childhood sexual abuse. *Applied Cognitive Psychology, 8,* 281–338.

Mullen, P. E., Martin, J. L., Anderson, J. C., Romans, S. E., & Herbison, G. P. (1993). Child sexual abuse and mental health in adult life. *British Journal of Psychiatry, 163,* 721–732.

Myers, N. A., Clifton, R. K., & Clarkson, M. G. (1987). When they were young: Almost-threes remember two years ago. *Infant Behavior and Development, 10,* 123–132.

Nash, M. (1987). What, if anything, is regressed about hypnotic age regression? A review of the empirical literature. *Psychological Bulletin, 102,* 42–52.

Neisser, U., & Harsch, N. (1993). Phantom flashbulbs: False recollections of hearing the news about *Challenger*. In E. Winograd & U. Neisser (Eds.), *Affect and accuracy in recall: Studies of "flashbulb" memories. Emory Symposia in Cognition, 4,* (pp. 9–31). New York: Cambridge University Press.

O'Connell, D. N., Shor, R. E., & Orne, M. T. (1970). Hypnotic age regression: An empirical and methodological analysis. *Journal of Abnormal Psychology, 76,* 1–31.

Sargant, W. (1967). *The unquiet mind*. London: Heinemann.

Stein, J. A., Golding, J. M., Siegel, J. M., Burnam, M. A., & Sorenson, S. B. (1988). Long-term psychological sequelae of child sexual abuse: The Los Angeles Epidemiologic Catchment Area study. In G. E. Wyatt & G. J. Powell (Eds.), *Lasting effects of child sexual abuse* (pp. 135–154). Newbury Park, CA: Sage.

Terr, L. (1991). Childhood traumas: An outline and overview. *American Journal of Psychiatry, 148,* 10–20.

Usher, J. A., & Neisser, U. (1993). Childhood amnesia and the beginnings of memory for four early life events. *Journal of Experimental Psychology, 122,* 155–165.

# INDEX

Repressed memories (continued)
228, 238, 263, 269, 281, 302, 313, 350,
355, 380

## S

Schemas, 98, 169, 207, 318
Self *(see Autobiographical memory, self concept and)*
Sexual abuse, 4, 30, 41, 238, 267, 279, 297, 313, 325, 342, 349, 355, 374
Sexual assault *(see Rape)*
Social influences *(see Family influences)*
Source misattribution, 225, 227, 306, 314
Stressful events *(see Traumatic events)*

Suggestibility, 30, 152, 165, 171, 176, 187, 197, 211, 216, 225, 247, 289, 314, 317, 318, 328, 343, 379

## T

Therapists, therapy *(see Psychotherapy)*
Trace strength theory, 200, 203, 215, 347
Traumatic events *(see also Memory, for traumatic events)*, 4, 47, 69, 81, 97, 169, 173, 175, 184, 214, 239, 279, 313, 325, 342

## V

Value system, 177
VCUG, 9, 214, 240, 315, 318, 331

## DATE DUE

| | | | |
|---|---|---|---|
| APR 2 4 1997 | | | |
| APR 0 6 1998 | | | |
| DEC 1 1 1999 | | | |
| MAY 2 9 2001 | | | |
| APR 0 3 2002 | | | |
| JUN 1 3 2002 | | | |
| OCT 2 4 2002 | | | |
| MAY 0 3 2011 | | | |
| NOV 1 6 2011 | | | |
| JAN 0 6 2012 | | | |
| | | | |
| | | | |
| | | | |
| | | | |
| | | | |
| | | | |
| | | | |
| GAYLORD | | | PRINTED IN U.S.A |